Clinical Handbook
of Sleep Disorders

Antonio Culebras, M.D.

*Professor of Neurology, State University of New York
College of Medicine; Chief, Neurology Service, Veterans
Affairs Medical Center; Consultant, The Sleep Center,
Community General Hospital, Syracuse, New York*

Butterworth–Heinemann

Boston•Oxford•Johannesburg•Melbourne•New Delhi•Singapore

Library of Congress Cataloging-in-Publication Data

Culebras, A.
    Clinical handbook of sleep disorders / Antonio Culebras.
       p.   cm.
    Includes bibliographical references and index.
    ISBN 0-7506-9644-3 (alk. paper)
    1. Sleep disorders--Handbooks, manuals, etc.   I. Title.
    [DNLM: 1. Sleep Disorders--physiopathology.   WM 188 C967c 1996]
    RC547.C85   1996
    616.8'498--dc20
    DNLM/DLC
    for Library of Congress   96-23960
                                             CIP

British Library Cataloguing-in-Publication Data
A catalogue record for this book is available from the British Library.

The publisher offers discounts on bulk orders of this book.
For information, please contact:
Manager of Special Sales
Butterworth–Heinemann
313 Washington Street
Newton, MA 02158–1626
Tel: 617-928-2500
Fax: 617-928-2620

For information on all medical publications available, contact our World Wide Web home page at http://www.bh.com/med

10 9 8 7 6 5 4 3 2 1

Printed in the United States of America

*To my wife Susan and my daughters Katerina and Andrea,
for providing the unending source of motivation
that spurred the work*

Contents

Contributing Authors

Antonio Bové-Ribé, M.D.
Adjunct, Department of Internal Medicine, Hospital Sant Pau i Santa Tecla, Tarragona, Spain

Antonio Culebras, M.D.
Professor of Neurology, State University of New York College of Medicine; Chief, Neurology Service, Veterans Affairs Medical Center; Consultant, The Sleep Center, Community General Hospital, Syracuse, New York

Mark Eric Dyken, M.D.
Assistant Professor of Neurology and Director, Sleep Disorders Center, Department of Neurology, University of Iowa College of Medicine, Iowa City

Deborah C. Lin-Dyken, M.D.
Assistant Professor of Clinical Pediatrics, Department of Pediatrics, University of Iowa College of Medicine; Staff Physician, University of Iowa Hospitals and Clinics, Iowa City

Robert E. Westlake, Jr., M.D.
Clinical Assistant Professor, Department of Internal Medicine, State University of New York Health Sciences Center; Director of Medicine and the Sleep Center, Department of Internal Medicine, Community General Hospital, Syracuse, New York

Foreword

Sleep is a metaphor for death, but dreaming is confirmation that the breath of life endures within us when we lose consciousness on falling asleep. Because of its mysterious nature, sleep has long attracted the attention of priests, philosophers, and poets and has been a guiding force for leaders and heroes. Psychoanalysis, which has had such a great influence on modern humans, is based on the interpretation of dreams. Yet it is only since the turn of this century that experimental medicine and technological advances have explored the anatomofunctional mechanisms of wakefulness and sleep and their cyclic alternation. Systematic research into sleep disorders began even later, in the 1960s, following the discovery of REM sleep. Since then, a tumultuous branch of medical science, known as sleep medicine, has developed.

The first international meeting on sleep disorders was held in Bologna, Italy, in May 1967 and was attended by Dement and Rechtschaffen (United States), Gastaut, Passouant, and Oswald (Europe), and Hishikawa (Japan). On that occasion, scientists with different cultural backgrounds, coming from all over the globe, presented the results of their studies on insomnia, hypersomnia, and parasomnias. After that meeting, there was a general consensus that we had ventured into unknown territory. This led many of the participants to devote their studies to sleep and sleep disorders. Two decades later, light had been shed on many clinical problems. Just think how the study of breathing during sleep disclosed the enormous impact of snoring and obstructive apneas on physical and psychological well-being and on patients' personal relationships.

Insomnia and daytime somnolence affect millions of people all over the world. The impact of these health problems is enormous and warrants in-depth study and diagnosis to devise appropriate treatment.

It was largely thanks to the advent of audiovisual recording equipment relatively recently that sleep-related motor events could be documented for the first time, revealing a far wider and more complex sphere of disorders than was previously envisaged. REM sleep behavior disorder and nocturnal frontal lobe epilepsy are sleep-related paroxysmal disorders that deserve to be treated seriously and not simply labeled "pavor" or "somnambulism."

Sleep disorders is a field of medicine in which scientific knowledge has been acquired rapidly and on a great scale. The wealth of new information has been skillfully laid out in this volume by Dr. Culebras and his co-authors. Despite the literature already available, a topic subject to constant flux deserves a textbook reviewing some fields and dwelling further on problems tackled only in part elsewhere. Sleep involves the organism as a whole, so that any disorder of sleep affects an individual's inner equilibrium and his or her relations with the outside world. Antonio Culebras has been studying sleep medicine for many years, and as a neurobiologist, he is used to investigating both the somatic and neurologic components of disease. The book will be useful both for those embarking on the study of sleep medicine for the first time and for those sleep experts who are keen to learn the views of other colleagues in this fascinating field.

Elio Lugaresi, M.D.
Director, Instituto di Clinica Neurologica,
Bologna, Italy

Preface

Not so long ago, sleep was the patrimony of poetry and psychodynamic psychiatry. With the advent of neurophysiologic techniques derived from the electroencephalographic laboratory that records and measures human brain waves at night, sleep gradually evolved into the medical sciences, becoming a domain in which surprising physiologic phenomena and vast pathologic alterations subject to study and analysis were found. In the last three decades the discipline of sleep medicine has experienced an exponential growth in response to the richness of the biological phenomena encountered and to satisfy the demand for services by an increasingly sophisticated community that requires peak function of cerebral abilities. Fatigue, the most common complaint in medicine, along with loss of attention and concentration, poor memory, lack of drive, and somnolence—that cuddlesome villain—may be manifestations of an underlying sleep disorder amenable to alleviation, if not cure.

Sleep centers and laboratories are the cornerstone and pivot of modern sleep medicine. Recordings of patients while asleep in the controlled environment of the sleep laboratory under the careful watch of a polysomnographic technologist and the supervision of a sleep specialist, are the only reliable methods of uncovering or confirming sleep apnea syndrome, nocturnal epilepsy, leg myoclonus, narcolepsy, or other pathologies too extensive to list. Multidisciplinary teams of professionals, each with a particular inclination, enrich the medical atmosphere of the sleep center and provide cross-referenced knowledge to the well-integrated group. Sleep medicine is clearly a discipline in its own right. Specialists come from the ranks of neurology, pulmonary medicine, psychiatry, and internal medicine, as if their vocation were an afterthought. Not until sleep medicine is taken seriously in medical school curricula will there be primary sleep specialists formed as such from the start.

Sleep medicine is a segment of real growth in the clinical medical sciences. Physicians are now discovering that the explanation for many heretofore mysterious discomforts of their patients may be found in an undiscovered sleep apnea syndrome, periodic leg movements of sleep, or monosymptomatic narcolepsy. Increasingly educated patients demand respite from insomnia, alleviation of hypersomnia, control of parasomnias, and a cure for fatigue. Concerned spouses inquire about sleep apnea, and both bedmates request that something be done to muffle snoring. Sufferers request testing for sleep conditions after reading or listening to their description in the popular media. Ironically, many are right in their initial diagnosis because it is not so difficult to suspect the presence of sleep apnea or to determine that something is definitely wrong when the person does not sleep night after night or hurts the spouse while asleep. What takes a specialist's expertise is to determine not only that the condition exists but to measure its severity and decide what to do.

A new frontier between science and the law is looming on the horizon for sleep medicine. Forensic sleep medicine is a new branch of study of sleep disorders that assists in determining where sanity ends and insanity starts, when a crime is committed while the perpetrator is allegedly asleep. In addition, some people are falling asleep while driving on the highway, in command of an airplane, at the helm of a boat, operating machinery, or taking an academic course. Traffic officers are becoming increasingly worried about fatigue and driving, while executives, administrators, and educators are more aware of the loss of work productivity and the decline in academic achievement that lurks behind mental fatigue and chronic somnolence. Such mishaps are perhaps more common than is documented, but the measuring stick is out to tabulate the reality while deciding how to integrate it with what is known in sleep medicine. More research is needed but the march is on. Sleep hygiene, the executor of preventive medicine in sleep medicine, is a neglected practice that should stand on the same pedestal as balanced nutrition and regular exercise.

The primary care physician is destined to be the gatekeeper in most branches of medicine; this prediction may also hold true for sleep medicine. Becoming acquainted with the basics of clinical sleep medicine will be a requirement for directing the patient and conducting a professional and effective patient examination. This handbook has been devised to serve as a readable manual for the medically literate professional who requires information and education in sleep medicine. The book has been written in response to the growth of sleep study as a medical discipline, with the objective of filling the gap between the dense encyclopedic texts and the facile manual intended for popular consumption. It covers the clinical and practical aspects of sleep medicine as practiced in the United States. The text contains enough information to satisfy the needs of the interested physician while providing sufficient scientific background to facilitate the comprehension of clinical manifestations and management strategies in sleep medicine. Tables, algorithms, and case studies are included to illustrate passages of clinical importance. The book also includes illustrations of laboratory recordings of human sleep (polysomnograms and hypnograms) to educate the reader in the best uses of recording protocols and technical interpretations. The references at the end of each chapter are a limited account of the relevant literature in each topic without losing perspective of historical developments. The glossary of terms assists the newcomer to sleep medicine in the understanding of new and idiosyncratic words. The book has been written mostly by myself to provide uniformity to the style of the text and balanced contents to the chapters.

I want to heartily thank my collaborators: Dr. Antonio Bové-Ribé, Dr. Robert E. Westlake, Jr., Dr. Deborah Lin-Dyken, and Dr. Mark E. Dyken for their expert contributions to specific chapters. The multidisciplinary team of the Sleep Center at Community General Hospital of Syracuse, New York, where most of the clinical material came from, provided invaluable help in the selection of case studies, polysomnograms, and hypnograms that grace and enhance the text.

Antonio Culebras, M.D.

Clinical Handbook of Sleep Disorders

1

Introduction and Overview of Sleep Medicine

> Somnus, vigilia, utraque modum excedentia, morbus.
> *Disease exists, if either sleep or watchfulness be excessive.*
>
> Hippocrates, Aphorism LXXI [1]

In the beginning, sleep was a time for quiet and peaceful restoration of depleted mental energies and of exhausted physical powers of the body. It was a passive period in our existence and a time of respite from our maladies. In sleep, pain disappeared, anguish atoned, insanity vanished, shakes stopped, shortness of breath abated, and the individual appeared reconciled with health. Why explore the desert if it was barren? Only dream interpreters maintained interest in a part of our lives that was the traditional domain of visionaries and poets. And yet, from the dawn of civilization there was concern for the interpretation of dreams as paradigms of devilish pathology and, more recently, of unexplained psychopathology [2]. The subject of sleep remained in focus among a few. In the preface to his book, Sigmund Freud began with an apology, "In attempting a discussion of the *Interpretation of Dreams,* I do not believe that I have overstepped the bounds of neuropathologic interest," expressing the conventional state of mind of his peers who perceived sleep as a physiologic retirement not worthy of pursuit.

The use of electroencephalography (EEG) techniques to investigate the sleeping brain revealed a wealth of electrical activity in a seemingly passive body. This finding was followed by the discovery of periods of sleep when the EEG resembles the awake state, as the eyes move in the orbits under closed eyelids, a state that was called paradoxic sleep.

Dreams were linked to paradoxic sleep, and the apparent incongruence of so much inner activity in a paralyzed body caught the fancy of investigators, triggering an unprecedented interest in sleep research. Despite a great deal of investigation and progress in understanding the biology of sleep, the "paradox of an active brain in a sleeping body remains one of the great mysteries of human neurobiology" [3].

Curiosity for the unexpected and the avid search for an explanation of the bizarre phenomena prevailing in sleep fostered the application of polygraphic techniques to the sleeping human, which led to the discovery of insufficient and irregular respirations in sleep. Sleep apnea briskly came to the fore as a rather common syndrome that accounted for symptoms that were previously unexplained but that most importantly could be reversed, yielding a remarkable improvement in the quality of life of sufferers. Sleep alterations became a clinical discipline with its own classification of disorders; a unique mode of testing; and respectability high enough in the medical establishment to warrant professional associations, board certifications, specialized journals, and worldwide attention.

The discipline of sleep is still evolving. The sociopathology and medicolegal implications of a cloudy mind in a modern society, and the demand for increasing alertness, agility of thought, and mental stamina are now beginning to take root and can offer only glimpses of their future projection. We still do not know how far the study of sleep as a neurophysiologic function will take us, or what twists and turns will be made by the results of the investigation of sleep disorders and circadian biopathology, with their attachments to neuroendocrinology, learning and memory, behavior and moods, emotions, and psychopathology. Paradoxic, mysterious, unexpected, and unexplained are qualifiers that will remain attached to sleep for many years.

History of Sleep as a Medical Discipline

Sleep is the only voluptuousness offered liberally and abundantly to humans by nature. When absent, humans suffer and are resentful. Sleep has been a pivotal part of human existence since time immemorial, and one could use sleep as the centerpiece in a general history of civilization. It is only in recent years that sleep and its disorders have become a medical discipline, in part because of growing research into the sources of sleep as a function of the brain, and in part because of recent therapies that restore quality to nocturnal sleep and the ensuing daytime vigilance. The historic revolution is yet to be completed pending the realization by sociologists, administrators, and community leaders that job performance, work productivity, and transportation safety depend primarily on alertness, an attribute of consciousness that is subsidiary to nocturnal sleep.

Preoccupation with sleep can be traced back to biblical writings. Following the destruction of the second temple of Jerusalem, the Hebrew priests ordered the scribes to put into writing all the oral traditions known to humankind. The result was the Babylonian Talmud, a recompilation of teachings and traditions containing several medical observations and recommendations. Sleep was classified in three stages, one of them being "eye-lid sleep," perhaps the first reference to rapid eye movement (REM) sleep [4]. Hippocrates of Cos, the founder of Greek medicine who lived in the fifth century B.C., recorded in his aphorisms that "Somnus, vigilia, utraque modum excedentia, morbus" (Disease exists, if either sleep or watchfulness be excessive) [5]. In the midst of the tenth century, when Europe was still engulfed in the Dark Ages, Avicenna, the intellectual physician of Bokhara, "prince of physicians," and exponent of Saracen medicine, wrote in his monumental *Canon of Medicine* about sleep hygiene with recommendations that are as sound today as they were centuries ago [6]. Avicenna remarked on sleepiness and sleeplessness; on sleep and food, fasting, and purgation; the best time for sleep; physiologic effects of sleep; and the effects of sleep on pulse. There were no contributions to sleep as a medical science until the late nineteenth century, when Jean Baptiste E. Gélineau published work based on 14 instances of excessive somnolence, in which he distinguished primary from secondary hypersomnia, a condition that he termed *narcolepsy* [7]. The Spanish histologist and Nobel laureate Santiago Ramón y Cajal and his disciple Francisco Tello observed thickening of neurofibrils in neurons of the brain stem and encephalon in reptiles during hibernation [8, 9], a phenomenon that disappeared when the reptiles returned to full activity. These observations appeared to confer a morphologic basis to sleep and gave new impetus to neurodynamic theories of dendritic retraction and neuronal disconnection underlying sleep. The understanding of the neurologic basis of sleep that had thus begun to take shape was furthered by the encephalitis epidemic of 1917. Clinical and neuropathologic observations made by Constantin von Economo in patients dying from encephalitis suggested the existence of cerebral centers controlling sleep [10]. Von Economo's neuropathologic studies suggested that the mesencephalic tegmentum and posterior hypothalamus maintained vigilance, since lesions of those centers caused excessive somnolence, whereas a center for sleep might exist in the basal forebrain and anterior hypothalamus, where damage gave rise to insomnia. This work constituted a turning point in sleep science, attracting the interest of neuroscientists and focusing the attention of sleep researchers on the hypothalamus. Gonzalo Rodríguez Lafora, working in Spain after his sojourn in the Government Hospital for the Insane of Washington, D.C. (where he described the now famous Lafora cytoplasmic bodies), delivered a discourse entitled "The Physiology and Pathology of Sleep" [11] on his inception into the Spanish National Academy of Medicine in 1933. His thesis summarized his work and that of contemporaries, showing a depth of neuropathologic knowledge solid enough to support the neurophysiologic research of the ensuing decade.

In 1930, Hans Berger published his recordings of cerebral electrical activity in sleep showing tracings that were different from the ones appearing in the vigil state [12]. Alfred Loomis et al., in 1937, described brain wave patterns of sleep that could be measured continuously [13]. It was not until after World War II that implantable brain electrodes facilitated the recording of the electrical activity of the brain in laboratory animals. In the late 1940s, a major breakthrough occurred with Giuseppe Moruzzi and Horace Magoun's discovery of the relation between the reticular formation of the brain stem and activation of the EEG in transitions from sleep to wakefulness, interrupting the synchronized discharges of sleep. In their seminal paper, these authors showed that activation of the upper brain stem produced desynchronized, low-voltage patterns of electrical activity along with behavioral arousal. A critical correlation was then made between EEG activation, wakefulness, and arousal on the one hand, and EEG synchronization, sleep, and decreased level of consciousness [14] on the other.

In the 1950s, Nathaniel Kleitman in Chicago was interested in investigating eye movements as an index of sleep, following reports that slow rolling eye movements were observed in sleep [15]. Working in the laboratory with Eugene Aserinsky, they used a Grass Model III oscillograph to record rapid eye movements occurring regularly during nocturnal sleep and related them to dreaming. This information was published in a momentous paper in 1953 in *Science* [15] that revolutionized sleep research. William Dement, then a medical student in the same laboratory, recounts in his paper "Personal History of Sleep Disorders Medicine" [16] that he was asked to gather data on dream recall during awakenings from episodes of REM and non–rapid eye movement (non–REM) sleep. Dement also recorded continuous brain waves during the night, coming to realize with his coworkers that the electrical brain activity of sleep was a highly organized and predictable phenomenon appearing in an orderly pattern, which they termed the architecture of sleep [17]. Central to this architecture was the occurrence of 90-minute cycles of changing EEG activity in conjunction with rapid eye movements. REM sleep was also observed in human infants and in animals. Dement's experimental research in the cat led to the discovery of desynchronized, seemingly activated, brain wave activity during REM sleep [18] that had been considered artifactual by some. This neurophysiologic paradox was difficult to accept because sleep had been associated with synchronized patterns, and the discordance went counter to current theories of reticular activation. In France, Michel Jouvet [19] confirmed the presence of activated sleep in cats and described controlling neural centers in the brain stem that conferred a solid neuroanatomic status to the generation of REM sleep. Jouvet clarified the role of pontine centers and described muscle atonia in REM sleep [20], contributing information that clearly separated REM sleep as a distinct form of sleep.

The medical science of sleep received a considerable impetus with the 1968 publication of the *Manual of Standardized Terminology, Techniques and Scoring System for Sleep Stages of Human Subjects*, by Allan Rechtschaffen and Anthony Kales [21], which is still used and is the required reference book in every sleep laboratory. Narcolepsy was further characterized by Robert Yoss and David Daly, who introduced methylphenidate hydrochloride (Ritalin) for the treatment of the disorder [22]. In 1963, Rechtschaffen described sleep onset REM periods in this condition [23], establishing the link with REM sleep pathology that would later unravel the known pathophysiology of this disorder. Sleep apnea was independently described by Henri Gastaut, Carlo Tassinari, and B. Duron in Marseilles [24] and by Richard Jung and Wolfgang Kuhlo in Germany [25] in 1965. Tassinari went to join Elio Lugaresi in Bologna, and 3 years later, they and their Italian coworkers provided a full description of the sleep apnea syndrome, pointing out loud snoring as a marker of the condition [26].

The development of sleep centers for the clinical evaluation of sleep disorders was pioneered by the opening of a sleep center at Stanford University in 1970 for the evaluation of patients at night. Shortly thereafter, Elliot Weitzman opened the Montefiore Hospital sleep center for the study of chronobiology, endocrine relations, and clinical sleep disorders. The Association of Sleep Disorders Centers (ASDC) was formed in 1976 to standardize the clinical practice of sleep medicine. The first examinations toward the certification of clinical polysomnographer were given in 1977, and the laboratory accreditation standards were

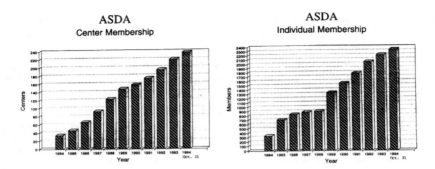

Figure 1-1. Sleep center and individual membership in the American Sleep Disorders Association (ASDA) from 1984–1994, showing impressive growth over a decade. (Reprinted with permission from the American Sleep Disorders Association, ASDA Update, Vol. 5, No. 5, November 1994, 1610 14th Street NW, Suite 300, Rochester, MN 55901.)

published in 1978 [27]. In 1979, the first classification of sleep disorders was published in *Sleep* [28], a journal that had appeared the year before as the official publication of the ASDC.

The first tracheotomies for the alleviation of obstructive sleep apnea were performed in the late 1970s, and uvulopalatopharyngoplasty was introduced in 1981 [29]. The continuous positive airway pressure apparatus was introduced by Colin Sullivan in 1981 [30], changing drastically the mode of treatment of sleep apnea and spearheading the phenomenal proliferation of evaluations and diagnoses of a condition that had remained virtually occult until then. These changes contributed to a demand for more sleep laboratories and specialists flourishing in a solidly established medical discipline with an expanding professional society, annual scientific meetings, specialty board certification, and diagnostic center accreditation. In 1994, the American Sleep Disorders Association (ASDA) listed 240 center members in the United States and 2,300 individual members (Figure 1-1).

Overview of Sleep Medicine

The modern sleep laboratory is used to perform nocturnal and diurnal polysomnography; the sleep center is an expanded version of the laboratory where sleep specialists clinically evaluate patients with sleep disorders. Thus, the sleep center incorporates ambulatory clinic and

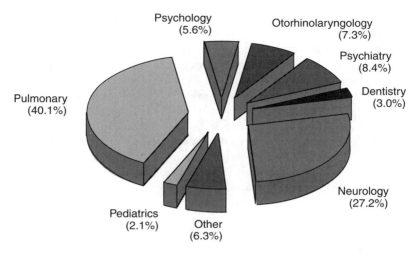

Figure 1-2. 1995 composition of ASDA membership by primary specialties. (Reprinted with permission from the American Sleep Disorders Association, ASDA Update, Special Issue, May 1995, 1610 14th Street NW, Suite 300, Rochester, MN 55901.)

polysomnographic laboratory functions. Sleep medicine revolves around the sleep center. Patients from all walks of medicine come to the sleep center for specialized management. The largest contingent is referred for evaluation of snoring or of suspected sleep apnea. In our sleep center, this group constitutes 69% of all patients. Other patients are referred for evaluation of excessive somnolence (10%), insomnia (10%), and miscellaneous conditions among which parasomnias and alleged seizure disorders predominate. Erectile impotence is no longer studied in our sleep center, whereas in centers where urologists have strong input, this evaluation remains important. Pediatric sleep medicine is a highly specialized section that can be practiced only under the leadership of a trained pediatrician. The assortment of patients is best served by sleep specialists with different backgrounds. In 1995, the ASDA documented the following breakdown of primary specialization for sleep specialists: pulmonary medicine, 40.1%; neurology, 27.2%; psychiatry, 8.4%; otorhinolaryngology, 7.3%; psychology, 5.6%; dentistry, 3.0%; pediatrics, 2.1%; and other, 6.3% (Figure 1-2).

A number of professional societies have developed in recent years in North America. The ASDA was founded in 1975 and reorganized into its present form in 1987 [31]. Its membership includes sleep disorders centers and individuals. The orientation is clinical, establishing standards of clinical care and providing a forum for the exchange of professional and scientific information. It also promotes education, training, and research in sleep disorders medicine. The ASDA reviews the standard diagnostic classification of sleep disorders and serves as an advocate and representative of the specialty in relation to health professional organizations, federal and local regulatory bodies, and third-party payers.

The Sleep Research Society (SRS) was initially organized in 1961 by a small group of researchers with varied interests, ranging from psychology to biochemistry. Initially, it was called the Association for the Psychophysiological Study of Sleep. The society promotes and fosters research in the basic sciences related to the functions of sleep.

The ASDA and the SRS in conjunction with the Association of Polysomnographic Technologists sponsor the Annual Meeting of the Associated Professional Sleep Societies [32], which is the high event for sleep medicine in North America. The eighth meeting, held in Boston in June 1994, received over 500 abstracts for review.

Today, sleep centers are accredited by the ASDC. Sleep specialists are certified by the American Board of Sleep Medicine [33]. Polysomnography technologists receive their certification through the Board of Registered Polysomnographic Technologists [34].

The journal *Sleep*, founded in 1978 by William Dement and Christian Guilleminault, is published ten times per year and is the official publication of the ASDA [35]. The ASDA also publishes a quarterly newsletter with notices about the association and trends in the field of sleep [36]. The American Electroencephalographic Society has published guidelines for the polygraphic assessment of sleep-related disorders [37].

Justification

Is there a need for sleep medicine and sleep centers? The specialty of sleep medicine has experienced an exponential growth. Outsiders view with skepticism the growth of a discipline that is fully appreciated only by sleep specialists and patients. Hospital administrators question whether limited resources should be invested in the development of a costly sleep center when there are people dying of coronary heart disease, trauma, and cancer. The answer to that dilemma depends on the orientation of the medical center. If the goal is exclusively to meet the challenge of critical care medicine, then there is little room for a sleep center. However, if the objective of the medical center encompasses the centuries old hippocratic pledge of curing disease, alleviating suffering, and preventing malady, then there is a great deal of clinical activity and justification for a sleep center because sleep disorders cause chronic misery and reduction in quality of life that can be ameliorated in many instances. Serious social decline and poor scholastic performance are commonplace for persons with intrinsic hypersomnias. Indirect morbidity and mortality are also a cause for concern in sleep pathology. Severe sleep apnea can be a risk factor for vascular disease. A large percentage of highway accidents and work-related accidents (see Chapter 14) are the result of sleepiness and loss of vigilance that could probably have been eradicated with the help of sleep specialists. In addition, some parasomnias provoke bizarre and violent behavior with resultant accidents. Thus, loss of work productivity, reduced income, poor health, and even risk of dying as a result of sleep disorders or of poor sleep hygiene are considerations to be made when evaluating the need for sleep medicine.

The Future

Sleep medicine will not remain static within the confines of the dyssomnias, parasomnias, and allied disorders. The future calls for a pivotal intervention of sleep centers and specialists in the prevention of sleep-related accidents; development of countermeasures where there is loss of work productivity resulting from poorly designed work shifts; as well as active participation in the correction of family pathology, social disruption, and general loss of quality of life that afflicts people in a state of subvigilance and chronic somnolence. In the United States, statewide studies are uncovering the endemic somnolence that underlies automobile and commercial vehicle accidents, and the pervasive sleep deprivation that undermines shift workers, people who work an excessive number of hours, and, in general, individuals who do not follow a proper sleep hygiene. Prevention, education, and research are the future frontiers of the sleep center.

References

1. The Aphorisms of Hippocrates (special ed). Birmingham, AL: The Classics of Medicine Library, Division of Gryphon Editions Ltd., 1982.

2. Freud S. The Interpretation of Dreams (special ed). Birmingham, AL: The Classics of Medicine Library, Division of Gryphon Editions Ltd., 1982.
3. Goodale MA. Active minds, sleeping bodies. Lancet 1994;344:1036.
4. Junger SS, Schwartz DB. Talmudic classification of sleep. Neurology 1990;40:Cl231.
5. Hippocrates. Aphorisms: Section II:3. Birmingham, AL: The Classics of Medicine Library, Division of Gryphon Editions Ltd., 1982.
6. The Canon of Medicine of Avicenna (special ed). Birmingham, AL: The Classics of Medicine Library, Division of Gryphon Editions Ltd., 1984.
7. Gélineau JBE. De la narcolepsie. Gaz Hôp 1880;53:626.
8. Tello F. Sobre la existencia de neurofibrillas colosales en las neuronas de los reptiles. Trab Lab Invest Biol 1903.
9. Cajal SR. Variaciones morfológicas normales y patológicas del retículo fibrilar. Trab Lab Invest Biol 1904; tomo III.
10. Von Economo. Sleep as a problem of localization. J Nerv Ment Dis 1930;71:249.
11. Lafora GR. La Fisiología y Patología del Sueño. Academia Nacional de Medicina. Madrid: Talleres Espasa-Calpe, 1933.
12. Berger H. Ueber das Elektroenkephalogramm des Menschen. J Psychol Neurol 1930;40:160.
13. Loomis A, Harvey E, Hobart G. Cerebral states during sleep as studied by human brain potentials. J Exp Psychol 1937;21:127.
14. Moruzzi G, Magoun HW. Brain stem reticular formation and activation of the EEG. Electroencephalogr Clin Neurophysiol 1949;1:455.
15. de Toni G. I movimenti pendolari dei bulbi oculari dei bambini durante il sonno fisiologico, e in alcuni stati morbosi. Pediatria 1933; 41:489.
16. Dement WC. Personal history of sleep disorders medicine. J Clin Neurophysiol 1990;7:17.
17. Dement WC, Kleitman N. Cyclic variations in EEG during sleep and their relation to eye movements, body motility and dreaming. Electroencephalogr Clin Neurophysiol 1957;9:673.
18. Dement WC. The occurrence of low-voltage, fast electroencephalogram patterns during behavioral sleep in the cat. Electroencephalogr Clin Neurophysiol 1958;10:291.
19. Jouvet M, Michel F, Courjon J. Sur un stade d'activité électrique cérébrale rapide au cours du sommeil physiologique. Compt Rend Seanc Soc Biol 1959;153:1024.
20. Jouvet M. Recherches sur les structures nerveuses et les mécanismes responsables des differentes phases du sommeil physiologique. Arch Ital Biol 1962;100:125.
21. Rechtschaffen A, Kales A. A Manual of Standardized Terminology, Techniques and Scoring System for Sleep Stages of Human Subjects. Los Angeles: Brain Information Service, 1968.
22. Yoss RE, Daly DD. Treatment of narcolepsy with Ritalin. Neurology 1959;9:171.
23. Rechtschaffen A, Wolpert E, Dement W, et al. Nocturnal sleep of narcoleptics. Electroencephalogr Clin Neurophysiol 1963;15:599.

24. Gastaut H, Tassinari C, Duron B. Etude polygraphique des manifestations episodiques (hypniques et respiratoires) du syndrome de Pickwick. Rev Neurol 1965;112:568.
25. Jung R, Kuhlo W. Neurophysiological studies of abnormal night sleep and the pickwickian syndrome. Prog Brain Res 1965;18:140.
26. Lugaresi E, Coccagna G, Mantovani M. Hypersomnia with Periodic Apneas. New York: Spectrum, 1978.
27. Certification Committee. Certification Standards and Guidelines for Sleep Disorders Centers. Association of Sleep Disorders Centers (ASDC), 1978.
28. Association of Sleep Disorders Centers (ASDC). Diagnostic classification of sleep and arousal disorders. Sleep 1979;2:1.
29. Fujita S, Conway W, Zorick F, et al. Surgical correction of anatomic abnormalities in obstructive sleep apnea syndrome: Uvulopalatopharyngoplasty. Otolaryngol Head Neck Surg 1981;89:923.
30. Sullivan CE, Issa FG, Berthon-Jones M, et al. Reversal of obstructive sleep apnea by continuous positive airway pressure applied through the nares. Lancet 1981;1:862.
31. American Sleep Disorders Association, 1610 14th Street N.W., Suite 300, Rochester, MN 55901-2200.
32. APSS Annual Meeting Office, 1610 14th Street N.W., Suite 300, Rochester, MN 55901-2200.
33. American Board of Sleep Medicine, 1610 14th Street N.W., Suite 300, Rochester, MN 55901-2200.
34. Board of Registered Polysomnographic Technologists, 1610 14th Street N.W., Suite 300, Rochester, MN 55901-2200.
35. Sleep. 1610 14th Street N.W., Suite 300, Rochester, MN 55901-2200.
36. ASDA News. 1610 14th Street N.W., Suite 300, Rochester, MN 55901-2200.
37. American Electroencephalographic Society. Guidelines for the Polygraphic Assessment of Sleep Related Disorders (Polysomnography). Bloomfield, CT: American Electroencephalographic Society, 1991.

2

The Biology of Sleep

I shall furthermore endeavor to explain the processes which give rise to the strangeness and obscurity of the dream, and to discover through them the nature of the psychic forces which operate, whether in combination or in opposition, to produce the dream. This accomplished, my investigation will terminate, as it will have reached the point where the problem of the dream meets with broader problems, the solution of which must be attempted through other material.

Sigmund Freud, *The Interpretation of Dreams* [1]

Functional Neuroanatomy and Neurophysiology of Sleep

As a function of the brain, sleep is based on neuroanatomic structures, and as is the case for other brain functions, sleep is orchestrated to produce highly predictable, well-organized electrophysiologic patterns that form the basis of behavioral sleep. The neural centers that intervene in the production and regulation of sleep are located in the brain stem, diencephalon, and thalamus, with ample secondary expression in the cortex of the cerebral hemispheres. Hormones, neurotransmitters, and active peptides exert a strong modulating influence over the neuroanatomic substrates that generate sleep, and in turn modify the physiology of most body organs.

Wakefulness and sleep compete for the domain of brain activity. The cyclic alternations of waking and sleep are controlled by neuronal mechanisms contained in the brain stem, hypothalamus, and basal forebrain, with relay nuclei in the thalamus and terminals in the cortex. Sleep is further subdivided in two distinct states, non–rapid eye movement (non-REM) and rapid eye movement (REM) sleep, each with anatomic, electrophysiologic, and behavioral characteristics that are distinct enough to render their study separate.

Wakefulness

People who are awake are aware of themselves and of the environment. Incoming stimuli are acknowledged, processed, and responded to. People who are asleep are not aware and hence incapable of consciously processing stimuli coming from external or internal sources. However, unlike an individual in a state of coma, a sleeping person can be awakened and restored to a state of full responsiveness.

Neurons involved in promoting wakefulness constitute a linked system located in the reticular formation of the brain stem (ventral medullary, central pontine, and midbrain reticular formation), posterior hypothalamus, and basal forebrain (nucleus basalis of Meynert or substantia innominata, nucleus of diagonal band, and septal nucleus, subthalamus, and reticular nuclei of the thalamus (ventromedial, intralaminar, and midline thalamic nuclei). Wakefulness is maintained by tonic activity in the reticular activating system reinforced via collaterals by sensory input. The most powerful influences are acoustic and painful stimuli. Reticular system activation ascends via the brain stem reticular formation into the nonspecific thalamic system from which it is transmitted to the cortex of the forebrain (Figure 2-1). An alternate extrathalamic route originates in the subthalamus, posterior hypothalamus, and basal forebrain from where it projects to the entire cortical mantle [2].

The electrophysiologic expression of wakefulness is desynchronization of cortical electrical activity manifested in the electroencephalogram (EEG) by predominantly low-amplitude, fast, intermixed waveforms. Desynchronization of EEG rhythms is also observed in REM sleep. Both waking and REM sleep are activated states in which neuronal networks are ready to receive afferent information. In wakefulness, afferent stimuli come from the exterior, whereas in REM sleep, afferent input is generated within the nervous system.

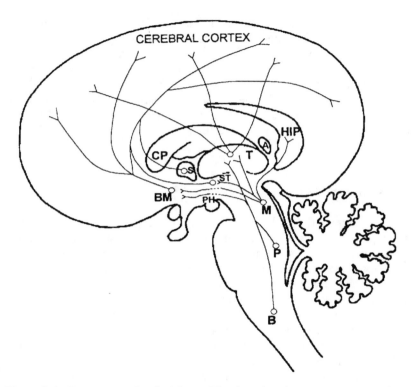

Figure 2-1. Generators of wakefulness. The dorsal pathway originates in the brain stem and reaches the cortex via the thalamus. An alternate extrathalamic ventral route originates in the subthalamus, posterior hypothalamus, and basal forebrain (nucleus basalis of Meynert, septal nuclei, and diagonal band) from where it projects to the entire cortical mantle. (B = medulla; P = pons; M = midbrain; PH = posterior hypothalamus; BM = nucleus basalis of Meynert; T = thalamus; S = septal nuclei; CP = caudate, putamen; ST = subthalamus; A = amygdala; HIP = hippocampus.)

There is overlap between the autonomic nervous system and systems generating wakefulness. Stimulation of the posterior hypothalamus and midbrain reticular formation simulates sympathetic activation with increases in blood pressure and heart rate, along with pupillary mydriasis plus behavioral and EEG signs of arousal.

Tonically active catecholamine- and acetylcholine-containing neurons modulate the activity of subcortical and cortical neurons during wakefulness. Wakefulness is also enhanced by histamine-containing neurons of the posterior hypothalamus and by other neurons containing certain neuropeptides (substance P, corticotropin-releasing factor [CRF], thyrotropin-releasing factor [TRF], and vasoactive intestinal peptide [VIP]). Glutamate-containing neurons located in the brain stem, thalamus, and cortex are excitatory and contribute to wakefulness.

Chemical substances borne by the cerebrospinal fluid (CSF) such as substance P, CRF, TRF, and VIP facilitate wakefulness. Blood-borne chemicals including epinephrine, histamine, and glucocorticoids can enhance wakefulness.

Synchronized Sleep

Sleep occurs as the wakefulness-maintaining mechanism wanes and sleep-promoting neurons become active. Light transitional sleep leading to synchronized sleep normally follows wakefulness. Synchronized sleep expresses the unified activity of many neuronal networks and is characterized by an EEG that shows high-voltage K complexes, sleep spindles, and in deep sleep, high-voltage slow waves. Neurons involved in the generation of synchronized sleep are found in the solitary tract nucleus of the medulla, raphe nuclei of the brain stem, reticular thalamic nuclei, anterior hypothalamus, preoptic area, basal forebrain, and orbitofrontal cortex (Figure 2-2).

Suppression of activity in the reticular arousal system releases the synchronous spindle oscillations of the thalamus. Sleep spindles are characterized by waxing and waning waveforms with a frequency of 7–14 Hz and a duration of 1–2 seconds. They are associated with the blockade of synaptic transmission of afferent impulses through the thalamus in parallel with loss of consciousness. The reticular nucleus of the thalamus is the synchronizing pacemaker of EEG spindle oscillations (Figure 2-3) [3]. This nucleus forms a neuronal sheet that covers the rostral, lateral, and ventral surfaces of the thalamus. Bursts of activity in the thalamocortical networks generate potentials and spike discharges within the spindle frequency in target neocortical neurons that can be recorded with the surface EEG. This neuronal system is GABAergic. Brain stem reticular cholinergic activation has a dampening effect on sleep spindle generation, and thus sleep spindles are erased during activation of the cholinergic system that is associated with desynchronized REM sleep and wakefulness. The functional significance of sleep spindles is unknown; an increase has been associated with pathologic hypersomnia [4].

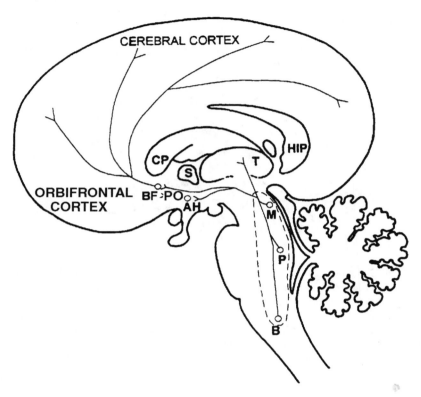

Figure 2-2. Generators of slow wave sleep. Slow wave sleep facilitatory stimuli originate in raphe nuclei that project rostrally to the anterior hypothalamus, thalamus, and basal forebrain nuclei. From these centers projections reach the cortical mantle. (B, P, M = raphe nuclei; B = medulla; P = pons; M = midbrain; AH = anterior hypothalamus; BF = basal forebrain; S = septal nuclei; CP = caudate, putamen; T = thalamus; HIP = hippocampus; PO = preoptic area.)

Serotonin-containing neurons of the brain stem raphe dampen sensory input and inhibit motor activity, promoting the emergence of slow wave cortical activity. The thalamus also plays an important role in the genesis of EEG delta waves. The resonant thalamocortical loop transfers to the cortex action potentials and in turn drives thalamic cells by backward volleys. Note, however, that slow waves persist in athalamic animals, perhaps because of autochthonous generation in cortical layers II, III, and IV [5].

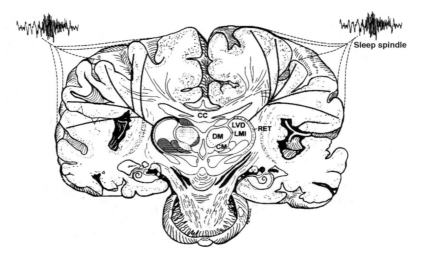

Figure 2-3. Sleep spindle generation. The reticular nucleus of the thalamus is the synchronizing pacemaker of EEG spindle oscillations. This nucleus forms a neuronal sheet that covers the rostral, lateral, and ventral surfaces of the thalamus. Bursts of activity in thalamocortical networks generate potentials and spike discharges within the spindle frequency in target neocortical neurons that can be recorded with surface EEG. (RET = reticular nucleus; CC = corpus callosum; DM = dorsomedial nucleus; LVD = lateral ventral nucleus; CM = centromedian nucleus; LMI = internal medullary lamina.)

Synaptic transmission through the thalamus is obliterated during drowsiness and blocked during synchronized sleep. The thalamus is the first relay station where afferent information is blocked at sleep onset. This blockade prevents the cortex from elaborating a response. However, incoming stimuli that are powerful enough (e.g., loud noise or intense pain) bypass the thalamic blockade, causing cortical arousal. Synaptic transmission through the thalamus is enhanced during wakefulness and in REM sleep.

There is overlap between sleep-generating centers and parasympathetic activity. Stimulation of the anterior hypothalamus and preoptic region elicits decreases in blood pressure and heart rate with pupillary miosis plus behavioral and EEG signs of sleep.

In the early part of the twentieth century, Piéron [6] introduced the concept that hypnogenic substances promote sleep after he observed that CSF extracts removed from sleep-deprived animals promoted sleep when injected into the ventricular system of a normal animal.

Serotonin is contained in cells of the brain stem raphe nuclei (midline rostral and caudal midbrain, pontine and medullary tegmentum, and dorsolateral medulla) that provide diffuse innervation to the brain and spinal cord. Lesions of this system produce insomnia. Serotonin antagonists such as parachlorphenylalanine (PCP, which prevents serotonin synthesis by blocking the enzyme tryptophan hydroxylase) produce severe insomnia that is reversed by the serotonin precursor 5-hydroxytryptamine, which bypasses tryptophan hydroxylase.

Substances found in brain cells such as adenosine, GABA (gamma-aminobutyric acid), opiates, somatostatin, and alpha-melanocyte–stimulating hormone facilitate sleep. Adenosine neurons are located in the hypothalamus, and adenosine receptors are blocked by caffeine and xanthines in general. Benzodiazepines binding with receptors enhance the postsynaptic action of GABA and thus promote sleep. Neurons of the reticular nucleus of the thalamus and neurons of the anterior hypothalamus and basal forebrain are GABAergic.

CSF-borne factors such as the substance proposed by Piéron and opiate peptides including beta-endorphin, enkephalin, and dynorphin have a role in sensory modulation and analgesia that could be important in initiating and maintaining sleep. Somatostatin found in CSF causes analgesia, akinesia, and depression of EEG activity. Other possible modulators of sleep are prostaglandin D_2 and uridine.

Several blood-borne factors that promote sleep have been identified. Insulin produces slow wave sleep when injected intravenously. Cholecystokinin is released in the gut after food ingestion and is called the satiety hormone because it suppresses appetite for food. Bombesin is released after food ingestion and promotes slow wave sleep. Both hormones are responsible for postprandial sleep either by direct action on periventricular brain organs or via vagal afferents to the solitary tract nucleus of the brain stem. Muramyl peptides originate in the gut from internal bacteria and have sleep-inducing properties. Interleukin-1 is stimulated by muramyl peptides and promotes sleep. No single chemical substance with a neurotransmitter, neuromodulator, or neurohormonal role has been identified that is critical or sufficient for the initiation and maintenance of sleep. Instead, it appears that multiple factors and systems are involved.

Desynchronized Sleep

REM sleep, also known as desynchronized, paradoxic, active, and dream sleep, originates in brain stem centers. It is characterized by an apparently unrelated constellation of phenomena that are generated in different areas of the pons and caudal midbrain. No center has been shown to function as the unique neural orchestrater, although according to some authors [7], the lateral portion of the nucleus reticularis pontis oralis, ventral to the nucleus locus ceruleus, is the brain region most critical for the production of REM sleep. As discussed later in this chapter, the purpose of REM sleep remains unknown. However, a correlation between active brain growth, brain development, and complexity of REM sleep has been observed. Fetal sleep is mostly REM, or active sleep, and the percentage of REM sleep observed in infancy (50%) is much higher than in the adult years (25%). Some authors have postulated that REM sleep generation is associated with the consolidation of memories.

Each of the following events occurring in REM sleep are discussed individually: (1) cortical desynchronization, (2) hippocampal synchronization, (3) muscle atonia, (4) ponto-geniculo-occipital (PGO) spikes, (5) rapid eye movements, (6) myoclonia, (7) cardiorespiratory fluctuations, (8) penile erection, (9) dream generation, (10) thermoregulatory suspension, and (11) other miscellaneous phenomena.

1.   Desynchronization of cortical EEG rhythms arise as a result of activation of large nerve cells in the central midbrain reticular formation.

2.   Hippocampal theta rhythms characterized by highly synchronized 4- to 10-Hz theta waves present continuously through the REM stage. Studies with deep electrodes have shown that theta rhythms are generated in the pyramidal cells of CA1 in the dentate gyrus and in the medial entorhinal cortex of the hippocampus. Input comes from the medial septal nucleus and from the nucleus pontis oralis in the brain stem.

3.   Muscle atonia is a pronounced reduction in postural tone sparing the oculomotor muscles and the diaphragm, which persists during REM sleep. Cells in the perilocus ceruleus area, ventral to the nucleus locus ceruleus, become active and stimulate via the tegmentoreticular tract the inhibitory nerve cells of the magnocellular reticular nucleus in the medial medulla (Figure 2-4), probably the same inhibitory area described by Magoun and Rhines [8]. This region is a well-known

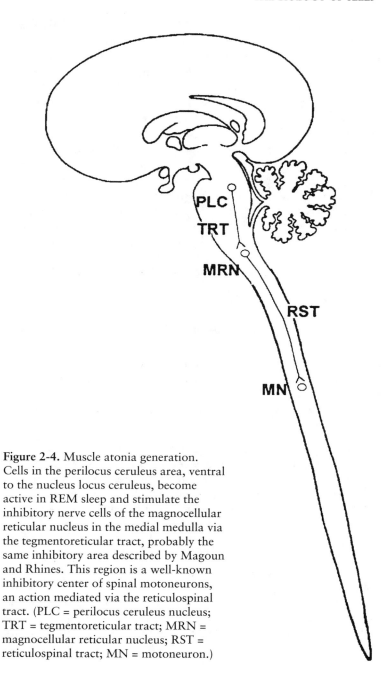

Figure 2-4. Muscle atonia generation. Cells in the perilocus ceruleus area, ventral to the nucleus locus ceruleus, become active in REM sleep and stimulate the inhibitory nerve cells of the magnocellular reticular nucleus in the medial medulla via the tegmentoreticular tract, probably the same inhibitory area described by Magoun and Rhines. This region is a well-known inhibitory center of spinal motoneurons, an action mediated via the reticulospinal tract. (PLC = perilocus ceruleus nucleus; TRT = tegmentoreticular tract; MRN = magnocellular reticular nucleus; RST = reticulospinal tract; MN = motoneuron.)

inhibitory center of spinal motoneurons, an action that is mediated via the reticulospinal tract. Postsynaptic inhibition is the principal mechanism responsible for atonia of the somatic musculature during REM sleep. The network of brain stem nuclei that mediate suppression of muscle tone in REM sleep uses acetylcholine and glutamate as the principal neurotransmitters.

The abolition of muscle atonia during REM sleep has been studied experimentally in the cat [9] and recognized clinically in humans. Bilateral interruption of the tegmentoreticular tract in the pons leads to REM sleep without atonia, a condition that facilitates dream enactment and the release of stereotypical behaviors in the experimental animal and in humans. The reverse condition, atonia without REM sleep, has been provoked experimentally by injecting carbachol, a potent cholinergic substance, in the same region of the dorsal pons that when injured causes REM sleep without atonia. More extensive injections can cause REM sleep. Activation of atonia without REM sleep can underlie the clinical phenomenon of cataplexy. Induction of cataplexy with laughter and other emotions in narcolepsy, and the occurrence of symptomatic cataplexy in individuals with circumscribed lesions of the posterior hypothalamus and midbrain [10] suggest that the REM sleep–muscle atonia system is modulated by supranuclear centers.

Experimentally, it has been shown that medullary stimulation normally producing atonia will paradoxically enhance muscle excitation when blood pressure is lowered as little as 10–20 mm Hg [11], an observation that might be related to the clinical association of Shy-Drager syndrome and REM sleep without atonia.

    4.   Ponto-geniculo-occipital (PGO) spike generation accompanies rapid eye movements and other phasic motor events of REM sleep [12]. PGO spikes originate in the dorsolateral pontine tegmentum bordering the brachium conjunctivum, also known as the peribrachial X area (Figure 2-5), reaching the lateral geniculate nucleus. Each half of the pons functions as an independent generator of PGO spikes, and the pathway for propagation can be interrupted unilaterally by lesions in the rostral pons. PGO spikes can be triggered by cholinergic stimulation in the absence of other REM sleep phenomena. Serotonin inhibits PGO waves, and serotonin depletion, such as produced by PCP, can trigger continuous PGO activity. PGO spikes facilitate rapid eye movements in the waking state and in REM sleep. PGO waves can eventually reach cortical areas and trigger fragmentary imagery that we recognize as dreams.

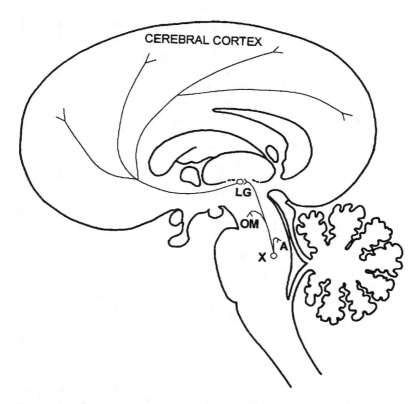

Figure 2-5. Ponto-geniculo-occipital (PGO) spike pathway in REM sleep. PGO spikes originate in the dorsolateral pontine tegmentum bordering the brachium conjunctivum, also known as the peribrachial X area, reaching the lateral geniculate nucleus and cortical areas, where they stimulate fragmentary imagery that we recognize as dreams. (LG = lateral geniculate nucleus; OM = oculomotor nucleus; A = abducens nucleus; X = peribrachial X area.)

    5.   Rapid eye movements are rapid, saccadic, conjugate eye movements in the horizontal, vertical, and oblique planes that represent the phenomenon par excellence of REM stage. Horizontal eye movements originate in the periabducens area of the dorsomedial pons, and vertical eye movements are generated in the midbrain reticular formation. Both appear phasically through REM sleep, at times in conjunction with other phasic motor events. PGO waves precede rapid saccadic eye movements in REM sleep and during waking.

6.   Myoclonia, or muscle twitches, are brief clonic contractions of facial and acral extremity muscles (and of the tail in animals) that appear throughout REM sleep. Inhibition responsible for muscle atonia is the predominant input reaching motoneurons during REM sleep. However, at irregular intervals, for reasons as yet unknown, overpowering breakthrough excitatory potentials reach motoneurons, causing group unit discharges that are manifested by myoclonic jerks and rapid eye movements [13]. Muscle twitches and jerks in humans and in animals predominate in distal segments of the extremities and face, are more evident in flexor muscles, and reach peak intensity during episodes of phasic REM activity. It has been suggested that the reticulospinal tracts are involved in phasic muscle twitches, with the stimulus originating in cells located in the reticular nucleus pontis caudalis and nucleus gigantocellularis [14], areas that project monosynaptically to forelimb and hindlimb motoneurons and the facial nucleus. Myoclonic twitches might represent remnants of heightened motor activity incompletely blocked by spinal inhibition.

7.   Cardiorespiratory fluctuations such as respiratory rhythm increases, heart rate acceleration, and blood pressure variations occur as a result of the phasic activation of centers in the medial and lateral parabrachial nuclei of the pons. These centers exert a modulatory influence over bulbar neurons. Respiratory fluctuations of REM sleep are not dependent on peripheral changes (oxygen saturation, CO_2 content, pH of blood) but instead are controlled directly by neural mechanisms originating in the pneumotaxic centers of the brain stem.

8.   Penile erections occur during REM sleep, from infancy (2–4 months) to senescence, even though most dreams are not sexually oriented. Similarly, female subjects have clitoral erections during REM sleep. The purpose remains unknown, although some have speculated that frequent periodic activation of the complex neurovascular mechanism involved in erections is important for its maintenance. In adolescence, tumescence time equals or surpasses REM sleep duration and occupies more sleep time than at any other age. Electrical stimulation of ventral tegmental points in the midbrain and of ventrolateral sites in the pons have elicited erections in the squirrel monkey [15].

9.   Dream generation has been reported in 85% of subjects awakened from REM sleep. PGO waves that originate in the pontine area travel to lateral geniculate nuclei and forebrain systems, providing exci-

tation of the forebrain (Figure 2-5). Autoradiographic experiments during REM sleep have shown increases in glucose metabolism in the visual cortex. This input might represent the substrate for visual dream experiences.

Sensory system activation during dream experiences always includes the visual system [16]. Auditory experiences appear in 65% of dreams. Spatial experiences such as flying, floating, or sinking, presumably associated with vestibular excitation, are considerably less common, whereas experiences involving perceptions of touch, taste, or smell are rare. Pain is almost never incorporated into dreams.

Motor system excitation during dream mentation generates complex motor commands that are consistent with the dream experience. However, motor commands are not executed because of the powerful inhibition of motoneurons prevalent during REM sleep. Should this neurologic curfew be lifted, complex motor behaviors would result as in the syndrome of REM sleep without atonia. Experimental evidence indicates that cortical and subcortical motor structures that mediate complex organized movements are activated during dream generation [17]. Organized activity in the lower extremities appears in 78% of dreams. The activation-synthesis hypothesis of Hobson and McCarley [18] proposes that (motor ineffectual) nonrandom excitation of brain stem generators of complex motor activity, such as walking or running, incorporates as a corollary subjective experiences elaborated in the forebrain.

10.   Thermoregulatory suspension occurs during REM sleep. Ongoing thermoregulatory responses cease, and the animal enters a poikilothermic state [19]. The major thermoregulatory integrative structures of the central nervous system are the preoptic-anterior hypothalamic nuclei. The dominant feedback signal to these structures is the local hypothalamic temperature. Cutaneous vasodilation and thermal polypnea, which are normal responses to hypothalamic heating, are absent or weak and unstable during REM sleep. The origin of thermoafferent impulses to hypothalamic structures remains conjectural, although there is evidence that midbrain and pontine electrical stimulation affect preoptic-anterior hypothalamic function. Humans do not display physiologic patterns indicative of complete cessation of thermoregulation as observed in nonhuman mammals. Nonetheless, there is evidence in humans of two separate processes of temperature regulation linked with non-REM and REM sleep.

11.   Other phenomena occur during REM sleep. Cerebral blood flow, flow velocities [20], and metabolism increase; waves of increased intracranial pressure occur; cardiac output decreases; urine volume decreases; phasic changes in parasympathetic output appear; sympathetic tone is lost; and sweating decreases or disappears. The arousal threshold is highest in REM sleep.

Integrated Anatomic Overview of Brain Stem Structures Involved in Sleep

Although all sections of the brain stem intervene in maintaining wakefulness and promoting sleep, the integrated anatomic overview reveals a multisegmental core of nuclei important to all states and an aggregate of centers in the pons critical to the development of REM sleep. From brain stem areas, ascending and descending fibers carry the nervous impulses that execute all functions of sleep and maintain wakefulness. Transection at the mesencephalic level causes permanent synchronization of the EEG and a state that resembles behavioral sleep.

The reticular formation is the system that is central to sleep. It is a phylogenetically old part of the brain made up of diffuse aggregates of cells of different sizes traversed by fibers going in all directions [21]. In general, large cells are restricted to the medial part, whereas small cells occupy the lateral regions of the formation. The largest cells are found only at certain levels, such as the nucleus reticularis gigantocellularis of the medulla, and more rostrally, the nucleus reticularis pontis caudalis. Along the brain stem midline, there are congregations of nerve cells collectively known as the raphe nuclei.

Nerve cells of the reticular formation project their axons rostrally and caudally, suggesting a close integration between ascending and descending impulses. Their dendrites spread out in a plane perpendicular to the long axis of the brain stem. The axons pass to the spinal cord from medullary and pontine nuclei in descending bundles known as the reticulospinal tract, and in ascending formations to the thalamus, while ascending and descending tracts reach other nuclei within the brain stem. Ascending fibers originate in the medulla, the lower pons–upper medulla, and the mesencephalon, the latter reaching targets that go beyond the targets of fibers coming from more caudal regions. Medullary and pontine fibers end in nonspecific thalamic nuclei, whereas projections from the mesencephalic formation pass under the thalamus and reach the hypothalamus, preoptic area, and medial septal nucleus.

Afferent connections to the reticular formation come from the spinal cord via the spinoreticular tract and terminate primarily in the nucleus reticularis gigantocellularis of the medulla and in the nuclei reticularis pontis caudalis and oralis. The reticular formation also receives input from cranial nerve nuclei, the cerebellum, lateral hypothalamus, pallidum, superior colliculus, and even sensorimotor cortex.

In general, the executive functions are mediated by nerve cells in the medial two-thirds of the reticular formation, whereas the lateral third works as an association area. There are also differences between levels, some acting preponderantly on the spinal cord and other levels on more rostral parts of the brain.

General Physiology

The function of organs and the homeostasis of body systems shift in sleep to different physiologic equilibriums, with activation of new mechanisms in some instances and modification of the level of activity in others. Each stage of sleep has individual peculiarities, but for practical purposes, it is sufficient to study the physiology in non-REM and REM states.

Respiration

Even the novice is aware that breathing changes during sleep. A parent listening to the baby or a bedmate hearing the partner breathe can identify when the individual falls asleep, and even if deep sleep has taken hold by gauging the depth and frequency of the respirations. The control of breathing is of paramount importance while the animal or human being is asleep and unconscious, and thus unable to introduce voluntary variations. During sleep, there are powerful mechanisms that control ventilation and ultimately awaken the animal or human if an overpowering impediment occurs. The control of breathing is different in non-REM and REM sleep.

The respiratory muscle groups that include the diaphragm, intercostal muscles, and upper respiratory dilator muscles receive appropriate signals from a medullary respiratory center. Three types of stimuli modulate the activity of the medullary center: chemical, chest/lung mechanical, and behavioral. Chemical stimuli arise from chemoreceptors that are responsive to $PaCO_2$, PaO_2, and pH. $PaCO_2$ receptors are located in the carotid body and medulla, responding to increases in $PaCO_2$ by stimulating a hyperventilatory response. PaO_2 receptors located in the carotid body trigger a hyperventilatory response via the glossopharyngeal nerve when the PaO_2 descends below 60 mm Hg. Very low PaO_2 levels depress the respiratory center. Mechanical receptors in the chest wall and lungs respond to inflation and deflation. Signals are transmitted centrally via the vagus nerve, causing shallow and rapid respirations. Behavioral control of breathing is exerted in the awake state and is involved with functions in which air flow is necessary (e.g., speaking, singing, crying, and laughing). Supramedullary signals originating in cerebral centers override chemical stimuli.

Hypoxia and hypercapnia stimulate arousals independently, but when combined, hypoxia increases the sensitivity to arousals caused by PCO_2. Increased airway resistance and occlusions of the airway cause arousals in all stages of sleep, and these arousals are more rapid during REM sleep. Cough is suppressed during sleep and can occur only after an arousal. Laryngeal stimulation during sleep causes reflex apnea that is longer in REM than in non-REM sleep.

Non–Rapid Eye Movement Sleep

In light non-REM sleep, which includes stage 1 and early stage 2, the respirations are dependent on stimuli originating in chemoreceptors responsive to PCO_2 and PaO_2, but the ventilatory response to hypoxia and to hypercapnia is decreased, a phenomenon that is more marked in men. Respirations are irregular, with periodic variations in amplitude, and therefore some authors use the label periodic breathing. The respiratory rate does not change. As age advances, periodic breathing becomes increasingly prominent approaching the pattern of Cheyne–Stokes respiration, with increasing and decreasing amplitudes terminating in a brief apnea. If an arousal occurs, the respiratory rhythm resumes stability and depth, revealing the change in the level of vigilance. The wakefulness stimulus [22] is of primordial importance in sustaining breathing through changes in chemical stimulation and when obstructions to respiration occur in sleep. There is no satisfactory explanation for periodic breathing during light non-REM sleep. It has been proposed that as the individual falls asleep and hypoventilation with hypoxia progresses, a higher sleep-dependent tolerance (gain set level) to CO_2 permits a relative increase in PCO_2 that triggers over-breathing should the individual be awakened. Hyperventilation can eliminate enough CO_2 to trigger a posthyperventilation apnea that eventually signals the resumption of respirations through a hypoxic stimulus. Hypoxia and hypercapnia are arousal stimuli contributing early on to respiratory and sleep-wake instability. Sighs are deep ventilations that occur more frequently during light non-REM sleep, sometimes associated with arousals. Their function is unknown, although the very nature of their depth suggests that they assist in maintaining ventilatory balance during irregular or shallow respirations.

For reasons that remain obscure, respiratory stability is achieved as stage 2 deepens. Breathing becomes regular, in amplitude and frequency, resulting in decreased minute ventilation, which can be the consequence of a decrease in respiratory rate and in tidal volume. Overall, ventilation is lower during non-REM sleep, and this relation continues as non-REM sleep progresses to deeper stages. Electromyographic (EMG) activity increases in intercostal muscles as the ventilatory rate decreases, suggesting increased upper airway resistance that reflects a partial impediment to air flow. Studies have shown that in some individuals, the upper airway resistance (measured behind the palate) during non-REM sleep, can be twice that of (up to 20 cm H_2O) waking levels [23]. Detailed studies of pharyngeal EMG activity during light non-REM sleep have shown a decrease in activity in dilator muscles that likely contributes, if not determines, the upper airway resistance encountered in this stage. During non-REM sleep, the metabolic rate decreases approximately 20%, and alveolar ventilation decreases. In consequence, arterial PCO_2 increases and saturation of oxygen decreases slightly.

Rapid Eye Movement Sleep

Since the discovery of REM sleep, it has been known that respirations become not only faster but also irregular with changes in amplitude and rate. During phasic REM, as the eyes shift rapidly, respirations cease for brief periods of time or become shallow. The irregularity persists through hypoxia, hypercapnia, and metabolic alkalosis, suggesting a strong neural influence. As in non-REM sleep, there is an overall decrease in ventilation and in responsiveness to chemical stimuli, with minute ventilation being the lowest during phasic REM. During REM sleep, muscle atonia reduces the activity of intercostal muscles without affecting diaphragmatic muscle tone, which can even be increased to compensate for the intercostal loss. Upper airway resistance is also higher during REM sleep [24], contributing to a decreased efficiency of the ventilatory effort that results in mild hypoxemia.

In pregnancy, progesterone stimulates respirations, whereas hypopneas and apneas are less frequent. Contrary to all expectations, there is no hypoxemia in sleep. Drugs that depress central nervous system function, notably benzodiazepines and alcohol, have a dampening effect on respiratory drive and protective arousals during all phases of sleep, while decreasing further pharyngeal dilator muscle activity. This decrease results in shallower respirations, increased ventilatory instability, and increased upper airway resistance. In consequence, snoring increases, the apnea-hypopnea index increases, and hypoxemia and hypercapnia tend to augment.

Cardiovascular System

Profound changes in cardiovascular activity during non-REM and REM sleep are tied to changes in autonomic outflow. Sympathetic activity decreases during non-REM and REM sleep, whereas parasympathetic activity increases during non-REM sleep. In REM sleep, there is variability in autonomic outflow, with phasic oscillations of parasympathetic activity against a background of low sympathetic activity.

Non–Rapid Eye Movement Sleep

Blood pressure decreases as a result of decreases in cardiac output and peripheral vascular resistance. Heart rate tends to decrease also, with some individual variability. These changes are consistent with the decreased metabolic rate and downward regulation of body temperature observed in non-REM sleep. Cerebral blood flow is decreased in non-REM sleep, with regional changes ranging from 3–12% relative to the waking state [25].

Rapid Eye Movement Sleep

Systemic arterial blood pressure in REM sleep is lower than in the waking state but higher relative to the pressure during non-REM sleep, with transient increases as high as 40 mm Hg that are at times independent of the conventional cardiovascular variables of heart rate, cardiac output, and stroke volume [26]. This change suggests a direct neural influence during REM sleep that is supported by the cutaneous vasoconstriction observed during bursts of eye movement.

The blood pressure variability with brief increases might be the result of central changes in neural outflow in association with phasic bursts of REM activity and myoclonic twitches. Heart rate is also variable, with a tendency to increase. Cerebral blood flow is increased, with phasic increases occurring in association with bursts of rapid eye movements; this increase is accompanied by significant increases in intracranial pressure, appearing as pressure waves. Experiments in cats have shown hindlimb skeletal muscle vasoconstriction that might be dependent on central mechanisms, supporting the concept of a strong central neural influence prevailing during REM sleep. Reduced blood flow to muscle is also tied to the metabolic decrease imposed by atonia; both central and peripheral mechanisms might play a role in this phenomenon.

Digestive System

The alimentary tract also participates in the widespread changes of function that occur during sleep. Some pathologic conditions might be related to alterations that are intrinsic to sleep. For instance, gastric acid secretion shows circadian oscillations that reach a peak between 10 P.M. and 2 A.M. During the entire 24-hour cycle, individuals with a duodenal ulcer can have enhanced gastric acid secretion that can be increased as much as 20 times during sleep [27]. Vagal control is important for circadian variation, a notion supported by the fact that vagotomy suppresses circadian oscillations. There is some evidence that gastric emptying is retarded during sleep, but it is not clear whether this delay is part of an overall circadian design or a phenomenon idiosyncratic to sleep.

Salivary flow, swallowing—primarily a volitional process—and esophageal motility decrease during sleep. The presence of acid in the distal esophagus normally triggers an arousal response followed by swallowing, which initiates the process of acid clearance. When the arousal response fails to occur, swallowing is not stimulated and acid clearance is delayed, leading to esophageal reflux and esophagitis [28].

Waves of intestinal motility occur periodically during the 24-hour cycle against a background of intestinal tonic motor activity. There is some evidence that these periodic contractions decrease during sleep and can be modified by a late evening meal. Some disorders tend to enhance the contrast in motility between sleep and wakefulness. Patients with irritable bowel syndrome exhibit many more intestinal symptoms during the day with a respite at night [29].

The effects of intestinal activity on sleep have been investigated since the provocative studies of Alvarez [30] showed that distention of the jejunum with an inflated balloon caused sleepiness in human subjects. Others have induced prolonged cortical synchronization in the cat by mechanical and electrical stimulation of the intestine [31]. These observations support the notion of a hypnogenic effect originating in the intestine and consistent with the assertion that postprandial sleepiness is a genuine physiologic phenomenon. Human studies have shown individual variations, but social customs (e.g., an afternoon siesta) strongly suggest, and indirect evidence in drivers confirms, the presence of postprandial sleepiness that at times overpowers the individual's ability to stay awake and continue functioning. Increased colonic motility and decreased external anal sphincter tone during REM sleep reduce continence and can facilitate the passage of gases.

Renal System

The glomerular filtration rate and the excretion of electrolytes are reduced in sleep, with the maximum reduction occurring during REM sleep. The decrease is partly the consequence of several secretory pulses of antidiuretic hormone not linked to any specific stage. Tonic decrease in sympathetic activity can help explain the REM sleep-related reduction of urinary excretion. Hormonal changes such as increased aldosterone and parathyroid hormone secretion might modulate the decreased excretion of sodium, chloride, potassium, and calcium observed in sleep.

Thermoregulation

Temperature regulation by the hypothalamus is driven by circadian rhythms that exhibit powerful interactions with sleep. The lowest body temperatures are achieved during the early morning hours (Figure 2-6), whereas thermoregulation is nearly suspended during REM sleep. In turn, ambient and body temperatures affect sleep architecture. These phenomena indicate that there is a continuous exchange of influences between the basal circadian rhythm, sleep, and ambient-induced temperature regulation.

Body temperature is regulated at a lower level during non-REM sleep concurrently with prospective circadian changes. Conservation of energy during non-REM sleep, when motor activity is low and hypometabolism dominates, is obviously best achieved by setting the body ther-

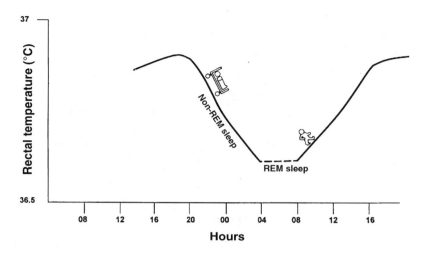

Figure 2-6. Twenty-four-hour core body temperature curve. Conventional time to go to bed coincides with the time when core body temperature begins to decline. Individuals remain asleep through the entire period of low and declining temperature and tend to get up when the body temperature begins to increase. The lowest body temperatures are achieved during the early morning hours, whereas thermoregulation is inhibited during REM sleep.

mostat at a lower level, a notion that retains teleologic sense. In fact, hibernation, which is clearly designed to conserve energy while the coldest months are bridged, might be a corollary phenomenon of non-REM sleep. However, the primordial function of non-REM sleep is probably beyond the control of temperature and energy conservation. That function remains to be uncovered. Shivering occurs during light non-REM sleep if the ambient temperature is excessively cool. The perspiration rate is higher during deep than during light non-REM sleep and lowest during REM sleep.

In REM sleep, there is inhibition of thermoregulatory mechanisms, a state similar to that of poikilothermia. The perspiration rate is decreased, but increases can be observed during phasic REM events. Shivering is abolished, perhaps because of widespread muscle atonia. Low ambient temperatures tend to decrease body temperature, and the opposite effect is observed in higher ambient environments during REM sleep. These observations support the premise that thermoregulatory mechanisms are virtually lost during REM sleep [32].

Ambient temperatures influence REM sleep. Experiments in rats have shown that the duration of REM sleep peaks at an ambient temperature of 29°C and decreases at higher and lower temperatures. Studies in humans have also shown that maximum amounts of REM and non-REM sleep are achieved at the ambient temperature of 29°C, decreasing when the temperature deviates in either direction. At excessively high and low temperatures, there is significant fragmentation of sleep.

Fever has specific effects on sleep, causing pronounced reductions of stage 4 and REM sleep, and compensatory increases of wakefulness and stage 1 [33]. Aspirin reduces stage 4 in healthy subjects, perhaps through a reduction of body temperature. It is interesting to note that some drugs can influence sleep through their effect on body temperature.

The core body temperature in humans is strongly dependent on circadian periodicity, which in turn powerfully influences sleep onset and continuity. The temperature rhythm can become uncoupled from the sleep-wake cycle in free-running environments. This concept has helped researchers study and better understand the influence of core body temperature on sleep. Conventionally, individuals go to bed at the time that their core body temperature begins to decline [34] and remain asleep throughout the entire period of low and declining temperature. Most individuals get up at the time that their body temperature begins to increase. In free-running subjects, sleep duration is longest when sleep is initiated during the peak of body temperature and is shortest when individuals go to sleep at a time that coincides with the temperature trough. REM sleep is also influenced by body temperature. When individuals go to bed during the postpeak temperature segment, the habitual timing, most REM sleep occurs during the second half of the sleep period, whereas if they go to sleep during the trough, REM sleep tends to shift toward the first half.

Sleep Architecture

The delicate neurobiological process that takes hold of the brain during sleep follows a predetermined pattern of well-organized sequential stages and cycles known as the architecture of sleep (Figure 2-7).

Sleep Stages

As wakefulness fades, posterior alpha activity disappears and slow activity in the theta (4–7 Hz) and delta ranges (2–3 Hz) of relatively

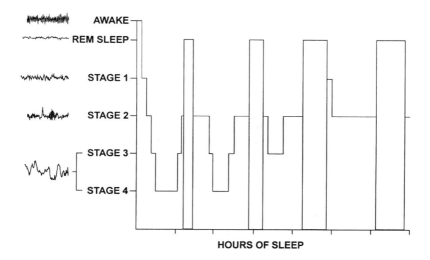

Figure 2-7. Sleep architecture. The organized temporal sequence of sleep stages produces a graphic display that has been compared to an architectural profile, thus the name *architecture of sleep*. Electrographic traces of each stage of sleep are represented to the left of the figure.

low voltage emerges in a temporal and central location intermixed with occasional vertex waves [35]. This period is stage 1, a form of light sleep that lasts only a few minutes and can recur briefly during the night in the transitions from wakefulness to other sleep stages or after brief body movements. Slow eye movements are recognized during stage 1 and tonic EMG levels are present but are below the levels of the waking state.

Stage 2, which follows, is recognized by the development of an increasing number of symmetric high-voltage vertex waves with a negative and positive sharp component (K complex) that can be associated with sleep spindles. These waves are waxing and waning events of fast activity in the 12- to 14-Hz range, lasting at least 0.5 seconds and occurring maximally in a vertex location. K complexes can occur spontaneously or in response to sudden stimuli such as a loud noise. At times, they are even associated with a sudden extremity jerk (hypnic jerk). After 15–30 minutes in stage 2, high-voltage waves (> 75 mV) in the delta range (< 2 Hz) gradually appear in a quasisymmet-

Sleep tends to occur in the late evening when the lights are dim and the core body temperature begins to decline. During sleep, most hormones show important individual patterns of secretion that modify the homeostasis of body systems. Two distinct states of being dominate brain activity during sleep: non-REM sleep associated with quiescence, repose, low body temperature, and hypometabolism; and REM sleep, a state of neural instability and high cerebral activity that recurs at 90-minute intervals and dominates the second half of the night. Uncoupling of these two states from each other and from other circadian rhythms normally linked to them leads to poorly understood pathology that reduces the quality of the awake and sleep states.

Ontogeny of Sleep

Sleep, being a cerebral function, is subject to a maturation and evolution similar to that of other cerebral functions. Predictable changes in sleep architecture parallel the epochs of growth, maturation, and decline of the brain in the life of the individual. In infancy, sleep is divided into two alternating phases: active and quiescent [36]. During active sleep, slow eye movements can be observed under closed lids along with muscular contractions, frowns, facial grimaces, sucking efforts, and writhing movements of hands and fingers. Vocalizations including grunts, whimpers, and cries are also noted. Penile erections can be observed very early in life during active sleep. Muscle tone is reduced when the infant is not moving, the electro-oculogram detects bursts of rapid eye movements, and the EEG shows a low-voltage, intermixed pattern that manifests a state equivalent to the adult REM stage.

The quiescent phase is characterized by scarcity of body movements, regularity of physiologic activity, presence of muscle tone in the EMG channel, and slow EEG waveforms. Respirations are regular, and eye movements do not occur. Indeterminate sleep refers to epochs when the polysomnogram does not meet any of the previously mentioned criteria. Such epochs can appear at sleep onset, at stage transitions, and on slow arousal. Abnormal sleep in infants with cerebral pathology might include increased amounts of indeterminate sleep that persist in later months and even years.

In the 30-week-old fetus, 80% of sleep is active sleep, dropping after birth to 50% of the 16–18 hours per 24 hours that the newborn sleeps. Sleep is not consolidated to the nocturnal period in the first weeks of life, but is broken up in approximately 4-hour segments that recur quasiperiodically as the day progresses, a phenomenon well known by nursing mothers.

Infants exhibit REM sleep at sleep onset, an event that is considered abnormal in the adult. Non-REM sleep is poorly developed because the EEG parameters that define it are not observable in the newborn. Vertex waves, K complexes, sleep spindles, and high-amplitude slow waves are not present until the age of 3 months, so that before that age it is not possible to score sleep using adult polysomnographic criteria.

As the weeks progress, quiet sleep increases in duration, active sleep loses vigor, and the total duration of sleep decreases relative to the 24-hour period. At 3–4 months of age, sleep tends to consolidate to the nocturnal period [37], although some large segments of sleep persist during daytime hours. Sleep spindles, K complexes, and high-amplitude slow waves appear and are increasingly better defined, translating the maturation of thalamoneocortical connections and structures.

The brain stem, where REM sleep is generated, develops earlier than the cerebral hemispheres. The optimal expression of slow wave sleep, with abundant high-amplitude slow wave activity, starts at 3–4 months of age and is the consequence of the development of synaptic precision in neocortical telencephalic structures [38].

At 1 year of age, the baby sleeps 12–13 hours, primarily at night, with one or two long naps during the day. Well-defined non-REM sleep alternates with REM sleep, which constitutes 30% of total sleep time in recurring cycles very similar to those of the adult. At 2 years of age, the proportion of REM sleep becomes fixed at approximately 23% of nocturnal sleep time and will remain at that proportion until very old age, despite a gradual reduction in total sleep that is experienced with advancing age.

Non-REM slow wave sleep acquires its maximal expression in duration and depth during the first decade of life, coinciding with telencephalic maturation. It is difficult to awaken a child from the first cycle of deep sleep. During the second decade of life, slow wave sleep decreases by approximately 40%, continuing its gradual descent until old age, when it is common to observe scarce or no deep sleep of stage 4, particularly in men. During deep non-REM sleep, growth hormone is secreted in large amounts at any age to assist in growth and maturation of tissues. Deprivation of deep sleep interferes with proper secretion of growth hormone and ultimately with corporal growth, a phenomenon that has immediate clinical correlation; children who fail to sleep well might not attain optimal growth.

The elderly and very elderly person rarely sleeps more than 6 or 7 hours at night. REM sleep is very resistant to age-related changes, maintaining a relation to total sleep that is similar to that observed in earlier decades of life. In the elderly, fragmentation of nocturnal sleep is common because of an increased number of arousals, which leads to more time in bed and a lower sleep efficiency [39].

The line between maturation and degeneration of sleep mechanisms is at times difficult to define, as is the case with other cerebral functions such as memory, motor performance, and sexual drive, to name a few. The changes in sleep architecture observed in the healthy elderly individual are predictable and the expression of an evolutionary pattern dependent on modifications of cerebral structure and function that occur as age advances.

Phylogeny of Sleep

Sleep in Animals

It is intuitively evident that animals exhibit behavioral changes that indicate sleep. The higher the level attained in the phylogenetic scale, the more compelling the evidence for sleep. On the lower tier, it becomes increasingly difficult to label as true sleep those periods of quiescence and repose that are unquestionably evident in fish and even invertebrates. The study of sleep in animals has uncovered cardinal facts of sleep anatomy and physiology that would have remained unattainable otherwise. Were it only for that achievement, the effort expended in the investigation of sleep in animals would have been sufficiently amortized. As facts continue to surface, a global design of sleep as a function of evolution, linked with the increasing complexity of the brain, is beginning to emerge that will perhaps answer the question, why do we sleep? The study of sleep in mammals like the dog, cat, and rat has acquired major scientific interest and is the subject of experimental laboratory work that is defining the neurophysiology of sleep.

Sleep in Mammals

The neurobiology of sleep is better known in cats than in humans. It is safe to say that all mammals sleep, although only 10% of animal species have been studied up to this point. Avians and reptiles sleep, and probably amphibians, fish, insects, and other invertebrates sleep as well. As one descends in the phylogenetic scale, sleep criteria become increasingly blurred. Some animals, for instance the dog, suffer sleep pathology, such as narcolepsy, that is very similar to the human ailment. Others, such as the cat, are unique for the study of the physiology of sleep.

Sleep can be defined according to the behavior displayed and as a function of the EEG record. Principal characteristics in all animals are the prompt reversibility to the waking stage plus the presence of cycles and endogenous periodicity. Sleep behavior is characterized by quiescence and the adoption of defined postures that are typical of each animal. Sleep EEG criteria are dominated by slowing of the cerebral background activity and by the periodic occurrence of paradoxic sleep (PS) or REM sleep linked in a bimodal pattern to non-REM sleep, with variations typical for each species. Based on behavioral and EEG criteria, all mammal species studied to date sleep, although there are significant variations. It is particularly important when studying sleep in animals to maintain prompt reversibility as a fundamental criterion to differentiate this state of being from hibernation, estivation, and coma.

The behavior displayed in sleep differs from one species of mammal to another [40]. Dogs, cats, and other felines lie down and close their eyes to sleep, whereas horses sometimes sleep while standing. Dolphins can sleep while swimming against the current, and sea otters sleep belly-up attached to floats of seaweed. Vampire and other bats sleep upside down hanging from a branch. Some species sleep during the day, and others prefer the night. There are major variations in the shape of the den, haunt, lair, or nest; temperature environment; and spatial location. Overall, sleep is dominated by a common pattern of quiescence, repose, and cognitive reduction.

The EEG tracing helps distinguish non-REM from REM sleep as these states alternate and conform to the basic cyclical unit of mammalian sleep. Non-REM sleep is characterized by the presence of spindles and slow waveforms of high amplitude that vary considerably interspecies. Carnivores, ungulates, and insectivores show a tracing of light non-REM sleep, interspersed with prolonged episodes of wakefulness, as if in continuous lethargy. Perhaps this is the reason that large felines spend so much time behaviorally asleep, sometimes as many as 18 hours of the 24-hour cycle.

PS is characterized by an EEG record of relatively low voltage and mixed frequency similar to the background prevalent in the awake state, and by postural muscle atonia, rapid eye movements, and myoclonia of acral body parts. In some mammals, it is possible to identify PGO spikes (what are dreams made of in animals?), synchronous theta waves of the hippocampus, and suppression of temperature regulation. PS alternates with non-REM sleep at intervals that vary from one species to another, depending on the total amount of sleep. A common trait is the great abundance of PS in the newborn animal (as much as 90% in the cat) and its gradual decline in parallel with the development of the telencephalon, which determines an increase in non-REM sleep.

As a function generated in the brain stem, PS is ontogenically more primitive than synchronized non-REM sleep, which depends on cortical development. Nonetheless, PS is a relatively recent acquisition in the phylogenetic scale. Only mammals—except the primitive monotreme echidna (Australian echidna)—and avians experience PS. The Australian echidna is an egg-laying mammal that is evolutionary closer to reptiles than to eutherian mammals. Since reptiles do not exhibit PS, some authors have hypothesized that perhaps this is why the echidna has failed to acquire it [40], but its absence also suggests that PS developed in mammals after the echidna had emerged in the phylogenetic scale. Because avians have a rudimentary form of PS and presumably developed from dinosaurs and reptiles after the mammal track had diverged, it has been suggested that PS has evolved independently more as a function of the complexity of brain organization than of evolutionary tracks. PS has not been identified in dolphins, which sleep with alternating hemispheres [41]. Some believe that this difference is an evolutionary strategy to allow surface breathing while asleep, but whales and manatees exhibit PS. More research is needed to provide a satisfactory explanation.

The total amount and distribution of sleep in 24 hours varies from 18 hours in the opossum with 5 hours of PS, to 2 hours in the giraffe with only 0.5 hour of PS [40].

Sleep in Avians

There are two types of sleep in avians: quiet sleep and active sleep [42]. In quiet sleep, the EEG shows synchronized slow activity, although not as slow as in mammals, with occasional sleep spindles while the animal is behaviorally immobile. Active sleep is the equivalent of PS. It is characterized by a desynchronized EEG occupying 5–10% of the total sleep tracing. Arousal thresholds are high, eyes are closed, and the head tends to droop, but the presence of muscle atonia is scarce although variable between species. PGO waves do not appear, suggesting absence of dreaming.

Intermediate forms of sleep include peculiar stages such as drowsiness and cataleptic immobility in owls, characterized by open eyes, reduced responsiveness, a slow EEG, and a cataleptic neck that stays in the posture imposed. Other species show gaze wakefulness with partly open eyes; a desynchronized EEG; hypotonia; and slow, phasic eye movements. Alternatively, they can exhibit vigilant sleep, which is a fragmented quiet sleep, sometimes occurring in segments lasting only seconds, that allows quick resumption of sleep after episodes of open-eye scanning. Like dolphins, some birds exhibit great hemispheric independence, sleeping with one hemisphere and alternating sides. The EEG shows a quiet, unilateral sleep pattern probably generated in the thalamus while the contralateral eye is closed.

The postures adopted in sleep are different across species. A common posture is characterized by a bill buried under the scapular feathers (known as "under the wing"). Birds can stand, perch, or even swim while asleep, and perhaps some migrating species are capable of flight while asleep.

Experimental studies in birds have revealed a neurochemical organization that is similar to that of mammals, with cholinergic, catecholaminergic, and serotonergic neurotransmitters playing a critical role. Sleep in birds is modified by the characteristic anatomy of the avian brain, but the overall design observed in mammals is also appreciated in birds. The brain stem, hypothalamus, and thalamus are the centers generating sleep, with neurophysiologic influences reaching all ends of the nervous system. In birds, even more so than in mammals, there is evidence that ecological forces on the nervous system have taken advantage of the enormous plasticity of cerebral functions and have molded the phylogenetic pathway with peculiar variations in behavioral and electrophysiologic sleep patterns that meet the needs and circumstances of each species. Nonetheless, as in mammals, sleep in birds preserves a grand design that matches or is adapted to the relatively advanced evolution and organization of the brain, but still the ultimate function is unknown.

Sleep in Reptiles, Amphibians, Fish, and Insects

As the distance from mammalian species augments, sleep becomes increasingly difficult to define according to criteria used for mammals. Behavioral sleep is present in virtually all forms studied, but electrophysiologic correlates are difficult to record and recognize. Despite the diversity, a common trait has been uncovered in electrophysiologic recordings of nonmammalian species [43]. A high-amplitude spike measuring up to 300 mV and lasting 150 msec is abundant during behavioral sleep in fish, amphibians, and reptiles. This waveform is equivalent to limbic spikes observed in depth recordings of the ventral hippocampus in mammals. The thinness of neocortical layers in nonmammalian species allows the surface expression of this peculiar discharge, which is not observed in surface recordings of sleep in mammals.

Reptiles, in general, and alligators, in particular, show high-voltage spikes during episodes of quiescence and higher arousal thresholds. Sleep can be temperature dependent, with an increasing number of spikes appearing with higher temperatures. Lizards and snakes exhibit behavioral sleep, and spikes are also present. Slow wave activity and PS, such as observed in mammals, have not been convincingly identified. Amphibians, salamanders, and frogs exhibit behavioral sleep and difficult-to-interpret changes in electrophysiologic tracings that show activity that is more similar to lethargy and torpor than sleep.

Intermittent behavioral quiescence and stereotypic postures in fish have been interpreted as the equivalent of sleep. Electrophysiologic recordings during episodes of rest have uncovered some variations in background activity, with a relative increase in spikes in some species of fish. Waveforms suggestive of slow wave sleep or PS have not been detected in fish.

Behavioral quiescence with stereotypic postures such as head tilt and downward posturing of antennae have been identified in bees, wasps, flies, butterflies, and moths. Arousal thresholds are increased during rest. The reduced volume of the brain in insects and arachnids precludes, for now, electrophysiologic recordings.

Hibernation

Some animals have developed the strategy of hibernation to bridge the winter months and conserve energy when temperatures are extremely cold and food is difficult to find. In such hostile environments, animals retire to a seeming sleep that is characterized by downregulation of body temperature and metabolic rate proportionate to the ambient temperature. Despite a close resemblance between non-REM sleep and hibernation, the restorative function of deep non-REM sleep does not occur during hibernation [44]. During deep hibernation, the preoptic-anterior hypothalamus, which regulates body temperature and metabolic rate, responds only to lower temperatures, indicating that the thermostat set point for temperature regulation has been lowered. Acidosis helps maintain the profound metabolic reduction that prevails, whereas on arousal, hyperventilation contributes to the elimination of

CO_2 as a prerequisite to a return to the euthermic acid-base equilibrium. During hibernation, the animal experiences spontaneous periodic arousals, rewarming to an active temperature, which makes little sense from a pure energy-economic perspective. Why periodic arousals occur is the subject of a great deal of scientific speculation, and the answers are elusive [45]. Although some consider hibernation to be a prolongation or extension of slow wave sleep (SWS), the aroused animal must sleep in a conventional way before entering another period of hibernation. Perhaps eating, eliminating excreta, and conventional sleeping are mandatory functions that need to be accomplished periodically in order to sustain a winter-long hibernation.

Functions of Sleep

We still do not know why humans and animals sleep. It is tempting to advance teleologic explanations of repose and quiescence necessary to restore vital energies and the powers of the body. However, this intuitive rationale fails to accommodate the periodic output and rich variety of high-amplitude brain electrical activity manifesting not repose but a switch to another set of systems that must have a vital purpose, or else " . . . it is the biggest mistake the evolutionary plan has made" [46]. Nonetheless, restoration must be a significant component of the assigned functions, because sleep is preceded by feelings of tiredness and followed by sensations of satisfaction and replenishment. Most neurologic deficits tend to worsen by day's end and appear improved in the morning. Myasthenic fatigability increases and pyramidal motor deficits are more pronounced in the evening, suggesting depletion of neurotransmitter agents, whereas morning foot dystonia in Parkinson's disease hints at replenishment of dopamine stores.

The overview of the ontogeny and phylogeny of sleep provides insights into possible functions of a grand design. REM sleep is linked to a highly organized brain stem such as develops in mammals and to a lesser extent in avians. It is also present in large proportions early in life, implying a function attached to active growth and development of the nervous system. Perhaps the high electrical activity of REM sleep accomplishes a trophic function and is necessary for the rapid growth of the brain in the fetus and newborn. REM sleep is also resistant to changes imposed by age, further supporting the important role in maintenance of nervous system functions. Some authors have hypothesized that REM sleep intervenes in the consolidation of memories. Recent experiments have shown that perceptual skills such as the ones that are learned through repeated practice improve overnight and are disrupted if there is selective interruption of REM sleep [47]. Others believe that the periodic cessation of discharge of locus ceruleus cells occurring in REM sleep is necessary to prevent desensitization of norepinephrine receptors, which would reduce their effectiveness [7]. Any theory of REM sleep function would have to take into account the consequences of REM sleep deprivation and the phenomenon of REM sleep rebound following deprivation.

SWS develops in parallel with the growth and maturation of the telencephalon. Only animals with an advanced neocortex exhibit SWS as we know it in humans in whom the neocortex acquires maximal development. SWS appears in infants during the third or fourth month after birth when neocortical structures and thalamoneocortical connections take shape. In reptiles and other vertebrates with scarce development of the cortical mantle, SWS is undetectable. Instead, sleep is associated with the output of high-amplitude spikes presumably originating in the limbic area, a more primitive structure. Recent experiments in rats have shown that in SWS there is reactivation of hippocampal networks whose synapses had been temporarily modified during the waking experience. Nocturnal replay of memories as expressed by high-voltage synchronized bursts might serve to transfer and eventually consolidate in neocortical structures declarative memories initially stored in the hippocampus, such as the ones involved in learning spatial references [48].

SWS is also related to repose and restitution. During SWS, growth hormone is secreted in large amounts. Animals, as well as perhaps humans, deprived of SWS and, therefore, growth hormone fail to thrive. In later years, SWS tends to decline and even disappear, coinciding with a reduced growth of tissues. It is likely that the low amounts of growth hormone still secreted in conjunction with SWS in the aged person or animal are necessary to promote repair of tissues and delay aging [49]. Any theories of the function of SWS need to consider the important neuroendocrine phenomena associated with it and the effects of its deprivation.

Sleep Deprivation

Many of the early studies used sleep deprivation as the main instrument to investigate the functions of sleep. More recently, sleep deprivation has become the subject of studies targeting the social and labor-related ramifications of insufficient sleep. As a result, a large body of work has accumulated describing the consequences of the acute and chronic loss of sleep in animals and in humans.

Sleep loss can be total, partial, or stage-specific; the immediate manifestation is sleepiness. Over time, the person deprived of total sleep develops a decrease in alertness and performance that is modulated by the circadian rhythm. Mood changes including irritability, fatigue, difficulty in concentration, and disorientation are commonly reported. Short-term memory alterations also occur as a result of decreased attention, concentration lapses, decreased motivation, and general difficulty to encode elements presented to memory. Early manifestations of psychopathology are more pronounced in individuals with a premorbid personality. Illusions, hallucinations, visual misperceptions, and paranoid ideation are thus observed with sleep loss. Subtle neurologic manifestations such as horizontal nystagmus, intermittent slurring of speech, hand tremor, increased deep tendon reflexes, and increased sensitivity to pain have been described following more than 205 hours of sleep deprivation [50]. Under such conditions, the EEG has shown unsustained alpha rhythms [51] and lack of facilitation of alpha activity with eye closure, along with modest increases of intermixed slowing in the theta and delta ranges. Microsleeps have been identified by performance errors associated with episodes of slowing of the EEG.

Some studies have reported increased appetite and eating in humans who are sleep deprived. Minor decreases in body temperature have also been noted. Humans at any age tolerate the loss of sleep better than animals do. Extrapolation of results obtained in rats suggest that a person would have to be totally deprived of sleep for 7 months before death [52], whereas rats die after 11–22 days of continued sleep loss. Severely sleep deprived rats develop clumped fur, skin lesions, and weight loss despite increases in food intake before dying [53]. Humans and rats allowed to sleep recover completely, without lasting signs or manifestations of dysfunction.

Studies of partial sleep loss in humans suggest that the main sleep requirement can be accomplished with 4–5 hours of sleep every 24 hours. Further decrements of sleep accumulated over several weeks begin to erode motor and mental performance. There is a difference between the required amount of sleep, perhaps 4–5 hours, and the desired amount, which in most individuals revolves around 8–9 hours per 24 hours.

Workers in some occupations are at higher risk of developing partial sleep deprivation syndrome. Shift workers, hospital staff, and commercial drivers commonly show signs of sleep deprivation, which

31. Kukorelli T, Juhasz G. Sleep induced by intestinal stimulation in cats. Physiol Behav 1977;19:355.

32. Glotzbach SF, Heller HC. Temperature Regulation. In MH Kryger, T Roth, WC Dement (eds), Principles and Practice of Sleep Medicine (2nd ed). Philadelphia: Saunders, 1994;260.

33. Karakan I, Wolff SM, Williams RL, et al. The effects of fever on sleep and dream patterns. Psychosomatics 1968;9:331.

34. Henana R, Buguet A, Roussel B, et al. Variations in evaporation and body temperature during sleep. J Appl Physiol 1977;42:50.

35. Rechtschaffen A, Kales AA. A Manual of Standardized Terminology, Techniques and Scoring System for Sleep Stages of Human Subjects. Washington, D.C.: U.S. Government Printing Office Public Health Service, 1968.

36. Anders T, Emde R, Parmelee A (eds). A Manual of Standardized Terminology, Techniques and Criteria for Scoring of States of Sleep and Wakefulness in Newborn Infants. Los Angeles: UCLA Brain Information Service, 1971.

37. Pollack CP. Regulation of sleep rate and circadian consolidation of sleep and wakefulness in an infant. Sleep 1994;17:567.

38. Feinberg I. Schizophrenia: Caused by a fault in programmed synaptic elimination during adolescence? J Psychiatr Res 1983;17:319.

39. Hoch CC, Dew MA, Reynolds CF, et al. A longitudinal study of laboratory and diary-based sleep measures in healthy "old old" and "young old" volunteers. Sleep 1994;17:489.

40. Zepelin H. Mammalian Sleep. In MH Kryger, T Roth, WC Dement (eds). Principles and Practice of Sleep Medicine (2nd ed). Philadelphia: Saunders, 1994;69.

41. Mukhametov IM, et al. Interhemispheric asymmetry of the electroencephalographic sleep patterns in dolphins. Brain Res 1977;124:581.

42. Amlaner CJ Jr, Ball NJ. Avian Sleep. In MH Kryger, T Roth, WC Dement (eds), Principles and Practice of Sleep Medicine (2nd ed). Philadelphia: Saunders, 1994;81.

43. Hartse KM. Sleep in Insects and Non-Mammalian Vertebrates. In MH Kryger, T Roth, WC Dement (eds), Principles and Practice of Sleep Medicine. Philadelphia: Saunders, 1994;95.

44. Kilduff TS, Krilowicz B, Milsom WK, et al. Sleep and mammalian hibernation: Homologous adaptations and homologous processes? Sleep 1993;16:372.

45. Lyman CP. The Mystery of Periodic Arousal. In CP Lyman, JS Willis, A Malan, et al (eds), Hibernation and Torpor in Mammals and Birds. New York: Academic, 1982;32.

46. Rechtschaffen A. Cited by Coleman RM. "Why sleep." In RM Coleman (ed), Wide Awake at 3 A.M.: By Choice or by Chance? New York: Freeman, 1986;87.

47. Karni A, Tanne D, Rubenstein BS, et al. Dependence on REM sleep of overnight improvement of a perceptual skill. Science 1994;265:679.

48. Wilson MA, McNaughton BL. Reactivation of hippocampal ensemble memories during sleep. Science 1994;265:676.

49. Culebras A. Thalamic Lesions and the Endocrine System. In C Guilleminault, et al (eds), Fatal Familial Insomnia: Inherited Prion Diseases, Sleep, and the Thalamus. New York: Raven, 1994.
50. Kollar EJ, Namerow N, Pasnau RO, et al. Neurological findings during prolonged sleep deprivation. Neurology 1968;18:836.
51. Naitoh P, Kales A, Kollar EJ, et al. Electroencephalographic activity after prolonged sleep loss. Electroencephalogr Clin Neurophysiol 1969;27:2.
52. Bonnet MH. Sleep Deprivation. In MH Kryger, T Roth, WC Dement (eds), Principles and Practice of Sleep Medicine (2nd ed). Philadelphia: Saunders, 1994;58.
53. Everson CA, Bergmann BM, Rechtschaffen A. Sleep deprivation in the rat, III: Total sleep deprivation. Sleep 1989;12:13.
54. Agnew HWJ, Webb WB, Williams RL. Comparison of stage four and 1-REM sleep deprivation. Percept Mot Skills 1967;24:851.
55. Agnew HWJ, Webb WB, Williams RL. The effects of stage 4 sleep deprivation. Electroencephalogr Clin Neurophysiol 1964;17:68.

3

Cardinal Manifestations, Pathophysiology, and Clinical Evaluation of Sleep Disorders

And finally every medical student should remember that his end is not to be made a chemist or physiologist or anatomist, but to learn how to recognize and treat disease, how to become a practical physician.

Sir William Osler, *The Practical in Medicine* [1]

Patients with sleep disorders usually manifest one or two cardinal symptoms: excessive sleepiness or protracted sleeplessness. Excessive sleepiness is characterized by a tendency to fall asleep, with attempts to fight the inclination to sleep resulting in a decline of vigilance and an uncomfortable struggle when the sleepiness is inopportune. Excessive and inappropriate sleepiness, if persistent, can lead to social decline, scholastic disruption, and decreased quality of job performance. It can even result in accidents and increase the risk of death in situations in which full alertness is critical for survival, such as when driving or operating heavy machinery and equipment. Sleeplessness, or insomnia, is the inability to initiate or maintain during conventional hours sleep of sufficient quality and duration to satisfy the requirements of full daytime vigilance. Patients with sleeplessness might have secondary excessive daytime sleepiness as a preponderant manifestation of their alteration. Excessive sleepiness and insomnia are the axis around which the disorders of sleep and alertness revolve. Independently or in combination, both manifestations color most sleep-related alterations.

The parasomnias are abnormal motor or sensory phenomena occurring during sleep because sleep is there. Each of the parasomnias is characterized by a peculiar event that is motor, sensory, or dream-like in nature, disrupting the quality of sleep, and often leading to complaints of insomnia or excessive sleepiness. However, neither sleepiness nor insomnia is an obligatory accompaniment of the parasomnias.

Patients with sleep disorders do not experience physical pain as a result but have manifestations that are commonly associated with feelings of anguish and mental suffering. The practice of medicine has been built on the need to alleviate pain, explaining in part why sleep alterations devoid of physical suffering have been ignored by conventional medicine for most of its history. With the virtual conquest of pain in modern times, more attention is being diverted to elusive complaints of mental fatigue, global tiredness, decreased motor performance, and chronic misery that typically plague the patient with an advanced sleep-wake disorder. The realization that such complaints are markers of family pathology, as well as poor scholastic and job performance, leading to social decline and even accidents, has brought increasing focus and respectability to their clinical evaluation. Labels of laziness applied to patients with excessive daytime sleepiness are gradually being discarded by physicians who understand sleep disorders. Patients with insomnia are no longer automatically treated with a sleeping pill. Professional attitudes are beginning to prevail in the approach to patients with sleep disorders in the wake of public education and medical sophistication in matters of sleep medicine.

The proliferation of sleep centers and specialists requires that general practitioners become increasingly versed in sleep pathology. Physicians need to learn to refer a patient with a sleep-wake problem to the sleep center and to integrate the diagnostic interpretation of the sleep alteration with the overall condition of the patient. Available treatment modalities require understanding of the pharmacologic side effects of the medicines administered and of their long-term consequences. Tolerance, interaction with other products, and loss of efficacy are common occurrences for medicines given to patients with excessive or insufficient sleep. For all these reasons, medical practitioners should be acquainted with the cardinal manifestations of sleep-wake disorders, their potential interpretation, clinical evaluation, treatment options, and follow-up.

Excessive Daytime Sleepiness

Sleepiness is a normal manifestation of the periodic want for sleep, just as hunger signals the need to eat, and thirst is a bodily claim to drink. Humans ordinarily feel sleepy when it is customary to go to bed, and many experience a transient episode of sleepiness around midday after lunch. Sleepiness is characterized by a tendency to fall asleep and is the unavoidable consequence of the unsatisfied need for sleep. When excessive or inappropriate, sleepiness constitutes a cardinal manifestation of the sleep-wake disorders, whether intrinsic, acquired, or behavioral in nature. Sleepy individuals do actually fall asleep, engage unavoidable naps, and remain asleep for variable periods of time. The term *hypersomnia* should be reserved for situations in which excessive amounts of sleep predominate.

A common accompaniment of sleepiness is the fight to stay awake when falling asleep is inopportune. Individuals experience the uncomfortable sensation of a losing struggle to remain aware and connected with the environment. Fluctuations in the level of alertness occur in response to a variable intent to stay awake. In this transitional period, attention wanes, learning declines, and memory fails to record accurately data from the moment. Reaction time is prolonged, and the individual might fail to respond promptly and accurately to unexpected occurrences. A vacant expression, reduced ocular convergence, droopy eyelids, yawning, eye-rubbing, and intermittent restlessness are signs that betray sleepiness and the inner struggle to stay awake. Electroencephalographic (EEG) signs of sleepiness commonly observed following all-night sleep deprivation consist of increased theta activity in behaviorally awake subjects. Physical activity helps maintain alertness, but tranquil environments with background noise (such as waiting rooms, lecture halls, and theaters) where the individual is occupied by a passive monotonous activity unmask the tendency to sleep. Watching TV, reading the newspaper, and driving a vehicle are common precipitating factors.

As sleepiness persists, some individuals enter a state of automatic behavior where reaction time is decreased, memory is weak and defective, perceptions become distorted, and lapses of attention occur. Under these circumstances, the individual carries on with simple motor tasks such as walking, marching, washing dishes, or driving a car. However, ability is compromised, and unexpected variations can increase the incidence of errors and the risk of accident. Without a notion of the time elapsed, these individuals continue performing the task in a trance; they will have only fragmentary recollection of their acts. Distorted perceptions and erroneous reactions can lead to altered behaviors. During such instances, individuals can drive a car for many miles, take the wrong turn, trespass properties, wander, and even commit delictive acts or criminal deeds. Automatic behavior is common in patients with narcolepsy, advanced sleep apnea syndrome, and severe sleep deprivation.

Prevalence

Sleepiness is pervasive in modern society. It is estimated that up to 5% of individuals complain of being excessively sleepy. A recent survey conducted by the New York State Task Force on Sleepiness/Fatigue and Driving discovered that 2.5% of surveyed drivers very often drove while drowsy, and that 54.6% had driven while drowsy some time during the year preceding the interview [2]. Young adults, elderly people, and shift workers have more complaints of sleepiness than other population subgroups. The causes are different, however (Table 3-1). Commonly, young adults are sleepy because the quantity of their sleep is insufficient as a result of poor sleep hygiene. Elderly people are sleepy because the quality of their sleep is poor, and shift workers are sleepy because of repeated violations of the circadian rhythm. Others can be sleepy for reasons that fall within the realm of pathology, whether primary, as in the intrinsic disorders of sleep, or secondary to a psychiatric, neurologic, or medical condition.

Clinical Forms

The amount of nocturnal sleep that an individual requires to allay daytime sleepiness is the measure of that person's needs on a 24-hour basis. Sleep deprivation, whether total, partial, or chronic, is perhaps the most common source of daytime sleepiness, particularly in young adults who acquire poor sleep habits and exhibit irregular bedtime behaviors. Even

Table 3-1. Causes of Excessive Daytime Sleepiness

Insufficient sleep
Sleep apnea
Narcolepsy
Idiopathic hypersomnia
Periodic limb movements
Irregular sleep-wake schedule
Withdrawal from stimulants
Hypnotics and sedatives
Neuroanatomic lesions
Psychiatric conditions
Kleine-Levin syndrome

modest sleep deprivations of 1 hour nightly will accumulate over time. Individuals who are sleep deprived show normal architecture of nocturnal sleep when allowed to sleep. They also exhibit a tendency to oversleep on weekends. The most compelling demonstration that sleepiness is caused by sleep deprivation is the total eradication of sleepiness when the individual is permitted to sleep sufficiently.

Excessive daytime sleepiness can also be the consequence of sleep of poor quality, commonly a function of fragmentation and discontinuity of sleep caused by awakenings and arousals. Awakenings are defined in the polysomnogram as alerting episodes of more than 30 seconds' duration; they are recorded in memory if they last more than 3 minutes. Awakenings can occur for a variety of internal or external reasons, from idiopathic to an urge to urinate, or in response to a loud noise. Arousals are brief alerting responses lasting less than 30 seconds. They are not recorded in memory, and thus individuals are unaware of their occurrence. Arousals are manifested in the polysomnogram by a brief (1–3 seconds) burst of cortical activity interrupting the continuity of the ongoing stage of sleep. Arousals typically occur at the termination of sleep apnea episodes and in relation to episodes of periodic leg movements. Awakenings can occur dozens of times and arousals hundreds of times during the night, altering the continuity of sleep and its homeostatic value. In consequence, patients with advanced sleep apnea syndrome, or with severe periodic leg movements syndrome typically exhibit excessive daytime sleepiness. Sleep can also be interrupted and rendered of poor quality for other reasons that are studied in the section on insomnia.

Sleepiness, like many other sleep-wake parameters, shows a circadian pattern. Sleepiness manifested by shorter latencies to sleep is more marked with body temperature reductions. Bedtime normally coincides with the initiation of the body temperature downturn and an increase in sleepiness. As the nocturnal period progresses, body temperature continues to decline, and sleepiness becomes increasingly marked, as noted when patients are awakened and allowed to fall asleep again [3]. A modest midday body temperature reduction is also associated with mild sleepiness in most people.

Patients with intrinsic forms of excessive sleepiness are sleepy for reasons as yet unknown. In narcolepsy, sleepiness is persistent and can occur in attacks over which the patient has little control. Short naps satisfy temporarily though partially the pressure to fall asleep, unlike idiopathic hypersomnia in which sleepiness is chronic and never satisfied by sleep. Pathologic sleepiness differs from excessive sleepiness secondary to sleep deprivation or nocturnal fragmentation in that it cannot be eliminated to the patient's satisfaction by sleep, regardless of how prolonged the sleep is. Sleepiness in the morning, following a full night in bed allegedly asleep is suggestive of sleep-wake pathology.

Clinical Significance

In a recent report, 24.7% of drivers admitted having fallen asleep at the wheel sometime in their life [2]. The rate of traffic accidents increases considerably between 1:00 and 7:00 A.M., ironically when road traffic is most scarce but vigilance is at its lowest. A recent study by the National Transportation Safety Board linking 750 to 1,500 annual road deaths to truck drivers falling asleep at the wheel was reported in the national press, with the additional comment that sleepiness is more of a safety problem among commercial drivers than drugs or alcohol [4]. Not surprisingly, job-related accidents are more common during the night shift when alertness is low. Twenty percent of shift workers have fallen asleep on the job, as shown by continuous EEG ambulatory recordings performed at night [5]. Excessive sleepiness can also interfere with the learning process in children and can lead to family pathology in adults.

Physiologic Basis

Sleepiness is a function of the central nervous system, but the neuro-physiologic or neurochemical basis of sleepiness remains unknown. It is unclear whether sleepiness represents a passive response to the reduction of alert mechanisms, indicates the engagement of active neurogenic processes, or expresses the accumulation of sleep-promoting substances. Compelling evidence implicates several neurotransmitters in sleepiness. The hypnotic effect of benzodiazepines and alcohol is probably mediated through facilitation of gamma-aminobutyric acid receptors, the most widespread inhibitory complex in the nervous system. Antihistamines promote sleepiness through blockade of histamine, a neurotransmitter that facilitates the generation of alertness. The adenosine receptor is also inhibitory and possibly intervenes in facilitating sleepiness because the antagonist methylxanthines, which include caffeine and theophylline, are potent stimulants of alertness.

Assessment and Measurement

Excessive sleepiness can be assessed and quantified in various ways. Clinical assessment is initially carried out by the physician during history taking. The clinician should be mindful of several markers of severity. It has been said that one glass of wine leading to uncomfortable sleepiness suggests sleep deprivation. Sleepiness in the morning following an alleged night of sleep indicates failure of reversal by nocturnal sleep, a common manifestation of the intrinsic disorders of sleep, narcolepsy, and idiopathic hypersomnia. Sleepiness that interferes with job performance, social and family activities, or scholastic achievement is another marker of severity that needs management. Sleepiness that the patient associates with occupational or automobile accidents should always be considered serious, requiring urgent attention and immediate counseling pending a full work-up. Chronic severe sleepiness is associated with a relative loss of awareness of sleepiness and inability or unwillingness to struggle to stay awake. Under these circumstances, patients can fall asleep without warning in what have been called sleep attacks.

The differential diagnosis needs to be made with mental fatigue, physical fatigue, lack of attention, loss of motivation, and even depression. Patients are often elusive and not specific with the usage of words. Sleepiness is best identified when it actually leads to sleep, particularly at inopportune times such as occasionally while driving, eating, talking on the phone, talking to others, and when it persistently occurs while reading the paper, watching TV, or attending meetings, shows, and religious services.

Excessive sleepiness can be documented with the Stanford Sleepiness Scale, which is a subjective rating scale of sleepiness [6]. Patients rate their daytime state of alertness every 2 hours using various levels of vigilance: full, high but not at peak, decreased, cannot stay awake, and asleep. The Epworth Sleepiness Scale [7] identifies sleep propensity by asking how likely would the subject be to fall asleep in everyday situations such as watching TV, reading, talking to others, riding as a passenger in a vehicle, or sitting in a vehicle waiting for the traffic light to turn green. The Visual Analogue Scale (VAS) [8] is quick to administer and asks questions about mood and subjective activation. Individuals are asked to view a line representing their range of feeling and mark to the right or left of center their very high or very low point. This scale can inquire about alertness, sleepiness, weariness, fatigue, motivation, and other feelings and perceptions that could be of interest to the physician.

The objective measurement of sleepiness has been standardized with the Multiple Sleep Latency Test (MSLT) [9]. Following nocturnal polysomnographic recording in the sleep laboratory, patients are asked to return to bed at 2-hour intervals during the daytime starting at 8:00 A.M. Four or five segments of sleep are recorded, each segment lasting 20 minutes or less. The objective is to identify the average time it takes to engage stage 1 of sleep, defined by a reduction of 50% or more in alpha activity over 50% or more of the epoch. An average daytime sleep latency of 5 minutes or less indicates excessive sleepiness, whereas a score between 5 and 9 minutes is suggestive but not indicative of excessive sleepiness. The MSLT has the advantage of detecting episodes of daytime REM sleep in patients with narcolepsy, allowing confirmation of this diagnosis.

Insomnia

The inability to initiate or maintain sleep is called insomnia. The condition is not a disease but a symptom of the failure to engage timely, satisfying sleep. The patient unable to fall asleep is commonly troubled by anxiety or develops a state of increasing anguish as precious time is consumed waiting for sleep to occur. The anticipation of a difficult entry into sleep heightens the tension, aggravating the condition. Some patients might have no difficulty falling asleep but 1 or 2 hours later wake up, and from that point on either are unable to continue sleeping or enter a state in which sleep comes and goes at brief intervals, finally driving the patient out of bed. The inability to initiate and the difficulty to maintain sleep can occur independently or, more often, be associated in the same person, disturbing the quality and quantity of nocturnal sleep. Some patients with insomnia report that they sleep better away from home, suggesting neurotic mechanisms underlying their complaint. In general, insomnia occurs against a background of psychopathology that interacts with sleep mechanisms, creating feedback loops of reinforcement that make it difficult to differentiate cause and effect.

Insomnia can take various clinical forms and have multiple causes. Transitional insomnia is a common complaint. Loss of a loved one, financial stress, job-related difficulties, and family pathology are examples of factors that can affect transiently the ability to initiate and maintain sleep. Once the problem is resolved, the insomnia tends to disappear. If the difficulty with sleep persists beyond 3 weeks, the clinician should suspect covert underlying factors and conditioned mechanisms responsible for sleeplessness. A peculiar form of insomnia is characterized by relatively sound sleep during the first part of the night followed by inability to continue sleep. When persistent, early morning awakenings are generally associated with depression. There is yet another group of patients who report that they sleep no longer than 2 or 3 hours per night. However, when tested in the laboratory, their sleep appears relatively well preserved and of good quality. This condition is called sleep state misperception, suggesting a basic disturbance of poorly known subconscious mechanisms that record the presence and chronology of sleep. Most persons are quite accurate in estimating the length of their sleep, but these patients seem to have lost that ability. Insomnia in childhood is commonly associated with other developmental disorders of brain function including learning disabilities, dyslexia, and hyperactivity, suggesting an underlying pathophysiologic mechanism that remains elusive. In recent years, fatal familial insomnia, a condition of extreme insomnia leading to death, has been described in patients with degeneration of the thalamus, drawing attention to the involvement of this important central nucleus in the production of sleep.

The differential diagnosis of insomnia needs to be made with circadian rhythm abnormalities that mimic the condition. Sleep phase delays, by retarding the appearance of sleep beyond conventional hours of the night, can resemble an insomnia. If the rhythm disorder is a sleep phase advance, the early consumption of sleep can awaken the patient early, giving the appearance of an early morning awakening. Finally, the clinician needs to remember that there are patients who fail to sleep well and sufficiently because of external factors such as environmental noises, temperature elevations, or traffic that continuously interrupts sleep. Somatic complaints can also cause insomnia, the paramount example being chronic pain that prevents the entry into sleep or arouses the individual.

Prevalence

Insomnia is a common complaint. Epidemiologic studies conducted in the United States [10] have shown that 35% of persons reported trouble with their sleep sometime during the year before the interview, but only half of the sample complained of having serious problems with sleep. Insomnia is not only common but also worthy of serious consideration when persistent. An often quoted study performed in 1979 [11] indicated that men sleeping less than 4 hours per night had a mortality 2.8 times higher than men sleeping more regularly. The study did not reveal the underlying factors affecting longevity, but one can surmise that patients afflicted with advanced medical conditions who do not sleep well, or patients with severe sleep apnea syndrome, hypertension, and allied vascular conditions might have a shortened lifespan.

Insomnia is more common among lower socioeconomic classes, older subjects, the chronically infirm, women, individuals with a high level of stress, and patients with psychiatric conditions.

Effects

Individuals who complain of insomnia are also distressed by the inability to function properly during waking hours. These subjects report being tired and irritable and having a loss of motivation, poor memory, decreased concentration, and vague physical manifestations. Muscle aches are common, particularly during morning hours. Despite sleepiness, patients are unable or unwilling to take naps because they are worried about the effect of daytime slumber on nocturnal sleep. Preoccupation about the ensuing night struggle to fall asleep heightens the tension surrounding the entire process and contributes importantly to sleeplessness, closing a vicious circle that loops anxiety and insomnia.

Assessment and Measurement

Polysomnographic evaluation of patients with insomnia can reveal several patterns of insomnia. In some patients, the study merely confirms prolongation of the latency to sleep and fragmentation of sleep architecture. In others, the study documents early morning awakenings. Polysomnography is justified when sleep state misperception is suspected. This condition can be demonstrated only by performing nocturnal polysomnography and comparing the scores with the declarations of the morning questionnaire. Major inconsistencies suggest the diagnosis. There is also justification to proceed with expensive testing when sleep apnea syndrome or severe periodic leg movements syndrome is a suspected factor underlying sleeplessness. In most other situations, the 14-day evaluation chart (see Chapter 5) is sufficient to document the presence and pattern of insomnia.

Snoring and Apnea

Snoring is the act of breathing with a rough, hoarse noise during sleep. Most individuals, particularly men past the age of 45, snore in their sleep, but pathologic or obnoxious snoring is more persistent and loud, disturbing the sleep of others. Commonly, the spouse or bedmate describes irregular breathing as another characteristic that is as disturbing as the noise itself. Snoring occurs with the turbulent passage of air through a narrow oropharynx, causing vibration of soft tissues. During sleep, the muscles that keep the pharyngeal wall taut tend to relax, narrowing the straits behind the tongue. In individuals with anatomic narrowing of any cause, such as large tonsils, accumulation of adipose tissue, or a large tongue, the stenosis creates increasing air turbulence and eventually might reach the point of collapse, interrupting the respiratory process. Thus, snoring of loud intensity, persistent occurrence, or irregular quality can be a marker of the sleep apnea syndrome and in consequence a manifestation of disease.

Snoring is aggravated while sleeping on the back because the weight of a relaxed tongue tends to choke even further the narrowed oropharyngeal passage, although individuals with severe disease snore in all positions. Snoring is also made worse by smoking, drinking alcohol, taking central nervous system depressants, and being sleep deprived. It acquires maximal intensity in stage 4 of sleep and tends to be softer during REM sleep, a paradoxic phenomenon since sleep apnea episodes are more prolonged; perhaps this situation occurs because the negative pressures exerted by the diaphragm are less forceful during the REM stage. A similar dissociation occurs in certain patients with muscular disorders who have severe sleep apnea syndrome but not loud snoring.

Individuals who snore intensely are not only embarrassed by the reports of partners and others but also often have to endure marital friction when they are asked to leave the bed or are abandoned at night by a sleepless spouse. Snoring can alter the sleep of other persons in the household and even of neighbors who complain of the incessant noise at night. These reports are valuable indicators of the intensity of snoring, the loudness of which has been measured in some individuals at 80 db, a level comparable to that of a pneumatic hammer. In patients with severe sleep apnea syndrome, snoring can be associated with grunts, gasps, whole body jerks, and arm flailing. A report of improvement in a snorer with severe sleep apnea syndrome suggests that the respiratory interruptions have become so long and predominant that there is hardly any opportunity left for snoring.

The incessant vibration of soft tissues produced by pathologic snoring can cause irritation of the oropharynx and a sensation of sore throat on awakening. Snoring has been considered an independent risk factor for stroke and myocardial infarction, perhaps because of the profound vascular alterations that appear with the increased negative intrathoracic pressures of inspiration.

Motor Episodes of Sleep

In some individuals, sleep is punctuated by motor activity that ranges from incessant restlessness to episodic complex behaviors that unwillingly drive the patient out of bed. Such phenomena can disturb the sleep of the patient and others, but more importantly, they create a risk of injury to the patient and bedmate. Often, nonepileptic motor phenomena of sleep have been confused with seizure episodes, and in this regard they have acquired major importance as well because the differential diagnosis poses a vexing clinical problem that can be resolved only with proper evaluation and testing in the sleep laboratory.

When evaluating motor episodes of sleep, it is important to record the subjective recollection offered by the patient, along with possible descriptions by others. These reports are complemented at a later time with polygraphic objective findings and nocturnal videotape recordings. Patients might have no remembrance of what happened at night but might glean indirect evidence from bruises, painful injuries, or disturbed bedroom furniture. Episodes occurring during REM sleep are usually recorded in memory as an occurrence attached to a dream, whereas events appearing in other stages of sleep are not remembered, or perhaps only partially and with little precision, unless the patient is awakened from sleep. Dream content suggests a REM sleep–related episode, whereas no dream association is more likely an event of non-REM sleep. The time of night when the episode occurred provides a clue to the related stage of sleep. Episodes occurring repeatedly during the first third of the night strongly suggest a link to slow wave sleep (SWS), whereas events appearing in the last third suggest an association with REM sleep.

The age of onset is similarly important. Episodes commencing in childhood tend to be related to SWS, such as nocturnal terrors and sleep walking. Paroxysmal dystonia, nocturnal wandering, and seizures, commonly associated with light non-REM sleep, are more frequent in youth and middle age, whereas REM sleep–related behavior disorder is usually a disorder of old age. A family history can have additional diagnostic value; sleepwalking and nocturnal terrors are typically familial, whereas REM sleep behavior disorder is usually acquired. Rhythmic movements of the head or body at the onset of sleep are almost exclusively seen in childhood, whereas stereotypic periodic movements of the lower extremities occur in non-REM sleep and are common in old age.

Predisposing and precipitating factors of motor events are varied but identifiable if one searches for them. Sleep deprivation is a well-known precipitating factor of seizures. Unusually deep SWS following sleep deprivation can precipitate nocturnal terrors and sleepwalking in children, as well as confusional episodes in adults. REM sleep deprivation followed by REM sleep rebound can trigger nightmares, hallucinations, and prolonged episodes of REM sleep behavior disorder. Factors modifying the quality, duration, and distribution of sleep architecture (such as alcohol, psychoactive medications, stress, fever, noise, heat, and cold) can facilitate the occurrence of motor episodes through varied mechanisms.

The polysomnographic study is necessary to document electrographically the episode (if it occurs during the nights of testing), serves to identify the stage of sleep in which it appears, and reveals allied signs of pathology. Interictal phenomena such as spikes in seizure disorders or REM stage without atonia in REM sleep behavior disorder have diagnostic value even in the absence of bona fide events. The videotaped registration is useful to analyze in detail the behavior of the patient during the episode, while procuring a correlation with electrographic phenomena. There is good specificity between certain events and stages of sleep. Thus, REM sleep behavior disorder occurs by definition during REM sleep. Nightmares are also associated with REM sleep, whereas seizure activity generally vanishes during segments of REM stage. Night terrors, somnambulism, confusional episodes, and paroxysmal awakenings are linked to SWS. Nocturnal wanderings and paroxysmal dystonia are more common in stage 2, whereas hypnic jerks and rhythmic head banging are typical of stage 1. Epileptiform discharges characteristically appear in light non-REM sleep, diminish in deep non-REM sleep, and disappear in REM sleep.

The response to treatment has diagnostic value also. Episodes responding to anticonvulsants such as carbamazepine are usually epileptic, or epileptoid in nature, a term applied to quasiepileptic phenomena such as paroxysmal dystonia and nocturnal wanderings. REM sleep behavior disorder specifically responds to clonazepam, and SWS-associated events such as somnambulism and nocturnal terrors disappear with low doses of benzodiazepines. Arousals linked to motor events can disappear differentially with benzodiazepines, improving the quality of sleep while having no effect over the motor event. This phenomenon is illustrated by the ameliorating effects that clonazepam has on the sleep of patients with periodic leg movements and fragmented sleep. Clonazepam eliminates event-associated cortical arousals but does not affect leg movements.

Often, the only evidence of a nocturnal epileptic seizure is the testimony of a bedmate, an episode of nocturnal incontinence, a disturbed bed, bruises, or a cut in the tongue. A sleep laboratory study with an extended cerebral montage over 2 or more consecutive nights might offer the only means of diagnosing the condition. The sleep of epileptics is commonly fragmented, but decidedly abnormal sleep patterns indicate underlying brain damage or toxic medication effect. Interictal epileptiform discharges, particularly in patients with complex partial seizures, tend to increase during early non-REM sleep, and virtually disappear during REM sleep [12]. Sleep deprivation increases the rate of focal interictal epileptiform discharges most markedly in stage 2.

Cataplexy and Sleep Paralysis

Cataplexy and sleep paralysis refer to the loss of tone in voluntary striated muscles along with inability to move, except in the diaphragm and oculomotor muscles. Cataplexy occurs while the individual is alert and therefore constitutes an intrusion of muscle atonia in wakefulness, expressing a partial generation of REM stage. The phenomenon is most common in patients with narcolepsy, and it has also been described in patients with lesions of the floor of the third ventricle and tegmentum of the midbrain. Cataplectic attacks are typically provoked by excitement or emotions, although idiosyncratic variations are common. Severe episodes are characterized by global paralysis with muscle atonia and areflexia. Less intense attacks produce drawing of the face, drooping of the eyelids, or sagging of the jaw. Nodding of the head, weakness of the hands, and buckling of the knees are also common occurrences in light attacks. Most attacks are rapid in onset and of brief duration without loss of consciousness; severe, prolonged episodes can be associated with hallucinations and followed by sleep. The frequency of episodes is quite variable and can be from 3–4 per day to 1 a month. Patients recover promptly and fully, but episodes can pose a serious hazard if they occur while the patient is driving, swimming, or engaged in situations in which maintenance of erect posture and balance are critical.

Sleep paralysis refers to episodes of muscle atonia that occur during the transitions from wakefulness to sleep and sleep to wakefulness. Typically, patients awaken at night or in the morning to find that they are unable to move for several minutes; some episodes are accompanied by hallucinations. The events disturb patients and if undiagnosed, lead to fear of dying. Sleep paralysis is common in patients with narcolepsy, although the condition has been described as an isolated symptom sporadically or in families without narcolepsy. Sometimes sleep paralysis precedes the onset of pathologic sleepiness in patients with narcolepsy.

Abnormal Dreaming

Eighty-five percent of subjects awakened from REM sleep report a dream experience. Ponto-geniculo-occipital (PGO) waves that originate in the pontine area travel to lateral geniculate nuclei and forebrain systems, providing nonrandom excitation of the forebrain. This input might represent the substrate for dream visual experiences and provides a rationale to comprehend partial or dissociated generation of dream phenomena outside REM sleep. Abnormal generation of dream experiences during wakefulness might underlie some hallucinatory phenomena. The transitions from sleep to wakefulness and vice versa are particularly vulnerable, especially in patients with narcolepsy. Hypnopompic hallucinations occur on awakening and hypnagogic hallucinations at onset of sleep.

Peduncular hallucinosis is the term given to a condition in which intense dreamlike experiences appear during wakefulness in patients with midbrain lesions [13]; excessive sleepiness is commonly found. The syndrome is undistinguishable from symptomatic narcolepsy.

Nightmares are dream-anxiety attacks that generally end in an awakening without motor enactment. They are more prevalent in younger patients, can be familiar, and tend to occur in persons with borderline personality disorders. Polysomnography fails to show the typical abnormalities of REM without atonia.

Motor system excitation during dream mentation generates complex motor commands that are consistent with the dream experience. Experimental evidence indicates that cortical and subcortical motor structures that mediate complex organized movements are activated during dream generation. However, motor commands are not executed, because of the powerful inhibition of motoneurons prevalent during REM sleep. If this neurologic barrier were lifted, complex motor behaviors would result in response to the dream as in the syndrome of REM sleep without atonia. In this condition, muscle atonia fails to occur, and patients are free to enact their dreams, resulting in punching, screaming, running, and other behaviors that translate a physical response to the dream content. In some individuals, lesions are found in the brain stem in the region of the perilocus ceruleus area responsible for generation of REM sleep–related muscle atonia.

Dissociated States

Dissociated states are intrusions of one state of being (wakefulness, non-REM sleep, and REM sleep) into another, resulting in mixed states, poorly defined states, or only partially developed states [14]. These phenomena are relatively common in patients with sleep disorders and can result in extraordinarily bizarre behaviors that are otherwise difficult to explain. Pathologic dissociated states such as cataplexy, hypnagogic hallucinations, and sleep paralysis occur commonly in patients with narcolepsy. Intense dream mentation following REM sleep deprivation might explain the vivid hallucinations encountered in the withdrawal phase of drugs that suppress REM sleep, such as anticholinergics and alcohol (i.e., delirium tremens), or conditions that inhibit REM sleep, such as metabolic coma. Episodes of confusional arousal or sleep drunkenness can occur in patients with severe sleep deprivation or in hypersomniacs who try to conform to a conventional sleep-wake schedule. During such episodes, patients engage in complex behaviors, even driving a car, without conscious awareness or critical judgment of the appropriateness of the act, suggesting that all vigil mechanisms have not been activated. Lucid dreaming might be another example of state dissociation. Individuals are aware of dreaming and guide their own dreams while in REM stage, as demonstrated by suppression of the H-reflex, a phenomenon typical of REM sleep [15].

Altered States of Mind Similar to Sleep

Acute Confusional States: Delirium

Delirium is defined as a transient global disorder of cognition and attention, associated with reduced level of consciousness, psychomotor agitation or retardation, and prominent sleep-wake cycle disturbance [16] (see Chapter 8).

The elderly are especially prone to develop delirium as a consequence of a variety of predisposing and precipitating factors that include dementia, structural brain disease, medical illness, drug use, sensory deprivation, psychosocial factors, and sleep loss. Delirium is frequently superimposed on dementia, and 25% of persons who are delirious have dementia [17].

Delirium is a transient disorder, usually lasting less than 1 month. Symptoms fluctuate during the daytime and reach a peak at night. The sleep-wake cycle disturbance is an essential disturbance of delirium. During daytime hours, patients are lethargic and tend to nap; at night, sleep is short, fragmented, and punctuated with hallucinations. Agitation, restlessness, and wakefulness dominate the nocturnal period in clear contrast with the subdued and drowsy state that prevails during the day. Cholinergic deficiency seems to be a major mechanism in delirium, and thus patients with Alzheimer's disease are particularly vulnerable.

Hypothermia

Hypothermia is defined as a core body temperature of 35°C or lower, affecting central nervous system functions in predictable ways. As the rectal temperature drops below 34°C, individuals exhibit psychomotor retardation, lethargy, and confusion, which can appear as sleepiness to the untrained eye. Dysarthria develops when the temperature descends to 33.5°C; below 28°C most patients are unresponsive or make unintelligible sounds in response to questions. In hypothermia, pupillary size is unaffected, but the pupillary response to light can be sluggish with core temperatures below 32°C. This sign is important in the differential diagnosis with true sleep because individuals who are asleep have small pupils unresponsive to light, which dilate with an alerting stimulus and become briskly responsive in the awake state. In early hypothermia, the EEG shows increased beta and theta activities and reduced alpha activity [18]. As the temperature continues to descend, there is progressive slowing of cerebral electrogenesis, followed by a burst-suppression pattern and eventually an isoelectric record with temperatures below 20°C. Survival is associated with full recovery of neurologic functions.

Hypothermia could also be a symptom of hypothalamic dysfunction. Patients with localized lesions in or near the hypothalamus can exhibit hypothermia along with other manifestations of hypothalamic dysfunction that include somnolence, hypogonadism, diabetes insipidus, and obesity. In the young, the most common pathology underlying unexplained hypothermia is neoplasia. In middle age, advanced alcoholism with Wernicke's encephalopathy should be considered as well as neoplasia, whereas in the elderly, hypothermia is generally the result of hypothyroidism.

Anesthesia

Induced general anesthesia causes an altered level of consciousness superficially resembling sleep, particularly if spontaneous respiration is preserved. During the intraoperative act under controlled circumstances, there is no room for mistaking the condition for natural sleep, although some patients report dreaming [19]. Postoperative confusion and lethargy are relatively common in elderly people. The differential diagnosis with natural sleep can be significant as patients come out of the induced anesthetic state. Risk factors for postoperative lethargy and confusion are preoperative sleep deprivation of any etiology, early dementia, depression, administration of anticholinergic medications, and alcoholism. Failure to awake as expected has been attributed to prolonged action of anesthetic drugs, metabolic encephalopathy, and cerebral injury. Idiosyncratic sensitivity to anesthetic drugs, causing failure to awaken will eventually resolve without a trail of focal neurologic deficits. Metabolic encephalopathy requires appropriate testing to exclude hypoglycemia, hypoxemia, hypercapnia, and electrolyte imbalances. Cerebral injury, exclusive of neurosurgical interventions, is virtually limited to high-risk operations such as aortic interventions and cardiac surgery that requires a cardiopulmonary bypass. Delayed awakening or prolonged lethargy with lateralizing signs of neurologic deficit suggest neurologic injury resulting from cerebral ischemia, hemorrhage, hypoxia, or cerebral edema. The incidence of cerebrovascular accident after general surgery is 0.2% in patients over 40 years of age [20].

Hypnosis

Hypnosis is a state that resembles sleep, generally induced by a hypnotizer or therapist. The hypnotized individual is in a condition of altered awareness associated with heightened concentration. Attention is restricted and highly focused without peripheral distractions. Although memory is variable and not dependable, perceptions are distorted and confabulation can occur. Hypnosis facilitates suggestibility, loss of executive control, and submission to the person inducing the state of hypnosis. Muscle tone is also variable, ranging from atonia to a cataleptic condition in which antigravitational bizarre postures can be maintained for many hours. Sensory obliteration during hypnosis has been used for medical applications like dentistry and minor surgery. Critical judgment is absent, and the behavior of the individual is unreliable, resembling that of the somnambulist or of the subject in a confusional arousal or in automatic behavior. Amnesia follows deep hypnosis.

Induction of hypnosis is attained in susceptible individuals by directing their attention to repetitive, monotonous tasks with a conditioned stimulus. Animals can also succumb to hypnosis by inducing forced postures for prolonged periods of time. EEG recordings during hypnosis have shown excessive, diffuse theta activity [21].

Automatic States

Occasionally, sleepy individuals exhibit a state of partial or intermittent arousal during which they are capable of performing complex motor acts that are characterized by greatly diminished critical judgment of their behavior followed by amnesia. These episodes can last several hours and put the individual at risk for accidents. They are usually induced by monotonous tasks such as driving, taking notes at lectures, riding a horse, or marching. Such incidents are relatively common in narcoleptics who can drive for miles and take the wrong exit, ending up in an unknown location without memory of the preceding events. Students in class might take notes that are unintelligible and incoherent, and soldiers can march in a state of subalertness. Automatic behavior is generally observed in patients with severe sleepiness of any cause, whether primary such as observed in narcolepsy and idiopathic hypersomnia [22], or secondary to sleep apnea syndrome, and behavioral sleep deprivation.

Electrographic recordings of these episodes have shown repeated "microsleeps" of REM sleep in narcoleptics, lasting 15–30 seconds, and non-REM microsleeps in others. The differential diagnosis needs to be made with fugue episodes of temporal lobe seizures, other ictal events of epileptic patients, and transient global amnesia. Automatisms associated with seizures are more stereotypic, are not associated with preceding drowsiness, and fail to respond to intense stimulation. Furthermore, anticonvulsants can prevent the occurrence of ictal events but have no effect on sleep-related automatic behavior. Patients with transient global amnesia are not drowsy or sleepy during the event.

Coma

Coma and sleep are similar in that consciousness has been suspended in both states. Consciousness has two components: wakefulness and awareness. Individuals who are asleep or in coma are neither awake nor aware. The patient in coma has lost sleep in addition to consciousness; is neither awake nor asleep; and the integrated sequence of awake, non-REM, and REM sleep fails to occur. The fundamental difference between coma and sleep is that the patient in coma cannot be aroused, and the polysomnogram fails to show the predictable architecture of sleep stages. Coma can result from a diffuse disorder of cerebral function or from a lesion interrupting the activity of the deep core of gray matter. Light coma, particularly if following a deeper level of coma, can overlap sleep. The patient seems to undergo a period of excessive sleepiness, while the clinical and electrographic differences between sleep and non-sleep cycles become increasingly pronounced. REM sleep rebound might be observed in patients recovering from hepatic or alcoholic coma [23], suggesting REM sleep deprivation during the coma. A parallel can be drawn with the hibernating animal that experiences sleep deprivation during the phase of hypothermic unresponsiveness, followed by sleep rebound on awakening. Early recovery of sleep spindles and REM sleep in coma patients suggests a favorable prognosis.

Spindle-coma refers to the coexistence of true sleep and coma. The presence of spindles, vertex waves, and K complexes indicates relative integrity of the cerebral hemispheres, whereas failure of arousal is attributable to impairment of the reticular activating system in the brain stem. Head trauma is the most common cause of this condition, but other etiologies have been described, including metabolic, infectious, and hypoxic alterations of the brain [24].

In the persistent vegetative state, patients remain unconscious because they lack awareness but might exhibit wakefulness and crude sleep cycles characterized by periodic immobility, changes in the respiratory pattern, and pinpoint pupils that do not react to light. During this time, the EEG might show abortive spindles and K complexes [25]. Outside sleep, patients appear restless with pupillary reactivity and a poorly developed EEG showing a diffusely slow and disorganized electrical pattern with increasingly intermixed faster rhythms. In akinetic mutism, resulting from a lesion of the upper brain stem and paramedian thalamic areas, cyclical electrographic changes suggest alternations of sleep and arousal.

Nocturnal Death

The ancestral fear of never waking up after falling asleep has found a tenuous basis in recent studies showing that indeed more deaths than allowed by coincidence occur between 5:00 and 9:30 A.M. [26]. Examination of death certificates in Massachusetts have shown a similar pattern of an increased number of deaths between the hours of 6:00 A.M. and 12:00 noon. Epilepsy and cardiorespiratory alterations modulated by circadian forces account for most of these deaths.

Epilepsy and Sudden Death

Sudden death during sleep has been associated with poorly controlled epilepsy, low anticonvulsant levels, and frontal or temporal lesions [27]. Typically, patients are found dead in bed or next to the bed, without evidence of a generalized convulsion, the assumption being that the nocturnal seizure precipitated a cardiorespiratory arrest [28].

Sleep Apnea and Sudden Death

Normally, ventricular ectopic activity during sleep is reduced as a consequence of vagal tone preponderance. However, in patients with advanced obstructive sleep apnea, cardiac arrhythmias occur when the oxyhemoglobin saturation decreases below 65%. At the time of the apneic episode, intermittent vasoconstriction along with a decrease in cardiac output and desaturation of oxyhemoglobin impose a considerable amount of stress on the cardiovascular system, particularly in elderly persons who show more abundant changes in cardiac rhythm in response to the apnea. Hypertension can occur with all its complications, including congestive heart failure. The results of untreated advanced obstructive sleep apnea are left ventricular hypertrophy, pulmonary hypertension, nocturnal myocardial ischemia, myocardial infarction, stroke, and eventually, vascular death.

Vascular Death

Most deaths occur between 5:00 and 9:30 A.M., whereas the incidence of cardiac death peaks between 8:00 and 11:00A.M. [25].The Framingham Study has revealed a circadian profile in the timing of sudden death in the morning that coincides remarkably well with the timing of myocardial infarction and stroke [29]. Coronary artery thrombosis appears to be the link between myocardial infarction, unstable angina, and sudden cardiac death. Histologic studies of occluded arteries have suggested that a thrombus forms over a ruptured atherosclerotic plaque. Several physiologic processes that increase their activity in the morning hours, such as blood pressure, blood viscosity, and platelet aggregability, along with a decrease in fibrinolytic activity could trigger plaque rupture and promote coronary artery thrombosis, thus explaining the circadian variation in vascular death.

Sudden Infant Death Syndrome

The inexplicable death of healthy infants while apparently peacefully asleep, or sudden infant death syndrome (SIDS), continues to confound physicians and bewilder parents (see Chapter 11). Infants are found dead in their cribs without signs of struggle, aspiration, or physical injury, and postmortem examinations fail to find a cause. Theories of the mechanism of death have ranged from inadvertent asphyxiation to unheralded cardiac arrest or respiratory failure. Death usually occurs between 2 and 3 months, a time that has been considered of particular vulnerability because it is the period when physiologic control of respiration during quiet sleep becomes dependent on timely maturation of forebrain-based homeostatic mechanisms [30]. The infant at risk appears unable to override the challenge imposed by the transition to different intrinsic respiratory drive mechanisms.

Eighty percent of deaths have occurred while the infant was asleep. There is some evidence that deaths have occurred in susceptible infants, and in certain instances, there has been a familial incidence, with subsequent siblings having a higher risk. The study of large groups of infants who have died of SIDS has revealed predisposing factors that increase the risk of such deaths. SIDS is more prevalent among infants with low birth weight and infants born to mothers in lower socioeconomic groups, particularly when the mothers are alcoholic, smoke, or suffer from drug addiction.

Sudden Unexplained Nocturnal Death

Mysterious sudden deaths during sleep have been reported in healthy young adults of Southeast Asian descent. The victims, usually men in their twenties or thirties, appeared to struggle briefly before dying, as if choking or gasping for breath. Autopsies failed to find a cause of death. In a few instances, individuals were successfully resuscitated and ventricular fibrillation was identified. Although exposure to offending chemical, pharmacologic, or biological agents has not been found, some authors have reported a higher incidence of nocturnal terrors in these individuals. Others have proposed hypokalemia, leading to cardiac arrhythmias in sleep as the mechanism of death [31].

History Taking, Examination, and Assessment

The patient with a sleep disorder is approached in the same way as the patient with any other medical disorder. The initial interview should gather all facts pertaining to the sleep-related problem as well as a comprehensive general anamnesis, review of systems, past medical-surgical history, medication use, family history, and social history.

History taking can be reinforced with a questionnaire previously sent to the patient but cannot be replaced by it. The history should contain the chief complaint, along with a description of the symptoms in the patient's own words. A detailed sleep-wake schedule is important to assess sleep hygiene and the presence of insomnia, hypersomnia, or sleep fragmentation. The schedule should list the time that the patient went to bed, the time that the patient fell asleep, the time of nocturnal awakenings and their duration, incidents during the night, restlessness or falling out of bed, dream content, and the presence of bizarre behavior. Falling out of bed is always a sign of sleep pathology in the adult. Snoring and the occurrence of respiratory interruptions is best described by the bed partner. Nocturnal leg movements, sleep talking, sleepwalking, and any form of bizarre behavior are also best described by witnesses rather than by patients who are unaware or have only fragmented recollection of the event. The testimony given by a bed partner, parents, or relatives is very important and should always be sought.

The time of awakening is also recorded, along with the time out of bed and a description of how the patient feels at that point, whether rested or still tired and sleepy. The presence of morning headaches can herald a sleep apnea syndrome, and diffuse muscle aches sometimes anticipate a fibromyalgia syndrome. Excessive sleepiness during the day, uncontrollable sleepiness, scheduled naps, inappropriate sleeping, and dream content during diurnal sleep should be carefully recorded. Patients should always be asked if they become sleepy driving, if they have ever fallen asleep at the wheel, and if they have been involved in accidents or "near-misses" such as drifting off the road. Examples of situations in which patients have fallen asleep might help estimate the severity of sleepiness. There are three graded tiers of severity: (1) falling asleep watching TV in the evening or reading the paper; (2) falling asleep at important meetings, at religious services, or consistently when attending a show; and (3) falling asleep while eating, talking on the phone, or waiting for a traffic light to turn green. Additional questions asked concern the quality of daytime vigilance, energy, motivation, affect, attention, concentration, memory, and sexual drive. Patients use the word "tired" indistinctly to indicate mental fatigue, physical tiredness, and sleepiness. These terms should be clearly differentiated because the clinical implications can vary. Sleepiness is the tendency to fall asleep. Mental fatigue is the state of drained mental energy with reduced motivation, unwillingness to continue, and decreased capacity to concentrate, not necessarily associated with sleepiness. Physical tiredness is the condition of fatigue, weariness, or lassitude stemming from the body. The history is completed with a review of systems, personal medical and surgical history, family history, and medications used. Tonsillectomy is an often forgotten surgical operation that has clear bearing on the diagnosis of sleep apnea syndrome. Patients should be asked about substances that affect sleep, specifying the amount consumed and the timing. These substances include coffee, tea, caffeine-containing sodas, chocolate, alcoholic beverages, cigarettes, and cigars.

Questions about the patient's mental and emotional status are important to identify components of primary or secondary anxiety in individuals with insomnia, or depression in patients with excessive daytime somnolence. Because most psychiatric disorders are associated with sleep alteration, any history thus obtained is critical to a full assessment of the condition. The family history might reveal whether siblings or close relatives suffer a similar disorder, which is sometimes the case in narcolepsy and rather common in sleepwalking. The social history adds details that help assess the severity of the problem as well as the impact on work and family life. Questions about declining job productivity, falling asleep on the job, and supervisory counseling are pertinent when excessive daytime sleepiness is the chief complaint. Family pathology resulting from poor participation in family affairs or marital stress when a spouse has to leave the bedroom because of snoring or bizarre behavior signals a serious condition.

The physical examination is conducted in the conventional way. The neck and oropharynx in patients with possible sleep apnea syndrome should be examined to search for anatomic obstructions or impediments to airflow and to assess the condition of the soft palate. In patients with severe obstructive sleep apnea syndrome, it is common to observe redundant, pendulous tissues crowding the oropharyngeal opening. The height and weight should always be recorded, particularly in patients suspected of having the sleep apnea syndrome.

After the clinical assessment, the physician should consider whether a polysomnographic study is indicated. When patients are suspected of having narcolepsy, or when narcolepsy is a principal disorder to be ruled out, they are referred to the sleep laboratory for overnight studies with the basic protocol followed by an MSLT. In instances in which sleep apnea is the principal working diagnosis, the sleep apnea protocol is ordered for the overnight evaluation. In our laboratory, an MSLT is a valuable adjunct to measure daytime sleepiness that serves as an indicator of the quality of nocturnal sleep. Bizarre behaviors and nocturnal epilepsy are studied with the seizure protocol that incorporates additional channels for electroencephalography and all-night video registration. Patients with insomnia are usually not studied in the laboratory unless there is compelling evidence of the presence of a physical condition altering sleep. Once in the sleep laboratory, patients are asked to complete a questionnaire before they go to sleep, addressing items that could affect nocturnal sleep such as recent medical or surgical conditions, and medications taken. This information complements the history obtained by the clinician and is incorporated into the record. The morning after, another questionnaire with entries about the patient's perception of the quality and duration of sleep in the laboratory is given to the patient. Sleep misperceptions are occasionally uncovered with this document.

The 14-day evaluation chart (see Chapter 5) is a valuable addition to the armamentarium of the sleep specialist. It is a detailed account of the sleep-wake schedule over a period of 14 days and can reveal patterns of sleep that are suggestive of any of the major forms of insomnia: difficulty initiating or maintaining sleep and early morning awakenings. The circadian rhythm disorders featuring advanced or delayed onset of sleep are best revealed with this chart.

The results of the clinical and laboratory evaluations are best conveyed to the patient at a subsequent early follow-up visit. The results are explained thoroughly and recommendations are given with the necessary emphasis on important points. Relatives are also invited so that everyone understands the nature of the problem and the solutions offered. These meetings serve to alleviate misgivings, false interpretations, and other misperceptions of the abnormal behavior and affect that usually accompany a sleep disorder. The response to treatment is assessed at a subsequent visit 3–6 months later.

Segmental Neurology of Sleep

Sleep is a neurogenic function with origin in centers of the brain stem, diencephalon (hypothalamus and thalamus), and basal forebrain. The hemispheric cortex also intervenes in the development of sleep as a resonating organ, but has no primary functions. Lesions of any nature affecting these segments of the nervous system will be reflected in a sleep disturbance that also alters vigilance. In recent years, a variety of neuroanatomic correlates have been revealed that confirm the findings of experiments involving localization in animals. Many sleep disorders resist explanation on a neuroanatomic basis, suggesting neurochemical alterations that remain to be uncovered.

Neuroanatomic Correlates

Brain Stem

Bremer's seminal experiments in the cat [32] served to localize sleep-generating structures in the brain stem. Bremer indicated that a transection of the midbrain immediately caudal to the third nerve nuclei (cerveau isolé) initially produced slow wave synchronized sleep without alternation between sleep and waking, loss of response to painful stimuli, and continuous spindles in the EEG. Observations made later with a similar preparation showed absent REM sleep [33]. When the transection was made lower in the brain stem, in the junction between the spinal cord and medulla (encephale isolé), wakefulness gradually returned, and after a few days spontaneous periods of EEG desynchronization could be identified. Later observers noted the appearance of REM sleep without atonia with this preparation [33]. Bremer's experiments set the stage for the future investigation of sleep-wake localizations in the brain stem that led to the development of the concept of the reticular activating system, synchronized and desynchronized states, and the discovery of REM sleep centers.

Mesencephalon

The medial midbrain contains the rostral segments of the reticular activating system in close proximity to the third nerve nuclei, so that lesions in this region almost invariably cause a reduction in the level of alertness, paresis of vertical gaze, and pupillary abnormalities. These manifestations occur in "top of the basilar" occlusion, a vascular syndrome with infarction of the paramedian midbrain territory, in which persistent sleepiness is associated with pupillary dilatation, paresis of vertical gaze, and loss of convergence [34]. Some patients develop hallucinations called "peduncular hallucinosis," which are characterized by colorful, intense, visual figments of the content of consciousness, probably related to the dream phenomena of REM sleep. Lesions of the pars reticulata of the substantia nigra have also been associated with hallucinations [35]. Peduncular hallucinosis always occurs in patients with sleep alterations, confirming the notion that its genesis lies in lesions of the midbrain adjacent to centers and pathways of the reticular system.

Symptomatic cataplexy characterized by muscle atonia associated with sleep paralysis and sleep attacks has been described in patients with rostral brain stem lesions invading the floor of the third ventricle [36]. Recent reports indicate that a lesion of the midbrain without hypothalamic involvement would be sufficient to trigger cataplexy and sleep paralysis [37]. Such lesions can disengage the atonia-generating system of the perilocus ceruleus area from rostral brain stem inhibition.

Lesions of the lower mesencephalon–upper pons tegmentum involving the perilocus ceruleus area are responsible for the syndrome of REM sleep without atonia. This syndrome is a partial alteration of REM sleep generation that facilitates excessive motor activity during the REM stage and is associated with a behavioral disorder characterized by bizarre acts during sleep that suggest dream enactment. Motor behavior driven by a dream is called phantasmagoria. Full expression of the syndrome occurs with bilateral pontine lesions involving the perilocus ceruleus area or the tegmentoreticular tract. In REM sleep behavior disorder, there is failure of muscle atonia development during the REM stage as a result of the destruction of the atonia generator in the perilocus ceruleus area or its disconnection from the muscle tone inhibitory center of Magoun and Rhines (nucleus reticularis magnocellularis) in the medulla. This nucleus transmits muscle atonia impulses to the spinal motoneurons via the ventrolateral reticulospinal tract.

Pons

Extensive lesions of the pontine tegmentum cause reduction in total sleep time and profound alterations or abolition of non-REM and REM sleep in humans [38]. Not uncommonly, sleep alterations are associated with lateral conjugate gaze paresis [39]. Patients with "locked-in" syndrome of vascular origin in whom the lesion extends into the pontine tegmentum experience loss of REM and non-REM stages.

There are reports of loss of non-REM sleep in patients with lesions involving the median raphe in the pons and midbrain. This loss is consistent with cat experiments in which damage to serotonergic nuclei of the median raphe causes persistent insomnia.

Medulla

Isolated lesions of the medulla are either incompatible with life or so scarce in clinical practice that meaningful studies of nocturnal sleep are few. Medullary lesions affect the ability to breathe during sleep. Bilateral medullary damage can result in complete failure of automatic respiration that is indistinguishable from Ondine's curse. Medullary centers involved in respiration can be affected in the Arnold-Chiari malformation resulting in nonobstructive sleep apnea, or obstructive sleep apnea if pharyngeal motor centers are also involved [40].

In poliomyelitis and in the postpolio syndrome, there can be extensive damage to the reticular formation at all brain stem levels with respiratory rhythm alterations, including the syndrome of sleep apnea [41]. It is likely that in this disease the pneumotaxic centers of the pons and the respiratory centers of the medulla are involved, in addition to reticular nerve cells maintaining tonic wakefulness in the midbrain region [42, 43].

Spinal Cord

The complaint of disordered sleep is common in patients with high spinal cord lesions [44]. Obstructive sleep apnea has been reported in patients with cervical cord damage. The alteration in breathing has been attributed to the excessive workload imposed on the diaphragm, which is the only source of ventilation, as shown by paradoxic retraction of the ribcage [45]. Alveolar hypoventilation, obesity, and medications such as baclofen are contributing factors.

In general, lesions of the rostrocentral midbrain tegmentum cause intense sleepiness associated with vertical gaze palsies and hallucinations. Lesions of the dorsal pontine tegmentum cause a profound reduction of sleep along with horizontal gaze palsies. Lesions of the pontomedullary junction or medulla cause cardiorespiratory alterations and loss of muscle atonia in the REM stage.

Diencephalon

Hypothalamus

Lesions to nerve cells of the posterior hypothalamus decrease wakefulness. Similar observations have been made in cell destructions of the basal forebrain nuclei (substantia innominata or nucleus basalis of Meynert, and nuclei of the diagonal band and septum), indicating the existence of a genuine waking center in the posterior hypothalamus and basal forebrain that projects to the cortical mantle.

The classic studies by von Economo [46] suggested that lesions of the anterior hypothalamus caused insomnia, whereas lesions of the posterior hypothalamus and mesencephalic tegmentum provoked lethargy and hypersomnia. Von Economo's studies were done in patients dying of encephalitis, and brain lesions were too diffuse to draw conclusive results. Nevertheless, the observations attracted attention to the hypothalamus as a brain area important to sleep and waking mechanisms.

The suprachiasmatic nucleus of the hypothalamus, connected with the outside world through the retinohypothalamic tract, plays a leading role in the organization of circadian rhythmicity. Declining function of this nucleus in old age or degeneration of its cells in Alzheimer's disease might underlie altered sleep-wake cycles in these conditions. Neuroendocrine rhythms related to sleep are modulated by structures as diverse as the amygdaloid nuclei, thalamus, midbrain, and the limbic system, but are integrated at the hypothalamic level. There is clinical evidence indicating that hypothalamic damage in humans results in various neuroendocrine dysfunctions that are usually manifested by loss of the adrenocorticotropic hormone–cortisol rhythm, hyperprolactinemia, and absence of SWS-associated growth hormone secretion [47].

Hypothalamic tumors are associated with hypersomnia. Symptomatic narcolepsy can occur in lesions of the floor of the third ventricle involving the hypothalamus. Patients with diencephalic lesions have genuine sleep attacks (and not prolonged subalertness), abnormal presence of REM sleep episodes in daytime sleep latency tests, and cataplexy. There is some evidence that the dopaminergic tone of the hypothalamus is reduced during the symptomatic phase of the Kleine-Levin syndrome [48], a periodic hypersomnia that is associated with hyperphagia and hypersexuality in young men.

Thalamus

Experiments in the cat have revealed that ablation of the thalamus leads to persistent and severe insomnia [49]. Diffuse lesions of the thalamus in humans lead to ipsilateral decrease or abolition of sleep spindles, a useful electrographic sign of thalamic injury [50]. Loss of stage 2 and sleep spindles after hemispheric stroke is a poor prognostic sign [51]. In patients with myotonic dystrophy, nerve cells of the dorsomedial nuclei contain cytoplasmic inclusion bodies that manifest neuronal damage that is probably responsible for hypersomnia, apathy, mental decline, and "slow alpha" rhythms [52]. Several clinical observations have linked lesions of the dorsomedial nuclei of the thalamus with loss of growth hormone secretion during SWS in patients with myotonic dystrophy [53] and in patients with stroke [54]. Lugaresi and coworkers described a familial occurrence of fatal insomnia with dysautonomia and a dreamlike state with dream enactments in patients with degenerative lesions of the dorsomedial and anterior nuclei of the thalamus [55]. Such observations suggest that the thalamus has an important role in integrating and expressing sleep [56].

Telencephalon

Cerebral Hemispheres

Although the cerebral hemispheres intervene in the expression of REM and non-REM sleep, they are not primordial in their generation or maintenance. Anencephalic infants without thalami have survived up to 85 days exhibiting periods of sleep and crude behaviors [57]. Patients with extensive cortical injury eventually exhibit cyclical changes in EEG activity suggestive of sleep-wake alternation [58]. Survivors of large hemispheric stroke have increased SWS while retaining normal percentages of REM sleep [59].

There is little clinical information on the effects of human lesions involving the basal forebrain area, a region that has been heavily implicated in sleep mechanisms in the cat. In humans, there are temporary increases in wakefulness following frontal leucotomy [60], but 10 years or more after the operation there is an increase in SWS [61].

Although cortical structures do not appear to play an executive role in sleep, it is likely that cortical modulating influences reach lower diencephalic and midbrain centers through systems such as the "limbic forebrain–midbrain circuit" of Nauta. Stimulation of this pathway promotes sleep, whereas damage causes insomnia along with neurovegetative disturbances [62].

Classification of Sleep Disorders

The original classification of sleep disorders (Diagnostic Classification of Sleep and Arousal Disorders) was published in 1979 in the journal *Sleep* [63]. This classification was a practical and usable one that revolved around the cardinal symptoms of insomnia and hypersomnia, with two additional sections to incorporate sleep phase disorders, and the phenomena that intrude in sleep because sleep is there, or parasomnias. The Diagnostic Classification served clinicians well and was followed in 1990 by the International Classification of Sleep Disorders [64] to update and revise the previous one. The International Classification is based on pathophysiologic processes, representing an advance from the previous classification, which was based on clinical descriptions. It purposefully avoids compartmentalization by organs and systems in deference to the multidisciplinary approach undertaken by sleep medicine. The new classification (Table 3-2) consists of four major

Table 3-2. International Classification of Sleep Disorders

Disorder	Diagnostic Code*
Dyssomnias	
Intrinsic sleep disorders	
Psychophysiologic insomnia	307.42-0
Sleep state misperception	307.49-1
Idiopathic insomnia	780.52-7
Narcolepsy	347
Recurrent hypersomnia	780.54-2
Idiopathic hypersomnia	780.54-7
Posttraumatic hypersomnia	780.54-8
Obstructive sleep apnea syndrome	780.53-0
Central sleep apnea syndrome	780.51-0
Central alveolar hypoventilation syndrome	780.51-1
Periodic limb movement disorder	780.52-4
Restless legs syndrome	780.52-5
Intrinsic sleep disorder not otherwise specified	780.52-9
Extrinsic sleep disorders	
Inadequate sleep hygiene	307.41-1
Environmental sleep disorder	780.52-6
Altitude insomnia	289.0
Adjustment sleep disorder	307.41-0
Insufficient sleep syndrome	307.49-4
Limit-setting sleep disorder	307.42-4
Sleep-onset association disorder	307.42-5
Food allergy insomnia	780.52-2
Nocturnal eating (drinking) syndrome	780.52-8
Hypnotic-dependent sleep disorder	780.52-0
Stimulant-dependent sleep disorder	780.52-1
Alcohol-dependent sleep disorder	780.52-3
Toxin-induced sleep disorder	780.54-6
Extrinsic sleep disorder NOS	780.52-9
Circadian rhythm sleep disorders	
Time zone change (jet lag) syndrome	307.45-0
Shift work sleep disorder	307.45-1
Irregular sleep-wake pattern	307.45-3
Delayed sleep phase syndrome	780.55-0

Disorder	Diagnostic Code*
Advanced sleep phase syndrome	780.55-1
Non–24-hour sleep–wake disorder	780.55-2
Circadian rhythm sleep disorder NOS	780.55-9
Parasomnias	
Arousal disorders	
Confusional arousals	307.46-2
Sleepwalking	307.46-0
Sleep terrors	307.46-1
Sleep-wake transition disorders	
Rhythmic movement disorder	307.3
Sleep starts	307.47-2
Sleep talking	307.47-3
Nocturnal leg cramps	729.82
Parasomnias usually associated with REM sleep	
Nightmares	307.47-0
Sleep paralysis	780.56-2
Impaired sleep-related penile erections	780.56-3
Sleep-related painful erections	780.56-4
REM sleep-related sinus arrest	780.56-8
REM sleep behavior disorder	780.59-0
Other parasomnias	
Sleep bruxism	306.8
Sleep enuresis	780.56-0
Sleep-related abnormal swallowing syndrome	780.56-6
Nocturnal paroxysmal dystonia	780.59-1
Sudden unexplained nocturnal death syndrome	780.59-3
Primary snoring	780.53-1
Infant sleep apnea	770.80
Congenital central hypoventilation syndrome	770.81
Sudden infant death syndrome	798.0
Benign neonatal sleep myclonus	780.59-5
Other parasomnia NOS	780.59-9
Sleep disorders associated with medical/psychiatric disorders	
Associated with mental disorders	290–319
Psychoses	292–299
Mood disorders	296–301

Table 3-2. (*continued*)

Disorder	Diagnostic Code*
Anxiety disorders	300
Panic disorder	300
Alcoholism	303
Associated with neurologic disorders	320–389
Cerebral degenerative disorders	330–337
Dementia	331
Parkinsonism	332–333
Fatal familial insomnia	337.9
Sleep-related epilepsy	345
Electrical status epilepticus of sleep	345.8
Sleep-related headaches	346
Associated with other medical disorders	
Sleeping sickness	086
Nocturnal cardiac ischemia	411–414
Chronic obstructive pulmonary disease	490–494
Sleep-related asthma	493
Sleep-related gastroesophageal reflux	530.1
Peptic ulcer disease	531–534
Fibrositis syndrome	729.1
Proposed sleep disorders	
Short sleeper	307.49-0
Long sleeper	307.49-2
Subwakefulness syndrome	307.47-1
Fragmentary myoclonus	780.59-7
Sleep hyperhidrosis	780.8
Menstruation-associated sleep disorder	780.54-3
Pregnancy-associated sleep disorder	780.59-6
Terrifying hypnagogic hallucinations	307.47-4
Sleep-related neurogenic tachypnea	780.53-2
Sleep-related laryngospasm	780.59-4
Sleep choking syndrome	307.42-1

*Numbers represent diagnostic codes.
Source: Adapted with permission from Diagnostic Classification Steering Committee, MJ Thorpy, Chairman. ICSD—International Classification of Sleep Disorders: Diagnostic and Coding Manual. Rochester, MN: American Sleep Disorders Association, 1990;15–17.

entries: (1) dyssomnias, (2) parasomnias, (3) medical/psychiatric sleep disorders, and (4) proposed sleep disorders, which leaves the door open for future developments.

The dyssomnias are classified in three categories: (1) intrinsic disorders, to accommodate primary sleep disorders that cause either insomnia or hypersomnia and are the consequence of internal alterations; (2) extrinsic sleep disorders, to include sleep disorders caused by factors external to the body; and (3) circadian rhythm sleep disorders, to include all alterations linked to a malfunction of the circadian rhythm, remaining much the same as in the old classification. The parasomnias, defined as undesirable physical phenomena that occur predominantly during sleep, have been subclassified in four major categories: (1) arousal disorders, in which the common link is a postulated impairment of arousal from sleep, such as would occur in sleepwalking, sleep terrors, and confusional arousals; (2) sleep-wake transition disorders, a group of events that occur in the transition from wakefulness to sleep; (3) REM-associated parasomnias; and (4) other parasomnias, a miscellaneous group of sleep-related phenomena. The medical/psychiatric sleep disorders are alterations of sleep associated with (1) mental disorders, (2) neurologic disorders, and (3) other medical disorders.

Each diagnosis has a code number in accordance with the International Classification of Diseases for coding diagnoses in clinical reports or for database purposes.

References

1. Osler W. The Practical in Medicine. Counsels and Ideals from the Writings of William Osler & Selected Aphorisms (special ed). Birmingham, AL: The Classics of Medicine Library, Division of Gryphon Editions, 1985;66.
2. Report of the New York State Governor's Task Force on Sleepiness/Fatigue and Driving. Albany, NY: 1994.
3. Carskadon MA, Dement WC. Daytime sleepiness: Quantification of a behavioral state. Neurosci Behav Rev 1987;11:307.
4. Wald ML. Sleepy truckers linked to many deaths. National Report. The New York Times. January 19, 1995;A16.
5. Akerstedt T. Sleepiness as a consequence of shift work. Sleep 1988;11:17.
6. Hoddes E, Zarcone V, Smythe H, et al. Quantification of sleepiness: A new approach. Psychophysiology 1973;10:431.
7. Johns MW. A new model for measuring daytime sleepiness: The Epworth Sleepiness Scale. Sleep 1991;14:540.

8. Folstein MF, Luria R. Reliability, validity, and clinical application of the visual analogue model scale. Psychol Med 1973;3:479.
9. Carskadon MA, Dement WC, Mitler MM, et al. Guidelines for the Multiple Sleep Latency Test (MSLT): A standard measure of sleepiness. Sleep 1986;9:519.
10. National Institute of Mental Health, Consensus Development Conference: Drugs and Insomnia: The use of medications to promote sleep. JAMA 1984;251:2410.
11. Kripke DF, Simons RN, Garfinkle L, et al. Short and long sleep and sleeping pills: Is increased mortality associated? Arch Gen Psychiatry 1979;36:103.
12. Rossi GF, Colicchio G, Pola P. Interictal epileptic activity during sleep: A stereo-EEG study in patients with partial epilepsy. Electroencephalogr Clin Neurophysiol 1984;58:97.
13. McKee AC, Levine DN, Kowall NW, et al. Peduncular hallucinosis associated with isolated infarction of the substantia nigra pars reticulata. Ann Neurol 1990;27:500.
14. Mahowald MW, Schenck CH. Dissociated states of wakefulness and sleep. Neurology 1992;42:44.
15. Brylowski A, Levitan L, LaBerge S. H-reflex suppression and autonomic activation during lucid REM sleep: A case study. Sleep 1989;12:374.
16. Lipowski ZJ. Delirium in the elderly patient. N Engl J Med 1989;320:578.
17. Erkinjuntti T, Wilkstrom J, Palo J, et al. Dementia among medical inpatients: Evaluation of 2,000 consecutive admissions. Arch Intern Med 1986;146:1923.
18. FitzGibbon T, Hayward JS, Walker D. EEG and visual evoked potentials of conscious man during moderate hypothermia. Electroencephalogr Clin Neurophysiol 1984;58:48.
19. Harris TJB, Brice DD, Hetherington RR, et al. Dreaming associated with anaesthesia: The influence of morphine premedication and two volatile adjuvants. Br J Anaesth 1971;43:172.
20. Larsen SF, Zaric D, Boysen G. Postoperative cerebrovascular accidents in general surgery. Acta Anaesthesiol Scand 1988;32:698.
21. Klemm WR. Electroencephalographic-behavioral dissociations during animal hypnosis. Electroencephalogr Clin Neurophysiol 1941;51:365.
22. Guilleminault C, Phillips R, Dement WC. A syndrome of hypersomnia with automatic behavior. Electroencephalogr Clin Neurophysiol 1975;38:403.
23. Parkes JD. The Anatomical and Physiological Basis of the Sleep-Wake Cycle. In JD Parkes (ed), Sleep and Its Disorders. London: Saunders, 1985;80.
24. Nogueira de Melo A, Krauss GL, Niedermeyer E. Spindle coma: Observations and thoughts. Clin Electroencephalogr 1990;21:151.
25. Danze F, Brule JF, Haddad K. Chronic vegetative state after severe head injury: Clinical study, electrophysiological investigations and CT scan in 15 cases. Neurosurg Rev 1989;12(Suppl):477.
26. Muller JE, Ludmer Pl, Willich SN, et al. Circadian variation in the frequency of sudden cardiac death. Circulation 1987;75:131.
27. Engel J Jr. Seizures and epilepsy. Philadelphia: Davis, 1980;251.

28. Annegers J, Hauser W, Shirts S. Heart disease mortality and morbidity in patients with epilepsy. Epilepsia 1984;25:699.
29. Willich SN, Levy D, Rocco MB, et al. Circadian variation in the incidence of sudden cardiac death in the Framingham Heart Study population. Am J Cardiol 1987;60:801.
30. Gould JB, Lee AFS, Morelock S. The relationship between sleep and sudden infant death. Ann N Y Acad Sci 1988;533:62.
31. Nimmannit S, Malasit P, Chaovakul V, et al. Potassium and sudden unexplained nocturnal death. Lancet 1990;1:116.
32. Bremer F. Cerveau isolé et physiologie du sommeil. C R Soc Biol (Paris) 1935;118:1235.
33. T Roth, WC Dement (eds), Principles and Practice of Sleep Medicine (2nd ed). Philadelphia: Saunders, 1994;125.
34. Caplan LR. Top of the basilar syndrome. Neurology 1980;30:72.
35. McKee AC, Levine DN, Kowall NW, et al. Peduncular hallucinosis associated with isolated infarction of the substantia nigra pars reticulata. Ann Neurol 1990;27:500.
36. Aldrich MS, Naylor MW. Narcolepsy associated with lesions of the diencephalon. Neurology 1989;39:1505.
37. Fernández JM, Sadaba F, Villaverde FJ, et al. Cataplexy associated with midbrain lesion. Neurology 1995;45:393.
38. Forcadas MJ, Zarranz JJ. Insomnio y alucinaciones tras lesiones vasculares del tegmento protuberancial en el hombre. Neurología 1994;9:211.
39. Autret A, Laffont F, Toffol B, et al. A syndrome of REM and non-REM sleep reduction and lateral gaze paresis after medial tegmental pontine stroke. Arch Neurol 1988;45:1236.
40. Balk RA, Hiller FC, Lucas EA, et al. Sleep apnea and the Arnold-Chiari malformation. Am Rev Respir Dis 1985;132:929.
41. Steljes DG, Kryger MH, Kirk BW, et al. Sleep in postpolio syndrome. Chest 1990;98:133.
42. Barnhart M, Rhines R, McCarter JC, et al. Distribution of lesions of the brain stem in poliomyelitis. Arch Neurol Psychiat (Chic) 1948;59:368.
43. Baker AB, Matzke HA, Brown JR. Poliomyelitis. III. Bulbar poliomyelitis, a study of medullary function. Arch Neurol Psychiat (Chic) 1950;63:257.
44. Bonekat HW, Andersen G, Squires J. Obstructive disordered breathing during sleep in patients with spinal cord injury. Paraplegia 1990;28:292.
45. Braun SR, Giovannoni R, Levin AB, et al. Oxygen saturation during sleep in patients with spinal cord injury. Am J Phys Med Rehabil 1982;61:302.
46. von Economo C. Sleep as a problem of localization. J Nerv Ment Dis 1930;71:249.
47. Culebras A, Magaña R. Neurologic disorders and sleep disturbances. Semin Neurol 1987;7:277.
48. Chesson AL, Levine SN, Kong LS, et al. Neuroendocrine evaluation in Kleine-Levin syndrome: Evidence of reduced dopaminergic tone during periods of hypersomnolence. Sleep 1991;14:226.
49. Villablanca J. Role of the Thalamus in Sleep Control: Sleep-Wakefulness Studies in Chronic Diencephalic and Athalamic Cats. In O Petre-

Quadens, JD Schlag (eds), Basic Sleep Mechanisms. New York: Academic, 1974;51.

50. Jurko MF, Andy OJ, Webster CL. Disordered sleep patterns following thalamotomy. Clin Electroencephalogr 1971;2:213.

51. Hachinski V, Mamelak M, Norris JW. Sleep Morphology and Prognosis in Acute Cerebrovascular Lesions. In JS Meyer, H Lechner, M Reivich (eds), Cerebral Vascular Disease. Amsterdam: Excerpta Medica, 1977.

52. Culebras A, Feldman RG, Merk FB. Cytoplasmic inclusion bodies within neurons of the thalamus in myotonic dystrophy. J Neurol Sci 1973;19:319.

53. Culebras A, Podolsky S, Leopold NA. Absence of sleep-related growth hormone elevations in myotonic dystrophy. Neurology 1977;27:165.

54. Culebras A, Miller M. Dissociated patterns of nocturnal prolactin, cortisol and growth hormone secretion after stroke. Neurology 1984;34:631.

55. Lugaresi E, Medori R, Montagna P, et al. Fatal familial insomnia and dysautonomia with selective degeneration of thalamic nuclei. N Engl J Med 1986;315:997.

56. Lugaresi E. The thalamus and insomnia. Neurology 1992;42:28.

57. Nielsen JM, Sedgwick RP. Instincts and emotions in an anencephalic monster. J Nerv Ment Dis 1949;110:387.

58. Autret A, Carrier H, Thommasi M, et al. Etude physiopathologique et neuro-pathologique d'un syndrome de décortication cérébrale. Rev Neurol 1975;131:491.

59. Culebras A, Miller M. Dissociated patterns of nocturnal prolactin, cortisol and growth hormone secretion after stroke. Neurology 1984;34:631.

60. Hauri P, Hawkins DR. Human sleep after leukotomy. Arch Gen Psychiatry 1972;26:469.

61. Culebras A. Update on disorders of sleep and the sleep-wake cycle. Psychiatr Clin North Am 1992;15:467.

62. Nauta WJ, Haymaker W. Hypothalamic nuclei and fiber connections. In W Haymaker, E Anderson, WJH Nauta (eds), The Hypothalamus. Springfield, IL: Thomas, 1969;136.

63. Association of Sleep Disorders Centers. Diagnostic Classification of Sleep and Arousal Disorders, First Edition, prepared by the Sleep Disorders Classification Committee, H.P. Roffwarg, Chairman, Sleep 1979;2:1.

64. Diagnostic Classification Steering Committee. MJ Thorpy, Chairman – ICSD–International Classification of Sleep Disorders: Diagnostic and Coding Manual. Rochester, MN: American Sleep Disorders Association, 1990.

4

Polysomnography

Polysomnography is the generic name for the body of recording methods and techniques used for the diagnosis of sleep disorders in the sleep laboratory [1, 2]. It borrows some of the neurophysiologic methodology applied in electroencephalogram (EEG) laboratories but differs in the focus of its parameters, placing emphasis on nocturnal recording. Polysomnography is complemented with video and sound recordings of the patient to assess nocturnal behaviors, vocalizations, and snoring. When applicable, the recording is extended to daytime hours. The recording of sleep parameters should be conducted in a properly equipped sleep laboratory by well-trained technologists with expertise in the technical aspects of polysomnography and basic knowledge of the nature of the disorders affecting the patients being tested. Sporadic recordings performed in an EEG laboratory by well-motivated though insufficiently trained technologists should be discouraged because invariably they are doomed to fail and will result in misleading test results.

Laboratory Evaluation of Sleep Disorders

Sleep studies, also known as polysomnography, allow the recording and temporal correlation of electrophysiologic phenomena important to sleep and its disorders. Polysomnographic recordings incorporate a combination of electrophysiologic parameters appropriate to the clinical condition under consideration. The most common problems studied are sleep-related respiratory syndromes, continuous positive airway pressure (CPAP) testing, excessive daytime somnolence, periodic movements of sleep, motor episodes of sleep, seizures, and insomnia. In some laboratories, testing for erectile impotence is also performed.

Temporal correlation of sleep-related events facilitates the interpretation of phenomena such as electrocardiographic (ECG) changes in relation to sleep apnea episodes, desaturations of oxygen in association with sleep stages and apneas, and depth and severity of sleep apnea episodes associated with body positions. These studies also allow temporal correlations of physiologic parameters with video recordings of the patient's behavior. Daytime recordings are interpreted as a continuum of nocturnal recordings. Isolated daytime recordings have little value since the characteristics of daytime sleep are modulated by nocturnal sleep.

To a certain extent, the sleep laboratory modifies the phenomena of sleep. The "first-night effect" is a well-known phenomenon that alters the architecture of sleep in certain individuals during the first night of adaptation to the laboratory [3]. Sleep latencies are prolonged, and fragmentation of sleep with frequent position changes reduces sleep efficiency and, in some instances, decreases the percentage of slow wave sleep (SWS). A second night of testing allows a return to a sleep cycle morphology that is more attuned to the patient's norm. The elimination of the first-night effect is not critical for the diagnosis of sleep apnea syndromes or for conditions in which the presence of a specific phenomenon determines the diagnosis. For instance, if paroxysmal dystonia or a nocturnal seizure occurs during the first night of testing with the seizure protocol, a second night of testing might not be necessary. Some motor phenomena, like somnambulism, do not occur nightly, and several nights of testing might be necessary to make a diagnosis, not so much to eliminate the "first-night effect" but to increase the chances of capturing the pathologic event.

In general, one night of testing followed by a daytime multiple sleep latency test (MSLT) is sufficient to diagnose most conditions commonly referred to the sleep center. CPAP testing requires a second night of study following a diagnosis of sleep apnea syndrome, for titration of pressures, assessment of tolerance, and global effect on sleep architecture. "Split night" testing, in which the first half of the night is dedicated to diagnosis of sleep apnea syndrome and the second half is used for testing with the CPAP machine, should be discouraged. This practice compromises the chances of diagnosing the severity of the sleep-related respiratory syndrome, since most of REM sleep occurs during the second half of the night, when sleep apnea episodes acquire their maximal expression. Titration of CPAP pressures might also be compromised because initial manipulation of the apparatus and pressures in the middle of the night can affect the full expression of REM sleep.

Polysomnographic Techniques

The basic polysomnogram is composed of the electroencephalogram (EEG), electro-oculogram (EOG), and electromyogram (EMG). Other physiologic parameters are added as needed. These parameters are recorded in independent polygraphic channels and arranged in a montage or study protocol that displays the electrophysiologic phenomena necessary for scoring the stages of sleep and for the assessment of the condition under consideration. Long leads are required to allow reasonable mobility during the night.

Electroencephalography

One or more channels are used for recording of cortical cerebral potentials. In our laboratory, we use three derivations that record cerebral electrogenesis from the right central region (C_3-A_1), left central region (C_4-A_2), and occipital region, the latter in a bipolar connection (O_1-O_2) (Figure 4-1). In some laboratories, the norm is to connect the paracentral region with the contralateral ear in a crossed arrangement that increases the amplitude of potentials but sacrifices laterality. The three-channel montage, as conducted in our laboratory, allows independent recordings from the central region of both hemispheres close to the vertex, where sleep phenomena such as vertex waves, sleep spindles, and K complexes acquire their maximal expression. It also records from the occipital region where alpha rhythms are best defined, facilitating the identification of changes in alpha activity that mark the transition from the alert state to stage 1 of sleep. In general, we use a sensitivity of 5 µV per mm or 7 µV per mm, an impedance of less than 5,000 Ω, and 70-Hz filters. The electrodes are perforated gold cups attached to the skin with collodion to ensure durability, and

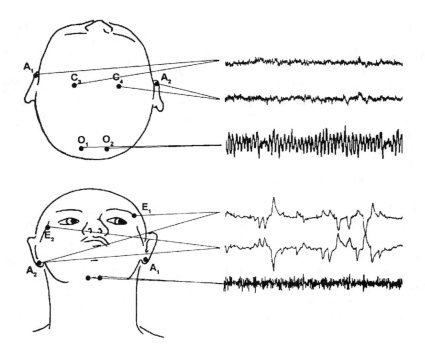

Figure 4-1. *The basic montage for polysomnography includes three channels for electroencephalography (EEG): C_3–A_1, C_4–A_2, and O_1–O_2 (10–20 System for electrode placement); two channels for electro-oculography (EOG): E_1–A_2 and E_2–A_2; and one channel for submental electromyography (EMG). The subject is awake and relaxed exhibiting desynchronized activity in central regions, alpha rhythm in occipital areas, rapid eye movements of wakefulness, and moderately active muscle tone. (E_1 = left eye; E_2 = right eye; A_2 = right ear lobe.)*

placed over the skull according to the 10–20 System to standardize anatomic localization.

Electro-Oculography

The eye globe acts as a small dipole where the retina is negative relative to the cornea. Eye movements create currents that are easily recorded as high-voltage potentials over the orbits or in anterior regions of the head. Electrodes (silver-silver chloride disposable) are placed 1 cm lateral and slightly superior to the lateral canthus of the left eye (E_1), and 1 cm lateral and slightly inferior to the lateral canthus of the right eye (E_2) (Figure 4-1). Both electrodes are connected in a monopolar arrangement with the right ear lobe (A_2). This montage differentiates EEG activity or artifacts that occur in-phase in both channels from true conjugate eye movements that appear as out-of-phase deflections. Amplitude will be slightly higher in the channel that crosses the midline. To make a distinction between vertical and horizontal conjugate eye movements, a third derivation with a supranasion electrode connection is required. The sensitivity used in EOG channels is 5 µV per mm or 7 µV per mm, the high-frequency filter is set at 35 Hz, and the time constant at 0.3 seconds, with an impedance of less than 5,000 Ω. The EOG channels are essential for gathering rapid eye movements of the alert state and of REM sleep, as well as slow rolling eye movements of early stage 1 of sleep.

Electromyography

One channel is sufficient to record EMG activity of submental muscles, using a bipolar arrangement of two electrodes (silver-silver chloride disposable) placed over the chin muscles (Figure 4-1). The EMG channel is used to recognize resting muscle tone changes in the different stages of sleep, in particular muscle atonia of REM sleep. In a variation of the EMG montage, electrodes are placed over the masseter muscle to record gnawing and masticatory activity in patients suspected of suffering bruxism. The sensitivity of the submental muscle channel is typically set at 20 µV per cm, although adjustments are required depending on the resting muscle tone activity of the individual. However, once the recording has commenced, changes in sensitivities might be confused with natural variations of muscle tone and should not be introduced. High filters are set at 70 Hz and low filters at 5 Hz (equivalent to a time constant of 0.035 seconds), and the impedance should be maintained below 5,000 Ω.

Electrocardiography

The ECG is not essential for scoring sleep stages but is very useful in assessing heart rhythm variations that occur during REM stage or in different pathologic situations, most notably in relation to profound sleep apnea events. One channel is sufficient to record activity gathered by electrodes (silver-silver chloride disposable) placed over the left subclavicular region and seventh intercostal space. Gain is set at 1 mV per cm and the filters between 1 and 15 Hz. This ECG recording is not useful for interpreting morphologic alterations of the QRS complex.

Respirations

The objective of respiratory monitoring is to identify apneas and hypopneas that are critical to the diagnosis of the sleep apnea syndromes. In addition, respiratory rhythm changes might be detected. The respiratory activity is monitored with thermistors or thermocouples that detect the subtle temperature changes caused by the exchange of air through the nose and mouth. One thermistor is placed over the side of the mouth and nose to record movement of air from all orifices. Chest excursions and abdominal movements related to the respiratory effort are best recorded with strain gauges placed around the thorax and abdomen. Two channels are necessary to monitor independently the effort of intercostal muscles and the diaphragm, and to identify paradoxic respirations that appear as out-of-phase deflections of the thoracic and abdominal efforts. Other methods include the esophageal balloon, a device inserted in the distal esophagus that measures pleural pressure variations. It is particularly useful to identify markedly negative pressures associated with obstructive apneas and differentiate them from the central apneas in which negative pressures do not occur in the absence of effort. Intercostal and diaphragmatic EMG tracings are useful adjuncts to record directly muscle activity in these groups.

Oximetry

Oxygen saturation of hemoglobin is continuously quantified with pulse oximeters that use a photoelectric cell to read changes in the color spectrum of oxyhemoglobin. Probes are attached to the earlobe or the fingertip. The tracing is calibrated to record 0–100% saturation where 1 mm deflection is equivalent to 2% saturation. Oximeters are relatively accurate when the saturation of oxygen is above 40%. Below that level, the figures obtained are inaccurate but might indicate a trend. Some laboratories prefer to improve the display over 40% saturation by sacrificing lower recordings and opening more space for recordings above.

The oximetry tracing in the polysomnogram is obtained by interfacing the output of the oximeter to a DC channel of the polygraph. Because probes are positioned in distal vascular territories, there is a delay of several seconds in the display of variations of oxyhemoglobin saturation relative to the respiratory effort and the ECG. Oximetry is a valuable component of the study of the sleep apnea syndromes.

Other Parameters

Leg or arm movement activity is recorded by means of surface EMG electrodes (silver-silver chloride disposable) attached to the anterior tibial muscle or the deltoid muscle. The recording channel obtains a tracing of the resting muscle tone and of any movement occurring during the recording period. A tracing of muscle activity in the extremities is necessary for the investigation of periodic movements of sleep and valuable for the study of bizarre behaviors and seizure activity at night.

Accelerometers and actigraphs can also be used for the detection of extremity and other body movements during the night. Most movement disorders of the waking state tend to disappear in sleep, so gains that are set while the patient is still awake should be kept at a low level.

Penile tumescence during sleep is recorded using mercury-filled ring electrodes that are placed around the base and tip of the penis [4]. An electrical current is generated when the ring is stretched, and the current can be recorded as a calibrated signal in a time-compressed graph of the night. Sleep-related tumescence studies for the study of organic versus psychogenic impotence have become less popular in recent years because of their relative inaccuracy and high expense, as well as evolution of therapeutic trends.

Endoesophageal pH tracings are used to identify esophageal reflux of acidic gastric contents while the patient is asleep. A pH-sensitive probe is inserted in the distal esophagus, and the output is interfaced with a DC channel of the polygraph. Deflections from a pH baseline of 6 indicate changes in the acid-base environment of the distal esophagus. Gastroesophageal reflux is identified when the pH falls below 4 for 30 seconds or more; the episode terminates when the pH returns to 4 or 5 [5].

The technologist notes the patient's body positions during sleep in the polysomnogram or uses a position monitor attached to the chest of the patient to generate appropriate electrical signals. Direct interface with the polygraph allows recording of position changes. Snoring and sleep apnea episodes can occur exclusively or become more intense and severe in the supine position, a phenomenon that has therapeutic implications.

Audio and Video Recording

The observation of the sleeping patient and the recording of all-night or of selected sleep segments is an important adjunct to polysomnography. The recording can be done using a closed-circuit television unit that uses a low-intensity light television camera with a pan-and-tilt mechanism, zoom lens focused on the bed, and remote controls in the equipment room. A small microphone is installed near the patient's head to record respiratory sounds and vocalizations. With this unit, the technologist can observe the patient on the television monitor and record annotations regarding sleep behavior, snores, body postures, incidents, and even accidents. Videotape recordings register visual and sound events for later analysis and interpretation by the specialist who is not present when they occur. Video and audio recordings are time-correlated with polysomnographic episodes using time-code generators with output to both systems.

Study Protocols

The arrangement of physiologic parameters in a montage of tracings appropriate for the study of sleep and its alterations is called a polysomnographic protocol. These protocols differ depending on the objective of the nocturnal study. The basic protocol for scoring the stages of sleep incorporates EEG, EOG, and EMG channels to which other parameters are added as needed. The only limitation is the channel capacity of the polygraph recorder. The following protocols are based on a 12-channel polygraph:

Basic Protocol

1. $C_3–A_1$
2. $C_4–A_2$
3. $O_1–O_2$
4. EOG left
5. EOG right
6. EMG

ECG is commonly added to the basic protocol. This montage is sufficient for the study of uncomplicated narcolepsy and other intrinsic hypersomnias. It is also used for recording the MSLT.

Sleep Apnea Protocol

1–6.   Basic

7.   ECG

8.   EMG anterior tibial

9.   Oronasal ventilation

10.   Thoracic excursions

11.   Abdominal excursions

12.   Oximetry

The apnea protocol (Figure 4-2) is also used for titration of CPAP and bilevel positive air pressure (Bi-PAP) units.

Periodic Leg Movements (Nocturnal Myoclonus) Protocol

1–6.   Basic

7.   ECG

8.   EMG anterior tibial (right or left)

9.   EMG contralateral anterior tibial

If sleep apnea is a consideration, two respiratory channels and oximetry can be added.

Erectile Impotence Protocol

1–6.   Basic

7.   ECG

8.   Tumescence base

9.   Tumescence glans

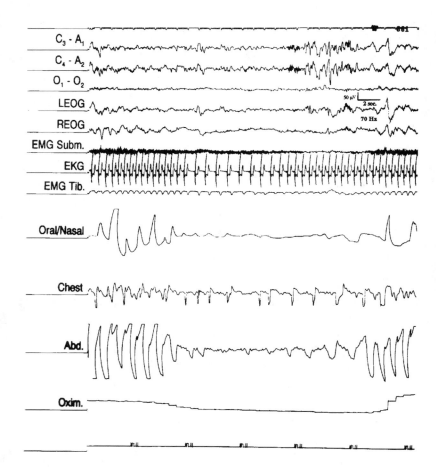

Figure 4-2. *Polysomnogram with the sleep apnea protocol illustrating a 30-second epoch representing one page of the record running at a speed of 10 mm per second. It shows an episode of mixed apnea with initial suspension of respiratory activity followed by abdominal effort ending in successful ventilation as noted in the oronasal channel. The oximetry channel shows a decline in oxygen saturation with recovery by the end of the apnea episode. The ECG channel reveals bradycardia during the apneic episode followed by tachycardia in the recovery phase. The EEG (C_3–A_1, C_4–A_2, and O_1–O_2) shows an arousal at the initiation of abdominal effort. (LEOG = left electro-oculogram; REOG = right electro-oculogram; EMG Tib = electromyogram tibialis muscle.)*

It is recommended that the studies for erectile impotence be performed over two consecutive nights to eliminate the first-night effect.

Seizure Protocol

1. T3–T4 (T3–P3 optional)
2. P3–P4 (T4–P4 optional)
3. C_3–A_1
4. C_4–A_2
5. O_1–O_2
6. EOG left
7. EOG right
8. EMG submental muscle
9. ECG
10. EMG left anterior tibial
11. EMG right anterior tibial
12. EMG deltoid (optional)

The seizure protocol is also used for the evaluation of the patient with a movement disorder or bizarre behavior during sleep. Two consecutive nights might be needed to capture the activity under question.

The paper speed typically used for polygraphic recording is 10 mm per second, although 15 mm per second can be used also. Higher speeds generate excessive amounts of paper and of epochs to be scored without adding more information, except when seizure activity needs to be analyzed. Time-compression to a paper speed of 5 mm per second or less decreases definition of high-frequency parameters such as sleep spindles and alpha activity. Polysomnograms are typically recorded on paper. In laboratories with computerized equipment, polygraphic signals are recorded in an optic disk for eventual display on a TV monitor or paper, or both.

Recording Procedure

The recording officially starts when the lights are turned off in the patient's bedroom and ends in the morning when the patient is awak-

Table 4-1. Filters and Gains

Channel	Low filter (Hz)	Time constant (secs)	High filter (Hz)	Sensitivities (μV/cm)
EEG	0.3	0.4	70	50
EOG	0.3	0.4	35	50
EMG	5	0.03	120	50
ECG	1	0.12	15	1
Respirations	0.15	1–2	15	50

EEG = electroencephalogram; EOG = electro-oculogram; EMG = electromyogram;
ECG = electrocardiogram.

ened by the technologist, who declares the procedure officially terminated. Both events, beginning and end, should be clearly defined in the record because scoring data are calculated relative to these two variables. Before and after the onset and cessation of the official recording, a series of routines are performed in the sleep laboratory that serve as a clinical adjunct to the record and improve the quality of the procedure.

Calibrations

Calibrations must be done at the beginning and end of the study. High and low filters of AC channels and low filters of DC channels are set at the beginning of the study (Table 4-1). The technologist should not use 50-Hz filters, except in extreme situations in which that artifactual frequency interferes with the record. Gain levels can vary from one individual to another, but once set at onset, they should not be modified unless some important occurrence requires a change. AC channels are reserved for EEG, EOG, EMG, and ECG recordings, whereas DC channels best serve electrical potentials with slow periodicity such as respirations, oximetry, and penile tumescence.

At 10 mm per second, each epoch or page of the tracing represents 30 seconds of recording, so that in a conventional 6-hour night, 720 pages are accumulated. Thus, chronic logistic problems in a sleep laboratory are the amortization of paper costs and records storage. Computerization and registration in optic disks has eased the pressure, but some recording on paper is still required to maintain quality control of studies.

Patient Preparation

The technologist receives the patient in the sleep laboratory at approximately 20.00 hours and initiates standard procedures that are intended to gather clinical information, put the patient at ease, and prepare the patient for the night recording. A description of the study is generally required to alleviate anxiety generated by the test. In some instances, patients are invited to tour the facility before the day of the testing.

The patient's collaboration is critical to obtain a good study. Well-informed patients who are at ease and mentally stable, without major concerns and anxiety triggered by the study, follow instructions and participate in a satisfactory manner. Information previously received in the form of brochures, letters, or telephone explanations prepare the patient for the initial encounter with the laboratory. This information should contain details about the precise timing of the test, its duration, and possible return visits to the laboratory for additional procedures. Patients should be told what toiletry accessories and clothing to bring for the night. Previous conversations with the specialist and with the laboratory personnel should have clarified what medications should be continued. Medications that modify cerebral electrogenesis are not allowed (Table 4-2) since they interfere significantly with the ability to score the record. Unauthorized medications must be discontinued 5–10 days before the procedure because of the prolonged half-life and activity of many products, such as the benzodiazepines, and to avoid a rebound effect. In special situations, a urine assay is indicated. Malingerers seeking stimulants for the alleged control of hypersomnia can precipitate daytime REM sleep, a sign of narcolepsy, by discontinuing abruptly (12 hours before the test) the administration of high doses of amphetamines.

The technologist should gather clinical information that is pertinent to the study, including a list of medications taken during the 10 days before the procedure. Questionnaires given before the beginning of the test procure information on sleep habits and schedules. A Zung test can be useful to screen for depression [6]. The application of electrodes can take up to 1 hour to complete (Figure 4-3). The application is followed by the pertinent calibrations to ensure that the equipment is in operating condition for the night. The patient is asked to move the eyes in all directions of gaze, blink, clench the teeth, breathe, and move the legs.

The patient is then invited to get into bed. Activities such as reading, watching television, and even smoking are permitted before the lights are turned off for the night. Excessive rigidity in laboratory procedures can prolong unnaturally the sleep latency. Children under 10 years

Table 4-2. Unauthorized Medications for Patients Undergoing Polysomnography

---

Barbiturates

Benzodiazepines

Zolpidem

Hypnotics in general

Antihistaminics

Chloral hydrate

Monoamine oxidase inhibitors

Amphetamines

Caffeine-containing preparations

Tricyclics*

Phenothiazines*

Haloperidol*

Cough preparations*

Psychoactive drugs in general*

---

*Authorized in special cases.

should be accompanied by one parent during the night. Polysomnography should not be performed in patients who are psychotic, delirious, demented, febrile, intoxicated, or under heavy sedation, except in particular circumstances or for clinical research.

During the night, the technologist tends the equipment, makes the appropriate entries on the record, and records information in the computer. An important task is to assist the patient at night. The independent function of the technologist requires maturity, knowledge, and experience. Decisions must be made in the absence of the specialist, and in case of need, calls are placed to the supervisory physician or even to the emergency team. Technologists are required to be trained in cardiorespiratory resuscitation for emergency application during the night, should it be required. Fortunately, despite a high-risk population and phenomena that raise concern, such occurrences are relatively rare.

Following the official termination of the study, the patient is asked to answer another questionnaire requesting personal perceptions and recollection of events occurring during the night, as well as a report on his or her satisfaction with sleep and with the laboratory. This

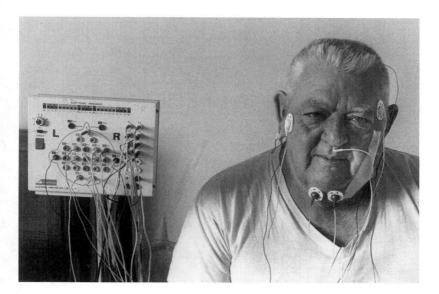

Figure 4-3. *Patient prepared for nocturnal polysomnography showing full complement of electrode attachments. Electro-oculogram electrodes are placed 1 cm lateral and slightly below or above the canthus of each eye. A nasal thermistor is in place for detection of nasal ventilation. Two submental electrodes are required for bipolar detection of muscle tone variations free of extraneous contaminations. Cables to the electrode junction box are long to permit movements in bed while the patient is asleep. Scalp electrodes are not visible. (Reprinted with permission from Culebras A. La Medicina del Sueño. Editorial Ancora. Barcelona, 1994.)*

information might help make a diagnosis of sleep misperception. The Zung test is then repeated. If an MSLT is to follow, the patient stays in the laboratory.

Multiple Sleep Latency Test

The MSLT was devised for the assessment of daytime sleepiness but also serves to identify daytime REM sleep, which is of critical value for the diagnosis of narcolepsy [7, 8]. The patient is put to sleep at 2-hour intervals starting at 8:00 A.M., and four or five segments are recorded. Each segment is allowed to last 20 minutes if there is no sleep recorded, or a maximum of 15 minutes after the first epoch of sleep. The objective is to identify the latency of sleep or time elapsed from lights out to the first epoch of sleep. This latency is defined as the point in the polysomnogram at which sleep occupies 50% or more of the epoch. A 50% reduction of alpha activity along with slow rolling eye movements and a subtle reduction in muscle tone indicate stage 1. REM sleep latency is defined as the time from the beginning of sleep to the onset of REM.

Four recording segments are sufficient, but some laboratories prefer to record five. The MSLT is scored according to general criteria and presented in a summary of values that contains total recording time, total sleep time, daytime sleep efficiency (percentage of time asleep relative to recording time), average proportion of each stage of sleep relative to total sleep time, mean sleep latency, and mean REM sleep latency.

It is generally assumed that a mean sleep latency of 5 minutes or less indicates a pathologic level of daytime sleepiness. The normal range starts at 10 minutes, and the interval that lies between (6–9 minutes) remains indeterminate and should be interpreted on a case by case basis. The presence of REM sleep in two or more segments of the MSLT is considered diagnostic of narcolepsy, except in instances in which the previous nocturnal sleep is highly disturbed by sleep apnea. In that event, a second MSLT test is necessary following successful treatment of the sleep apnea syndrome.

The MSLT should always be preceded by a nocturnal polysomnogram, and both should conform in time as closely as possible to the patient's real-life schedule. A morning MSLT in a patient who works nights has little value. REM sleep activity in the first segment of the morning is observed in patients who customarily sleep late. Daytime REM sleep can be precipitated by the abrupt discontinuation of drugs that suppress REM sleep. Occasionally, REM sleep occurs in one or more daytime segments in patients with sleep apnea that interfere with nocturnal generation of REM sleep.

Scoring

The quantification or scoring of the polysomnogram and MSLT is performed by the senior technologist using the criteria of Rechtschaffen and Kales for sleep staging [9] (Figures 4-4 through 4-7). Sleep apnea events are classified, measured, and tabulated along with oxygen desaturations, arousals, ECG changes, leg movements, and EEG abnormalities (Table 4-3). Other parameters noted include snoring; body positions; and

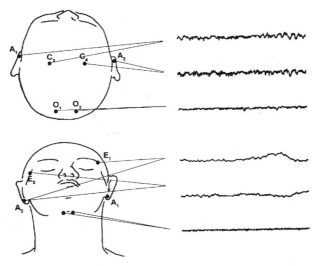

Figure 4-4. *Stage 1 of sleep manifested by presence of relatively low-voltage, mixed frequency electroencephalogram activity, slow rolling eye movements, reduction in muscle tone, and occasional vertex waves.*

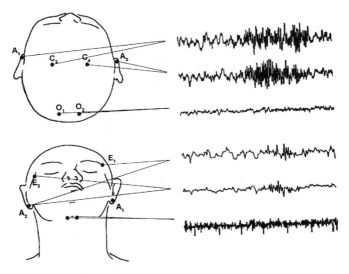

Figure 4-5. *Stage 2 of sleep manifested by presence of sleep spindles (12–14 Hz undulating waveforms shown in illustration), K complexes, and vertex waves (not shown).*

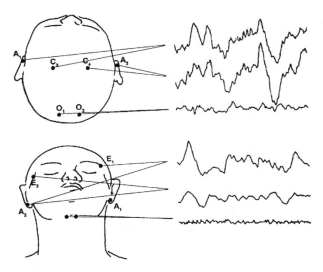

Figure 4-6. *Stage 3 of sleep manifested by slow wave activity of more than 75 µV amplitude and less than 2 Hz occupying 20–50% of the epoch. Stage 4 is characterized by slow wave activity occupying more than 50% of the epoch.*

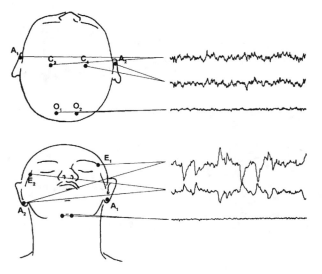

Figure 4-7. *Stage REM is characterized by the presence of rapid eye movements, markedly reduced muscle tone, and mixed low-voltage electroencephalogram. Sleep spindles and K complexes are not seen.*

behavioral alterations such as vocalizations, attempts to get out of bed, paroxysmal movements, and seizure activity. This process lasts approximately 1 hour and is carried out page by page on the paper tracing or on the computer monitor.

Table 4-3. Definition of Terms

Stage wake	Presence of alpha activity and low-voltage, mixed frequency activity
Sleep onset	Transition from wake to sleep marked by > 50% reduction in alpha activity and presence of stage 1. Transition to REM stage can be observed in some patients
Stage 1	Presence of relatively low-voltage, mixed frequency EEG activity, slow rolling eye movements, reduction in muscle tone, and occasional vortex waves (Figure 4-4)
Stage 2	Presence of sleep spindles, K complexes, and vertex waves (Figure 4-5)
Stage 3	Slow wave activity of > 75 μV amplitude and < 2 Hz occupying 20–50% of epoch (Figure 4-6)
Stage 4	Slow wave activity occupying > 50% of epoch (Figure 4-6)
Stage REM	Presence of rapid eye movements, markedly reduced muscle tone, and mixed low-voltage EEG. No sleep spindles or K complexes (Figure 4-7)
Sleep latency	Time elapsed from lights out to onset of sleep
REM sleep latency	Time elapsed from onset of sleep to beginning of first episode of REM sleep
Non-REM sleep latency	Time elapsed from onset of sleep to beginning of first episode of non-REM sleep
Total recording time	Time elapsed from lights out to lights on
Total sleep time	Time in sleep from onset of sleep to end of sleep
Sleep efficiency	Percent of time in sleep relative to recording time
Arousal	Partial awakening of < 30 seconds' duration characterized by increased muscle tone and movement activity
Awakening	Return to wake stage of > 30 seconds' duration
Movement time	Time consumed by artifact obscuring the record

Table 4-3. *continued*

Central apnea	Cessation of airflow and respiratory effort of > 10 seconds' duration
Obstructive apnea	Cessation of airflow without loss of respiratory effort of > 10 seconds' duration
Mixed apnea	Initial central apnea followed by obstructive apnea
Hypopnea	Reduction of > 50% of airflow of > 10 seconds' duration with desaturation of oxygen
Apnea and hypopnea index	Number of events per hour of sleep
Desaturation of oxygen	Reduction in oxygen saturation of > 4%

REM = rapid eye movement; EEG = electroencephalogram.

Computer-Assisted Scoring

Computer technology has changed the everyday operation of laboratories in which it has been installed. Computer equipment allows the registration and storage of data in optic disk, permits paperless scoring on a computer monitor, and facilitates printing of eloquent graphs highlighting different aspects of the process [10]. These capabilities have reduced, if not eliminated, the use of expensive paper and have resolved the storage problem of voluminous and heavy records. The retrieval of old records has been made very simple, and comparisons are immediately available.

There are two methods of applying computer technology to polysomnography: computer-assisted scoring and automated scoring. With assisted scoring, the technologist reviews the polysomnogram epoch by epoch on the monitor, staging sleep, and making annotations of artifacts and incidents that computers might not readily identify such as motor events, REM sleep without atonia, and seizures. Numerical data entered in the computer can be incorporated into the record. With automated scoring, standardization of the scoring system improves, and much unavoidable inter- and intraobserver variation is obviated. However, the specialist should be mindful that automated systems have difficulty recognizing transitions from wake to stage 1 to REM sleep, and fail to distinguish accurately between arousals, epileptiform activity, and parasomnias. The temptation is to rely excessively on the results provided by the computer at the expense of accuracy, and therefore, meticulous supervision is required.

There are several systems available to suit the idiosyncrasies and budget of each laboratory. Most recording systems accept more than one patient simultaneously. Some are more flexible than others in permitting changes in the diagnostic parameters and algorithms set by the manufacturer. Assisted scoring and automated scoring are optional features in most systems. Automated scoring systems process signals as they are being collected and allow almost immediate display of results after the study has been completed. The number of channels displayed simultaneously on the monitor can vary from one system to another, and the tables and graphics generated are also different.

Quality control should be performed frequently by scoring manually a paper polysomnogram obtained concurrently with the computer-assisted or computer-generated record and comparing results.

Hypnograms

Laboratories with computer-assisted scoring can display the events of the night in a computerized histogram, or hypnogram, that features temporal correlations prominently (Figure 4-8). Hypnograms facilitate immensely the diagnosis of sleep alterations. The typical hypnogram displays in a temporal sequence beginning with lights out, the stages of sleep (awake, REM sleep, stages 1–4, and movement time), the apnea or hypopnea index, saturation of oxygen curve, heart rate, positions of the body, arousals, awakenings, leg jerks, and CPAP/Bi-PAP pressure curves. Depending on the computer model and software used, different variations of temporal correlations can be obtained. Hypnograms form part of the documentation package submitted to the referring physician.

Interpretation

The scoring sheet with data from the epoch-by-epoch analysis along with the hypnogram are presented to the polysomnographist for clinical description and interpretation. The final report contains a detailed account of parameters tested and numerical results (Table 4-4). The final impression summarizes the key findings and provides a diagnosis with Current Procedural Terminology (CPT) codes that conform with the

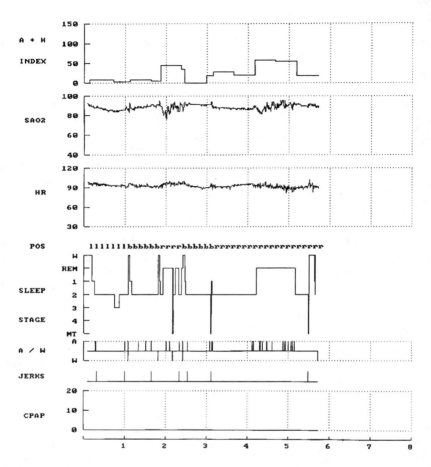

Figure 4-8. *A computer-generated hypnogram showing temporal correlation of sleep parameters. REM sleep is correlated with an increase in the apnea and hypopnea index and more profound desaturations of oxygen (SAO₂). Arousals (A) tend to cluster with episodes of apnea. (A + H index = apnea and hypopnea index; SAO₂ = saturation of oxygen; HR = heart rate; POS = body position; Sleep stage = architecture of sleep; W = wake; MT = movement time; A/W = arousals and awakenings; jerks = leg jerks; CPAP = mask pressures when continuous positive airway pressure apparatus is applied. Numbers at the bottom refer to nocturnal hours elapsed from lights out.)*

Table 4-4. Information Contained in the Polysomnographic Report

1. Parameters monitored
2. Start time and duration of study
3. Sleep stages with time and percent spent in each stage, total sleep time, sleep efficiency, number and duration of awakenings and arousals, latencies to sleep, REM sleep, and non-REM sleep
4. Respiratory patterns (central, obstructive, mixed), number, mean and duration, impact on saturation of oxygen, sleep stage, and body position in sleep. Associated arousals and other phenomena
5. Cardiac rhythm, rate changes, and effect of apneas on same
6. Behavioral observations
7. EEG and EMG abnormalities. Abnormal motor activities
8. MSLT description with mean sleep latencies per segment and account of REM sleep events if present

REM = rapid eye movement; EEG = electroencephalogram; EMG = electromyogram; MSLT = multiple sleep latency test.

International Classification of Sleep Disorders. The interpretation and a copy of the hypnogram are sent to the referring physician along with a covering letter offering additional comments and recommendations.

Satellite Systems

Some computerized units include the option of a satellite system that records data away from the laboratory in an optic disk. The location could be another ward within the hospital, another hospital in the same town or city, or a distant site. The disk can be delivered by overnight mail to the main laboratory for analysis and interpretation of data. The impression can then be returned by telephone communication or FAX transmission to the originator. Recordings are done in a satellite laboratory setting, attended by a trained technologist, using a full spectrum of channels and protocols. The attendant need not have the full qualifications of the technologists in the main laboratory, and the equipment required is limited to the satellite recorder and a closed-circuit television unit. The satellite laboratory is an acceptable compromise for centers that have a demand for sleep procedures, but which find it impractical to send their patients to the central laboratory and find it cost-ineffective to develop a fully operational laboratory.

Ambulatory Polysomnography

Portable devices are available to record sleep stages, cardiorespiratory functions, and oximetry outside the sleep laboratory in unattended settings. This recording can be done in the patient's home or in an intensive care unit, depending on circumstances. Recent acquisition of computerized systems to sample, store, retrieve, display, and analyze information has made it possible to replicate polysomnographic records outside the laboratory. Factors that decrease the practicality of laboratory-based polysomnography, such as limitations in patients' access, high cost, and extraneous environment, have stimulated the development of ambulatory polysomnography. However, since the studies are performed unattended, serious concerns have been raised about the intrinsic quality of records and the potential for acquiring spurious information in the absence of trained personnel.

Various systems with different recording capabilities are available [11]. Patients are instructed to come to the laboratory in the evening for the application of electrodes and system set up. The input cable from the recorder is camouflaged under the patient's shirt and attached to a neck collar, which holds the input jacks. The cassette recorder is lightweight and is carried around the waist or in a pocket. Chewing gum, baths, and showers are prohibited. The failure rate is 1.6% [12].

According to the ASDA Standards of Practice Committee [13], a comprehensive portable polysomnography system incorporates seven channels (EEG, EOG, EMG, ECG, airflow, respiratory effort, and oximetry) to which actigraphy can be independently added. A modified protocol incorporates four channels (respiratory effort, airflow, ECG, and oximetry). Obstructive sleep apnea is the most common condition targeted for assessment outside the laboratory. The recommendations given by the ASDA state that standard laboratory-based polysomnography is the accepted test for the diagnosis of sleep apnea syndrome. Unattended portable recordings can be performed when standard polysomnography is not available, for patients unable to undergo study in the sleep laboratory, and for follow-up studies when a diagnosis has been established by standard polysomnography. The ASDA discourages the use of the procedure by commercial testing companies in the absence of a physician-initiated order.

In centers in which normative data for ambulatory polysomnography have been acquired, this technique might be valuable in the assessment of patients with alleged insomnia who present a major first-night effect, or have excessive concerns about laboratory testing. Twenty-four-hour recordings are possible and can provide a more accurate assessment of daytime naps and nighttime vigils than what is recounted by the patient. Conditioned arousal stimuli developed by patients with psychophysiologic insomnia might be easier to identify with home recordings [12].

Actigraphy

Actigraphy involves documentation of the rest or activity cycle and use of motion as a diagnostic tool by means of a device that detects movement in all directions. The sensor is a piezoelectric beam incorporated in a wristwatch-type unit that collects data over several days. The unit can be interfaced with a computer system that accepts downloading of data into its memory for storage and analysis. Display of data and review are made in time-compressed graphs with a variety of retrieval and mobility options. The screen formats can be printed into report forms. Actigraphy can be used for documentation of circadian activity, leg movement activity during the day and night (restless legs and periodic movements of sleep), jet lag, pediatric sleep; for shift work studies; and for the identification of a variety of movement disorders in sleep, such as parkinsonian tremors.

Practice Guidelines

Laboratory-based polysomnography is an accepted technique for the objective assessment of sleep disorders. Patients are referred to the sleep center and laboratory by a variety of medical professionals or come on their own. Self-referred patients should always be evaluated clinically by a sleep specialist before the decision is made whether a sleep study in the laboratory is necessary. Ideally, patients referred by physicians and other professionals should also be evaluated initially by a sleep center specialist. Not uncommonly, patients are referred to the laboratory following a thorough assessment by outside knowledgeable specialists that leaves little room for improvement. In this situation, it is redundant and excessive to subject the patient to yet another clinical evaluation by the center specialist. In our center, we accept outside evaluations, but we make a point of reviewing all documentation submitted to determine its validity and the protocol to be applied. Direct referrals to the laboratory not backed by clear documentation become a potential source of confusion and should be discouraged.

Several professional organizations have published practice parameters and guidelines [14, 15] to guide clinicians in the proper use of this technique, as well as to standardize procedures and set limits to avoid abuse. The conditions with indication for laboratory study that are most commonly evaluated are sleep-disordered breathing, narcolepsy-cataplexy, sleep-related violent or injurious behaviors, periodic movements of sleep, and selected instances of insomnia. The evaluation of circadian rhythm and seasonal affective disorders in a sleep laboratory has been deemed promising by the Practice Committee of the American Academy of Neurology. The recording, scoring, and interpretation of sleep stages and respiratory parameters of neonates and infants requires special experience and training. Polysomnography for the evaluation of nighttime sleep and daytime sleepiness is considered a safe procedure.

The efficacy of sleep studies has been proven for the diagnosis of sleep-disordered breathing and for the evaluation and titration of subsequent treatment modalities such as CPAP. In addition, the MSLT has been proven effective to determine the degree of hypersomnia suffered by patients with sleep-disordered breathing. The application of CPAP and Bi-PAP units for the elimination of sleep-disordered breathing should be initiated in the sleep laboratory. Tolerance, titration of mask pressures, and effect on sleep parameters can be evaluated only in the sleep laboratory.

Formal sleep studies have also been proven effective for the diagnosis of narcolepsy and for its differentiation from other hypersomnias. The combination of a nocturnal polysomnogram followed by an MSLT is the optimal test to establish the diagnosis of narcolepsy and idiopathic CNS hypersomnia.

A variety of spells or ictal events that are harmful to the patient and bedmate can occur during the night and should be ultimately differentiated from epileptiform seizures. Many times, clinical evaluation is inconclusive because these conditions masquerade as each other; objective laboratory assessment becomes necessary with polysomnographic recording and direct video observation. Included in this category are somnambulism, sleep terrors, confusional arousals, sleep-related seizures, REM sleep behavior disorder, paroxysmal arousals, nocturnal dystonias, and psychogenic dissociative states.

Polysomnography is indicated when the diagnosis of periodic movements of sleep is suspected, to define the condition, and to assess the degree of excessive daytime somnolence, should it be present. A nocturnal test with the appropriate protocol followed by an MSLT is the combination of choice.

Although insomnia is the most common sleep-related complaint, the evaluation of this condition in the sleep laboratory is limited to situations in which a pathophysiologic cause is suspected, such as sleep-disordered breathing, periodic movements of sleep, and sleep misperception. In some studies, the yield of clinically useful information has been as high as 49% in patients with chronic insomnia [16]. According to the ASDA, sleep laboratory evaluation of insomnia is indicated when the condition has been present for more than 6 months, has not responded to therapy, and when a medical or psychiatric cause has been excluded.

References

1. McGregor PA. Updates in polysomnographic recording techniques used for the diagnosis of sleep disorders. Am J EEG Technol 1989;29:107.
2. Culebras A. The practice of neurosomnology. Arq Neuropsiquiatr 1990;48:138.
3. Browman CP, Cartwright RD. The first-night effect on sleep and dreams. Biol Psychiatry 1980;15:809.
4. Ware JC, Hirshkowitz M. Characteristics of penile erections during sleep recorded from normal subjects. J Clin Neurophysiol 1992;9:78.
5. Orr WC. Gastrointestinal Disorders. In MH Kryger, T Roth, WC Dement (eds), Principles and Practice of Sleep Medicine (2nd ed). Philadelphia: Saunders, 1994;861.
6. Zung WWK. A self-rating depression scale. Arch Gen Psychiatry 1965;12:63.
7. Carskadon MA, Dement WC, Mitler MM, et al. Guidelines for the Multiple Sleep Latency Test (MSLT): A standard measure of sleepiness. Sleep 1986;9:519.
8. Roehrs T, Roth T. Multiple sleep latency test: Technical aspects and normal values. J Clin Neurophysiol 1992;9:63.
9. Rechtschaffen A, Kales A (eds), A Manual of Standardized Terminology, Techniques and Scoring System for Sleep Stages of Human Subjects. Los Angeles: BIS/BRI, UCLA, 1968.
10. Burgess RC. Technology and equipment review. Computerized polysomnographic analysis systems. J Clin Neurophysiol 1990;7:145.
11. Zimmerman JT, Torch WC, Reichert JA. A comparison of sleep data-acquisition and analysis systems and computerized-paperless polysomnography. Journal of Polysomnography Technology 1992;44(June 30).

12. McCall MV, Erwin CW, Edinger JD, et al. Ambulatory polysomnography: technical aspects and normative values. J Clin Neurophysiol 1992;9:68.
13. Standards of Practice Committee of the American Sleep Disorders Association. Portable recording in the assessment of obstructive sleep apnea. Sleep 1994;17:378.
14. Therapeutics and Technology Assessment Subcommittee of the Practice Committee, American Academy of Neurology, Practice Handbook. Assessment: Techniques Associated with the Diagnosis and Management of Sleep Disorders. Minneapolis, MN, 1991;95.
15. American Electroencephalographic Society. Guideline fifteen: Guidelines for polygraphic assessment of sleep-related disorders (polysomnography). J Clin Neurophysiol 1994;11:116.
16. Coleman RM, Roffwarg HP, Kennedy SJ, et al. Sleep-wake disorders based on a polysomnographic diagnosis. JAMA 1982;247:997.

5

Insomnia

> *"If we don't ever sleep again, so much the better,"* José Arcadio Buendía *said in good humor. "That way we can get more out of life." But the Indian woman explained that the most fearsome part of the sickness of insomnia was not the impossibility of sleeping, for the body did not feel any fatigue at all, but its inexorable evolution toward a more critical manifestation: a loss of memory.*
>
> Gabriel García Márquez
> *One Hundred Years of Solitude,* 1970 [1]

Overview

Insomnia is not a diagnosis; it is a symptom that refers to the inability to initiate or maintain sleep. Insomnia encompasses disturbed, low-quality sleep, as well as sleep of reduced duration that is insufficient to restore full alertness. When chronic, insomnia is perhaps the most vexing problem in the clinical practice of somnology because of its resistance to therapeutic mediation and the considerable amount of human suffering that it causes. It has been estimated that 35% of the general population will suffer a bout of insomnia in the course of any given year and that half of that group will consider the episode serious enough to consult a physician [2]. And yet, insomnia remains an underreported, underdiagnosed, and inframanaged form of sleep disorder that lacks an organized program of health care [3]. One-fourth of insomniacs use alcohol ingestion to promote sleep, and approximately 30% resort to nonprescription, over-the-counter drugs [4]. The management of insomnia offered by primary care physicians is rather simple, reflecting lack of training, and usually taking the form of a reactive prescription for a sleeping pill. In recent years, negative publicity surrounding pharmacotherapy for insomnia has led to undertreatment and suspended motivation for administration of medications with genuine effect in the global management of the patient with insomnia.

Insomnia is commonly associated with anxiety, depression, psychological stress, psychopathology, and in some instances neurologic illness. Of patients consulting a physician for insomnia, 53% also have some psychiatric symptom [5], and 24% might have depression. An epidemiologic study has indicated that 57% of patients reporting insomnia develop a psychiatric condition within the year [6]. The profile of the patient with advanced insomnia is revealing and suggests that commonly patients are older women, who suffer other medical health problems, psychic distress, anxiety, or depression [7].

The absence of timely nocturnal sleep engenders frustration, increasing anxiety, and anger that dispel any hopes of attaining any meaningful rest. Lack of restoration and loss of the pleasant feeling of refreshment that is associated with a satisfying sleep are manifested by mental and physical fatigue, somnolence, and loss of motivation. The reaction to these symptoms generates some of the same manifestations of anxiety and depression that initiated the insomnia, closing a cycle of vicious circular course that is difficult to discontinue. Primary and secondary manifestations are often so enmeshed in patients in whom insomnia has become a stressor that an analysis of what came first might not be practical. Patients with inveterate insomnia are often plagued by subjective complaints that diminish their functional capacity, interfere with their social interactions, alter their family life, and limit their joie de vivre, inexorably diminishing the quality of their existence.

In a study conducted by the American Cancer Society, chronic sleeplessness of less than 4 hours per night was found to be associated with relative increased mortality of 2.8 for men and 1.5 for women [8]. A similar trend was noted by the California State Department of Health in persons who slept less than 6 hours per night. Long sleep length was also associated with increased mortality. Mortality was the lowest for persons sleeping 7–8 hours per night [9]. These results remain unexplained, particularly after adjusting for other risk factors, and suggest that duration of sleep serves as an index of general health.

The study of insomnia involves the identification and evaluation of all possible medical, physical, psychoaffective, psychophysiologic, and social factors that disturb sleep. Analysis and proper perspective of the weight of each factor in the global picture provide the clinical tools to approach rationally the symptom-complex of insomnia.

Definition

Insomnia, or agrypnia, is the lack of sleep at times when convention dictates that one should be asleep. The condition of sleeplessness might be temporary causing a transient insomnia, which by definition is a symptom occurring in persons who under normal circumstances sleep well. In general, the condition lasts less than 3 weeks. Many factors can trigger transient insomnia, but the common denominator is activation of the system that maintains alertness. Hyperactivity of this system occurs in response to alerting or stressing factors that can originate in the environment or be of a medical or psychogenic nature. Environmental extrinsic factors such as noise generated by airports, nearby highways, and busy city streets disturb sleep. A restless, snoring bedmate is another extrinsic cause of alteration. Admission to a hospital or moving to a new household produces enough stress and alters the conditioned responses of the individual sufficiently to disturb the ability to sleep. Pain at night (such as that caused by rheumatic disorders), a change in medication, and ingestion of large amounts of coffee are some of the common conditions that can cause temporary insomnia. A death in the family, a divorce, an important test, and an appearance in court are examples of stressors that can also temporarily affect sleep.

Most persons have suffered an episode of insomnia in response to a precipitating factor, but it remains to be explained why some persons suffer repeated bouts without being subjected to more intense stimuli. It is believed that vulnerable individuals have an intrinsic low threshold for the development of insomnia or possess stress-control mechanisms that fail to restore the baseline in a timely manner, creating the ingredients for the development of chronic insomnia.

Age is of paramount importance in the development of insomnia. Precipitating, coadjuvant, and conditioning factors differ as age advances, suggesting that there are forms of insomnia that are idiosyncratic to each age. The clinician should be cognizant of these variations to understand better the type of insomnia affecting the patient and to implement a more effective therapy. Sleeplessness in infancy should alert the clinician to a disorder affecting the maturation of the nervous system, since normal sleep development is an index of global brain function. Insomnia can dominate the manifestations of the child with minimal brain dysfunction. Sometimes a familial incidence is uncovered, and a diagnosis of idiopathic insomnia is entertained. However, not infrequently, insomnia in the child is instead a complaint of the parents who have perceptions, limits, and habits not conforming to reality. In middle age, psychiatric and mood disorders are common conditions affecting the insomniac. As age advances, physical, neurologic, and pharmacologic factors, combined with psychosocial problems inherent to advanced age, converge on a sleep architecture that tends to be increasingly vulnerable to disturbances.

The pattern of insomnia can provide clues to its origin. The inability to initiate sleep is generally caused by a heightened level of anxiety and can differ from the insomnia that occurs as a result of the inability to maintain sleep. Fragmentation of nocturnal sleep secondary to many awakenings can follow an apparently easy onset of sleep and could be the consequence of factors that develop as the night progresses, ranging from an insufficient bladder to medication effect. A rather typical pattern of insomnia occurs in patients with some forms of depression who have no major difficulty falling asleep but wake up 3 or 4 hours later, finding it difficult to return to sleep. This early morning awakening generally responds well to the satisfactory treatment of depression, attesting to its origin.

Thus, insomnia is a common, final pathway where a variety of factors converge. Insomnia can be transient or chronic, primary or secondary, somatic or psychogenic, extrinsic or intrinsic to the organism, with various recognizable clinical patterns. Insomnia can in itself precipitate psychopathology that makes the condition chronic.

Insomnia secondary to manipulation or alteration of the biological clock such as can occur with jet lag, shift work, or delayed phase syndromes is discussed in Chapter 9.

Classification

The original Classification of Sleep Disorders of 1979 [10] defines insomnia as the inability to initiate or maintain sleep, conceding equal weight to latency to sleep, duration of sleep, and quality of sleep. There are nine subtypes of insomnia categorized according to the alleged source of sleeplessness. The clinical forms of insomnia (Disorders of Initiating and Maintaining Sleep [DIMS]) listed are as follows:

1. *Psychophysiologic.* This type includes transient insomnia caused by acute emotional disturbances, and persistent insomnia engendered over the years by somatized tension-anxiety and negative conditioning to sleep. Apprehension about falling asleep constitutes a conditioned factor that might be one of the most common forms of insomnia related to repeated unsuccessful and excessive efforts to sleep. Patients with this condition sleep better away from home.

2. *Associated with psychiatric disorders.* This type of insomnia is related to behavioral disorders, affective disturbances, and psychotic alterations. Patients with depression exhibit a characteristic pattern of sleep characterized by easy onset, early morning awakening, and short REM sleep latency. In mania, there is sleep onset insomnia and short sleep. In patients with acute and chronic psychoses, sleep onset and continuity are seriously disturbed by feelings of anxiety, guilt, fear, suspiciousness, and pressure of thought.

3. *Associated with use of drugs and alcohol.* This form of insomnia is related to tolerance of or withdrawal from psychoactive and central nervous system depressants. Tolerance is related to an escalation of doses to achieve the same effect. Loss of pharmacologic effect in the middle of the night, such as can occur when tolerance develops or with short-acting hypnotics, leads to rebound insomnia. Very active dreaming can occur during the second part of the night in patients suffering withdrawal effects when the drug has an inhibitory action over REM sleep of the first part of the night. Sustained use of stimulants that are taken in excessive amounts or too late in the day is also a cause of sleeplessness. The drugs listed in Table 5-1 have sleep-interfering effects. Acute intoxication with alcohol induces sleep that is followed by withdrawal effects and insomnia in the second half of the night. Chronic alcoholism disintegrates sleep architecture, whereas withdrawal from drinking causes slow wave sleep (SWS) and REM sleep rebound. Severe, inveterate alcoholism can cause permanent alteration of sleep generation.

4. *Associated with sleep-induced respiratory impairment.* When predominant, central sleep apnea syndrome causes disturbance of nocturnal sleep maintenance with awakenings characterized by sensations

Table 5-1. Drugs That Interfere with Sleep

Phenylethylamines (ephedrine, amphetamines)
Xanthines (theophylline, caffeine)
Antimetabolites
Cancer chemotherapeutic agents
Thyroid preparations
Phenytoin
Monoamine oxidase inhibitors
Adrenocorticotropic hormone
Oral contraceptives
Alpha methyldopa
Propranolol
Cocaine

of gasping for breath or choking associated with anxiety. Central apneas are recognized as episodes of cessation of breathing during REM and non-REM sleep. Only some of the apneic episodes lead to a full awakening. Central sleep apnea syndrome is more common in the elderly and can occur in isolation or in association with diffuse degenerative neurologic disorders. Patients with central sleep apnea snore intermittently and not as loudly as patients with obstructive sleep apnea; neither type of patient complains of respiratory trouble during the day. Obstructive sleep apnea syndrome is typically associated with daytime somnolence. Some patients derive benefit from the application of a continuous positive airway pressure (CPAP) apparatus, and others respond to the administration of oxygen, as discussed in Chapter 7. True Ondine's curse is the inability to breathe while asleep; most often this syndrome takes the form of primary alveolar hypoventilation with prominent hypoxemia. Choking sensations that awaken the patient and are associated with gasping for breath and a feeling of anxiety should also suggest the sleep-related abnormal swallowing syndrome and gastroesophageal reflux. Polysomnography is required to diagnose central sleep apnea syndrome, its severity, and the impact caused in sleep architecture and oxygen saturation levels. It is also necessary to differentiate the condition from other disorders causing awakenings associated with gasping for breath and anxiety.

5. *Associated with sleep-related (nocturnal) myoclonus and "restless legs."* Periodic episodes of repetitive stereotypical leg jerks while the patient is asleep, known as nocturnal myoclonus syndrome, or periodic limb movement disorder, can be associated with insomnia when leg jerks are followed by arousals. The movement disorder consists of flexion of the knee and hip associated with dorsiflexion of the ankle and dorsal extension of the first toe. Each movement lasts less than 5 seconds and does not have the jerky quality that its name implies. Periodicity occurs at 20- to 40-second intervals in clusters of many minutes. Sometimes the movement disorder affects one leg, other times there is alternation of sides. The condition is rather common in the elderly and associated with a variety of neurologic disorders. It has been estimated that 13% of patients complaining of insomnia have nocturnal periodic limb movement syndrome as a primary condition [11]. Polysomnography is required to make the diagnosis. Benzodiazepines, opioids, levodopa/carbidopa and carbamazepine are useful in the treatment of this condition, sometimes in combination. Further details are discussed in Chapter 10.

Restless legs syndrome is generally associated with periodic leg movements of sleep and is characterized by creeping, uncomfortable dysesthesias in the legs, which forces the individual to shift position continuously. It interferes with sleep onset when it occurs in the evening. Treatment is similar to that for periodic leg movements syndrome.

6. *Associated with other medical, toxic (Table 5-2), and environmental (Table 5-3) conditions.* This category includes medical, neurologic, environmental, and toxic factors and parasomnias interfering with onset and continuity of sleep. Removal of the cause restores sleep.

7. *Childhood-onset DIMS.* This type involves developmental insomnia without explanation that starts before puberty and persists into adulthood.

8. *Associated with other DIMS conditions.* This category includes conditions involving repeated REM sleep interruptions with awakenings recurring in almost every REM sleep period. It does not include conditions in which somatic phenomena, such as headache or angina, evoked in REM sleep cause the awakening. Nonrestorative sleep is a poor-quality light sleep associated with atypical polysomnographic features such as alpha sleep or alpha-delta sleep characterized by alpha waves occurring in non-REM sleep.

9. *No DIMS abnormality.* This category includes healthy insomniacs with short sleep who need less than the conventional amount of

Table 5-2. Toxic Factors That Interfere with Sleep

Arsenic

Mercury

Copper

Heavy metals

Carbon monoxide

Radiation

Tobacco

Table 5-3. Environmental Factors That Interfere with Sleep

Heat

Cold

Noise

Light

Excessive movement of bed partner

Danger

Allergens

Hospitalization

Unfamiliar surroundings

sleep, for instance 2 or 3 hours in the 24-hour cycle. It also includes individuals who complain of insomnia that is at variance with laboratory evidence of normal architecture of sleep, clearly reflecting a sleep misperception.

The International Classification of Sleep Disorders (ICSD) [12] (see Chapter 3) seeks a pathophysiologic organization acknowledging that the pathology is unknown for most sleep disorders. In this classification, the primary insomnias are further subdivided into intrinsic, caused by a factor from within the body; extrinsic, caused by a factor external to the body; and the ones that are the consequence of a circadian rhythm disorder. The primary insomnias are separated from the large group of insomnias that are secondary to a medical, neurologic, or psychiatric disorder.

The ICSD lists three degrees of severity for the cardinal symptom of insomnia, as follows:

1.   Mild insomnia is a complaint of insufficient sleep along with a feeling of not being rested, without impairment of daily functions. It can be associated with mild anxiety, frustration, and fatigue.

2.   Moderate insomnia is insufficient sleep along with feelings of not being rested occurring nightly and associated with moderate impairment of functioning. It always generates irritability, anxiety, and fatigue.

3.   Severe insomnia involves insufficient sleep and feelings of not being rested occurring nightly with severe impairment of social and occupational functioning. It is associated with irritability, anxiety, and fatigue.

The ICSD offers a list of differential diagnoses extracted from the main classification that serves to place the insomnias in the context of the global overview of sleep disorders (Table 5-4).

Table 5-4. Differential Diagnosis of the Insomnias

1. Associated with behavioral/psychophysiologic disorders
    a. Adjustment sleep disorder
    b. Psychophysiologic insomnia
    c. Inadequate sleep hygiene
    d. Limit-setting sleep disorder
    e. Sleep-onset association disorder
    f. Nocturnal eating (drinking) syndrome
    g. Other
2. Associated with psychiatric disorders
    a. Psychoses
    b. Mood disorders
    c. Anxiety disorders
    d. Panic disorder
    e. Alcoholism
    f. Other

Table 5-4. *continued*

3. Associated with environmental factors
   a. Environmental sleep disorder
   b. Food allergy insomnia
   c. Toxin-induced sleep disorder
   d. Other
4. Associated with drug dependency
   a. Hypnotic-dependent sleep disorder
   b. Stimulant-dependent sleep disorder
   c. Alcohol-dependent sleep disorder
   d. Other
5. Associated with sleep-induced respiratory impairment
   a. Obstructive sleep apnea syndrome
   b. Central sleep apnea syndrome
   c. Central alveolar hypoventilation syndrome
   d. Chronic obstructive pulmonary disease
   e. Sleep-related asthma
   f. Altitude insomnia
   g. Other
6. Associated with movement disorders
   a. Sleep starts
   b. Restless legs syndrome
   c. Periodic limb movement disorder (nocturnal leg myoclonus)
   d. Nocturnal leg cramps
   e. Rhythmic movement disorder
   f. REM sleep behavior disorder
   g. Nocturnal paroxysmal dystonia
   h. Other
7. Associated with disorders of the timing of the sleep-wake pattern
   a. Short sleeper
   b. Time zone change (jet lag) syndrome
   c. Shift work sleep disorder
   d. Delayed sleep phase syndrome
   e. Advanced sleep phase syndrome

    f. Non–24-hour sleep-wake syndrome

    g. Irregular sleep-wake pattern

    h. Other

8. Associated with parasomnias (not otherwise classified)

    a. Confusional arousals

    b. Sleep terrors

    c. Nightmares

    d. Sleep hyperhidrosis

    e. Other

9. Associated with central nervous system disorders (not otherwise classified)

    a. Parkinsonism

    b. Dementia

    c. Cerebral degenerative disorders

    d. Sleep-related epilepsy

    e. Fatal familial insomnia

    f. Other

10. Associated with no objective sleep disturbance

    a. Sleep-state misperception

    b. Sleep choking syndrome

    c. Other

11. Idiopathic insomnia

12. Other causes of insomnia

    a. Sleep-related gastroesophageal reflux

    b. Fibrositis syndrome

    c. Menstrual-associated sleep disorder

    d. Pregnancy-associated sleep disorder

    e. Terrifying hypnagogic hallucinations

    f. Sleep-related abnormal swallowing syndrome

    g. Sleep-related laryngospasm

    h. Other

Source: Reprinted with permission from Diagnostic Classification Steering Committee, Thorpy MJ, Chairman. The International Classification of Sleep Disorders: Diagnostic and Coding Manual. Rochester, MN: American Sleep Disorders Association, 1990;331.

Common Patterns

Sleep-onset insomnia, or the inability to fall asleep at a conventional time with waiting periods of 30 minutes or more from bedtime, is common and can occur on several occasions throughout life. This form of sleeplessness also appears in individuals experiencing anxiety and is seen in association with acute grief, environmental changes, hospitalization, loss of a job, examinations, bereavement of any kind, and even with positive emotions such as anticipation of a wedding day or having the first baby. Insecure individuals with low emotional thresholds are particularly vulnerable.

Inability to maintain sleep suggests fragmentation caused by extrinsic agents such as environmental noise (Figure 5-1); excessive light; a hot or cold environment; and a restless, snoring bed partner. However, loss of continuity can result from the action of pathophysiologic factors such as the sleep apnea syndrome, nocturnal myoclonus, asthma, or painful osteoarthritis. It is also common in individuals with psychiatric disorders or psychophysiologic insomnia. Individuals with constitutional light sleep are more severely affected by extraneous factors whether extrinsic or intrinsic.

The pattern of early morning awakening is typical of individuals with psychoaffective depression. Successful treatment of the depression improves the ability to maintain sleep all night long.

Cyclical insomnia is observed in patients with bipolar psychoaffective disorders, in alcoholics with a tendency to binge, in individuals with anorexia and bulimia nervosa, and in patients with drug addiction.

Circadian rhythm disorders are the consequence of a misalignment of the biological clock with external geocosmic rhythms. In the delayed-phase syndrome, the inability to fall asleep at a conventional time might mimic a sleep-onset insomnia. However, individuals with this condition eventually fall into a deep, long sleep from which they cannot be aroused easily.

Clinical Forms

Psychophysiologic Insomnia

This form of insomnia is the consequence of a complex series of factors combining a premorbid tendency to light sleep and precipitating events of an emotional nature. The persistence of these factors can even-

Figure 5-1. *The City From Greenwich Village at night illustrates eloquently the many sources of disturbance that can afflict the sleep of the urban dweller. (Reprinted with permission from John Sloan, 1922, Oil on canvas. National Gallery of Art, Washington, D.C.)*

tually induce a negative conditioned behavior that perpetuates a chronic aversion to engage in sleep. Psychophysiologic insomnia can be transient and situational, such as when it is caused by acute emotional conflicts that disrupt not only the ability to fall asleep but also the continuity of sleep. Patients under the influence of acute emotional stress who fail to sleep properly at night are seldom sleepy during the day but complain of being fatigued and drained of energy. Typically, they are unable to take daytime naps for the same reason that their nocturnal sleep is disturbed. Uncomplicated transient and situational insomnia disappears once the precipitating emotional factors are eliminated.

The persistence of psychoaffective elements in individuals with a tendency to somatize tension and anxiety can produce over time a negative reinforcement or conditioned response to their sleeplessness. The failure to engage in sleep causes apprehension about the acts of going to bed and entering sleep that is charged with negative emotions and anxiety. Excessive and unsuccessful efforts to sleep stimulate arousal responses that guarantee sleeplessness night after night, reinforcing apprehension and closing the vicious circle of psychophysiologic insomnia. Individuals with these kinds of worries have no difficulty falling asleep when not trying, such as when reading, waiting, or watching a show. Furthermore, they sleep better away from home where the objects of the conditioned response (such as furniture, sounds, and rituals) are not present. Patients with anxiety fueled by their daily activities also sleep better during vacations away from home because the stressors of work and school are probably inoperative. Unfortunately, the negative conditioning developed by some individuals remains as a negative learned behavior long after the stressors and objects of their conditioning have disappeared. Under such influence, insomnia can persist unless steps are taken to eliminate the learned behavior. Poor sleep habits picked up in response to the disturbance create a subsidiary set of negative factors that need to be resolved by retraining the individual in proper sleep hygiene.

Individuals with psychophysiologic insomnia commonly exhibit other traits of somatized tension (such as muscle contraction headaches, vague aches, low back pain, and dizziness) that are mixed with the effects of longstanding sleeplessness (such as fatigue, irritability, poor memory, and reduced concentration). Somatized symptoms and subjective negative perceptions interfere with the ability to function and decrease work productivity, adding elements to the patient's fears and worries. The sleep of the anxious individual is of short duration and marred by intrusive thoughts, restlessness, excessive muscular tension, and poor restorative quality. Polysomnography has revealed alpha activity infiltrating a record punctuated by many awakenings and postural shifts. In less anxious individuals, all stages of sleep are reached with a relatively good distribution. A recent study shows that when insomniacs with psychophysiologic factors are studied in the laboratory with polysomnography and the multiple sleep latency test (MSLT), they do not exhibit a heightened level of daytime sleepiness, perhaps because chronic physiologic hyperarousal prevents both sleep and sleepiness [13].

Patients with a heavy load of conditioned behavior sleep better in the sleep laboratory than at home, a phenomenon that they acknowledge in the morning questionnaire. Consecutive night studies in the sleep laboratory have uncovered in some patients a "reverse first-night effect," indicating better sleep on the initial night than on subsequent studies [14]. On the other hand, patients with sleep misperception who complain of insomnia exhibit a quasinormal sleep in the laboratory, but when they complete their morning questionnaire, they claim to have slept poorly or not at all.

A sleep laboratory study can also serve to uncover pathophysiologic causes of insomnia such as sleep apnea and nocturnal myoclonus.

Depression

The primary affective disorders are subdivided into major depressive and bipolar disorders. Both conditions alter sleep but in different ways. Patients with depression secondary to other psychiatric conditions or medical and neurologic disorders can also have insomnia but less pronounced and of a different pattern. Sleep alteration is so common in patients with depression that it is considered a diagnostic manifestation. Insomnia predominates, but 15–20% of patients have a bipolar disorder with hypersomnia [15].

Patients with a major depressive disorder have a profound alteration of mood without a clear precipitating factor. In the unipolar type, insomnia is characterized by minor difficulty falling asleep with a pattern of early morning awakening 2–4 hours after sleep onset that disturbs severely the continuity of sleep. Elderly patients have more difficulty than younger ones. The polysomnographic evaluation confirms reduced total sleep and usually uncovers a short REM sleep latency (20–40 minutes) that is considered a biological marker of depression [16]. Stages 3 and 4 are also reduced relative to baseline tracings. REM sleep percentages are elevated in patients with depression and shifted toward the first part of the night, a phenomenon that is the result of combining reduced SWS and REM sleep episodes of equal duration, in contrast with normal individuals, who exhibit lengthening of successive REM periods as the night progresses. Density of rapid eye movements, or frequency of eye movements per unit of time, is increased, a phenomenon that is also observed in narcolepsy. Short REM sleep latency can be seen in the early stages of the disorder and in masked depression, contributing to the clinical diagnosis. Patients with agitated depression or with a strong component of anxiety also exhibit sleep-onset insomnia.

In bipolar depression, mania alternates with major depression. During the depressive phase, patients report daytime somnolence and experience increased duration of nocturnal sleep with the characteristic feature of short REM sleep latency. Despite increased duration of total sleep, patients continue to complain of unrefreshed vigilance. During the manic phase, sleep is abbreviated with a drastic reduction in the 24 hours that fails to provoke complaints of fatigue or tiredness in the hypervigilant patient.

Patients with secondary depression also experience early morning awakenings and short REM sleep latency, but these are less pronounced than in patients with primary depression.

Chronic Anxiety

The personality disorder predominantly displaying anxiety, in a patient without affective or psychotic disorder, is associated with sleep-onset and sleep maintenance insomnia. In generalized anxiety disorder, there are no specific clinical characteristics other than the persistent anxious mood. Anxiety can also be a prominent feature of other conditions that embody functional alterations commonly labeled as neurotic. These conditions can present various clinical forms that include panic and phobic disorders, hypochondriasis, obsessive-compulsive disorder, and posttraumatic stress disorder. In phobic and obsessive-compulsive disorders, there is an object of fear and anxiety that is not present in panic disorders, in which the individual develops sudden unexplained episodes of acute anxiety with somatic symptoms, sometimes awakening the patient at night. The posttraumatic stress disorder is easily diagnosed when the precipitating factor can be identified. Sleep continuity suffers as the individual experiences repeated dreams loaded with anxiety recollecting the traumatic event.

Uncontrolled anxiety along with poor stress-control mechanisms dominate the clinical picture in these conditions in which worries, fear, guilt, competitiveness, checking and rechecking, concerns with health, and excessive pre-bed rituals prevent falling asleep. Such psychological conflicts disrupt repeatedly the continuity of sleep, altering considerably its architecture. Tiredness and fatigue during the day are common complaints, but napping is unrewarding or not possible.

Polysomnographic evaluation is seldom necessary although occasionally performed when the clinician orders the test to exclude other conditions such as seizures, night terrors or nightmares in sleep-related panic disorders, or leg myoclonus and sleep apnea in generalized anxiety disorder with fragmentation of sleep. As expected, the laboratory studies in patients with generalized anxiety show long sleep latencies, interruption of sleep by long awakenings, decreased sleep efficiency, increased stage 1, reduced SWS, and reduced REM sleep. The MSLT shows hypervigilance without evidence of excessive daytime somnolence. REM sleep latency is not decreased, in contrast with the phenomenon typically observed in patients with depression. Patients with panic attacks have relatively well-preserved sleep architecture; nocturnal panic attacks occur during non-REM sleep. In general, the laboratory findings in anxiety disorders are nonspecific, showing a degree of abnormality that correlates with the intensity of the clinical manifestations.

Insomnia associated with chronic anxiety can be difficult to differentiate from persistent psychophysiologic disorders with negative conditioning. Although the manifestations of sleeplessness are similar, patients with psychophysiologic insomnia have features of anxiety that are more severe or only manifest in relation to sleep; patients lack the anxious mood during the waking hours.

Successful management of the anxiety disorder considerably improves the ability to initiate and sustain sleep. Insight-oriented psychotherapy and behavioral treatment programs have been successful. Benzodiazepines are the anxiolytic agents par excellence with the additional advantage of a hypnotic effect. Long-acting benzodiazepines (chlordiazepoxide, diazepam, flurazepam) given at bedtime combine a desired early hypnotic effect with a residual anxiolytic action during the ensuing day. Propranolol has a beneficial effect on prominent somatized cardiovascular symptoms, and buspar has a nonsedating anxiolytic action that has been used in patients with sleep-related respiratory difficulties. Panic attacks respond to alprazolam.

Idiopathic Insomnia

Occasionally, one encounters patients with a lifelong form of insomnia, starting in childhood, that is unexplained in its causation and relentless in its progression. These individuals recount being short sleepers in childhood or even problem sleepers in infancy. It appears as if they never had enjoyed a normal sleep. And yet, there are no apparent factors to be blamed for their sleeplessness, even though psychopathology and poor sleep habits eventually add to their insomnia. Patients with idiopathic insomnia also complain of daytime tiredness, irritability, depressive mood, increased tension, and sleepiness as a result of their sleeplessness. When obtaining a clinical history in patients with idiopathic insomnia, the clinician is struck by the continuum of the struggle with sleep from the early years to youth to middle age, evolving from a relatively pure inability to sleep to an existence dominated by a core of unyielding insomnia loaded with psychophysiologic complaints.

In patients with idiopathic insomnia, it is relatively common to find parallel manifestations of minimal brain damage, attention deficit disorder, or a developmental learning disability. This peculiar association elicits the suspicion of an unidentified basic neurologic deficit, perhaps developmental in origin, affecting the centers for the generation of sleep. Current diagnostic techniques have failed to uncover an underlying lesion or a pathophysiologic mechanism responsible for the symptom association. It is worthwhile to note, however, because its elucidation would uncover the common ground between insomnia and the neurologic fabric of the brain.

The polysomnographic study of patients with idiopathic insomnia shows increased sleep latency, and reduced sleep efficiency with sleep fragmentation. In one study, REM sleep was characterized by scarcity of rapid eye movements [17].

The diagnosis is made on the basis of a lifelong history of insomnia starting before puberty in an individual without obvious causes of sleeplessness or evidence of preponderant psychopathologic, psychophysiologic, or psychoaffective disorder. Treatment is remarkably unsuccessful in changing the course of the insomnia. Maladaptive factors added to the primary core of insomnia are more amenable to treatment. Symptomatic medication can be tried with occasional limited success using tricyclic antidepressants, neuroleptics, or opiates.

Sleep State Misperception

Some individuals are convinced that their sleep is of poor quality and too short to satisfy them. They go on to explain how their disturbed sleep is the cause of daytime fatigue that prevents them from functioning at a peak. In extreme instances, they report virtual absence of nocturnal sleep night after night [18]. However, when one tests them in the sleep laboratory the architecture of sleep is close to normal with acceptable latencies, percents of sleep stages, and few interruptions. These individuals have a peculiar form of pseudoinsomnia that is called sleep state misperception. They are not malingerers because their complaints are genuine and have no evidence of psychopathology, but they seem to have lost the ability to keep track of their sleep while asleep, a function that is present in most individuals.

The polysomnographic evaluation shows a normal or quasinormal sleep in contrast with a morning questionnaire indicating a gross miscalculation of perceived time asleep and of sleep latency. Normal polygraphic sleep is characterized by a sleep latency of less than 20 minutes, with a total sleep duration of more than 6.5 hours, devoid of major interruptions [19]; the MSLT shows an average daytime sleep latency of more than 10 minutes. The polysomnographic results showing a marked discrepancy between subjective complaints and objective findings serve to demonstrate to patients that their sleep has near normal parameters despite their claims, an action with therapeutic value.

The condition is distinguished from psychophysiologic insomnia in that patients with sleep misperception carry over complaints of sleeplessness to nights spent in the sleep laboratory, whereas subjects with psychophysiologic insomnia who sleep better away from home and have a near normal sleep in the laboratory will admit the improvement in the morning questionnaire. Patients with atypical polysomnographic features will manifest subtle abnormalities in the polygraphic record such as alpha-delta and alpha-REM complexes that are not present in sleep misperception.

Treatment revolves around the demonstration of a normal or relatively normal nocturnal sleep to the patient. Behavioral modification and psychotherapy might be necessary for patients who have developed secondary symptoms of anxiety and depression.

Childhood Insomnia

Most alterations of sleep in childhood are generated by environmental, familial, or social factors [20]. Poor sleep habits, limit setting failures, family pathology, and excessive parental concerns are the common sources of alleged insomnia in childhood. Complaints of insomnia do not usually come from the child but from the parents. Investigation of the circumstances might show that the parents channel the complaint of insomnia through the impact that the child's behavior has on their own sleep. Such conditions need to be distinguished from the lifelong poor sleeper with secondary psychopathology and the child with physical alterations ranging from sleep apnea to nocturnal asthma to muscular dystrophy.

When evaluating an infant or child for insomnia, it is of foremost importance to determine whether there is a neurologic disorder altering the development of the child, in which case sleeplessness is just another manifestation of the syndrome. For example, a blind child or a child with a hypothalamic disorder will present important alterations of the circadian rhythm with disturbance of the sleep-wake schedule.

Infants with neurologic disorders exhibit poor sleep consolidation in the nocturnal period as an early marker of dysfunction. By the third month of life, when non-REM sleep organization coincides with the development of the cerebral hemispheres, sleep begins to coalesce and consolidate in the hours of the night guided by environmental and social cues. Between the ages of 3 and 6 months, sleep spindles and K complexes take shape and stages 2, 3, and 4 become increasingly better defined. The total amount of sleep in 24 hours decreases and most is confined to the night period, although two or three naps are still necessary. At the age of 6 months, the infant sleeps a total of 14 hours and two naps in 24 hours; at the age of 1.5 years, total nocturnal sleep occupies a mean of 11.5 hours, along with two naps; by the age of 5 years, the child sleeps 11 hours at night; and by the age of 14 years, nocturnal sleep is limited to an average of 9 hours. In non-Mediterranean countries naps are usually abandoned between the ages of 3 and 5 years.

Chaotic sleep hygiene, as observed in some families, engenders a learned behavior in the child that translates into an irregular sleep schedule with the capacity to become chronic and even autonomous. Lack of discipline and inadequate enforcement of bedtimes by the caretaker along with the child's resistance to go to bed at specified times can result in the limit-setting sleep disorder of childhood that produces relative deprivation of sleep. Introduction of discipline restores a regular sleep schedule.

Children who suffer psychological trauma or are physically abused sleep poorly. At times of family tension or social strife, children fear falling asleep or are kept up by their parents as a shield against quarrels.

Intrinsic circadian rhythm disorders such as the delayed phase syndrome can become evident when the child starts attending school. The near impossibility of getting the child out of bed at defined times in the morning can create serious family and school problems, as discussed in Chapter 9.

The treatment of sleep disorders in childhood is usually effective once the causes and mechanisms have been uncovered and all precipitating and determinant factors have been identified and understood by caretakers. Training in proper sleep hygiene, elimination of environmental stress, imposition of caretaker and parental authority, as well as family involvement produce excellent results when organic pathology is not the cause of insomnia.

Secondary Insomnia

Sleeplessness can occur as the result of medical or psychiatric disorders. Painful syndromes such as rheumatism, osteoarthritis, gastroduodenal ulcer, and nocturnal angina are examples of medical disorders that commonly affect sleep [21]. Insomnia can also occur as a result of the breathlessness caused by asthma, chronic obstructive pulmonary disease, or cardiovascular disorders not associated with the sleep apnea syndrome. Patients with chronic renal failure or undergoing dialysis frequently complain of insomnia, and in fact they commonly exhibit fragmentation of sleep perhaps because of the central dysfunction caused by the metabolic derangement [22]. Endocrinologic disorders such as hyperthyroidism cause disorganization and reduction of sleep, whereas hypothyroidism is associated with hypersomnia. Patients with acromegaly and some patients with hypothyroidism develop a form of obstructive sleep apnea syndrome that responds to successful treatment of the primary cause. Some neurologic disorders are associated with a sleep disturbance that can feature insomnia as the main complaint. This situation is particularly notable in Parkinson's disease, a disorder in which patients complain profusely about sleeplessness that can dominate the clinical picture when it is severe.

Virtually all psychiatric disorders are associated with some manifestation of sleep alteration, either insomnia or hypersomnia, as mentioned previously. Some sleep alterations can be intrinsic to the psychiatric disorder, such as in manic psychosis, in which the drastic reduction of sleep causes no daytime effects; or in depression, which is a condition with prominent REM sleep changes. However, other alterations are clearly secondary and the direct result of the psychiatric disease. This situation is particularly obvious in patients with obsessive-compulsive disorders with many nocturnal rituals in whom sleep is displaced and reduced in duration.

The ingestion of alcohol has a profound effect on sleep. In small amounts, alcohol has a sedative effect; this desirable action facilitates sleep, particularly in individuals who are sleep deprived, perhaps in disproportion to a genuine hypnotic effect. Moderate drinking promotes sleep and augments stages 3 and 4, but the effect lasts less than 4 hours, disappearing when the blood alcohol levels decrease. Under the influence of alcohol, REM sleep decreases during the first half of the night, creating the conditions for a REM sleep rebound on the second half. Acute intoxication is associated with inhibition of REM sleep and increase of non-REM sleep, along with heavy snoring and worsening of sleep apnea syndrome in susceptible individuals. With sustained drinking, sleep architecture disintegrates and REM sleep appears reduced and fragmented. Eventually, the unrelenting heavy consumption of alcohol causes an insomnia characterized primarily by the inability to maintain sleep.

Acute withdrawal after sustained heavy drinking precipitates a REM sleep rebound with short REM sleep latency, many episodes of REM sleep, and enhanced muscle tone, as in the syndrome of REM sleep without atonia. The vivid hallucinations of delirium tremens in the acute toxic withdrawal syndrome can be related to an intense REM sleep rebound breaking through the alert but agitated state. In the acute and chronic phases of alcohol withdrawal, patients manifest difficulty initiating sleep as well as maintaining its continuity [23]. Sleep efficiency is low at the expense of non-REM sleep that is mostly composed of stages 1 and 2 with virtual absence of stages 3 and 4. Sleep stages lose their distinctive features, and the polysomnogram becomes difficult to score, as in patients with subcortical neurologic deficit. Some patients fail to recover a normal sleep pattern and continue to be plagued with complaints of sleeplessness and daytime fatigue for many years [24]. Depression and anxiety, commonly occurring in the dry alcoholic, can play important roles in maintaining manifestations of insomnia.

The use of alcohol to induce sleep is a tempting action for some patients with insomnia. Alcohol is consumed at sleep onset and also during the night after prolonged awakenings. The self-prescription of alcohol can be habit forming with all its consequences.

The treatment of nonrestorative sleep in dry alcoholics is a vexing problem. Benzodiazepines and other sedatives with hypnotic effect are not recommended because of the potential for abuse and dependence. Strict sleep hygiene and cognitive relaxation therapies have some beneficial effect and should be tried.

Fibromyositis Syndrome

In some individuals, fragmented, nonrestorative sleep of poor quality can be associated with complaints of stiff, painful, achy muscles when awakening in the morning [25], a disorder that has been termed fibromyositis, fibrositis, fibromyalgia, and rheumatic pain modulation syndrome. The discomfort is centered around the neck and shoulder muscles, with specific points of tenderness over the upper border of the trapezius muscles, medial border of the scapula, lateral aspect of the elbows, second costochondral junction, and upper outer quadrant of the buttock. It tends to improve as the day progresses and is not associated with other signs of joint or muscle inflammation, such as increased sedimentation rate. Patients complain of light sleep that fails to satisfy their need for rest, even after spending the conventional 7 or 8 hours in bed apparently sleeping. In consequence, they feel tired and unmotivated during vigil hours but not excessively sleepy. The polysomnogram shows alpha waves intruding in stages 3 and 4, riding on delta waves, but not appearing in REM sleep, a peculiar polysomnographic pattern termed atypical in the old classification. Short arousals are also common, and sleep spindles tend to be scarce and rachitic, contrary to what occurs in idiopathic hypersomnia, a condition in which sleep spindles are abundant and prominent. The polysomnographic pattern of alpha-delta sleep can be seen in individuals taking stimulants or hypnotic medication, but in fibromyositis the atypical pattern continues to be observed even after withdrawal of the medication. Nevertheless, the presence of alpha-delta sleep in the polysomnogram is a rather nonspecific finding. Epstein-Barr virus titers are not elevated in fibromyositis.

The course of the disorder is protracted and relapsing, lasting many months if not years. It is more common in women with onset in early adulthood. Treatment of fibromyositis is not always gratifying. In some instances, patients respond well to small doses of tricyclic antidepressants (10–50 mg) or chlorpromazine (50–100 mg) at bedtime. Associated psychophysiologic features and nocturnal myoclonus syndrome should be treated accordingly.

Chronic Fatigue Syndrome

The outstanding feature of this condition, also known as Icelandic disease, neuromyasthenia, and benign myalgic encephalitis, is the presence of chronic, unrelenting, overwhelming fatigue that is not relieved by rest. Regardless of how much time patients spend in bed trying to recuperate from fatigue and restore their strength, the feeling of tiredness and lack of energy fails to resolve. Sleep is characterized by delayed sleep onset and poor sleep efficiency. Patients complain of somnolence during daytime hours without objective findings in the MSLT. Associated manifestations can include a low-grade fever, sore throat, tender lymph nodes that the patient may point out to the physician, headaches, muscle tenderness, and excessive fatigability after exercise; depression is common [26] along with alleged poor memory and inability to concentrate. The relatively abrupt onset of symptoms has led investigators to hypothesize a viral origin. Laboratory studies have revealed a high titer of Epstein-Barr virus antibodies in most patients with this syndrome, but this can be a nonspecific finding. Other viral infections have been implicated but without verification.

The differential diagnosis with fibromyositis syndrome can be difficult to achieve. Elevated Epstein-Barr virus antibody titers are not commonly seen in fibromyositis syndrome, a condition in which the polysomnogram reveals the characteristic pattern of alpha-delta activity. Treatment with tricyclic antidepressants and nonsteroidal anti-inflammatory agents can offer some relief. Fluoxetine and monoamine oxidase inhibitors have been tried with variable although scanty success. Chronic fatigue syndrome tends to improve gradually independently of therapeutic manipulations.

Rapid Eye Movement Sleep Interruptions

This is a relatively rare condition that is characterized by repeated interruptions of sleep during episodes of REM sleep. Although patients report dreams, awakenings are not caused by dream anxiety attacks or by a motor disorder. The condition is exclusively a maintenance disorder of sleep with a characteristic pattern of awakenings starting 90 minutes from sleep onset and recurring at approximately 90-minute intervals coinciding with episodes of REM sleep. Awakenings can be of long duration, decreasing the sleep efficiency and causing patients to complain of nonrestorative sleep and daytime fatigue. Associated psychopathology is common and the condition needs to be distinguished from cluster headache, angina, and paroxysmal nocturnal dyspnea occurring in REM sleep. Polysomnography is required to make the diagnosis; in some instances, alpha activity is observed during otherwise typical REM sleep, a pattern called alpha-REM, suggesting partial intrusion of wakefulness into REM sleep. Stimulant medications can cause a similar alpha-REM pattern. Propranolol and tricyclic antidepressants that inhibit REM sleep have been reported to benefit some patients with this disorder.

Fatal Familial Insomnia

This is a familial disorder with progressive loss of neuroendocrine regulation and of vegetative circadian rhythms starting in middle age [27]. Prominent manifestations are severe progressive insomnia with frequent awakenings, impotence, loss of libido, orthostatic sweating, lacrimation, salivation, and increased body temperature; daytime stupor alternates with wakefulness. In the terminal stages of the disease, there is increasing agitation, confusion, disorientation, progressive stupor from which the patient is only transiently arousable, coma, and death. At autopsy, there is severe degeneration and gliosis of the anterior and dorsomedial nuclei of the thalamus. Recent investigations have shown that this is a prion disease [28], akin to Creutzfeldt-Jakob disease, with presence of an abnormal protein containing the infectious agent and encoded by a gene located in human chromosome 20.

Altitude Insomnia

Most individuals who are exposed acutely to an altitude of 4,000 meters (12,000 feet) or more will develop sleep disturbances and sleep-related respiratory alterations. Subjects studied during the first nights of exposure exhibit periodic breathing, marked reduction of stages 3 and 4, many arousals related to termination of sleep apnea episodes, and near normal duration of total sleep. Individuals complain of subjective poor sleep, restless sleep, feelings of suffocation, and gasping for air. The disturbance of sleep occurs in the context of the high altitude syndrome or acute mountain sickness that is manifested by poor appetite, nausea, vomiting, headache, decreased mental acuity, and insomnia. In rare instances, individuals slip into a coma that is resolved only by a return to low altitude.

The respiratory alteration is characterized by alveolar hypoxia and arterial hypoxemia in the context of a low barometric pressure where oxygen tension is reduced. The early physiologic response is an increase in ventilation and cardiac output, and the late response consists of a relative polycythemia with increase in red blood cell concentration.

Insomnia and other manifestations of mountain sickness tend to improve with acclimatization. Administration of acetazolamide, a carbonic anhydrase inhibitor, 250 mg twice per day, has prophylactic effects when given 3 or 4 days before the ascent and through the stay at high altitude. It reduces respiratory alkalosis and increases ventilation and oxygenation.

Clinical Approach

When a patient comes to the office complaining of insomnia, the symptom should be approached in the same manner as pain, paralysis, nausea, or any other manifestation of dysfunction. A detailed history, physical and mental examination, and appropriate laboratory evaluations including polysomnography, if indicated, are necessary to evaluate the patient. The history should contain details of the following items: sleep hygiene; social habits such as smoking, drinking alcohol, and drinking coffee and caffeine-containing sodas; the sleep-wake pattern; other medical or neurologic disorders; an account of psychiatric, behavioral, or mood disturbances; and medications taken.

The history and general physical examination should emphasize the identification of conditions that could disturb sleep such as rheumatic disorders causing pain at night, heart disease provoking chest pain, congestive heart failure, asthma or chronic pulmonary disease producing shortness of breath, and neurologic deficits preventing turns in bed as occurs in Parkinson's disease.

The laboratory tests ordered should be guided by the clinical findings. For instance, computed tomography scanning or magnetic resonance imaging of the head might be necessary to complete the study of a patient with initial dementia, REM behavior disorder secondary to brain stem strokes, or posttraumatic stress disorder. An electroencephalogram is necessary if the patient is suspected of suffering nocturnal epilepsy.

The 14-day evaluation log of sleep and wakefulness (Figure 5-2) is particularly helpful to document reports of fragmented sleep and to define the pattern of insomnia. It also serves to identify circadian rhythm disorders and to assess sleep hygiene. The quality of sleep cannot be evaluated except by the patients' own assertion of dissatisfaction with their sleep. A sleepiness scale on the reverse side of the chart provides a subjective assessment of patients' own perceptions relative to somnolence. The 14-day chart should be given to all patients complaining of insomnia. In a cost-effective way, it documents complaints that are many times elusive, providing some form of objective measurement for subjective manifestations; it also helps follow the evolution of the effect of treatment.

A psychological evaluation by a specialist well versed in sleep disorders is indicated in many instances, not only to uncover psychiatric, behavioral, or mood disturbances but also to evaluate the secondary effect of insom-

Figure 5-2.▶ *The 14-day sleep-wake evaluation chart. Over a period of 14 days, the chart serves to log information provided by the patient hourly on the following items: time in bed, time the patient fell asleep, time of awakenings during the night, time of awakening in the morning, time out of bed, and time of naps. By the end of each day, the following questions are answered: How long did it take you to fall asleep last night? Did you take any sleeping pills or alcohol at bedtime? How many times did you wake up? How much sleep did you get last night? By what time did you have to be up this morning? How did you awaken? How did you feel immediately after getting up? Were you alert all day yesterday? The reverse (not shown) records the sleepiness scale on any two typical consecutive days of the 14-day study period. (Reprinted with permission from Metrodesign Associates/Charles Pollak, MD, Homer, NY, 1979.)*

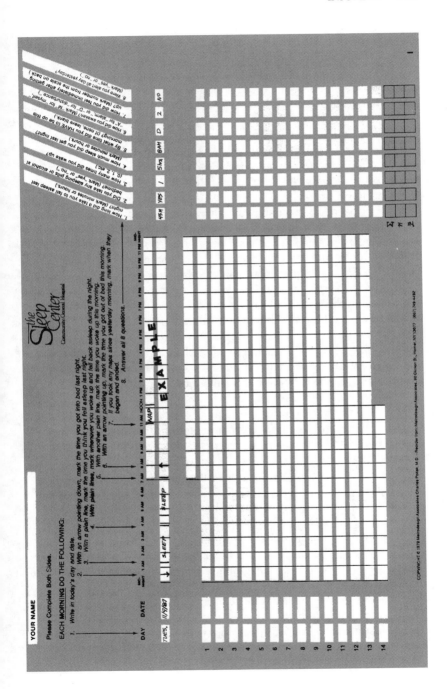

nia, regardless of its cause, on the patient's frame of mind and mood. Because many patients with insomnia exhibit mental alteration [29], the psychological evaluation serves to put it in perspective and assess the weight of such a component. It also assists in the decision to perform a polysomnographic study when the psychophysiologic or psychoaffective contribution is subsidiary or negligible, and helps define a therapeutic plan. Most sleep centers have a staff psychologist or psychiatrist with secondary specialization in sleep disorders, precisely to help evaluate patients with insomnia and to provide specialized team management.

The polysomnographic study of the patient with insomnia has attracted unnecessary debate [30, 31] and has been excluded by many third-party payers. Some patients with insomnia need to be studied in the sleep laboratory so that a precise diagnosis can be reached. This necessity is the case in sleep misperception; suspected sleep apnea syndrome; periodic limb movements disorder; parasomnias disturbing sleep; repeated REM sleep interruptions; epilepsy; and neurologic conditions associated with severe insomnia, such as Parkinson's disease, progressive supranuclear palsy, other degenerative disorders of the nervous system, and the rare fatal familial insomnia. In a national cooperative study of patients with a primary complaint of insomnia, sleep apnea was diagnosed in 6.2%, sleep myoclonus and restless legs syndrome in 12.2%, and no insomnia abnormality in 9.2% [32]. Other authors have found a higher proportion (34%) of abnormalities diagnosed by polysomnography in patients with insomnia, but the criteria used were less strict [33]. Unexpected findings in polysomnographic studies are relatively scarce and prior expectations versus polysomnographic results yield a low but not negligible index of diagnostic recovery that increases substantially when adding expected diagnoses not confirmed [33]; unsuspected findings are more common in elderly patients.The MSLT performed following nocturnal polysomnography is a powerful tool to measure the patient's complaint of daytime hypersomnia secondary to insomnia. In some instances, there is no objective verification of the sleepiness alleged by the patient, as in the nonrestorative sleep disorders associated with psychopathology in which chronic anxiety predominates. Failure to confirm hypersomnia can allay the temptation to administer controlled stimulant medication to increase daytime alertness. The Standards of Practice Committee of the American Sleep Disorders Association has given recommendations for the use of polysomnography in the evaluation of insomnia (Table 5-5) [34]. In recent years, wrist actigraphy has been proposed as a method of evaluating insomnia that is more objective than self-reporting sleeplessness in sleep logs and less expensive than

Table 5-5. Clinical and Technical Indications for the Use of Polysomnography in Insomnia

Clinical

1. Indicated when sleep-related disorders or periodic limb movement disorder are suspected. These conditions are most likely to cause insomnia in middle-aged or elderly patients.

2. Indicated when the initial diagnosis is uncertain or when the treatment, either behavioral or pharmacologic, is unsuccessful.

3. Indicated for the diagnosis of precipitous arousals or violent behavior in sleep when the clinical diagnosis is uncertain.

4. May be indicated for the diagnosis of persistent circadian rhythm disorders, such as delayed sleep phase syndrome, when the clinical diagnosis is unclear.

5. Not indicated for the routine evaluation of transient or chronic insomnia.

Technical

1. A single night of study is sufficient to identify sleep-related breathing disorder or periodic limb movement disorder.

2. Two nights of consecutive recording may be necessary when:

    a. Sleep latency, sleep efficiency, arousal frequency, and sleep-stage distribution need to be well established;

    b. A parasomnia under evaluation does not occur on the first night;

    c. The first night of testing is insufficient or inadequate.

polysomnography. Proponents argue that motor restlessness associated with insomnia can be unobtrusively recorded in the patient's home night after night, yielding sleep patterns of diagnostic value [35]. Wrist actigraphy provides a rough estimate of sleep time but no data concerning sleep stages or brief arousals. Its value as a method of diagnosing insomnia needs further clinical validation relative to the more established methods of recording sleep and wake patterns. Actigraphy can be valuable as a measure of sleep in studies of treatments of insomnia [36].

The differential diagnosis of the insomnias is facilitated when the factors intervening in their causality are properly assessed. It is helpful to stratify risk factors in the following categories: precipitating, predisposing, contributing, conditioning, and determinant. Precipitating factors include all extrinsic causes of insomnia such as noise, light, heat, cold, acute illness, and acute emotional stress. Predisposing factors are elements of the constitutional background of the individual that provide a fertile background such as age, family history of insomnia, and neurologic alterations such as Parkinson's disease. The neurotic fabric of many insomniacs can be categorized as a predisposing constitutional factor in many instances. Contributing factors are coadjuvant elements usually in the form of medical conditions that disturb sleep such as nocturia, dyspnea, and rheumatic diseases. Conditioning factors are the learned behaviors that help make insomnia chronic once it has developed, such as apprehension of going to bed, frustration, and anger. Determinant factors are the dominant constituents of insomnia, such as idiopathic insomnia in childhood. Some factors, such as anxiety, can enter the picture as contributing elements and later become precipitating factors, or factors can be initially determinant, such as idiopathic insomnia in childhood, and become a predisposing factor in the adult years when psychophysiologic and even psychiatric elements dominate the picture. The concept is to identify and assess the weight of as many factors as possible to categorize their participation in the development of insomnia. This strategy helps chart a therapeutic plan of action directed at eliminating as many factors as can be identified and to prioritize the effort.

Circadian rhythm disorders, in particular the delayed phase syndrome, can mimic protracted insomnia. Patients complain of being unable to sleep at conventional times, and when trying to conform to socially accepted schedules sleep fails to occur, leading to a complaint of insomnia. Unlike the genuine patient with insomnia, individuals with circadian rhythm alterations can maintain deep sleep for many hours once they reach their time for sleep. This syndrome is studied in Chapter 9.

The primary care physician should consider referring the patient with insomnia to the sleep specialist when the condition fails to be resolved by simple means and affects the social interactions, lifestyle, and work habits of the patient.

General Management

Transient, situational, and short-term insomnias, such as caused by grief, jet lag, or acute emotional conflict, are short lived, lasting by definition less than 3 weeks, and require no major diagnostic effort or complex treatment. When the condition causes severe sleeplessness or is predictable in its occurrence, a short-acting hypnotic can be beneficial. Triazolam, 0.125–0.250 mg, and zolpidem, 10 mg, at bedtime over a period not to exceed 5 days, can be repeated in two or three cycles, depending on the duration of the insomnia.

Management of chronic insomnia is a difficult clinical exercise that frequently frustrates both the therapist and the patient. A common strategy is to attempt to eliminate or decrease the effect of detrimental factors, a process that when performed step by step can take many months to complete. Patients should be advised that the process of reversing many years of insomnia with a heavy load of learned behaviors, psychophysiologic components, and medical disturbances is long and fails to respond to a simple prescription. Not all patients are ready to accept a form of treatment that can occupy many hours, is expensive, and introduces unwanted lifestyle changes. This situation is particularly true for the impatient individual frustrated with the medical establishment who might seek consolation in parallel treatments, a phenomenon that explains the explosive growth of some forms of therapy for insomnia that are being based on slim and unproven evidence that has proliferated in recent years. Such has been the case with the amino acid tryptophan, precursor of serotonin, and more recently with the promising hormone melatonin, modulator of the circadian rhythm. Both are dispensed over the counter in health stores, although they have not undergone previous clinical trials.

The management of the patient with insomnia has a three-prong approach: sleep hygiene, behavioral therapy, and pharmacotherapy.

Sleep Hygiene

A surprising number of people have no instruction in or respect for the rules of proper sleeping. Violations of sleep hygiene are as common as violations of the diet, except that perhaps the general population is even less well instructed in sleep regulations. Adherence to the rules of proper sleeping is basic to the initiation of therapy in a patient complaining of insomnia. Patients should be instructed to follow the norms given in Table 13-1.

Behavioral Therapy and Psychotherapy

The goals of psychotherapy in insomnia are generally multifaceted (see Table 13-2) and directed at the different components converging on the symptom insomnia. Stress management is paramount in patients with emotional and cognitive arousal under real or perceived psychological stress. Several methods of mental relaxation are commonly used [37], including progressive relaxation techniques that teach patients how to recognize and control inner tension, and biofeedback techniques that do the same using electromyography. Meditation and cognitive refocusing are taught to patients with persistent rumination of thought preventing sleep onset. Learned habits and conditioning to the bedroom and its environment can be reformed with stimulus control techniques that attempt to interrupt the negative bond between patients and their bedrooms [38]. The procedure requires that patients leave the bedroom when not sleepy and use the bedroom exclusively for sleep. Sleep restriction therapy, by producing a daily modest sleep debt, can help some individuals with a weak homeostatic drive to initiate sleep [39]. It has been stated that the efficacy of behavioral therapy for insomnia occurs beyond any placebo effect, although polysomnographic objective measures have failed to show a difference [40]. Cognitive and behavioral therapies would be more effective with a better understanding and ability to diagnose the various subtypes of insomnia.

Several specific measures are helpful in patients with certain contributing and coadjuvant factors. Addiction to sleeping pills, alcohol, and other drugs should be treated to bring the patient under better control; this step includes management of occult withdrawal states from doses that are insufficient to carry the patient into the second half of the night. The treatment of medical, neurologic, or psychiatric conditions causing a secondary insomnia is satisfying because successful control of these disorders delivers the best results in the therapy of the insomnias. Chronotherapy and light therapy for the alleviation of circadian rhythm disorders is covered in Chapter 9.

Pharmacotherapy

Pharmacotherapy continues to be the cornerstone of the treatment of insomnia once the proper assessment of the condition has been established and defined goals have been determined. Therapy with hypnotics is perfectly adequate for the control of transient insomnias. Patients with chronic forms of insomnia can use hypnotic medication as an adjunct to therapy, administering the minimum effective dose for short periods of time, and only when cognizant of the adverse reactions [41]. Sometimes periods of severe insomnia are predictable in susceptible individuals, and these times can be targeted for treatment with hypnotics. Dose escalation and frequency of use, which are markers of dependency, can be controlled with close supervision, although most specialists would agree that risk of dependency is related to the personality of the patient and not so much to the medication. Both the patient and the prescriber need to have a clear understanding of the duration of activity of the medication administered in order to achieve the desired effect at night and during the day, avoiding unwanted actions. Duration of activity is a function of distribution and elimination, and half-life is a relative estimate of the duration of activity but fails to predict accumulation, a factor that underlies toxicity (see Chapter 13).

Ultrashort-acting compounds with a half-life of 3 hours or less initiate sleep and do not accumulate in the body. Compounds with a half-life of 5 hours or more maintain sleep better than short-acting preparations but can show a tendency to accumulate and cause toxicity over many days of administration in susceptible individuals and elderly persons with slow metabolism. Before recommending a hypnotic, it is desirable to establish the goals of therapy. Three different actions can be sought: facilitate initiation of sleep, maintain sleep, and produce daytime sedation following sleep.

Ultrashort- and short-acting benzodiazepines (midazolam, 7.5 mg; triazolam, 0.125 mg) facilitate the onset of sleep and do not cause daytime sedation. The dose of ultrashort- and short-acting benzodiazepines should not be increased in search of a more potent effect, because higher doses can indeed cause a desirable short latency to sleep but pose the risk of rebound insomnia during the second half of the night once the effect is gone. Intermediate-acting benzodiazepines (temazepam,10 mg) are effective to initiate, maintain, and consolidate fragmented sleep. Long-acting benzodiazepines (diazepam, 2.5 mg; flurazepam,15 mg; clorazepate, 7.5 mg; quazepam, 7.5 mg ; estazolam, 2 mg) have a sedative effect beyond the nocturnal period and serve to consolidate sleep as well as to bring sedation the following day to anxious patients. Clonazepam (0.5 mg) is used to eliminate the cortical arousals of periodic limb movements. All benzodiazepines should be administered in interrupted doses, for instance 5 days of the week, followed by 2 days of rest, in cycles not to exceed 1 month. Some patients use the hypnotic only on nights before important events, although there is no proof that the quality of alertness improves following a better night sleep.

All benzodiazepines aggravate the sleep apnea syndromes and should not be administered to patients unless the respiratory syndrome is controlled with nasal CPAP or bilevel positive air pressure (Bi-PAP). In elderly persons, benzodiazepines should be used with great caution because of untoward reactions including increased number of falls, memory alteration, and confusion. The adverse effects of benzodiazepines popularized in the lay press can occur with abuse of the preparation, when given too long in too high doses, or when administered to susceptible individuals, such as the elderly and very elderly, the medically infirm, and the mentally disturbed. Judicious use by knowledgeable physicians will preempt development of anterograde amnesia, frequent falls, and dependence. These drugs are not indicated for the treatment of insomnia in patients with a history of alcohol or drug abuse, or patients with untreated depression or psychosis. As with most other preparations, the use of hypnotics is not indicated during pregnancy.

The tricyclic antidepressants administered at night have shown some efficacy in patients with idiopathic insomnia, Parkinson's disease, and depression. Antihistamine preparations with a hypnotic effect are useful in Parkinson's disease because of the added mild antiparkinsonian action.

Zolpidem (10 mg), a benzodiazepine receptor ligand imidazopyridine, is a new hypnotic that has received a great deal of attention. It potentiates deep sleep and has an ultrashort half-life of 2–3 hours, which prevents accumulation in the body. Zolpidem, like triazolam and flurazepam, can improve insomniacs' perception of being asleep [42].

Barbiturates are no longer used for the treatment of insomnia. Although effective in initiating and maintaining sleep, their potential for toxicity is such that they have been displaced by the benzodiazepines and more recently by zolpidem.

References

1. Márquez GG. One Hundred Years of Solitude. New York: Harper & Row, 1970.
2. National Institute of Mental Health, Consensus Development Conference: Drugs and Insomnia: The use of medications to promote sleep. JAMA 1984;251:2410.
3. Walsh JK, Hartman PG, Kowall JP. Insomnia. In S Chokroverty (ed), Sleep Disorders Medicine. Boston: Butterworth, 1994;219.
4. Gallup Organization. Sleep in America. Princeton: Gallup Organization;1991.
5. Charon F, Dramaix M, Mendlewicz J. Epidemiological survey of insomniac subjects in a sample of 1,761 outpatients. Biol Psychiatry 1989;21:109.
6. Ford DE, Kramerow DB. Epidemiological study of sleep disturbances and psychiatric disorders. JAMA 1989;262:1479.
7. Mellinger GD, Balter MB, Uhlenhuth EH. Insomnia and its treatment. Arch Gen Psychiatry 1985;42:225.
8. Kripke DF, Simons RN, Garfinkle L, et al. Short and long sleep and sleeping pills: Is increased mortality associated? Arch Gen Psychiatry 1979;36:103.

9. Wingard DL, Berkman LF. Mortality risk associated with sleeping patterns among adults. Sleep 1983;6:102.

10. Association of Sleep Disorders Centers, Sleep Disorders Classification Committee. Diagnostic classification of sleep and arousal disorders. Sleep 1979;2:1.

11. Coleman RM, Bliwise DL, Sajben N, et al. Epidemiology of Periodic Movements of Sleep. In C Guilleminault, E Lugaresi (eds), Sleep/Wake Disorders: Natural History, Epidemiology and Long-Term Evolution. New York: Raven, 1983;217.

12. Diagnostic Classification Steering Committee, Thorpy MJ, Chairman. The International Classification of Sleep Disorders: Diagnostic and Coding Manual. Rochester, MN: American Sleep Disorders Association, 1990.

13. Lichstein KL, Wilson NM, Noe SL, et al. Daytime sleepiness in insomnia: Behavioral, biological and subjective indices. Sleep 1994;17:693.

14. Hauri PJ, Olmstead EM. Reverse first night effect in insomnia. Sleep 1989;12:9.

15. Reynolds CF III, Shipley JE. Sleep in Depressive Disorders. In RE Hales, AJ Frances (eds), Psychiatry Update: The American Psychiatric Association Annual Review, Vol 4. Washington, DC: American Psychiatric Press, 1985;341.

16. Cartwright RD. Rapid eye movement sleep characteristics during and after mood-disturbing events. Arch Gen Psychiatry 1983;40:197.

17. Hauri P, Olmstead E. Childhood-onset insomnia. Sleep 1980;3:59.

18. McCall MV, Edinger JD. Subjective total insomnia: An example of sleep state misperception. Sleep 1992;15:71.

19. Diagnostic Classification Steering Committee, Thorpy MJ, Chairman. The International Classification of Sleep Disorders: Diagnostic and Coding Manual. Rochester, MN: American Sleep Disorders Association, 1990;332.

20. Ferber RA. Behavioral "insomnia" in the child. Psychiatr Clin North Am 1987;10:641.

21. Coccagna G, Lugaresi E. All-night polygraph in patients with painful disease. EEG EMG 1982;13:149.

22. Karacan I, Williams RL, Bose J, et al. Insomnia in hemodyalitic and kidney transplant patients. Psychophysiology 1972;9:137.

23. Benca RM, Obermeyer WH, Thisted RA, et al. Sleep and psychiatric disorders: A meta-analysis. Arch Gen Psychiatry 1992;49:651.

24. Adamson J, Burdick JA. Sleep of dry alcoholics. Arch Gen Psychiatry 1973;28:146.

25. Moldofsky H, Scarisbrik P, England R, et al. Musculoskeletal symptoms and non-REM sleep disturbance in patients with "fibrositis syndrome" and healthy subjects. Psychosom Med 1975;37:341.

26. Moldofsky H. Non-restorative sleep and symptoms after a febrile illness in patients with fibrositis and chronic fatigue syndrome. J Rheumatol 1989;16:150.

27. Lugaresi E, Medori R, Montagna P, et al. Fatal familial insomnia and dysautonomia with selective degeneration of thalamic nuclei. N Engl J Med 1986;315:997.

28. Medori R, Tritschler HJ, LeBlanc A, et al. Fatal familial insomnia is a prion disease with a mutation at codon 178 of the prion disease. N Engl J Med 1992;326:444.

29. Buysse DJ, Reynolds CF II, Kupfer DJ, et al. Clinical diagnoses in 216 insomnia patients using the International Classification of Sleep Disorders (ICSD), DSM-IV and ICD-10 categories: A report from the APA/NIMH DSM-IV field trial. Sleep 1994;17:630.
30. Jacobs EA, Reynolds CF III, Kiupfer DJ, et al. The role of polysomnography in the differential diagnosis of chronic insomnia. Am J Psychiatry 1988;145:346.
31. Aldrich MS. Polysomnographic assessment of insomnia. Sleep 1990;13:188.
32. Coleman RM, Roffwarg HP, Kennedy SJ, et al. Sleep-wake disorders based on a polysomnographic diagnosis: a national cooperative study. JAMA 1982;247:997.
33. Edinger JD, Holescher TJ, Webb MD, et al. Polysomnographic assessment of DIMS: Empirical evaluation of its diagnostic value. Sleep 1989;12:315.
34. American Sleep Disorders Association, Standards of Practice Committee. Practice parameters for the use of polysomnography in the evaluation of insomnia. Sleep 1995;18:55.
35. Hauri PJ, Wesbey J. Wrist actigraphy in insomnia. Sleep 1992;15:293.
36. Brooks JO, Friedman L, Bliwise DL, et al. Use of the wrist actigraph to study insomnia in older adults. Sleep 1993;16:151.
37. Spielman AJ, Caruso LS, Glovinsky PB. A behavioral perspective on insomnia treatment. Psychiatr Clin North Am 1987;10:541.
38. Bootzin RR, Epstein D, Wood JM. Stimulus Control Instruction. In PJ Hauri (ed), Case Studies in Insomnia. New York: Plenum, 1991;19.
39. Spielman AJ, Saskin P, Thorpy MJ. Treatment of chronic insomnia by restriction of time in bed. Sleep 1987;10:45.
40. Stepansky EJ. Behavioral Therapy for Insomnia. In MH Kryger, T Roth, WC Dement (eds), Principles and Practice of Sleep Medicine (2nd ed). Philadelphia: Saunders, 1994;535.
41. National Institute of Mental Health, Consensus Development Conference: Drugs and Insomnia: The use of medications to promote sleep. JAMA 1984;251:2410.
42. Mendelson WB. Effects of flurazepam and zolpidem on the perception of sleep in insomniacs. Sleep 1995;18:92.

6

Primary Hypersomnias

*He even fell asleep kneeling at the altar at our wedding
ceremony.*

The wife of a patient with narcolepsy

Overview

Sleepiness is the normal tendency to fall asleep and the physiologic consequence of sleep deprivation. When sleepiness is excessive, undesirable, inappropriate, or unexplained, it often indicates a clinical
disorder that is generically termed hypersomnia. Technically, the word
hypersomnia indicates excessive sleep, but by extension it is also used
to indicate a strong tendency to fall asleep, a condition that would be
best described as hypersomnolence or excessive sleepiness. Patients
with hypersomnia tend to be passive and compliant, although concerned about their plight, unlike patients with insomnia who are angry
and vocal about the frustration with sleep. Inappropriate and excessive somnolence erodes professional achievement, reduces productivity, disturbs social liaisons, affects family life, and prevents academic
advancement. Furthermore, it can lead to traffic accidents and increase
the risk of work-related injuries. Hypersomnia should be considered
a serious manifestation of neurologic dysfunction and of psychosocial
disturbance that can be identified, quantified, and qualified by
polysomnography and the multiple sleep latency state (MSLT). A per-

son whose sleep needs have been satisfied and does not have a pathologic tendency to fall asleep fails to sleep during daytime hours, whereas patients with hypersomnia will fall asleep over 30% or more of the testing time, with an average sleep latency of less than 10 minutes.

The sleep specialist tends to see more patients with excessive daytime sleepiness than with insomnia, although the prevalence of the insomnias is higher. This situation is probably an indication of patients' concern about their ability to function, the chronic discomfort suffered, and the perceived danger when driving. It has been estimated that the prevalence of excessive daytime sleepiness is 2–10% of the population or 5 million persons in the United States [1]. This figure is probably conservative because there is a large body of evidence that the "vast majority of Americans with sleep disorders remain undiagnosed and untreated" [2]. A survey conducted in France among 58,162 draftees between 17 and 22 years of age [3] showed that 14.1% had occasional episodes of sleepiness, 3.8% reported one or two daily episodes, and 1.1% had more than two episodes of daily somnolence. Factors related to sleepiness were snoring, use of hypnotics, and sleep deprivation.

Some patients suffer excessive daytime sleepiness and appear to need more sleep than the norm for reasons that are not obvious. Their hypersomnia is the result of some disorder of the central nervous system (CNS) that eludes us. These patients have primary hypersomnia, which should be distinguished from other disorders also featuring hypersomnia that are clearly the consequence of a factor external to the sleep mechanisms. Narcolepsy, idiopathic hypersomnia, and the periodic hypersomnias are examples of primary conditions, whereas the hypersomnia of the sleep apnea syndrome and the hypersomnia associated with sleep deprivation are classic examples of secondary hypersomnias.

Chronic sleep deprivation as a result of insufficient nocturnal sleep can be the most common cause of subtle and even moderately excessive somnolence in the productive years of life. A poor sleep hygiene, continued detraction of nocturnal sleep, and lack of respect for sleep needs eventually lead to a state of sleep debt that is manifested by chronic fatigue and sleepiness. Narcolepsy, on the other hand, is a genetically determined, sometimes familial disorder, that causes daytime sleepiness, dream generation during daytime sleep, and in more severe forms is responsible for sleep attacks, cataplexy, hypnagogic and hypnopompic hallucinations, sleep paralysis, automatic behavior, and psychosocial decline. Idiopathic CNS hypersomnia is a subtle disease with the cardinal symptom of hypersomnia, commonly associated with excessive fatigue, poor drive, and great difficulty in attaining immediate and full alertness from sleep that

Table 6-1.   Diagnostic Symptoms Associated with Sleepiness

Symptom/cause	Diagnosis
Sleep deprivation	Poor sleep hygiene
Very loud snoring	Sleep apnea
Nap dreaming	Narcolepsy
Cataplexy	Narcolepsy
Unrefreshing naps	Idiopathic hypersomnia
Intermittent sleepiness	Periodic hypersomnia
Very late hours	Phase-delayed syndrome
Head trauma	Posttraumatic hypersomnia
Neurologic disorder	Secondary hypersomnia
Psychiatric alteration	Secondary hypersomnia
Medical disorder	Secondary hypersomnia
Pharmacologic abuse	Secondary hypersomnia

continues to elude clinicians. Hypersomnia secondary to nocturnal disruption caused by the sleep apnea syndrome can dominate the clinical picture and constitute the principal manifestation of the sleep-related respiratory disorders. Other forms of secondary hypersomnia are studied in subsequent chapters. Some are associated with psychiatric disorders such as depression; others develop in conjunction with well-defined medical disorders such as myxedema; and another group is the result of injury to the brain such as in posttraumatic hypersomnia, viral encephalitis, or disruption caused by a brain tumor or a neurodegenerative disorder.

The clinician confronted with a patient complaining of or manifesting excessive pathologic sleepiness must consider these diagnoses (Table 6-1) in the differential diagnosis and resort to polysomnography for a proper resolution of the diagnostic dilemma. Each of the principal conditions mentioned has a distinct form of therapy so that a precise diagnosis is critical to the appropriate management of the patient with hypersomnia.

Clinical Evaluation of Sleepiness

The evaluation and measurement of sleepiness, as commonly performed in sleep centers today, was a landmark development in the evolution of

Table 6-2.   Stanford Sleepiness Scale

---

1. Alert, wide awake, energetic.

2. Functioning at high level, but not at peak. Able to concentrate.

3. Awake, but not fully alert.

4. A little foggy, let down.

5. Foggy. Beginning to lose interest in remaining awake. Slowed down.

6. Sleepy. Prefer to be lying down. Woozy.

7. Cannot stay awake. Sleep onset soon.

---

the discipline of sleep disorders. Sleepiness can be measured with the Stanford Sleepiness Scale (SSS) with pupillography, or with the MSLT.

The SSS presents seven statements to the patient who makes a choice of his or her current state by checking the statement that matches best his or her subjective feelings. The exercise can be performed at 2-hour intervals as the day progresses, obtaining a 24-hour profile of the patient's state of vigilance. The SSS can be combined with the 14-day evaluation chart, by listing the scale in the reverse of the form (see Chapter 3). Subjects who are fully alert will check the statement "Feeling alert, wide awake, energetic" (number 1), whereas subjects who are on the verge of falling asleep will check "Cannot stay awake, sleep onset soon" (number 7) (Table 6-2). Statements 2 through 6 define gradations of alertness that fall between numbers 1 and 7. For patients who are chronically sleepy and have forgotten how it feels to be fully awake, the reliability of the scale might be questionable.

Pupillography measures the pupillary diameter; this diameter is dependent on the level of peripheral autonomic tone that fluctuates in accordance with the state of arousal. During sleep, there is a fixed constriction of the pupil, whereas an individual who is fully alert will maintain a stable dilated pupil measuring 7 mm or more while sitting in the dark over a period of 10 minutes [4]. Sleepy individuals show pupillary fluctuation with a tendency to constriction soon after the lights are turned off. Limitations of the test include lack of collaboration, eyelid closure, neurologic alterations, and dark irises. Pupillography does not distinguish among the different forms of excessive sleepiness.

The MSLT has been described in Chapter 4. The test consists of four or five segments of sleep recorded at 2-hour intervals starting at 8:00 A.M., each segment lasting 20 minutes or less. The MSLT should be done following nocturnal polysomnography to control for nocturnal sleep that has a critical influence on daytime vigilance. In theory, a normal person who has completed a fully satisfactory night of sleep should not fall asleep during the 20-minute segments of subsequent daytime recording. Average daytime sleep latencies of 10 minutes or more, should some sleep emerge, are not considered abnormal. Mean scores of 6–10 minutes constitute a gray zone, whereas average sleep latencies of 5 minutes or less are considered pathologic and expressive of excessive somnolence. Subjects must not be under the influence of medications that could affect sleep. In our laboratory, we routinely request discontinuation of these medications 10 days before the test is conducted, except under very specific circumstances (see Chapter 4). Drugs such as methylphenidate or benzodiazepines are incompatible with the proper interpretation of the MSLT, whereas some psychoactive preparations (i.e., fluoxetine and phenothiazines) are permitted if their discontinuation would pose a threat to the individual's mental health. A sleep diary conducted 10–14 days before testing is desirable, although not mandatory. The MSLT also identifies REM sleep periods, a critical finding for the diagnosis of narcolepsy.

Continuous polysomnographic recording over a period of 36 hours is the ideal way of recording all episodes of sleep and, in the opinion of some [5], the only objective test that allows a diagnosis of idiopathic hypersomnia or true hypersomnia. However, this prolonged recording is excessively expensive, not practical, and not performed routinely in clinical practice.

Narcolepsy

Narcolepsy is a disorder of sleep par excellence. It is dominated by persistent, unrelenting, daytime sleepiness that can be alleviated transiently by short naps. In addition, patients with narcolepsy can have other peculiar manifestations that include cataplexy or sudden bouts of generalized muscle weakness, hallucinations on falling asleep or waking up, and sleep paralysis.

History

Gélineau, a French neuropsychiatrist, described the condition in 1880 and gave it the name of narcolepsy, from the Greek, meaning "seized by somnolence." In a series of articles appearing in the French medical literature [6], Gélineau recognized that somnolence occurred at short intervals and was relieved by naps. Furthermore, he indicated how emotions influenced the occurrence of sleep attacks that were sometimes associated with "astasias" or falls. He reported that the collapse of patients with narcolepsy was preceded and induced by sleep, whereas in epilepsy sleep followed the fall and was associated with loss of memory of the event. Gélineau reported patients of his own and mentioned others gathered from previous reports of "sleep sickness" that he recognized as pertaining to narcolepsy.

Following the outbreak of encephalitis lethargica in the 1920s, there was renewed interest in narcolepsy and in the identification of sleep brain centers, but the lack of appropriate clinical methodology to distinguish the various sleep syndromes as we know them today diluted the precise diagnosis of sleep entities. Yoss and Daly's concise description of the narcolepsy tetrad [7]—excessive daytime sleepiness, cataplexy, hypnagogic hallucinations, and sleep paralysis—along with the introduction of methylphenidate for its treatment added a strong impetus to the clinical definition of the disorder. The discovery of REM sleep and the identification of narcolepsy as a REM sleep disorder provided the foundation for the development of electrophysiologic tests that advanced considerably the ability to diagnose the condition in sleep laboratories. Today, narcolepsy is diagnosed with a high degree of specificity using polysomnographic techniques, opening the way to a better understanding and management. The recent discovery of an association between specific HLA antibodies in serum and narcolepsy has uncovered a biomedical marker that will allow further pathophysiologic characterization of the disorder.

Epidemiology

Narcolepsy is a relatively common neurologic disorder with a prevalence estimated at 1 in 3,000 individuals in North America, suggesting that it is more common than multiple sclerosis. The condition can remain underdiagnosed despite expanding publicity and increasing general perception of sleepiness as a medical alteration. Most sleep laboratories have diagnosed narcolepsy in elderly persons who recount a history of sleepiness going back to their teenage years. Narcolepsy is more commonly diagnosed in North America where sleep laboratory evaluation is more available. Men and women are equally affected, and onset occurs in the second or third decade of life.

Etiology

Physical and mental stresses such as head trauma, pregnancy, or an infection are common alleged precipitants, although it is unclear whether the association is a coincidence or a genuine pathophysiologic phenomenon. Otherwise, the etiology of narcolepsy remains unknown.

Clinical Manifestations

The full tetrad of symptoms as described by Yoss and Daly [7]—excessive sleepiness, cataplexy, sleep paralysis, and hypnagogic hallucinations—is suffered by only a minority of patients with narcolepsy. Sleepiness and cataplexy are by far the most important complaints. Other manifestations include automatic behavior, disturbed nocturnal sleep, memory disturbance, and visual-ocular symptoms.

Excessive daytime sleepiness dominates and characterizes the condition. Patients with narcolepsy have a chronic, sometimes irresistible, tendency to fall asleep that unlike mental fatigue, weakness, or nonspecific tiredness, is relieved only by sleep. Sleepiness is inappropriately excessive. Patients tend to become inordinately sleepy in situations in which most individuals develop some somnolence, such as at lectures, driving for long distances, watching dull shows, or after lunch. The difference is that patients with narcolepsy become dysfunctional with sleepiness and actually fall asleep against their desire, creating a risk of accident or contravening common rules of etiquette and civility. Falling asleep while at work, talking on the phone, eating at the table, or kneeling at the altar during a wedding ceremony defy all explanation and generate embarrassing circumstances at best and antisocial mishaps at worst, with unfortunate lasting consequences. Two-thirds of patients with narcolepsy have fallen asleep driving and four-fifths have fallen asleep at work.

Sudden bouts of sleep occur after a preamble of increasing drowsiness that the patient might not remember. In fact, sleep attacks generally considered a classic manifestation of narcolepsy are a mere marker of intensity of sleepiness and can occur in other conditions in which the pressure to fall asleep is strong, such as severe sleep deprivation and advanced sleep apnea syndrome. Somnolence in narcolepsy is transiently alleviated by physical activity, but unlike other conditions it is not fully relieved by daytime or nocturnal sleep. Despite persistent hypersomnolence, patients with narcolepsy do not exhibit excessive time asleep.

Chronic sleepiness is responsible for poor job performance, scholastic failure, and family pathology. Like other individuals with unsatisfied sleep needs, patients with narcolepsy show irritability, lack of motivation, unexplained mood changes, and general social decline. Patients with severe forms of sleepiness can continue functioning at a low level of performance or with semipurposeful behavior, lacking proper wisdom of the consequences and ramifications of their acts. This condition, termed automatic behavior, has been associated with ongoing drowsiness punctuated with brief episodes of sleep or "microsleeps" lasting 10–20 seconds that interrupt repeatedly the trend of consciousness, derailing the finality of thought and judgment. Automatic behavior can underlie the nonsensical notes taken by a sleepy student in class, the unexplained packing of laundry in the dishwasher by a housewife, the frightful driving of many miles without recollection, or the eerie nocturnal marching of a soldier while asleep. Automatic behavior is not exclusive of narcolepsy but is a common experience in untreated patients.

Cataplexy is the sudden loss of muscle tone associated with weakness involving all voluntary muscles of the body except the oculomotor muscles and diaphragm. Episodes last a few seconds to several minutes and are not accompanied by loss of consciousness. Physical examination during the attack reveals flaccid paralysis along with facial twitching, reactive pupils, and generalized areflexia. Typically, cataplectic events are precipitated by excitement, emotion, stress, and startle. Laughter is the most common precipitant, and patients learn to control or avoid laughing at jokes or hilarious situations. In normal individuals without evidence of narcolepsy, intense laughter can be associated with perceived weakness of leg muscles, a phenomenon that has been acknowledged in vernacular expressions such as "rolling on the floor with laughter." Severe cataplectic events involve all muscles and force the patient to fall or slump to the floor, whereas mild episodes are manifested by sagging of the jaw, buckling of the knees, transient head drop, or dysarthria. Severe events are followed by sleep and vivid dreaming. Patients can suffer as many as four or five episodes daily, or as few as one or two per month.

Cataplexy is a manifestation unique to narcolepsy, although in rare instances it has been identified in patients with brain stem lesions. It represents a partial REM sleep manifestation that is no different in its clinical expression than the muscle atonia of REM sleep. The primary difference is that cataplexy occurs in isolation and outside the context of REM sleep while the individual is awake. It appears commonly several months after the onset of manifestations of sleepiness, although in some instances it has been reported to occur before sleepiness was identified. Patients with sleepiness and electrophysiologic evidence of narcolepsy might not have cataplexy, a condition that is known as monosymptomatic narcolepsy; some patients might still develop cataplexy as many as 40 years after the onset of sleepiness. A peculiar condition of persistent cataplexy, or status cataplecticus, has been described in patients who abruptly discontinue anticataplectic medication.

Sleep paralysis is the inability to move during sleep or on awakening, lasting a few seconds to a few minutes. Patients are aware of their plight and struggle mentally to extricate themselves to escape the uncomfortable feeling. Sleep paralysis can be associated with hallucinations that are called hypnagogic if they occur at sleep onset and hypnopompic if at termination of sleep. Both phenomena represent a residue of partial REM sleep generation, particularly if appearing in the morning following the last episode of REM sleep. Sleep paralysis and to a lesser extent hallucinations can occur in normal individuals under extreme circumstances of sleep deprivation or sleep disruption, being more common in normal juveniles than in older persons. Sleep paralysis has also been reported as an isolated finding in some families.

Insomnia is ironically and paradoxically common in patients with narcolepsy. Nocturnal sleep is fragmented and unrefreshing in many, to the extent that, in the opinion of some specialists, if sleep were better consolidated at night patients with narcolepsy would be less sleepy during daytime hours. In fact, some therapeutic strategies, such as treatment with gamma-aminobutyric acid, that promote sleep are based on this thesis. Not uncommonly, patients with narcolepsy complain of restlessness at night, and some show early REM sleep without atonia that facilitates motor activity and acting out of dreams.

Memory disturbance may be the result of poor concentration, attention lapses, and microsleeps. One half of patients complain of memory impairment that contributes to poor work performance and declining academic achievement.

Visual and ocular symptoms are also common, ranging from double vision to burning eyes. Some complaints like blurry vision and even double vision might be attributable to the exophoria of the transition to sleep, but others like burning eyes popularly associated with sleep deprivation are of unknown origin.

Psychopathology, depression, and behavioral disorders are also observed in patients with narcolepsy. Some manifestations such as depression reflect the deficits imposed by the narcoleptic symptoms, but others, for instance, behavioral disorders, might be inherent to the disease. When hallucinations are prominent, complaints have been taken for symptoms of schizophrenia.

Differential Diagnosis

Persistent tiredness and mental fatigue such as occur in the chronic fatigue syndrome or following viral illnesses are distinguishable from sleepiness by careful questioning. The patient with severe fatigue does not fall asleep inappropriately and does not have a tendency to sleep as readily as the patient with true excessive somnolence. The sleepiness of other disorders of sleep is not qualitatively different from the sleepiness of narcolepsy, except that in the latter condition it can be associated with dreaming during daytime sleep. Some patients with narcolepsy claim to fall asleep suddenly, perhaps because they have no memory of the preceding drowsiness, and the differential diagnosis needs to be entertained with other neurologic conditions in which consciousness is lost, such as syncope or epilepsy. Patients with syncope are not sleepy between episodes, and patients with seizure disorder cannot be "awakened" from the spell; drowsiness and some degree of confusion occur following the event. Narcoleptic patients show a pattern of falling asleep in situations devoid of physical activity; during the episode they are arousable and complain of sleepiness between events.

Cataplectic attacks should be distinguished from transient cerebral ischemia, myasthenia gravis, periodic paralysis, syncope, atonic seizures, and hyperekplexia. The cataplectic event is usually triggered by a known precipitant, generally laughter, and careful questioning reveals that there is no loss of consciousness during the episode, although it can be followed by sleep. Most patients will acknowledge having interictal sleepiness. Facial myokimias and unsustained trembling during generalized cataplexy can superficially resemble an epileptic event. However, memory of the episode precludes loss of consciousness, which would be obligatory in an epileptic fit affecting both sides of the body. In hyperekplexia, there is loss of strength with hypertonia and myoclonic jerking of the extremities in response to a startling stimulus, but not an emotion. Therefore, there is some potential for confusion with cataplexy [8], but the combined polysomnogram should clearly differentiate both conditions by showing no relation to partial REM sleep generation in hyperekplexia.

Cataplexy is differentiated from syncopal episodes in that there is no loss of consciousness. In transient cerebral ischemia, focal lateralizing neurologic deficits dominate the picture. Akinetic seizures and drop attacks are not associated with excessive sleepiness. In hypoglycemia, altered consciousness prevails. More rarely, the differential diagnosis needs to be made with vestibular conditions that are associated with vertigo and the rare form of familial sleep paralysis, an isolated manifestation of sleep alteration. The objective polysomnographic evaluation is critical to differentiate some of these disorders from narcolepsy.

The hallucinations of patients with narcolepsy are dreamlike visual fabrications sometimes associated with auditory and tactile perceptions that occur in the transitions from and into sleep. They differ from genuine dreams in that the static nature of their figment is devoid of a theme or unfolding story. Patients are aware of the fantastic nature of the imagery and generally feel uncomfortable, disconcerted, or frightened. Hypnagogic and hypnopompic hallucinations differ from peduncular hallucinosis in that the latter are usually associated with neurologic deficits of midbrain origin, such as vertical gaze palsy or pupillary abnormalities that are absent in narcolepsy. In the sundown syndrome and in delirium, there is associated confusion and agitation with no recognition of the fictional quality of the hallucinations. Patients with epileptic seizures of posterior temporal or occipital origin might describe stereotypical hallucinatory imagery associated with drowsiness, forcing a differential diagnosis in which the presence of EEG epileptiform activity plays a critical role.

Sleep paralysis can be mistaken for epileptic seizures and periodic paralysis. The occurrence of the event at sleep onset or termination and the preservation of some consciousness throughout the episode assists in making the distinction. Furthermore, patients with sleep paralysis are easily aroused to full consciousness and movement by touch or noise.

Pathophysiology

Narcolepsy is a disorder of REM sleep. Disordered linkage of REM sleep to non-REM sleep results in untimely appearance of manifestations of REM sleep such as early dreaming at night and recording of sleep-onset REM periods (SOREMP) in polygraphic recordings. The well-timed and predictable cycles of consolidated REM sleep at night terminating in the morning on arousal in the normal individual are not well defined in the narcoleptic patient. This results in poor sleep state definitions with expression of REM activity in the MSLT recorded in the morning and afternoon hours. However, REM sleep is also qualitatively abnormal. Partial generation and abnormal expression are common, resulting in fragments of REM sleep phenomena breaking through consciousness, causing muscle atonia (cataplexy), dreams (hallucinations), or muscle atonia lingering in the morning after awakening (sleep paralysis). The overall picture suggests that sleep state boundaries are impaired in narcolepsy and that REM sleep generators are poorly coordinated among themselves and with non-REM sleep modulators.

Cholinergic agonists exacerbate cataplexy whereas cholinergic antagonists inhibit cataplexy and in general reduce the intensity of symptoms related to partial generation of REM sleep, such as sleep paralysis and hallucinations. There is evidence that monoaminergic regulation of cholinergic activity is impaired in narcolepsy [9]. Amphetamines that increase synaptic availability of norepinephrine are effective in alleviating sleepiness, and tricyclic compounds such as protriptyline that inhibit reuptake of norepinephrine and therefore increase monoaminergic availability at the synaptic level are effective in controlling cataplexy; this evidence supports the notion of a REM sleep inhibitory role for monoamines. Compounds that block reuptake of serotonin, such as fluoxetine [10], are also effective in controlling cataplexy, further suggesting a role for serotonergic systems in the pathophysiology of narcolepsy.

The family history is commonly positive for excessive daytime sleepiness, but when relatives are objectively tested, only 3% show polygraphic evidence of narcolepsy [11]. The risk of narcolepsy developing in children with one narcoleptic parent is 1%. Some patients with narcolepsy have associated diseases of an immunoallergic nature such as asthma and lupus erythematosus, leading to the theory that narcolepsy is also an autoimmune disorder. This hypothesis was fueled by the discovery of the linkage between narcolepsy and the antigen HLA-DR2 (human leukocyte antigen), the strongest association between this antigen and any disorder so far discovered [12]. European patients with narcolepsy-cataplexy and with monosymptomatic narcolepsy carry the antigen HLA-DR2 and the subtype DRw15 in more than 90% of instances; African-Americans have this antigen in 65% of instances, but HLA-DQ1 and its subtype DQw6 are carried by more than 90% [13]. There are patients with narcolepsy without either antigen, indicating that it is not necessary for expression of the disease.

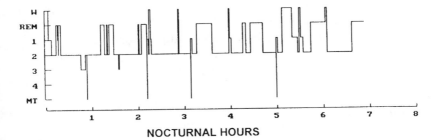

Figure 6-1. *Architecture of sleep in a 42-year-old man with narcolepsy. The first episode of REM sleep occurs 10 minutes after sleep onset. There are eight cycles of REM sleep in the course of 7 hours of nocturnal sleep, representing 25% of total sleep time. The subsequent MSLT showed episodes of REM sleep in two of the four segments tested with a mean latency of 11 minutes.*

Laboratory Diagnosis

Polysomnography is the principal test for the evaluation and diagnosis of narcolepsy. Patients should undergo a nocturnal polygraphic evaluation followed by an MSLT. The nocturnal evaluation is intended as a control of the night before the MSLT. Theoretically, a savvy individual yearning for controlled stimulants could stay up all night before the daytime test, forcing the appearance of a REM sleep rebound in the MSLT that could lead to the spurious diagnosis of narcolepsy. Nocturnal polysomnography can uncover other conditions contributing to or determining excessive daytime somnolence, such as sleep apnea syndrome and periodic leg movements. In many instances, SOREMP is found along with excessive cycles of REM sleep (Figure 6-1). The MSLT shows SOREMPs in two or more segments with an average latency of 15 minutes or less. Using more strict criteria, namely, two or more SOREMPs with an average latency of 5 minutes or less, the MSLT has a 61% sensitivity for the diagnosis of narcolepsy, being similar for narcolepsy with and without cataplexy [14]. Patients clinically suspected of having narcolepsy who do not meet diagnostic criteria on initial polysomnography should undergo additional testing at a subsequent time. Repeat MSLT will sometimes demonstrate two or more SOREMPs in untreated patients. SOREMPs can also occur in other conditions such as depression, severe sleep deprivation, circadian rhythm disorder, drug and alcohol withdrawal, and severe sleep apnea with REM sleep deprivation. In one series of patients with two or more

SOREMPs on MSLT and a latency of 5 minutes or less, the specificity for the diagnosis of narcolepsy was 97% [15].

Other tests such as sleepiness scales and pupillometry, which identifies pupillary constriction in drowsiness and sleep, are more useful to assess the severity of sleepiness than the nature of the disease.

Clinical Diagnosis

Narcolepsy should be differentiated from most other conditions that cause excessive daytime sleepiness. The diagnosis of narcolepsy is made when there is a complaint of excessive sleepiness or sudden muscle weakness and the patient exhibits sleep paralysis, hypnagogic hallucinations, automatic behaviors, and a disrupted major sleep episode [16]. In addition, there should be polysomnographic evidence of two or more of the following: sleep latency of less than 10 minutes, REM sleep latency of less than 10 minutes, MSLT mean sleep latency of less than 5 minutes, and two or more sleep-onset REM periods in the MSLT. The patient should also be free of psychiatric or medical conditions that could account for the symptoms. The criteria allow the diagnosis of narcolepsy without history of cataplexy, a condition that has been termed monosymptomatic narcolepsy. It is unclear whether monosymptomatic narcolepsy is a fixed variant of the disorder or an incompletely expressed form of narcolepsy that given the proper circumstances or sufficient time would eventually emerge with the full complement of cataplectic manifestations. HLA typing supports but does not determine the diagnosis of narcolepsy when positive for DR2 and DQ1 antigens and respective subtypes Drw15 and DQw6.

Complications

There is a high risk of falling asleep at the wheel and being involved in a traffic accident, an occurrence acknowledged by two-thirds of patients with narcolepsy. In a 1984 comparison of driving records, narcoleptics had poorer outcomes than epileptics [17]. Some legislations have regulated the conditions under which patients with narcolepsy may drive commercial and noncommercial vehicles. There is some concern that states might impose mandatory reporting of narcolepsy before issuing or renewing a driver's license. Some believe that this move would deter patients from admitting that they have excessive sleepiness or could delay treatment particularly for individuals who, being poorly controlled, would need it most. In California, a driver's license can be revoked if narcolepsy is out of control. In seven states (California, Maine, Maryland, North Carolina, Oregon, Texas, and Utah), there are regulations for all drivers regarding narcolepsy. Commercial drivers with a history of narcolepsy are prohibited from operating a vehicle in Texas, and Oregon's regulations state that patients may not drive until the condition has been satisfactorily controlled as judged by a physician. The legislation regarding sleepiness and specifically narcolepsy is in a state of flux and concerned drivers should check the Motor Vehicles Department in their respective state for accurate information. Outside the United States, regulations regarding driving by patients with narcolepsy are in effect in many countries (see Chapter 14).

Failing grades, work impairment, a history of falling asleep on the job, and loss of productivity punctuate the history of psychosocial decline or arrested advancement, so common in patients with narcolepsy. Depression has a prevalence of 30% [18], perhaps as a corollary of the psychosocial ramifications of suffering the condition. Patients with narcolepsy can be misdiagnosed as schizophrenics if the complaints of hallucinations are taken out of context or figure prominently in the list of symptoms.

Management

The management of narcolepsy includes social aspects, behavioral modification, and pharmacologic treatment. Patients and relatives should be made aware that excessive sleepiness is a medical condition and not a negative attitude or a depraved behavior indicating laziness. This revelation is often of great consolation for patients who have been derided and punished over the years for failing to achieve in school and at work, or have been unable to accomplish family and social obligations. Realizing that a force beyond them, in this instance a medical condition, has been responsible for their failures alleviates some of the mental anguish and depression that accompanies the disorder. An accurate diagnosis is therefore of great importance, to enable the physician to counsel the patient and relatives from a position of authority. It is also important to document the diagnosis to avoid difficulty obtaining stimulant treatment from reluctant physicians and to overcome patient resistance to receiving controlled drugs. Occupational and career counseling should be offered to young patients so that they understand to avoid sedentary, monotonous tasks and jobs that involve hazard should they fall asleep.

Behavioral counseling should include a discussion on vehicle driving and sleep hygiene. Patients should understand that if they are adequately treated, driving is permitted, but only for short distances and limited to daytime hours. Should the need arise to drive a long distance, patients are authorized to increase the administration of stimulant medication and make highway stops at 1-hour intervals to take naps if necessary. There is evidence that after 1 hour of driving, normal individuals begin to show signs of mental fatigue [19] that presumably becomes more pronounced if the subject is afflicted with excessive sleepiness. Narcoleptics more than any other individuals need to keep rigorous sleep/wake schedules to improve nocturnal consolidation of sleep and avoid sleep deprivation, which would contribute to daytime sleepiness. Some patients with narcolepsy have fragmented nocturnal sleep and prefer to be active at night, taking nocturnal jobs that camouflage their inadequate cycles. The ideal schedule includes 7–8 hours of sleep at night, aided with medication if necessary, and assisted by short naps during daytime hours. Naps of 15–20 minutes are refreshing for most narcoleptics when taken at times when the pressure to fall asleep is most intense, such as mid-morning, after lunch, in mid-afternoon, and after dinner. Napping regularly cuts down on the amount of stimulant medication required and decreases unscheduled episodes of falling asleep, introducing some control over sleep. If needed, naps should be prescribed formally in a prescription form so that patients can present it to their supervisors.

Pharmacologic treatment is the cornerstone of management of excessive daytime sleepiness and cataplexy. Excessive daytime sleepiness responds best to the administration of CNS stimulants. Some practitioners are resistant to prescribe these medications for fear of inducing habituation. However, the risk to the physical, mental, and emotional well-being of patients with uncontrolled narcolepsy is much higher than the risk of drug dependency. In the absence of controlled clinical therapeutic trials, the treatment of narcolepsy is primarily based on consensus of opinions and to a certain extent on the results of a few small studies assessing the effect of drugs on the MSLT and Maintenance of Wakefulness Test (MWT) [20].

In the United States, excessive daytime sleepiness is most commonly treated with methylphenidate (Ritalin), dextroamphetamine (Dexedrine), and pemoline (Cylert). According to objective MSLT and MWT assessments [21], pemoline is less effective in controlling somnolence but has the advantage of being a Schedule IV drug. It is therefore administered to patients with mild to moderate forms of excessive sleepiness. Some authors prefer to initiate treatment with pemoline before considering more potent stimulants. The initial dose of 18.75 mg can be increased to a total of 112.5 mg given in the morning. The *Physicians' Desk Reference* recommends checking the level of liver enzymes during the first 3 months of treatment to detect any changes premonitory of rare, potentially fatal liver damage.

Methylphenidate, a piperidine derivative related to amphetamine, is perhaps the most commonly prescribed drug for narcolepsy, at least in the United States. It is administered orally in doses ranging from 10–65 mg per day. Higher doses provide more stimulant effect but can cause dose-dependent behavioral changes, irritability, and insomnia. Tolerance tends to develop with prolonged use of the medication; it is delayed by starting at the lowest possible dose and escalating slowly over the ensuing months or years. Drug holidays are effective in decreasing tolerance but can pose a risk of accident should the patient fall asleep inappropriately and are an annoyance to implement in most patients. To implement a drug holiday, patients are asked to decrease and eventually discontinue the administration of the drug over a period of 7–10 days. In most individuals, resumption of administration at a much lower dose provides a level of efficacy that was reached before only with high doses. When methylphenidate is insufficient, dextroamphetamine sulfate can be tried, starting at 10 mg per day and increasing the dosage slowly to a maximum of 60 mg per day. In some patients, 5–15 mg of the sustained release form of dextroamphetamine administered in the morning can be sufficient. Other drugs that are useful in the treatment of excessive sleepiness are methamphetamine, which has good CNS penetration but is more expensive than dextroamphetamine; selegiline, an MAO-inhibitor that is converted to levoamphetamine and is also used in the treatment of Parkinson's disease; and protryptiline, a tricyclic derivative also effective in cataplexy. Outside the United States, modafinil, an $alpha_1$-receptor agonist with alerting properties but no effect on cataplexy, is used successfully [22].

Although the goal of therapy in narcolepsy is to maintain patients free of symptoms and side effects, this goal is rarely achieved in clinical practice. The physician might have to use clinical judgment to strike a compromise that fits the patient's needs. Increased levels of alertness can be achieved by increasing the dose of CNS stimulant, but this alertness might come with the price of increased side effects. CNS stimulants combined with 15-minute naps help to reduce the patient's tendency to develop side effects. I recommend an early morning dose of stimulants, followed by a mid-morning dose, a nap after lunch, a mid-afternoon dose, a nap after work, and a late afternoon dose. Stimulants taken after 5:00 P.M. can affect nocturnal sleep in persons who retire early to bed. Depending on the severity of symptoms and response to medication, this regimen can be reinforced at times when alertness is most needed, such as with long-distance driving, or when symptoms are most obstructionist.

When taken in large doses, CNS stimulants can cause side effects that include insomnia, irritability, headache, and in some instances paranoid behavior with rare delusions indistinguishable from paranoid psychosis. It is important that the physician treating patients with CNS stimulants be able to recognize these symptoms, to lower the dose, impose a drug holiday, or switch to another drug. CNS stimulants suppress REM sleep and can cause a REM sleep rebound with shortened REM sleep latency when discontinued. The sympathomimetic effects of the amphetamines and derivatives include systolic and diastolic hypertension; variations in heart rate; cardiac arrhythmias, rarely; mydriasis; and hyperthermia. At therapeutic doses, these side effects are uncommon [23]. Intracranial hemorrhage, brain infarction, myocardial infarction, and hypertensive crisis have been reported in drug abusers [24].

Cataplexy is most effectively controlled with tricyclic antidepressants that probably inhibit cataplexy and sleep paralysis through blockade of serotonin and norepinephrine reuptake in addition to their well-known anticholinergic effect. Protryptiline (5–15 mg in divided doses) is a powerful REM sleep suppressant with moderate cholinergic effect, well tolerated by most patients and the treatment preferred by many specialists in the United States. In Europe, clomipramine (25–200 mg per day) is the treatment of choice; this compound abolishes cataplectic attacks without affecting daytime sleepiness but can potentiate the alerting effect of amphetamines. Imipramine (10–200 mg in divided doses) can be efficacious if protryptiline is not tolerated or fails to work. Fluoxetine, a relatively specific blocker of serotonin reuptake, is often useful particularly if dry mouth, constipation, impotence in men, and other anticholinergic side effects of the tricyclic compounds are intolerable; the recommended dose is 20 mg administered in the morning to avoid nocturnal disruption. Gamma-hydroxybutyrate [25], reported to be effective in consolidating nocturnal sleep and in increasing daytime alertness, is also effective in reducing cataplexy; it has not been commercialized in the United States and remains a difficult medication to manage because of the variable range of responses. Abrupt discontinuation of anticataplectic drugs can lead to a rebound increase in cataplexy or even to continuous incapacitating cataplexy also known as status cataplecticus.

Nocturnal disruption of sleep is a common complaint of many narcoleptics. Muscle twitches and nocturnal myoclonus that keep patients awake can be related to the effect of tricyclic medications. If the complaint is not resolved by reducing the dose of medication, carbidopa-levodopa 10/100, carbidopa-levodopa 25/100 in patients with more intense symptoms, or clonazepam, 0.5 mg, might be helpful taken at bedtime. In some patients with severely disrupted nocturnal sleep, zolpidem (5–10 mg) at bedtime can be tried for short periods of time in an attempt to consolidate nocturnal sleep. Gamma-hydroxybutyrate appears to control nocturnal disruption of sleep better than other medications, but the effect is irregular and the substance is not available in the United States.

Symptomatic Narcolepsy

This form of narcolepsy is associated with lesions of the upper brain stem and floor of the third ventricle. Patients with symptomatic narcolepsy have excessive daytime sleepiness appearing abruptly and overwhelmingly in boring situations, along with cataplexy triggered by laughter, hallucinations, and sleep paralysis, a syndrome indistinguishable from idiopathic narcolepsy. Excessive daytime sleepiness and REM sleep alteration have been documented by polygraphic evaluation in most instances diagnosed since 1976 [26, 27]. Imaging studies have shown a variety of lesions invading the diencephalon, affecting variably the hypothalamus, third ventricle, midbrain, pituitary gland, and chiasma. The nature of the lesions has been diverse including glioma, glioblastoma, gliosis, multiple sclerosis, sarcoidosis, surgical ablation of craniopharyngioma, adenoma, colloid cyst of the third ventricle, and infarct. Following the epidemic of encephalitis lethargica described by von Economo, many reports appeared in the literature describing narcolepsy as a result of encephalitis. However, the absence of proper laboratory evaluations and imaging procedures along with the vogue of the time to ascribe all sleep pathology to encephalitis, disallows many of the reports, although some might have been genuine instances of symptomatic narcolepsy. A recent case report of arteriovenous malformation invading the third ventricle and affecting the hypothalamus described symptomatic improvement following successful treatment of the malformation [28]. HLA typing has shown presence of DR2 and DQ1 antigens in only a few of the patients tested suggesting that the antigen is not necessary for the expression of symptomatic narcolepsy.

Excessive somnolence and inappropriate daytime sleep can occur in patients with multiple sclerosis. Based on the remitting course of sleep attacks exhibited by some patients with multiple sclerosis, investigators have hypothesized that this condition can cause symptomatic narcolepsy [29]. In some individuals, excessive daytime sleepiness and sleep attacks occur in conjunction with cataplexy, sleep paralysis, and hypnagogic hallucinations leading to a diagnosis of narcolepsy. Excessive somnolence and other narcoleptic symptoms can appear before or after the onset of multiple sclerosis, and the age of presentation has varied widely. Chronic fatigue is common in multiple sclerosis and can confound the interpretation of sleep disturbances. Sleep laboratory evaluations in patients with multiple sclerosis have revealed that sleep disturbance is common and that its etiology is multifactorial involving both physical and psychological features [30]. The susceptibility to multiple sclerosis is coded by genes within or close to the HLA-DR-DQ subregion, a coincidence of genetic susceptibility between multiple sclerosis and narcolepsy that has led some authors to postulate a common immunogenetic etiology [31]. The presence of midbrain plaques in the hypothalamic periventricular region is an often cited but rare occurrence of narcolepsy in multiple sclerosis [32].

Narcolepsy featuring both excessive daytime somnolence and cataplexy can develop following a closed head injury in previously asymptomatic patients, a condition that has been termed secondary narcolepsy [33]. The laboratory evaluation of patients has shown genetic susceptibility, suggesting a dormant condition brought to full clinical expression by the head trauma. However, there are patients who develop excessive daytime somnolence following head trauma who do not have narcolepsy and the specter of litigation obscures the diagnosis [34].

All newly diagnosed patients with narcolepsy should undergo a full neurologic examination. Brain imaging studies are indicated if focal or lateralizing signs of neurologic alteration are present, or when the natural history of the disease takes an unconventional course. Associated conditions such as epilepsy, excessive headaches, true syncope, vertical double vision, and abnormal EEG warrant brain imaging, preferably magnetic resonance imaging.

Canine Narcolepsy

A condition very similar to human narcolepsy featuring excessive sleepiness and cataplexy has been discovered in some breeds of dogs, including Labrador retrievers, Dobermans, and poodles. Affected dogs exhibit episodes of muscular weakness when shown food, playing, or attempting sexual intercourse, displaying a clear relation between emotion and cataplexy. During the attack, there is loss of deep tendon reflexes but no loss of alertness, and polygraphic recordings show evidence of REM sleep. Affected dogs have short sleep latencies and respond to the same medications that are used for the treatment of human narcolepsy. The availability of an animal model has facilitated genetic, pharmacologic, and neurochemical studies of the condition. In some breeds of dogs, a familial tendency appears when both parents have narcolepsy. Investigation of the pedigree suggests a recessive autosomal mode of transmission with full penetrance [35]. In poodles, familial transmission has not been successful, suggesting etiologic factors other than genetic. Pharmacologic studies in dogs suggest that $alpha_{1b}$-noradrenergic blockade (i.e., prazosin) worsens cataplexy and therefore should be contraindicated in patients with narcolepsy [36], whereas stimulation (i.e., amphetamine or tricyclics) improves it. $Alpha_2$-receptors can be involved too, as well as central dopamine D_2-receptors that suppress cataplexy when stimulated. Brain tissue analysis has shown elevated concentrations of dopamine and dihydroxyphenylacetic acid, suggesting alteration of the intracellular metabolism of these compounds. Muscarinic cholinergic receptors are increased in the brain stem of narcoleptic dogs [37].

Idiopathic Central Nervous System Hypersomnia

This disorder is characterized by the inability to obtain sufficient sleep despite prolonged sleep episodes. Patients with this condition might sleep 8 or more hours without interruption and yet feel insufficiently rested during waking hours. Episodes of daytime sleepiness are associated with prolonged nonrestorative naps devoid of dream content. Sleepiness dominates the life of affected individuals and modifies their behavior. Situations that demand continued attention such as lectures, shows, reading, or watching television enhance sleepiness. Some patients are difficult to arouse from sleep and might appear confused initially on awakening. Attacks of sleepiness are common and are preceded by long episodes of drowsiness. Complaints suggestive of autonomic imbalance are also common; they include nonspecific headaches, orthostatic syncope, and Raynaud's phenomenon.

The cause of the disorder is unknown, and its prevalence is variable depending on the criteria used to diagnose it. Some clinics estimate that 10% of patients referred with a complaint of sleepiness have idiopathic hypersomnia, whereas other specialists indicate that they rarely observe the condition. Idiopathic CNS hypersomnia usually starts in adolescence or early adult life, equally affecting men and women. Laboratory determination of HLA typing shows a normal prevalence of HLA-DR2 antigen contrary to the observed very high prevalence in narcolepsy. The frequency of HLA-Cw2 is increased in families of patients with idiopathic hypersomnia [38]. Some authors [39] distinguish various clinical subgroups of the disorder: I, a familial form with the presence of HLA-Cw2 antigen and symptoms suggestive of autonomic imbalance; II, patients who report a viral illness at the beginning of their disorder, most commonly infectious mononucleosis, atypical pneumonia, or even Guillain-Barré syndrome; III, patients with no family history and no antecedent viral disorder, thus it appears to be truly idiopathic. The rate of the familial to the sporadic cases remains unknown.

The diagnosis is made with the help of polysomnography. Nocturnal sleep architecture is normal, showing proportions of sleep stages that are well balanced, the only anomaly being a short sleep latency and a sleep period of longer than average duration. In our laboratory, we have observed excessive amounts of sleep spindle generation with high sleep spindle density in both hemispheres [40]. In contrast to normal individuals, patients with idiopathic hypersomnia show an increase in sleep spindle density at the beginning and most peculiarly at the end of the sleep period, as if the expected dwindling activity of the thalamic generator had failed to occur. The MSLT demonstrates a sleep latency of less than 10 minutes with abundant daytime sleep but no evidence of sleep-onset REM periods that rule out narcolepsy. Polysomnographic monitoring also serves to exclude sleep apnea syndrome, upper airway resistance syndrome, periodic leg movement activity, and disorders associated with sleep fragmentation.

The differential diagnosis with sleepiness associated with depression is less well defined, requiring psychological evaluation and long-term observation of the patient. In some patients with depression, a short REM sleep latency at night supports the diagnosis of depression. Patients with idiopathic hypersomnia can develop secondary psychophysiologic manifestations, including depression, that complicate the diagnostic definition. Posttraumatic hypersomnia can be clinically indistinguishable from idiopathic hypersomnia. The age of the individual and the antecedent of significant head trauma occurring in temporal association with the onset of the sleep alteration should assist in making the diagnosis. Neuroimaging procedures are indicated when there is suspicion of a structural brain lesion causing hypersomnia, as in children with hydrocephalus and individuals with midbrain lesions.

The management of idiopathic hypersomnia follows the same clinical guidelines as in narcolepsy. Counseling is desirable for this life-long disorder, which can be disabling and poorly responsive to treatment. CNS stimulants including pemoline, methylphenidate, and dextroamphetamine provide relief of sleepiness, but the response is more irregular and less predictable than in narcolepsy. Occasionally, patients develop headaches and report more side effects such as tachycardia and irritability. Naps are not refreshing, but in their absence the patient might feel more sleepy and uncomfortable; proper rules of sleep hygiene should be followed to avoid worsening.

Periodic Hypersomnias

These are rare but well-defined conditions of sleep/wake abnormality featuring episodes of recurrent hypersomnia typically occurring weeks or months apart. The best known disorder is the Kleine-Levin syndrome [41], an alteration characterized by heavy sleepiness and true hypersomnia associated with hyperphagia and hypersexuality. The episodes appear in early adolescence in boys, rarely in girls, and last several days or at the most 2 or 3 weeks [42]. Bouts of sleepiness appear daily, forcing the individual to sleep up to 18 hours per day, unable to achieve full vigilance when awake. Commonly, patients appear confused and capable of performing only simple tasks such as eating, which they might do voraciously, and voiding. Social withdrawal, negativism, incoherence, and memory disturbances are common; hallucinations have also been reported. Overeating and excessive sleeping lead to weight gain of several kilograms during episodes. Hypersexuality in the form of social disinhibition, repeated masturbation, or uncharacteristic sexual overtures completes the triad of manifestations in the florid form of the disorder. Some individuals develop only hypersomnia with irritability, poor memory, disorientation, and depression while awake, but no hyperphagia or hypersexuality. Polysomnographic evaluation is nonspecific; some authors have described excessive theta activity in the awake EEG,which probably reflects the subvigilant state. During intervals, patients act normally and are free of hypersomnia.

The condition is of unknown etiology. A hypothalamic dysfunction has been suggested by some, but neuroimaging studies and serum hormone levels are normal. Bouts of hypersomnia and behavioral deviation are incapacitating. Treatment is symptomatic and limited to CNS stimulants such as pemoline, dextroamphetamine, or methylphenidate during attacks of hypersomnia. Some authors advocate the prophylactic use of lithium carbonate to reduce the frequency and intensity of episodes.

The menstrual-associated hypersomnia is characterized by excessive sleepiness in temporal association with the days that precede menstruation [43]. At other times, the individual is free of symptoms. The etiology is unknown and polysomnography shows normal architecture of nocturnal sleep, whereas the MSLT reveals excessive sleepiness during the symptomatic stage. Hormonal assays are normal and show the expected changes consistent with the temporal profile of the menstrual cycle. Treatment is symptomatic with CNS stimulants.

References

1. Lemmi H. Excessive daytime sleepiness: Is it narcolepsy? Sleep Medicine Review 1995;3:3.
2. National Commission on Sleep Disorders Research. Wake up America: A National Sleep Alert. Submitted to the U.S. Congress and to the Secretary of the U.S. Department of Health and Human Services, January 1993.
3. Billiard M, Alperovitch A, Perot C, et al. Excessive daytime somnolence in young men: Prevalence and contributing factors. Sleep 1987;10:297.
4. Schmidt HS, Fortin LD. Electronic Pupillography in Disorders of Arousal. In C Guilleminault (ed), Sleep and Waking Disorders: Indications and Techniques. Menlo Park: CA, Addison-Wesley, 1981;127.
5. Billiard M. Personal communication.
6. Gélineau J. De la narcolepsie. Gaz Hôp (Paris) 1880;53:626 and 1880;54:635.
7. Yoss RE, Daly DD. Criteria for the diagnosis of the narcoleptic syndrome. Proc Staff Mayo Clin 1957;32:320.
8. Hochman MS, Chediak AD, Ziffer JA. Hyperekplexia: Report of a non-familial adult onset case associated with obstructive sleep apnea and abnormal brain nuclear tomography. Sleep 1994;17:280.
9. Foutz AS, Delashaw JB, Guilleminault C, et al. Monoaminergic mechanisms and experimental cataplexy. Ann Neurol 1981;10:369.
10. Langdon N, Shindler J, Parkes JD, et al. Fluoxetine in the treatment of cataplexy. Sleep 1986;9:371.
11. Guilleminault C, Mignot E, Grumet FC. Familial patterns of narcolepsy. Lancet 1989;2:1376.

12. Kramer RE, Dinner DS, Braun WE, et al. HLA-DR2 and narcolepsy. Arch Neurol 1987;44:853.
13. Neely S, Rosenberg R, Spire JP, et al. HLA antigens in narcolepsy. Neurology 1987;37:1858.
14. Aldrich MS, Chervin RD, Malow BA. Sensitivity of the multiple sleep latency test (MSLT) for the diagnosis of narcolepsy. Neurology 1995;45(Suppl. 4):A432.
15. Chervin RD, Aldrich MS. Specificity of the multiple sleep latency test (MSLT) for the diagnosis of narcolepsy. Neurology 1995;45(Suppl 4):A432.
16. Diagnostic Classification Steering Committee. ICSD–International Classification of Sleep Disorders: Diagnostic and Coding Manual. Rochester, MN: American Sleep Disorders Association, 1990;42.
17. Broughton R, Guberman A, Roberts J. Comparison of the psychosocial effects of epilepsy and narcolepsy/cataplexy: A controlled study. Epilepsia 1984;25:423.
18. Kales A, Soldatos CR, Bixler EO, et al. Narcolepsy-cataplexy. II. Psychosocial consequences and associated psychopathology. Arch Neurol 1982;39:169.
19. Knipling RR, Wierwille WW. Vehicle-based drowsy driver detection: Current status and future prospects. Proceedings of the Fourth Annual Meeting of IVHS America. IVHS America, Altanta, GA, April 17–20, 1994.
20. Mitler MM. Evaluation of treatment with stimulants in narcolepsy. Sleep 1994;17:S103.
21. Billiard M, Besset A, Montplaisir J, et al. Modafinil: A double-blind multicentric study. Sleep 1994;17:S107.
22. Mitler MM, Hajdukovic R, Erman MK. Treatment of narcolepsy with methamphetamine. Sleep 1993;16:306.
23. Derlet RW, Rice P, Horowitz BZ, et al. Amphetamine toxicity: Experience with 127 cases. J Emerg Med 1989;7:157.
24. Mamelak M, Scharf MB, Woods M. Treatment of narcolepsy with gamma-hydroxybutyrate. A review of clinical and sleep laboratory findings. Sleep 1986;9:285.
25. Poirier G, Montplaisier J, Decary F, et al. HLA antigens in narcolepsy and idiopathic central nervous system hypersomnolence. Sleep 1986;9:153.
26. Bonduelle M, Degos C. Symptomatic Narcolepsy: A Critical Study. In C Guilleminault, WC Dement, P Passouant (eds), Narcolepsy. New York: Spectrum, 1976:313.
27. Aldrich MS, Naylor MW. Narcolepsy associated with lesions of the diencephalon. Neurology 1989;39:1505.
28. Clavelou P, Tournilhac M, Vidal C, et al. Narcolepsy associated with arteriovenous malformation in the diencephalon. Sleep 1995;18:202.
29. Berg O, Hanley J. Narcolepsy in two cases of multiple sclerosis. Acta Neurol Scand 1963;39:252.
30. Potolicchio SJ, Calderon ET, Richert J. Periodic limb movements of sleep and chronic fatigue in multiple sclerosis: Correlations between diagnosis and treatment. Neurology 1991;41(Suppl 1):320.
31. Younger DS, Pedley TA, Thorpy MJ. Multiple sclerosis and narcolepsy: Possible similar genetic susceptibility. Neurology 1991;41:447.

32. Castaigne P, Escourolle R. Étude topographique des lesions anatomiques dans les hypersomnies. Rev Neurol 1967;116:547.
33. Lankford DA, Wellman JJ, Ohara C. Post-traumatic narcolepsy in mild to moderate closed head injury. Sleep 1994;17:S25.
34. Guilleminault C, Faull KF, Miles L, et al. Post-traumatic excessive daytime sleepiness: A review of 20 patients. Neurology 1983;33:1548.
35. Foutz AS, Mitler MM, Cavalli-Sforza LL, et al. Genetic factors in canine narcolepsy. Sleep 1979;1:413.
36. Guilleminault C, Mignot E, Aldrich M, et al. Prazosin is contraindicated in patients with narcolepsy. Lancet 1988;2:511.
37. Kilduff TS, Bowersox SS, Kaitin KI, et al. Muscarinic cholinergic receptors and the canine model of narcolepsy. Sleep 1986;9:102.
38. Guilleminault C. Idiopathic central nervous system hypersomnia. In MH Kryger, T Roth, WC Dement (eds), Principles and Practice of Sleep Medicine (2nd ed). Philadelphia: Saunders, 1994; 562.
39. Bové A, Culebras A, Moore JT, et al. Relationship between sleep spindles and hypersomnia. Sleep 1994;17:449.
40. Levin M. Periodic somnolence and morbid hunger. Brain 1936;62:494.
41. Critchley M. Periodic hypersomnia and megaphagia in adolescent males. Brain 1962;85:627.
42. Billiard M, Guilleminault C, Dement WC. A menstruation-linked periodic hypersomnia. Neurology 1975;25:436.

7

Sleep Apnea Syndromes

> *Everybody was excited, except the fat boy, and he slept as soundly as if the roaring of cannon were his ordinary lullaby..."Sleep!" said the old gentleman, "he's always asleep. Goes on errands fast asleep, and snores as he waits at table."*
>
> Charles Dickens (1812–1870)
> *The Posthumous Papers of the Pickwick Club* [1]

Overview

There is a special and intimate relationship between sleep and respiration, so much so that even ancient Greek civilizations remarking on this unique association created the myth of Ondine, the goddess unable to breathe while asleep. The damnation of Ondine is the archetype of a group of alterations of the respiratory function only recently described. There is a strong liaison between sleep and breathing, such that while the individual is asleep, the pneumotaxic centers of the brain stem assume total control of respiration. Were this to fail, the individual would die from asphyxiation in a matter of minutes, an extraordinarily rare occurrence in the adult person. The central nervous system (CNS) has a series of safeguard mechanisms destined to preserve vital functions, among which prevails immediate awakening should respiration be threatened. Ironically, these same mechanisms that are guarantors of respiration and life reduce the quality of sleep while activating awakenings in individuals predisposed to the development of sleep-related respiratory dysfunction.

Sleep apneas, whether complete or partial, occur in virtually all men past the age of 45 years and in many women. A great deal has been said about the threshold between normal and abnormal, tolerable and intolerable interruptions. There is consensus in acknowledging disease whenever the frequency and depth of respiratory alterations is such that sleep architecture becomes disturbed, oxygen saturation of circulating hemoglobin is modified, the cardiac function is altered, or the quality of subsequent alertness is reduced. In the opinion of Guilleminault and colleagues [2], five or more episodes of apnea, lasting 9 seconds or more, per hour of nocturnal sleep, would constitute the threshold beyond which normalcy disappears. However, most patients fail to exhibit clinical manifestations until the frequency of apnea events reaches or surpasses 30 episodes per hour of sleep.

The study of the sleep apnea syndromes, in particular obstructive sleep apnea, has stimulated the proliferation of sleep laboratories and centers, especially in the United States, where the diagnosis is commonly made. The ancestral fear of dying in sleep, the insufficient quality of nocturnal sleep attributable to sleep apneas, and the increasing evidence that advanced obstructive sleep apnea syndrome constitutes a risk factor for the development of cardiovascular and cerebrovascular diseases, justify fully the evaluation of patients suspected of harboring the disorder. Furthermore, available treatments are efficacious, and their administration cannot be ignored or missed whenever the opportunity arises.

Physiology of Respiration in Sleep

A series of factors converge in sleep to permit rhythmic, calm, and sufficient respiration. The pontine pneumotaxic centers in REM sleep and the reflexes depending on bulbar and carotid sinus chemoreceptors during non-REM sleep activate the respiratory muscles that conform the inspiratory-expiratory respiratory pump. The control of this pump involves neural and chemical mechanisms. In order for the air to flow smoothly, the respiratory airways require a certain diameter that is appropriate to the negative pressures generated. When these conditions fail or are altered, the respiratory function ceases or becomes insufficient, activating, without delay, alerting mechanisms that partially or fully arouse the sleeping individual.

Three elements integrate the control of respiration: a neural controller, mechanical sensors and chemoreceptors, and an effector system. The neural control is located within the brain stem and spinal cord and is responsible for maintaining the involuntary reflexes while integrating sensory inputs. The sensors can be found in the upper airways, lungs, and thorax. The effectors are the muscles of respiration, which include the diaphragm and the thoracic and auxiliary muscles of respiration.

The rhythmic contraction of respiratory muscles is activated by a pattern generator system located in the brain stem that activates two normally well-coordinated outputs, inspiration and expiration. The neuronal centers that integrate the system are located in the pons and medulla with extensions to the spinal cord. The region in the pons that is responsible for respiratory activity is found in the dorsolateral rostral area (coinciding with the nucleus parabrachialis medialis) and is called the pneumotaxic center; a lesion of this center causes breath-holding spells or apneusis. Two neuronal aggregations integrate the medullary centers: a dorsal respiratory group (DRG) associated with the ventrolateral nucleus of the solitary tract, and a ventral respiratory group (VRG) associated with the nucleus ambiguus. The DRG is mainly involved in inspiration, and its lesions cause a reduction of phrenic nerve activity. The VRG is involved with expiration, as shown by bulbospinal expiratory projections that reach the thorax from this region. Lesions of the VRG cause a reduction in the amplitude of respiratory motor activity, suggesting that this nucleus is not critical for maintenance of the respiratory cycle.

A wide range of centers located in the sensorimotor cortex, orbital frontal cortex, limbic lobe, amygdala, hypothalamus, and even mesencephalon modify the respiratory cycle when electrically excited. These suprapontine centers intervene in the modification of respiration while individuals are awake during activities such as phonation, swallowing, emotions, temperature regulation, and so on.

Spinal respiratory motoneurons located in the cervical cord receive descending and local inputs. Medullary impulses descending in the ventral and lateral columns are separate from corticospinal tract input that descends in the dorsolateral columns. The phrenic motor nucleus extends from the third through the fifth cervical segments, whereas the intercostal motor column that innervates intercostal muscles extends the entire length of the thoracic spinal cord. Respiratory motor units have properties similar to those of other alpha-motoneurons innervating skeletal muscles. Motoneurons are actively inhibited during the portion of the respiratory cycle in which they are not firing.

Sensors located in the upper airways and lungs are mechanoreceptors and chemoreceptors that respond to lung inflation and hyperinflation, as well as to exogenous and endogenous agents, including prostaglandins and histamine. These receptors are responsible for reflexes such as bronchodilation, bronchoconstriction, hyperpnea, tachycardia, bradycardia, cough, mucus secretion, and hypotension. Chest wall receptors are found in muscle spindles and serve as sensors of respiratory load change. The density of muscle spindles is high in intercostal muscles and low in the diaphragm.

Physiologic stresses such as hypoxia and hypercapnia alter breathing through appropriate chemoreceptors located peripherally in the carotid body and aortic bodies, and through central chemoreceptor areas located in the ventral surface of the medulla. The carotid bodies are situated at the bifurcation of the common carotid artery. De Castro [3], working in Cajal's laboratory in Madrid, first suggested that the rich vascularity and innervation of the glomus caroticum was an indicator that this body might serve as a sensor of the chemical composition of the blood. Afferent fibers from the carotid bodies are carried by the nerve of Hering, or carotid sinus nerve, which also contains baroreceptor afferents from the carotid sinus and ultimately joins the glossopharyngeal nerve. Similar bodies are found in the aortic arch with afferent fibers joining the vagus nerves. Carotid bodies respond to decreases in arterial PO_2 rather than reductions in arterial O_2 content or desaturation of oxyhemoglobin, and also to increases in arterial PCO_2. Hypoxia and hypercapnia are therefore the changes that trigger stimuli in the carotid body, but their combination produces more than a simple additive effect, a phenomenon that explains the excessive increase in ventilatory activity that is observed in hypoxic subjects when carbon dioxide increases.

Central chemoreceptors in the medulla respond to hypercapnia independently of peripheral chemoreceptors, causing an increase in ventilation through appropriate reflex mechanisms. In a hyperoxic environment, central chemoreceptors are primarily responsible for carbon dioxide responsiveness. As the oxygen level decreases, peripheral chemoreceptor activity takes over and the response augments. Hypocapnia can trigger hypopnea and apnea in the anesthetized and asleep individual. Hypoxia stimulates ventilation through peripheral carotid body receptors. In humans, a response is obtained only with alveolar PO_2 of 60 mm Hg or less, if PCO_2 remains constant. Should hyperventilation appear, the resultant hypocapnia might offset the effect of hypoxia on peripheral chemoreceptors. Denervation of the carotid body chemoreceptors causes failure of ventilatory response in acute hypoxia.

Acute metabolic acid-base changes also stimulate chemoreceptors. In systemic metabolic acidosis, there is an increase in ventilation because of peripheral chemoreceptor stimulation that can be partly offset by a decrease in central chemoreceptor stimulation caused by posthyperventilation hypocapnia. The blood–brain barrier is poorly permeable to acid-base changes but not to carbon dioxide, therefore central chemoreceptors respond quickly to peripheral PCO_2 changes but not to acid-base metabolic changes.

During synchronized slow wave sleep (SWS), breathing is regular with an increase in tidal volume and a decrease in frequency. In contrast, breathing in desynchronized REM sleep is irregular, exhibiting a decrease in average tidal volume and an increase in average frequency. In SWS, the ventilatory response to carbon dioxide shows little change, whereas in REM sleep the response is reduced. The response to hypoxia in both REM and non-REM sleep is approximately equal to that in the alert state, although there is some evidence that in men it can be reduced.

Habitual Primary Snoring

Snoring is the act of breathing during sleep with a rough hoarse noise. Most individuals, particularly men past the age of 45, snore softly or even intermittently loudly in their sleep, but only some exhibit pathologic or obnoxious snoring that is more persistent and loud, disturbing the sleep of others. Although the prevalence of snoring depends greatly on how it is defined, some population studies indicate that habitual snoring occurs in 9–24% of middle-aged men and 4–14% of middle-aged women [4]. Many snorers are not aware of their snoring unless informed by a bedmate, so epidemiologic studies need to include spouses, housemates, and bedmates in their questionnaires; nevertheless 13% of individuals reporting that they did not snore were simply unaware [5]. Snoring occurs with the turbulent passage of air through a narrow oropharynx, causing vibration of soft tissues. During sleep, the muscles that maintain the pharyngeal wall taut tend to relax, narrowing the straits behind the tongue. In individuals with anatomic narrowing of any cause, such as large tonsils, accumulation of adipose tissue, or a large tongue, the reduced cross-sectional area creates increasing air turbulence. Eventually it can reach the point of collapse, interrupting the respiratory process. There is a continuum between heavy snoring and obstructive sleep apnea syndrome. The factors that force the passage from asymptomatic snoring to sleep apnea have not been determined. However, there is strong evidence that weight gain, alcohol ingestion, drug administration, and progressive age play significant roles. Snoring of loud intensity, persistent occurrence, and irregular quality can be a marker of the sleep apnea syndrome and in consequence a manifestation of disease. Paradoxically, snoring can become intermittent and more sparse as the sleep apnea syndrome worsens and episodes of obstruction become increasingly prolonged.

Snoring is aggravated while sleeping supine because the weight of a relaxed tongue tends to choke even further the narrowed oropharyngeal passage, although individuals with severe disease snore in all positions. Snoring is also made worse by rhinitis, smoking, alcohol, CNS depressants, and sleep deprivation. It acquires maximal intensity in stage 4 of sleep and tends to be softer during REM sleep, a paradoxic phenomenon since sleep apnea episodes are more prolonged; perhaps this situation occurs because the negative pressures exerted by the diaphragm are less forceful during REM stage. A similar dissociation occurs in certain patients with muscular disorders who have severe sleep apnea syndrome but not loud snoring.

Individuals who snore intensely are not only embarrassed by the taunting reports of others but also often have to endure marital friction when asked to leave the bed or when abandoned at night by a sleepless spouse. Snoring can alter the sleep of other persons in the household and even of neighbors who complain of the incessant noise at night. These reports are valuable indicators of the intensity of snoring, the loudness of which has been measured in some individuals at 80 decibels, a level comparable to that of a pneumatic hammer.

The incessant vibration of soft tissues that is produced by pathologic snoring can cause irritation of the oropharynx and a sensation of sore throat on awakening. An association between habitual snoring and hypertension was noted in epidemiologic studies conducted in the republic of San Marino [6]. When snoring was combined with other risk factors such as male sex, smoking, and obesity, the risk for hypertension was 4.2 times greater and for heart disease 2 times greater [7]. Snoring has been considered an independent risk factor for stroke and myocardial infarction, perhaps because of the profound vascular alterations that appear with the increased negative endothoracic pressures of inspiration [8].

The clinical assessment of snoring can be done by recording the sounds at the bedside with a simple tape recorder. A more formal evaluation in the sleep laboratory is conducted by the technician who documents the rhythm, intensity, and variations with sleep stage and posture. Quantitative assessment can be obtained by a sound level meter connected to a microphone placed next to the patient. Some laboratories print the sounds recorded by the microphone directly on the polygraph.

The treatment of snoring first addresses all risk factors that intervene. A recommendation is given to reduce weight, increase regular exercise, quit smoking, reduce alcohol ingestion, and discontinue drugs that have a sedative and hypnotic effect. Patients with hypothyroidism and acromegaly should be adequately controlled, and patients with epilepsy on phenytoin should be switched to another anticonvulsant, if possible. If there is chronic rhinitis, a nasal decongestant can be useful. For individuals who snore predominantly while sleeping on their back, a snore ball is recommended. It consists of a tennis ball within a pocket or sock sown to the back of the pajama top that trains individuals to sleep on their side. Oral appliances (vide infra) can be tried in individuals who do not respond to more conservative measures of risk factor control, such as weight loss and cessation of smoking and drinking alcohol.

Laser-Assisted Uvulopalatoplasty

Laser-assisted uvulopalatoplasty (LAUP) is an office-based procedure introduced recently for the treatment of habitual snoring. The carbon dioxide laser beam is used to vaporize the uvula and adjacent soft-palate tissue with linear incisions of the palate; only topical anesthesia is used. LAUP does not excise the tonsils or the lateral pharyngeal tissues. The intervention is done in a series of one to five sessions spaced at weekly or biweekly intervals. The procedure is not indicated for patients with snoring and obstruction at sites other than the pharynx, for instance the nose or hypopharynx. LAUP has a limited role in the treatment of obstructive sleep apnea because the obstruction is often located at multiple sites, a concept that is also applicable to conventional uvulopalatopharyngoplasty (UPPP). Patients with obstructive sleep apnea syndrome might need treatment with continuous positive airway pressure (CPAP) following LAUP if symptoms of nocturnal sleep fragmentation and excessive daytime sleepiness persist despite the successful eradication of snoring. There are few objective results recorded in the literature. Complications relate to pain that can last up to 8 days, but because of postoperative inflammation and further limitation of airflow patients should be cautioned about the use of analgesic drugs with sedative and narcotic action. For the same reason, alcohol is proscribed until the swelling subsides. The Standards of Practice Committee of the American Sleep Disorders Association has published the following recommendations [9]:

1. LAUP is not recommended for the treatment of obstructive sleep apnea syndrome because there is a lack of validated data.

2. Surgical candidates for LAUP as a treatment for snoring should undergo nocturnal polysomnography to detect underlying sleep-related breathing disorders.

3. Patients should be informed that the risks, benefits, and complications have not been established.

4. Patients should be informed that snoring is a marker of sleep apnea and its elimination might reduce the chances of diagnosing the disorder at a future time, unless evaluations are performed periodically.

5. The use of narcotics, alcohol, sedatives, and sleeping pills can be hazardous to patients following the operation; the hazard becomes more pronounced in the immediate postoperative period.

Some authors recommend UPPP for the alleviation of primary uncomplicated snoring in patients who have not responded to other less invasive procedures. In fact, this procedure was initially introduced for the treatment of snoring and later extended to treatment of obstructive sleep apnea syndrome. The success rate in asymptomatic snorers varies from study to study and can depend on the choice of candidates. In general, we discourage this form of treatment in the absence of sleep apnea syndrome, unless there is clear evidence of isolated anatomic obstruction in the oropharynx that might not be amenable to LAUP. Polysomnography is recommended before the intervention to assess for the presence and severity of obstructive sleep apnea. In children with loud snoring and tonsillar and adenoidal hypertrophy, tonsillectomy and adenoidectomy are followed by a satisfactory and lasting response. Maxillofacial reconstruction is reserved for special circumstances of retrognathia, micrognathia, and stenosis of the hypopharynx with inveterate loud snoring.

Sleep Apnea Syndromes

Pathophysiology

The most common alteration determining a sleep apnea syndrome is the partial or complete obstruction of the upper respiratory airway during sleep. Most patients with sleep apnea syndrome breathe without difficulty while awake. On falling asleep, one or more factors converge to occlude the upper airway, usually at the oropharyngeal level (Figure 7-1).

Some patients exhibit structural anomalies that can be congenital in origin, such as stenosis of the oropharyngeal opening that diminishes the pharyngeal lumen, or retrognathia that reduces the diameter of the hypopharynx. In other instances, the obstructive anatomic lesion is acquired, such as tonsillar hypertrophy in children, or redundant soft palate and pharyngeal tissues in obese adults. A recent anatomic study with magnetic resonance imaging (MRI) suggests that patients with sleep apnea have more adipose tissue adjacent to the airway than normal subjects, contributing to compression and narrowing of the upper airway [10]. Sometimes macroglossia, as observed in hypothyroidism or in acromegaly, can determine the occlusion. However, even in the face of anatomic lesions or anomalies, one has to explain why the manifestations of obstruction occur exclusively at night while the individual is asleep. Clearly, there is failure of the neurophysiologic mechanisms that normally maintain an adequate upper airway opening during sleep, among which the dilation of pharyngeal muscles during the inspiratory act occupies a dominant spot.

Inspiration generates a negative airway pressure that depends on the force of muscular activity and on the dimensions of the upper airway. The negative pressure tends to collapse the soft walls of the pharynx, which remain open because of tonic contraction of the dilator muscles of the pharynx activated through specific neurogenic reflexes. A stenotic lesion located at any level of the upper airway, be it the nose, oropharynx, or hypopharynx, increases disproportionately the negative pressure generated during inspiration. The tension of the pharyngeal muscles maintains the walls in a rigid state; should that contraction fail or become too weak to counteract the negative pressure, the walls would collapse and cause obstruction.

During sleep, there is a generalized tendency to muscular relaxation that includes the pharyngeal muscles and becomes more pronounced during REM sleep. Normally, the dilation of the pharyngeal

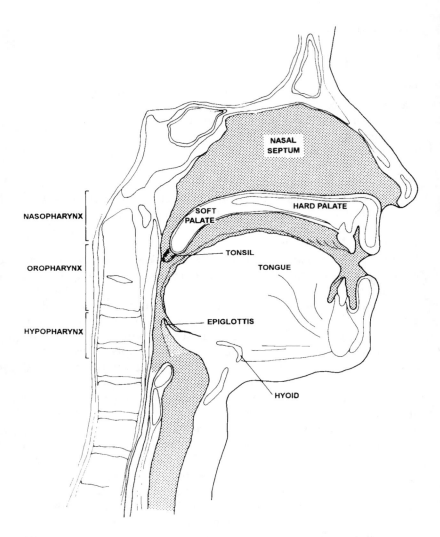

Figure 7-1.   *Diagram of the median section of the face and neck showing the anatomic relations of the soft palate, tongue, and pharyngeal structures. The oropharynx is the narrowest segment and thus the most vulnerable to obstruction during sleep.*

wall is maintained by activity of accessory inspiratory muscles that respond to central reflexes. The central stimulus for inspiration and for the associated pharyngeal muscle dilation originates in bulbar chemoreceptors sensitive to hypercapnia, and in the carotid body sensitive to hypoxia, the latter being the most potent stimulus. It is assisted in sleep by receptors sensitive to postural changes located in neck, mouth, and chin, as well as by pressure receptors located in the upper airway. The tone of the genioglossus muscle increases through the same mechanism. In sleep, there is a reduction of the ventilatory response to hypercapnia and to hypoxia, particularly in men, that partially explains why men have a higher propensity to develop sleep apnea syndrome. In a hypercapnic environment, the carotid body receptor becomes more sensitive to hypoxia. In hypoxia, the reflex hyperventilation causes ensuing hypocapnia that eventually reduces the sensitivity of the carotid body to hypoxia. Under these circumstances, such as occurs in a high-altitude environment, the individual ceases to breathe because of loss of sensitivity to both stimuli, until the accumulation of carbon dioxide or the deepening hypoxia reaches a threshold sufficient to stimulate the chemoreceptors. Thus, in normal individuals, a periodic respiratory pattern appears in high altitude during sleep, resembling the central sleep apnea syndrome and Cheyne-Stokes respiration. The notable difference with genuine sleep apnea syndrome is that the periodic pattern of respiration at high altitude becomes regular during REM sleep, whereas the obstructive sleep apnea syndrome worsens. During REM sleep, inspiration is activated through neurogenic mechanisms that are independent of chemoreceptor stimuli, whereas in non-REM sleep, activation is dependent on reflexes initiated in chemoreceptor stimuli. In high altitude, hypocapnic alkalosis is the predominant factor responsible for periodic respiration, whereas hypoxia is the precipitating factor.

In addition to stimuli generated by chemoreceptors, there are neurogenic reflexes that originate in pharyngeal pressure receptors. These reflexes form a first line of defense to guard against foreign bodies, but in addition serve to regulate respiratory activity, providing modulation to the rhythm and respiratory depth. Pharyngeal reflexes that are partially inhibited during sleep normally stimulate pharyngeal dilation and prolong the inspiratory time, compensating for the need to increase the negative pressure in the face of partial obstruction of the upper airway. In normal subjects, the negative pressure necessary to collapse the pharyngeal wall is of the order of 30 cm H_2O, whereas in patients with obstructive sleep apnea syndrome the pharynx can collapse with a small pressure of 0.5 cm H_2O. This finding suggests that in obstructive sleep apnea syndrome there is failure of neurogenic stimulation of dilating pharyngeal muscles, or that the reflex is insufficient to maintain open a lumen overloaded with pendulous, inflamed, flaccid, soft tissues typically observed in patients with obstructive sleep apnea syndrome. In habitual snorers, without overt obstructive sleep apnea syndrome, a similar phenomenon is observed with closure of the pharynx at low pressures of 5 cm H_2O. In these individuals, intense vibrations of the pharyngeal wall productive of the snore and snort might mechanically stimulate dilating pharyngeal reflexes and protect against sleep apnea syndrome [11]. The loss of these reflexes would determine the transition from habitual snoring to obstructive sleep apnea.

Substances that depress cerebral function, such as the benzodiazepines, barbiturates, and alcohol, also depress bulbar and carotid body centers, worsening the sleep apnea syndromes. On the contrary, tricyclic compounds such as protriptyline that activate the neurogenic stimuli that keep the pharynx dilated during sleep, tend to alleviate obstructive sleep apnea.

Failure of inspiratory pharyngeal dilation during sleep is the final common pathway on which the factors that determine obstructive sleep apnea syndrome converge. Concurring anatomic factors such as pharyngeal stenosis of any cause, or coadjuvant factors such as age and sex, and precipitating factors of pharmacologic or environmental origin, are also important. The specialist should endeavor to determine the specific weight of each factor and the sequence of events whenever possible.

Clinical Forms

There are two major forms of sleep apnea: obstructive sleep apnea and nonobstructive, or central, sleep apnea. Mixed sleep apnea refers to the combination of both clinical forms. Hypopnea is a less intense form of respiratory alteration that can occur in combination with the full form.

Obstructive Sleep Apnea Syndrome

This form is characterized by repetitive episodes of respiratory interruption that occur during sleep and are generally associated with a decrease in oxygen saturation of the oxyhemoglobin (Figure 7-2). Respiratory pauses lasting 20–30 seconds are associated with inspiratory effort but without passage of air to the lungs caused by obstruction of the upper airway. Eventually, the blockage is overcome by the increasing respiratory struggle, allowing a column of air to irrupt precipitously in the upper airway. The turbulence causes vibration of soft pharyngeal tissues that like a sail flapping in the wind generates a loud rapping noise that is recognized as snoring. Thus, the typical pattern of obstructive sleep apnea is characterized by loud snores and brief gasps alternating with episodes of silence. Virtually all adults make some noise while asleep; if it is transient or not loud, it is devoid of clinical significance. However, when snoring is habitual and so loud that it disturbs the sleep of the bed partner, it might be a manifestation of obstructive sleep apnea. Usually, patients are unaware of their own snores and partial arousals, although occasionally they might wake up gasping for air, choking, or unable to sleep, a complaint that becomes increasingly common as age advances. The bed partner provides a better description and might relate alarming respiratory pauses, which if prolonged provoke the urge to nudge the patient to restart breathing. The termination of the sleep apnea episode is marked by loud gasps and moans associated with whole body shaking that further discomforts the bed partner. Motor restlessness in sleep is a hallmark of the advanced sleep apnea syndrome, and patients sometimes fall out of bed, an event that is virtually unique to the condition. Bed partners usually move out of the bedroom to regain the ability to sleep, a situation that leads to family pathology. Ingestion of alcohol, CNS sedatives, and all hypnotics aggravate all nocturnal manifestations of the patient with sleep apnea syndrome.

In advanced forms, patients might get out of bed and walk to the bathroom or another area of the house in a state of automatism. Some are found asleep in uncomfortable positions in sections of the house where they do not belong at night. Profuse nocturnal perspiration is common in patients with morbid obesity.

In the morning, patients have difficulty waking up and feel lethargic and unrefreshed. Morning headaches lasting 30–60 minutes are reported by some patients with severe forms of sleep apnea syndrome. Some patients complain of a sore throat, perhaps caused by the incessant snoring, and others of dry mouth that leads to repetitive drinking at night. During daytime hours, patients are plagued by excessive somnolence that is hardly satisfied with naps and leads to inappropriate episodes of falling asleep, particularly during monotonous sequences. As the condition advances, patients relate falling asleep in situations increasingly inopportune and bizarre, such as when talking

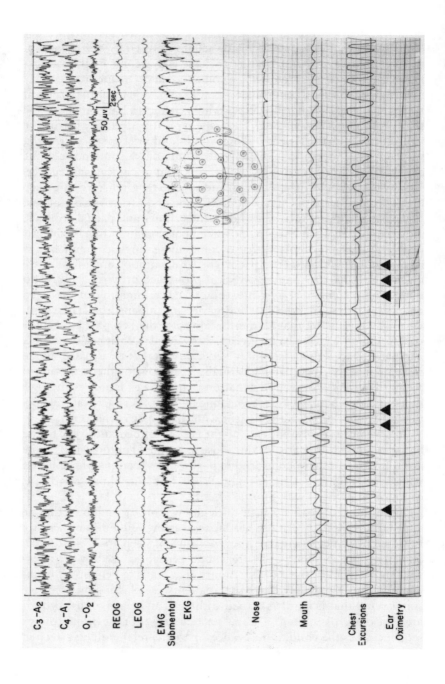

to clients, speaking on the phone, eating at the table, or more ominously, while driving their car. Lethargy and sleepiness are aggravated by apathy and depression, which interfere with productivity at work and with family life at home. Inability to concentrate and poor memory force patients to stop reading documents, books, and even newspapers and to cease in their studies. Finally, an automobile accident, the loss of a job, or a determined spouse induce reluctant patients to seek consultation while they remain unconvinced that their troubles are medical in nature.

The medical examination is rather revealing. Typically, patients are obese men, with a protuberant abdomen and a short, thick neck with a double chin (Figure 7-3) . Examination of the oropharynx shows a narrow opening partially occluded by redundant, pendulous, and occasionally inflamed tissues conforming the soft palate and pillars. In children, tonsillar enlargement usually determines the occlusion. Structural obstruction can also be caused by macroglossia in patients with hypothyroidism, acromegaly, or Down's syndrome, or by anatomic anomalies such as a shallow anteroposterior pharyngeal diameter in individuals with retrognathia and craniofacial malformations. Special examination of the upper airway with fiberoptic techniques, fluoroscopy, CT, or MRI might be necessary to demonstrate stenosis of the hypopharynx. Obstructive sleep apnea syndrome in a patient with normal body weight should suggest a structural occluding lesion of the pharynx.

In patients with advanced sleep apnea syndrome, systemic hypertension with an elevated diastolic component might be found. Cardiac

◀ **Figure 7-2.**   *Obstructive sleep apnea is characterized by respiratory interruption generally associated with a decrease in oxygen saturation of the oxyhemoglobin. Respiratory pauses are associated with inspiratory effort but without passage of air to the lungs because of obstruction of the upper airway. The polysomnogram shows (arrowhead) chest excursions with no or insignificant ventilation, followed by a brief recovery phase (double arrowheads), and a subsequent mixed apnea (triple arrowheads) characterized by initial inhibition of respiratory effort followed by increasing chest excursions and failed ventilation because of obstruction. The oximetry curve shows a delayed decrease in oxygen saturation after each episode of apnea. Note partial arousal during the recovery phase. (C_3–A_2, C_4–A_1, O_1–O_2 = EEG, 10–20 international electrode placement system; REOG = right electro-oculogram; LEOG = left electro-oculogram; EMG = electromyogram; ECG = electrocardiogram; nose, mouth = ventilation through nose and mouth.)*

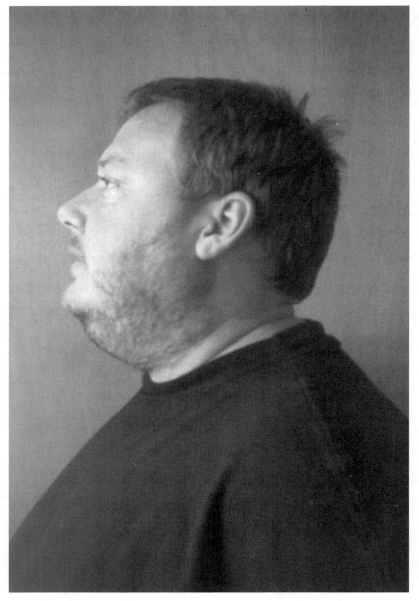

Figure 7-3. *A 36-year-old obese man with advanced obstructive sleep apnea syndrome exhibiting a thick, short neck and a double chin.*

dysrhythmias (predominantly at night), cor pulmonale, and heart failure are occasionally observed. Advanced sleep apnea syndrome and habitual snoring are potential risk factors for the development of ischemic heart disease and stroke, so a careful evaluation focusing on these conditions is required.

Concurrent features in some patients with sleep apnea are gastroesophageal reflux and more rarely laryngospasm. Recent weight gain in overweight or morbidly obese patients is a common phenomenon that can be associated with a recent worsening of symptoms, perhaps the same that brought the patient to the attention of the physician. Sexual impotence along with affective depression are common findings in patients with advanced disorder.

Recent population-based studies conducted in North America indicate that the prevalence of sleep-disordered breathing, defined as an apnea-hypopnea score of five or more events per hour of sleep, is 9% for women and 24% for men [12]. The combination of sleep-disordered breathing and daytime hypersomnia constitutes the sleep apnea syndrome that occurs in 2% of women and 4% of men [12]. Most patients are men (8 to 1) past the age of 45 years. In some instances a familial occurrence has been noted possibly because of the inheritance of pharyngeal structural anomalies, but most cases are sporadic. In some patients, a neuromuscular disorder is suspected or obvious.

Children with sleep apnea syndrome are commonly afflicted by apathy that can be mistaken for laziness, and show difficulty with concentration and poor memory, leading to low grades in school and behavioral changes. Their condition is often misdiagnosed as attention deficit disorder or minimal brain defect. Habitual and loud snoring is not as universal as in adults, making the diagnosis more difficult, although nocturnal sleep is marked by unusual postures and motor agitation that should suggest the diagnosis. An "adenoidal facies" with long thin facial structures, open mouth, receding chin, and vacant stare (Figure 7-4) is commonly found along with pectus excavatum and rib flaring. Mouth breathing and poor speech articulation with a nasal twang might be additional features.

Sleep Apnea and Cardiovascular Disease
The sleep apnea syndrome of the obstructive variety can have serious cardiovascular consequences. In patients with five episodes or more of apnea-hypopnea per hour of sleep, mean blood pressures are significantly higher both during wakefulness (>9/5 mm Hg) and in sleep (>9/4 mm Hg) [13]. The variability of blood pressure is greater during sleep,

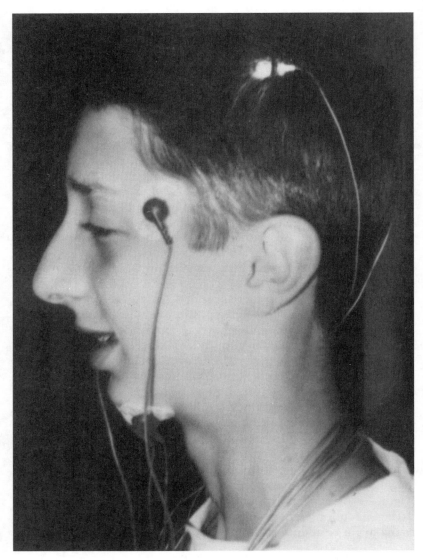

Figure 7-4. *Habitual and loud snoring in children and adolescents is sometimes associated with "adenoidal facies" characterized by long, thin facial structures, open mouth, receding chin, and vacant stare. Pectus excavatum and rib flaring are commonly found along with mouth breathing and poor speech articulation with a nasal twang. (Reprinted with permission from A Culebras. La Medicina del Sueño. Barcelona, Spain: Editorial Áncora, 1994.)*

and changes are independent of obesity, age, and sex. Transient elevations of blood pressure lasting 3.5 seconds during the recovery phase from apnea can reach high levels, with measurements recorded above 200 mm Hg in REM sleep. This phenomenon has been attributed to the arousal at the termination of the apnea. During the apnea episode, there are high negative intrathoracic pressures, progressive desaturation of oxyhemoglobin, and even hypercapnia that contribute to elevate the blood pressure. Repeated bouts of hypertension, night after night, in patients with untreated sleep apnea can eventually lead to sustained hypertension through unknown mechanisms [14]. It has been postulated, however, that repetitive hemodynamic oscillations can result in neurohumoral, renovascular, or structural vascular changes that sustain an elevated blood pressure even during waking hours. Compelling evidence of the relationship between sleep apnea and hypertension comes from studies showing that the successful treatment of obstructive sleep apnea with tracheostomy or nasal CPAP results in a stepwise reduction of blood pressure levels [15, 16]. Circulating epinephrine levels decrease after tracheostomy, and sympathetic tone decreases in patients treated with nasal CPAP [17].

The cardiac response to prolonged apnea consists of a reduction of stroke volume, decreased heart rate, and reduced cardiac output [18]. At the termination of the apnea episode, there is acceleration of the heart rate, so that the entire episode results in a characteristic pattern of brady-tachyarrhythmia (Figure 7-5). Normally, ventricular ectopic activity during sleep is reduced as a consequence of vagal tone preponderance. However, in patients with advanced obstructive sleep apnea, cardiac arrhythmias occur when the oxyhemoglobin saturation decreases below 65%.

All these pathophysiologic changes can result in significant cardiovascular morbidity in patients with sleep apnea. At the time of the apnea episode, intermittent vasoconstriction along with a decrease in cardiac output and desaturation of oxyhemoglobin impose a considerable amount of stress on the cardiovascular system, particularly in older persons who show more abundant changes in cardiac rhythm in response to the apnea. Hypertension can become sustained with all its complications including congestive heart failure. Other consequences of untreated obstructive sleep apnea are left ventricular hypertrophy, pulmonary hypertension, nocturnal myocardial ischemia, myocardial infarction, stroke, and vascular death. Increased mortality in patients with sleep apnea syndrome has been attributed to the development of hypertension [19].

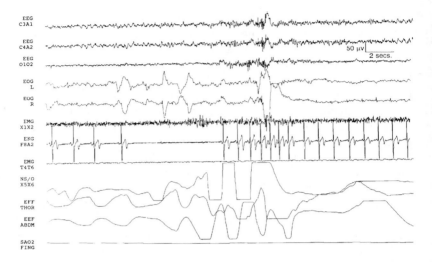

Figure 7-5. *Brady-tachyarrhythmia in relation to an obstructive sleep apnea event observed in the patient shown in Figure 7-3. Note bradycardia and brief asystole during phasic REM and obstructive apnea, followed by heart acceleration in the subsequent recovery phase along with brief arousal. Not shown is the decrease of oxyhemoglobin saturation under 65%.*

Polysomnography

In patients with habitual loud snoring who are suspected of having obstructive sleep apnea syndrome, nocturnal polysomnography and MSLT are critical to confirm the diagnosis, determine the degree of severity, and assess the presence of complications including the impact of sleep apnea in daytime vigilance. A baseline test is needed to proceed with therapeutic options that require additional polysomnographic testing, such as CPAP or bi-level positive airway pressure (Bi-PAP) application. The protocol for sleep apnea monitoring (as described in Chapter 4) incorporates three channels for EEG, two channels for EOG, one channel for EMG, one channel for ECG, one channel for leg movement activity, one channel for oronasal ventilation, one channel for thoracic excursions, one channel for abdominal excursions, and one channel for oximetry. Abdominal excursions are the only respiratory activity identified during REM sleep.

The objective of respiratory monitoring is to identify apneas and hypopneas that are the cornerstone of the diagnosis of the sleep apnea

Table 7-1.   Diagnostic Criteria for Obstructive Sleep Apnea Syndrome

1. Excessive daytime sleepiness
2. Obstructed breathing during sleep
3. Loud snoring that can be associated with morning headaches and motor agitation in adults, or chest retraction during sleep in children
4. More than five obstructive apneas, greater than 10 seconds in duration, per hour of sleep
5. Additional features are frequent arousals associated with apneas, brady-tachycardia, oxygen desaturation with apnea episodes, and MSLT showing mean sleep latency of less than 10 minutes

syndromes. An apnea is defined as a respiratory pause with cessation of airflow through the nostrils and mouth lasting 10 seconds or longer, although some authors accept a duration of 9 seconds or longer. Obstructive apneas show concurrent inspiratory effort in the thoracic or abdominal channels, or both (see Figure 7-2); nonobstructive, or central, apneas appear in the polysomnogram as a total cessation or inhibition of the inspiratory effort. Mixed apneas are characterized by an initial central component followed by an obstructive apnea. A hypopnea is defined as an episode of shallow breathing, with respiratory effort reduced by at least 50%, lasting 10 seconds or longer. The apnea index refers to the number of apnea episodes per hour of sleep and the apnea-hypopnea index refers to the tabulation of both apnea and hypopnea episodes per hour of sleep. The diagnostic criteria for obstructive sleep apnea syndrome require the presence of five or more episodes of obstructive apnea per hour of sleep (Table 7-1).

Respiratory activity is monitored with thermistors or thermocouples that detect the subtle temperature changes caused by the exchange of air through the nose and mouth. Chest excursions and abdominal movements related to the respiratory effort are recorded with strain gauges placed around the thorax and abdomen. Two channels are necessary to monitor independently the effort of intercostal muscles and diaphragm, and to identify paradoxic respirations that appear as out-of-phase deflections of the thoracic and abdominal efforts. Other methods include the esophageal balloon and intercostal and diaphragmatic EMG tracings to record directly muscle activity.

Obstructive apneas typically last 20–40 seconds but can be as long as 1 minute in duration. Episodes are more common during stages 1 and 2 of sleep and in REM sleep. In severe obstructive sleep apnea syndrome, the apnea index surpasses 60 per hour, and the total for the night can reach 600–800 episodes (Figure 7-6). In patients with diaphragmatic insufficiency caused by abdominal obesity or neuromuscular disorder, episodes of sleep apnea can worsen or occur predominantly, if not solely, during REM sleep.

Oxygen saturation of hemoglobin is continuously quantified with pulse oximeters that use a photoelectric cell to read changes in the color spectrum of oxyhemoglobin. Probes are attached to the earlobe or to the fingertip. Oximeters are relatively accurate when the saturation of oxygen is above 40%; below that level the figures obtained are inaccurate but can indicate a trend. Hypoxemia is common in association with episodes of obstructive apnea and is a typical feature of the disorder. Oxygen saturation returns to a normal value at the termination of the apnea except in patients with chronic obstructive pulmonary disease or alveolar hypoventilation who show low baseline values of oxygen saturation even in the awake state.

The ECG channel is required to identify cardiac arrhythmias that can indicate the severity of the disease. These arrhythmias are particularly common in adults with severe sleep apnea syndrome and increase in number and severity as age advances. Cardiac arrhythmias range from sinus arrhythmia to premature ventricular contractions, all varieties of atrioventricular block and even sinus arrest, the latter occurring predominantly during phasic REM sleep. In patients with severe

Figure 7-6. ▶   A. *Hypnogram illustrating severe obstructive sleep apnea syndrome in a 40-year-old obese man. The apnea-hypopnea index (A + H) fluctuates between 80 and 100 episodes per hour of sleep with profound and sustained episodes of oxygen desaturation (SAO$_2$) accompanied by instability of heart rate (HR). The sleep architecture shows poor generation of sleep stages with virtual absence of slow wave sleep (SWS) and poor development of REM sleep. The bottom graph (A/W) shows innumerable arousals illustrated by vertical lines. B. For comparison, the hypnogram from the subsequent night of the same patient, treated with CPAP apparatus, showing an improved pattern of sleep following successful elimination of sleep respiratory interruptions. Episodes of apnea and hypopnea have virtually disappeared, while oxygen saturation remains at 90% and heart rate appears more stable. Sleep architecture shows early generation of SWS and remarkable REM sleep rebound; arousals have been eliminated. The bottom graph shows the CPAP pressures applied. REM sleep rebound appears at 8 cm of H$_2$0. (Reprinted with permission from A Culebras. La Medicina del Sueño. Barcelona, Spain: Editorial Áncora, 1994.)*

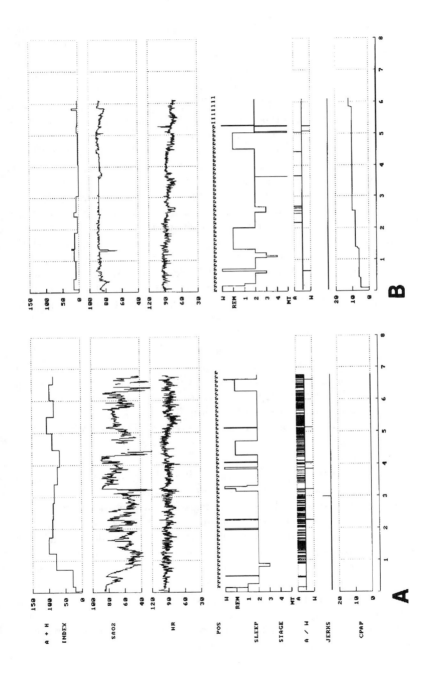

obstructive sleep apnea syndrome and profound hypoxemia, brady-cardia might be observed during the apneic phase, followed by tachy-cardia during recovery of respiration at the termination of the apnea.

Arousals, which are common at the termination of each apnea episode, are defined as an increase in EEG frequency or the presence of EMG artifacts in the EEG lasting longer than 2 seconds, along with enhanced tone in the submental muscle recording, and acceleration of the heart rate. The arousal index, which refers to the number of arousals per hour of sleep, determines the quality of nocturnal sleep and is indirectly related to the subsquent presence of excessive somnolence in the MSLT.

The sleep architecture is very disrupted in patients with severe obstructive sleep apnea syndrome. Stages 3 and 4 are much reduced or absent, and REM sleep is similarly reduced. However, when stages 3 and 4 are present, episodes of apnea are reduced or absent. In some instances, motor agitation and other forms of artifact interfere with the proper scoring of the polysomnogram so that the analysis is reduced to a REM–non-REM score. The MSLT typically shows the presence of sleep in daytime segments with an average latency of 10 minutes or less and presence of brief REM sleep in some individuals with marked dis-ruption of nocturnal sleep architecture.

Nonobstructive (Central) Sleep Apnea Syndrome

Central, or nonobstructive, sleep apnea is characterized by the cessa-tion of respiration, which can be associated with hypoxemia. In con-trast with obstructive sleep apnea, there is no inspiratory effort during the respiratory pause. Patients complain of choking and gasping at night with insomnia and prolonged awakenings. During daytime hours, they complain of lassitude and fatigue, and exhibit excessive somno-lence (Table 7-2).

Nonobstructive sleep apnea can be combined with obstructive and mixed forms of sleep apnea. The central, nonobstructive, sleep apnea syndrome is considerably less frequent than the obstructive form. Per-haps only 10% of patients attending sleep centers with complaints referable to sleep-disordered respiration have central sleep apnea. It is somewhat more common in men and tends to increase in prevalence as age advances. Habitual, loud snoring is not as common or manifest, but cardiac dysrhythmias are present. Patients afflicted with central sleep apnea are not obese and the physical examination fails to reveal occluding lesions in the oropharynx. Occasionally, patients are not symptomatic and are referred to the physician by a concerned bedmate who has observed respiratory interruptions at night.

Table 7-2.   Diagnostic Criteria for Nonobstructive Sleep Apnea Syndrome

1. Excessive daytime sleepiness or insomnia
2. Shallow or interrupted breathing during sleep
3. Frequent gasps, grunts, choking episodes, and body movements that disturb sleep and contribute to insomnia
4. More than five central apneas, greater than 10 seconds in duration, per hour of sleep. Oxygen desaturation events in association with episodes of apnea, and cardiac dysrhythmias. Frequent partial arousals at the termination of apneas
5. MSLT with a mean sleep latency of less than 10 minutes

In patients with predominant or pure forms of central sleep apnea syndrome, the physician should suspect a CNS or neuromuscular disorder affecting the neural control of sleep respiration. Such is the case in patients with autonomic dysfunction as in the Shy-Drager syndrome, familial dysautonomia, and diabetes mellitus. Brain stem disorders of any nature, damaging the pontine pneumotaxic or more commonly the bulbar centers of respiration, can affect the automatic control of respiration in sleep without disturbing the wake-related system, as occurs in mild forms of bulbar poliomyelitis [20] and in the early postpolio syndrome. The bulbar centers of ventilation can also be altered by other structural lesions such as stroke [21], encephalitis, and tumor. In cervical cordotomy, the ventilatory reflex arc driven by metabolic stimuli is interrupted, explaining the common occurrence of sleep-related respiratory dysrhythmia and central sleep apnea following the procedure, in the absence of damage to the brain stem centers. Patients with advanced neuromuscular disorders such as myasthenia gravis suffer a failure of the effector mechanism of the reflex arc resulting in alveolar hypoventilation and central sleep apnea episodes. In neurologic and neuromuscular disorders affecting ventilation, the sleep-related function is affected much earlier than the awake system of respiration, a phenomenon to be taken into consideration when assessing the global diagnosis.

Central sleep apnea syndrome in association with obstructive sleep apnea can be temporarily observed in patients with acute nasal obstruction, as in the common cold and in allergic rhinitis. This temporary condition can result from dampening of local sensors that normally contribute to the ventilatory drive, or to potentiation of oropharyngeal collapse as a result of increased negative inspiratory pressures when the nasal passage is partially occluded.

Cardiac dysrhythmias are similar to the ones found in the obstructive sleep apnea syndrome. Sinus arrhythmia, bradycardia, and sinus arrest can be the consequence of intense vagal stimulation resulting from hypoxemia, a condition that can be reversed with the administration of oxygen [22]. Some studies suggest that central and obstructive sleep apneas are frequently found in patients with congestive heart failure, adding to the poor quality of sleep commonly observed in these patients.

Some patients with severe disease report morning headaches. In the central sleep apnea syndrome, several concurrent manifestations are similar to the ones found in the obstructive variety and include depression, cognitive deficits, sexual impotence, and hemodynamic complications.

Polysomnography

In patients with nonobstructive sleep apnea syndrome, the use of the sleep apnea protocol demonstrates the presence of repetitive respiratory pauses lasting 10–30 seconds, associated with moderate hypoxemia. At times, a postapneic period of hyperventilation lasting up to 60 seconds contributes to a pattern that mimics Cheyne-Stokes respiration. Contrary to events in the obstructive sleep apnea syndrome, episodes of respiratory interruption are not more pronounced or prolonged during REM sleep. Indeed, the respiratory effort becomes more regular during REM sleep, a phenomenon also observed in the high-altitude syndrome. The ECG channel might show cardiac dysrhythmias that in general are not as severe as in the obstructive sleep apnea syndrome. The MSLT shows daytime hypersomnia of variable severity depending on the number of nocturnal arousals. In some patients, narcolepsy and central sleep apnea syndrome coexist; REM sleep can be found in MSLT segments.

Other Clinical Variants

Mixed Sleep Apnea

Strictly speaking, this is not a clinical form but a polysomnographic finding that can have clinical implications. The combination of a respiratory alteration consisting of a central apnea followed by an obstructive apnea is called a mixed apnea. These events are common in patients with obstructive sleep apnea syndrome and serve to distinguish the polysomnographic pattern from that of central sleep apnea. However, the presence of many episodes of mixed apnea might herald the conversion of obstructive sleep apnea to a nonobstructive form when CPAP is applied. In turn, this development can require Bi-PAP application, as discussed later.

Positional Sleep Apnea Syndrome

Sleeping in the supine position aggravates the signs of obstructive sleep apnea. The relaxation of the genioglossus muscle facilitates the posterior displacement of the tongue while the patient is supine, a phenomenon that contributes to the collapse of the oropharynx. Bedmates of patients with habitual loud snoring and obstructive sleep apnea commonly relate that when the individuals sleep on their back manifestations appear or become much worse, and further report that nudging the patients to turn on their side is followed by improvement of the noise. The polysomnographic evaluation confirms these observations and occasionally identifies individuals who present snoring and sleep apnea episodes solely when sleeping on their back. Treatment with various devices, such as the snore ball, that force and eventually train patients to sleep on their side are relatively successful in mild forms of sleep apnea.

Upper Airway Resistance Syndrome

Patients with loud snoring and excessive daytime sleepiness can exhibit many nocturnal arousals in the polysomnogram despite minimal polygraphic evidence of obstructive sleep apnea and few, if any, oxygen desaturations. This combination of findings suggests the upper airway resistance syndrome [23]. Patients tend to be nonobese with a triangular face, malocclusion, and retrognathia indicative of a small space behind the base of the tongue. In the polysomnogram, patients exhibit many short arousals in relation to snoring but no changes in oxygen saturation. Some patients do not snore, and the polysomnogram with the esophageal balloon to evaluate esophageal pressures documents repetitive brief alpha EEG arousals as short as 3 seconds immediately following increases in negative esophageal pressure, translating increased resistance in the upper airway. However, this technique is cumbersome and not readily available in many sleep centers. Alternatively, a therapeutic trial with a CPAP mask and a pressure between 4 and 8 cm H_2O can have diagnostic value if the arousals disappear and the sleepiness comes under control.

Differential Diagnosis

Excessive daytime somnolence is the principal manifestation of the sleep apnea syndromes, a diagnosis that needs to be considered in most situations presenting with excessive sleepiness. Furthermore, it is not uncommon to find that obstructive sleep apnea syndrome and to a lesser extent the nonobstructive variety are components of other disorders that have excessive sleepiness as the principal manifestation, as is the case in narcolepsy. The assessment of the sleep apnea component is important because its therapeutic elimination reduces proportionately the tendency to excessive sleepiness.

Obstructive sleep apnea syndrome should be suspected if there is a history of disruptive habitual loud snoring, particularly if the bedmate reports respiratory pauses. The nonobstructive variety is suspected in individuals who complain of respiratory alteration and choking episodes at night and do not present the typical body habitus that is commonly observed in the obstructive form. All-night polysomnography with the sleep apnea protocol and MSLT are required for the appropriate evaluation of the sleep apnea syndromes. A particular diagnostic dilemma can arise when the MSLT shows REM sleep in daytime segments. This phenomenon suggests narcolepsy but can also be caused by REM sleep deprivation, which is common in patients with advanced sleep apnea syndrome. A follow-up test after 2 or more months of therapy for the sleep apnea syndrome is generally required to exclude the diagnosis of narcolepsy.

In some patients, panic attacks, choking events, gastroesophageal reflux, and the rare sleep laryngospasm and sleep-swallowing syndrome can lead one to suspect a diagnosis of sleep apnea syndrome. Polysomnography easily excludes or confirms the diagnosis of sleep apnea, if present.

Central Hypoventilation Syndromes

Central hypoventilation syndromes are characterized by the appearance of hypoxemia, sometimes with hypercapnia, during sleep in patients without pulmonary disease. The principal alteration is the marked decrease of the sleep-related respiratory effort because of reduction or loss of the central neurogenic drive. The alteration becomes worse during REM sleep, a time when ventilation depends exclusively on neurogenic activity. Commonly, patients are afflicted by insomnia, daytime hypersomnia, and morbid obesity. The syndrome of alveolar hypoventilation can be combined with the various forms of sleep apnea (obstructive, central or mixed), making it important to assess the relative contribution of these forms of sleep apnea to the overall clinical picture. The differential diagnosis needs to be established with the restrictive pulmonary disorders that appear in association with neuromuscular disorders, hypothyroidism, and structural chest deformities. Drugs that depress cerebral function and alcohol precipitate or aggravate the condition. In contrast to sleep apnea, the central hypoventilation syndrome can appear in infancy and youth, progressing toward cardiopulmonary insufficiency with pulmonary hypertension. Pulmonary function studies show a reduced response to hypercapnia and hypoxia during wakefulness and in sleep, a phenomenon that suggests dysfunction of chemoreceptors in the carotid body or the medulla.

In the acquired forms of central hypoventilation syndrome, consideration should be given to bulbar dysfunction as observed in poliomyelitis, vascular lesions, and tumors. Following bilateral cordotomy to reduce pain in cancer patients, a bilateral lesion of ventrolateral tracts in the upper cervical cord could result in profound hypoventilation, apneas, carbon dioxide retention, and even death in sleep [24]. In the absence of a background disorder, a rare idiopathic form with central dysfunction is postulated, particularly if the disorder presents in adolescence or early adulthood.

In patients with the central hypoventilation syndrome, nocturnal polysomnography using the sleep apnea protocol shows a saturation of oxygen below 85% in the absence of apnea episodes, with shallow respiratory excursions and decreased tidal volume. Hypoxemia is most marked during REM sleep and carbon dioxide measurements of arterial blood show progressive hypercapnia. During the night, numerous arousals associated with episodes of hypoventilation interrupt sleep repeatedly, leading to insomnia and secondary daytime hypersomnia. Profound oxygen desaturation in sleep can trigger cardiac dysrhythmias and eventually lead to pulmonary hypertension and heart failure.

In the congenital hypoventilation syndrome [25], abnormal respiratory pauses are noted immediately after birth each time the newborn falls asleep. In this syndrome, there is dysfunction of central chemoreceptors, with preserved function of peripheral chemoreceptors, so that ventilation is apparently normal during wakefulness. Hypoxemia and carbon dioxide retention increase in non-REM sleep, whereas ventilation improves during REM sleep through the direct activity of the pontine pneumotaxic centers.

Neuromuscular Disorders

Neuromuscular disorders interfere with the effector mechanism of the ventilatory system, causing failure of respiration that becomes more marked in sleep. Patients with neuromuscular disorders are at high risk for the development of sleep-related respiratory disorders and respiratory failure. In these patients, a variety of concurring abnormalities converge that explain their vulnerable status. Diaphragmatic weakness and failure is the most important determinant of sleep-related respiratory insufficiency. Chest wall weakness along with restrictive pulmonary disease such as caused by chest wall deformities and kyphoscoliosis contribute to hypoventilation both in REM and non-REM sleep. Weakness of the pharyngeal wall compounded with obesity of sedentary origin and craniofacial maldevelopment can facilitate the development of obstructive sleep apneas. Some patients with neuromuscular disorder exhibit nocturnal hypoventilation in excess of muscular weakness or of diaphragmatic failure, suggesting an alteration of central respiratory drive.

Poliomyelitis and Postpolio Syndrome

Poliomyelitis can affect the brain stem neuronal centers that control respiration. In REM sleep, apneas are of longer duration and breathing is shallower as a result of the concurrence of muscle atonia of respiratory muscles and a weak central neurogenic drive to the diaphragm. In the postpolio syndrome, some patients present progressive deterioration of nocturnal sleep as sleep apnea episodes and oxygen desaturation events become increasingly frequent. Most apneas are of the obstructive variety or mixed with favorable response to CPAP applications [26]. Patients with kyphoscoliosis secondary to poliomyelitis often develop restrictive respiratory dysfunction, particularly if there is associated weakness of thoracoabdominal and respiratory accessory muscles.

Myasthenia Gravis

In myasthenia gravis, respiratory function can be altered during sleep, with carbon dioxide retention and respiratory failure serious enough to require ventilatory assistance [27]. The most profound alterations are observed during REM sleep. Patients suffering generalized myasthenia gravis complain of waking up with a sensation of breathlessness, morning headaches, and daytime somnolence. Muscle fatigability can involve the diaphragm and accessory respiratory muscles with resulting respiratory failure. Polygraphic studies in treated patients show increased duration of stage 1 and decreased proportion of stages 3 and 4 and REM sleep. The sleep apnea index can climb at the expense of predominantly mixed and obstructive sleep apnea episodes, associated with oxygen desaturations of moderate severity. This finding is particularly evident during REM stage when the diaphragm is the only muscle that remains active in the exchange of air. Respiratory muscles can be focally affected in patients with myasthenia gravis [28]. Older patients with increased body mass index and abnormal daytime blood gas concentration are more vulnerable to the development of a diaphragmatic form of sleep apnea syndrome with oxygen desaturation. Daytime somnolence in a patient with myasthenia gravis should suggest abnormal breathing during sleep, even in the absence of abnormal daytime functional activity. The dysfunction usually responds to the administration of slow-release pyridostigmine at night, although patients receiving appropriate treatment, with satisfactory daytime functional capacity, can still have abnormal breathing during sleep.

In the myasthenic syndrome, dysfunction of respiratory muscles can cause sleep hypoventilation and sleep apnea, to the point of requiring assisted ventilation.

Myotonic Dystrophy

In patients with myotonic dystrophy, nonobstructive sleep apneas and sleep-related alveolar hypoventilation are common [29] contributing to excessive daytime somnolence, a clinical manifestation frequently observed in these patients. Sleep-related breathing abnormalities are the result of central neuronal lesions and declining muscular function. Hypersomnia can remain despite reversal of sleep apnea with CPAP applications [30], suggesting an independent origin, probably linked to dysfunction of the dorsomedial nuclei of the thalamus.

In myotonic dystrophy, weakness of inspiratory effort during REM sleep and increased upper airway resistance during non-REM sleep [31] are the main mechanisms for the development of sleep-related respiratory disturbance. Early muscular weakness in these patients affects craniofacial and mandibular growth that contribute to the development of obstructive sleep apnea by increasing airway resistance through a stenotic oropharynx.

Congenital and Metabolic Myopathies

Severe nocturnal respiratory failure has been described in nemaline myopathy [32], a congenital myopathy with a relatively benign prognosis that affects all skeletal muscles including the diaphragm. Patients develop marked sleep inertia in the morning with headaches, vomiting, and daytime lethargy with marked hypoxia, hypercapnia, and cor pulmonale. Breathing at night is irregular with progressive hypercapnia. Nocturnal respiratory failure is not caused by muscular weakness or obstructive sleep apnea but is attributed to a disturbance of central respiratory control with poor sensitivity to carbon dioxide inhalation. This condition is also detected in relatives of affected individuals. Nocturnal mechanical ventilation reverses respiratory failure and permits a return to daytime activities including school attendance.

Patients with Duchenne's muscular dystrophy develop restrictive pulmonary disease as muscle weakness progresses and rib cage deformities appear. A study of patients with moderately advanced disorder reported nocturnal hypoventilation with profound desaturation during REM sleep despite normal awake minute ventilation [33].

Neuropathy and Phrenic Nerve Paralysis

Phrenic nerve damage resulting in diaphragmatic paralysis can be part of the spectrum of involvement in some diffuse neuropathies and in motoneuron disease. Unilateral paralysis can be asymptomatic or cause manifestations of ventilatory insufficiency that might remain undiagnosed; bilateral paralysis is invariably symptomatic and can be life-threatening. Bilateral paralysis causes orthopnea with severe difficulty on inspiration that is out of proportion to the cardiopulmonary status. In the supine posture, patients complain of profound difficulty breathing that is the result of a reduction in lung volume and increased inspiratory effort as the abdominal contents rise into the thorax. In severe or acute instances, patients present with nocturnal orthopnea, cyanosis, and fragmented sleep followed by morning headaches, vomiting, and daytime lethargy. Polysomnography reveals hypoventilation that is particularly profound during REM sleep. As the desaturation event frequency increases in REM sleep, arousals and secondary daytime somnolence become increasingly prominent so that the condition resembles the sleep apnea syndrome. The severity of hypoventilation and the depth of oxygen desaturation in non-REM sleep is determined by the degree of involvement of chest wall and accessory respiratory muscles. Undiagnosed bilateral diaphragmatic paralysis of any cause can lead to acute cardiopulmonary failure and death. Some reports describe the unexplained failure to wean patients from respirators as the presenting manifestation of diaphragmatic paralysis in patients with undiagnosed motoneuron disease [34] or myopathies.

Phrenic nerve paralysis has been reported in patients with Charcot-Marie-Tooth disease (hereditary motor and sensory neuropathy) complicated with diabetes mellitus [35]. Other conditions in which diaphragmatic paralysis has been observed include spinal cord injury, poliomyelitis, Guillain-Barré syndrome, diabetes, diphtheric neuropathy, beri-beri, alcoholic neuropathy, brachial plexus neuropathy, lead neuropathy, trauma, amyotrophic lateral sclerosis, myotonic dystrophy, Duchenne's muscular dystrophy, and paraneoplastic syndrome [34, 35].

The diagnosis of diaphragmatic paralysis is suspected when paradoxic respirations appear in patients in the supine posture along with major discrepancies in vital capacity between the erect and supine postures. Phrenic nerve stimulation studies, nerve conduction measurements, and EMG of selected muscles can aid in the diagnosis, along with fluoroscopy and CT studies of the chest. Nocturnal polysomnography is of critical importance to evaluate the presence and degree of sleep-related respiratory dysfunction in patients with suspected paralysis of the diaphragm.

General Approach and Management of Neuromuscular Disorders

Patients with neuromuscular disorder developing a sleep-related respiratory alteration present a variety of symptoms and signs that include nocturnal restlessness, frequent unexplained awakenings, and loud snoring punctuated by occasional episodes of awakening gasping for breath. Paradoxical low-intensity snoring suggests advanced weakness of respiratory muscles. Subjects report difficulty awakening in the morning and prolonged sleep inertia that interferes with morning activities. During the day, these patients can present somnolence, fatigue, and inappropriate napping, which underlie failure to thrive in the very young and poor school grades or work performance at later ages. Some patients develop nocturnal cyanosis, severe insomnia, morning lethargy, headaches, vomiting, and leg edema that indicate the insidious and relentless occurrence of acute respiratory failure and cor pulmonale.

Polysomnographic evaluation with the sleep apnea protocol followed by an MSLT is necessary to distinguish among the different causes of sleep disturbance and to assess the severity of the disorder.

The study might show obstructive, central, and mixed sleep apneas, hypoventilation with oxygen saturations under 85%, or profound REM sleep-related desaturation of oxygen indicative of diaphragmatic failure. The sleep architecture might reveal fragmentation of sleep with numerous arousals and awakenings, many of them associated with episodes of respiratory interruption.

Nocturnal disruption can occur as an independent abnormality translating nocturnal postural discomfort in a weak, incapacitated, sometimes deformed patient. The daytime test can show excessive daytime somnolence proportionate to the nocturnal alteration, or as in myotonic dystrophy, can show excessive daytime somnolence that is not explained by the nocturnal findings. This situation suggests an intrinsic form of hypersomnia that has been associated with REM sleep abnormalities in some instances.

Therapeutic goals should define whether therapy is directed at elimination of excessive daytime somnolence, improvement of nocturnal desaturation, reconstruction of sleep architecture, or correction of respiratory and heart failure. Positive pressure breathing corrects obstructive sleep apnea, improves hypoventilation, and assists diaphragmatic failure. Supplemental oxygen is recommended when positive air pressure therapy is insufficient to overcome mean levels of hypoventilation of 85% or less. Bi-PAP is better tolerated by patients with weak chest muscular effort who cannot overcome expiratory forces. Supplemental oxygen via nasal cannula can be sufficient to correct REM sleep-related desaturations in some instances.

Patients with advanced restrictive pulmonary disease, severe chest wall muscle weakness, loss of sleep-related respiratory drive, and diaphragmatic paralysis pose special problems that might need to be resolved individually with a combination of therapeutic maneuvers. Tracheostomy can be indicated in a few instances, but dependence and complications have to be weighed against the benefits obtained. Ethical considerations might have to be addressed in patients with terminal neuromuscular disease. Children under the age of 6 years tolerate nasal ventilation poorly; other therapeutic measures, including temporal use of tracheostomy, might have to be considered.

Protriptyline at bedtime improves muscle tone and is of some value in patients with obstructive sleep apnea with weak pharyngeal walls. It is also indicated to reduce REM sleep-related hypoventilation. Methylphenidate can serve as an adjunct for the control of hypersomnia in patients with myotonic dystrophy who do not respond to the application of CPAP.

Cognitive Function and Sleep-Disordered Breathing

Patients with sleep apnea syndrome commonly report poor memory, confusion, and irritability along with daytime sleepiness. These cognitive changes can lead to low scholarly achievement and poor job performance, contributing to reduce the quality of life of the patient. In normal individuals, memory ability after sleep decreases as a function of the depth of sleep [36] and improves as a function of the duration of time transpired since awakening. Poor performance immediately following arousal is called sleep inertia and ranges from a few seconds to 30 minutes [37] and is worse after awakening from stage 4 of sleep. It has been suggested that the sleep disturbance of patients with sleep apnea can be equated with the disturbance of individuals subjected to frequent sleep interruptions that result in sleep deprivation. Under such circumstances, cognitive processes deteriorate leading to nocturnal confusion and poor long-term memory for events occurring during the night. Sleep deprivation also increases sleep inertia with deficits in short- and long-term memory throughout the day [36]. Mitler [38] used the maintenance of wakefulness test to make an interesting observation: Among patients with excessive somnolence, patients with sleep apnea syndrome were the most impaired in their ability to perform cognitive tasks. Sleep apnea syndrome represents a potentially treatable factor contributing to mental decline in old age.

Treatment

The treatment of the sleep apnea syndromes (Figure 7-7) can be subdivided into three sections: (1) medical, (2) physical, and (3) surgical.

Medical Treatment

It is important to address the management of risk factors contributing to the sleep apnea syndrome. Obesity is a prime factor that contributes importantly to the development and progression of obstructive sleep apnea; unfortunately, it responds poorly to treatment. Nevertheless, weight reduction should remain a long-term therapeutic goal that in most instances requires professional supervision to achieve. Patients should be referred to the hospital dietitian and enrolled in a weight-reduction program.

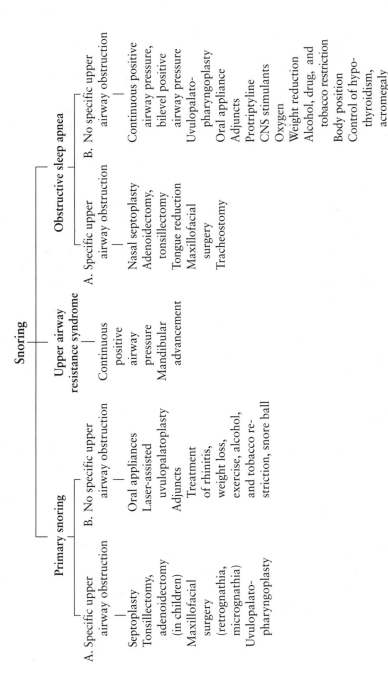

Figure 7-7.   *Algorithm for the treatment of snoring and sleep apnea.*

In the sleeping individual, alcohol diminishes the neural input to the dilator pharyngeal muscles via the hypoglossal nerve, augmenting the pharyngeal wall's tendency to collapse with negative inspiratory pressures. Furthermore, as a sedative, alcohol reduces the cortical arousal triggered by hypoxemia. For all these reasons, patients with obstructive sleep apnea should discontinue or considerably reduce consumption of alcohol-containing beverages in the evening, at least 3 hours before going to bed. For similar reasons, medications with a sedative effect should be discontinued, reduced, or replaced by other less sedating compounds. Smoking irritates the oropharynx and causes some tissue inflammation that contributes to reduce the oropharyngeal opening. Its elimination eradicates another contributing factor and improves the general health outlook of the patient. In patients with epilepsy, phenytoin can promote soft tissue growth with resultant long-term aggravation of the obstructive component; therefore, a switch to another anticonvulsant is recommended. Hypothyroidism is associated with macroglossia and other risk factors such as weight gain, neurogenic dysfunction, and muscle weakness that promote obstructive sleep apneas. The syndrome responds well to thyroid hormone replacement.

Protryptiline has a modest stimulant effect on neurogenic mechanisms that intervene in the maintenance of dilator glossopharyngeal muscle tone during sleep. This action contributes to the reduction of snoring and of sleep apnea [39]. Furthermore, protriptyline reduces REM sleep, a time when sleep apneas increase in duration and desaturations are more profound. The beneficial effect of protriptyline tends to disappear gradually in 2–3 months, thereby serving only as an adjunct to the management of mild to moderate forms of obstructive sleep apnea that do not respond to other more efficacious forms of treatment.

Oxygen administration, 1 or 2 liters per minute, via nasal cannula should be considered for patients with a mean nocturnal saturation of oxygen of 85% or less despite other forms of treatment.

In patients with nonobstructive central sleep apnea syndrome, diamox (250 mg at bedtime) can be tried. This medication is a carbonic anhidrase inhibitor that stimulates chemoreceptors and also has a beneficial effect on high-altitude sickness, perhaps through the same mechanism. There are instances in which episodes of central sleep apnea disappear with the administration of oxygen via nasal cannula, perhaps because of relief of hypoxic ventilatory depression of the central respiratory centers [40]. Therefore, this mode of treatment should be considered and tested in the sleep laboratory. Medroxyprogesterone is a hormone that among its many effects stimulates nocturnal ventilatory drive in pregnant women.

It might have a similar effect in patients with sleep apnea syndrome, but there is no evidence that clinical manifestations improve.

Central stimulants such as methylphenidate, pemoline, or dextroamphetamine might be required to maintain safe levels of alertness in patients with any form of sleep apnea. Stimulants provide temporary help and should serve only as an adjunct to the main treatment. The rules of treatment of hypersomnia with central stimulants described in Chapter 6 should be followed.

Physical Treatment

The application of CPAP during sleep is the treatment of choice for obstructive sleep apnea syndrome. The goal is to eliminate apneas, hypopneas, oxygen desaturations, arousals, and snoring (see Figure 7-6). The apparatus consists of a mask adapted to the face, covering the nose but not the mouth (Figure 7-8), that delivers air through a flexible hose connected to a compressor that generates air flow at a continuous specified pressure. The objective is to overcome the negative pressures created during inspiration that tend to collapse the upper airway and produce apneas in sleep. The airway remains open in most patients with pressures of 5–20 cm H_2O. Exceptionally, higher pressures are needed, but the physical impact of the strong air current tends to arouse the patient. The system functions primarily as a pneumatic splint [41]. Other mechanisms have been proposed to explain the therapeutic action including increase of end-expiratory lung volume, traction on mediastinal and upper airway structures, and stimulation of the oropharyngeal dilator reflex.

Patients require an overnight study in the sleep laboratory for proper titration of pressures and to assess tolerance to the mask. A pressure that is lower than the necessary minimum might be insufficient to eliminate snoring and alleviate apneas, whereas excessive pressure might arouse the patient and prevent continuation of sleep. On the following morning, patients who respond favorably describe a sensation of well-being and of satisfaction with sleep that had not been experienced in years. Excessive daytime somnolence disappears or improves considerably with only 1 night of therapeutic effect, but progressive improvement in alertness can be seen over the ensuing weeks [42]. Sleep architecture changes relative to the baseline study, showing large amounts of REM sleep (REM sleep rebound) of up to 30% and 40% of total sleep, with short latency and distribution in several cycles (see Figure 7-6B). SWS also increases at the expense of light non-REM sleep.

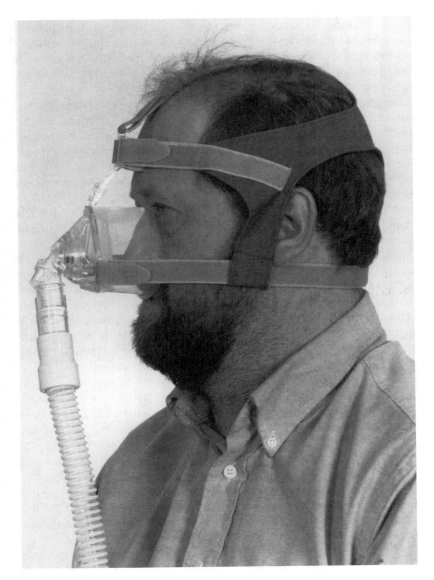

Figure 7-8. *CPAP application has revolutionized the treatment of the obstructive sleep apnea syndrome. The system consists of a mask that adapts snugly over the face, covering the nose. An air compressor delivers air at a specified pressure through a flexible hose connected to the mask. Oxygen and a humidifier can be added as needed.*

Complications, adverse reactions, and side effects are benign but annoying to patients. Poorly fitting masks can cause leakage of air toward the eyes and skin abrasions over the bridge of the nose. As the mask pressure increases, the risk of leakage also increases. Different mask sizes and models might overcome inconveniences caused by an inadequate mask adaptation. Nasal and upper respiratory dryness are also common complaints, which respond favorably to the addition of a humidifier to the unit or a vaporizer in the bedroom. Rhinorrhea is a less common but perhaps more vexing problem that occurs in some patients and responds variably to nasal sprays containing steroid preparations. Temporary nasal congestion and rhinorrhea such as caused by a cold can be controlled with the application of a nasal spray with vasoconstrictor effect. Rare epistaxis has been reported in relation to the use of CPAP [43]. CPAP application should be discontinued following head trauma until there is assurance that cerebrospinal fluid (CSF) leakage is not present.

Successful elimination of apneas and hypopneas with the application of a CPAP mask is sometimes associated with the emergence of periodic leg movements during non-REM sleep variably associated with arousals [44]. Whether this situation is a de novo occurrence or the unveiling of a subclinical phenomenon is unclear. If the clinical judgment is that periodic leg movements affect the quality of sleep, drug treatment might be warranted. Under the influence of CPAP, it is safe to administer medications, such as clonazepam, if necessary, that reduce cortical arousals and otherwise prolong apneas.

The application of CPAP to patients with sleep apnea syndrome and advanced chronic obstructive pulmonary disease or congestive heart failure should be carefully monitored in the laboratory. There is one report of worsening nocturnal hypoventilation and oxygen desaturation in a patient with hypercapnia and cor pulmonale [45] treated with CPAP. Increased thoracic pressure and consequent diminished venous return might have compromised further the cardiac function and output. Extreme caution should be exercised in patients with bullous emphysema or cystic lung lesions that might be ruptured by the delivery of external air pressures.

The apparatus is dispensed with medical prescription only; the script shows the pressure required and the size of the mask. In the modern era of managed care and third-party payments, it is desirable to attach a copy of the polysomnographic evaluation documenting the favorable response and the pressure required. The equipment weighs 7–9 lbs and is perfectly portable in an executive briefcase. Current versions are adaptable to most power sources including camp outlets, car and boat plugs, and currents used outside the United States. It is prudent to check the equipment periodically along with its expected favorable effect by performing home overnight oximetry to assess nocturnal saturations of oxygen. If conditions change (e.g., a drastic loss of weight) or if the patient reports snoring or loss of response despite mask adjustments, a follow-up polysomnographic test in the laboratory is suggested.

When nocturnal oxygen saturations remain under 85% despite satisfactory function of the CPAP apparatus, consideration should be given to supplying additional oxygen via the mask. Administration can be done by bleeding 1 or 2 liters of oxygen per minute into the mask.

Tolerance is good or excellent in 80% of patients with moderate or advanced obstructive sleep apnea syndrome. Compliance declines in 25–30% of all patients treated who show an initial good response. Approximately 20% of patients drop the use of the apparatus within the first year of therapy, and 30% report that applications are not taken nightly [46]. Young patients tend to be disgusted with the idea of life-long dependency on the apparatus, especially if they are unattached and socially active. However, they might accept its temporary use as a compromise while they lose weight and explore other therapeutic modalities. In children with obstructive sleep apnea syndrome secondary to structural anomalies, CPAP application might be the only viable therapeutic alternative until craniofacial growth has been completed and surgical reconstruction is acceptable. In general, tolerance and compliance to CPAP increase with severity of the sleep apnea syndrome and daytime sleepiness. Some sleep centers have organized support groups so that patients can share complaints, problems, and solutions.

Consistent use on consecutive nights is recommended and desirable since there is suggestive evidence of continued improvement of various parameters after several weeks of optimal use of CPAP [42]. Indeed, blood pressure measurements tend to decrease after several weeks of treatment [47]. However, interruption of therapy for only 1 night decreases the level of daytime alertness as measured with MSLT even though patients might not complain of sleepiness [48].

The conventional mask covering the nose can be substituted by a full face mask in patients who are unable to keep their mouth closed while asleep. The mask should not be used if there is a risk of vomiting leading to aspiration of gastric contents, a consideration particularly important in weakened individuals or patients with neuromuscular disorders. The apparatus should have an incorporated safety system to deliver fresh air in case of power failure.

Another useful variation involves nasal pillars or prongs, a device adapted to the nares with silicon rubber, avoiding the use of the mask. Some patients find this modality more acceptable and less cumbersome than the nasal mask, whereas others find the sensation of nose plugs intolerable. Patients should know that there are different modalities available, each with a particular advantage. For instance, patients with excessively sensitive skin over the bridge of the nose or with a tendency to leak air in the direction of the eyes should consider nasal prongs.

Some patients complain of delayed initiation of sleep because of discomfort caused by the strong air current, in particular when the pressure delivered is high. Initial ramp pressures alleviate this problem. The ramp mechanism delivers pressure increments during an initial period of time prescribed by the technician, permitting initiation of sleep before the pressure reaches its maximal vigor. However, since pressures are not optimal at inception of sleep it is expected that during this period patients will show desaturations and apneas. "Ramping" has been introduced in practice but not validated formally. Although it appears useful, caution should be exercised in patients with severe forms of sleep apnea syndrome.

The Bi-PAP apparatus delivers differential inspiratory positive air pressure (IPAP) and expiratory positive air pressure (EPAP). Thus, an optimal positive pressure can be applied during inspiration only and lowered during expiration to prevent excessive expiratory effort. Inspiratory pressure sufficient to maintain airway patency is triggered by a low inspiratory airflow, whereas the expiratory level is reached when the inspiratory airflow decreases below a set value. Modern devices have a safety feature that provides a timed trigger of IPAP in case of total failure of inspiratory airflow and of triggered delivery; this feature is particularly useful in patients with neuromuscular disorders or predominantly central apneas of long duration. The combination of spontaneous and timed trigger allows comfortable physiologic breathing while the patient is awake and avoids frightening long-duration respiratory arrests in asleep patients with central sleep apnea. The differential pressures provide a more physiologic delivery of air that is more comfortable and helpful in a variety of clinical situations. Thus, the Bi-PAP apparatus is useful in patients with restrictive neuromuscular disorders or kyphoscoliosis, or in whom CPAP is indicated but not tolerated. The latter can be the case in patients who complain of chest pain while taking CPAP applications but have no evidence of ischemic heart disease.

Titration of pressures for both CPAP and Bi-PAP should be done in the sleep laboratory, at night, under the close supervision of an experienced technician. Titration is achieved by introducing small increments of pressure of 2.5 cm H_2O until the optimal pressure is reached. Occasionally, there is a fine border zone between virtual elimination of apneas and hypopneas and arousals caused by excessive airflow and pressure, forcing a compromise between less than optimal goal achievement and patient comfort. When this circumstance arises using CPAP, a trial on Bi-PAP might be warranted. Future versions of the CPAP apparatus will incorporate sensors of airflow to drive ongoing autoadjustments of mask pressure, accommodating subtle differences generated by shifts in body posture and sleep stage changes. Optimal pressures should be checked in various stages of sleep, particularly in REM sleep, and with the patient supine. Alcohol and medications that suppress cortical arousals should be discontinued unless their suspension is not indicated or poses a hazard. Along these lines, if the patient is going to sleep nightly under the influence of sedatives or alcohol, it is practical to check pressures under such influence to avoid introduction of unusable levels. Bi-PAP should always be considered in patients with neuromuscular conditions and kyphoscoliosis who exhibit a weak expiratory effort insufficient to overcome the high CPAP pressure. Similarly, it is indicated in bullous and cystic lung conditions in which high pressures could traumatize the lungs. Finally, Bi-PAP is the alternative of choice when the expiratory effort against CPAP pressure causes discomfort and arousals, or prevents sleep.

Patients with nonobstructive central sleep apnea syndrome deserve a trial on CPAP and Bi-PAP. Typically, they tolerate CPAP less well or not at all, and might even complain of suffocation and claustrophobia while the mask is in place. Bi-PAP is indicated in patients with central sleep apnea who are intolerant of CPAP and in patients exhibiting a prominent central apnea component after elimination of the obstructive portion of the apneas with CPAP. The immediate goal is to eliminate apneas and hypopneas along with arousals, but the ultimate goal, the one that will determine the usefulness of the apparatus, is to reduce excessive daytime sleepiness.

Patients with loud snoring, daytime sleepiness, and many nocturnal arousals despite minimal polygraphic evidence of obstructive sleep apnea might have the upper airway resistance syndrome [23]. The instability caused by large negative pressures and loud snoring suggestive of increased upper airway resistance might trigger arousals that disrupt sleep sufficiently to cause daytime sleepiness. The polysomnographic finding of an increased arousal index in a snorer with excessive sleepiness of unknown etiology should raise the question of the upper airway resistance syndrome [49]. Under these circumstances, a CPAP test is warranted with the goal of eliminating nocturnal arousals and snoring and eventually excessive sleepiness. Guilleminault and colleagues [50] go as far as to advocate maxillofacial surgery in selected instances.

Surgical Treatment

The presence and severity of sleep apnea should be determined with polysomnography before initiating surgical therapy. There are several forms of surgical intervention applied to patients with obstructive sleep apnea syndrome, all intended to alleviate or correct the obstruction.

Tracheostomy

Tracheostomy was originally performed in patients with advanced obstructive sleep apnea to bypass the pharyngeal obstruction. It consists of creating an artificial opening in the anterior trachea immediately below the larynx (Figure 7-9). The stoma is maintained open with a silver prosthesis that is plugged during the day to allow conversation and regular respiration; at night the stoma is reopened. The operation is technically simple, the rationale unassailable, and the immediate results surprisingly positive. However, tracheostomy is socially unacceptable and difficult to maintain free of complications, posing a risk of chronic infection. Today, tracheostomy is rarely used, remaining as a back-up intervention for severe cases with a high risk of death.

Nasal Reconstruction

Nasal obstruction contributes to increase the negative pressures generated more distally in the airway during inspiration and can constitute an impediment for the use of CPAP. Septal deviation and turbinate hypertrophy interfering with the adequate passage of air might have to be corrected surgically.

Tonsillectomy

Hypertrophic tonsils are the most frequent cause of sleep apnea syndrome in children and young adults and the most common determinant of tonsillectomy in children. In our practice, a 13-year-old girl presented with sleep apnea syndrome and hypertrophic tonsils so severe that an emergent tonsillectomy was performed before polysomnography could be arranged.

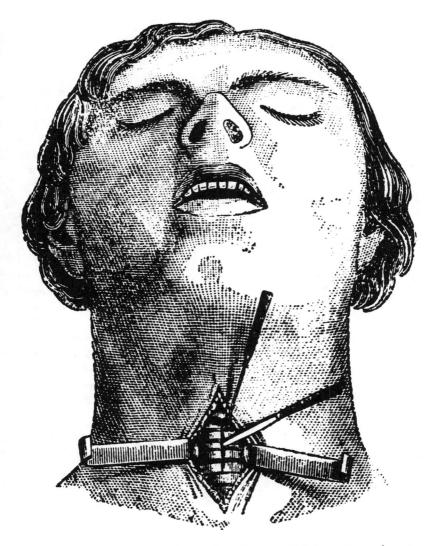

Figure 7-9.   *Tracheostomy consists of creating an artificial opening on the anterior trachea immediately below the larynx to bypass the pharyngeal obstruction. The operation is technically simple, the rationale unassailable, and the immediate results surprisingly favorable. However, tracheostomy is socially unacceptable and difficult to maintain free of complications, creating a risk of chronic infection. (Reprinted with permission from JD Bretos [ed]. Medicina e Historia. N° 54, Tercera Época. Barcelona, Spain: Publicación Médica Uriach, 1994.)*

Uvulopalatopharyngoplasty

UPPP was originally introduced to alleviate snoring by reducing the tissues of the soft palate and uvula along with residual tonsillar tissue. Later, the indications were extended to obstructive sleep apnea syndrome. The initial enthusiasm was considerably toned down by the irregular results obtained, the pain associated with the intervention in adults, and the risk of potential complications with development of permanent deficits, some of which are serious. However, the selection of patients improves the results, and in the hands of experienced surgeons the discomfort and hospital stay are reduced considerably with few complications. The intervention causes local pain and difficulty swallowing that can last for up to 8 days. The patients who benefit most are the ones with obstructive sleep apneas and large tonsils, redundant lateral pharyngeal walls, and the ones with long soft palate. Some centers report that with careful selection, 87% of patients experience at least a 50% reduction in respiratory events [51]; others indicate that less than 50% of patients show at least a 50% reduction in the sleep apnea–hypopnea index following the intervention [52]. Complications usually relate to postoperative swelling or excessive reduction of tissue and include nasal reflux that is transient in most patients developing this complication [53], partial wound dehiscence, and, rarely, palatal incompetence. When attempting to understand how this operation works, one should remember that the cross-sectional area of the pharynx does not increase with the intervention. Failure occurs in patients with multiple sites of obstruction that had remained occult before the operation, a phenomenon that has introduced the concept of a stepwise approach in the surgical treatment of obstructive sleep apnea [54].

Mandible, Tongue, and Hyoid Reconstructions

Interventions at this level are intended to improve the airflow at the base of the tongue in the hypopharyngeal level. There are several degrees of complexity in these operations that range from genioglossus advancement including hyoid bone myotomy in some instances, to mandibular advancement. Patients are selected on the basis of radiographic analysis and cephalometric measurements showing stenosis of the hypopharynx. Advancement of the mandible 1 or 2 mm can be sufficient to improve airflow. Patients who benefit most from these operations are young, with moderate-to-severe sleep apnea syndrome and loud snoring caused by hypopharyngeal stenosis, frequently with associated craniofacial malformations, retrognathia, or malocclusions.

The procedures are specialized maxillofacial interventions available only in selected centers. Complications appear to be small in number and range from surgical edema of the floor of the mouth to mental nerve dysesthesias. Contraindications are psychiatric disorders, advanced age, and drug dependency.

Oral Appliances

Oral appliances are used to eliminate snoring and improve sleep apnea by modifying the anatomy and changing the dynamics of the mandible, intraoral cavity, and upper airway sufficiently to improve the passage of air while the subject is asleep. There is some evidence that the cross-sectional area of the tongue increases and the cross-sectional area of the oropharynx decreases with the supine posture [55]. Furthermore, the volume of the tongue and of the soft palate increase with the body mass index [56]. On the basis of these observations, there appears to be some rationale for the modification of the intraoral anatomy in obese patients with sleep apnea syndrome. Oral appliances have been devised to move the mandible forward, lift the soft palate, move the tongue forward, or accomplish a combination of these changes. One of these appliances, sleep and nocturnal obstructive apnea reductor (SNOAR), is an acrylic appliance adapted to the teeth that repositions and advances the mandible up to 9 mm. This alteration in turn repositions the tongue more anteriorly and frees additional space posteriorly. Early results indicated a reduction in the respiratory disorder index from 45.5–9.7 along with elimination of snoring [57]. Another device, Snore Guard, covers the front teeth only and is easy to fit. It has been marketed for the treatment of snoring only. Snoring is reduced in 60% of patients and eliminated in 40% [58], and compliance appears to be acceptable. The tongue-retaining device is a custom-made appliance that holds the tongue forward by means of negative pressure. Polysomnographic studies have shown an improved respiratory disorder index and sleep architecture exhibiting more REM sleep and delta-wave sleep [59, 60]. The tongue-retaining device might be useful in some patients with macroglossia.

As many as 13 oral and dental appliances have been introduced in clinical practice [61]. In general, oral appliances are safe and can be considered in individuals with snoring and in patients with obstructive sleep apnea syndrome of any degree of severity who refuse or do not tolerate CPAP and show anatomic reductions in the posterior space and oropharynx. Oral appliances should be fitted by qualified personnel and cephalometric evaluations performed when deemed necessary by trained professionals, although it does increase the cost of the application. The ASDA recommends [62] that patients with moderate-to-severe obstructive sleep apnea receive follow-up polysomnography or another objective measure of respiration during sleep with the appliance in place, to ensure satisfactory therapeutic benefit. The precise indications for dental appliances have not been validated with reliable clinical studies. Dental appliances are not indicated in patients with temporomandibular arthrosis or in uncooperative individuals.

References

1. Dickens C. The Posthumous Papers of the Pickwick Club. New York: Pollard and Moss, 1884.
2. Guilleminault C, Partinen M. Introduction. In C Guilleminault, M Partinen (eds), Obstructive Sleep Apnea Syndrome. New York: Raven, 1990.
3. de Castro F. Sur la structure et l'innervation de la glande intercarotidienne (glomus caroticum) de l'homme et des mammiferes, et sur un nouveau système d'innervation autonome du nerf glossopharyngien. Trav Lab Rech Biol (Univ Madrid) 1926;24:365.
4. Koskenvuo M, Kaprio J, Partinen M, et al. Snoring as a risk factor for hypertension and angina pectoris. Lancet 1985;1:893.
5. Telakivi T, Partinen M, Koskenvuo M, et al. Periodic breathing and hypoxia in snorers and controls: Validation of snoring history and association with blood pressure and obesity. Acta Neurol Scand 1987;76:69.
6. Lugaresi E, Cirignotta F, Coccagna G, et al. Some epidemiological data on snoring and cardiocirculatory disturbances. Sleep 1980;3:221.
7. Mondini S, Zucconi M, Cirignotta F, et al. Snoring as a Risk Factor for Cardiac and Circulatory Problems: An Epidemiological Study. In C Guilleminault, E Lugaresi (eds), Sleep/Wake Disorders: Natural History, Epidemiology and Long-term Evolution. New York: Raven, 1983;99.
8. Palomaki H, Partinen M, Erkinjuntti T, et al. Snoring, sleep apnea syndrome, and stroke. Neurology 1992;42(Suppl 6):75.
9. Standards of Practice Committee of the American Sleep Disorders Association. Practice parameters for the use of laser-assisted uvulopalatopharyngoplasty. Sleep 1994;17:744.
10. Shelton KE, Woodson H, Gay SB, et al. Adipose tissue deposition in sleep apnea. Sleep 1993;16:S103.
11. Sullivan CE, Grunstein RR, Marrone O, et al. Sleep Apnea—Pathophysiology: Upper Airway and Control of Breathing. In C Guilleminault, M Partinen (eds), Obstructive Sleep Apnea Syndrome. Clinical Research and Treatment. New York: Raven, 1990; 49.
12. Young TB, Palta M, Dempsey J, et al. The occurrence of sleep-disordered breathing among middle-aged adults. N Engl J Med 1993;328:1230.

13. Hla MK, Young TB, Bidwell T, et al. Sleep apnea and hypertension. Ann Intern Med 1994;120:382.
14. Millman RP, Redline S, Caelisle CC, et al. Daytime hypertension in obstructive sleep apnea. Prevalence and contributing risk factor. Chest 1991;99:861.
15. Guilleminault C, Simmons FB, Motta J, et al. Obstructive sleep apnea syndrome and tracheostomy. Long-term follow-up experience. Arch Intern Med 1981;141:985.
16. Rauscher H, Pormanek D, Popp W, et al. The effects of nasal CPAP and weight loss on daytime hypertension in obstructive sleep apnea [Abstract]. Am Rev Respir Dis 1992;145:442A.
17. Waravdekar N, Leueberger U, Sinoway L, et al. Impact of nasal continuous positive airway pressure therapy on muscle sympathetic nerve activity in sleep apnea syndrome. Am J Respir Crit Care Med 1994;149:808.
18. Garpestad E, Katayama H, Parker JA, et al. Stroke volume and cardiac output decrease at termination of obstructive apneas. J Appl Physiol 1992;73:1743.
19. Lavie P, Herer P, Peled R, et al. Mortality in sleep apnea patients: A multivariate analysis of risk factors. Sleep 1995;18:149.
20. Plum F, Swanson AG. Abnormalities in central regulation of respiration in acute and convalescent poliomyelitis. Arch Neurol Psychiatr 1958;80:267.
21. Levin B, Margolis G. Acute failure of autonomic respirations secondary to unilateral brainstem infarct. Ann Neurol 1977;1:583.
22. Zwilich C, Delvin T, White D, et al. Bradycardia during sleep apnea: Its characteristics and mechanisms. J Clin Invest 1982;69:1286.
23. Guilleminault C, Stoohs R. Upper airway resistance syndrome. Am Rev Respir Dis 1991;143:A589.
24. Krieger AJ, Rosomoff HL. Sleep-induced apnea: A respiratory and autonomic dysfunction syndrome following bilateral percutaneous cervical cordotomy. J Neurosurg 1974;32:277.
25. Guilleminault C, Challamel MJ. Congenital Hypoventilation Syndrome (CCHS): Independent Syndrome or Generalized Impairment of the Autonomic Nervous System? In R Korobkin, C Guilleminault (eds), Progress in Perinatal Neurology, Vol 1. Baltimore: Williams & Wilkins, 1981;197.
26. Steljes DG, Kryger MH, Kirk BW, et al. Sleep in postpolio syndrome. Chest 1990;98:133.
27. Quera-Salva MA, Guilleminault C, Chevret S, et al. Breathing disorders during sleep in myasthenia gravis. Ann Neurol 1992;31:86.
28. Mier-Jedrejowicz A, Brophy C, Green M. Respiratory muscle function in myasthenia gravis. Am Rev Respir Dis 1988;138:867.
29. Hansotia P, Frens D. Hypersomnia associated with alveolar hypoventilation in myotonic dystrophy. Neurology 1981;31:1336.
30. Park YD, Radtke RA. Hypersomnolence in myotonic dystrophy. Neurology 1992;42(Suppl 3):352.
31. Guilleminault C, Cumminskey J, Motta J, et al. Respiratory and hemodynamic study during wakefulness and sleep in myotonic dystrophy. Sleep 1978;1:19.

32. Maayan Ch, Springer C, Armon Y, et al. Nemaline myopathy as a cause of sleep hypoventilation. Pediatrics 1986;77:390.
33. Smith PEM, Edwards RHT, Calverly PMA. Ventilation and breathing pattern during sleep in Duchenne muscular dystrophy. Chest 1989;96:1346.
34. Parhad IM, Clark AW, Barron KD, et al. Diaphragmatic paralysis in motor neuron disease. Neurology 1978;28:18.
35. Chan CK, Mohsenin V, Loke J, et al. Diaphragmatic dysfunction in siblings with hereditary motor and sensory neuropathy (Charcot-Marie-Tooth disease). Chest 1987;91;567.
36. Bonnet MH. Cognitive effects of sleep and sleep fragmentation. Sleep. 1993;16:S65.
37. Dinges DF. Napping Patterns and Effects in Human Adults. In DF Dinges, RJ Broughton (eds), Sleep and Alertness Chronobiological, Behavioral, and Medical Aspects of Napping. New York: Raven, 1989;171.
38. Mitler MM. Daytime sleepiness and cognitive functioning in sleep apnea. Sleep 1993;16:S68.
39. Brownell LG, West P, Sweatman P, et al. Protriptyline in obstructive sleep apnea. A double blind trial. N Engl J Med 1982;307:1037.
40. Gold AR, Schwartz AR, Bleecker ER, et al. The effect of chronic nocturnal oxygen administration upon sleep apnea. Am Rev Respir Dis 1986;134:925.
41. Abbey NC, Cooper KR, Kwentus JA. Benefit of nasal CPAP in obstructive sleep apnea is due to positive pharyngeal pressures. Sleep 1989;12:420.
42. Lamphere J, Roehrs T, Wittig R, et al. Recovery of alertness after CPAP in apnea. Chest 1989;96:1364.
43. Strumpf DA, Harrop P, Dobbin J, et al. Massive epistaxis from nasal CPAP therapy. Chest 1989;95:1141.
44. Fry JM, DiPhillipo MA, Pressman MR. Periodic leg movements in sleep following treatment of obstructive sleep apnea with nasal continuous positive airway pressure. Chest 1989;96:89.
45. Krieger J, Weitzenblaum E, Monassier JP, et al. Dangerous hypoxemia during continuous positive airway pressure treatment of obstructive sleep apnea. Lancet 1983;2:1429.
46. Nino-Murcia G, McCann CC, Bliwise DL, et al. Compliance and side effects in sleep apnea patients treated with continuous positive airway pressure. West J Med 1989;150:165.
47. Mayer J, Becker H, Brandenburg U, et al. Blood pressure and sleep apnea: results of long-term nasal continuous positive airway pressure therapy. Cardiology 1991;79:84.
48. Sforza E, Lugaresi E. Daytime sleepiness and nasal continuous positive airway pressure therapy in obstructive sleep apnea syndrome patients: Effects of chronic treatment and 1-night therapy withdrawal. Sleep 1995;18:195.
49. Shepard JW. Excessive daytime sleepiness, upper airway resistance, and nocturnal arousals. Chest 1993;104:665.
50. Guilleminault C, Stoohs R, Clerk A, et al. A cause of excessive daytime sleepiness. The upper airway resistance syndrome. Chest 1993;104:781.
51. Sher AE, Thorpy MJ, Shrintzen RJ, et al. Predictive value of Muller maneuver in selection of patients for uvulopalatopharyngoplasty. Laryngoscope 1985;95:1483.

52. Pelausa EO, Tarhis LM. Surgery for snoring. Laryngoscope 1989;99:1006.
53. Powell NB, Guilleminault C, Riley RW. Surgical Therapy for Obstructive Sleep Apnea. In MH Kryger, T Roth, WC Dement (eds), Principles and Practice of Sleep Medicine (2nd ed). Philadelphia: Saunders, 1994;706.
54. Nordlander B. Long-term studies addressing success of surgical treatment for sleep apnea syndrome. Sleep 1993;16:S100.
55. Pae E, Lowe A, Sasaki K, et al. A cephalometric and electromyographic study of upper airway structures in the upright and supine position. Am J Orthod Dentofacial Orthop 1994;106:52.
56. Lowe A, Fleetham J, Adachi S, et al. Cephalometric and CT predictors of apnea index severity. Am J Orthod Dentofacial Orthop 1995;107:589.
57. Viscomi V, Walker J, Farney R, et al. Efficacy of a dental appliance in patients with snoring and sleep apnea [abstract]. Sleep Res 1988;17:266.
58. Schmidt-Nowara W, Meade T, Hays M. Treatment of snoring and obstructive sleep apnea with a dental orthosis. Chest 1991;99:1378.
59. Shepard HW. Excessive daytime sleepiness, upper airway resistance and nocturnal arousals. Chest 1993;104:665.
60. Cartwright R, Samelson C, The effects of a non-surgical treatment for obstructive sleep apnea—The tongue retaining device. JAMA 1982;248:705.
61. Lowe AA. Dental Appliances for the Treatment of Snoring and Obstructive Sleep Apnea. In MH Kryger, T Roth, WC Dement (eds), Principles and Practice of Sleep Medicine (2nd ed). Philadelphia: Saunders, 1994;722.
62. American Sleep Disorders Association. Practice parameters for the treatment of snoring and obstructive sleep apnea with oral appliances. Sleep 1995;18:511.

8

Sleep Disorders Associated with Psychiatric, Medical, and Neurologic Disorders

And thus with little sleeping and much reading, his brains dried up to such a degree that he lost the use of his reason. His imagination became filled with a host of fancies he had read in his books—enchantments, quarrels, battles, challenges, wounds, courtships, loves, tortures, and many other absurdities. So true did all this phantasmagoria from books appear to him that in his mind he accounted no history in the world more authentic.

Miguel de Cervantes Saavedra
Don Quixote of La Mancha [1]

Sleep and wakefulness are functions of the brain and thus subject to alterations of the nervous system. Each state, although antagonistic in its domain, determines the viability and quality of the other so that affections of sleep will alter wakefulness and vice versa. The determinants of sleep are the circadian rhythm, behavior, homeostasis, and age. The circadian rhythm, served by its pacemaker, the suprachiasmatic nucleus, is the orchestrater of sleep. Behavior can override the other determinants to a certain point beyond which the forces that induce or dispel sleep take over. Homeostatic drives include a wide variety of factors that range from hypnogenic substances to duration of the domain. All determinant factors work in an integrated manner to generate the neurologic processes that produce sleep and its counterpart wakefulness. Psychiatric, medical, and neurologic disorders can alter profoundly the integratory mechanisms of sleep and wakefulness causing deficit, excess, or distortion of sleep. This chapter reviews the pathologic conditions that lead to secondary insomnia or hypersomnia. There is a fine conceptual distinction between secondary and symptomatic disorders. From a purist's perspective, a secondary disorder is the indirect result and distant consequence of an etiologic factor, whereas symptomatic refers to the direct and immediate manifestation of a known etiology. In this handbook, the term secondary is used to encompass both concepts because there is little practical gain in maintaining the distinction.

A good number of medical, neurologic, and psychiatric disorders have an associated sleep disorder that can be considered secondary. With relative frequency, the sleep alteration, either insomnia or hypersomnia, is the presenting manifestation or dominates the clinical picture, and its correct diagnosis leads to the discovery of the background disorder. Knowledge of these associations has practical importance since proper management of the medical, neurologic, or psychiatric disorder will improve or eradicate the sleep alteration.

Psychiatric Disorders with Sleep Alteration

Affective Depression

Affective depression is characterized by a depressed mood, markedly diminished interest in most activities, significant weight loss or weight gain, insomnia or hypersomnia, psychomotor agitation or retardation, loss of energy or fatigue, feelings of worthlessness or guilt, diminished ability to think or concentrate, recurrent thoughts of death, or recurrent suicidal ideation [2]. The primary affective disorders are subdivided into major depressive and bipolar disorders. Both conditions alter sleep but in different ways. A sleep alteration is so common in patients with depression that it is considered a diagnostic manifestation. Insomnia predominates, but 15–20% of patients have a bipolar disorder with hypersomnia [3].

Patients with major depressive disorder have a profound alteration of mood without a clear precipitating factor. In the unipolar type, insomnia is characterized by minor difficulty falling asleep with a pattern of early morning awakening 2–4 hours after sleep onset that severely disturbs the continuity of sleep. Elderly patients have more difficulty than younger ones. The polysomnographic evaluation confirms reduced total sleep and usually uncovers a short REM sleep latency (20–40 minutes) that is considered a biological marker of depression [4]. Stages 3 and 4 are also reduced relative to baseline tracings. REM sleep percents are elevated in patients with depression and shifted toward the first part of the night, a phenomenon that is the result of combining reduced slow wave sleep (SWS) and REM sleep episodes of equal duration as the night progresses. Density of rapid eye movements, or frequency of eye movements per unit of time, is increased, a phenomenon that is also observed in narcolepsy. Short REM sleep latency can be seen in the early stages of the disorder and in masked depression, facilitating the clinical diagnosis. Patients with agitated depression or with a strong component of anxiety also exhibit sleep onset insomnia.

In bipolar depression, mania alternates with major depression. During the depressive phase, patients report daytime somnolence and experience increased duration of nocturnal sleep with the characteristic feature of short REM sleep latency. Despite increased duration of total sleep, patients continue to complain of unrefreshed vigilance. During the manic phase, sleep is abbreviated with a drastic reduction during the 24 hours that fails to provoke complaints of fatigue or tiredness in the hypervigilant patient.

Patients with secondary depression also show early morning awakenings and short REM sleep latency, but they are less pronounced than in patients with primary depression.

The diagnosis of affective depression can be complicated by the common denial expressed by patients. Another complicating factor in making a proper diagnosis is the confounding high prevalence of some degree of secondary depression manifested by patients with serious medical illnesses. Depression is treated with psychotherapeutic intervention, pharmacologic treatment, or a combination of both. Serious illness usually warrants administration of medication. Tricyclic antidepressants and the newer generation of antidepressant drugs have approximately the same efficacy in reversing depression with prominent melancholia and early morning awakening. The choice is made according to accompanying symptoms. For instance, patients with agitated depression and sleep onset insomnia benefit more from the administration of a drug with associated sedative effects (tricyclic antidepressants and trazodone) given in divided doses and at bedtime. Monoamine oxidase (MAO) inhibitors constitute second-line therapy and are also useful in patients with hypersomnia. Antipsychotic medication can be used in combination with antidepressants when delusional manifestations or psychotic features are present. Electroconvulsive therapy is reserved for severely depressed patients who fail to respond appropriately to medication.

Bipolar disorders are generally treated with lithium carbonate in combination with a neuroleptic agent during the severely manic phase, as well as with an antidepressant agent if the patient is severely depressed.

Most antidepressant medications have potent REM suppressant effects, an action that can underlie their antidepressant effect. Cessation of antidepressants is associated with REM sleep rebound. Fluoxetine and MAO inhibitors can increase insomnia and should be administered in the morning. Tricyclic antidepressants increase or activate periodic leg movements of sleep. In general, sleep problems resolve as the psychiatric illness disappears, but it is important to consider that the psychiatric illness should be treated with full therapeutic doses for a minimum of 3 weeks (Table 8-1).

Sleep hygiene should be reviewed and disciplined sleep-wake measures instituted for patients with disorderly patterns. Selective deprivation of REM sleep and sleep deprivation have an antidepressant effect [5], but this therapy is not practical and seldom recommended by sleep specialists. Light therapy can be considered as an adjunct for patients with winter-related depression.

Pseudodementia

Cognitive impairment in depressed elderly patients occurs in 10–20% of instances with symptoms of such severity that the patient appears to be demented. Conversely, patients with a primary degenerative dementia can exhibit secondary symptoms of depression. Since "pseudodementia" of a predominantly affective nature can be correctable, it is important to determine whether depression is causing the symptoms.

Patients with pseudodementia have less severe symptoms of dementia at baseline and show significant improvement following sleep deprivation [6], whereas patients with degenerative dementia and depression show no change, or get worse with sleep deprivation. Polysomnographic studies in pseudodemented patients reveal higher REM sleep percent and phasic REM sleep activity. REM sleep rebound is more prominent in pseudodemented patients following sleep deprivation.

The sleep of elderly depressed patients [7] is characterized by reduced REM sleep latency, increased REM sleep percent and first REM sleep period density, and altered temporal distribution of REM sleep. In contrast, demented patients show reduced REM sleep percent, and loss of spindles and K complexes. A more favorable outcome has been associated with initially greater depressive symptomatology,

Table 8-1.   Commonly Prescribed Antidepressant Drugs

Medication	Dosage Range (mg)
With sedative effect	
Tricyclics and heterocyclics	
Amitryptiline	150–300
Protriptyline	20–60
Imipramine	150–300
Doxepin	150–300
Nortriptyline	50–150
Desipramine	75–200
Trazodone	150–600
Produce insomnia	
Fluoxetine	20–60
Bupropion	225–450
Monoamine oxidase inhibitors	
Isocarboxacid	10–30
Tranylcypromine	10–30

higher cognitive function, and moderate sleep continuity disturbance or early morning awakening [8].

REM sleep latency of elderly demented patients can be prolonged, whereas the REM sleep latency of depressed elderly patients can be reduced, an observation that requires verification to be clinically useful [9].

Schizophrenia

The first sleep studies produced in patients with schizophrenia failed to reveal any sleep abnormalities, despite the apparent similarity between the schizophrenic state (with hallucinations, distortion of reality, and bizarre thoughts) and the dream state. Later, more advanced and detailed polysomnographic studies [10] showed that REM sleep rebound normally found following suppression of REM sleep does not appear during the acute phase of schizophrenia, whereas chronic schizophrenics show an exaggerated REM sleep rebound. These curious observations gave way to interesting hypotheses that are still being debated. Some believe that the absence of REM sleep rebound would be the consequence of a REM sleep exhaustion caused by the continuous generation and intrusion of REM sleep in alertness and non-REM stages of sleep. Intrusion of REM sleep in the alert state would explain the hallucinations typically exhibited by schizophrenics, a pathogenetic mechanism that remains to be confirmed. Some experimental observations have lent support to this notion. Serotonin-depleted cats using parachlorophenylalanine (PCP) exhibit intrusion of ponto-geniculo-occipital (PGO) waves in non-REM stages of sleep as well as in alertness, a phenomenon that has been associated with hallucinatory behavior observed in these cats. REM sleep suppression in PCP-treated cats is not followed by REM sleep rebound unless they are treated with chlorpromazine, which eliminates the hallucinatory behavior. In humans, PGO waves cannot be identified directly, as routinely done in cats, although EMG activity of middle ear muscles is a detectable PGO equivalent. Such activity is not increased in schizophrenics, an observation that is counter to the REM sleep hypothesis.

Schizophrenic patients also show SWS decrease with amplitude reduction [11], a phenomenon that is corrected with neuroleptic administration [12].

Anxiety Disorders

The overriding characteristic of general anxiety is the excessive worry and unrealistic apprehension about common life situations. In generalized anxiety disorder, there are no specific clinical characteristics other than the persistent anxious mood. Patients manifest somatic features such as trembling, muscle tension, palpitations, shortness of breath, fatigability, difficulty swallowing, excessive sweating, dry mouth, dizziness, and difficulty concentrating. The personality disorder predominantly displaying anxiety, in a patient without affective or psychotic disorder, is associated with sleep onset and sleep maintenance insomnia. Frequent awakenings disturb sleep, and acute anxiety episodes appear during wakefulness. Generalized anxiety is more common in women, tends to run in families, and appears in early adulthood lasting for many years, if not the patient's entire life.

Anxiety can also be a prominent feature of other conditions that embody functional alterations commonly labeled as neurotic. These conditions can present various clinical forms that include panic and phobic disorders, hypochondriasis, obsessive-compulsive disorder, and posttraumatic stress disorder. In phobic and obsessive-compulsive disorders, there is an object of fear and anxiety.

Patients with panic disorder develop sudden, unexplained discrete episodes of acute anxiety with intense fear, a feeling of impending doom, and somatic symptoms such as choking, palpitations, trembling, chest pain, and discomfort causing nocturnal awakenings. Postictal hyperarousal prevents subsequent sleep. Patients also suffer daytime attacks of acute anxiety and agoraphobia, or fear of open spaces, that prevents them from being in crowds, shopping malls, or situations from which escape is difficult such as elevators, bridges, and vehicles. Panic episodes are common in patients with depressive disorders, tend to run in families, and are more frequent in women. They should be differentiated from sleep terrors that are usually of childhood onset, begin with a loud scream, and are not generally associated with daytime anxiety. Nightmares are easily distinguished by the intense dream content and early morning occurrence.

Posttraumatic stress disorder is easily diagnosed when the precipitating factor can be identified. Sleep continuity suffers as the individual experiences repeated dreams loaded with anxiety recollecting the traumatic event.

Uncontrolled anxiety along with poor stress-control mechanisms dominate the clinical picture in these conditions in which worries, fear, guilt, competitiveness, checking and rechecking, concerns with health, and excessive prebed rituals prevent the patient from falling asleep. Such psychological conflicts repeatedly disrupt the continuity of sleep, altering considerably its architecture. Tiredness and fatigue during the day are common complaints; however, napping is unrewarding or not possible.

Polysomnographic evaluation is seldom necessary, although occasionally performed when the clinician orders the test to exclude other conditions such as seizures, night terrors or nightmares in sleep-related panic disorder, or periodic limb movements and sleep apnea in generalized anxiety disorder with fragmentation of sleep. As expected, the laboratory studies in patients with generalized anxiety show long sleep latencies, interruption of sleep by long awakenings, decreased sleep efficiency, increased stage 1, reduced SWS, and reduced REM sleep. The multiple sleep latency test (MSLT) shows hypervigilance without evidence of excessive daytime somnolence. Nocturnal REM sleep latency is not decreased, in contrast with the phenomenon typically observed in patients with depression. Nocturnal panic attacks occur during non-REM sleep, and patients have relatively well-preserved sleep architecture. In general, the laboratory findings in anxiety disorders are nonspecific, showing a degree of abnormality that correlates with the intensity of the clinical manifestations.

Successful management of the anxiety disorder considerably improves the patient's ability to initiate and sustain sleep. Insight-oriented psychotherapy and behavioral treatment programs are successful. Benzodiazepines are the anxiolytic agents par excellence with the additional advantage of having an hypnotic effect. Long-acting benzodiazepines (chlordiazepoxide, diazepam, and flurazepam) given at bedtime (see Table 13-3) combine a desired early hypnotic effect with a residual anxiolytic action during the ensuing day. Propranolol (80–120 mg in two divided doses) has a beneficial effect on prominent somatized cardiovascular symptoms, and buspirone hydrochloride (15–60 mg in three divided doses) has a nonsedating anxiolytic action that has been used in patients with sleep-related respiratory difficulties. Panic attacks respond to alprazolam (0.5–4 mg two or three times daily, with a maximum dosage of 10 mg per day).

Alcoholism

Alcoholism is the term applied to the condition of excessive alcohol intake, abuse, and dependency. Acute alcoholism is characterized by sleepiness that starts 30 minutes after intake and lasts for approximately 4 hours. Under the influence of alcohol, patients show exacerbation of snoring and sleep apnea, bed wetting, sleep terrors, and sleep walking. Thereafter, sleep becomes increasingly fragmented with a surge of dreams and even nightmares.

Chronic alcoholism is a risk factor for the development of Korsakoff psychosis, liver cirrhosis, and alcoholic encephalopathy, which in themselves disrupt sleep. In general, the pattern of disruption is characterized by increasing fragmentation except when the patient comes under the influence of alcohol [13]. Abstinence is marked by profound disturbance of sleep patterns, awakenings, and nightmares. Sleep generation improves after 2 weeks, but patients tend to develop light sleep easily interrupted by myriad factors generally dependent on associated depression and chronic anxiety. Total recovery of sleep generation and satisfaction is never achieved in some patients.

Polysomnographic studies in patients under the influence of toxic levels of alcohol show a decreased sleep latency and REM sleep reduction with an increase in SWS during the first 4 hours. REM sleep rebound in the last 2 or 3 hours of the night underlies excessive dreaming and nightmares. Chronic alcohol consumption is associated with fragmentation of sleep, indistinct sleep stages, alpha-delta pattern, and slow eye movements during stage 2 of sleep. Abstinence is characterized by REM sleep rebound during the first few days and absence of SWS. Abstinence with delirium tremens is characterized by initial insomnia followed by hallucinations that represent an intense REM rebound phenomenon invading wakefulness. After the acute hallucinatory phase, some patients develop hypersomnia. During the long recovery phase, "dry alcoholics" complain of nocturnal awakenings and daytime somnolence; REM sleep percents tend to decrease and SWS shows gradual recovery. Fragmentation of nocturnal sleep is prominent. A few patients develop REM sleep without atonia, phantasmagorias, and periodic limb movements of sleep.

Alcohol-dependent sleep disorder refers to the bedtime use of alcohol with which the individual is seeking a hypnotic effect to assist the initiation of sleep [14]. Alcohol is self-prescribed by patients with underlying syndromes that interfere with their ability to initiate sleep. Sustained use results in tolerance and partial withdrawal that lead to arousals at night, sometimes associated with uncomfortable dreams. Patients might increase the bedtime dose of alcohol or add other drugs with hypnotic effect, such as the benzodiazepines, that potentiate the effect of alcohol. Discontinuation of the use of alcohol is followed by insomnia.

The treatment and rehabilitation of alcoholism is a long-life proposition that incorporates counseling, motivation, and involvement of family members. Drugs with antianxiety and sedative effects should not be used despite the prevalence of accompanying anxiety, because of risk of addiction to cross-tolerant medications such as the benzodiazepines. Antidepressants have been preconized by some, if used under controlled circumstances. Good sleep hygiene is paramount, although difficult to sustain.

Medical Disorders with Sleep Alteration

Nocturnal Angina

Nocturnal angina is characterized by manifestations that are typical of myocardial ischemia during nocturnal sleep. Patients complain of chest pressure or pain radiated to shoulder, left arm, or mandible. Angina episodes are more common during REM sleep, which is when the heart rhythm and the arterial pressure are more unstable. Changes in autonomic tone can be important in the causation of nocturnal ischemia. Commonly, patients also present effort angina during daytime hours.

Predisposing risk factors are coronary artery disease and valvular heart disease. Contributing factors are uncontrolled arterial pressure, smoking, obesity, and nocturnal hypoxemia. Patients with advanced obstructive sleep apnea are at higher risk for the development of nocturnal angina. Complications are serious since nocturnal myocardial ischemia can precipitate ventricular arrhythmias and sudden death [15].

The polysomnographic study shows depression of the ST segment of more than 1 mm that can appear independently of chest pains. In contrast to typical angina, patients with Prinzmetal's variant angina have nocturnal manifestations more frequently and show elevation of the ST segment [16]. The polysomnographic study is important to identify hypoxemia secondary to apneas, a condition easily corrected with continuous positive airway pressure (CPAP), bilevel positive air pressure (Bi-PAP), and administration of oxygen via nasal cannula, when necessary. The differential diagnosis needs to be made with nocturnal paroxysmal dyspnea, gastroesophageal reflux, and peptic ulcer.

Myocardial Infarction

Myocardial infarction is three times more likely to begin in the morning than in the evening, according to information [17] based on initial elevations of creatine kinase in plasma, or using onset of pain as the marker for the start of the myocardial infarction. Unmedicated patients with stable angina show a peak incidence of episodes of transient myocardial ischemia with ST segment depression between the hours of 6:00 A.M. and 12:00 noon. Adjusting for wake time, it has been possible to determine that the increase in frequency occurs in the first 4 hours after awakening [18], a pattern similar to that exhibited by myocardial infarction. These phenomena suggest that circadian triggers of transient ischemia can eventually cause irreversible damage in the presence of a vulnerable coronary artery plaque. Such events might be mediated by a combination of transient coronary vasoconstriction and transient increases in heart rate and systemic arterial pressure.

In patients with coronary atherosclerosis, physiologic phenomena that increase in intensity in the morning might increase the risk of myocardial ischemia. The systemic arterial pressure elevation observed in the morning could initiate coronary plaque rupture. Contributing factors such as enhanced blood viscosity, platelet aggregability, and coronary vasoconstriction could produce a state of relative hypercoagulability in a compromised vessel, increasing the likelihood of coronary occlusion following rupture of the plaque. A confounding factor is the interaction with the rest-activity cycle that increases platelet aggregability and systemic arterial blood pressure.

Cardiac Arrhythmias

Cardiac arrhythmias dependent on changes in the balance between parasympathetic and sympathetic tones occur more commonly during sleep, and in relation with the various sleep stages, than during wakefulness. Periods of asystole are sometimes associated with episodes of sinus bradycardia. Asystolic periods of up to 2.5 seconds in duration during nocturnal recording of heart activity with a Holter monitor are considered within normal limits; episodes of asystole lasting up to 9 seconds during REM sleep have been observed in otherwise asymptomatic healthy young adults [19]. The cardinal observation has been that all episodes occurred during REM sleep and most appeared during phasic REM sleep. It has been hypothesized that increased parasympathetic tone during REM sleep reduces heart rate and plays an important role in inducing asystole (Figure 8-1), a phenomenon that might be linked to unexplained sudden nocturnal death.

Chronic Obstructive Pulmonary Disease

Patients with chronic obstructive pulmonary disease (COPD) suffer a severe and persistent alteration of gaseous exchange at the pulmonary level that leads to cardiorespiratory alteration during sleep with severe insomnia [20]. Patients complain of difficulty initiating sleep, with abundant awakenings, dyspnea, cough, morning headache, and physical fatigue. Polysomnographic studies show prolonged sleep latency; fragmentation of sleep architecture; oxygen desaturation, in particular during REM sleep segments; and central sleep apnea episodes. Some patients have associated obstructive sleep apnea syndrome. REM sleep and SWS percents are reduced. Theophylline administration contributes to sleeplessness.

Complications include cardiac arrhythmias, cor pulmonale, and sudden death. Many patients present chronic anxiety, depression, and

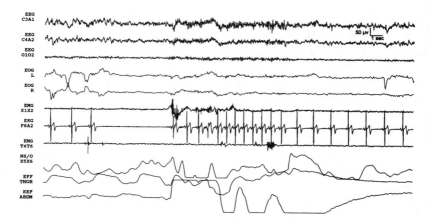

Figure 8-1.   *Nocturnal polysomnogram in a 35-year-old patient with severe obstructive sleep apnea syndrome and phasic REM sleep asystole. Note the tachycardia during partial arousal associated with apnea recovery. (Reprinted with permission from A Culebras. Stroke and Sleep Disorders. In M Fisher, J Bogousslavsky [eds], Current Review of Cerebrovascular Disease. Philadelphia, Current Medicine: 1996.)*

hypersomnia during daytime hours. Obesity, commonly observed in these sedentary patients, tends to aggravate all nocturnal manifestations.

When studying patients with COPD, it is important to evaluate the contribution of psychophysiologic components and of obstructive sleep apnea syndrome. Both conditions respond to proper management, and their correction alleviates nocturnal manifestations of insomnia and daytime symptoms of hypersomnia. Some patients might have underlying conditions such as poliomyelitis, muscular dystrophy, kyphoscoliosis, or debilitating neurologic disorders that produce restrictive pulmonary insufficiency and contribute to the development of central sleep apnea syndrome.

Asthma

Nocturnal asthma causes individuals to awaken in the middle of the night with acute respiratory distress, enhanced inspiratory effort, prolonged expiration, wheezing, cough, cyanosis, perspiration, and fast pulse. Mild nocturnal hypoxemia is also observed. Poor sleep quality leads to daytime fatigue and excessive somnolence. Ingestion of xanthines, which are frequently prescribed to asthmatic patients, contributes to sleeplessness. Two-thirds of patients suffer nocturnal attacks, some every night. Contributing factors are excessive bronchial resistance that normally increases in the early morning hours, exposure to allergens in the bedroom, and decreased levels of circulating norepinephrine and cortisol; sleep-synchronized circadian rhythm in airway caliber might be an influential factor [21]. Allergic reactions are important in the development of nocturnal asthma but do not explain all episodes of bronchoconstriction. Another contributing factor is the decrease of therapeutic levels of antiasthmatic medication as the night progresses. The eosinophil count is increased. The most feared complication is sudden death.

Polysomnographic studies show that asthmatic episodes tend to occur following the first cycle of sleep [22] without sleep stage predilection. The differential diagnosis should be made with paroxysmal nocturnal dyspnea of cardiac origin, sleep apnea syndrome, gastroesophageal reflux, sleep choking syndrome, alveolar hypoventilation, nocturnal laryngospasm, and nocturnal angina.

The treatment of nocturnal asthma is initially directed at improving daytime function with conventional maintenance therapy, by the inhalation of bronchodilators at bedtime and whenever the patient is awakened by wheezing. The effect lasts approximately 4 hours so that some patients require long-acting inhaled bronchodilators such as salmeterol and formoterol. Oral theophyllines can be used as well but have a tendency to impair sleep. A few patients might need oral steroid therapy and even immunosuppression.

Gastroesophageal Reflux

Esophagitis caused by reflux of gastric contents produces nocturnal manifestations that are characterized by sudden awakenings with heartburn, chest pain, and prolonged interruption of sleep. Some patients have dysphagia, laryngospasm, laryngopharyngitis, and even aspiration pneumonia, which can occur when gastric acid enters the pharynx and upper respiratory airway. Generally, patients have daytime symptoms that suggest gastroduodenal ulcer or esophagitis. The most serious complication is ulceration with esophageal stenosis. Predisposing factors are a gastroesophageal sphincter pressure of less than 10 mm, hiatal hernia, obesity, and pregnancy. Symptoms worsen as age advances.

Endoesophageal pH tracings are used for the identification of esophageal reflux of acidic gastric contents while the patient is asleep. A pH-sensitive probe is inserted in the distal esophagus, and the output is interfaced with a DC channel of the polygraph. Deflections from a pH baseline of 6 indicate changes in the acid–base environment of the distal esophagus. Gastroesophageal reflux is identified when the pH falls below 4 for 30 seconds or more.

Treatment of gastroesophageal reflux includes elevation of the head of the bed, which produces a major improvement in the acid clearance time, although the number of reflux episodes remains the same [23]. Administration of H_2-receptor antagonists (ranitidine, 150 mg twice a day) to suppress acidic gastric secretion relieves heartburn and controls the symptoms. Metoclopramide (10–15 mg four times a day, 30 minutes before each meal and at bedtime) accelerates acid clearance time. Improvement of gastroesophageal reflux has been reported in patients with and without obstructive sleep apnea syndrome using CPAP [24]. Sedating drugs and alcohol should be avoided because they prolong acid clearance time during sleep, worsening the condition [25].

Peptic Ulcer

Gastric peptic ulcer and the more common duodenal peptic ulcer produce epigastric pain that awakens the patient between 1 and 4 hours after going to bed. Pain is of low intensity and spasmodic in character, with a deep, boring localization; acute and intense pain suggests perforation. Associated manifestations are heartburn, and pain radiated to the chest, substernum, and back that leads to confusion with angina and other painful conditions. Food ingestion eliminates pain transiently, to reappear 15–30 minutes later. Predisposing risk factors are smoking; alcoholism; and ingestion of aspirin, corticosteroids, nonsteroidal anti-inflammatory medications, and analgesics. Peptic ulcer disease should be suspected in patients with insomnia caused by epigastric pain in relation to stress, whether of a psychological, medical, or surgical nature.

The polysomnographic study of patients with active peptic ulcer shows awakenings during the first half of the night, associated with epigastric pain. Gastric pH indicates lower acidity during awakenings and wakefulness than during SWS. Evaluation of circadian rhythmicity has shown that the highest levels of acidic gastric secretion occur between 9:00 P.M. and 12:00 midnight.

The differential diagnosis must be made with other conditions that provoke epigastric or abdominal pain at night including gastric cancer, cholelithiasis, pancreatitis, irritable bowel syndrome, and gastroesophageal reflux. Nocturnal angina might have to be excluded in some patients. Appropriate radiographic and endoscopic procedures confirm the diagnosis by demonstrating an ulcer crater. Treatment should be directed at eliminating all contributing factors and reducing nocturnal gastric acidity.

Neurologic Disorders with Sleep Alteration

The structures that intervene more directly in the generation of sleep and wakefulness are the pons, midbrain, hypothalamus, thalamus, and cortex, which serves as a target organ. Structural, pathophysiologic, and neurochemical abnormalities of these anatomic sites have a profound effect on sleep. To better understand how brain alterations affect sleep, it is important to remember that two distinct states, REM and non-REM, conform nocturnal sleep. The generators of the REM state are primarily cholinergic and aminergic nuclei located in the tegmentum of the pons and midbrain, whereas the non-REM state is mediated by serotonergic nuclei of the upper brain stem tegmentum and the anterior hypothalamus. The reticular nucleus of the thalamus is the generator of sleep spindles and the gatekeeper of the functional blockade of transmission toward the cortex that prevails in non-REM sleep. Tonic wakefulness is maintained by aminergic and cholinergic systems of the reticular nuclei of the brain stem, with the assistance of histaminergic centers in the posterior hypothalamus and glutamate containing neurons of the brain stem, thalamus, and cortex. Any pathologic alterations of these brain structures will have a profound effect on sleep and wake mechanisms.

Sleeping Sickness

This is a meningoencephalitis caused by the protozoan *Trypanosoma brucei*. The parasite is transmitted to humans through the sting of the tsetse fly that generally feeds on wild animals in tropical Africa. Approximately 20,000 new cases are reported each year. The acute phase of the disease starts 1–2 weeks after the bite, with local painful inflammation (chancre) followed by fever, lymphadenopathy, and headache. A circinate rash might appear around the orbits and in distal segments of the extremities as other manifestations of systemic disease such as malaise, weight loss, arthralgias, hepatosplenomegaly, and tachycardia take hold. Phase II of the disease with CNS invasion is characterized by nocturnal insomnia and daytime hypersomnia. Indifference, mental torpor, and psychomotor retardation progress relentlessly along with ataxia, extrapyramidal manifestations, and gait disorder that can resemble Parkinson's disease. Seizures, tremors, and ophthalmoplegia can be observed in some patients. The final phase is marked by advanced neurologic impairment, coma, and death.

The diagnosis is made with identification of the parasite in blood, or in fluid aspirates from the initial chancre or lymph nodes. Cerebrospinal fluid analysis shows an increase in cell count, high protein content, and increased IgM levels. Patients with advanced disease have demyelinating lesions in the cerebral hemispheres and the brain stem. The polysomnographic study shows loss of electrophysiologic markers such as vertex waves, sleep spindles, and K complexes with loss of definition of non-REM sleep, suggestive of a diffuse encephalopathy. The electroencephalogram (EEG) reveals high-amplitude slow waves in all stages of non-REM sleep that can acquire a pseudoperiodic pattern, but curiously there is relative preservation of REM sleep parameters until the final phases of the disease [26]. The differential diagnosis should be made with other infectious encephalitides that course with symptomatic hypersomnia. The intrinsic hypersomnias are readily excluded because they are not associated with manifestations of inflammation, systemic disease, or encephalopathy. The infection with *Trypanosoma cruzei*, also known as American trypanosomiasis or Chagas' disease, rarely causes encephalopathy with hypersomnia.

The disease is treated with suramin, pentamidine, or organic arsenicals before the CNS invasion occurs. If neurologic manifestations are present before treatment begins, the prognosis worsens but there is still a chance of treatment with melarsoprol, an arsenical that crosses the blood–brain barrier. The dosage is 2.0–3.6 mg per kg given intravenously in three divided doses over a period of 3 days, followed by another course 1 week later and another 21 days later. The product is highly toxic and neurologic complications have been reported in 18% of patients thus treated.

Stroke

An inversion of the sleep-wake rhythm is commonly observed in the days that follow a large hemispheric stroke. This inversion is manifested by lethargy during daytime hours and wakefulness, with some agitation, during the night. Patients with acute stroke can develop sleep apnea of the obstructive and nonobstructive variety. Low amounts of oxygen through a nasal cannula might be needed to counteract nocturnal desaturations of oxygen. Patients who survive a large hemispheric infarction exhibit months later normal percentages of REM stage and increased amounts of SWS [27] that are more pronounced when the lesion affects the right hemisphere [28]. Loss of sleep spindle activity following a hemispheric stroke suggests dysfunction of thalamic structures and carries a poor prognosis for survival [29].

REM sleep behavior disorder has been observed in patients with lacunar strokes of the brain stem involving the midbrain and pons [30]. The disturbance is characterized by bizarre behavior during REM stage that suggests enactment of a dream. Magnetic resonance imaging studies in some older individuals with risk factors for stroke have shown the presence of ischemic lesions in the tegmentum of the pons in a location that suggests damage to the muscle tone inhibiting system, which normally generates muscle atonia during REM stage. This system originates in the peri-locus ceruleus area of the rostral tegmentum of the pons and activates the medullary inhibitory zone of Magoun and Rhines via the tegmentoreticular tract. This action, in turn, produces neuronal hyperpolarization by way of the reticulospinal tracts. Pathologic loss of atonia during REM sleep facilitates motor behaviors that range from simple limb movements to complex quasi-purposeful acts, depending on the extent of the infarcted pontine area. REM sleep behavior disorder presenting in an older person with risk factors for stroke should suggest vascular lesions of the brain stem. Clonazepam, 0.5 mg taken at bedtime, reduces or eliminates the episodes.

Sleep can be a risk factor for stroke. Various studies have shown that the time of onset of stroke occurs more commonly between 6:00 A.M. and 12:00 noon than at any other time of the 24-hour cycle, with the most critical period occurring 1 hour after awakening [31]. The onset of stroke is least likely to occur in the late evening, before midnight [32]. Low blood pressure at night in vulnerable patients with altered vasomotor reflexes has been implicated as a conditioning factor for the development of thrombotic stroke [33], whereas the blood pressure elevation observed in the morning has been associated with hemorrhagic stroke. Some authors negate the existence of periodicity in the occurrence of intracerebral hemorrhage [34]. The administration of aspirin does not modify the circadian pattern of onset of stroke in the morning [31].

Homeostatic variables linked to the circadian rhythm are a source of increased risk. The incidence of myocardial infarction, thrombotic stroke, and vascular death shows a peak between 6:00 and 10:00 A.M., suggesting the presence of underlying factors potentiating these conditions. Indeed, blood pressure elevations and heart rate increases occur at these times along with changes in other parameters, including increased platelet aggregability, fibrinogen activity, blood viscosity, and level of circulating epinephrine [35]. There appears to be a circadian interplay, as yet poorly understood and studied, between hemodynamic, coagulation, and homeostatic factors at specified times of the 24-hour cycle that increase the vulnerability to stroke occurrence.

Retinal infarction of embolic origin occurred during sleep at an unexpectedly high rate in one study of 24 consecutive patients [36]. The authors hypothesized that embolism appears commonly during sleep and that the retina might be especially susceptible to infarction during sleep. There are scarce reports of patients being awakened from sleep with transient manifestations of neurologic deficit suggestive of transient ischemic attacks [37]. The incidence of silent brain infarction occurring during sleep in patients with risk factors for stroke remains to be studied.

Snoring and sleep apnea syndromes might be important risk factors for the occurrence of stroke [38]. A constellation of satellite factors are involved in this association because of the profound changes that severe sleep apnea syndrome can entail. Secondary factors are arterial hypertension and coronary heart disease with confounding factors being age, obesity, smoking, and alcohol consumption. According to Palomaki and colleagues [38], snoring can increase the risk of cerebrovascular disease independently of the other factors. Alleged mediators between snoring, sleep apnea syndrome, and stroke are cardiac arrhythmias, hemodynamic disturbances, increased levels of catecholamines, disturbances of cerebral blood flow, and periods of hypoxemia. The brief arousal observed at the termination of obstructive sleep apneas is receiving increasing attention because of the pronounced sympathetic surges and acute hypertension noted during the 3- to 5-second period of recovery from apnea [39]. Repeated bouts of hypertension at night, although brief, might eventually chronify the condition and facilitate sustained hypertension with vascular structural changes.

Restless Legs Syndrome and Periodic Limb Movements of Sleep

Since the seminal account by Ekbom in 1945 [40] and subsequent review of 175 cases in 1960 [41], restless legs syndrome (RLS) has been a relatively well-known, although poorly understood, neurologic condition. Later descriptions and reports noted a familial incidence and the association with various metabolic, neurologic, and vascular disorders. In 1953, the term *nocturnal myoclonus* was coined by Symonds [42], who described myoclonic jerks on falling asleep that persisted through the night. In 1965, Lugaresi and colleagues [43] performed polysomnographic evaluations of patients with these conditions and established the association between RLS and nocturnal myoclonus. Further studies by Coleman and colleagues in 1980 [44] defined nocturnal myoclonus in more detail. They proposed the term *periodic movements in sleep* to separate the disturbance from true myoclonic alterations. In the past decade, periodic limb movements of sleep (PLMS) has been the preferred term to incorporate the occasional occurrence of upper limb involvement; PLMS is considered a common cause of sleep disturbance, particularly in the elderly.

RLS is characterized by uncomfortable, unpleasant, crawling sensations localized in both legs, occasionally asymmetric and alternating extremities. The shin and calf are more often affected than the foot, thigh, and buttock, or rarely the lower back. Occasionally, a patient reports similar symptoms involving the arm. The sensations are felt deep in the leg and typically are described as aching, creeping, burning, or stretching; pain is an atypical component. Symptoms occur only while the patient is at rest, particularly in the evening and at night. Long periods of rest at any time during the day precipitate symptoms, such as when the patient rides as a passenger in a car, is confined to a cramped seat in an airplane, or attends a show. The symptoms worsen with fatigue. The discomfort can continue or reappear after the patient goes to bed, provoking sleeplessness. Massaging the legs, taking hot or cold baths, and moving around are some of the activities patients have devised to alleviate the unpleasant sensations. The urge to move the limbs and pace the floor for as long as 30 minutes can, in fact, become irresistible.

On falling asleep, patients with RLS commonly exhibit involuntary, repetitive PLMS characterized by a partial flexion at the ankle, knee, and sometimes the hip with extension of the big toe, followed by slow recovery of the extended posture. The entire movement lasts anywhere between 0.5 and 5 seconds, most typically 1.5–2.5 seconds, and is sometimes initiated by a small amplitude jerk of the foot or toes. The limb displacement is not classically myoclonic and thus the reticence by authors to call it myoclonus. Electromyographic recordings of tibialis muscles (Figure 8-2) demonstrate rhythmic activity occurring at 20- to 40-second intervals involving one or both lower limbs, symmetrically or alternating as if pedaling. Clusters of movements lasting many minutes appear predominantly during light non-REM sleep; they become less common in stages 3 and 4, and virtually disappear in REM sleep. K complexes in stage 2 or alpha activity marking arousals might be associated with PLMS. Patients are generally unaware of the disturbance; it is brought to their attention by the awakened bedmate who hears the rumble under the sheets.

RLS plus PLMS disturbs sleep considerably either by preventing its occurrence or by provoking multiple awakenings. Consequent sleep deprivation causes excessive daytime somnolence and tiredness. Sleep latency can be prolonged, even for several hours; sleep efficiency is decreased; light non-REM sleep is increased; and the time spent in deep sleep is reduced. PLMS at night contributes to increase the number of arousals and awakenings. Insomnia and daytime somnolence can be complicated with the occurrence of depression, emotional distress, and other psychological dysfunctions.

One-third of the patients in the original series described by Ekbom had a family history of RLS. Families with many affected members have been reported by various authors and as many as half of the instances might be of familial origin [45].

A variety of neurologic, metabolic, and vascular disorders are associated with RLS and PLMS, although the latter can occur in otherwise healthy individuals who remain asymptomatic. Iron deficiency anemia and folate deficiency have been reported with RLS plus PLMS, and indeed the correction of the hematologic disorder can improve the condition. RLS plus PLMS has also been observed in pregnancy, chronic renal failure, hypothyroidism, rheumatoid arthritis, and in neurologic disorders such as poliomyelitis, peripheral neuropathy (particularly of diabetic origin), chronic myelopathy, and Parkinson's disease. Caffeine abuse was originally cited by Ekbom, and subsequently it was shown that the ingestion of a variety of drugs, including antidepressants, phenothiazines, lithium, and calcium-channel blockers, is a risk factor for development of RLS plus PLMS. Barbiturate withdrawal is a risk factor as well. PLMS is commonly observed in patients treated with tricyclic compounds. RLS is considered idiopathic when there are no

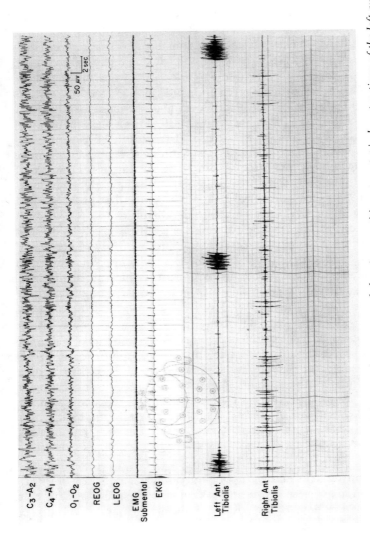

Figure 8-2. *Polysomnogram with leg myoclonus protocol showing repetitive, stereotypical contractions of the left anterior tibialis muscle lasting 2–2.2 seconds and occurring at 23-second intervals in stage 2 of sleep, indicative of periodic limb movements of sleep. The activity involves the left leg only and is not associated with an arousal.*

other associated disorders known to cause or increase the risk of developing the alteration.

The pathogenesis of RLS and PLMS is unknown. It has been suggested that a CNS oscillator drives the motor activity at night overcoming the motor inhibition that naturally exists in non-REM sleep. The presence of PLMS in patients with total spinal cord transection at a high level suggests that the oscillator might be located in the spinal cord [46].

The prevalence of RLS is unknown primarily because of the absence of diagnostic criteria for research and epidemiologic studies, and the fluctuations exhibited by the disorder through the lifetime of the individual. Ekbom cited a prevalence of 5% [40] of the general population including all ranges of symptom intensity. RLS plus PLMS occurs in any age group but increases in frequency without sex preference as age advances. Although longitudinal studies are lacking, it is known that RLS plus PLMS persists during the lifetime of the individual with fluctuations in intensity and variations in the course that progress with remissions and exacerbations without identifiable cause.

The general and neurologic examination is normal except in patients with associated disorders. A careful search for evidence of peripheral neuropathy and degenerative CNS disorders including pertinent blood tests (Table 8-2) should be conducted in susceptible and elderly individuals. The diagnosis can be made from the description provided by the patient and is confirmed with polysomnography. The nocturnal study with videotape recording reveals awakenings in which the patient typically sits at the edge of the bed and massages the legs or paces the floor to alleviate the suffering. The polysomnographic record reveals PLMS characterized by repetitive, stereotypical EMG activity recorded from the anterior tibialis muscle, lasting 1.5–5 seconds, occurring at 20- to 40- second intervals (range, 5–120 seconds, depending on the author consulted), affecting one or both lower limbs, and in clusters that are more prominent during light non-REM sleep [47]. Five or more contractions within the time frame of 5- to 120-second intervals define a cluster. Contractions outside that range are considered independent aperiodic movements and are not counted toward the index of movements per hour of sleep. Most authors consider the presence of five or more PLMS per hour of sleep to be abnormal. Arousals can be seen with some or all the events.

Rarely, patients with RLS fail to show PLMS in the polysomnogram, and PLMS can occur in healthy individuals independently of RLS. The general prevalence of PLMS reaches a peak of 29% by the age of 50 years. A high rate is usually associated with chronic insomnia, daytime

Table 8-2. Suggested Diagnostic Studies in Patients with Restless Legs Syndrome Plus Periodic Limb Movements of Sleep

Blood tests
- Complete blood count
- Sedimentation rate
- Iron content
- Folate level
- Vitamin B_{12}
- Blood glucose
- BUN
- Creatinine
- Sodium, potassium, chloride
- Magnesium, calcium, and phosphorus

Polysomnography
- Leg myoclonus protocol with videotape recording
- Multiple sleep latency test

Neurophysiology
- Electromyography and nerve conduction velocity studies of lower extremities

Sleep log
- 14-day evaluation chart

Predisposing drug/medication checklist
- Caffeine, neuroleptics, lithium, L-dopa, tricyclic antidepressants. Withdrawal from barbiturates, other sedatives and narcotics

somnolence, and fatigue, but the correlation has been questioned by others who have reported high rates of occurrence in asymptomatic patients [48].

RLS should be distinguished from a variety of repetitive movement disorders affecting the limbs during wakefulness, most notably akathisia that is induced by neuroleptics or associated with Parkinson's disease. In akathisia, patients shift and move their lower extremities in response to inner restlessness but not to alleviate an irresistible sensory discomfort. Furthermore, akathisia is not aggravated by rest or drowsiness as RLS is, but worsens with progressive deprivation of the offending neuroleptic. Patients with akathisia might have other motor dysfunctions, such as marching in place, that do not occur in association with RLS.

The differential diagnosis of PLMS is made with sleep starts that are aperiodic movements of early drowsiness. Also, with epileptic conditions, genuine myoclonic jerks and several forms of waking myoclonus occur in association with CNS degenerative disorders. The periodic, repetitive nature of PLMS, heightened in light non-REM sleep, is the cornerstone of the diagnosis.

The treatment of RLS revolves around pharmacotherapy with benzodiazepines, dopaminergic drugs, and opioids, individually or in combination. Tolerance, habituation, and even addiction are risks that can be decreased by rotating medications or administering interrupted doses in mild cases. Clonazepam is a popular choice at a starting dose of 0.5 mg at bedtime, increasing to 4 mg if warranted. This preparation, like other benzodiazepines, can cause excessive sedation and should be used sparingly and in the minimum amount necessary to produce a therapeutic effect. Other short- and ultrashort-acting benzodiazepines can have a similar therapeutic benefit. Long-acting benzodiazepines such as diazepam should be avoided to prevent accumulation of sedating effects.

Opioids are also effective, particularly if the component of RLS is more intense than PLMS. Propoxyphene (65–130 mg), oxycodone (5 mg, can be combined with acetaminophen), and codeine (30 mg) are usually effective when given in the evening or at bedtime. Escalating doses up to the maximum allowed might be necessary in some patients but should be discouraged because of the addictive potential of these compounds. Methadone (15–20 mg in a single dose) has been successful in the hands of the few who have used it.

Carbidopa-levodopa (Sinemet) preparations starting at 10/100 can be increased in subsequent weeks; the dosage should not exceed 400 mg of levodopa daily in divided doses. Carbidopa-levodopa CR, 25/100 or 50/200, has a longer period of action, and when given at bedtime might preempt resurgence of symptoms in the middle of the night. A peculiar restless legs augmentation syndrome can be observed in some patients who receive escalating doses of levodopa exceeding 400 mg per day. Bromocriptine (2.5–5.0 mg at bedtime) has also been used successfully.

Carbamazepine is a second-choice drug to be administered in amounts equivalent to antiseizure therapeutic doses. It can add therapeutic efficacy when combined with first-choice preparations in resistant patients. Other drugs that have been tested and proposed by some are baclofen, clonidine, and propranolol.

Parkinson's Disease

Early manifestations of Parkinson's disease are insomnia and nocturnal sleep of poor quality. Patients' difficulty initiating sleep is related to anxiety, but most patients frequently complain of interrupted sleep with multiple prolonged awakenings that contribute to sleepiness in the morning [49]. Parkinsonian tremors disappear in sleep to reappear occasionally in association with arousals and body movements. In REM sleep, muscle tone can be increased, and REM sleep behavior disorder is occasionally observed; alpha-REM might be noted along with occasional REM-onset blepharospasm [50]. Sleep spindles are decreased in amplitude and frequency [51], a phenomenon reversed by therapy with dopaminergic agents [52]. Nocturnal myoclonus and apneas of the nonobstructive and obstructive variety are common and more severe in patients with autonomic disturbances.

Sleep-related abnormalities can be idiopathic or coincidental in patients of advanced age. However, there are a number of factors inherent in Parkinson's disease that cause, mediate, or aggravate the sleep disturbance. Lack of mobility in bed, pervasive depression, and dementia contribute importantly while complicating the management of the alteration.

Management of sleep abnormalities in patients with Parkinson's disease is a vexing problem. Dopaminergic medications tend to improve sleep disturbances, although in some patients the same medication is the cause of sleep alteration. In general, large amounts of levodopa in the evening have an alerting effect. On the other hand, moderate amounts of sustained release carbidopa-levodopa given at bedtime, for instance, CR 25/100 or CR 50/200, are useful in patients with nocturnal immobility but have the risk of enhancing nocturnal hallucinations and nightmares [53]. Selegiline and amantadine can have alerting effects and should not be given past noon in patients who complain of insomnia [54]. The old antihistaminic medication diphenhidramine hydrochloride has a mild antiparkinsonian effect while providing a soft hypnotic component, if given at bedtime (50–75 mg). When administered in the evening, tricyclic antidepressants have a dual clinical beneficial action through the anticholinergic effect and by inducing sleepiness. Episodes of REM behavior disorder respond to the administration of clonazepam (0.5 mg at bedtime); however, the cumulative and cognitive effects of the benzodiazepines might limit usefulness. Restorative sleep has a therapeutic antiparkinsonian effect. Overall, patients report improvement of rigidity and bradykinesia in the morning immediately after getting up, and some describe transient episodes of dystonia after daytime naps. Both observations suggest spontaneous increase of the cerebral dopamine pool following sleep.

Patients treated with levodopa report the return of dreams that are sometimes vivid and on occasions become genuine nightmares. Reduction of nocturnal doses of levodopa might alleviate the intensity of nocturnal dreaming. When nightmares and frank hallucinations plague the patient despite adjustments in levodopa treatment, clozapine can be administered if clinical judgment dictates that levodopa doses should be continued to maintain optimal motor function. Low-dose clozapine administration (12.5–25.0 mg at night) can be of great benefit, although weekly monitoring of the white blood count is mandatory to identify neutropenia, should it occur.

RLS and PLMS are common accompaniments of Parkinson's disease. Patients complain of uncomfortable crawling sensations in the legs in the evening that force them to continuously shift leg position, and bed partners report excessive nocturnal motor restlessness in bed. When PLMS becomes intense, sleep architecture can suffer, contributing to complaints of insomnia. The response to levodopa administration (carbidopa-levodopa CR, 25/100 or 50/200 at bedtime) can be dramatic, suggesting a direct effect on the phenomenon. Other dopaminergic agents have a beneficial effect too. Tricyclic antidepressants should be discontinued, since they aggravate the nocturnal phenomenon.

Daytime sleepiness can be the consequence of relentless insomnia, but some patients report excessive sleepiness as the dose of levodopa takes effect. Levodopa-induced sleepiness is a relatively rare phenomenon that tends to occur more commonly with sustained-release carbidopa-levodopa; switching to a short-acting form of carbidopa-levodopa might alleviate the problem. Depression can be a factor contributing to daytime sleepiness. Administration of tricyclic compounds or alerting antidepressants such as bupropion, 75–300 mg per day in divided doses, along with counseling, increased daytime activities, and other psychotherapeutic techniques is of great assistance. Should daytime sleepiness become a dominant factor, consideration can be given to the administration of methylphenidate, 5–10 mg daily.

Shy-Drager Syndrome

This is a multisystem degeneration syndrome with parkinsonian features, orthostatic hypotension, and other manifestations of failure of the autonomic nervous system. The occurrence of obstructive and nonobstructive sleep apnea syndromes [55, 56], as well as dysrhythmic patterns of respiration during sleep—and even in wakefulness—confer a particular profile to the sleep alteration [57]. Laryngeal stridor, manifested by a peculiar loud noise likened to a donkey's braying when inspiratory and expiratory, has been described [58], whereas alveolar hypoventilation and respiratory arrest at night have been cited as causes of death [59]. Patients tend to have lower systemic arterial blood pressures during sleep, and multi-infarct dementia is a risk. An increased incidence of REM sleep behavior disorder [60] has also been reported; we have observed [61] that the manifestations of REM sleep behavior disorder and REM sleep without atonia can precede the onset of typical neurologic deficits by 2 or 3 years. Sleep-associated manifestations can be related to nocturnal hypotensive events, or to lesions found in the pontine tegmentum, reticular formation, nucleus ambiguus, hypoglossal nucleus, and anterior horn cells of the cervical and thoracic spinal cord, causing sympathetic and parasympathetic denervation in combination with variable forms of motoneuron disease.

The management of the sleep-related disturbances in Shy-Drager syndrome is the same as that of the disorder itself and includes measures to elevate the blood pressure with administration of salt and fluids, compression stockings, and fludrocortisone to prevent hypotensive episodes during sleep. REM behavior disorder is managed with clonazepam, 0.5 mg at bedtime, but care should be taken to avoid further lowering of the blood pressure.

Progressive Supranuclear Palsy

Progressive supranuclear palsy is characterized by vertical palsy of voluntary gaze, axial rigidity, gait disturbance, and subcortical dementia. At times, the clinical picture is confused with Parkinson's disease. Histologic lesions are found in subcortical nuclear structures, heavily involving the central gray of the pons and mesencephalon. Patients exhibit the sleeplessness that one would expect with injury to the tegmental nuclei of the rostral half of the brain stem, subthalamus, and medial thalamus. Polygraphic studies show reduction of total sleep time, fragmentation of nocturnal sleep, disorganization of non-REM stages with poor development of sleep spindles, markedly reduced REM sleep [62], and abnormal rapid eye movements. Electrographic features of wakefulness can occur in association with behavioral sleep (ambiguous or indeterminate sleep), a phenomenon that coupled with poor definition of sleep stages interferes with the proper interpretation of the polysomnogram when conventional scoring criteria are applied. Sleep disturbance is greatest in patients with the most severe disease [63]. Therapy with levodopa and amantadine is often tried to overcome the relentless progression of motor abnormalities, with hardly any effect on sleep abnormalities.

Olivopontocerebellar Degeneration

From the perspective of sleep pathology, olivopontocerebellar degeneration is another interesting neurologic condition that affects brain stem structures involved in sleep mechanisms. Although there is some experimental evidence that the cerebellar system has a modulating effect on sleep-wake mechanisms, the clinical changes observed in this disorder are adequately explained by brain stem lesions. Patients with olivopontocerebellar degeneration exhibit reduction of phasic eye movement density in REM sleep that is not explained by reduced proportions of REM and non-REM sleep [64]. Obstructive and nonobstructive sleep apnea syndromes related to autonomic dysfunction [65] sometimes dominate the picture. There is one report of normalization of respiratory rhythm disturbance with trazodone [66]. Increased duration of indeterminate sleep suggests progressive involvement of sleep generators in pontine tegmental structures. REM sleep without atonia has also been found [67], a phenomenon that might be related to degeneration of tegmentoreticular tracts.

Spinocerebellar Degeneration

Patients with spinocerebellar degeneration have widespread neurologic dysfunction that is the result of damage to various systems including brain stem structures. Polygraphic investigations have revealed absence of REM sleep, reduced non-REM sleep, and indeterminate sleep [68]. Sleep-related breathing irregularities are common and potentially serious because of associated autonomic dysfunction and cardiac dysrhythmias. Nocturnal sudden death is a risk in bedridden patients who exhibit snoring, breathing abnormalities, and bulbar symptoms [69].

Huntington's Chorea

This is a progressive and eventually fatal autosomal dominant condition characterized by choreic movements, personality disturbance, and dementia. The responsible gene is located on chromosome 4, locus G8. In advanced disease, there is global brain atrophy with changes most marked in the caudate nucleus and putamen. Patients with Huntington's disease might complain of insomnia very early in the course of the disease, sometimes even before other manifestations of neurologic impairment become evident. Unexplained and persistent insomnia in a patient at risk of developing the disorder should elicit the suspicion that the individual is afflicted. Polysomnographic evaluation shows reduced sleep efficiency, increased sleep latency, sleep fragmentation, decreased SWS, reduced REM sleep, and an increase in density and amplitude of sleep spindles. Spindle density and amplitude are increased (Figure 8-3) in contrast with reduced amplitude or loss in Parkinson's disease. This electroclinical phenomenon suggests that a high level of cerebral dopamine, as observed in Huntington's disease, increases spindle amplitude and density, a notion supported by the fact that in Parkinson's disease, spindle activity is enhanced with levodopa administration [70].

Multiple Sclerosis

In some patients with multiple sclerosis, the observation of excessive and inappropriate daytime sleepiness in conjunction with cataplexy, sleep paralysis, and hypnagogic hallucinations has led to a diagnosis of narcolepsy. It remains unresolved whether narcolepsy-cataplexy is the manifestation of demyelination of appropriate structures in diencephalic systems and the brain stem, or an associated condition. Excessive somnolence and other narcoleptic symptoms can appear before or after the onset of multiple sclerosis [71], with the age of presentation varying widely. Chronic fatigue is common in multiple sclerosis and can confound the interpretation of sleep disturbances.

Susceptibility to multiple sclerosis is coded by genes within or close to the HLA-DR-DQ subregion. Patients with narcolepsy exhibit the highest known association between a disease entity and the HLA-DR2 and DQw1 antigens, estimated at 95% or greater in most series [72, 73]. The coincidence of genetic susceptibility between multiple sclerosis and narcolepsy has led some authors to speculate that there is a common immuno-

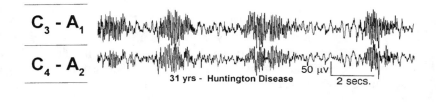

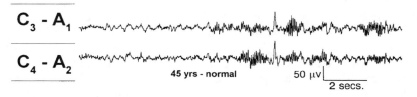

Figure 8-3. *Sleep spindles developing in stage 2 in a 31-year-old patient with insomnia of recent onset and family risk factors of Huntington's chorea (top tracing). Spindles are dense and of high voltage in comparison with the spindles of a slightly older, normal person (bottom tracing).*

genetic etiology [74]. Other authors have indicated that sleep disturbance is relatively common in patients with multiple sclerosis, suggesting a multifactorial etiology that ranges from depression to lesion site [75, 76].

Based on the remitting course of sleep attacks exhibited by some patients, some authors have hypothesized that multiple sclerosis can cause symptomatic narcolepsy [77]. Castaigne and colleagues [78] observed midbrain plaques in the hypothalamic periventricular region of a patient with bouts of excessive sleep and multiple sclerosis, an often cited but rare occurrence as estimated by literature reports. There is no clear difference in sleep latencies between DR2 positive patients and controls [79], suggesting that by themselves the genes coding for HLA-DR2 and DQw1 are not sufficient to cause sleep alteration. Nonetheless, the association between multiple sclerosis and sleep disturbance is higher than expected, and other pathogenetic mechanisms have been investigated. Patients with multiple sclerosis engage in more daytime napping than control subjects (53% versus 21% of controls) [74] that could be related in part to nocturnal and early morning awakenings caused by bladder problems. Patients with multiple sclerosis report difficulty falling asleep, restless sleep, nonrestorative sleep, and early morning awakenings more frequently than control subjects [80].

Sleep laboratory evaluations suggest that the etiology is multifactorial, involving both physical and psychological features [81]. Polysomnography and MSLT are required to distinguish narcolepsy from other causes of excessive daytime sleepiness.

Antidepressant medication has been suggested for the management of sleep disorders in multiple sclerosis [81]. Clonazepam (0.5 mg at bedtime) has been advocated for the treatment of PLMS, and amantadine (100 mg twice per day) for chronic fatigue [81]. A welcome increase in evening wakefulness has been reported by patients treated with selegiline [82].

Myotonic Dystrophy

In patients with myotonic dystrophy, clinical manifestations of nervous system degeneration occur in parallel with progressive skeletal muscle changes. Hypersomnia, apathy, mental decline, and "slow alpha" rhythms in patients with moderately advanced myotonic dystrophy have been linked to dysfunction of the dorsomedial nucleus of the thalamus [83]. Nerve cells of the dorsomedial nucleus contain eosinophilic cytoplasmic inclusion bodies that manifest neuronal damage [83]. In addition, in this disorder, lesions of the dorsomedial nucleus have been related to loss of integration of growth hormone secretion with SWS [84]. Nonobstructive sleep apneas and sleep-related alveolar hypoventilation are common [85] and can contribute to increased somnolence. Sleep-related breathing abnormalities are the result of central neuronal lesions and declining muscular function. Hypersomnia remains despite reversal of sleep apnea with CPAP applications [86], suggesting an independent origin, probably linked to dysfunction of the thalamic dorsomedial nuclei. The loss of SWS-related growth hormone secretion in patients with myotonic dystrophy might be related to signs of premature aging generally observed in patients with damage of thalamic dorsomedial nuclei [87].

Myasthenia Gravis

Sleep-related complaints in patients with myasthenia gravis include waking up with sensations of breathlessness, morning headaches, and daytime somnolence. Fatigability can involve the diaphragm and accessory respiratory muscles with resulting respiratory failure in the awake and sleep states. Polygraphic studies in treated patients show increased stage

1 and decreased proportions of stages 3, 4, and REM sleep. Patients also exhibit an increased sleep apnea index with predominantly mixed and obstructive sleep apnea episodes, along with oxygen desaturation of moderate severity. This finding is particularly evident during REM stage when the diaphragm is the only muscle that remains active in the exchange of air. Respiratory muscles can be focally affected in patients with myasthenia gravis [88]. Older patients with an increased body mass index and abnormal daytime blood gas concentration are more vulnerable to the development of a diaphragmatic form of sleep apnea syndrome with oxygen desaturation [89]. Daytime somnolence in a patient with myasthenia gravis should suggest abnormal breathing during sleep, even in the absence of abnormal daytime function. Patients receiving appropriate treatment, and with satisfactory daytime functional capacity and activity level, might still have abnormal breathing during sleep.

In the myasthenic syndrome, dysfunction of respiratory muscles can cause sleep hypoventilation and sleep apnea to the point that the patient requires assisted ventilation.

Brain Tumors

Tumors of the brain can cause sleep-wake disruption directly by virtue of their location, or indirectly through the development of intracranial hypertension or hydrocephalus, or both. Symptomatic narcolepsy characterized by brief sleep attacks and sometimes cataplexy has been described in association with craniopharyngioma compressing the floor of the third ventricle (Figure 8-4); glioma, sarcoidosis, and colloid cyst of the third ventricle; pituitary adenoma, midbrain glioma, and cerebral sarcoidosis [90]. Lower brain stem tumors can cause severe hypoventilation and respiratory failure during sleep, requiring tracheostomy [91]. Persistent subalertness and lethargy are more typical of patients with increased intracranial pressure. Some patients with obstructive hydrocephalus exhibit a similar condition. Intracranial pressure shows fluctuations during sleep along with increases in REM stage and stage 2 [92].

Head Trauma and Sleep

Closed head injuries that cause loss of consciousness can produce alterations of the sleep-wake cycle. In patients with traumatic coma and stupor, the occurrence of EEG patterns resembling sleep carry

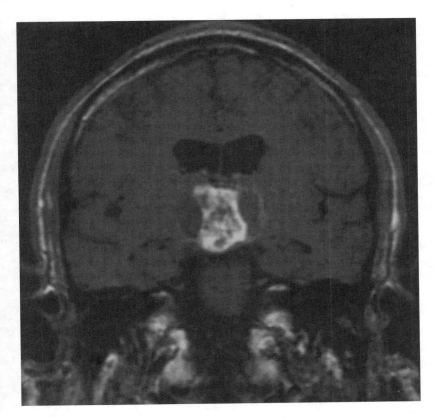

Figure 8-4.   *Computed tomographic scan of the head of a 55-year-old man presenting with excessive daytime somnolence. The cystic mass compressing the diencephalon was found at operation to be a craniopharyngioma.*

a favorable prognosis [93]. In the initial phase of recovery, while the patient is coming out of the coma, hypersomnia is common with reduction of or poor recollection of dreams. The organization of sleep tends to become normalized as the rehabilitation progresses; there is a parallelism between improving percentages of REM sleep and cognition [94]. Adult patients with postconcussion syndrome complain of a variety of neurovegetative disturbances that include anorexia, bulimia, depression, memory alteration, loss of libido, nonrestorative sleep, and hypersomnolence. Polysomnographic studies show increased fragmentation of nocturnal sleep [95].

Post-traumatic hypersomnia is characterized by a prolonged major sleep episode followed by frequent daytime sleepiness and sleep episodes. Hypersomnia is most prominent initially, associated with other complaints of a neurovegetative nature, and tends to resolve over the ensuing weeks or months following the trauma, sometimes persisting after 1 year. The specific neuroanatomic substrate remains unknown. Lesions have been described around the third ventricle, posterior hypothalamus, midbrain, and pons. Polysomnographic studies reveal excessive daytime somnolence but fail to show a specific pattern of alteration; they are useful to exclude other disorders of sleep associated with hypersomnia, namely, sleep apnea syndrome and narcolepsy. After careful neurologic evaluation to exclude structural brain lesions that need further management, patients can be treated with CNS stimulants such as pemoline and methylphenidate in the usual doses. Depression might require independent management.

Coma and Sleep

Coma can result from a diffuse disorder of cerebral function or from a lesion interrupting the activity of the deep core of gray matter. The patient in coma has lost both consciousness and sleep; is neither awake nor asleep; and the integrated sequence of awake, non-REM, and REM sleep fails to occur. The fundamental differences between coma and sleep are that the patient in coma cannot be aroused, and the polysomnogram fails to show the predictable architecture of sleep stages. During the recovery phase, lighter coma and sleep can overlap. The patient seems to undergo a period of undue sleepiness, whereas the clinical and electrographic differences between sleep and nonsleep cycles become more pronounced. A pronounced REM sleep rebound can be observed in patients recovering from hepatic or alcoholic coma [96]. Early recovery of sleep spindles and REM sleep indicates a favorable evolution.

Spindle-coma refers to the coexistence of true sleep and coma. The presence of spindles, vertex waves, and K complexes indicates relative integrity of the cerebral hemispheres, whereas failure of arousal is attributable to impairment of the reticular activating system in the brain stem. Head trauma is the most common cause of this condition, but other etiologies have been described including metabolic, infectious, and hypoxic alterations of the brain [97].

In the persistent vegetative state, patients remain unconscious because they lack awareness but can exhibit wakefulness and crude sleep cycles characterized by periodic immobility, changes in the respiratory pattern, and pinpoint pupils that do not react to light; the EEG might show abortive spindles and K complexes [98]. When not asleep, patients appear restless, pupillary reactivity returns, and the EEG shows a poorly developed, diffusely slow, and disorganized electrical pattern with increasingly intermixed faster rhythms. In akinetic mutism resulting from a lesion of the upper brain stem and paramedian thalamic areas, cyclical electrographic changes suggest alternations of sleep and arousal. Patients in persistent vegetative state with severe thalamic damage have loss of cognition, thought, emotion, and awareness but not of arousal mechanisms, suggesting preservation of extrathalamic pathways involved in arousal phenomena. A recent neuropathologic observation [99] supports the notion that the cerebral cortex can be directly activated by cholinergic, serotonergic, noradrenergic, and histaminergic arousal systems originating in the brain stem, basal forebrain, and hypothalamus that bypass the thalamus.

Headache and Sleep

Cluster headache, paroxysmal hemicrania, and chronic mixed headache are the types of primary headache most commonly seen during sleep. Secondary sleep-related headaches are observed in patients with intracranial hypertension caused by brain tumors, cerebral edema, obstructive hydrocephalus, and benign intracranial hypertension.

Migraine attacks characterized by premonitory manifestations, unilateral headache, photophobia, nausea, vomiting, and sometimes scintillating scotoma and other visual field defects, and transient neurologic deficits, can be provoked by sleep, although most patients find relief in sleep. Excessive sleep triggers migraine attacks in some sufferers. Patients with sleep terrors, somnambulism, and enuresis have a high incidence of migraine attacks [100].

Current theories of migraine suggest that neural stimuli originating in the hypothalamus or brain stem provoke changes in cerebral and extracranial circulation. Stimulation of the noradrenergic locus ceruleus decreases regional cerebral blood flow [101], whereas stimulation of the serotonergic raphe nuclei increases cerebral blood flow [102].

The trigeminovascular system that promotes vasodilatation and release of calcitonin gene-related peptide and substance P [103] has been implicated in the mechanism of migraines because calcitonin gene-related peptide is elevated in the jugular venous blood of migraine sufferers during the attack [104]. Serotonin is released from platelets during migraine headaches and 5-hydroxyindolacetic acid, the main metabolite of serotonin, is excreted in excess in the urine following a migraine attack [105]. Sumatriptan, an agonist of the $5-HT_1$ receptor found in cerebral arteries where it has an inhibitory effect, aborts the migraine headache, whereas methysergide, antagonist of the $5-HT_2$ receptor found primarily in temporal arteries where it has an excitatory effect, also terminates migraines. Serotonin, implicated in mechanisms of non-REM sleep, is a possible neurotransmitter bridge between migraine and sleep.

Proper sleep hygiene is paramount to aid in the prevention of sleep-related headaches in general and migraines in particular. Daily administration of preventive therapy is considered when migraine attacks occur more than twice a month or when they are prolonged and refractory to acute therapy. All effective headache medications interact with the serotonergic system and thus probably have some corollary effect on sleep. Patients with migraine should be instructed in a good sleep hygiene and should avoid such potential precipitating factors as sleep deprivation, excessive sleep, stress, trauma, and ingestion of certain idiosyncratic foods including alcohol.

Preventive treatment includes beta-blockers; calcium-channel blockers; serotonin receptor antagonists (methysergide, only for use in periods not to exceed 4 weeks) and $5-HT_2$ antagonists cyproheptadine and methylergonovine; antidepressants that interact with serotonergic receptors such as tricyclics, MAO inhibitors, and serotonin reuptake inhibitors (fluoxetine and sertraline); anticonvulsants, particularly in children with an abnormal EEG; and, nonsteroidal anti-inflammatory agents. Sumatriptan, a $5-HT_1$ selective agonist, administered via subcutaneous injection (6 mg, can repeat after 1 hour; limit two injections in 24 hours) is a new and effective abortive medication for migraine attacks. Other abortive medications include ergotamine derivatives, acetaminophen, corticosteroids, and nonsteroidal anti-inflammatory derivatives. Symptomatic treatment for migraine attacks includes nonsteroidal anti-inflammatory derivatives, mixed barbiturate and analgesics, antiemetics (promethazine, 50 mg), and in special circumstances of severity, meperidine (50 mg) or codeine sulfate (30 mg).

Cluster headaches are typically more intense than migraine attacks. They occur in 0.4% of men and 0.08% of women [106], being a predominantly nocturnal disorder; 75% of cluster headaches appear between 9:00 P.M. and 10:00 A.M. [107], and one-half of them are associated with REM sleep [108]. Patients complain of unilateral periorbital pain, lacrimation, rhinorrhea, stuffy nose, and redness of the cheek. Seventy-five percent of cluster headache attacks occur in sleep, predominantly although not exclusively in relation to REM stage; they can occur daily for several weeks, each attack lasting no more than 2 hours. Cluster headache shows a remarkable periodicity in its occurrence, suggesting a linkage to the circadian rhythm. The neurovascular hypothesis suggests excitation of autonomic fibers of the greater superficial petrosal nerve that would be responsible not only for lacrimation and conjunctival injection but also for edema of the wall of the internal carotid artery with pain and ipsilateral Horner's syndrome. Cluster headache and migraine can awaken the patient during the night, but episodes also occur during daytime hours. Cluster headaches are prevented with ergotamine derivatives at bedtime (1–3 mg sublingual), amitriptyline (150 mg daily), methysergide (6–8 mg daily), prednisone (40 mg daily) and lithium carbonate (initial dose, 250 mg). An acute attack can be terminated with inhalation of oxygen.

Paroxysmal hemicrania characterized by the occurrence of unilateral attacks of pain lasting 30 minutes or less is very regular in its appearance every night. It is commonly associated with REM sleep, and thus it has been called "REM sleep–locked headache" [109]. It responds remarkably well to indomethacin, 50 mg at bedtime or 25 mg three times per day. Cluster headaches are prevented with avoidance of triggering factors foremost of which is alcohol consumption. Sleeping late in the morning has been cited as a precipitating factor that should be avoided by patients with cluster headache.

Headache on awakening is a relatively nonspecific symptom observed in patients with systemic hypertension, depression, muscle-contraction headache, brain tumor, alcohol intoxication, and sinus inflammation. In the sleep apnea syndrome, patients often complain of diffuse headache in the morning, but the incidence is not related to the severity of the disease [110]. Thirty-six percent of patients with sleep apnea have headache on awakening [111]. Nocturnal hypoxemia, hypercapnia, and sleep deprivation can contribute, and typically the headaches disappear gradually within 30–60 minutes after the patient gets out of bed. Successful treatment of sleep apnea syndrome with nasal CPAP, Bi-PAP, or tracheostomy eliminates associated headaches on awakening.

Chronic headache patients with a high level of anxiety and depression have atypical sleep patterns including decreased sleep efficiency and frequent awakenings. Early morning awakenings and sleep fragmentation can also be the result of medication taken for chronic headache. In some epileptic patients, nocturnal headaches are postictal in origin and mark the occurrence of a sleep-related seizure.

The exploding head syndrome is characterized by flashing lights and sounds during the night that terrify patients [112]. Polysomnographic studies have shown that the attacks occur during awakenings, without evidence of epileptogenic discharges [113]. Reassurance and clomipramine (25 mg that can be increased gradually to 100 mg at bedtime) are curative in most instances. Hypnic headache is a benign headache disorder of the elderly, characterized by regular awakenings at a consistent time of night [114]. The headache is diffuse, lasts 30–60 minutes, and is sometimes associated with a dream.

Bruxism, or clenching and grinding of the teeth during sleep, occurs predominantly in stage 2 of sleep, although it has also been noted in REM sleep. Hundreds of events occurring during the night can lead to abnormal wear of the teeth, temporomandibular joint disorder, and jaw pain [115]. Some patients with bruxism develop or have associated muscle-contraction headaches. Episodes of bruxism can be reduced with stress management and are eliminated with diazepam, 5 mg given at bedtime, although the latter might not be a therapeutic option. A mouth guard or an intraoral occlusal splint [116] reduces the tooth-grinding activity.

Headaches occurring at night disturb patients and concern physicians. Nocturnal migraine and cluster headaches need to be differentiated from other acute severe headaches such as the ones associated with intracranial brain tumors, ruptured aneurysm, and meningitis. Patients with intracranial tumors can be awakened at night by headache that improves on getting out of bed. Headaches on awakening, as observed in sleep apnea patients, are also seen in patients with severe hypertension, depression, intracranial tumor, muscle-contraction headache, alcohol intoxication, and craniofacial sinus disease. Neurologic consultation, neuroimaging studies, and lumbar puncture are indicated in patients who exhibit the following causes for concern: first or worst-ever headache, associated neurologic symptoms or signs, progressive worsening of headache over days or weeks, intractable nausea or vomiting, associated fever, lethargy, confusion, and stiff neck. Lightning-type head pains that can be pinpointed with one finger by the patient are usually benign.

Polysomnography is indicated when sleep apnea syndrome is suspected. Patients with seizures or in whom the differential diagnosis requires exclusion of a seizure disorder should undergo polysomnography with the seizure protocol. In general, polysomnography fails to yield specific findings unless a headache occurs during the night of testing. Most often, it helps to resolve the diagnostic dilemma by excluding objective pathologies while reassuring patients and physicians.

Neurologic Disorders with Cognitive Impairment

Acute Confusional State: Delirium

Delirium is defined as a transient organic mental syndrome characterized by a global disorder of cognition and attention, a reduced level of consciousness, psychomotor agitation or retardation, and prominent sleep-wake cycle disturbance [117]. The elderly are especially prone to developing delirium as a consequence of a variety of predisposing and precipitating factors that include dementia, structural brain disease, medical illness, use of drugs, sensory deprivation, psychosocial factors, and sleep loss. Delirium is frequently superimposed on dementia, and 25% of individuals who are delirious have dementia [118].

Delirium is a transient disorder, usually lasting less than 1 month. Symptoms fluctuate during the daytime and reach a peak at night. The sleep-wake cycle disturbance is an essential disturbance of delirium. During daytime hours, patients are lethargic and tend to nap, whereas at night sleep is short, fragmented, and punctuated with hallucinations. Agitation, restlessness, and wakefulness dominate the nocturnal period in clear contrast with the subdued and drowsy state that prevails during the day. Cholinergic deficiency seems to be a major mechanism in delirium, and thus patients with Alzheimer's disease are particularly vulnerable. Treatment is directed to removal of the cause whenever possible, correction of homeostatic imbalances, and control of symptoms. Haloperidol in small doses (0.5–2.0 mg, two or three times per day) can be used as a tranquilizer, whereas benzodiazepines are the drugs of choice in withdrawal from alcohol and sedative-hypnotic agents. Medications with anticholinergic effects should be avoided.

Dementia and Sleep

Brain insufficiency, being a common occurrence in the elderly, contributes importantly to the deterioration of sleep-wake rhythms. Approximately 10% of the elderly population suffers cognitive decline of a pathologic nature. Dementia is a major contributing factor to the degradation of sleep in the elderly, and several studies have shown more sleep disruption in demented patients than in normal elderly control subjects. In turn, the loss of sleep-wake rhythms adds to mental decline.

The clinician's responsibility is to analyze all the detrimental factors contributing to sleep of poor quality in the demented patient in an effort to identify the ones that might be corrected, thus providing a window of opportunity to ameliorate the deficit.

Typical findings in demented patients are decreased sleep efficiency, increased stage 1, and excessive fragmentation by arousals and awakenings. Specific patterns of sleep-wake alteration have not as yet emerged in relation to the different varieties of dementia, and no studies have related sleep patterns to specific areas of brain pathology. However, suggestive signs and symptoms of sleep-wake alteration might be uncovered.

Alzheimer's Disease

One-half of demented elderly patients suffer Alzheimer's disease (AD), a condition of unknown cause that is associated with progressive degeneration of cortical and subcortical cerebral structures. Sleep in AD is characterized by profound disturbance of the sleep-wake rhythm, fragmentation of sleep, nocturnal insomnia, and nocturnal wandering. Disruption of the sleep-wake rhythm occurs early in the disease [119] and progresses as the disease advances [120]. Observation of the 24-hour sleep pattern in patients with AD reveals prominent fragmentation of the diurnal/nocturnal rhythm with frequent daytime napping, and prolonged nocturnal awakenings. Time in bed spent awake increases as the disease progresses from a mild to severe form. Patients with AD might spend up to 40% of their bedtime hours awake and 14% of their daytime hours asleep. The cognitive decline is paralleled by a decline in the percentage of time spent in SWS and REM sleep. These changes might represent a progressive loss of the neuronal mechanisms responsible for the generation of non-REM and REM sleep.

In AD, there is a profound disturbance of the central cholinergic system centered in the nucleus basalis of Meynert in the basal forebrain. This finding is of interest because the cholinergic system is heavily involved in the generation of REM sleep. Some studies have shown that REM sleep percentage is decreased in patients with AD [121], as one would expect in a cholinergic deficit. Others have found that REM sleep latency is prolonged in AD patients [122]. This finding is also of interest because if confirmed, it could help differentiate AD from pseudodementia caused by affective depression, in which the REM latency is shortened. However, in at least one study, REM sleep percentages were increased and REM latency shortened in a neuropathologically verified patient with AD [123]. Nonetheless, the evidence strongly suggests that neuronal degeneration underlies the profound disturbances in sleep and sleep-wake rhythms in AD, serving as a biological marker of its severity.

Sleep-related respiratory disturbances are not more abundant in AD patients than in elderly controls, but this association is important since sleep-related respiratory disturbances and oxygen desaturations could contribute to cognitive dysfunction [124]. Although few data are available, it appears that periodic limb movements are increased in AD. Central dopamine depletion and cholinergic deficit might contribute to this clinical phenomenon.

Sundown Syndrome

Many patients with AD exhibit "sundown" syndrome, a poorly understood clinical phenomenon characterized by nocturnal confusion, wandering, agitation, and in instances of advanced disease, delirium. In hospitals and nursing homes, the sundown syndrome might be manifested by loud vocalizations and vigorous attempts to remove restraints or climb over bed rails, an activity highly disturbing to other patients and nursing personnel. The syndrome has not been characterized with precision as yet. Some use the term *sundowning* when the disturbance appears in the early evening, whereas others include all events occurring during the period of darkness. Sundowning and delirium share many common features but are separate clinical phenomena. Sundowning is the description of a behavior and not a diagnosis, and refers to the nocturnal exacerbation of disruptive behaviors and agitation. Delirium, on the other hand, is an acute confusional state with transient global disorder of cognition and attention commonly aggravating the sundowning phenomenon. Sundowning has been related to REM sleep behavior syndrome, and to severity of nocturnal desaturations in patients with sleep apnea syndrome. Degeneration of the suprachiasmatic nucleus in AD with temperature rhythm disregulation might contribute importantly to the profound fragmentation of nocturnal sleep and development of the sundown syndrome [125].

Nocturnal agitation and wandering can be the most common causes of institutionalization of the elderly. Management includes improvement of sleep hygiene, restriction of daytime napping, exposure of patients to daytime sunlight, maintenance of a stable nocturnal environment, use of a bedroom soft light, and in instances of severe agitation, administration of haloperidol (0.5–1.0 mg at bedtime) or thioridazine (25 mg at bedtime).

Down's Syndrome

Patients with Down's syndrome who live long enough develop a degenerative form of dementia that neuropathologically is undistinguishable from AD [126]. Daytime sleepiness and disturbed nocturnal sleep are relatively early manifestations of this form of dementia. Other early symptoms are apathy, withdrawal from social interactions, and loss of self-help skills. Obstructive sleep apnea syndrome has been observed in patients with mongolism. A patient we studied had a very large tongue that was considered to be the probable cause of obstructive sleep apnea.

Fatal Familial Insomnia

In this familial disorder, there is loss of neuroendocrine regulation and of vegetative circadian rhythms [127]. Prominent manifestations are severe progressive insomnia with frequent awakenings, impotence, loss of libido, orthostatic sweating, lacrimation, salivation, and increased body temperature. Daytime stupor alternates with wakefulness. In the terminal stages of the disease, there is increasing agitation, confusion, disorientation, progressive stupor from which the patient is only transiently arousable, coma, and death. At autopsy, there is severe degeneration and gliosis of the anterior and dorsomedial nuclei of the thalamus. Fatal familial insomnia is a prion disease with distinctive genotypic features located in the short arm of human chromosome 20, with a mutation at codon 178 resulting in substitution of asparagine for aspartic acid in the prion protein [128].

Vascular Dementia and Sleep Disturbance

Nocturnal polygraphic studies in patients with multi-infarct dementia have shown sleep-related apneas and hypopneas [129]. These changes have led to the hypothesis that nocturnal hypoxemia could worsen the intellectual capacity of patients, causing hemodynamic changes, such as cardiac dysrhythmias, hypotension, and decreased cardiac index, that would perpetuate the risk of additional brain damage [130].

In patients with lacunar infarctions involving the tegmentum of the pons, particularly when associated with periventricular white matter damage, the syndrome of REM sleep without atonia and phantasmagorias (REM sleep behavior disorder) can develop [131]. Periventricular white matter lesions, also of an ischemic nature, contribute to the syndrome, perhaps by damaging a supratentorial system that modulates REM sleep–related muscle atonia and inhibits stereotypic behaviors originating in brain stem structures. Patients with ischemic subcortical leukoencephalopathy, or Binswanger's disease, can have an increased risk of developing REM sleep behavior disorder. Patients with Shy-Drager syndrome can develop REM sleep behavior disorder through nocturnal hypotensive episodes and brain stem ischemia.

References

1. Miguel de Cervantes Saavedra, Don Quixote of La Mancha. Translated by Walter Starkie. New York: The New American Library, 1964.
2. DSM-III Diagnostic Criteria for Major Depressive Episode. American Psychiatric Association: Diagnostic and Statistical Manual of Mental Disorders (3rd ed). Washington, DC: American Psychiatric Association, 1987.
3. Reynolds CF III, Shipley JE. Sleep in Depressive Disorders. In RE Hales, AJ Frances (eds), Psychiatry Update: The American Psychiatric Association Annual Review (Vol. 4). Washington, DC: American Psychiatric Press, 1985;341.
4. Cartwright RD. Rapid eye movement sleep characteristics during and after mood-disturbing events. Arch Gen Psychiatry 1983;40:197.
5. Schilgen B, Tolle R. Partial sleep deprivation as therapy for depression. Arch Gen Psychiatry 1980;37:267.
6. Buysse DJ, Reynolds CF, Kupfer DJ, et al. Electroencephalographic sleep in depressive pseudodementia. Arch Gen Psychiatry 1988;45:568.
7. Reynolds CF, Kupfer DJ, Taska LS, et al. EEG sleep in elderly depressed, demented and healthy subjects. Biol Psychiatry 1985;20:431.
8. Reynolds CF, Kupfer DJ, Hoch CC, et al. Two-year follow-up of elderly patients with mixed depression and dementia. J Am Geriatr Soc 1986;34:793.
9. Bliwise DL, Tinklenberg J, Yesavage JA, et al. REM latency in Alzheimer's disease. Biol Psychiatry 1989;25:320.
10. Zarcone V, Azumi K, Dement W, et al. REM phase deprivation and schizophrenia. II. Arch Gen Psychiatry 1975;32:1431.
11. Traub AC. Sleep stage deficits in chronic schizophrenia. Psychol Rep 1972;31:815.
12. Kaplan J, Dawson S, Vaughn T, et al. Effect of prolonged chlorpromazine administration on the sleep of chronic schizophrenics. Arch Gen Psychiatry 1974;31:62.
13. Zarcone VP. Sleep and Alcoholism. In M Chase, ED Weitzman (eds), Sleep Disorders: Basic and Clinical Research. Advances in Sleep Research. New York: Spectrum, 1983;6:319.
14. Diagnostic Classification Steering Committee. ICSD—International Classification of Sleep Disorders: Diagnostic and Coding Manual. Rochester, MN: American Sleep Disorders Association, 1990;111.
15. Verrier RL, Kirby DA. Sleep and cardiac arrhythmias. Ann N Y Acad Sci 1988;533:238.

16. Araki H, Koiwaya Y, Nakagaki D, et al. Diurnal distribution of ST segment elevation and related arrhythmias in patients with variant angina: A study by ambulatory ECG monitoring. Circulation 1983;67:995.

17. Muller JE, Stone PH, Turi ZG, et al, and the MILIs Study Group. Circadian variation in the frequency of onset of acute myocardial infarction. N Engl J Med 1985;313:1315.

18. Rocco MB, Barry J, Campbell S, et al. Circadian variation of transient myocardial ischemia in patients with coronary artery disease. Circulation 1987;75:395.

19. Guilleminault C, Pool P, Motta J, et al. Sinus arrest during REM sleep in young adults. N Engl J Med 1984;311:1006.

20. Guilleminault C, Cumminsky J, Motta J. Chronic obstructive airflow disease and sleep studies. Am Rev Resp Dis. 1980;122:397.

21. Douglas NJ. Asthma. In MH Kryger, T Roth, WC Dement (eds), Principles and Practice of Sleep Medicine (2nd ed). Philadelphia: Saunders, 1994;748.

22. Montplaisir J, Walsh J, Malo JL. Nocturnal asthma features of attacks, sleep and breathing patterns. Am Rev Respir Dis 1982;125:18.

23. Johnson LF, DeMeester TR. Evaluation of the effect of elevation of the head of the bed, bethanecol, and antacid foam tablets on gastroesophageal reflux. Dig Dis Sci 1981;26:673.

24. Kerr P, Shoenut P, Millar T, et al. Nasal CPAP reduces gastroesophageal reflux in obstructive sleep apnea syndrome. Chest 1992;101:1539.

25. Vitale GC, Cheadle WG, Patel B, et al. The effect of alcohol on nocturnal gastroesophageal reflux. JAMA 1987;258:2077.

26. Schwartz BA, Escande C. Sleeping sickness: Sleep study of a case. Electroencephalogr Clin Neurophysiol 1970;29:83.

27. Culebras A, Miller M. Absence of sleep-related elevations of growth hormone level in patients with stroke. Arch Neurol 1983;40:283.

28. Korner E, Flooh E, Reinhart B, et al. Sleep alterations in ischemic stroke. Eur Neurol 1986;25(Suppl 2):104.

29. Hachinski V, Mamelak M, Norris JW. Sleep Morphology and Prognosis in Acute Cerebrovascular Lesions. In JS Meyer, H Lechner, M Reivich (eds), Cerebral Vascular Disease. Amsterdam: Excerpta Medica, 1977.

30. Culebras A, Moore JT. Magnetic resonance findings in REM sleep behavior disorder. Neurology 1989;39:1519.

31. Marsh EE, Biller J, Adams HP, et al. Circadian variation in onset of acute ischemic stroke. Arch Neurol 1990;47:1178.

32. Marler JR, Price TR, Clark GL, et al. Morning increase in onset of ischemic stroke. Stroke 1989;20:473.

33. Argentino C, Toni D, Rasura M, et al. Circadian variation in the frequency of ischemic stroke. Stroke 1990;21:387.

34. Pasqualetti P, Natali G, Casale R, et al. Epidemiological chronorisk of stroke. Acta Neurol Scand 1990;81:71.

35. Muller JE, Tofler GH, Stone PH. Circadian variation and triggers of onset of acute cardiovascular disease. Circulation 1989;79:733.

36. Bruno A, Biller J, Adams HP, et al. Retinal infarction during sleep and wakefulness. Stroke 1990;21:1494.

37. Rivest R, Reiher J. Transient ischemic attacks triggered by symptomatic sleep apneas. Stroke 1987;18:293.

38. Palomaki H, Partinen M, Erkinjuntti T, et al. Snoring, sleep apnea and stroke. Neurology 1992;42(Suppl 6):75.
39. Ringler J, Basner RC, Shannon R, et al. Hypoxia alone does not explain blood pressure elevations after obstructive apneas. J Appl Physiol 1990;69:2143.
40. Ekbom KA. Restless legs: A clinical study. Acta Med Scand Suppl 1945;158:1.
41. Ekbom KA. Restless legs syndrome. Neurology 1960;10:868.
42. Symonds CP. Nocturnal myoclonus. J Neurol Neurosurg Psychiatry 1953;16:166.
43. Lugaresi E, Coccagna G, Montovani M, et al. Some periodic phenomena arising during drowsiness and sleep in man. Electroencephalogr Clin Neurophysiol 1972;32:701.
44. Coleman RM, Pollak CP, Weitzman ED. Periodic movements in sleep (nocturnal myoclonus): Relation to sleep disorders. Ann Neurol 1980;8:416.
45. Godbout R, Montplaisir J, Poirier G. Epidemiological data in familial restless legs syndrome. Sleep Research 1987;16:338.
46. Yokota T, Hirose K, Tanabe H, et al. Sleep-related periodic leg movements (nocturnal myoclonus) due to spinal cord lesion. J Neurol Sci 1991;104:13.
47. Coleman RM. Periodic Movements in Sleep (Nocturnal Myoclonus) and Restless Legs Syndrome. In C Guilleminault (ed), Sleeping and Waking Disorders: Indications and Techniques. Menlo Park, CA: Addison-Wesley, 1982;265.
48. Bixler EO. Nocturnal myoclonus and nocturnal myoclonic activity in the normal population. Res Comm Chem Pathol Pharmacol 1982;36:129.
49. Nausieda P, Weiner W, Kaplan L, et al. Sleep disruption and psychosis in chronic levodopa therapy. Clin Neuropharmacol 1982;5:183.
50. Mouret J. Differences in sleep in patients with Parkinson disease. Electroencephalogr Clin Neurophysiol 1975;39:653.
51. Emser W, Brenner M, Stober T, et al. Changes in nocturnal sleep in Huntington's and Parkinson's disease. J Neurol 1988;235:177.
52. Puca FM, Bricolo A, Turella G. Effect of L-DOPA and amantadine therapy on sleep spindles in parkinsonism. Electroencephalogr Clin Neurophysiol 1973;35:327.
53. Rodnitzky RL. Discussion. In Role of controlled-release formulation of carbidopa-levodopa in the treatment of Parkinson disease. William C. Koller, Supplement Editor. Neurology 1992;42:59
54. Koller WC, Silver DE, Lieberman A (ed). An algorithm for the management of Parkinson's disease. Neurology 1994;44(Suppl 10);43.
55. Castaigne P, Laplane D, Autret A, et al. Syndrome de Shy et Drager avec troubles du rhythme respiratoire et de la vigilance; à propos d'un cas anatomo-clinique. Rev Neurol (Paris) 1977;133:455.
56. Briskin JG, Lehrman KL, Guilleminault C. Shy-Drager Syndrome and Sleep Apnea. In C Guilleminault, W Dement (eds), Sleep Apnea Syndromes. New York: Alan R. Liss, 1978;317.
57. Chokroverty S. Sleep Apnea and Respiratory Disturbances in Multiple System Atrophy with Progressive Autonomic Failure (Shy-Drager Syn-

drome). In R Bannister (ed), Autonomic Failure (2nd ed). London: Oxford University Press, 1988;432.

58. Bannister R, Gibson W, Michaels L, et al. Laryngeal abductor paralysis in multiple system atrophy. Brain 1981;104:351.
59. Lockwood AH. Shy-Drager syndrome with abnormal respirations and antidiuretic hormone release. Arch Neurol 1976;33:292.
60. Sforza E, Zucconi M, Petronelli R, et al. REM sleep behavioral disorders. Eur Neurol 1988;28:295.
61. Culebras A. Update on disorders of sleep and the sleep-wake cycle. Psychiatr Clin North Am 1992;15:467.
62. Gross RA, Spehlmann R, Daniels JC. Sleep disturbances in progressive supranuclear palsy. Electroencephalogr Clin Neurophysiol 1978;45:16.
63. Aldrich MS, Foster NL, White RF, et al. Sleep abnormalities in progressive supranuclear palsy. Ann Neurol 1989;25:577.
64. Neil JF, Holzer BC, Spiker DG, et al. EEG sleep alterations in olivopontocerebellar degeneration. Neurology 1980;30:660.
65. Chokroverty S, Sachdeo R, Masdeu J. Autonomic dysfunction and sleep apnea in olivopontocerebellar degeneration. Arch Neurol 1984;41:926.
66. Salazar-Grueso EF, Rosemberg RS, Ross RP. Sleep apnea in olivopontocerebellar degeneration: Treatment with trazodone. Ann Neurol 1988;23:399.
67. Quero-Salva MA, Guilleminault C. Olivopontocerebellar degeneration, abnormal sleep, and REM sleep without atonia. Neurology 1986;36:576.
68. Osorio I, Daroff RB. Absence of REM and altered NREM sleep in patients with spinocerebellar degeneration and slow saccades. Ann Neurol 1980;7:277.
69. Katayama S, Hirano Y, Yoyama S. Nocturnal sudden death in cases with spinocerebellar degeneration. Sleep Research 1987;16:483.
70. Puca FM, Bricolo A, Turella G. Effect of L-DOPA and amantadine therapy on sleep spindles in parkinsonism. Electroencephalogr Clin Neurophysiol 1973;35:327.
71. Schrader H, Gotlibsen OB, Skomedal GN. Multiple sclerosis and narcolepsy/cataplexy in a monozygotic twin. Neurology 1980;30:105.
72. Langdon N, Welsh K, van Dam, et al. Genetic markers in narcolepsy. Lancet 1984;2:1178.
73. Marcadet A, Gebuhrer L, Betuel H, et al. DNA polymorphism related to HLA-DR2 Dw2 in patients with narcolepsy. Immunogenetics 1985;22:679.
74. Younger DS, Pedley TA, Thorpy MJ, et al. Multiple sclerosis and narcolepsy: Possible similar genetic susceptibility. Neurology 1991;41:447.
75. Leo GJ, Rao M, Bernardin L, et al. Sleep disturbances in multiple sclerosis. Neurology 1991;41(Suppl 1):320.
76. Clark CM, Fleming JA, Li D, et al. Sleep disturbance, depression, and lesion site in patients with multiple sclerosis. Arch Neurol 1992;49:641.
77. Berg O, Hanley J. Narcolepsy in two cases of multiple sclerosis. Acta Neurol Scand 1963;39:252.
78. Castaigne P, Escourolle R. Étude topographique des lésions anatomiques dans les hypersomnies. Rev Neurol 1967;116:547-584.
79. Rumbach L, Tongio MM, Warter JM, et al. Multiple sclerosis, sleep latencies and HLA antigens. J Neurol 1989;236:309.

80. Saunders J, Whitham R, Schaumann B, et al. Sleep disturbance, fatigue, and depression in multiple sclerosis. Neurology 1991;41(Suppl 1):320.

81. Potolicchio SJ, Calerón ET, Richert J, et al. Periodic limb movements of sleep and chronic fatigue in multiple sclerosis: Correlations between diagnosis and treatment. Neurology 1991;41(Suppl 1):320.

82. Desrouleaux R, Weinreb HJ. Fatigue in multiple sclerosis: Pilot trial with selegiline. Neurology 1991;41(Suppl 1):321.

83. Culebras A, Feldman RG, Merk FB. Cytoplasmic inclusion bodies within neurons of the thalamus in myotonic dystrophy. J Neurol Sci 1973;19:319.

84. Culebras A, Podolsky S, Leopold NA. Absence of sleep-related growth hormone elevations in myotonic dystrophy. Neurology 1977;27:165.

85. Hansotia P, Frens D. Hypersomnia associated with alveolar hypoventilation in myotonic dystrophy. Neurology 1981;31:1336.

86. Park YD, Radtke RA. Hypersomnolence in myotonic dystrophy. Neurology 1992;42(Suppl 3):352.

87. Culebras A. Thalamic Lesions and the Endocrine System. In C Guilleminault, E Lugaresi, P Montagna, et al (eds), Fatal Familial Insomnia: Inherited Prion Diseases, Sleep and the Thalamus. New York: Raven, 1994;87.

88. Mier-Jedrejowicz A, Brophy C, Green M. Respiratory muscle function in myasthenia gravis. Am Rev Respir Dis 1988;138:867.

89. Quera-Salvo MA, Guilleminault C, Chevret S, et al. Breathing disorders during sleep in myasthenia gravis. Ann Neurol 1992;31:86.

90. Aldrich MS, Naylor MW. Narcolepsy associated with lesions of the diencephalon. Neurology 1989;39:1505.

91. Chokroverty S. Sleep, Breathing and Neurological Disorders. In S Chokroverty (ed), Sleep Disorders Medicine. Boston: Butterworth, 1994;307.

92. Cooper R, Hulme A. Changes of the EEG, intracranial pressure and other variables during sleep in patients with intracranial lesions. Electroencephalogr Clin Neurophysiol 1969;27:12.

93. Chatrian GE, White LE, Daly D. Electroencephalic patterns resembling those of sleep in certain comatose states after injuries to the head. Electroencephalogr Clin Neurophysiol 1963;15:272.

94. Harada M, Minami R, Hattori E, et al. Sleep in brain damaged patients; an all-night study of 105 cases. Kumamoto Med J 1976;29:110.

95. Prigatano GP, Stahl ML, Orr WC, et al. Sleep and dreaming disturbances in closed head injury patients. J Neurol Neurosurg Psychiatry 1982;45:78.

96. Parkes JD. The Anatomical and Physiological Basis of the Sleep-Wake Cycle. In JD Parkes (ed), Sleep and Its Disorders. London: Saunders, 1985;80.

97. Nogueira de Melo A, Krauss GL, Niedermeyer E. Spindle coma: observations and thoughts. Clin Electroencephalogr 1990;21:151.

98. Danze F, Brule JF, Haddad K. Chronic vegetative state after severe head injury: clinical study, electrophysiological investigations and CT scan in 15 cases. Neurosurg Rev 1989;12(Suppl):477.

99. Kinney HC, Korein J, Panigrahy A, et al. Neuropathological findings in the brain of Karen Ann Quinlan. N Engl J Med 1994;330:1469.

100. Dexter JD. The relationship between disorders of arousal from sleep and migraine. Headache 1986;26:322.

101. Lance JW, Lambert GA, Goadsby PJ, et al. Brain stem influences on the cephalic circulation: Experimental data from cat and monkey of relevance to the mechanisms of migraine. Headache 1983;23:258.

102. Goadsby PJ, Lance JW. Brain Stem Effects on Intra- and Extra-Cerebral Circulations. Relation to Migraine and Cluster Headache. In J Olesen, L Edvinsson (eds), Basic Mechanisms of Headache. Amsterdam: Elsevier, 1988;413.

103. Moskowitz MA, Buzzi MG, Linnik M, et al. Pain mechanisms underlying vascular headaches: Progress report. Rev Neurol 1989;145:181.

104. Goadsby PJ, Edvinsson L, Ekman R. Vasoactive peptide release in the extracerebral circulation of humans during migraine headache. Ann Neurol 1990;28:183.

105. Sicuteri F, Testi A, Anselmi B. Biomedical investigations in headache: Increase in hydroxiindoleacetic acid excretion during migraine attacks. Int Arch Allergy Immunol 1961;19:55.

106. Kudrow L. Cluster Headache: Mechanisms and Management. Oxford: Oxford University Press, 1980.

107. Russell D. Cluster headache: Severity and temporal profile of attacks and patient activity prior to and during attacks. Cephalalgia 1981;1:209.

108. Pfaffenrath V, Pollman W, Ruther E, et al. Onset of nocturnal attacks of chronic cluster headache in relation to sleep stages. Acta Neurol Scand 1986;73:403.

109. Kayed K, Goadtlibsen OB, Sjaastad O. Chronic paroxysmal hemicrania. IV. "REM sleep locked" nocturnal headache attacks. Sleep 1978;1:91.

110. Aldrich MS, Chauncey JB. Are morning headaches part of obstructive sleep apnea syndrome? Arch Intern Med 1990;150:1265.

111. Guilleminault C, Hold J, Mitler MM. Clinical Overview of the Sleep Apnea Syndromes. In C Guilleminault, WC Dement (eds), Sleep Apnea Syndromes. New York: Alan R. Liss Inc., 1978;1.

112. Pearce JMS. Exploding head syndrome. Lancet 1988;ii:270.

113. Sachs C, Svanborg E. The exploding head syndrome: Polysomnographic recordings and therapeutic suggestions. Sleep 1991;14:263.

114. Raskin NH. The hypnic headache syndrome. Headache 1988;28:534.

115. Rugh JD, Harlan J. Nocturnal Bruxism and Temporo-Mandibular Disorders. In J Jankovic, E Tolosa (eds), Advances in Neurology (Vol. 49): Facial Dyskinesias. New York: Raven, 1988.

116. Holmgren K, Sheikholeslam A, Riise C. Effect of full arch maxillary occlusal splint on parafunctional activity during sleep in patients with nocturnal bruxism and signs and symptoms of craniomandibular disorders. J Prosthet Dent 1993;69:293.

117. Lipowski ZJ. Delirium in the elderly patient. N Engl J Med 1989;320:578.

118. Allen SR, Seiler WO, Ståhelin HB, et al. Seventy-two hour polygraphic and behavioral recordings of wakefulness and sleep in a hospital geriatric unit: Comparison between demented and nondemented patients. Sleep 1987;10:143.

119. Prinz PN, Vitaliano P, Vitiello M, et al. EEG and mental function changes in mild, moderate and severe senile dementia of the Alzheimer's type. Neurol Aging 1982;3:361.

120. Vitiello MV, Bliwise DL, Prinz PN. Sleep in Alzheimer's disease and the sundown syndrome. Neurology 1992;42(Suppl 6):83.

121. Reynolds CF, Kupfer DJ, Hoch CC, et al. Sleep deprivation as a probe in the elderly. Arch Gen Psychiatry 1987;44:982.

122. Vitiello MV, Bokan JA, Kukull WA, et al. REM sleep measures of Alzheimer's-type dementia patients and optimally healthy aged individuals. Biol Psychiatry 1984;19:721.

123. Bliwise DL, Nino-Murcia G, Forno LS, et al. Abundant REM sleep in a patient with Alzheimer's disease. Neurology 1990;40:1281.

124. Bliwise DL, Yesavage JA, Tinklenberg JR, et al. Sleep apnea in Alzheimer's disease. Neurobiol Aging 1989;10:343.

125. Evans LK. Sundown syndrome in institutionalized elderly. J Am Geriatr Soc 1987;35:101.

126. Evenhuis HM. The natural history of dementia in Down syndrome. Arch Neurol 1990;47:263.

127. Lugaresi E, Medori R, Montagna P, et al. Fatal familial insomnia and dysautonomia with selective degeneration of thalamic nuclei. N Engl J Med 1986;315:997.

128. Gambetti P, Medori R, Manetto V, et al. Fatal Familial Insomnia: A Prion Disease with Distinctive Histopathological and Genotypic Features. In C Guilleminault, E Lugaresi, P Montagna, et al (eds), Fatal Familial Insomnia: Inherited Prion Diseases, Sleep, and the Thalamus. New York: Raven, 1994;27.

129. Erkinjuntti T, Partinen M, Sulkava T, et al. Sleep apnea in multiinfarct dementia and Alzheimer's disease. Sleep 1987;10:419.

130. Palomaki H, Partinen M, Erkinjuntti T, et al. Snoring, sleep apnea syndrome, and stroke. Neurology 1992;42(Suppl 6):75.

131. Culebras A. Neuroanatomic and neurologic correlates of sleep disturbances. Neurology 1992;42(Suppl 6):19.

9

Disorders of the Circadian Rhythm

Below lay stretched the boundless Universe!
There, far as the remotest line
That limits swift imagination's flight,
Unending orbs mingled in mazy motion,
    Immutably fulfilling
    Eternal Nature's law.
    Above, below, around,
    The circling systems formed
A wilderness of harmony.

Percy Bysshe Shelley
Demon of the World [1]

Since antiquity, humans have been aware of the behavioral regularity of living beings. Plants such as the heliotrope open their leaves to receive the light of day and close them at night; the salmon returns at a specific time of the year to the river of its birth to lay its eggs; birds migrate to the mandates of the seasons; the squirrel hoards nuts in the fall; and the marmot hibernates during the winter. These behaviors respond to external markers as obvious as day and night, winter and summer, and the tides of the ocean. Intuitively, it is easy to accept without questions their objective and remain content with their familiar regularity. However, in the fifteenth century, Dortous de Mairan, a

French scientist, noted in what has become a classic observation that if the heliotrope were maintained in complete darkness, the leaves would open and close with the same regularity as if light and obscurity had fallen on them. In the absence of a stimulus-action binomial equation one had to hypothesize the existence of an internal force marking periodic behavior, perhaps a biological clock, sufficient and autonomous but capable of linking biological mechanisms with the outside world.

For the next 250 years, little progress was made in the understanding of biological rhythms, until 1960 when a major conference on chronobiology took place in Cold Springs Harbor, New York. It became clear that biological rhythms dictate many functions of life, not only in plants but also in the animal world. An observation concerning humans added another basic principle to the natural periodic behavior of living beings. Jurgen Aschoff, director of the Max Planck Institute for Behavioral Physiology in Bavaria, studied subjects in total isolation from external markers [2]. He remodeled a bunker and turned it into living quarters isolated from the external world except for a dumb-waiter. The subjects of his experiments were able to exist in this environment for many weeks without a clue to the time of day, the weather conditions, or other markers of the external environment. Motor activity traced by sensors on the floor and the record of rectal temperatures indicated the evolutions of the person. As time progressed, the subject went to sleep on the average 1 hour later every day, de facto extending the subject's day by 1 hour; days lasted 25 hours instead of the conventional 24 hours. On the sixteenth day of the experiment, the sleep-wake cycle had shifted 12 hours, and on the twenty-fifth day, the subject had sleep-phased only 24 times; the subject had lived through only 24 days. The sleep-wake ratio remained constant at approximately two-thirds to one-third, reflecting an extension of daytime hours and also of nocturnal sleep.

Detailed analysis of sleep stages has shown that humans in isolation distribute REM sleep more evenly throughout the night while reducing the REM sleep latency, a pattern reminiscent of that seen in narcolepsy. By the end of several months, individuals have the subjective impression of having spent less time in isolation than they actually did. Some individuals extend their days longer than others, and each person appears to have a different cycle that is constant from day to day. The human experiments have demonstrated the existence of a remarkably stable and well-organized internal chronology independent of the timing set by geocosmic markers, suggesting the existence of an autonomous internal clock responsible for orchestrating biological rhythms. When exposed to the exterior, the internal clock shows the ability to couple once again with external markers and to synchronize biological mechanisms to the natural evolutions of day and night, winter and summer, and other geo-cosmic phenomena.

Subsequent studies were devised to investigate the precise location of the internal biological clock, the exact nature of the natural phe-nomena influencing biological rhythms, and the clinical implications of these experiments.

Chronobiology

All living beings show periodicity of functions in cycles of varying length and amplitude. Physiologic cycles can be coupled with internal or external markers that are called *zeitgebers*, a German term meaning marker of time. Many cycles are tied to the unending geocosmic cycle of day and night, recurring periodically every 24 hours in periods that are called circadian—near 24 hours. Subsidiary cycles, like entrained cogwheels, occur in compliance with the primary circadian sleep-wake rhythm, and these in turn trigger other cycles in a chain of events that touches virtually every aspect of the biological economy.

Circadian rhythms have been extensively investigated in many liv-ing beings to identify their source and biological purpose. The rest-activity behavior of rodents lends itself well to this objective. It can be studied by placing sensors on the bottom of the cage and recording graphs over a period of many days (Figure 9-1, left). In the figure, hor-izontal bars indicate activity, and silence indicates rest. The graphs show clusters of horizontal bars where motor activity was prominent followed by silence where the animal was at rest. Since the rat is a noc-turnal animal, much of the activity occurs in darkness while the resting behavior coincides with times when the light is on. Modification of the light-dark conditions changes the rest-activity cycle, strongly suggest-ing that light or its absence is the specific stimulus that controls the mechanisms orchestrating the motor rhythm of the rat. When the rat is maintained in total darkness and in a soundproof environment, the cir-cadian rhythm tends to drift to longer cycles, just as it does in humans in the bunker experiment of free-running conditions.

Stephan and Zucker [4] performed experiments in the early 1970s in rats to locate the brain center controlling biological rhythms. These authors reported that lesions of the interbrain or hypothalamus of the rat eliminated the rest-activity cycle of the animal along with the peri-

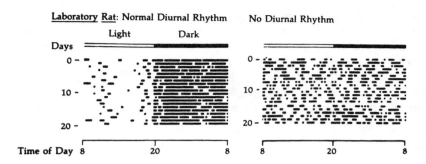

Figure 9-1. *The rest-activity cycle of the rat before and after the ablation of the interbrain. Horizontal bars indicate activity, and interruptions indicate rest. On the left, normal circadian rhythm; on the right, random distribution of rest-activity following ablation of controlling suprachiasmatic nuclei in the interbrain. (Reprinted with permission from A Borbély. Secrets of Sleep. New York: Basic Books, 1986;183.)*

odic drinking behavior that thereafter became chaotic and random throughout the day. The area of the hypothalamus critical for this behavior was localized to a small cluster of hypothalamic cells situated above the optic chiasm and thus called the suprachiasmatic nucleus (SCN). When the SCN was obliterated bilaterally, the rats continued to move and drink, but the periodicity of the functions organized in accordance to the light-dark cycles or on a free-running basis disappeared entirely; they became erratic and failed to show any vestiges of rhythmicity (Figure 9-1, right). Non-REM and REM sleep were still generated, but their occurrence failed to show periodicity or coupling with external cues.

SCN of the anterior hypothalamus is the principal pacemaker of the circadian system. SCN rhythmicity is intrinsically generated as shown by isolation studies and by recording of SCN activity in vitro. SCN activity can be entrained with light stimuli and can be modified with electrical stimulation of SCN neurons with resetting of circadian rhythms and induction of phase shifts [5]. Afferent projections to the SCN come primarily from retinal photoreceptors, and also from brain stem serotonergic raphe nuclei, cholinergic forebrain neurons, and pedunculopontine tegmental nuclei. Efferent projections from the SCN reach the area ventral to the paraventricular nucleus in the hypothalamus by way of a dorsal pathway that appears to be the major efferent tract. From the paraventricular nucleus, efferents reach secondarily many other areas of influence of the SCN, including the pineal gland. Other efferent projections terminate in the preoptic area of the hypothalamus and in the anterior hypothalamic area.

Using autoradiographic techniques, Moore and Lenn [6] demonstrated neural projections linking the retina to the SCN that were capable of conveying direct photic information to the suprachiasmatic pacemaker. Thus, photic entrainment is achieved through the mediation of retinal photoreceptors. This system is unique to mammals since birds and lizards have encephalic photoreceptors that permit direct photic entrainment. Transection of the retinohypothalamic tract or elimination of the retinal photoreceptors by enucleation abolishes circadian rhythms, showing the critical role of this projection in synchronizing the circadian pacemaker with the light-dark cycle. Congenitally blind mammals do not respond to light-dark cycles. Further studies have shown that light intensity, duration of the light pulse, light spectrum, and clock time of exposure determine the characteristics of the phase shift [7]. There are segments of the 24-hour cycle during which the circadian system is highly responsive to light and other times when it appears to be resistant. Exposure to light in the evening phase-delays, or lengthens, the cycle, whereas exposure in the early morning causes a phase-advance or shortening. However, during the middle of the day, there is no circadian response to light cues.

Excitatory amino acids appear to mediate transmitter responses in the retinohypothalamic tract, but the actual amino acid has not been identified yet. Various active peptides and neurotransmitters have been identified in SCN cells, including vasoactive intestinal neuropeptide, peptide histidine isoleucine, and gastrin-releasing peptide. A reduction in SCN volume has been observed with progressive age, and in humans, a shrinkage of the SCN has been identified in senile dementia, perhaps in connection with the major circadian dysrhythmia observed in this condition [8]. In homosexual men, the SCN is twice the size it is in the reference study group, an observation that is difficult to interpret [9].

Another pathway, the geniculohypothalamic tract, links the lateral geniculate body of the thalamus with the SCN. This pathway mediates nonphotic entrainment but might also respond to photic stimuli through indirect routes.

Hormones have a modulatory influence on the structures controlling circadian rhythms. Studies in rats have shown that the estrous cycle has an important influence on daily motor activity, whereas ovariectomy abolishes the effect, suggesting that estradiol exerts a strong influence. In male animals, steroids modulate circadian timing of motor activity. Castration and injection of male hormones both influence free-running rhythm periods. Seasonal variations in motor activity might be related to gonadal fluctuations in function.

Melatonin, secreted by the pineal gland, is the hormone that exerts the most potent regulatory effect on the SCN rhythm independently of the sleep-wake rhythm. It might act by synchronizing uncoupled rhythms. Light inhibits melatonin secretion, whereas darkness promotes its secretion, indicating that light stimuli relayed via the retino-hypothalamic tract and the SCN play a critical role in the photoendocrine reflex (Figure 9-2). Melatonin reduces sleep latency and promotes sleep; its deficiency may have an important role in the development of insomnia among elderly people in whom controlled-release melatonin replacement therapy improves sleep quality [11]. In the summer when days are longer, melatonin secretion is reduced; westbound flights, which prolong daylight hours, also reduce melatonin secretion, and the adjustment can take up to 11 days. The SCN is the target organ for melatonin not only in adults but also in the fetus where most of the hormone appears concentrated. Pinealectomy reduces the coupling effect among SCN oscillators and the amplitude of their oscillations, de facto reducing the leadership role of the SCN pacemaker. Melatonin secretion is increased in individuals with pinealoma and appears to be free-running in the blind. Given the biological effects of melatonin, it is not surprising that this hormone has been sought for therapeutic actions. It has been proposed that substances inhibiting the production of melatonin, including bright light, might be useful for the alleviation of the lethargy that overcomes the traveler in the jet lag syndrome or to reverse the somnolence in the seasonal affective disorder (SAD) syndrome.

The earliest presence of SCN in humans occurs during the eighteenth week of gestation [12]. It is unclear whether the SCN plays an executive autonomous role before birth, since there is evidence that circadian rhythms present in the fetus might be driven by the mother. Melatonin, which crosses the placental barrier, mediates the entrainment of the fetal SCN to the circadian rhythm of the mother. After birth, entrainment to external factors, mainly light, occurs gradually over the first weeks and months of postnatal development. This change is expressed by the eventual consolidation of sleep to the nocturnal period [13] (Figure 9-3). The daily sleep-wake cycle is one of the most prominent manifestations of circadian rhythmicity, and its correct development in

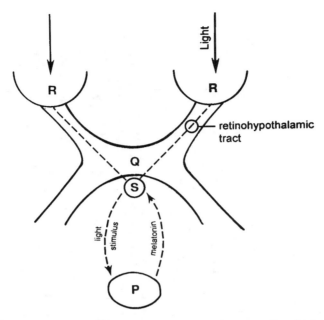

Figure 9-2. *The retinohypothalamic tract and photoendocrine reflex. Light striking on the retina generates stimuli that reach the suprachiasmatic nucleus (SCN) through the retinohypothalamic tract, independently of the visual pathways. A photoendocrine reflex originating in the SCN controls melatonin secretion by the pineal gland. Light inhibits and darkness stimulates melatonin secretion. R = retina; Q = optic chiasm; S = suprachiasmatic nucleus; P = pineal gland. (Reprinted with permission from A Culebras. Stroke and sleep disorders. In M Fisher, J Bogousslavsky [eds], Current Review of Cerebrovascular Disease. Philadelphia: Current Medicine, 1996.)*

compliance with expected parameters over the first few months of life suggests a healthy integrated biological system.

Ideally, all cogs of the circadian wheel should rotate in perfect harmony and synchronization. However, there is evidence that uncoupling can occur and that some rhythms can rotate independently of others. There are physiologic functions that oscillate with a rather rigid periodicity of circa 24 hours and resist abrupt changes. Such is the case with core body temperature, REM sleep, and cortisol secretion; other functions, such as slow wave sleep (SWS), are more malleable and can shift with relative ease to longer cycles dissociated from the main cir-

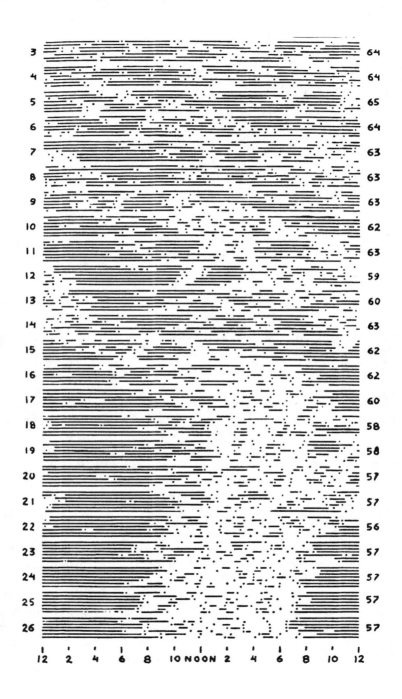

cadian rhythm. Desynchronization is evident in situations such as jet lag and shift work, and in conditions, such as narcolepsy, in which REM sleep is dissociated from non-REM sleep.

The circadian rhythm exhibits variability in response to stimuli, depending on the time when the stimulus is applied. This phenomenon was discovered by DeCoursey [14] when testing identical stimuli in free-running animals at different times of the circadian cycle and observing the phase shifts. DeCoursey constructed a phase-response curve that was later recognized as a universal property of circadian rhythmicity with clinical applicability. The basic principles of the phase-response curve are as follows:

1. Stimuli applied early in the night produce a phase-delay shift.

2. Stimuli late in the night cause a phase-advance shift.

3. The system is not responsive during most of the day.

Sleep tends to occur in the late evening when the lights are dim and the core body temperature begins to decline (Chapter 2). During sleep, most hormones show important individual patterns of secretion that modify the homeostasis of body systems. Two distinct states of being dominate brain activity during sleep: (1) non-REM sleep associated with quiescence, repose, low body temperature, and hypometabolism, and (2) REM sleep, a state of neural instability, cortical readiness, and high cerebral activity that recurs at 90-minute intervals and dominates the second half of the night. Uncoupling of these two states of being from each other and from other circadian rhythms normally linked to them leads to poorly understood pathology that reduces the quality of both the awake and sleep states.

◀ **Figure 9-3.**   *Sleep, wakefulness, and feeding in an infant from the 11th to the 182nd day of life. Each line represents a calendar day. Horizontal bars indicate sleep periods, interruptions indicate wakefulness, and dots represent feedings. A double blank space separates weeks, which are indicated with the numbers on the left. Percentage of sleep time is indicated on the right. Bottom figures indicate time of day in 2-hour intervals. Note the progressive consolidation of sleep time to the nocturnal period. (Reprinted with permission from N Kleitman, TG Engelmann. Sleep characteristics of infants. J Appl Physiol 1953;6:269.)*

Hormonal Circadian Rhythms

Cortisol

Cortisol secretion, a marker of adrenocorticotropic hormone release, occurs during the night, peaking in the early morning. It declines during daytime hours, reaching a nadir shortly before the individual retires to bed. Cortisol secretion is very resistant to change and persists even if sleep is eliminated, such as in coma, or delayed, as in the jet lag syndrome.

Growth Hormone

The largest bursts of growth hormone (GH) secretion, representing approximately 80% of the 24-hour secretion, occur in normal individuals at night in association with the first cycle of SWS [15], approximately 60 minutes after falling asleep. If sleep onset is delayed, the nocturnal increase of GH is also delayed. Not all episodes of SWS are accompanied by GH secretion, and dissociations can occur, suggesting that both events are temporally related but not strictly interdependent. The sleep-related rise of GH is resistant to peripheral metabolic variations and fails to respond to pharmacologic interventions that modify the waking state response. SWS-related GH secretion increases with vigorous exercise the evening before [16] (Figure 9-4), is larger in children than in adults, and tends to disappear in the elderly [17]. The evidence suggests that SWS-related GH secretion is regulated by neural pathways that are different from the ones intervening in the wake-state release [18] and independent of metabolic influences. It has been proposed that a subcortical center is responsible for integrating SWS, a cortical event, with the hypothalamic-pituitary function of GH release and that the dorsomedial nucleus of the thalamus could play such a role [19]. In acromegaly, sleep-related peaks of GH are abolished and episodic secretion is lost. Sleep deprivation in children can cause disruption of sleep-related GH release with ominous consequences for normal growth. In fact, emotionally deprived children with poor sleep tend to be of short stature [20]. Sleep laboratory investigation of patients with myotonic dystrophy and others with vascular or surgical lesions involving the dorsomedial nucleus of the thalamus or thalamocortical connections, or both, shows paucity or loss of plasma GH increases that normally are associated with the slow wave phase of sleep. Patients with frontal leucotomy, presumably with retrograde

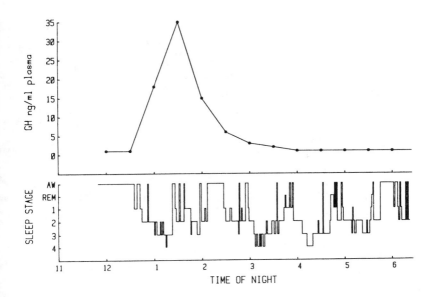

Figure 9-4. *A graph showing slow wave sleep (SWS)-associated growth hormone (GH) release in a 40-year-old athlete. There is a large burst of GH release in relation to the first cycle of SWS. (Reprinted with permission from A Culebras. La Medicina del Sueño. Barcelona, Spain: Editorial Áncora, 1994.)*

degeneration of thalamic parvocellular dorsomedial nuclei, exhibit erratic elevations of plasma GH during the night. The dorsomedial nucleus of the thalamus is anatomically connected with suprahypothalamic centers involved with neuroendocrine regulation, and with the hypothalamus (Figure 9-5). Thus, the clinical and experimental evidence indicates that the dorsomedial nucleus of the thalamus intervenes in the neuroendocrine regulation of sleep-associated GH secretion [21]. SWS-related GH release is a biological phenomenon of unknown significance unique to humans and to the higher primates, perhaps linked to what is also unique to humans, the large size of the brain.

Prolactin

In normal individuals, prolactin secretion begins within 60 minutes of falling asleep and continues to increase during the night, reaching peak

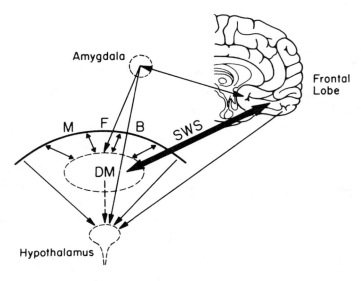

Figure 9-5. *Hypothetical neural circuitry involved in nocturnal growth hormone (GH) release. The dorsomedial nucleus of the thalamus is anatomically connected with suprahypothalamic centers related to neuroendocrine regulation, and with the hypothalamus. Clinical and experimental evidence indicates that the dorsomedial nucleus modulates the neuroendocrine regulation of slow wave sleep-associated GH secretion. (DM = dorsomedial nucleus; MFB = medial forebrain bundle; SWS = slow wave phase of sleep.)*

values between 5:00 and 7:00 A.M. [22]. It is not specifically related to any of the stages of sleep. The brain's predominant effect on prolactin secretion is inhibitory, and the major hypothalamic mechanism for the control of prolactin is also inhibitory, mediated by dopaminergic receptors. The mechanism of nocturnal release of prolactin is probably independent of neural pathways involved in the release of GH.

Other Hormones

Sleep inhibits thyroid-stimulating hormone release. Circadian patterns of thyroid stimulating hormone show high levels in the evening before sleep onset. Sleep deprivation has no effect on thyroid-stimulating hormone secretion. Gonadotrophins (luteinizing hormone and testosterone) are released during the day and the night in pulses that vary with age. At puberty, luteinizing hormone (LH) is released during the night in large amounts both in girls and in boys. In women, LH secretion varies with the menstrual cycle but tends to surge during the late hours of sleep, whereas in men, LH is secreted in random peaks both during the day and the night. Testosterone secretion in men occurs primarily during sleep and tends to peak by the end of the night. It has been suggested that this peak is the result of increased testicular blood flow by the end of the night [23], perhaps in relation to REM sleep.

Sleep-related hormonal secretion depends on neuroendocrine systems that interface with neurogenic mechanisms responsible for sleep generation. Little is known about these mechanisms in humans, since it appears that there is great interspecies variation. Brain and cerebrospinal fluid (CSF) serotonin increase during nocturnal sleep [24], as much as 20 times in the rhesus monkey, has been proposed as a mediator. In fact, when serotonin is administered during daytime waking hours, a surge in plasma and CSF prolactin levels is observed [25]. The endorphin system might be responsible for driving or at least modulating some of the mechanisms responsible for GH secretion through its influence on intermediary hypophyseal and hypothalamic factors that release GH [26]. The endorphin system is primarily concentrated in the hypothalamic area and several extrahypothalamic sites, one of which is the thalamic dorsomedial nucleus.

Chronobiopathology

The most fundamental alteration in chronobiopathology is a dissociation between the internal circadian pacemaker and conventional time, giving rise to overwhelming sleepiness in daytime hours, contrasting with overflowing wakefulness during the night. The causes might be extrinsic, as in jet lag, or intrinsic. In turn, the intrinsic causes can be categorized as primary, as in the delayed sleep phase syndrome, or secondary to a neurologic disorder, as in the sundown syndrome of Alzheimer's disease.

Jet Lag Syndrome

Increasing transcontinental travel aboard jet aircraft has brought to the fore the syndrome of jet lag. The condition appears when several time zones are crossed over in an eastward or westward direction. It does not occur in travel bound north or south. The manifestations of the jet lag syndrome include sleep fragmentation by awakenings, poor quality nonrestorative sleep, difficulty maintaining sleep, daytime fatigue, apathy, depression, moodiness, and malaise along with somatic complaints such as gastrointestinal changes, muscle aches, and headaches [27]. Some travelers complain of poor psychomotor coordination, decreased cognitive performance, and memory disturbance. The intensity of the manifestations is highly idiosyncratic, although as a general rule travelers past the age of 50 years suffer more intense complaints that take longer to dissipate.

Jet lag is the consequence of a misalignment of internal circadian rhythm drives with external cues. The traveler's circadian rhythms remain set to the external cues of the point of departure, although a shift to coincide with the external cues of the point of destination is almost always achieved if enough time is allowed. The intensity of the manifestations depends on the distance traveled, direction of flight, and idiosyncratic factors that determine the circadian rhythm inertia for each individual. Eastward flights shorten the day by as many hours as time zone changes are crossed, so that recovery is accomplished by a phase advance. In other words, it is the equivalent of going to bed very early in the day. Westward flights lengthen the day by as many hours as time zone changes, so that the effect resembles going to bed very late, an action that most people accomplish more easily if they are young. When traveling west, the symptoms of jet lag are milder, and the recovery is faster. Research into jet lag has confirmed that the internal circadian rhythm accepts a lengthening of its approximately 24-hour period more easily than a shortening. The rate of recovery, which is dependent on the direction of flight, is 1 hour per day in westward passengers, and 1.5 hours per day in eastward passengers.

Desynchronization of circadian internal rhythms can also play a role. Researchers have described almost 100 rhythms that respond to the mandates of the internal biological clock in the SCN of the hypothalamus. The disturbance caused by an abrupt misalignment with the external world can release some rhythms from the tight internal schedule that binds them all together, contributing to somatic manifestations. Some rhythms have more inertia than others and take longer to recover their synchrony. There is evidence that some rhythms adjust by phase advance, whereas others recover by phase delay.

Temperature regulation is one of the most important and independent rhythms. It exhibits a trough at approximately 1:00 A.M. and a peak at 8:00 P.M., with a difference of 0.80°C between both levels. The body temperature begins to decline at 9:00 P.M. and continues to descend during the night until the trough is reached. Shortly thereafter, it climbs to near peak levels at 9:00 A.M. and remains high during daytime hours

Table 9-1.   Jet Lag Syndrome Countermeasures

Eastward flights

Retire to bed and get up 30 minutes *earlier* each day for 5 days before flight

Westward flights

Retire to bed and get up 30 minutes *later* each day for 5 days before flight

On board all flights

a. Drink only small amounts of alcoholic beverages
b. Avoid regular coffee and caffeine-containing beverages
c. Reset watch to time of point of arrival
d. Sleep only if it falls within new schedule

On arrival, first day

a. Stay awake in accordance with new schedule
b. Take a short nap, 1 hour maximum, only if necessary
c. Expose yourself to bright daylight
d. Avoid staying in the hotel room during daytime hours
e. Follow new meal schedules
f. Avoid alcohol and caffeine-containing beverages
g. Initiate new dosage schedule for chronic medications
h. Do not drive a vehicle
i. Retire to bed at conventional time, i.e., 22:00 hours
j. Triazolam, 0.125 mg, or zolpidem, 5 mg, at bedtime to consolidate
sleep, if no exclusions apply

until the peak is reached at 8:00 P.M. Some authors claim that sleep is facilitated when the temperature begins to descend in late evening hours. The interesting point is that under jet lag conditions, temperature continues its rhythm independent of sleep-wake cycles and external cues, although showing a slow drift that can last several days before the point of alignment is reached [27].

Individual differences are also important. In a conventional eastward 6–8 hour time zone travel to Europe, some passengers will be free of complaints, most will recover within 2–6 days, and a few will have lingering symptoms for 10 days.

Countermeasures (Table 9-1) include modification of daily routines, restriction of alcohol and caffeine consumption, and administration of hypnotics in selected circumstances. Passengers taking eastward flights are advised to train themselves to go to bed early and rise early several days before travel. The reverse change is recommended in westward flights. The rationale is to start shifting circadian rhythms toward the external cues at the point of destination. During the flight, passengers should abstain from drinking excessive amounts of caffeine to stay awake or alcohol to induce relaxation. On the first day of arrival, passengers should force themselves to adopt immediately the meal and sleep routines of the point of destination. Prolonged sleep should be avoided, and only a nap not to exceed 2 hours is permitted during daytime. Exposure to bright external light, particularly in the morning, is important to retrain the biological clock [28]. Caffeine and heavy exercise should be avoided for at least 6 hours before retiring, and bedtime should be accomplished between 10:00 P.M. and 12:00 midnight. On the first and second nights, some passengers find it useful to take a short-acting hypnotic (e.g., triazolam, 0.125 mg, or zolpidem, 5 mg) at bedtime to consolidate nocturnal sleep. Individuals sensitive to benzodiazepines and elderly persons might experience excessive apathy and memory alteration on days following the administration of triazolam. Passengers on medications that require a specific dose or schedule should consult with their family physician to avoid toxic effects or transient deprivation.

Case Study 9-1

Transatlantic passenger Susan, a 25-year-old college student, leaves New York City at 6:30 P.M. bound for a European capital. Following dinner at 9:00 P.M., she reads a few pages of a favorite book, watches the movie projected overhead, and by 11:00 P.M. decides to unroll the blanket, remove her shoes, reposition the pillow, and close her eyes. She spends the night shifting postures, turning on the cramped seat, and peeking occasionally out the window. After what appears to be the longest night, a thin sunrise over the ocean heralds the new day. Soon after, the lights go on and a flurry of activity within the cabin announces breakfast. The traveler consults a watch and is surprised to note 1:00 A.M. while the flight attendant offers a breakfast tray. An announcement over the loudspeaker indicates that the local time is 7:00 A.M. and that the expected arrival time is 7:45 A.M. Broad daylight has taken over. On arrival, a sense of anxious expectation is followed by continuous physical and mental activity to recover baggage, pass customs, arrange transportation, and reach a hotel downtown. By 11:00 A.M., Susan checks into the hotel room, unpacks a few items, resets her watch from 5:00 A.M. to local time, and looking at the inviting bed decides to take a short nap. Before slumping on the bed, she draws shut the heavy window drapes to block the bright morning light pouring into the room. Within no time she is asleep.

Hours later, the phone rings insistently while Susan takes many seconds to regain full orientation of self and surroundings. Wearily, she picks up the phone as a foreign voice finally comes through with half intelligible language. She has missed lunch, and the tour bus is about to leave. Can she be ready in 5 minutes? Having regained full consciousness, Susan jumps out of bed and in no time joins the group. The remainder of the day is spent sightseeing over mounting traffic, mixed emotions, and tour guide admonitions. Dinner at 9:00 P.M. is early by local standards, and she is not hungry. Retiring at 11:30 P.M., the traveler is exhausted, with last thoughts recalling that back home the time is 5:00 P.M. and folks are getting ready for supper. Falling asleep does not take long, but 3 hours later, Susan wakes up and thereafter remains fully awake unable to fall back to sleep. The following day, she feels relatively well despite the lack of sleep, but as the day progresses, declining mental and physical vigor somewhat impair social interactions and decrease the drive to participate. She is not sleepy but feels fatigued and prefers to retire early. The second night is somewhat different. Initially, there is some difficulty falling asleep but Susan is able to remain asleep for more time, although waking up more frequently than at home. At 5:00 A.M., she gets up refreshed but not at peak. The second day in town is a bit more organized, but the sensation of weariness, combined with vague depression and light fatigue, seems to fill every quiet moment. Nonetheless, her enthusiasm about this first trip to Europe helps overcome transient deficiencies. On the sixth day, Susan has fully recovered and she is enjoying the European schedule.

The pattern of activities depicted in the case study is characteristic of many passengers but should be avoided. Prolonged daytime sleep and light avoidance on the day of arrival delays retraining of the biological clock. Preservation of external cues such as leaving a watch set for the point of departure can also delay recovery.

Shift Work

In the United States, 20% of the work force is engaged in shift work. Shift work disturbs sleep, circadian rhythms, and social and family structures. Most shift workers are partially sleep deprived and therefore will complain of sleepiness. In addition, their circadian rhythms can be out of synchrony, leading to complaints of malaise, gastrointestinal upset, and poor work performance. Not uncommonly, shift workers visit their physician's office complaining of a series of vague manifestations that can be traced back to sleepiness and circadian misalignment; gastrointestinal dysfunction takes a prominent place among these manifestations. Although adaptation to a new shift is accomplished within 1 or 2 weeks, depending on individual factors, it is easy to fall back on the conventional routine; most shift workers do that by catching up on days off. Thus, internal circadian rhythms are almost never totally adapted to new schedules, particularly if rotations are frequent. Family life and social interactions are commonly disturbed. The daytime sleep of individuals is easily disturbed by household activity, adding to sleep deprivation, irritability, and accusations. Family obligations are not met, sexual behaviors are altered, and spouses can feel isolated and lonely on nights without their mate.

Some factors decrease the tolerance and aggravate the manifestations of shift work. Individuals older than 50 years adapt poorly to rotating shifts. Even subjects who have been in the shift work force for many years can find that after the age of 50 years they become increasingly intolerant of their work schedules. Individuals who have a tendency to retire and arise early (early birds), have more difficulty adapting than night owls, who retire late and consequently tend to prefer getting up late. Other factors that make adaptation more difficult are sleep disorders, psychiatric disorders, alcohol abuse, chronic diseases, intake of medication that affects CNS function, and being overworked or working several jobs.

Shift workers are chronically sleep-deprived by approximately 7 hours per week at the expense of stage 2 and REM sleep, whereas SWS appears to be relatively well preserved [29]. Sleep loss is usually recovered on weekends and days off.

In order to develop countermeasures that ease tolerance of shift work, one has to remember that circadian periods change slowly. Bright light at work and a dark environment during sleep help the process of adaptation. Going forward in the rotation of shifts—night → morning → evening—is tolerated better than other rotating schedules. External cues should be minimized during the time set aside for sleep to avoid falling back on the baseline rhythm. In Europe, shifts are rotated every 2 days, causing disruption of sleep but preserving circadian rhythmicity. In special circumstances, short-acting benzodiazepines can be used for a few days to consolidate a better quality sleep. However, work performance might be affected, a consideration that should be taken into account in high-risk jobs or when the task demands continuous attention and dexterous moves. Contrary to previous belief, there is no evidence that benzodiazepines help reset the biological clock. Melatonin, the pineal hormone that facilitates natural resetting of suprachiasmatic rhythms, is being investigated as a potential substance to improve adaptation to shift work.

Intrinsic Asynchronous Sleep Phase Disorders

All internal circadian rhythms are normally linked to the 24-hour cosmic cycle through the myriad stimuli that reach the pacemaker located in the SCN. In the bunker experiment in which individuals are kept in isolation from external cues, circadian rhythms become loose from cosmic links and tend to become longer, reaching a duration of 25 hours in most but as many as 30 hours in some individuals. Weeks later, these subjects exhibit a sleep-wake rhythm as if they lived on a distant planet where cosmic evolutions dictated nights lasting as long as 12 hours followed by days of 18 hours. When returned to the conventional world full of engaging stimuli, subjects recover a 24-hour circadian rhythm with relative ease because of an eager internal pacemaker that has plasticity and adaptability.

Delayed Sleep Phase Syndrome

For reasons that remain unknown, some individuals fail to adapt to external changes. Their internal pacemaker does not link to the external world, and their rhythms remain out of order. These individuals fail to fall asleep at the conventional nighttime for lack of sleep. Despite their efforts to comply with a standard schedule, wakefulness does not abandon them and sleepiness fails to surge, until early morning hours when they finally drift into a sleep that remains profound and continuous for 10–12 hours. Sleep architecture is usually normal with cycles of SWS alternating with REM sleep. Individuals with this behavior are afflicted by a condition that is termed delayed sleep phase syndrome (DSPS) [30] to emphasize the late appearance of sleep. The condition has also been described following head trauma [31].

The most serious problem affecting patients with DSPS is psychosocial in nature. Patients believe they have insomnia because of their inability to initiate sleep at conventional times. Others accuse them of laziness when they miss socially demanding wake up calls, and in the perception of some, they slip slothfully through the better part of valuable mornings abandoned in deep sleep. Unable to get up on time, they lose work continuity and in consequence are sanctioned, counseled, or expelled from their job. Students arrive late to school, omit important classes, skip examinations, and suffer considerable decline in grades and scholarly production. Unable to cope with the pressures of a rigid schedule, they quit their jobs or drop out of school. Social life also suffers when their schedule strays out of line with that of family members and friends. Their rhythm is truly that of the night wanderer; they find their strength in the late evening and night, while succumbing to the call of unavoidable sleep as the core of the day progresses.

Typically, subjects fall asleep past 2:00 A.M. despite strenuous attempts to follow a more conventional schedule. Even hypnotics or sedatives are insufficient to summon sleep. The most motivated patients get up with great effort at a regular time to go to work or school where they function in a state of subalertness, not exempt of irascibility and irritability as is habitual in people deprived of sleep. When the weekend finally arrives, they indulge in a profound slumber for many hours, finally getting up well beyond noon, while savoring renewed energy in the wee hours of the early morning.

One-half of adults with DSPS have associated psychopathology similar to the alteration affecting patients with chronic insomnia. DSPS makes its debut in adolescence, persisting for many years until the changes brought on by advanced age shorten the circadian cycle and lighten sleep. Some patients can identify a precipitating factor causing a change in their habitual rhythm, such as a shift in their work schedule, staying up all night studying, or vacation time propitiating long nocturnal hours. Some travelers in arctic regions have reported a similar condition, as days grew shorter and the long polar winter night set in.

The prevalence of DSPS is unknown; in sleep centers, it represents less than 5% of patients complaining of insomnia. The condition should be distinguished from sleep phase delay caused by poor sleep hygiene and sometimes intended to avoid social contacts. Individuals who voluntarily stay up late and shorten their nighttime sleep are chronically sleep deprived and exhibit a short sleep latency at night, regardless of the time they go to bed. Daytime somnolence usually appears in the afternoon in sleep-deprived individuals, whereas patients with DSPS are sleepy and subalert in the mornings, should they manage to get up.

Non–24-Hour Sleep-Wake Syndrome

On rare occasions, DSPS must be differentiated from a rarer condition that is manifested by a progressive asynchrony with conventional clock times caused by a greater than 24-hour sleep-wake period length, usually 25 hours. When out of synchrony, the aberrant cycle causes insomnia along with inability to remain awake during the day, whereas complaints disappear when the rhythm is in phase with the external cycle of 24 hours. This condition is called the non–24-hour sleep-wake syndrome and is also known as the hypernycthemeral syndrome [32]. When patients attempt to conform to conventional schedules, the result is progressive sleep deprivation that causes secondary hypersomnia and consequent difficulty at work and school. Should the patient continue to enforce a schedule in synchrony with conventional hours, a time will come every few weeks when the progressively incremental internal rhythm reaches a period in phase with external hours during which time the patient will report freedom of symptoms, although for a short length of time. This finding is significant and should alert the physician to the presence of this relatively rare condition. Schizoid personality predisposes to the disorder.

Advanced Sleep Phase Syndrome

The advanced sleep phase syndrome (ASPS) occurs less commonly than its antagonist DSPS. Typically, patients complain of evening sleepiness that forces them to retire early; in consequence, they wake up excessively early [33] believing that they should sleep longer. This condition rarely triggers a medical complaint but is a habitual finding in elderly persons. The major problem is the inability to keep up with the social beat. Work and scholarly productivity do not suffer, and in fact, some individuals find solace and enhancement of their academic production during early morning hours when quiescence reigns in their household. In severe forms of the advanced sleep phase syndrome, individuals retire to bed between 6:00 and 8:00 P.M., and get up between 1:00 and 3:00 A.M., hardly a time to engage in activities other than the ones that are desk-bound. Sleep is continuous without awakenings.

Irregular Sleep-Wake Pattern

In the irregular sleep-wake pattern, sleep occurrence and waking behavior are variable, disturbing considerably the standard sleep-wake pattern. Patients present to their physician complaining of insomnia and reporting frequent daytime naps at irregular times with inadequate length of nocturnal sleep. Waking intervals are characterized by some sleepiness. The cornerstone of the disturbance is severe fragmentation of sleep without clear consolidation to the nocturnal period. In advanced instances, even meal times are altered, and processes such as temperature regulation and endocrinologic functions show flattening of the normal periodic cycling. The alteration has been observed as an idiopathic condition but also in association with CNS disorders including Alzheimer's disease, head injury, developmental disabilities, and hypothalamic tumors [34]. It should be differentiated from behavioral sleep fragmentation and from disruption caused by frequent rotation of shift work schedules by obtaining a careful history of precipitating factors. Narcolepsy coursing with fragmentation of nocturnal sleep and frequent daytime napping can resemble this disorder.

Seasonal Affective Disorder

SAD is a recurrent winter depression affecting predominantly women as nights grow longer. It is characterized by a depressive mood, phase-delayed sleep, morning hypersomnia, fatigue, and increased appetite for carbohydrates with consequent weight gain [35]. Patients with SAD, usually women between the ages of 20 and 40 years, have increased sleep duration and signs of DSPS such as morning hypersomnia; some complain of menstrual irregularities. Sleep architecture shows decreased SWS and increased REM sleep with normal REM sleep latency [36]. Spontaneous remissions occur in late winter and spring; in summer months, patients show increased delta sleep and decreased sleep time. The prevalence of SAD is greater in northern latitudes, increasing as the distance from the equator lengthens. Craving for carbohydrates, weight gain, and seasonal variation distinguish this disorder from other forms of recurrent depression. Patients with SAD respond favorably to exposure to bright light (2,500 lux) in the mornings. In one study [37], patients improved after 1 week of morning therapy with bright light; the antidepressant effect was accompanied by a 1.5-hour advance in the onset of melatonin production, indicating a biological effect on circadian timing.

Clinical Approach

Patients with circadian dysrhythmias complain to their physicians of either insomnia or hypersomnia. In DSPS, the common complaint is an inability to sleep at conventional times, a phenomenon that patients translate into insomnia; in ASPS and SAD, patients are more concerned about an inappropriate feeling of lethargy and sleepiness. A detailed history reveals that once asleep patients are able to maintain continuity of sleep that is usually deep, although not necessarily restorative. Morning lethargy in DSPS, afternoon sleepiness in ASPS, and seasonal variations in SAD are manifestations that reveal the diagnosis. Patients with DSPS and SAD are young or middle aged; patients with ASPS are elderly.

The 14-day sleep-wake chart (Chapter 3) is valuable to document sleep-wake schedules and confirm the diagnosis. Actigraphy is also a valuable adjunct since it can be loaned to the patient to take home and records the rest-activity cycle over a period of several days. Polysomnography is not indicated except when it is necessary to exclude diagnoses such as narcolepsy, periodic limb movements of sleep, or sleep apnea syndrome.

A psychiatric history is also relevant to uncover schizoid personalities in the non–24-hour sleep-wake syndrome, or the beginning of a schizophrenic decompensation or bipolar disorder in some patients with DSPS. Persistence of DSPS after remission of psychiatric manifestations might be observed in patients with both conditions in whom DSPS was revealed by the psychiatric disorder. The distinction between SAD and other forms of depression can be facilitated by finding carbohydrate craving, increased appetite, weight gain, and seasonal variation in SAD. Polysomnography can reveal alterations of REM sleep latency and distribution in true affective depression that are not present in SAD.

Chronobiotherapy

Three techniques have been developed to manipulate circadian rhythms: chronotherapy, luminotherapy, and chronopharmacotherapy.

Chronotherapy

This form of therapy was devised to treat patients with DSPS and later adapted to treat patients with ASPS. It is an attempt to reset the circadian clock by inducing a drift of sleep times over a period of days until an acceptable match is obtained between the internal and external cycles. In DSPS, sleep is scheduled later and later each day [38]. The therapeutic goal of chronotherapy is to achieve and maintain a desired phase in the 24-hour cycle. The method is to impose a 27-hour day on successive days by delay-shifting scheduled bedtimes and wake times until the desired position is reached. For instance, patients are instructed to enforce a schedule as follows: day 1, 3:00 to 11:00 A.M.; day 2, 6:00 A.M. to 3:00 P.M.; day 3, 9:00 A.M. to 5:00 P.M.; day 4, 12 noon to 8:00 P.M.; day 5, 3:00 to 11:00 P.M.; day 6, 6:00 P.M. to 2:00 A.M.; day 7, 9:00 P.M. to 5:00 A.M. Thereafter, patients are maintained on the final schedule allowing less than 1-hour deviations from the time frames. Naps are not permitted, and patients are instructed to maintain the discipline every day including weekends and days off. Keeping a log book or diary is helpful, and strengthening of time cues along with enforcement of strict schedules is critical to maintain a socially acceptable timetable.

Moldofsky and colleagues reported the successful phase-advance of schedules in a patient with ASPS [39]. Their technique was similar to that used in phase-delay, except that the patient was asked to go to bed and wake up 3 hours earlier each day until a desired schedule was reached.

Luminotherapy

Luminotherapy, or bright light treatment, for circadian dysrhythmias with sleep-wake alteration has been in use since the discovery that bright light is a more effective zeitgeber than ordinary indoor light. The intensity of light is measured in lux units of illumination. Indoor light has approximately 150 lux, whereas therapeutic bright light has a potency of 2,500 to 10,000 lux. Bright light of any source is an effective suppressor of melatonin [40]. Commercially available light boxes (information can be obtained from ad hoc societies) [41] emit fluorescent cool white light with ultraviolet rays filtered out to prevent damage to the lens and retina. An effective regimen has a range of 2,500 lux for 2 hours to 10,000 lux for 30 minutes. The light box is placed at eye level at a distance of 3 feet. Treatment overdose is manifested by headache, dizziness, and hyperactivity.

Following the principles of the phase response curve hypothesis, bright light can be applied in the morning or in the evening to achieve maximal therapeutic value. In DSPS, exposure to bright light is scheduled immediately on awakening to prevent morning lethargy, between 6:00 and 8:00 A.M., for a duration of 2 hours daily for 1 week; in some instances, light restriction past 4:00 P.M. can be a useful adjunct. In ASPS, light exposure 2 hours before scheduled bedtime can energize the individual and achieve a desired delay of bedtime to a more socially acceptable hour. Luminotherapy might be useful in idiopathic cases of non–24-hour sleep-wake disorder and in the irregular sleep-wake pattern, but controlled studies and large series of patients are lacking. In SAD, treatments are given in the morning for 2 hours and sometimes in the evening for 30 minutes to reduce the hours of darkness. Adjustments in the dose and duration of treatment are made according to individual response.

Light therapy can be useful in the future management of shift work schedules [42], jet lag syndrome [43], and space flights [44]. Further work is needed before it becomes a standard form of treatment for these situations.

Chronopharmacotherapy

Chronopharmacotherapy is also used to modify circadian schedules. The entrainment of the circadian rhythm with short-acting benzodiazepines was the subject of considerable speculation and work in the 1980s [45]. Administration of triazolam in small amounts (0.125 mg at bedtime) can produce high-quality sleep in individuals who wish to reset their biological clock immediately following a long transmeridian flight [46]. This can be the case in travelers with important business to conduct within the first 48 hours following arrival, or when the anticipated stay is intended to be short. However, prudence demands that medication administration should not exceed 4 or 5 days and should always be given in small doses to avoid rebound phenomena, accumulation, and even idiosyncratic adverse effects primarily centered around memory mechanisms. More recently, melatonin has been advocated as a natural product capable of resetting the circadian rhythm in individuals with jet lag syndrome, DSPS, and SAD. Administered at the beginning of the night, melatonin advances the sleep phase, an effect similar to that obtained with bright light [47]. Melatonin tablets are available over-the-counter in health stores in the United States and are promoted as a product to help initiate and maintain sleep. Unfortunately, there is no scientific validation of this claim, and there is no quality control of the product.

References

1. Shelley PB. Demon of the World. Quoted by Sir William Osler in The Evolution of Modern Medicine (1921). The Classics of Medicine Library, Special edition. Birmingham, AL: Division of Gryphon Editions, Ltd., 1982;1.
2. Aschoff J. Circadian rhythms in man: A self-sustained oscillation with an inherent frequency underlies human 24-hour periodicity. Science 1965;148:1427.

3. Borbély A. Secrets of Sleep. New York: Basic Books, 1986;183.
4. Stephan F, Zucker I. Circadian rhythms in drinking behavior and locomotor activity of rats are eliminated by hypothalamic lesions. Proc Natl Acad Sci U S A 1972;69:1583.
5. Rusak B, Groos G. Suprachiasmatic stimulation phase shifts in rodent circadian rhythm. Science 1982;215:1407.
6. Moore RY, Lenn NJ. A retino-hypothalamic projection in the rat. J Comp Neurol 1972;146:1.
7. Czeisler CA, Kronauer RE, Allan JS, et al. Bright light induction of strong (Type O) resetting of the human circadian pacemaker. Science 1989;244:1328.
8. Swaab DF, Fliers E, Partiman TS. The suprachiasmatic nucleus of the human brain in relation to sex, age, and senile dementia. Brain Res 1985;342:37.
9. Swaab DF, Hofman MA. An enlarged suprachiasmatic nucleus in homosexual men. Brain Res 1990;537:141.
10. Culebras A. Stroke and Sleep Disorders. In M Fisher, J Bogousslavsky (eds), Current Review of Cerebrovascular Disease. Philadelphia: Current Medicine, 1996.
11. Garfinkel D, Laudon M, Nof D, et al. Improvement of sleep quality in elderly people by controlled-release melatonin. Lancet 1995;346:541.
12. Reppert SM, Weaver DR, Rivkees SA, et al. Putative melatonin receptors in a human biological clock. Science 1988;242:78.
13. Kleitman N, Engelmann TG. Sleep characteristics of infants. J Appl Physiol 1953;6:269.
14. DeCoursey P. Daily light sensitivity in a rodent. Science 1960;131:33.
15. Takahashi Y, Kipnis DM, Daughaday WH. Growth secretion during sleep. J Clin Invest 1968;47:2079.
16. Adamson L, Hunter WM, Ogunremi OO, et al. Growth hormone increase during sleep after daytime exercise. J Endocrinol 1974;62:473.
17. Prinz P, Blenkarn D, Linnoila M, et al. Growth hormone levels during sleep in elderly males. Sleep Research 1976;5:87.
18. Sassin JF, Parker DC, Mace JW, et al. Human growth hormone release: relation to slow-wave sleep and sleep-waking cycles. Science 1969;165:513.
19. Culebras A, Podolsky S, Leopold NA. Absence of sleep-related growth hormone elevations in myotonic dystrophy. Neurology 1977;27:165.
20. Powell GF, Hopwood NJ, Barrett ES. Growth hormone studies before and during catch-up growth in a child with emotional deprivation and short stature. J Clin Endocrinol Metab 1973;37:674.
21. Culebras A. Thalamic Lesions and the Endocrine System. In C Guilleminault, E Lugaresi, P Montagna, et al (eds), Fatal Familial Insomnia: Inherited Prion Diseases, Sleep and the Thalamus. New York: Raven,1994;87.
22. Sassin JF, Frantz AG, Kapen S, et al. The nocturnal rise of human prolactin is dependent on sleep. J Clin Endocrinol Metab 1973;37:436.
23. Weitzman ED. Circadian rhythms and episodic hormone secretion in man. Ann Rev Med 1976;27:225.
24. Taylor PL, Garrick NA, Burns RS, et al. Diurnal rhythms of serotonin in monkey cerebrospinal fluid. Life Sci 1982;31:1993.

25. Kalin NH, Insel TR, Cohen RM, et al. Diurnal variation in cerebrospinal fluid prolactin concentration in the rhesus monkey. J Clin Endocrinol Metab 1981;52:857.
26. Rivier C, Vale W, Ling N, et al. Stimulation in vivo of the secretion of prolactin and growth hormone by beta-endorphin. Endocrinology 1977;100:238.
27. Gander PH, Myhre G, Graeber RC, et al. Crew factors in flight operations, I: Effects of 9-hour time zone changes on fatigue and the circadian rhythms of sleep/wake and core temperature. NASA Technical Memorandum 88197. Moffett Field, CA: NASA Ames Research Center, 1985.
28. Daan S, Lewey AJ. Scheduled exposure to daylight: A potential strategy to reduce "jet lag" following transmeridian flight. Psychopharmacol Bull 1984;20:566.
29. Ackerstedt T. Adjustment of Physiological Circadian Rhythms and the Sleep-Wake Cycle to Shift Work. In S Folkard, TH Monk (eds), Hours of Work—Temporal Factors in Work Scheduling. New York: Wiley, 1985;199.
30. Weitzman ED, Czeisler CA, Coleman RM, et al. Delayed sleep phase syndrome: A chronobiologic disorder with sleep onset insomnia. Arch Gen Psychiatry 1981;38:737.
31. Patten SB, Lauderdale WM. Delayed sleep phase disorder after traumatic brain injury. J Am Acad Child Adolesc Psychiatry 1992;31:100.
32. Wollman M, Lavie P, Peled R. A hypernycthemeral sleep-wake syndrome: A treatment attempt. Chronobiol Int 1985;2:277.
33. Kamei R, Hughes L, Miles L, et al. Advanced-sleep phase syndrome studied in a time isolation facility. Chronobiologia 1979;6:115.
34. Cohen RA, Albers HE. Disruption of human circadian and cognitive regulation following a discrete hypothalamic lesion: A case study. Neurology 1991;41:726.
35. Rosenthal NE, Sack DA, Gillin JC, et al. Seasonal affective disorder: A description of the syndrome and preliminary findings with light therapy. Arch Gen Psychiatry 1984;41:72.
36. Skwerer RG, Jacobsen FM, Duncan CC, et al. Neurobiology of seasonal affective disorder and phototherapy. J Biol Rhythms 1988;3:135.
37. Lewy AJ, Sack RL, Miller S, et al. Antidepressant and circadian phase-shifting effects of light. Science 1987;235:352.
38. Czeisler CA, Richardson GS, Coleman RM, et al. Chronotherapy: Resetting the circadian clocks of patients with delayed sleep phase insomnia. Sleep 1981;4:1.
39. Moldofsky H, Musisi S, Philipson EA. Treatment of a case of advanced sleep phase syndrome by phase advance chronotherapy. Sleep 1986;9:61.
40. Lewy AJ, Wehr TA, Goodwin FK, et al. Light suppresses melatonin secretion in humans. Science 1980;210:1267.
41. Society for Light Treatment and Biological Rhythms. P.O. Box 478, Wilsonville, Oregon 97070.
42. Czeisler CA, Johnson MP, Duffy JF, et al. Exposure to bright light and darkness to treat physiologic maladaptation to night work. N Engl J Med 1990;322:1253.

43. Czeisler CA, Allan JS. Acute circadian phase reversal in man via bright light exposure: Application to jet lag. Sleep Research 1987;16:605.
44. Czeisler CA, Chiasera AJ, Duffy JF. Research on sleep, circadian rhythms and aging: Applications to manned spaceflight. Exp Gerontol 1991;26:217.
45. Nicholson AN, Pascoe PA, Spencer MB, et al. Sleep after transmeridian flights. Lancet 1986;1:1205.
46. Cohen AS, Seidel WF, Yost D, et al. Triazolam used in the treatment of jet lag: Effects on sleep and subsequent wakefulness. Sleep Research 1991;20:61.
47. Lewy AJ, Ahmed S, Jackson JML, et al. Melatonin shifts human circadian rhythms according to a phase-response curve. Chronobiol Int 1992;9:380.

10

Parasomnias and Motor Disorders of Sleep

When the night was far advanced, Mary awoke with a sudden start. A vivid dream had latterly involved her in its unreal life, of which, however, she could only remember that it had been broken in upon at the most interesting point. For a little time, slumber hung about her like a morning mist, hindering her from perceiving the distinct outline of her situation.

Nathaniel Hawthorne
"The Wives of the Dead" from *Tales and Sketches* [1]

Bizarre behaviors and unusual motor acts can appear during the night because sleep is there; were sleep to go away, the acts would cease. Sometimes, the events occur when arousal is incomplete or insufficient, or they surge in association with REM sleep; other times, the episodes appear in transitions from wakefulness to sleep, from sleep to wakefulness, or from one sleep stage to another. In all instances, the events are undesirable and translate some form of nervous system activation that when frequent and intense can put the patient and bedmate at risk of physical, emotional, or social injury. These phenomena are called parasomnias, and in the International Classification of Sleep Disorders they are subdivided into arousal disorders, sleep-wake transition disorders, parasomnias of REM sleep, and other parasomnias. Polysomnography with video recording has advanced enormously the clinical evaluation and knowledge of these events by providing images of the motor activities along with detailed information of their occurrence in relation to sleep and its stages. Treatment varies depending on the condition, and the response is clearly the function of a precise diagnosis.

Arousal Disorders

These are alterations of the waking mechanism that impede full control of volitional motor activity. Sleep inertia is prolonged, and when awakened, the individual appears slow with memory impairment, poor judgment, and inappropriate behavior. Three disorders are included in this section: confusional arousals, sleep terrors, and sleepwalking.

Confusional Arousals

Confusional arousals, or sleep drunkenness, are phenomena that occur in the process of waking up in predisposed individuals who are deprived of sleep or whose sleep is so profound and intense that full vigilance fails to take hold with the required diligence. As a result, in a transition to wakefulness generally out of deep sleep in the first third of the night, the person remains in a state of confusion and subalertness. The individual appears disoriented, incoherent, hesitant, and slow, responding precariously to questions and commands. Memory for the event is fragmented or nonexistent despite a duration that can last from minutes to hours. Patients do not recall a dream content, although flashbacks of recollection can be evoked more in connection with the activity itself than with an oneiric experience.

While in a state of confusional arousal, subjects can walk, climb stairs, move about, open and close drawers, get dressed, and even drive a car. It is not inconceivable that violence and assault driven by a distorted perception of reality can take place [2], but planning and premeditation are not possible. The fine edge of judgment is blunted, and critical analysis of the situation is absent, so that acts appear more irrational than malicious if crime is a consideration. Rarely, homicides have been committed during confusional arousals [3]. Most often, however, the episodes of confusion are limited to simple acts such as picking up a lamp instead of a ringing phone or mumbling incoherently in response to a question. Children under 5 years of age forcefully awakened from deep sleep during the first third of the night are universally prone to develop a confusional arousal. As age advances, the frequency diminishes, and in the adult years, confusional arousals are limited to susceptible individuals who are severely sleep deprived as a result of shift work or their voluntary behavior, or whose sleep deprivation has been primed by alcohol or CNS depressant drugs. Patients with sleep apnea, narcolepsy, and idiopathic hypersomnia are especially vulnerable and can develop confusional arousals with more frequency than the rest of the population. Encephalopathies that depress global mental function such as the ones that are of hepatic, renal, or toxic origin can facilitate confusional arousals, although in these situations, a distinction between confusional arousal and delirium would have to be made. In all instances, drifting into a deep, prolonged sleep is a risk factor, and forcing an awakening out of this state is a triggering process.

The polysomnographic evaluation shows an arousal out of slow wave sleep (SWS) usually in the first third of the night, although in children and in patients with idiopathic hypersomnia, confusional arousals can appear during forced awakenings at any time. In susceptible individuals, these events have also been recorded during afternoon naps. The electroencephalogram (EEG) channels show residual slow wave activity in the delta and more commonly the theta range despite behavioral evidence of concurrent motor activity. Repeated microsleeps and poorly reactive alpha rhythm have also been described in association with confusional arousals [4].

The differential diagnosis should be made with sleep terrors that course with manifestations of excessive autonomic discharge such as dilated pupils, a frightened appearance, and inconsolable crying. A distinction should also be made with sleepwalking, a condition that can resemble confusional arousal because of complex motor activity appearing in a subvigilant state; however, the somnambulist is generally docile and returns promptly to bed when requested, whereas the individual in a state of confusional arousal can become aggressive if challenged. Episodes of REM sleep behavior disorder (RSBD) are best differentiated by polysomnography or when obtaining a history of unquestionable dream enactment with dream content driving the motor behavior. Fugues, episodic wandering, and other forms of epileptic activity require polysomnography or EEG telemetry for proper differentiation, although a history of seizures and elimination of episodes with anticonvulsant medication weighs heavily in favor of an epileptic phenomenon. There is some debate whether seemingly complex motor behaviors, particularly if associated with violence, represent confusional arousals or prolonged episodes of reticent somnambulism. A sleepwalking event can turn into a confusional arousal, and both are the result of an arousal disorder in which a subvigilant state is associated with motor activity, so that the argument might be moot. In any event, it is difficult to characterize episodes in which the individual drives a car and commits other acts that are beyond the ability to walk as somnambulism [5]. Such states are perhaps better categorized as confusional arousals.

Treatment is best achieved by instituting measures that prevent the patient from falling into deep, prolonged, SWS. Susceptible individuals should avoid sleep deprivation and CNS depressants such as alcohol, antihistaminic preparations, hypnotics, sedatives, and tranquilizers. Awakenings during the first third of the night should be prevented.

Sleep Terrors

Sleep terrors, pavor nocturnus, or incubus, are virtually the patrimony of children between the ages of 4 and 12 years. The prevalence is 3% in children, is more frequent in boys than in girls, and sometimes shows a familial incidence. Episodes are characterized by a sudden awakening out of deep sleep, heralded by a chilling scream that abruptly interrupts the sleep of parents. Rushing to the bedside, they find the child sitting up in bed crying inconsolably, agitated, sweaty, exhibiting dilated pupils and goose bumps, while breathing heavily with a rapid pulse. Oblivious to the pleads and caresses of the parents, the child continues in such a desperate state for 10–15 minutes, showing increased muscle tone and resisting any physical contact. If forcibly awakened, the child appears confused and incoherent but soon falls asleep and has no recollection of the event the following morning. With the passage of time, episodes of pavor nocturnus disappear spontaneously; however, the parents need to know that the phenomena are not the result of some terrible mishap but a simple autonomic discharge without major consequences except for sleep interruption and the fright of the parents.

Deep and prolonged SWS is a predisposing factor, whereas fever, sleep deprivation, and CNS depressants are precipitating factors. The polysomnogram shows an abrupt awakening out of stage 3 or 4 of sleep with generation of alpha activity, usually during the first third of the night. Partial arousals out of SWS, as many as 10–15 in the course of 1 night, are more common in sleep terror sufferers and could represent the only indication of recorded abnormality.

Sleep terrors should be differentiated from nightmares (Table 10-1), which are intense dreams loaded with anxiety occurring during REM

Table 10-1. Differential Diagnosis of Sleep Terrors and Nightmares

Item	Terror	Nightmare
Behavior	Piercing, chilling scream, inconsolable crying, autonomic discharge, sitting up in bed, confused, appears frightened	Minimal motor activity
Response	No response or resists	Docile, responds without confusion
Sleep stage	Stage 3/4, 90–120 minutes following sleep onset	Stage REM, last third of night
Frequency	One or more night episodes	One episode per night
Dream content	Absent, fragmentary	Vivid with anxiety
Memory	Amnesia	Intense recollection
Age	4–12 yrs	Starts at 6 yrs
Sex	Male predominates	Female predominates in adult age
Predisposing factors	Slow wave sleep	Schizoid personality, psychopathology in adult
Precipitating factors	Fever, sleep deprivation, CNS depressants	Stress, mental trauma, dopaminergic meds, REM sleep suppressors, REM sleep rebound
Family history	Positive	Uncertain
Polysomnography	Awakening from stages 3 and 4	10 minutes of REM sleep followed by awakening
Electroencephalogram	Normal	Normal
Pharmacologic treatment	Benzodiazepines	Protryptiline, propranolol, clonidine

stage, commonly awakening the patient. Nightmares tend to occur during the last third of the night when REM sleep is more abundant, leaving a vivid recollection of the dream content. Nightmares are not associated with motor activity or autonomic discharge. The individual awakened from a nightmare is not confused or incoherent, realizing immediately the nature of the anxiety dream. Sometimes the clinician has to differentiate sleep terrors from epileptic events, but their association with ictal epileptiform discharges appearing in the EEG channels settles the diagnosis.

When sleep terrors occur one or more times per week, management consists of eliminating precipitating factors while reducing the level of daytime stress and reassuring the parents of the benign character of the condition. In some instances, benzodiazepines (e.g., diazepam, 2–5 mg) that reduce the cortical arousal component can be administered at bedtime. Sleep terrors that persist into adulthood are commonly associated with psychopathology, and the response to treatment is weaker, requiring a psychotherapeutic complement in many instances.

Somnambulism

Somnambulism, or sleepwalking, is a common automatism among children over 4 years of age, characterized by an episode of walking during SWS in the first third of the night. Sleepwalking occurs among 30% of children with sleep terrors; a sex predominance is not identified but a familial incidence is commonly observed [6]. It has been estimated that up to 15% of the general population has had at least one episode of sleepwalking during childhood. Peak prevalence occurs between the ages of 4 and 8 years, tending to disappear spontaneously by the age of 15 years; only 0.5% of adults have occasional sleepwalking episodes.

In the typical episode, the child sits up in bed, opens the eyes, moves around without purpose, tries to get out of bed and frequently fails to do so, walks around the bedroom with slow indecisive steps, avoids obstacles, and sometimes even handles objects like bathroom items or kitchen utensils. The child gets partially dressed or undressed and generally exhibits incoherent somniloquy; if awakened, the child appears confused and disoriented. The child returns without resistance to bed, falls easily asleep, and has no recollection of the episode the following day. The event can provoke serious accidents such as a fall down the stairs or an exit through a window. Motor activity is never organized, intentional, or planned. Dream content, when present, is scarce, fragmented, and without theme or story. The polysomnogram shows an EEG typical of light non-REM sleep; sometimes immediately preceding the episode, the EEG shows hypersynchrony of generalized high-voltage delta waves, without epileptiform morphology.

Table 10-2.   Differential Diagnosis of Somnambulism and Episodic Wandering

Item	Somnambulism	Episodic Wandering
Behavior	Walks slowly, appears sleepy, mumbles (sometimes inappropriate)	Walks fast, aggressive, appears awake, quizzical facial expression, loud voice, incoherent
Response	Docile	No response or resists
Sleep stage	Stages 3/4, 90–120 minutes from sleep onset	Stage 2, second half of the night
Frequency	One episode per night	Two or more episodes
Dream content	Absent	Fragments
Memory	Amnesia	Amnesia
Predisposing factors	Prolonged deep sleep	Epilepsy
Precipitating factors	Sleep deprivation, stress, sedatives, hypnotics, sleep apnea, noises, full bladder	Epileptic discharge?
Age	4–15 yrs	12–25 yrs
Sex	Equal	Males predominate
Family history	Positive	Negative
Polysomnography	Delta hypersynchrony	Uncertain
Electroencephalogram	Normal	2/3 epileptiform
Pharmacologic treatment	Benzodiazepines	Carbamazepine

The causes of somnambulism are unknown. During an episode, there is cortical blockade without motor inhibition, resulting in a state of confused subalertness or light non-REM sleep, from which it is difficult to arise. In consequence, some authors consider somnambulism an arousal disorder. Precipitating factors are all the ones that promote deep sleep, including sleep deprivation, fever, excessive tiredness, hypnotics, and some neuroleptics. Psychopathology is common in the adult sleepwalker but not in the child. In the young adult, the differential diagnosis needs to be made with episodic wandering (Table 10-2); in the third and fourth

Table 10-3. Differential Diagnosis of Somnambulism and Rapid Eye Movement Sleep Behavior Disorder (Phantasmagoria)

Item	Somnambulism	Phantasmagoria (RSBD)
Behavior	Walks slowly, appears sleepy, mumbles (sometimes inappropriate)	Gesticulates, waves hands, punches, gets out of bed, walks or runs frightened, agile
Response	Docile	Awakens rapidly without confusion
Sleep stage	Stages 3/4, 90–120 minutes from sleep onset	REM sleep, any segment
Frequency	One episode per night	Several episodes per week
Dream content	Absent	Intense, persecutory
Memory	Amnesia	Remembers
Predisposing factors	Prolonged deep sleep	Neurologic disorder
Precipitating factors	Sleep deprivation, stress, sedatives, hypnotics, sleep apnea, noises, full bladder	REM sleep rebound, dopaminergic agents
Pathology	Unknown	Ponto-mesencephalic tegmental lesions
Age	4–15 yrs	65 yrs
Sex	Equal	Males predominate
Family history	Positive	Rarely positive
Polysomnography	Delta hypersynchrony	REM sleep without atonia
Electroencephalogram	Normal	Normal
Pharmacologic treatment	Benzodiazepines	Clonazepam

RSBD = REM sleep behavior disorder.

decades with epileptic fugues; and, in the elderly person with RSBD (Table 10-3). Special consideration should be given when an elderly or very elderly individual starts walking at night. Nocturnal wandering as part of the sundown syndrome in dementia, or in the context of nocturnal confusion caused by a variety of factors such as medication or change to another bedroom, is addressed in Chapter 12.

Violence in the course of sleepwalking occupies a special category [5]. It is conceivable that the sleepwalker has the potential to drift into a confusional arousal, a state in which violence and assault are likely when prolonged and if given the adequate circumstances. The differential diagnosis should also include other conditions in which violence related to sleep is a risk, such as RSBD, fugue states, and episodic wandering. Malingering can be ruled out when the violent act appears irrational without malicious or premeditated intent and there is an immediate past history supporting the facilitation of an arousal disorder. These situations are discussed in Chapter 14.

Management consists of protecting the patient from harm by closing windows, locking doors, blocking stairs, and securing balconies. Travelers should request accommodations on the ground or first floor. Diminishing daytime stress and engaging in relaxation therapies help reduce the frequency of events. It is important to avoid sleep deprivation by maintaining a regular sleep hygiene. The somnambulist responds favorably to administration of small doses of benzodiazepines such as diazepam (2–10 mg at bedtime), depending on weight and age, a step taken only when episodes are frequent and pose a risk to the patient.

Rapid Eye Movement Sleep–Related Parasomnias

Two cardinal phenomena characterize REM sleep: dream content and muscle atonia. Abnormalities of these phenomena determine most of the parasomniac experiences of REM sleep. Excessive dreaming precipitates intense oneiric experiences loaded with anxiety that disturb the patient. Dream activity can drive motor acts when the muscle atonia that normally overpowers the individual in REM sleep is abolished. Other parasomnias are provoked by the rich and diverse peculiar phenomena of REM sleep, and it is conceivable that alterations remain to be described.

Nightmares

Nightmares are intense dream anxiety attacks that frighten patients. The cornerstone of the condition is the dream experience, and thus nightmares occurring during REM sleep are more common during the second half of the night. The oneiric content is generally a long, complex, and disturbing imagined perception (Figure 10-1) ending in an awakening without confusion. The element of fright is consubstantial with the nightmare and not a mere reaction to the dream experience. Memory of the event is vivid and independent of awakenings terminating the sequence. Nightmares are rarely associated with overt motor activity despite the intense dream experience, a characteristic that serves in the differential diagnosis.

Starting at the age of 3 years, children might suffer nightmares, and it is likely that up to one-half of the population has such an experience at some point [7]. By the age of 6 years, nightmares start to subside and gradually disappear. The few adolescents and adults who continue to report nightmares are often women harboring a schizoid or border-line personality disorder with fragile emotional structure and suscep-tibility to develop mental illness [8]. Frightening and intense real-life experiences can constitute the precipitating factor of recurrent night-mares in vulnerable adults, as is the case in the posttraumatic stress syn-drome seen in military personnel exposed to war [9].

The polysomnographic correlate is characteristic of REM sleep, showing increased REM density lasting at least 10 minutes terminated by an awakening. Heart and breathing rate variability can occur but not as intensely as observed during a sleep terror.

The differential diagnosis with sleep terrors (see Table 10-1) is rel-atively simple when the child reports a well-remembered dream expe-rience, loaded with fear, occurring during the last third of the night. Nightmares are distinguished from RSBD by the lack of motor activity despite the intense dream experience. On the other hand, RSBD tends to be more common in the elderly and is frequently associated with a neurologic disorder. Polysomnography shows REM sleep without ato-nia that is not present in nightmare sequences.

Treatment is unnecessary unless nightmares are frequent, recurrent, and disturbing to the patient and parents or immediate relatives. Stress avoidance and discontinuation of drugs that can promote nightmares, such as beta-adrenergic blockers and dopaminergic compounds, should be considered first along with a well-regimented sleep hygiene. Psy-chotherapy is helpful in individuals with borderline personality disor-ders. Medications that suppress REM sleep, such as tricyclics and monoamine oxidase (MAO) inhibitors, also suppress nightmares. A useful regimen is the administration of protryptiline, 10 mg at bedtime. Discontinuation of these drugs should be done gradually to avoid REM sleep rebound and more nightmares. A similar phenomenon can occur

Figure 10-1. *The age-old dream of flying can turn into the frightening nightmare of falling in space. This engraving was done by the Spanish painter, Francisco de Goya y Lucientes (1746–1828) from the series* Sueños *(dreams), also known as* Disparates *(follies). Nightmares occur in REM sleep typically during the second half of the night. The oneiric content is generally a long, complex, and disturbing imagined perception that ends in an awakening without confusion. The element of fright is consubstantial with the nightmare and not a mere reaction to the dream experience. (Bequest of Horatio G. Curtis by exchange and the Harvey D. Parker Collection by exchange. Courtesy of the Museum of Fine Arts, Boston.)*

with large amounts of alcohol, which has a mild REM sleep suppressant effect.

Rapid Eye Movement Sleep Behavior Disorder

RSBD is characterized by a history of bizarre acts during nocturnal sleep associated with polygraphic evidence of loss of muscle atonia. Clinical manifestations range from aperiodic motor hyperactivity such as muscle twitches, jerks, and restlessness to complex forms of organized motor activity in REM stage, such as flailing of arms, pointing with a finger, waving with the hand, punching, kicking, vocalizing, sitting up or getting out of bed, walking, running, screaming, and jumping. Motor overactivity can lead to physical injuries to the patient or spouse. If awakened, patients report having a dream that drove them to act in their sleep. The character of the dream is usually violent, featuring persecutions and confrontations with persons or animals; repetitive themes are common. It has been suggested that quasi-intentional motor activity might be an attempted enactment of the dream content, which is frequently violent, vivid, and confrontational. Such a figment of the senses leading to physical endeavor, seemingly the response to a complex succession of things imagined during a dream experience, is termed phantasmagoria, to distinguish it from the common nightmare in which perceived motor action is physically ineffectual.

The frequency of episodes ranges from one or more times nightly to once per month. Since episodes are associated with REM sleep, they appear 60–90 minutes after sleep onset without apparent preference for any of the REM cycles.

RSBD predominates in older persons and in men; the average age of presentation is between 56 and 59 years, as observed in a series of 11 patients studied in our center and in 70 patients studied by Schenck and Mahowald [10]. In our series of older patients, risk factors for stroke were predominant, and two patients with remarkably low blood pressure for age at presentation eventually developed Shy-Drager's syndrome. In Schenck and Mahowald's series, neurologic disorders were identified in 42.9% of patients who underwent neurologic examination. Schenck and Mahowald noted the following conditions associated with RSBD: olivopontocerebellar degeneration, ischemic cerebrovascular disorder, multiple sclerosis, Parkinson's disease, Guillain-Barré syndrome, brain stem astrocytoma, narcolepsy, dementia, Shy-Drager syndrome, and alcoholism.

Patients with RSBD typically show REM sleep without atonia in polysomnographic studies (Figure 10-2). Myoclonia of limb muscles and generalized motor restlessness are common during REM sleep, although they are also observed in non-REM sleep. The architecture of sleep is generally well preserved, and epileptiform discharges are not seen. Nocturnal video recordings reveal motor overactivity.

Five out of six consecutive patients studied in our series with magnetic resonance imaging (MRI) of the head [11] exhibited increased signal intensity lesions in periventricular white matter and three in the tegmentum of the pons, all suggestive of ischemic lesions secondary to small vessel arteriopathy. One patient with a normal study subsequently developed Shy-Drager's syndrome. In Schenck and Mahowald's series,

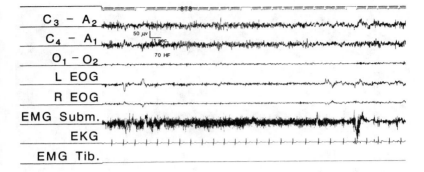

Figure 10-2.   *Polysomnographic recording of REM sleep without atonia in a patient with REM sleep behavior disorder. Note the presence of well-defined electromyographic activity in the submental channel (EMG) in association with REM complexes (L and R EOG) and low-voltage, mixed, desynchronized activity in the occipital channel (O_1–O_2). The ECG shows relative bradycardia of 60 beats per minute. (EOG = electro-oculogram; EMG Subm. = electromyogram of muscles of submental region; EKG = electrocardiogram).*

42 patients were studied with MRI of the head, and the incidence of abnormalities of likely clinical importance was 14.6%.

Case Study 10-1

A 74-year-old woman had nocturnal episodes of arm flailing, screaming, getting out of bed, walking, and moving furniture. On one occasion, she fractured her hip when falling out of bed. She had vivid dreams nightly but felt well rested in the mornings. Risk factors for stroke included cigarette smoking, systemic hypertension, ischemic heart disease, and mitral annulus calcification. The neurologic examination was normal. A polygraphic study showed REM sleep without atonia (Figure 10-2), phasic myoclonia, talking, and restlessness during REM stage. An MRI of the head showed multiple foci of increased signal intensity in periventricular white matter of both hemispheres and in the posterior pons, suggestive of ischemia (Figure 10-3). Administration of clonazepam 0.5 mg at bedtime stopped the events.

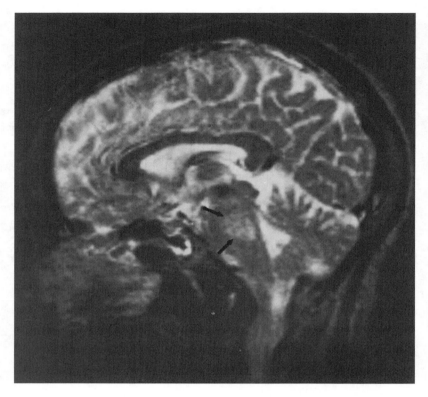

Figure 10-3. *Magnetic resonance imaging of the head of the patient referred to in Figure 10-2, illustrating pontine lesion (arrows) of probable ischemic origin affecting the tegmentum in the theoretical location of muscle atonia–generating centers. Compare this figure with Figure 10-4. (Reprinted with permission from A Culebras, JT Moore. Magnetic resonance findings in REM sleep behavior disorder. Neurology 1989;39:1519.)*

Experimental studies in the cat by Jouvet and Delorme [12] showed that discrete lesions in the dorsolateral rostral pons, in the region of the locus ceruleus, would eliminate muscle atonia during REM stage. The cats would develop REM stage but to the casual observer appeared awake, with orienting movements, standing up and even playing as if chasing a mouse, or displaying flight behavior. During such time, however, the animal would not respond to auditory or visual stimuli.

Subsequent experiments showed that the precise brain stem region responsible for muscle atonia during REM stage was the peri-locus ceruleus area. This center is linked by a direct tegmentoreticular tract to the inhibitory medullary area of Magoun and Rhines that is monosynaptically connected with spinal motoneurons by way of the reticulospinal tracts. Postsynaptic inhibition during REM sleep is the result of activity in this anatomic system that incorporates a cholinoceptive trigger zone in the dorsolateral pontine tegmentum (peri-locus ceruleus). Lesions of this pontine region cause the syndrome of REM sleep without atonia. Recent experiments have shown that lesions of the medial medullary region can also reproduce the syndrome of REM sleep without atonia in the cat [13].

It has been proposed that loss of muscle atonia during the REM stage facilitates motor overactivity, whether aperiodic jerks or complex organized behaviors. Hendricks et al. [14] have indicated that the location and extent of the pontine lesion determines the type of behavior exhibited by the cat, suggesting that in addition to causing REM without atonia, the brain stem lesion releases stereotypic behaviors. This observation furthermore suggests that pontine lesions abolish inhibition of motor pattern generators located in the brain stem.

Similar phenomena might occur in humans following appropriate brain stem lesions. Structural damage to the pontine tegmentum as caused by vascular disease or multiple sclerosis, degenerative lesions in patients with olivopontocerebellar degeneration, or neurotransmitter deficiencies in Parkinson's disease and Shy-Drager's syndrome, likely causes dysfunction of the anatomic pontomedullary system responsible for the development of atonia during REM stage (Figure 10-4). Many instances remain etiologically unexplained, but the preponderant presentation of the disorder in the elderly strongly suggests an acquired multifactorial alteration of a defined anatomic brain stem system with specific neurotransmitter effectors.

Apparent dream enactment is a key feature of the phantasmagoric experience that requires further elaboration. Elimination of the atonia that paralyzes motor effort during REM sleep necessarily facilitates motor overactivity. But in RSBD, motor overactivity is associated with an oneiric experience that is not only exuberant but also concordant with the motor act. The activation-synthesis hypothesis of Hobson and McCarley [15] provides a framework for developing a biological bridge between mind and body that explains the phantasmagoria. It allows the notion that liberation of motor system generators in the brain stem stimulates corollary forebrain areas, presumably through ponto-

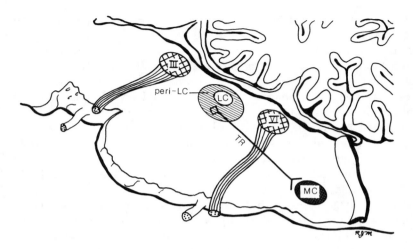

Figure 10-4.   *Diagrammatic representation of the pons in sagittal projection illustrating the location of muscle atonia–generating centers in REM sleep. The peri-locus ceruleus nucleus (peri-LC) in the pontine tegmentum is considered the principal generator of stimuli that travel through the tegmentoreticular tract to the magnocellular nucleus of Magoun and Rhines in the medulla and eventually reach the spinal motoneurons via the reticulospinal tract. III = N. oculomotoris; VI = N. abducens; LC = N. locus coeruleus; MC = N. reticularis magnocellularis; TR = F. tegmentoreticularis. (Reprinted with permission from A Culebras, JT Moore. Magnetic resonance findings in REM sleep behavior disorder. Neurology 1989;39:1519.)*

geniculo-occipital spike avenues. Activation of visual, affective, and amnestic circuits would synthesize a dream concordant and synchronous with the motor act, a phenomenon that McCarley [16] has characterized as dreaming out the act, as opposed to acting out the dream.

Recent clinical publications suggest that RSBD can appear in the absence of REM sleep without atonia. An enhancement of the system that generates phasic myoclonia in the presence of normal muscle atonia could in theory underlie such clinical observations [17]. Furthermore, it has been suggested that thalamic lesions could also release RSBD, suggesting that the thalamus normally exerts an inhibitory influence over motor activities during REM sleep [18].

The presentation of bizarre motor acts during sleep associated with a relevant dream in a middle-aged or elderly person, particularly if a man and with neurologic risk factors, should suggest a diagnosis of RSBD. Episodes commonly result in injury to the patient or spouse. The diagnosis is confirmed with polysomnography and video recording that show REM sleep without atonia; increased aperiodic motor activity in non-REM and REM sleep; and complex, organized motor activity during REM sleep segments, ranging from hand waving to running. Ratification comes when the administration of clonazepam results in the suppression of episodes.

RSBD should be distinguished from conventional nightmares (see Table 10-1) or dream anxiety attacks that generally end in an awakening without motor enactment. These events are more prevalent in younger patients, can be familiar, and tend to occur in persons with borderline personality disorders. Polysomnography fails to show the typical abnormalities of REM sleep without atonia. Sleep terrors and sleepwalking (see Table 10-3) occur in children or young adults. Both are more prevalent during non-REM sleep in the first third of the night and are not associated with dream content. Sleep terrors in adults are rare, but when they occur, there is a history of childhood events and evidence of psychopathology not present in RSBD. Sleepwalking in the adult is also relatively rare, while the childhood and family history are generally positive for the disorder. Nocturnal wanderings are episodes of complex, highly organized behavior during non-REM sleep characterized by ambulation associated with screaming and often violent automatisms (see Table 10-2). Dream content is absent or fragmented and static, as opposed to the complex, persecutory sequences of RSBD. Patients appear awake and wary although incoherent, resisting attempts to restrain them, which can result in violence and aggression. Patients are generally older adolescents and younger adults, occasionally with a history of epilepsy, which has led some to consider these episodes as epileptoid in nature. Polysomnography shows normal sleep architecture, but daytime and nighttime electrographic recordings occasionally reveal epileptiform activity. The condition responds favorably to the administration of carbamazepine. Confusional arousals are characterized by confused behavior immediately following an awakening from deep sleep. The patient appears awake but inquisitive, with motor acts that belie inappropriate cognition or incoherent language. Virtually universal in children before the age of 5 years, confusional arousals become increasingly rare as age advances. Sleep-related seizures occur in light non-REM sleep, are more common in children or young adults, and are sometimes associated with tongue biting and incontinence of urine. Electrographic tracings at night or during daytime hours generally show epileptiform discharges. Episodes respond to anticonvulsant medication but not to small amounts of clonazepam, in contrast to RSBD.

The diagnosis of RSBD in an older patient should elicit suspicion of an underlying cerebrovascular or neurologic degenerative disorder, so that an MRI of the head is recommended. RSBD could be the presenting complaint of small vessel arteriopathy involving the brain stem or of Parkinson's disease or Shy-Drager's syndrome [19]. Patients should be followed neurologically to detect potential neurologic problems as they develop.

Clonazepam, 0.5 mg at bedtime, is generally sufficient to suppress episodes and the associated violent dreams; in Schenck and Mahowald's series of 70 patients with RSBD, 89.5% responded favorably [10]. Clonazepam has no effect on REM sleep cycling or on the muscle tone alteration. Side effects are limited to morning sedation in susceptible individuals. Discontinuation of the treatment leads to recurrence of RSBD episodes. Clonazepam is not curative, but it should be administered to patients with RSBD to avoid nocturnal injury to the patient, along with spousal injury and sleeplessness. Other medications with reported RSBD-suppression effect in clonazepam-intolerant patients are carbidopa-levodopa, clonidine, and L-tryptophan.

Sleep Paralysis

Sleep paralysis refers to a condition in which individuals suffer the frightening perception of being unable to move, generally on awakening and occasionally on falling asleep. Patients are conscious and aware of their situation; however, the experience can be associated with hallucinatory imagery that belies its association with REM sleep. As is the case in REM sleep, subjects undergoing a sleep paralysis phenomenon are capable of breathing and moving their eyes. In fact, it has been reported that voluntary vigorous excursions with the eyes can break the spell and bring the individual out of the event. A sudden noise or a touch from a witness can also terminate the episode. Sleep paralysis events occur as an isolated phenomenon, although a familial incidence with a dominant trait bound to the X chromosome has been reported.

Sleep paralysis is clinically similar to the paralysis that occurs in patients with narcolepsy, and it very well might be that a number of individuals reporting sleep paralysis have narcolepsy or will develop the condition in later years. As an isolated episode occurring once in a life-time, the prevalence of sleep paralysis in the general population is high (40–50%) but very low as a recurrent condition outside narcolepsy. It has been reported with higher frequency in sleep-deprived individuals such as medical students [20], shift workers, and in individuals with jet lag syndrome.

Polysomnographic studies of narcoleptic individuals undergoing an episode of sleep paralysis show atonia in submental and other periph-eral muscles; presumably, muscle atonia continues as a dissociated residual phenomenon after the subject has awakened and the record already shows unequivocal desynchronized EEG with eye movements and blinking [21]. H-reflex activity is abolished during an episode of sleep paralysis, just as it is in REM sleep.

In awake individuals, cataplexy is triggered by emotions and appears in relation to a history of sleep attacks and hallucinations, whereas iso-lated sleep paralysis occurs in REM sleep-wake transitions unassoci-ated with other manifestations of REM sleep dysfunction. Recurrent attacks of paralysis in patients with hypokalemia appear during rest and on awakening, making the differential diagnosis with sleep paral-ysis difficult. Periodic hypokalemic sleep paralysis occurs in adolescents following a large carbohydrate meal and is reversed by correcting the low potassium level that can be identified in peripheral blood during attacks. A familial trait is generally uncovered.

Improving sleep hygiene might avert episodes of sleep paralysis in sleep-deprived individuals. In familial cases, clomipramine hydrochlo-ride, 25 mg at bedtime, has been recommended [22]. MAO inhibitors that are strong REM sleep suppressants can be effective, but the ben-efit should be measured against potential adverse reactions.

Sleep-Related Painful Erections

Sleep-related painful erections refers to a condition in which the sub-ject reports penile pain during erections associated with REM sleep [23]. The perception of pain usually awakens the patient, causing sleep loss along with other signs of sleep deprivation such as irritability, anx-iety, and excessive daytime sleepiness. Erections during daytime hours are not associated with pain. The condition is of unknown origin, although it is occasionally observed in association with Peyronie's dis-ease. Subjects with painful erections associated with phimosis also experience pain during daytime sexual arousal.

Rapid Eye Movement Sleep-Related Sinus Arrest

REM sleep-related sinus arrest is a nocturnal cardiac asystole that appears in relation to phasic REM sleep. The individual is generally unaware of the condition or at the most complains of vague chest pains during daytime hours and occasional lightheaded or even syncopal episodes on awakening and getting out of bed at night. It occurs primarily in young adults, and the prevalence is unknown because the disorder is asymptomatic.

The polysomnogram shows periods of asystole lasting up to 9 seconds in relation to phasic REM (see Figures 7-5 and 8-1) not necessarily associated with episodes of sleep apnea or of oxygen desaturation. Concurrent use of a 24-hour Holter monitor fails to show cardiac arrhythmias outside REM sleep. Guilleminault and colleagues [24] hypothesized that the powerful cholinergic output during phasic REM causes a vagotonic parasympathetic reduction of heart rate and inhibition of cardiac conduction in susceptible individuals with otherwise healthy hearts. This phenomenon might be linked to unexplained sudden nocturnal death so that installation of pacemakers has been recommended to prevent fatal cardiac arrest. Asystoles lasting up to 2.5 seconds are considered within normal limits in healthy young adults.

Sleep-Wake Transition Disorders

These alterations occur in the transitions from wakefulness to sleep, sleep to wakefulness, and from one sleep stage to another. When occurring with great frequency or severity, they can cause discomfort and social embarrassment, leading to a complaint of sleep abnormality. The following conditions are included in this section: rhythmic movement disorder, sleep starts, somniloquy, and nocturnal leg cramps.

Rhythmic Movement Disorder

Rhythmic movement disorder is the encompassing title for a series of relatively common repetitive motor phenomena affecting different parts of the body, variously known by the descriptive terms of jactatio capitis nocturna, head rolling, head banging, body rolling, and body rocking [25]. Movements are stereotypic and rhythmic, involving the head and sometimes the body, immediately preceding sleep and during early light sleep. In a typical situation, the child, usually a boy, lies in the crib face down, lifts up the head and sometimes the upper torso, and bangs the head onto the pillow. If supine, banging is done with the occiput against the pillow, mattress, or even headboard. Head rolling, as its name implies, consists of side-to-side movements of the head, whereas body rolling involves the entire body. Body rocking can assume bizarre postures such as when the child gets on his hands and knees and rocks forward and backward. The rhythm assumes a frequency of 0.5–2.0 movements per second; the movements occur in clusters with a duration of 10–15 minutes. Polysomnographic recordings show rhythmic movement artifact during light non-REM sleep without signs of epileptiform activity.

Episodes of head banging are primarily seen in infancy and generally resolve within the first 18 months of age, although occasionally they persist into early adulthood. Rhythmic movement activity of sleep appears in children of normal intelligence and no psychopathology, generally posing no danger. When present in older children or adults, it is usually characterized by violent rhythmic banging and associated with psychopathology. Sometimes, traumatic head injury results, including callus formation and hematomas where the banging is most persistent, as well as scalp lacerations and subdural hematoma. Rhythmic movement activity while awake is commonly observed in mentally retarded children. Treatment is unnecessary in most individuals. It might be required, however, when the motor activity causes traumatic head injury or the accompanying noise is disturbing to others or socially unacceptable. In such instances, benzodiazepines or tricyclics can be tried, but the success, particularly in adults, is variable.

Sleep Starts

Sleep starts, or hypnic jerks, are sudden, abrupt muscle group contractions independently involving the upper and lower extremities and sometimes the neck or the entire body, occurring at sleep onset. Jerks are aperiodic and asymmetric, appearing either spontaneously or induced by arousals. Individuals awakened by jerks can have a disconcerting impression of falling in space (siderealism) that, when intense and frequent, can lead to the nightly fear of drifting to sleep. Polysomnographic correlates show occasional vertex waves associated with electromyographic evidence of muscle contractions.

In contrast to its benign nature, the differential diagnosis of sleep starts is extensive and should be entertained with a variety of conditions that cause the extremities or parts of the body to move, jump, jerk, or convulse while the individual falls asleep. Such is the case with myoclonic jerks accompanied by epileptiform activity in the EEG, occurring in patients with epilepsy who might report seizures outside sleep. In the rare hyper-ekplexia syndrome [26], patients are easily startled and show myoclonic activity in response to minor stimuli either during wakefulness or in sleep. Fragmentary myoclonus [27] is characterized by involuntary brief muscle twitching that appears bilaterally in arms and legs and is of lesser ampli-tude than sleep starts. Fragmentary myoclonus is more common during non-REM sleep and is sometimes associated with a K complex discharge. Nocturnal leg myoclonus or periodic leg movements of sleep are repeti-tive, slow flexion-extension movements of the lower extremities that appear predominantly in light non-REM sleep. Nocturnal leg myoclonus is frequently associated with restless legs syndrome characterized by unavoidable leg posturing in response to an uncomfortable urge to move the lower extremities immediately before falling asleep.

Sleep starts are virtually universal and need no treatment other than reassurance in frightened individuals. Avoidance of caffeine, nicotine, and other stimulants can be helpful. In special circumstances, small amounts of clonazepam at bedtime have been successful in eliminating hypnic jerks.

Somniloquy

Somniloquy, or sleep talking, is a common parasomnia characterized by unintelligible mumbling or incoherent speech while asleep. The duration is brief, and the speech is generally devoid of meaning, uttered in short sentences without inflection or emotion. On rare occasions, emotionally charged long tirades with distinct pronunciation can be heard, their content related to the patient's occupation or preoccupa-tion [28]. Polyglots can have episodes of somniloquy in various lan-guages. Physical stimuli including talking to the sleeper can elicit somniloquy in susceptible individuals, a phenomenon that leads to the rare situation in which two sleepers talk to each other. Other para-somnias such as confusional arousals, sleep terrors, and RSBD are com-monly associated with sleep talking. In two-thirds of instances, the polysomnogram shows a brief partial arousal during light non-REM sleep; less commonly there is REM sleep, particularly if associated with dream content or when the patient suffers RSBD. The alteration is an annoyance to others, particularly if talking is abundant and occurs night after night. When associated with other sleep pathology, it should be considered a secondary disturbance.

Nocturnal Leg Cramps

Nocturnal leg cramps refers to sensations of painful tightness in the calf or muscle groups of the distal lower extremities that occur during sleep and awaken the patient [29]. One or two episodes per night can be sufficient to bring the condition to the attention of the primary physician who generally prescribes a compound with quinine to alleviate the discomfort. Further inquiry into the events reveals a poorly understood alteration, usually affecting the elderly, that disturbs nocturnal sleep in the context of a wide variety of medical conditions. These conditions include excessive muscular activity, dehydration, electrolyte imbalance, diabetes, peripheral neuropathy, neuromuscular disorders, arthritis, and Parkinson's disease. It is also seen in pregnancy, accounting for a higher prevalence in women. The differential diagnosis should be made with nocturnal periodic leg movements, which are painless but can coexist with leg cramps. Also it should be differentiated from muscle spasms occurring in patients with spasticity following strokes and other conditions damaging corticospinal tracts. In hemiparesis of any origin associated with spasticity, muscle spasms cause displacement of the affected limb, can be painful, and respond to benzodiazepines. If recurrent night after night, nocturnal leg cramps are best treated with quinine sulfate, 325 mg at bedtime. Massage, heat, and dorsiflexion of the foot are also palliative measures.

Other Parasomnias

The International Classification of Sleep Disorders sets aside a group of other parasomnias to incorporate phenomena that do not fit in the previous categories. In following the same order, we will study some of those parasomnias in this section. The parasomnias of infancy are found in Chapter 11.

Bruxism

Bruxism refers to repetitive grinding of the teeth during sleep, causing unpleasant noises that disturb the sleep of others. Grinding can be characterized by rhythmic chewing-like movements interspersed with periods of isotonic contraction of the jaw muscles. It is common in childhood and youth. The occurrence of bruxism in the adult suggests heightened stress as a predisposing factor and dental or mandibular disease as a precipitating factor. In a few persons, episodes of bruxism can occur hundreds of times during nocturnal sleep, leading to wearing down of teeth, periodontal damage, tooth mobility, and temporomandibular joint pains [30]. A familial tendency has been observed in some instances. Teeth grinding in wakefulness is associated with mental deficiency.

The polysomnogram shows brief but distinct episodes of muscle artifact lasting a few seconds, originating in facial muscles, and occurring in all stages of sleep but predominantly in stage 2. Treatment is necessary when the condition affects the integrity of the teeth and causes pain. Correction of dental, mandibular, maxillary, and malocclusion defects is recommended, while excessive stress is managed with the habitual measures of behavioral modification, psychotherapy, and sedatives in selected situations. Dental molds or mouth guards that prevent friction during sleep have been advocated by some.

Sleep-Related Abnormal Swallowing Syndrome

Sleep-related abnormal swallowing syndrome is a rare condition that results from pooled saliva in the hypopharynx overflowing into the upper airway provoking coughing, choking, and aspiration with arousal. The condition is more common in middle and advanced age and is brought to the attention of the physician when repeated episodes disrupt sleep. The abnormal swallowing syndrome is distinguished from gastroesophageal reflux by the absence of heartburn and chest pain, which are common in the latter disorder. The use of CNS depressants or hypnotic agents can be a predisposing factor.

Nocturnal Paroxysmal Dystonia

Nocturnal paroxysmal dystonia is a recently described parasomnia that has undergone various changes in its classification reflecting its as yet undetermined origin. It is characterized by an abrupt episode out of non-REM sleep in which the individual opens the eyes and displays a peculiar facial expression denoting surprise followed by dystonic posturing of the head, trunk, and limbs (Figure 10-5). The adventitious movements consist of head rotation, flexion of the neck and trunk, choreoathetoid movements of the limbs, and sometimes opisthotonus. Dystonic posturing is followed several seconds later by semipurposeful, stereotypic, and repetitive movements of the limbs. During the

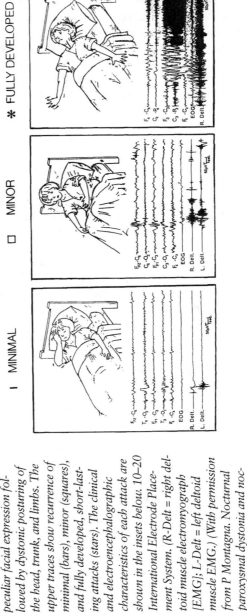

Figure 10-5. Sleep video-polysomnogram and hypnogram of a patient with nocturnal paroxysmal dystonia. The phenomenon is characterized by an abrupt episode out of non-REM sleep in which the individual opens the eyes and displays a peculiar facial expression followed by dystonic posturing of the head, trunk, and limbs. The upper traces show recurrence of minimal (bars), minor (squares), and fully developed, short-lasting attacks (stars). The clinical and electroencephalographic characteristics of each attack are shown in the insets below: 10–20 International Electrode Placement System. (R-Delt = right deltoid muscle electromyograph [EMG]; L-Delt = left deltoid muscle EMG.) (With permission from P Montagna. Nocturnal paroxysmal dystonia and nocturnal wandering. Neurology 1992;42:61.)

attacks, individuals vocalize unintelligible words with a tone of voice suggesting distress. After approximately 1 minute, subjects go back to sleep and the following day have no recollection of the event or at the most remember a few fragmented images.

Attacks can appear as often as 20 times per night [31], usually during stages 3 and 4 of sleep. The age of onset ranges from 3–47 years, and neurologic examination is usually normal; scalp EEG and imaging studies of the brain are likewise normal. Polysomnographic evaluation shows a paroxysmal arousal with autonomic activation such as tachycardia and tachypnea, followed by widespread muscle artifact, reflecting movement activity. During the paroxysmal arousal, there is no evidence of epileptiform discharges, but concomitant video recording shows stereotypic motor behavior as described. Patients displaying this activity have been considered hysterical or diagnosed as having atypical seizures. Tinuper and colleagues [32] have remarked that nocturnal paroxysmal dystonia has features resembling those of frontal lobe seizures of orbitomesial origin. In fact, some patients with nocturnal paroxysmal dystonia have reported daytime attacks of paroxysmal activity, and some authors have described interictal focal paroxysms in some of their patients [33]. In all instances, carbamazepine terminates the attacks, further suggesting a relation with an epileptiform process.

Long-lasting attacks of nocturnal paroxysmal dystonia with a duration of up to 50 minutes have been described in individuals with neurologic traits [34–36]. One subject developed Huntington's disease 20 years after the onset of attacks. The lack of therapeutic responsiveness to anticonvulsants suggests a nonepileptic origin.

Paroxysmal Arousals

Paroxysmal arousals are ultrashort attacks characterized by a sudden arousal out of SWS with a scream, opening of eyes, frightened facial expression, fleeting dystonic or athetoid limb movements, and autonomic activation [34]. Events last only a few seconds and are followed by sleep but no recollection. The polysomnogram reflects an arousal followed by movement artifact out of non-REM sleep without evidence of epileptiform discharges. Some authors [35] have suggested that attacks of paroxysmal arousal indeed represent epileptiform phenomena based on findings of highly synchronized activity appearing during non-REM sleep in some of their patients and subsequent relief with anticonvulsant medication.

Episodic Nocturnal Wandering

Episodic nocturnal wandering is the term given to attacks of extravagant behavior occurring at night characterized by abrupt arousal, violent ambulation, screaming, and utterance of unintelligible speech [37]. Individuals engage in complicated motor behavior such as running, leaping, kicking, and banging while displaying uncommon strength. The facial expression of subjects under such a spell reflects a wary, surprised look; if challenged, they resist advances with unusual violence, posing a risk of physical injury to themselves and to others. Patients are unaware of their nocturnal behavior and have no dream content or recollection of the episodes. The condition has been described in young men, and there is no evidence of a familial origin. Polysomnographic studies so far have failed to show abnormalities, but interictal EEGs have revealed focal epileptiform activity in anterior temporal areas [38]. Administration of carbamazepine has terminated the episodes, further suggesting an epileptic nature.

In many ways, episodic nocturnal wandering is similar to fugue states or poriomania observed in patients with temporal lobe epilepsy. In poriomania, patients wander aimlessly without recollection of the event. EEG recordings are abnormal, and anticonvulsants control the events, confirming their epileptic nature. The major difference is that poriomania appears during wakefulness, whereas episodic nocturnal wandering surges from light non-REM sleep. Other forms of nonepileptic nocturnal wandering such as observed in somnambulism, RSBD, and dementia with delirium or sundown syndrome are distinguished by the natural history of the disorder, the EEG characteristics, and the patient's response to anticonvulsants (see Tables 10-2 and 10-3).

Nocturnal Epileptic Seizures

Sleep and sleep deprivation are powerful activators of seizure activity. There is an intimate liaison between epilepsy and sleep; 25% of epileptics have seizures predominantly during sleep [39]. Sleep deprivation lowers the seizure threshold, increasing the tendency to develop recurrent seizures [40], which is the basis of the epileptic condition. Sleep deprivation is a well-known activator of epileptiform electrical discharges and of clinical seizures regularly used in the EEG laboratory. In general, non-REM sleep facilitates and REM sleep inhibits ictal activity.

The sleep of epileptics is commonly fragmented, but decidedly abnormal sleep patterns indicate underlying brain damage or toxic medication effect [41]. In patients with complex partial seizures, interictal epileptiform discharges tend to increase during early non-REM sleep, whereas in REM sleep, there is a marked reduction or disappearance of discharges. Sleep deprivation increases the rate of focal interictal epileptiform discharges, particularly during stage 2. At times, an episode of nocturnal incontinence is the only vestige of a seizure occurring at night while the individual is asleep; other signs are tongue biting and paroxysmal nocturnal headaches in epileptics. The unequal influence exerted on seizure activity by non-REM and REM sleep is also observed in the changing morphology of petit mal discharges in either state. In non-REM sleep, the typical 3-Hz discharges change to polyspike and wave complexes of varying frequency, whereas in REM sleep, discharges recover the standard 3-Hz frequency and morphology. REM sleep is not totally refractory to the development of other forms of paroxysmal activity since there are specific forms of complex partial seizures, particularly of limbic origin, that are more abundant or precipitated by REM sleep [42]. All ictal phenomena occurring during sleep suggest an epileptic event; however, the clinician should be mindful of other nonepileptic paroxysmal events as described in previous sections. To make the distinction, it is helpful to remember that genuine epileptic events are more common in children and young persons, appear more frequently in the transitions to wakefulness as well as in light non-REM sleep, and respond favorably to the administration of anticonvulsant medication. The diagnosis of an epileptic event is further suspected when the patient with nocturnal motor activity has associated incontinence of urine; the diagnosis is confirmed with the observation of ictal or interictal epileptiform discharges in the EEG channels of the polysomnogram. The video recording and analysis of ictal motor behavior facilitates the differential diagnosis, particularly if there are simultaneous electrical discharges observed in the EEG. In isolation, none of the previously described phenomena is genuinely epileptic. Thus, incontinence of urine might represent simple nocturnal enuresis, motor behavior might translate into somnambulism, a favorable response to anticonvulsants can reflect a nonspecific phenomenon, and headache might have another etiology.

The epileptic syndromes occurring predominantly in sleep are (1) juvenile myoclonic epilepsy (impulsive petit mal of Janz), (2) generalized tonic-clonic seizures on awakening, (3) benign childhood epilepsy with centrotemporal spikes (rolandic epilepsy), and (4) epilepsy with continuous spikes and waves during SWS. The first three syndromes have a benign prognosis, whereas continuous spikes and waves during SWS syndrome are associated with developmental neuropsychological alterations and dysphasia.

Juvenile Myoclonic Epilepsy

Juvenile myoclonic epilepsy, also known as myoclonic epilepsy of Janz [43], first occurs between the ages of 13 and 19 years and is characterized by bilateral, synchronous, myoclonic jerks of the extremities appearing in isolation or in multiple discharges. The jerks predominantly involve the upper extremities, forcing the patient to throw any objects held in the hands. When the contractions involve the lower extremities, the individual can lose stability and fall. Although consciousness is not lost, the subject appears confused when the paroxysms persist for some time. The crises appear more frequently in the morning on awakening, sometimes graduating into a secondary generalized convulsion; during the day they are occasionally associated with absence seizures. Sleep deprivation is an important precipitating factor. The EEG shows synchronous, bilateral 4- to 6-Hz spike and wave or polyspike and wave discharges localized in frontal areas sometimes in association with myoclonic motor activity. The neurologic and mental examinations are usually normal. Prevalence is similar in both sexes. Treatment with valproic acid is recommended, although primidone is also effective. Sleep deprivation and stress should be avoided. The prognosis is good if patients remain compliant with their treatment.

Generalized Tonic-Clonic Seizures on Awakening

Generalized tonic-clonic seizures [44] is a rather rare syndrome characterized by generalized convulsions on awakening from nocturnal sleep or following naps. Seizures appear in the second decade of life and sometimes are associated with myoclonic jerks resembling the myoclonic epilepsy of Janz. Photosensitivity is common in both conditions. The diagnosis is made when generalized seizures predominate. Treatment with phenytoin, carbamazepine, or valproate controls the seizures, but the rate of recurrence is high when the medication regimen is stopped.

Benign Childhood Epilepsy with Centrotemporal Spikes

Benign childhood epilepsy with centrotemporal spikes, also known as rolandic epilepsy and sylvian seizures [45], is characterized by generalized convulsions appearing at night in children between the ages of 3 and 13 years. Occasionally, patients suffer partial seizures with anarthria or aphasia during wakefulness, and clonic contractions of one side of the face with extension to the ipsilateral arm or leg without loss of consciousness. Febrile seizures are common in patients with rolandic epilepsy. Interictal EEG recordings show isolated negative spike or sharp wave and slow wave complexes in centrotemporal areas, alternating hemispheres, facilitated by light non-REM sleep. Centrotemporal spikes can be confused with temporal lobe discharges unless considered in the context of the clinical picture. Rolandic epilepsy shows a strong familial incidence with dominant autosomal traits; it can account for one-fourth of childhood epilepsies [46]. Prognosis is quite favorable, and treatment is carried out with phenytoin or carbamazepine if there are repetitive seizures. Interictal discharges and seizures disappear by the age of 15 years, and medication can be discontinued. Because episodes occur almost exclusively at night, the condition might be overlooked when events are scarce.

Epilepsy with Continuous Spike and Wave Activity During Slow Wave Sleep

Epilepsy with continuous spike and wave activity during SWS is a rare epileptic syndrome characterized by continuous spike and wave activity or electrical status during non-REM sleep [47]. The condition can be asymptomatic or associated with partial or generalized seizures during sleep as well as neuropsychological alterations. Some patients show absence spells during wakefulness. Neuropsychological alterations can persist despite successful therapeutic control of clinical epileptic phenomena that, nonetheless, have a tendency to disappear spontaneously in a few months or years. When epileptiform discharges affect the dominant hemisphere, the child might manifest deterioration of acquired language functions, a combination some label the Landau-Kleffner syndrome. Other authors prefer to reserve the term for the condition of developmental aphasia without epileptiform activity. Conventional anticonvulsants do not adequately control paroxysmal discharges occurring during SWS that according to some would be the cause of functional deterioration of the language centers. Adrenocorticotropic hormone can arrest progression of the disorder so that accurate diagnosis by means of polysomnography becomes important. This test might be indicated in all children presenting with behavioral changes, aphasia, and seizures [48]. Polysomnographic records show virtually continuous, partial, or generalized spike and wave activity at 2–2.5 Hz in non-REM sleep that disappears during REM sleep. In the absence of polysomnography, it becomes difficult to conduct a differential diagnosis with the Lennox-Gastaut syndrome.

Epilepsy and Sleep Apnea

Sleep apnea syndrome can occur with unusual frequency in epileptic patients. These subjects do not present the typical habitus of obesity, globular abdomen, and short, thick neck, suggesting that other factors might be important. Some epileptics treated for many years with phenytoin can develop dental malocclusion along with intraoral and velopalatine soft-tissue hypertrophy that might contribute to respiratory obstruction in sleep. Some patients exhibit a leonine facies with a large nose, as well as gingival hypertrophy and thick lips. In a few situations, epileptiform activity occurring at the termination of apnea events has led to the speculation of a triggering effect of unknown nature related to apnea [49].

Epilepsy and Nocturnal Death

Patients with epilepsy have a higher risk of dying in their sleep than nonepileptic individuals, partly because of the risk of developing status epilepticus. Generally, these patients are poorly controlled epileptics with low anticonvulsant levels and temporal or frontal cerebral lesion. Typically, patients are found in bed or near the bed without signs of convulsion. It has been hypothesized that the onset of a seizure provokes irreversible cardiorespiratory arrest or ventricular fibrillation that kills the patient [50].

References

1. Hawthorne N. The wives of the dead. In Tales and Sketches. New York: Literary Classics of the United States, 1982.

2. Bonkalo A. Impulsive acts and confusional states during incomplete arousal from sleep: Criminological and forensic implications. Psychiatry Q 1974;48:400.
3. Klawans HL. The Sleeping Killer. In Trials of an Expert Witness. Boston: Little, Brown, 1991;130.
4. Gastaut H, Broughton R. A clinical and polygraphic study of episodic phenomena during sleep. Rec Adv Biol Psychiatry 1965;7:197.
5. Broughton R, Billings R, Cartwright R, et al. Homicidal somnambulism: A case report. Sleep 1994;17:253.
6. Kales A, Soldatos CR, Bixler EO, et al. Hereditary factors in sleep walking and night terrors. Br J Psychiatry 1980;137:111.
7. Hartmann E. The Nightmare: The Psychology and Biology of Terrifying Dreams. New York: Basic Books, 1984.
8. Kales A, Soldatos CR, Caldwell AB, et al. Nightmares: Clinical characteristics and personality patters. Am J Psychiatry 1980;137:1197.
9. Lavie P, Hefez A, Halpern G, et al. Long-term effects of traumatic war-related events on sleep. Am J Psychiatry 1979;136:1175.
10. Schenck CH, Mahowald MW. Polysomnographic, neurologic, psychiatric, and clinical outcome report on 70 consecutive cases with REM sleep behavior disorder (RBD): Sustained clonazepam efficacy in 89.5% of 57 treated patients. Cleve Clin J Med 1990;57:9.
11. Culebras A, Moore JT. Magnetic resonance findings in REM sleep behavior disorder. Neurology 1989;39:1519.
12. Jouvet M, Delorme JF. Locus coeruleus et sommeil paradoxal. C R Soc Biol 1965;159:895.
13. Schenkel E, Siegel JM. REM sleep without atonia after lesions of the medial medulla. Neurosci Lett 1989;98:159.
14. Hendricks JC, Morrison AR, Mann GL. Different behaviors during paradoxical sleep without atonia depend on pontine lesion site. Brain Res 1982;239:81.
15. Hobson JA, McCarley RW. The brain as a dream state generator: An activation-synthesis hypothesis of the dream process. Am J Psychiatry 1977;134:1335.
16. McCarley RW. The Biology of Dreaming Sleep. In MH Kryger, T Roth, WC Dement (eds), Principles and Practice of Sleep Medicine. Philadelphia: Saunders, 1989;173.
17. Chase MH, Morales FR. The atonia and myoclonia of active (REM) sleep. Annu Rev Psychol 1990;41:557.
18. Lugaresi E, Medori R, Montagna P, et al. Fatal familial insomnia and dysautonomia with selective degeneration of thalamic nuclei. N Engl J Med 1986;315:997.
19. Sforza E, Zucconi M, Petronelli R, et al. REM sleep behavioral disorders. Eur Neurol 1988;28:295.
20. Penn NE, Kripke DF, Scharff J. Sleep paralysis among medical students. J Psychol 1981;107:247.
21. Nan'no H, Hishikawa Y, Koida H, et al. A neurophysiological study of sleep paralysis in narcoleptic patients. Electroencephalogr Clin Neurophysiol 1970;28:382.
22. Roth B. Narcolepsy and Hypersomnia. Basel: Karger, 1980.

23. Matthews BJ, Crutchfield MB. Painful nocturnal penile erections associated with rapid eye movement sleep. Sleep 1987;10:184.
24. Guilleminault C, Pool P, Motta J, et al. Sinus arrest during REM sleep in young adults. N Engl J Med 1984;311:1006.
25. Thorpy MJ, Govinsky P. Jactatio Capitis Nocturna. In MH Kryger, T Roth, WC Dement (eds), Principles and Practice of Sleep Medicine. Philadelphia: Saunders, 1989;648.
26. Gastaut H, Villeneuve A. The startle disease or hyperekplexia: Pathological surprise reactions. J Neurol Sci 1967;5:523.
27. Broughton R. Pathological Fragmentary Myoclonus, Intensified Hypnic Jerks and Hypnagogic Foot Tremors: Three Unusual Sleep-Related Movement Disorders. In WP Koella, F Obal, H Schulz, et al (eds), Sleep '86. Stuttgart: Gustav Fisher, 1988;240.
28. Arkin AM, Toth MF, Baker J, et al. The degree of concordance between the content of sleep talking and mentation recalled in wakefulness. J Nerv Ment Dis 1970;151:375.
29. Weiner JH, Weiner HL. Nocturnal leg muscle cramps. JAMA 1980;244:2332.
30. Ware JC, Rugh J. Destructive bruxism: Sleep stage relationship. Sleep 1988;11:172.
31. Montagna P. Nocturnal paroxysmal dystonia and nocturnal wandering. Neurology 1992;42:61.
32. Tinuper P, Cerullo A, Cirignotta F, et al. Nocturnal paroxysmal dystonia with short-lasting attacks: Three cases with evidence for an epileptic frontal lobe origin of seizures. Epilepsia 1990;31:549.
33. Sellal F, Hirsch E, Maquet P, et al. Postures et mouvements anormaux paroxystiques au cours du sommeil: dystonie paroxystique hypnogénique ou épilepsie partielle? Rev Neurol (Paris) 1991;147:121.
34. Montagna P, Sforza E, Tinuper P, Cirignotta F, et al. Paroxysmal arousals during sleep. Neurology 1990;40:1063.
35. Peled R, Lavie P. Paroxysmal awakenings from sleep associated with excessive daytime somnolence. A form of nocturnal epilepsy. Neurology 1986;36:95.
36. Lugaresi E, Cirignotta F, Montagna P. Nocturnal paroxysmal dystonia. J Neurol Neurosurg Psychiatry 1986;49:375.
37. Pedley TA, Guilleminault C. Episodic nocturnal wanderings responsive to anticonvulsant drug therapy. Ann Neurol 1977;2:30.
38. Maselli RA, Rosenberg RS, Spire JP. Episodic nocturnal wanderings in non-epileptic young patients. Sleep 1988;11:156.
39. Declerck AC. Interaction sleep and epilepsy. Eur Neurol 1986;25:117.
40. Logothetis J, Milonas I, Bostantzopoulou S. Sleep deprivation as a method of EEG activation. Eur Neurol 1986;25:134.
41. Baldy-Moulinier M, Touchon J, Besset A, et al. Sleep Architecture and Epileptic Seizures. In R Degen, E Niedermeyer (eds), Epilepsy, Sleep and Sleep Deprivation. Amsterdam: Elsevier, 1984;109.
42. Silvestri R, Domenico PD, Musolino R, et al. Nocturnal complex partial seizures precipitated by REM sleep. Eur Neurol 1989;29:80.
43. Janz D. Epilepsy with impulsive petit mal (juvenile myoclonic epilepsy). Acta Neurol Scand 1985;72:449.

44. Wolf P. Epilepsy with Grand Mal on Awakening. In J Roger, C Dravet, M Bureau, et al (eds), Epileptic Syndromes in Infancy, Childhood and Adolescence. London: John Libbey, 1985;259.

45. Lombroso CT. Sylvian seizures and midtemporal spike foci in children. Arch Neurol 1967;17:52.

46. Cavazzutti GB. Epidemiology of different types of epilepsy in school-age children of Modena, Italy. Epilepsia 1980;21:57.

47. Tassinari CA, Bureau M, Dravet C, et al. Epilepsy with Continuous Spikes and Waves During Slow Wave Sleep. In J Roger, C Dravet, M Bureau, et al (eds), Epileptic Syndromes in Infancy, Childhood and Adolescence. London: John Libbey, 1985;194.

48. Engel J Jr. Seizures and Epilepsy. Contemporary Neurology Series. Philadelphia: FA Davis, 1989;209.

49. Paroski MW, Fine EJ, Culebras A: Epileptiform discharges associated with sleep apnea. EEG and Clin Neurophysiol 1986;64:21P.

50. Jay GW, Leestma JE. Sudden death in epilepsy: A comprehensive review of the literature and proposed mechanisms. Acta Neurol Scand 1981;82:1.

11

Sleep in Infancy, Childhood, and Youth

Deborah C. Lin-Dyken and Mark Eric Dyken

Sleep in the pediatric population differs in many important ways from sleep in adults. In addition, the development of sleep and its concomitant clinical disorders varies greatly from infants to older children to adolescents. Sleep is an important aspect of every child's life. It is estimated that by the second year of life, a child will have spent 10,200 hours sleeping (approximately 14 months) [1], and by 5 years of age, approximately 50% of the time will have been consumed in sleep. Therefore, it is not surprising that sleep-related problems occur in approximately 25–30% of children seeking health care services [1]. This chapter explores the development of normal sleep as well as some common sleep problems in each of the pediatric age groups.

Infancy is defined as the period of life from the termination of the newborn period (first 4 weeks of life) to the time of assumption of erect posture (12–14 months); it is regarded by some to extend to the end of the first 24 months. Childhood is considered to be the period of life extending from infancy to puberty, and puberty is the period during which the secondary sex characteristics begin to develop and the capability of sexual reproduction is attained [2]. Age of onset is variable, but in general, puberty occurs in girls from ages 12–14, and in boys from ages 14–16 years [3].

Sleep in Fetal Life, Infancy, and Young Children

Development of Sleep and Wake Cycles

The exact mechanisms surrounding the development of sleep and wake cycles in fetal life are unclear. Spontaneous fetal movements can be appreciated at approximately 10 weeks' gestation with rhythmic cycling of motor activity generally occurring by 20 weeks. Much of the important information concerning sleep and waking physiology of the fetus has been obtained from electroencephalographic (EEG) studies performed on prematurely born infants. Before 24–26 weeks' gestation, there is a discontinuous burst-suppression EEG pattern called tracé discontinue, in which bursts of high-amplitude activity are interrupted by suppressed, flat, attenuated periods. This burst-suppression pattern represents 64% of the EEG tracing at 27–28 weeks and decreases to 45% by 31–32 weeks. From 29–40 weeks' gestation, the burst periods increase from 3.3–5.9 seconds, while the flat periods decrease from 9.3–4.4 seconds [4].

When comparing the respective sleeping and waking EEG recordings of premature and full-term infants of similar conceptual age, the findings are identical, with the exception that the degree of EEG organization is less pronounced in preterm infants. This difference might be caused by environmental effects since the extrauterine development of the premature newborn occurs in surroundings that are significantly different from the 24-hour darkness normally experienced in utero [5]. As a result, differentiating between sleeping and waking in the early preterm ages is based on both behavioral and physiologic measures. This practice is in contrast to the laboratory situation for older children and adults for whom such distinctions are generally based primarily on the EEG pattern alone [6].

At 28–32 weeks' gestation, the pattern becomes relatively unstable with alternating active periods associated with rapid eye movements, body movements, and irregular respiratory patterns, along with brief resting or quiet periods during which there are no significant body movements [7]. The waking and sleeping states for the first 3–6 months after birth are generally classified as wakefulness; active sleep, which is the correlate of REM sleep; and quiet sleep, the correlate of non-REM sleep [8]. In addition, periods that cannot be identified as one of the three already mentioned states are designated as indeterminate or transitional states. The indeterminate sleep state predominates in the early premature infant but represents only 3% of total sleep time in the full-term infant. Quiet sleep generally does not become significant until 36 weeks' gestation, after which it increases in amount, becoming the predominant sleep state at approximately 3 months of postnatal life [7].

Wakefulness in the full-term infant is characterized by open eyes with a bright, alert appearance, random body movements, vocalizations, irregular respirations, phasic electromyographic (EMG) activity, and an EEG that reveals uniformly distributed, low-voltage, irregular, mixed frequency activity.

At birth, the percentage of time spent in active sleep is greater than that spent in quiet sleep. Active sleep in a full-term infant has been estimated to account for anywhere from 35–80% of the total sleep time [9, 10]. Generally, by the time a child has reached approximately 6 months of age, this percentage decreases to 30% [11]. The active sleep state is associated with rapid eye movements and a generally suppressed EMG tracing that reveals occasional brief phasic body movements. The EEG during active sleep is desynchronized with predominantly theta activity intermixed with frequent delta waves and some alpha and faster rhythms. By 3 months of age, there is a resolution of the phenomena where active REM-like sleep appears during the onset of clinically apparent sleep.

During quiet sleep, rapid eye movements are not seen, the EMG activity is consistently elevated when compared with that of the active sleep state, and respiration is regular. Two major EEG patterns have been identified in quiet sleep: tracé alternant (TA) and high voltage slow (HVS). TA appears as 3- to 8-second bursts of slow waves, with a frequency of 0.5–3 Hz, that are occasionally associated with faster underlying activity and sharp waves (Figure 11-1). These bursts are separated by 4- to 8-second periods of EEG attenuation that are not as profound as the suppression periods associated with the tracé discontinue pattern seen in younger infants. This pattern generally resolves 3–4 weeks after term [12]. The HVS pattern can generally be appreciated by 36 weeks and replaces TA as the predominant quiet sleep pattern at 44–45 weeks postconceptional age.

By 9 weeks of age postpartum, one can usually appreciate the onset of sleep spindles and K complexes. These are EEG phenomena strongly associated with adult stage 2 non-REM sleep. Although sleep spindles are usually firmly established by 6 months, they generally appear in a relatively asynchronous manner across the cerebral hemispheres during the first year of life. By 3–6 months of age, all four stages of non-REM sleep can be appreciated. In general, by 6–12 months of age, sleep records can be scored using the adult Rechtschaffen and Kales criteria [13].

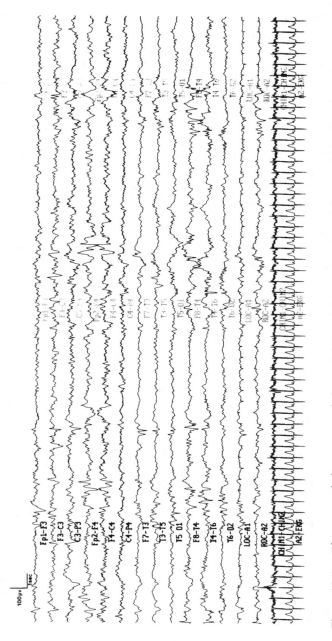

Figure 11-1. *Electroencephalogram recorded overnight in a behaviorally asleep, full-term newborn during quiet sleep. The tracing shows bursts of electrographic activity separated by periods of relative attenuation characteristic of tracé alternant. Paper speed, 15 mm per second; 10–20 International Electrode Placement System.*

Development of Circadian Rhythmicity

An important clinical consideration in the development of sleep in older infants is the gradual change in sleep pattern from ultradian rhythms to circadian rhythms. Ultradian rhythms are characterized by 3- to 4-hour periods of wakefulness that alternate with periods of sleep of similar length. In general, there is no day versus nighttime difference in the patterning of these episodes. In addition, the infant progresses through all four stages of non-REM sleep as well as REM sleep over a period of approximately 50 minutes [14–16], in contrast to the normal cycle of 90 minutes seen in adults and older children [17]. These rhythms can generally be appreciated between 6 and 12 weeks and of age, progressing to longer, more consolidated periods of wakefulness and activity during daytime hours and periods of rest and sleep during the night. Initially, the entrainment into the alternating patterns of behavior appears to be influenced more by feeding schedules than by cues of light and dark [18–20]. However, in later childhood and adulthood, the presence of other zeitgebers, which are environmental time cues such as sunlight, noise, meals, and social interactions, play a crucial role in maintaining these 24-hour cycles [21]. The development of circadian rhythms in young children leads to the concept of "settling" or sleeping through the night. This pattern generally begins between the ages of 3–6 months [22].

By 5–7 months of age, most infants should be able to sleep through the night without significant difficulty. A fairly common finding, however, is the reemergence of nighttime awakenings during the second 6 months of life [23, 24]. The exact cause of the redevelopment of these nighttime awakenings is unclear. Theories regarding this pattern indicate that this change might represent some type of developmental necessity on the part of the young child or might be a reflection of parent–child interactions. However, it is important to know that these awakenings do redevelop to avoid mishandling an otherwise benign situation and inadvertently causing chronic sleep difficulties.

Common Sleep Disorders

Sudden Infant Death Syndrome

Beginning shortly after birth and continuing through the first year of life, some of the most significant sleep problems in young infants are the ones associated with the controversial sudden infant death syndrome (SIDS). The syndrome is characterized by the unexpected death of apparently normal infants during nocturnal or daytime sleep. It is more common in lower socioeconomic classes, giving rise to hypotheses related to poor hygiene, parental ignorance, and alcoholism to explain the mysterious deaths, although no socioeconomic class has remained immune. SIDS occurs most frequently between the ages of 4 weeks and 6 months, with a seasonal predominance from October through March. Autopsy studies have shown few pathologic signs, and these were consistent with respiratory death. The syndrome has caused great public concern because of the drama surrounding the unexpected death of a child, sometimes with repeated incidence in the same family, which raises suspicions and accusations.

Various hypotheses concerning cardiorespiratory functions have been invoked to explain the pathophysiology of SIDS. Some newborns present ECG abnormalities such as prolongation of the Q-T interval, attributed to a sympathetic disequilibrium or to changes in heart rate caused by a variability in vagal tone. It has been suggested that the delay in the development of respiratory controls during non-REM sleep, when this state consolidates and acquires prominence by age 3 months, would increase the risk of sudden death [25]. This hypothesis would explain the temporal distribution of SIDS, which acquires its maximal incidence between 2 and 3 months of age [26]. Other pathogenic theories such as laryngospasm from laryngeal irritation and apneas of epileptic origin have been suggested. The role played by respiratory infections remains to be clarified, since there is suggestive evidence that it contributes to sudden death in some instances. Accidental suffocation and death in poorly designed cribs is another possibility.

The identification of infants with a tendency to develop SIDS continues to be a vexing problem. Risk factors are prematurity, complicated pregnancy, drug addiction during pregnancy, chronic disease, complicated delivery, history of admission to a neonatal intensive care unit, multiple pregnancies, very young mother, family history of SIDS, and developmental defects. Some authors recommend hospitalization of SIDS-prone infants until the high-risk period passes, particularly if there is evidence of prolonged episodes of apnea. Other authors recommend the home use of apnea alarms that are triggered when prolonged hypoxemia occurs. The home use of apnea alarms has been debated a great deal. These units do not reveal the cause when the alarm is triggered (for instance, prolonged hypoxemia or cardiac failure) and may provoke undue anxiety if sounding falsely. Parents need to be instructed in cardiopulmonary resuscitation in case an episode of prolonged apnea occurs. Although methylxanthines are useful for the treatment of the apneas in the premature infant, their role in the prevention of SIDS has not been established.

A recent decline in SIDS-related mortality has been attributed to the change in the generally accepted sleeping position recommendations that have been made by the medical profession for infants. Full-term, healthy infants with no craniofacial abnormalities are no longer encouraged to be placed in the prone sleeping position, but rather in the supine position. It has been noted that infants in the prone position sleep longer and have fewer arousals than infants placed in the supine position. Infants with "near-miss SIDS" might have differences in sleep development. In these infants, the amount of stage 2 sleep is lower at 3 months, the expected reduction in the amount of REM sleep with normal aging is delayed, and motility in sleep is decreased when compared with that of normal controls. As a result of these findings, one hypothesis for SIDS is that infants with faulty arousal mechanisms, which can be associated with abnormal sleep stage development, can in some way be more susceptible to sudden death when placed in the prone sleeping position. This theory has not been substantiated scientifically.

The relationship of near-miss SIDS to actual SIDS death also remains unclear. In a series of sleep studies on near-miss SIDS patients, some of whom eventually died from SIDS, there was one major common finding: SIDS victims had more mixed and obstructive apneas than normal when monitored immediately after their near-miss episodes. Some SIDS victims have upper airway abnormalities that can indicate a potential increased risk for the development of obstructive sleep apnea. However, it remains unknown how many SIDS victims die from apnea during sleep [27].

Case Study 11-1

B. B. is a 4-week-old male infant who was transferred for further evaluation and management of an apparently serious apnea event that occurred in the evening, 2 days before admission. B. B. weighed 2575 g when he was born at 36 weeks' gestation to a 24-year-old gravida 3, para 3 mother whose pregnancy was apparently uncomplicated except for preterm labor. B. B.'s father was caring for him one evening when he heard a squeaky noise from B. B.'s bassinet, went to check on him, and found him limp, dusky, blue, and not breathing. The father was able to revive B. B. by shaking him a bit. The local ambulance service was notified as the father turned B. B. over and suctioned mucus out of his mouth. When the ambulance arrived, B. B. again became apneic and required positive pressure oxygen by bag and mask. He was transported to the local emergency room where he continued to require positive pressure oxygen. The initial work-up including ECG, echocardiogram, and head computed tomography were normal. The physical examination showed no evidence of child abuse, and the parents adamantly denied this possibility. Overnight polysomnography revealed frequent central apneas, almost exclusively in active sleep. The overall apnea index was 64 events per hour, with a saturation of oxygen nadir of 82% in active sleep. The highest frequency of central apneas was approximately four per minute with the duration of apneas ranging from 6–12 seconds. No significant abnormalities were noted in the EEG monitor or in the ECG channel during the periods of apnea. B. B. was discharged on the third hospital day and was placed on continuous home monitoring. The parents were instructed on management of home monitoring and CPR technique.

Sleeplessness and Insomnia

When evaluating sleep problems in infants, it is important to remember that because the parents or caregivers are the providers of the history, it is subsequently their complaint, and not the child's, that must be evaluated. The complaint often refers to the effect that the child's symptoms are having on the parents' lives. The child might be happy with the status quo, whether it is sleeping with the parents, staying up late, waking up frequently at night, or waking up too early.

Sleeplessness in children is not the same as insomnia, a term that implies a strong desire to go to sleep but an inability to do so. Children might not actually want to go to sleep and might attempt vigorously to stay awake. The act of falling asleep has evolved so that it preferentially is temporally and physically limited to safe places. The consequence of this evolution is that perceived threats might induce a high state of vigilance that can delay sleep onset and impair sleep continuity, subsequently leading to significant sleep loss.

The most common sleep problems in young children occur from sleep-onset associations that can result from inappropriate environmental conditions that parents might provide during the period surrounding the bedtime hours [22, 28]. Symptoms of sleep-onset associations can be either positive, leading to the rapid onset of sleep, or negative, producing difficulties initiating and maintaining sleep. Problematic sleep-onset associations are often the result of inappropriate or excessive interventions that parents might use to induce sleep in their children; these interventions might include rocking, holding, patting, nursing, bottle feeding, the habitual use of a pacifier, and even car rides [29]. Several important points need to be kept in mind. First of all, everyone has sleep-onset associations, which can include reading, watching television, listening to music, or using an assortment of pillows and blankets to assume certain positions in bed. In most instances, these activities are initially under the control of the individual, and then become simply a matter of habit. Additionally, everyone wakes up briefly several times during the night. These "microarousals" occur almost unconsciously, and generally the return to sleep is quick and uncomplicated. Most people do not recollect these awakenings the next day. It is important to stress to parents whose children are experiencing frequent nighttime awakenings that their children's awakenings are in all probability normal. Parents frequently see nighttime awakenings as abnormal and feel it is their job to get their children back to sleep. To treat these problems, it is important to counsel parents that their children are experiencing a normal phenomenon of sleep and that they merely need to provide for conditions under which the children can initially get to sleep or return to sleep by themselves if nocturnal arousals occur.

Essentially, sleep-onset associations are self-comforting habits, which increase in response to stress and are highly rewarding since they decrease stress. Punishment is never recommended in dealing with sleep-onset associations. It heightens stress and anxiety, and therefore increases the drive toward further engagement in a particular behavior. Punishment also forces the child to override an intense drive to self-comfort and generally is not effective in the long run. Parents should be instructed to anticipate the "extinction burst," or initial worsening, of the behavior when the treatment plan is first implemented and to vigorously maintain the program. Just one night of regression can undermine weeks of effort. It can be helpful to have parents anticipate what will cause them to give in, so that alternative strategies can be planned in advance.

Once a child has developed a strong negative sleep-onset association that requires a parent's presence for sleep onset to occur, the cornerstone of the treatment plan is to first put the child into the crib while the child is drowsy and not completely asleep. This step essentially teaches the child how to fall asleep without assistance. If and when the child awakens at night, the parents should be counseled to wait progressively longer periods of time before going back into the child's room. When parents do enter the child's room, they should spend a brief amount of time making sure that the child is not sick, hurt, or in any type of physical discomfort. They can then briefly speak to the child and reassure the child that everything is all right. They should not pick up the child, and they should not stay in the room until the child is completely asleep. The parent should leave the room and allow the child to eventually fall asleep without assistance. It is generally recommended that this technique be used for children who are 5 months of age or older. Younger children might not be biologically ready to sleep through the night yet and on occasion can have real physiologic needs that are causing the nighttime awakenings [22, 28].

Another sleep problem in young children is the result of excessive nighttime feedings. Symptoms associated with this disturbance include frequent awakenings with return to sleep only with bottle feeding or nursing. Frequent feedings can result in arousals caused by excessive wettings, the child's expectation of feedings (a learned behavior), or secondarily acquired circadian rhythm effects. In general, at bedtime, body temperatures are low and the upper gastrointestinal tract is empty. Frequent nighttime feedings can lead to a daytime-like pattern of increased body temperature, enhanced gut motility, and higher insulin secretion that can in itself disrupt sleep continuity. The treatment for this disorder is to taper and then discontinue nighttime feedings. This process can be done by decreasing the volume of bottle feedings by an ounce every day or two, spacing out feedings, or watering down formula [22, 28].

Poor limit setting on the part of parents can lead to sleep problems, particularly in older children. Symptoms of these problems include bedtime refusals to go to sleep, stalling, and multiple nighttime demands. Typically, these are learned behaviors for which children derive secondary gain from parental attention. In effect, it is the child who is now given control of the bedtime situation. The appropriate treatment is parental education and counseling that it is correct to set limits. A child will feel more secure knowing that certain rules regarding acceptable and unacceptable behaviors exist and that parents are truly in charge. Parents often require concrete and specific instructions regarding how to set limits. Typically recommended strategies include timed door closings and the use of a safety gate for children who have difficulties staying in bed or persist in leaving the bedroom [22].

Case Study 11-2

M. E. is a 22-month-old girl who was evaluated for frequent nighttime awakenings. At approximately 1 year of age, the child fell out of her crib and became difficult to put to sleep. Her mother felt that the patient was a restless sleeper, because she was rolling up against the crib railings, so she took the child out of the crib and placed her to sleep on a mattress on the floor. However, the child continued to wake up during the night, beginning approximately 2 hours after she was put to sleep. The parents then became concerned that the child was afraid to fall asleep alone, so she was placed to sleep on several blankets on the living room floor, between 9:15 and 9:30 P.M., with the television on and with her parents sitting on a nearby sofa. She slept until 2:00 or 3:00 A.M., at which time she would wake up calling for her bottle. After a few swallows, she would throw the bottle down and go back to sleep within a few minutes. This routine was repeated approximately every 2 hours until 7:30 A.M., at which time she would awaken for the day. Afternoon naps were taken under the same conditions. Recommendations to the parents included immediate withdrawal of the bottle, and a stepwise approach to moving the blankets onto a mattress on an appropriately sized toddler bed in the child's own bedroom and placing the child to sleep on this bed. A safety gate was recommended for the bedroom doorway. Bedtime refusals and nighttime awakenings were to be managed with progressively longer periods of time between door closings and parental visits to the bedroom. Allowing the child to leave the bedroom was strongly discouraged. Naps were also to be taken in the bedroom. After approximately 2 weeks, the child was falling asleep in her own bed and sleeping through the night.

Difficulty in falling asleep at bedtime secondary to real fear and anxiety must be differentiated from stalling. For example, children who come from abusive, neglectful, or otherwise dysfunctional family environments can experience true emotional stressors in the evening hours, which can lead to anxiety disorders that can be associated with symptoms that are rational and situational or irrational and free floating. For such individuals, it can be inappropriate to use the previously discussed strategies of strict limit setting. Instead, therapy might center around interventions such as scheduled adjustments, relaxation of limits, behavior modification, gradual desensitization, periodic checking, temporary co-sleeping, and in severe instances, counseling and psychotherapy [22, 28].

Young children can also have difficulties sleeping at night because of a variety of medical problems, such as middle ear disease, gastroesophageal reflux, or milk allergies, which can all produce nighttime symptoms. In addition, medication side effects can lead to disrupted sleep. Commonly used medications with possible detrimental effects on sleep include theophylline preparations for asthma, anticonvulsants, and stimulant medications for hyperactivity.

Children with severe neurologic impairments can have markedly disrupted sleep. These children can exhibit extremely irregular sleep patterns, in addition to having low total sleep requirements. This problem might be caused by dysfunction of the central systems that control sleep and waking cycles. These situations are often difficult to manage, and the children might never achieve normal sleep. In general, it is recommended to treat coexisting medical, behavioral, environmental, and schedule or sleep hygiene problems first. If problems persist after these interventions, nighttime sedation might be necessary. Chloral hydrate, at times in large doses, has generally been the most effective for this population [22]. Recent reports indicate that melatonin might also be useful in this group of children under certain circumstances [30].

Scheduling problems are an example of sleep difficulties that appear when young children do not follow proper sleep hygiene (Table 11-1). In assessing a child's sleep schedule, two important concepts should be kept in mind: the "forbidden zone" and *schlafbereitschaft*. The forbidden zone is the period of best wakefulness and alertness, representing the most difficult time during the day for the child to actually fall asleep. This zone generally occurs in the early evening hours, just before the time the individual normally falls asleep. Children are often described as having their second wind in the forbidden zone. Schlafbereitschaft literally means sleep readiness and denotes a time when the child is both physiologically and psychologically ready for sleep. Often, bedtime struggles are encountered if the child is put to bed during the forbidden zone instead of the time during which sleep readiness occurs.

Children can have specific circadian tendencies toward either early or late sleep-phase disorders. The ones with an early sleep phase tend to

Table 11-1.   Sleep Patterns and Hygiene in Infancy and Childhood

Sleep is not linked to the cycle of day and night until the age of 3 months

Between the ages of 3 and 6 months, the infant sleeps 14–15 hours, mostly during the night, with two or three daytime naps

At the age of 6 months, total sleep time is 14 hours, with two daytime naps amounting to 3 hours

At 1 year of age, the infant sleeps 11.5 hours at night, and 2 hours during one daytime nap

At the age of 5 years, the child requires 11 hours of nocturnal sleep; at 9 years, 10 hours; at 14 years, 9 hours. Daytime naps are abandoned at 4 years of age depending on local customs

Sleep schedules should be regular and stable including weekends and holidays. Loss of discipline may lead to behavioral insomnia

Nocturnal feedings should be eliminated to avoid conditioned awakenings

Sleep in infancy and childhood should take place in an environment that is tranquil, relaxed, clean, comfortable, cozy, and safe. Loss of sleep may retard physical and mental development

fall asleep early, wake up early, and have early meal and nap times, whereas children with a late sleep phase generally stay up late, have difficulty falling asleep early, and have difficulty waking up early in the morning. Late-phase children also tend to have later meal times and nap times. In general, for the toddler and preschool group, gradual phase shift protocols are not required. The child can be moved directly to a new bedtime and wake time without significant difficulty, as long as the new schedule is maintained consistently over several days. It is important to realign the child's entire schedule, so that meal and nap times correlate with the new bedtime and morning waking time. Before aggressively attempting to correct a presumed sleep problem, it should be recognized that parents often overestimate their young child's sleep requirements.

The parental misperception concerning "too little sleep" might need to be distinguished from the short sleeper syndrome. Short sleepers require a relatively small total amount of sleep and subsequently experience no symptoms of daytime sleepiness. Although many parents complain that their children sleep an insufficient number of hours, the diagnosis of short sleeper is actually rare and essentially is a diagnosis of exclusion [21, 28].

Excessive Sleepiness

Excessive sleepiness in a young child is often expressed as behavioral problems, at home or in school, frequently associated with hyperactivity and irritability. Detailed sleep logs and sleep diaries generally indicate that most children sleep a similar total number of hours night after night. However, parents who misinterpret their child's needs might require the child to go to bed very early or spend much longer periods of time in bed. Their attempts to correct these problems can result in irregular sleep patterns with a combination of delayed sleep onset (there is nothing more difficult than getting a child to fall asleep the evening before a major holiday or birthday), extended nighttime arousals, and early morning awakenings with subsequent behavioral difficulties.

Childhood Years

In general, childhood is considered the gold standard of sleep quality; it is the period of life when humans achieve the best sleep that they will ever have. Several observations contribute to this belief. Children, for the most part, have very short sleep latencies; they usually fall asleep 5–10 minutes after lying down in bed. Children routinely obtain 8–10 hours of consolidated sleep per night, with very few spontaneous arousals, which results in excellent sleep efficiencies that are often greater than 95%. Arousal in the morning is usually spontaneous, and there are generally no difficulties with excessive daytime sleepiness. Despite this relatively protected phase, there are several important sleep disorders frequently seen in this age group that include parasomnias, partial arousals, enuresis, rhythmic movement disorders, and obstructive sleep apnea.

Parasomnias

There is a large list of parasomnias (see Chapter 10) headed by night terrors, sleep walking, and head banging [31]. The proposed pathophysiology of parasomnias is multifactorial and includes constitutional, precipitating, and perpetuating factors. Among the constitutional factors is the genetic predisposition with an increased incidence in affected families. Developmental changes in the CNS also appear to be important, and many parasomnias are associated with deep slow wave sleep (SWS), which in general occupies a greater percentage of total sleep time in children.

Although parasomnias can occur spontaneously, there are precipitating factors that can lead to a relative sleep deprivation that results in a rebound or more intense SWS when the child is allowed to recover sleep. Precipitating factors include psychological disorders, which are often associated with chaotic sleep-wake cycles; medical problems such as fever and gastroesophageal reflux; seizure disorders; administration of certain drugs such as lithium, major tranquilizers, and doxepin; intrinsic sleep pathologies including obstructive sleep apnea; and the many periodic and aperiodic movement disorders of sleep. It is believed that these phenomena can jolt the child from SWS into a lighter stage such as stage 1 or 2, and produce a partial arousal, which can often be recognized as one of the parasomnias. Perpetuating factors include conditioned responses to the arousals. It is believed that the combination of constitutional, precipitating, and perpetuating factors builds to a threshold level beyond which an arousal or parasomnia occurs [31].

The parasomnia evaluation can be difficult. An accurate history, including a relation of psychosocial and family factors that might predispose to parasomnias, should be obtained. It is important to determine the time of night when the arousals occur, and to obtain a description of the child's behavior, level of consciousness, and responsiveness during a spell. In addition, the physician should assess whether the child recollects the event the following morning. The general physical and neurologic examinations are almost always normal. The usefulness of a polysomnogram to assess parasomnias remains somewhat controversial; however, in general, it is believed that a sleep study can be helpful when the arousals are recurrent, stereotypic, or associated with injury. In such instances, a polysomnogram is used to rule out seizures, obstructive sleep apnea, gastroesophageal reflux, or sudden arousals of medical origin that might mimic a parasomnia. Because parasomnias often do not occur on a nightly basis, a series of consecutive sleep studies might be needed to capture an actual spell.

When partial arousals or suspected parasomnias are associated with specific disorders such as seizure, reflux, or apnea, the underlying problems should be treated first. If the arousal is a conditioned phenomenon, similar to the ones previously discussed, deconditioning techniques should be used. In night terrors or nightmares, a thorough search should be made for a possible precipitant factor, such as a recent frightening experience or watching a horror movie; subsequently, precipitant factors should be avoided to prevent future recurrences. Treatment begins with parental education and reassurance that parasomnias are generally benign phenomena, especially when certain guidelines are followed to ensure the child's safety. Family members should not try to vigorously awaken a child during spells because the child might perceive the attempt as a threatening act. As much as possible, the sleep environment should be protected from sources of inadvertent injury that could result from mishaps when encountering sharp or dangerous objects, falling down the stairs, or walking out of the house and into a street. Relaxation therapy, mental imagery, and psychological counseling can be helpful in some instances. Some medications including clonazepam and tricyclics have been used with varying success. The recommended dosage of clonazepam for children up to 10 years of age or 30 kg in weight is initially 0.01–0.05 mg per kg in 24 hours, divided into three doses, with increments of 0.25–0.5 mg per 24 hours every 3 days, up to a maximum maintenance dose of 0.1–0.2 mg per kg per 24 hours divided into three doses. In older children and adults, the initial dose of clonazepam is 1.5 mg per 24 hours, divided into three doses, with increments of 0.5–1.0 mg per 24 hours every 3 days, up to a maximum dosage of 20 mg per 24 hours [32]. The use of timed awakenings in which the child is awakened 15 minutes before the usual occurrence of the event, over a period of several nights, has been reported to be successful in some instances [31].

Case Study 11-3

R. B. is a 14-year, 4-month-old young man who was seen in the clinic for evaluation of sleepwalking. According to his mother, R. B. has been sleepwalking for years, approximately once a week. His mother recalls one episode during which she caught the patient sleepwalking into the backyard at 1:00 A.M. on a winter night. R. B. has no memory in the morning of the sleepwalking episodes. He has never sustained injuries secondary to the sleepwalking. His mother estimates that sleepwalking occurs most commonly between midnight and 2:00 A.M. R. B.'s usual bedtime is 10:00 P.M. He starts out in his bed, but might end up on the couch in the living room or on the floor. In addition, R. B. sleep talks several times a week and has complained of daytime sleepiness. There is a strong family history of parasomnias. The mother frequently walked in her sleep as an adolescent, and the father walked and talked in his sleep during his teenage years. R. B.'s older brother frequently walked in his sleep and reportedly once drove a car in his sleep. Two of R. B.'s older sisters had sleepwalked in childhood. An overnight polysomnogram revealed a sleep efficiency of 94%, with no apneas or hypopneas noted during the study. One brief episode of somniloquy occurred during stage 3. Comments the patient made during this episode could not be understood. No sleepwalking occurred. The patient and his family were advised to ensure a safe sleeping environment that would provide adequate protection from injury to the patient and others, encourage good sleep hygiene, and consider counseling and psychological or psychiatric assessment if stress in the patient's life or in the family exacerbated nocturnal symptoms.

Rhythmic Movement Disorder

This parasomnia includes behaviors such as head banging (jactatio capitis nocturna), body rocking, and leg banging. These behaviors occur with a high frequency in the normal population and typically begin between 6 and 9 months of age. Although the movements are generally benign and resolve over a relatively short period of time, they can persist into the grade school years and can be associated with injury and a variety of neuropsychological concomitants. Polysomnographic studies have shown that these behaviors can arise in drowsiness, stages 1 and 2, occasionally in SWS, and rarely in REM sleep. Rhythmic movement disorder can be associated with vocalizations and moaning, and at times can raise the suspicion of seizures. On average, the movement episodes last only 1–15 minutes, but they can persist for hours. Unfortunately, there is no good treatment for rhythmic movement disorders, other than protecting the sleeping environment and aggressively addressing any concomitant neuropsychological problems that might exist. However, a thorough neurologic and psychological assessment should be considered in patients with chronic severe head banging who are beyond the age of 3 years [33]. Injuries occur in patients with severe mental retardation and a variety of psychopathologies. Trauma is the result of violent head banging that generally happens while the individual is awake and can result in subdural hematoma [34], skull deformities [35], and eye injuries [36].

The use of helmets, behavior modification [37], and aggressive management of neuropsychological problems can be beneficial. Short-acting benzodiazepines, such as oxazepam, 10–20 mg taken at bedtime, and the tricyclic imipramine can reduce rhythmic movement disorder for days to weeks. Because tolerance to these medications can rapidly develop, they are not recommended for prolonged use and should be taken only on selected nights when the ensuing day's social activities demand a good night's rest. Anticonvulsants have been ineffective in treating the disorder.

Case Study 11-4

N. F. is an 8-year, 5-month-old girl admitted for evaluation and management of behavioral and learning problems. The family was also undergoing significant emotional and financial stressors, but the mother felt that N. F.'s sleep problems were a primary concern. According to the mother, N. F. requires a long period of time to fall asleep and awakens throughout the night. Sleep was assessed initially by videotaping nighttime behaviors. During the first 4 nights, N. F. slept through the night, but her sleep was restless. Beginning on the fifth night, an extremely restless pattern emerged, averaging five to six rocking episodes per night. An overnight polysomnogram revealed five discrete episodes of head banging, body rocking, or leg banging, generally arising from either stage 1 or stage 2 sleep. N. F. spent a total of approximately 85 minutes exhibiting rhythmic behavior. A multiple sleep latency test revealed no evidence of daytime sleepiness. At one time during the admission, N. F. sustained a nosebleed as a result of a head banging episode. Management recommendations included the use of a hospital bed at home, with side rails and padding to prevent potential serious injury; family counseling; consideration of short-term out-of-home respite care service; and implementation of an ongoing behavioral management program.

Enuresis

Enuresis is defined as three or more episodes of involuntary nocturnal wetting per week; it is usually a much greater problem in boys than in girls. The incidence decreases with age, with a 15% spontaneous cure rate per year. At the age of 6 years, approximately 25% of boys and 15% of girls will have enuresis; however, by the age of 12 years, only 8% of boys and 4% of girls will be enuretic. Enuresis can occur on a familial basis. Sometimes, dream content is related to the act of urination in association with the episode of enuresis. Predisposing factors are admission to a hospital and belonging to a lower socioeconomic group.

Primary enuresis refers to involuntary micturition during sleep past the age of 5 years when voluntary control is normally achieved. Patients with primary enuresis have no organic or psychological disorder so that a focal retardation of neurologic development is suspected. Idiopathic and familial enuresis fall into this group. Secondary enuresis refers to episodes of nocturnal micturition that appear after voluntary sphincter control has been achieved and maintained for at least 6 months. This form of enuresis can be secondary to anatomic anomalies, neurologic defects, or acquired disorders. Nocturnal incontinence during febrile episodes, in association with intense stress, following excessive ingestion of fluids, or related to the administration of sedative medications is not considered conventional enuresis. The differential diagnosis also needs to be made with organic disorders that cause nocturnal urinary incontinence. These disorders include diabetes, nephrogenic diabetes insipidus, decreased antidiuretic hormone secretion at night, and seizures.

Although the pathophysiology of primary enuresis remains largely unknown, a number of hypotheses born out of suggestive findings have been proposed. Some patients might have a small bladder, insufficient to retain all the urine produced during the prolonged nocturnal sleep of childhood. Control of the external sphincter might be incomplete, resulting in an uninhibited bladder for unknown reasons but related to CNS immaturity. Recurrent urinary tract infections can be both cause and consequence of enuresis: The irritation produced by the infection increases the number of episodes of enuresis, and perineal dampness promotes infections. When the infection is eliminated, enuresis disappears in one-third of instances [38]. Anatomic obstruction of the neck of the bladder, or stenoses of the ureter or meatus provoke nocturnal and daytime enuresis. There are also instances of enuresis associated with anomalies of the cordlike diastematomyelia and other structural lesions.

The evaluation should begin with a careful genitourinary history that includes presence of daytime wetting, characteristics of the stream, frequency, urgency, dysuria, hematuria, pyuria, or manifestations of a urinary tract infection. This history is complemented by an assessment of features suggesting organicity, such as weight loss, polyuria, polydipsia, snoring, seizures, constipation, and encopresis. In addition, an evaluation of the psychosocial situation, including the parents' and child's level of distress about the situation, should be conducted. The results of any previous therapeutic attempts should be reviewed. In girls, the physical examination should include an inspection of the genitourinary system to look for inflammation, exudate, adhesions, or the presence of an ectopic ureter. In boys, the voiding pattern should be observed. Palpation of the abdomen and a rectal examination should be performed to search for abnormal masses. The upper airway should be assessed for anything that might predispose the patient to nocturnal respiratory disorders, such as tonsillar or adenoidal hypertrophy, abnormalities in the craniofacial structures, and altered muscle tone. A neurologic assessment for a tethered cord should be performed, including inspecting for a sacral dimple and evaluating lower extremity sensation, muscle stretch reflexes, and gait. Laboratory evaluations include a urinalysis and a urine culture.

Polysomnography in children with primary enuresis shows a normal sleep architecture. Episodes can occur in any stage of sleep, although they tend to predominate during the first third of the night when SWS is prevalent. The polysomnographic study can help define the diagnosis and is important to exclude conditions, such as obstructive sleep apnea syndrome, that can be associated with enuresis, and seizures that cause incontinence of urine.

Treatment options cover a wide range of modalities. An expectant attitude can be justified by a spontaneous yearly cure rate of 15%. Interventions include fluid restriction; punishments or rewards, such as giving the child responsibility for cleaning the bed sheets, or using star charts; relaxation and mental imagery training, which has a success rate of approximately 75%; bladder exercises with techniques such as waking the child at a predetermined time of night to void; and the use of a wetness pad attached to an alarm, which is effective in about 70% of instances.

Pharmacologic treatment is considered when training, conditioning, and other psychotherapeutic methods fail and social life is disrupted. Imipramine completely eliminates enuresis in 50% of instances and partially in an additional 20%. The dose range varies between 25 and 75 mg (1 mg per kg) at bedtime. The initial dose is 10–25 mg at bedtime with increments of 10–25 mg at 1- to 2-week intervals until the maximum dose for age is achieved. Maximum doses are as follows: 6–8 years, 50 mg per 24 hours; 8–10 years, 60 mg per 24 hours; 10–12 years, 70 mg per 24 hours; and 12–14 years, 75 mg per 24 hours. The medication should be continued for 2–3 months and then tapered slowly. It should not be administered to children under the age of 6 years. Some authors recommend that imipramine be administered in short cycles or only at specific times such as sleepovers, campouts, journeys, and so forth. A rebound phenomenon has been described after discontinuation of the drug when taken for a prolonged period of time. It is thought that imipramine increases bladder capacity through a central inhibition of norepinephrine reuptake.

Oxybutynin hydrochloride (Ditropan) has an antispasmodic effect on smooth muscle at doses of 10–15 mg per day, allowing an increase in bladder capacity and decreasing the frequency of bladder contractions [39]. Nasal administration of synthetic vasopressin (antidiuretic hormone) at doses of 10–40 µg at bedtime are also efficacious, particularly in children over 8 years of age and in adults [40].

Obstructive Sleep Apnea

Obstructive sleep apnea is also an important consideration when addressing sleep disorders in children. However, there are several important distinctions between obstructive sleep apnea in the adult population and in the pediatric age groups. The evaluation of suspected obstructive sleep apnea begins with a clinical history, including investigation of both nocturnal and daytime symptoms. Frequently encountered nocturnal manifestations include snoring, apnea, diaphoresis, enuresis, many arousals with and without confusion, morning headaches, vomiting, belabored breathing, and unusual sleep positions. Waking symptoms suggestive of obstructive apnea include excessive daytime sleepiness and failure to thrive. It is not uncommon to find failure to thrive in infants who have obstructive apnea as opposed to obesity, which is more common in older children. Other manifestations include hyperactivity, irritability, developmental delay, school problems, loud or noisy respirations, nasal obstruction, mouth breathing, feeding difficulties, gastroesophageal reflux, and recurrent aspiration [41].

The airway in children is much smaller in diameter than in the adult, and it can be more sensitive to factors that might further affect its size. Along these lines, the physical examination should assess for craniofacial structural abnormalities such as mid-face hypoplasia, nasal obstructions, retrognathia or micrognathia, and deformities of the base of the skull. Other soft-tissue anomalies are tonsillar or adenoidal hypertrophy, an enlarged tongue, abnormal pharyngeal dimensions, altered palatal morphology, and fatty infiltrations. The structure of the trachea and bronchi should be studied for conditions such as laryngo-tracheobronchomalacia. Some neurologic features can predispose to obstructive sleep apnea, including peripheral nerve dysfunction, especially when involving the recurrent laryngeal nerve, neuromuscular transmission abnormalities, compression of the cervical spinal cord or medulla, as well as bulbar palsy and hydrocephalus resulting in pharyngeal incoordination [41]. The physical examination should also include a measurement of the blood pressure and growth percentiles including the height, weight, and head circumference.

The complications of untreated obstructive sleep apnea and hypoventilation in the child could be serious. These complications include hypoxemia, hypercarbia, pulmonary hypertension, cor pulmonale, systemic hypertension, cardiac arrhythmias, hypoxic brain damage, and possibly seizures.

It is inappropriate to use adult criteria for the diagnosis of sleep apnea in children because they have much smaller lung capacities and a higher respiratory rate. The definition of sleep apnea in the pediatric population includes an apnea-hypopnea index of greater than 1, a minimal baseline oxyhemoglobin saturation of less than 92% [42], and a drop in the oxygen saturation (SaO_2) of 4% or more [43]. In addition, the duration of the apnea episode in children can be less than 10 seconds, whereas in adults, the commonly used criterion is greater than 10 seconds [42].

In a child with a sleep-related respiratory disorder, several qualitative factors should be assessed, including any increases in respiratory rate or effort, or oxygen desaturations that might or might not be associated with electroencephalographic evidence of arousal. A comparison should be made of the severity of respiratory abnormalities that occur in non-REM and REM sleep, and between different sleeping positions. In general, the hypotonic, floppy, oropharynx that is normally associated with REM sleep and the gravitational effects of sleeping flat on the back (possibly causing the tongue to fall back over the oropharyngeal opening) tend to exacerbate obstructive sleep apnea. Ideally, before continuous positive airway pressure or bilevel positive airway pressure (CPAP/Bi-PAP) therapy can be considered completely successful, the patient's breathing pattern should normalize while lying flat on the back during REM sleep.

The differential diagnosis of obstructive sleep apnea, for which polysomnography can be considered, includes benign snoring, unexplained failure to thrive, cardiopulmonary abnormalities, behavioral disorders, and intrinsic sleep disorders that can lead to excessive daytime sleepiness. An overnight sleep study can identify populations who might be at high risk for postoperative upper airway obstruction and respiratory failure caused by the effects of anesthesia, sedating medications, and possibly the surgical procedure itself.

Other laboratory studies that might be ordered depending on the patient's clinical picture include radiographic cephalometric evaluations, fluoroscopy of the upper airway, cine-analysis of swallowing, and magnetic resonance imaging or computed tomography of the brain and brain stem [41]. However, a major drawback of these examinations is that they are generally performed while the patient is awake and therefore might not be representative of the pathophysiology relevant during sleep.

In children, enlarged tonsils and adenoids are commonly associated with obstructive sleep apnea. Their resection is often curative and is the treatment of choice [44]. The nonsurgical therapeutic mainstay of obstructive sleep apnea in older children, as it is in adults, is CPAP therapy. It is indicated in patients with tracheobronchomalacia, and other craniofacial and pharyngeal anomalies that are not amenable to surgery, and in patients with severe obesity who are not surgical candidates. It is also indicated in the preoperative management of severe obstructive apnea and hypoventilation. Postoperatively, CPAP should be applied if surgical interventions fail. When CPAP is titrated, the initial starting pressure is low, generally between 3.0 and 5.0 cm of H_2O pressure. This pressure is gradually increased in 0.5- to 1.0-cm increments until obstructive events resolve and associated desaturations and snoring are eliminated. In infants, even smaller increments might be needed, such as 0.3 cm. Bi-PAP might be more easily tolerated by infants and patients who require airway pressures greater than 10 cm of H_2O.

General counseling and discussing the many aspects of CPAP application with both the child and the parents can be helpful in increasing CPAP compliance. The patient should be allowed to choose between a mask or nasal pillow unit, and to use the different units on an alternating basis if so desired. Meticulous care should be taken to ensure that the mask or nasal pillow unit fits properly. Initially, the child should wear the apparatus during the day while watching television, listening to music, or playing a board game, with the pressure turned off. Desensitization is possible if slow, gradual increases in pressure are then made. Compliance can also be improved with the use of sticker charts, although in some situations straight arm splints might be required to prevent the unconscious or active removal of the mask at night. One major potential problem is that obstructive sleep apnea can be exacerbated by upper respiratory infections and certain drugs or medications to the point where the initially successful CPAP pressure might no longer be adequate. This situation can lead to persistent obstructions with clinical deterioration and possible respiratory failure, despite the use of CPAP. Other problems include difficulties with mask fit; drying of the nasal mucosa, which is treated with heated humidity; and rhinitis, which is managed with nasal steroids and decongestants.

Case Study 11-5

T. L. is a 4-year, 8-month-old girl with the diagnoses of cerebral palsy, mental retardation, seizure disorder, hydrocephalus with ventriculoperitoneal shunt, mild pulmonary hypertension, and biatrial and biventricular cardiac enlargement. During a hospitalization for positioning and feeding assessments, it was noted that she snored loudly and had frequent awakenings. Nighttime oximetry indicated frequent oxygen desaturations, which were worse when the patient was on her back. An overnight polysomnogram showed severe sleep apnea with an apnea-hypopnea index of 48.8 events per hour and oxygen saturations as low as 56%. CPAP at 10 cm of H_2O pressure eliminated all major apnea events, allowing the oxygen saturation to remain above 92%. It was recommended that the patient continue CPAP at 10 cm H_2O pressure. However, she had difficulty tolerating CPAP, and was referred for tonsillectomy and uvulopalatopharyngoplasty.

Adolescence

Sleep patterns change significantly during puberty and adolescence. In a series of sleep camp studies conducted by Mary Carskadon and her colleagues at Stanford University [45], 24 children were initially classified according to Tanner stages of pubertal development and followed longitudinally with studies of nighttime sleep and daytime sleepiness. Results of this study showed that when adolescents were given an adequate time-window to sleep (between 10:00 P.M. and 8:00 A.M.), their total sleep time remained constant from Tanner stage 1 to Tanner stage

5 and averaged approximately 9.25 hours per night. The sleep architecture changed at puberty showing a decrease of SWS by 40% without appreciable change in the amount of REM sleep. An increase in daytime sleepiness was noted despite constant total nighttime sleep. It was then postulated that all humans experience a midday tendency toward sleepiness, beginning in adolescence and persisting through adulthood. Daytime sleepiness might be a developmental inevitability, but it was also found that alertness returns later in the day independent of a midday nap [45].

In addition to such physiologic modifications, other behavioral and social changes occur during adolescence. The role of parental involvement in children's sleep changes significantly so that by the age of 13 years parents are no longer putting their children to bed but rather are playing an active role in waking them in the morning. Another significant factor is the involvement of adolescents in part-time work. Children who work 20 hours or less per week generally sleep approximately 7.5 hours, whereas children who work more than 20 hours per week generally sleep less than 7 hours per night. In junior high and high school, it is not uncommon for school schedules to begin earlier during the day, and if the adolescent is involved in sports or school organizations, there might be further obligations and practice sessions before the beginning of school. In addition, the adolescent is often exposed to increased social opportunities during the evening hours. Finally, although adolescents often claim that their academic obligations have increased, it has been found that they spend an average of less than 1 hour per day studying on weekdays and less than 2 hours per day on weekends.

The changes of adolescence can result in the most common pathology associated with the adolescent sleep pattern: inadequate sleep hygiene mimicking the delayed sleep phase syndrome. This condition typically begins in the summer between the eighth and ninth grades. The adolescent begins staying up later and later at night and sleeping later and later in the mornings. When school starts, the adolescent's biological pacemaker is overridden but not completely reset. In other words, the adolescent continues to stay up late during the week but is awakened early in order to attend school. As a result, the young person develops a sleep debt Monday through Friday that is repaid on the weekend or nonschool days in the form of recovery sleep, including sleeping until noon or beyond and taking naps. Recovery sleep allows the persistence of the delayed sleep phase cycles. The differential diagnosis should include insomnia and intrinsic erratic sleep-wake phases.

The assessment of this alteration requires a clinical history and a detailed sleep log. Overnight polysomnography is rarely required. General principles of treatment include making the consequences of persisting in this behavior greater than the advantages through the use of specific behavioral contracts, specifying target behaviors, and educating and counseling both the adolescent and the parents [1]. The specific methods of treatment of delayed sleep phase syndrome include phase advance chronotherapy and phase delay chronotherapy. Phase advance chronotherapy consists of shifting the adolescent's bedtime and waking time 15 minutes earlier each day until the desired sleep and wake times are achieved. The use of bright lights or sunlight and moderate activity is encouraged at awakening. The adolescent is not permitted to take naps, or consume caffeine, alcohol, drugs, or unnecessary medications. No deviations are allowed on weekends and school vacations. Behavioral contracts should state specific items regarding bedtime including time for lights out, no telephone, no radio, no television, no video games, and wake up times—opening the eyes, getting up and out of bed, moving around, turning lights on in the room, and getting dressed. After the desired bedtime and awakening time are achieved, the schedule should be rigidly maintained for 2 full weeks before a maintenance protocol is started.

Phase delay chronotherapy is similar to phase advance chronotherapy, except that the bedtime and wake up times are delayed by 3 hours per night until the schedule cycles around the clock and the desired bedtime and awakening time are achieved. Often, adolescents find this technique more acceptable because it allows them to feel like they are staying up later each night. Naps, caffeine, alcohol, drugs, and unnecessary medications are not allowed, and no deviations are allowed on weekends or nonschool days. Behavioral contracts should specify the bedtime and wake-time activities. Once the desired times are achieved, the schedule should be followed rigidly for 2 weeks before a maintenance protocol is instituted [1].

Following successful realignment by chronotherapy and 2 weeks of rigid scheduling, a maintenance protocol allows for some flexibility in the weekend and vacation schedule, but bedtime and awakening times should not deviate by more than 2 hours. If adolescents stay up very late for a special event, they must get up within 2 hours of their usual schedule with no naps on the following day. They should continue to follow good sleep hygiene practices, which include using the bed only for sleep, having a regular bedtime ritual, learning positive relaxing images to initiate sleep, and avoiding naps and caffeine. During the summer, if desired, the adolescent can go off this schedule but should resume chronotherapy and maintenance protocols 2 weeks before the beginning of school [1].

Case Study 11-6

J. W. is a 16-year-old boy seen in the clinic for assessment of daytime sleepiness. J. W. has difficulty getting up in the morning and as a result, has frequently been late for school. School personnel are threatening to remove him from the wrestling team as a consequence of his poor attendance. J. W. sleeps in his own room and often listens to music or watches television for a long time before falling asleep. J. W. could not identify a bedtime but admitted to frequently staying up past midnight, even on school nights. He also frequently sleeps past awakening time on weekends, and he takes naps in the early evening and on weekends. J. W. had large tonsils as a child, which led to loud snoring and recurrent infections and were surgically removed at 2 years of age. J. W. was evaluated by a psychiatrist 4 months ago and was started on an antidepressant. An overnight sleep study revealed no evidence of obstructive sleep apnea or other intrinsic sleep pathologies. Recommendations regarding phase advance chronotherapy were made to J. W. and his parents. J. W., however, did not like the strict schedule on weekends and preferred to maintain his current routine.

Another important clinical entity to consider in the adolescent population is narcolepsy (see Chapter 6). The symptoms of narcolepsy usually begin in adolescence, but typically the disorder is not diagnosed until much later in life. Classic symptoms include the tetrad of excessive daytime sleepiness or sleep attacks; cataplexy or loss of muscle tone lasting seconds or minutes, which can be precipitated by laughter, anger, or strong emotion; sleep paralysis, or loss of voluntary movement, when attempting to go to sleep or on awakening from sleep; and hypnagogic hallucinations, or vivid dreamlike imagery, that occurs while the patient is awake. It is believed that narcolepsy is a disorder of REM physiology. The differential diagnosis of narcolepsy includes chronic fatigue syndrome, poor sleep schedules, conversion reactions, sleep apnea syndrome, and seizures. The consequences of narcolepsy include fragmented sleep at night with decreased sleep efficiency, severe daytime sleepiness, and chronic sleep deprivation. The diagnosis is made with overnight polysomnography that shows a relatively short REM sleep latency, followed by a multiple sleep latency test that typically shows a mean sleep latency of less than 5 minutes, and sleep onset REM during two or more naps. Treatment of narcolepsy includes education and counseling of the patient, family, school, and employer; institution of good sleep habits, including regular nap times; the use of stimulant medications to reduce excessive sleepiness; and the use of tricyclics for cataplexy, sleep paralysis, and hypnagogic hallucinations [46].

References

1. Dahl RE. Child and Adolescent Sleep Disorders. In DM Kaufman, GE Solomon, CR Pfeffer (eds), Child and Adolescent Neurology for the Psychiatrist. Baltimore: Williams & Wilkins, 1992;169.
2. Dorland's Illustrated Medical Dictionary (25th ed). Philadelphia: Saunders, 1974.
3. Behrman RE, Vaughan VC. Nelson Textbook of Pediatrics (13th ed). Philadelphia: Saunders, 1987.
4. Parmelee AH, Wenner WH, Akiyama Y, et al. Sleep states in premature infants. Dev Med Child Neurol 1967;9:70.
5. Sheldon SA, Spire J-P, Levy HB. Normal Sleep in Children and Young Adults. In Pediatric Sleep Medicine. Philadelphia: Saunders, 1992;14.
6. Hoppenbrouwers T. Sleep in Infants. In C Guilleminault (ed), Sleep and Its Disorders in Children. New York: Raven,1987;1.
7. Sterman MB, Hoppenbrouwers T. The Development of Sleep-Waking and Rest-Activity Patterns from Fetus to Adult in Man. In MB Sterman, DJ McGinty, AM Adinolfi (eds), Brain Development and Behavior. New York: Academic, 1971;203.
8. Aserinsky E, Kleitman N. A motility cycle in sleeping infants manifested by ocular and gross bodily activity. J Appl Physiol 1955;8:11.
9. Roffwarg HP, Dement WC, Fisher C. Preliminary Observations of the Sleep-Dream Pattern in Neonates, Infants, Children, and Adults. In E Harms (ed), International Series of Monographs on Child Psychiatry. Problems of Sleep and Dreams in Children. New York: MacMillan, 1964;60.
10. Petre-Quadens O. On the different phases of the sleep of the newborn with special references to the activated phase, or phase d. J Neurol Sci 1966;3:151.
11. Williams RL, Gokcebay N, Hirshkowtz M, et al. Ontogeny of Sleep. In R Cooper (ed), Sleep. London: Chapman and Hall, 1994;60.
12. Spehlmann R. The normal EEG from premature age to the age of 19 years. In EEG Primer. Amsterdam: Elsevier, 1981;159.

13. Coons S. Development of Sleep and Wakefulness During the First Six Months of Life. In C Gulleminault (ed), Sleep and Its Disorders in Children. New York: Raven, 1987;17.
14. Lenard HG. Sleep studies in infancy. Acta Paediatr Scand 1970;59:572.
15. Stern E, Parmalee AH, Harris MA. Sleep state periodicity in prematures and young infants. Dev Psychobiol 1973;6:357.
16. Stern E, Parmalee AH, Akiyama Y, et al. Sleep cycle characteristics in infants. Pediatrics 1969;43:65.
17. Williams RL, Karacan I, Hursch CJ. Electroencephalography of human sleep: Clinical applications. New York: Wiley, 1974.
18. Kleitman N. Sleep and Wakefulness. Chicago: University of Chicago Press, 1939.
19. Kleitman N, Engelmann TG. Sleep characteristics of infants. J Appl Physiol 1953;6:269.
20. Ferber R, Boyle MP. Persistence of a free-running sleep-wake rhythm in a one-year-old girl. Sleep Res 1983;12:364.
21. Ferber R. Circadian and Schedule Disturbances. In C Guilleminault (ed), Sleep and Its Disorders in Children. New York: Raven, 1987;165.
22. Ferber R. The Sleepless Child. In C Gulleminault (ed), Sleep and Its Disorders in Children. New York: Raven, 1987;141.
23. Moore T, Ucko LE. Nightwaking in early infancy: Part 1. Arch Dis Child 1957;32:333.
24. Ragins N, Schachter S. A study of sleep behavior in two-year-old children. J Am Acad Child Adolesc Psychiatry 1971;10:464.
25. Gould JB, Lee AFS, Morelock S. The Relationship Between Sleep and Sudden Infant Deaths. In PJ Schwartz, DP Southall, M Valdés-Dapena (eds), The Sudden Infant Death Syndrome. New York: Ann N Y Acad Sci 1988;533:62.
26. Peterson DR, Van Belle G, Chinn NM. Epidemiologic comparisons of the sudden infant death syndrome with other major components of infant mortality. Am J Epidemiol 1979;110:699.
27. Gilleminault C. Sleep Apnea in the Full-Term Infant. In C Guilleminault (ed), Sleep and Its Disorders in Children. New York: Raven, 1987;195.
28. Ferber R. Solve Your Child's Sleep Problems. New York: Simon & Schuster, 1985.
29. Illingworth RS. Sleep problems in the first three years. Br Med J 1951;1:722.
30. Jan JE, Espezel H. Melatonin treatment of chronic sleep disorders. Dev Med Child Neurol 1995;37:279.
31. Rosen G, Mahowald MW, Ferber R. Sleepwalking, Confusional Arousals, and Sleep. In R Ferber, M Kryger (eds), Principles and Practice of Pediatric Sleep Medicine. Philadelphia: Saunders, 1995;99.
32. Greene MG. The Harriet Lane Handbook (12th ed). St. Louis: Mosby, 1991.
33. Kravitz H, Rosenthal V, Teplitz Z, et al. A study of headbanging in infants and children. Dis Nerv Sys 1906;21:203.
34. Robertson MM, Trimble RM, Less AJ. Self-injurious behavior and the Gilles de la Tourette syndrome: A clinical study and review of the literature. Psychol Med 1989;19:611.

35. Stuck KJ, Hernández RJ. Large skull defect in a head banger. Pediatr Radiol 1979;8:257.
36. Demporad JR. Cataracts following chronic head banging: A report of two cases. Am J Psychiatry 1968;125:245.
37. Thorpy MJ, Govinsky PB. Headbanging (Jactatio Capitis Nocturna). In MH Kryger, T Roth, WC Dement (EDS), Principles and Practice of Sleep Medicine. Philadelphia: Saunders, 1989; 648.
38. Jones B, Gerrard JW, Shokeir MK, et al. Recurrent urinary infections in girls: Relation to enuresis. Can Med Assoc J 1972;106:127.
39. Lovering JS, Tallett SE, McKendry JB. Oxybutynin efficacy in the treatment of primary enuresis. Pediatrics 1988;82:104.
40. Fjellestad-Paulsen A, Wille S, Harris AS. Comparison of intranasal and oral desmopressin for nocturnal enuresis. Arch Dis Child 1987;62:674.
41. Guilleminault C. Obstructive Sleep Apnea Syndrome in Children. In C Guilleminault (ed), Sleep and Its Disorders in Children. New York: Raven, 1987;213.
42. Marcus DL, Omlin KJ, Basinki DJ, et al. Normal polysomnographic values for children and adolescents. Am Rev Respir Dis 1992;146:1235.
43. Ali NJ, Pitson DJ, Stradling JR. Snoring, sleep disturbance, and behaviour in 4–5 year olds. Arch Dis Child 1993;68:360.
44. Ferber R. Sleep Disorders in Children. In R Cooper (ed), Sleep. London: Chapman and Hall, 1994;326.
45. Carskadon MA, Dement WC. Sleepiness in the Normal Adolescent. In C Guilleminault (ed), Sleep and Its Disorders in Children. New York: Raven, 1987;53.
46. Dahl RE, Holttum J, Trubnick L. A clinical picture of child and adolescent narcolepsy. J Am Acad Child Adolesc Psychiatry 1994;33:834.

Sleep in Old Age

> *There is a chronic disease, obligatory fatal, that we should all avoid, and that, however, we all desire: old age.*
> Santiago Ramón y Cajal [1]

With the passage of time, sleep, like other cerebral functions, undergoes predictable changes in the healthy individual that become increasingly noticeable as age advances. The evolution of sleep in senescence acquires characteristics that become gradually undistinguishable from degenerative alterations. In general, the changes tend to reduce the intensity, depth, and continuity of sleep, decreasing its quality and increasing its vulnerability to detrimental factors [2]. Survey data have indicated that the elderly are commonly dissatisfied with their sleep [3]. Sleep disturbances can contribute to increased risk of accidents, falls, and long-term care placement while causing chronic misery, impairing cognitive abilities, and affecting quality of life.

Involution of Sleep

Recent epidemiologic data from the United States [4] indicate that only 12% of noninstitutionalized persons 65 years of age or older report no sleep complaints, whereas 19% report difficulty initiating sleep, 29% have difficulty maintaining sleep, 18% have early morning awaken-

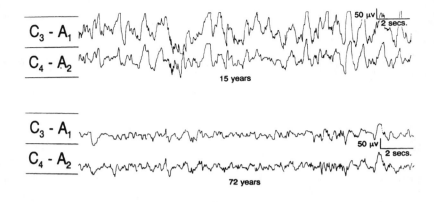

SWS

Figure 12-1. *Fragment of a polysomnogram comparing stages 3 and 4 slow wave activity in two healthy subjects aged (above) 15 and (below) 72 years, respectively. In the elderly person, slow wave sleep is reduced in amplitude; the proportion relative to total sleep is also decreased, determining a partial loss of stages 3 and 4. (10–20 International Electrode Placement System.)*

ings, and 28% report insomnia. Sleep disturbances are primarily associated with manifestations of poor health, while advanced age is not necessarily linked to more frequent complaints after adjusting for health status.

The sleep EEGs of elderly persons show that delta activity, a marker of stages 3 and 4 of slow wave sleep (SWS), decreases in amplitude by 75% relative to childhood (Figure 12-1). In addition, the proportion relative to total sleep decreases markedly, determining a partial loss of both stages. By 60 years of age, SWS represents no more than 10%, and past the age of 75 years, stage 4 virtually disappears. A study of men between 90 and 110 years of age conducted in the former Soviet Union showed negligible amounts of SWS [5]. These changes are more marked in men than in women.

In advanced age, sleep spindles decrease in amplitude, becoming more monotonous and less variable, whereas the frequency increases while the duration remains the same (Figure 12-2) [6]. Other authors have found decreased density of sleep spindles in old age [7].

As SWS decreases, the first cycle of sleep shortens, and the time-latency to the first episode of REM sleep is consequently reduced [8]. In advanced age, this latency measures 70–80 minutes, whereas in the young adult,

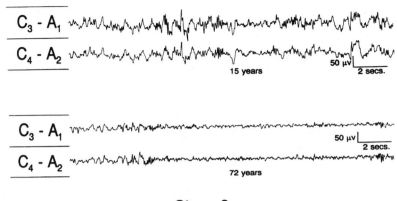

Stage 2

Figure 12-2. *Fragment of a polysomnogram comparing sleep spindle activity in the same two healthy subjects shown in Figure 12-1, aged (above) 15 and (below) 72 years, respectively. In the elderly person, sleep spindles are reduced in amplitude and density, becoming more monotonous and less variable; the duration remains the same. (10–20 International Electrode Placement System.)*

it typically measures 90–95 minutes. Perhaps as a result of the same phenomenon, the first episode of REM sleep lengthens so that the tendency is to observe REM sleep cycles of approximately equal duration throughout the night, although the proportion of REM sleep to total sleep time tends to remain stable during the life of the individual.

Another phenomenon observed in the elderly is an increase in the number and duration of nocturnal arousals causing fragmentation of nocturnal sleep [9, 10]. This change is the result of sleep that becomes increasingly light and vulnerable to external and internal arousing stimuli.

To obtain the same restorative satisfaction with sleep, the elderly person needs to remain in bed more time than at a younger age, so that sleep efficiency decreases to approximately 70% or 80% [11]. The percentage of stage 1 increases by a range of 8–15%, being less pronounced in older women. In view of a shortened nocturnal sleep, some claim that total sleep needs decrease in advanced age, but most studies have not taken daytime naps into account.

The reduction in the voltage and proportion of SWS might be related to an advanced age-related reduction of the mass of cortical nerve cells, where slow waves are generated. The pontomesencephalic reticular nuclei where REM sleep originates are phylogenetically older and more resistant to age, thereby explaining the relative preservation of REM sleep even in very elderly people.

Senile degeneration of the suprachiasmatic nuclei (SCN) of the hypothalamus might underlie the circadian rhythm alterations experienced by some elderly persons and observed in the degenerative dementias [12]. Some of the changes consist of a sleep phase advance manifested by a tendency to retire early and to wake up early. Loss of nocturnal consolidation facilitates fragmentation, poor restorative power, and the subsequent need to take daytime naps. Elderly individuals tolerate very poorly sleep shifts and time zone changes, suggesting a decreased plasticity in neuronal function. In advanced age, the ability, but not the necessity to sleep, is diminished. The evolutionary changes that transform sleep as age advances increase its vulnerability to factors that can disturb it, and that are also more abundant and powerful in the elderly. The overall tendency is in the direction of impaired sleep maintenance and reduced depth [13]. The analysis of these factors opens a window of opportunity for the management of sleep dysfunction in the elderly.

Detrimental Factors

Detrimental factors of sleep most commonly observed in the elderly and very elderly are sleep-related respiratory disturbances, periodic leg movements of sleep, medical-related disturbances, medications, depression, and changes in sleep hygiene consequent to psychosocial disturbances.

Sleep Apnea

Sleep apnea events of 10 or more seconds in duration increase with age and are more common in men [14]. Past the age of 65 years, 30–50% of men exhibit 20 or more episodes of apnea per night. The underlying causes are multiple and include degeneration of pneumotaxic centers in the brain stem, causing nonobstructive apnea; inspiratory obstruction of the upper airways, causing obstructive sleep apnea; and reduction of SWS with a proportional increase of light non-REM sleep when sleep apnea events are more intense. In elderly individuals, apneas and hypopneas occur frequently, but their effect on ill-health and mortality remains under debate. A study conducted in a nursing home found that obstructive sleep apnea predisposed individuals to death at night [15].

However, another study of nondemented seniors living in a retirement village complex in Australia [16] showed that a respiratory disturbance index of 15 or more per hour was not a predictor of mortality and that in general the prevalence of high levels of sleep apnea was low.

Snoring, a risk factor for obstructive sleep apnea and stroke [17], also increases as age advances and is more prevalent in men. The ingestion of drugs and alcohol can worsen a sleep apnea syndrome. Oxygen desaturation during profound apnea events can alter the cardiac rhythm, decrease the quality of sleep, and increase the number of partial arousals that reduce the restorative functions of sleep. In persons with advanced chronic obstructive pulmonary disease, hypoxemia can reach dangerous levels in REM stage.

Elderly persons with marginal cerebral reserve can suffer severe mental decompensation that mimics a dementia, or can exhibit symptoms of a subclinical dementia with sleep deprivation secondary to the sleep apnea syndrome. Consequently, some authors have advocated the vigorous treatment of obstructive sleep apnea syndrome in demented patients with evidence of nocturnal desaturations, cardiac dysrhythmias, partial arousals, and daytime hypersomnia. To this effect, continuous positive airway pressure (CPAP) or bilevel continuous positive airway pressure (Bi-PAP) applications are very effective in eliminating obstructive sleep apnea events and restoring normoxemia. The management should be supplemented with the suppression of other risk factors, including consumption of drugs and alcohol. Patient education in proper sleep hygiene is important. In some instances, administration of acetazolamide, which reduces nonobstructive sleep apneas, losing weight, avoiding sleeping on the back, and a course of protryptiline if mild obstructive apneas are present can have limited success. Surgical interventions to alleviate obstructive sleep apnea are considered only in instances of well-documented anatomic impediments.

Periodic Limb Movements of Sleep

Periodic limb movements of sleep (PLMS) are repetitive, stereotypic movements consisting mostly of extension of the large toe with flexion of the ankle, knee, and hip. The movements are sometimes paired, other times independent of each other, and when intense always disturb the patient's or spouse's sleep [18]. Although not exclusive of advanced age, PLMS tend to disturb sleep increasingly and can be more frequent as age advances [14]. Typically, they are associated with the restless legs syndrome, an uncomfortable crawling sensation in lower extremities that forces the patient to shift postures and move, and are common in patients with iron deficiency anemia, peripheral neuropathies, renal insufficiency, and diabetes. When PLMS provoke partial arousals, subjects complain of daytime hypersomnia. Treatment with benzodiazepines (e.g., clonazepam, 0.5 mg at bedtime) eliminates the cortical component of the partial arousal but depresses mental function in susceptible older individuals. Levodopa-carbidopa administered at night, not to exceed 200 mg of the sustained release form; and oxycodone administration, 2.5–4.5 mg; or codeine sulfate, 15–200 mg at bedtime, have been successful in mild to moderate instances. Oxycodone and codeine might be more effective for the relief of restless legs syndrome than PLMS; for restless legs, the medication should be taken 2 hours before bedtime. In severe forms of either condition, the addition of carbamazepine, 200 mg three or four times daily, or even methadone, 5–20 mg daily, might help.

Medical Disturbances

If grave enough, almost any medical disease will alter nocturnal sleep and reduce its restorative function. Chronic disorders that most frequently alter sleep in advanced age are rheumatic disorders that produce nocturnal pains, respiratory insufficiency, and nocturia of any origin. It has been estimated that 20% of nocturnal awakenings of more than 5 minutes in duration are caused by nocturia. Drugs used for the treatment of medical disorders might cause insomnia or hypersomnia. Neurologic disorders such as Parkinson's disease, stroke, multiple sclerosis, and the spinocerebellar degenerations can impair the patient's ability to turn in bed and can exert a direct effect on sleep mechanisms.

Management is directed at the discontinuation of drugs that might alter sleep, the suppression of pain with conventional analgesics, the administration of diuretics early in the day, and the avoidance late in the day of drugs with sympathomimetic action that interfere with the initiation of sleep. The heavy use of over-the-counter drugs with caffeine should be discouraged. In advanced age, the metabolism of hypnotics, sedatives, tranquilizers, and other substances with central action, such as antihypertensives, anticonvulsants, and antihistaminics, can be delayed with consequent risk of accumulation [19]. All these substances can aggravate sleep apnea, reduce the level of alertness, and decrease daytime functioning.

Circadian Rhythm Alterations

The older person is increasingly intolerant of circadian rhythm changes [20]. Past the age of 45 years, adaptation to work shifts becomes increasingly difficult, resulting in sleep deprivation with decreased attention, increased risk of accidents, and reduced quality of work. Jet lag syndrome is more pronounced and of longer duration in the elderly. Travelers should start to adapt before their journey by establishing a rhythm of going to bed early if contemplating a west-east journey, and vice versa if traveling from east to west. Circadian rhythms show a natural tendency to decrease in phase duration as age advances; this phenomenon might explain why elderly persons tend to retire early to bed and prefer to rise early in the morning.

Depression

A constellation of social, medical, and psychoaffective factors trigger or aggravate affective depression in advanced age. Multiple sleep-related manifestations can thus result, including short REM sleep latency, high REM density, and increased REM sleep duration in the first half of the night, along with decreased duration of total sleep, reduced sleep efficiency, and virtual disappearance of SWS [21, 22]. As a result, fragmentation of nocturnal sleep supervenes with reduced quality of sleep and daytime hypersomnolence. Early morning awakening, 3 or 4 hours after initiating sleep, is a typical manifestation. Suppression of REM sleep improves affective depression.

Chronic anxiety manifested by difficulty initiating sleep and by panic attacks during the night is commonly added. Some authors have associated these events with surges of circulating catecholamines [23].

Pseudodementia

Cognitive impairment occurs in 10–20% of depressed elderly patients. Symptoms can be of such severity that the patient appears to be demented. Conversely, patients with a primary degenerative dementia can exhibit secondary symptoms of depression. Since "pseudodementia" of a predominantly affective nature can be correctable, it is important to determine the contribution of depression to the causation of symptoms.

In one study, patients with pseudodementia had less severe symptoms of dementia at baseline than Alzheimer's disease (AD) patients did and showed significant improvement following sleep deprivation [24]. Patients with degenerative dementia and depression manifested no change, or even worsened with sleep deprivation. Polysomnographic studies in pseudodemented patients showed higher REM sleep percent and phasic REM sleep activity. REM sleep rebound was more prominent in pseudodemented patients following sleep deprivation.

In another study comparing elderly depressed and demented subjects [25], the sleep of depressives was characterized by reduced REM sleep latency, increased REM sleep percent, and enhanced density of the first REM sleep period, as well as altered temporal distribution of REM sleep. In contrast, demented patients showed reduced REM sleep percent, loss of spindles, and K complexes.

Patients who initially show greater depressive symptomatology with higher cognitive function, and only moderate sleep continuity disturbance or just early morning awakenings [26], have a more favorable outcome.

REM sleep latency of depressed elderly patients can be reduced, whereas in patients with AD, REM sleep latency can be prolonged. Confirmation of these differences would allow polysomnography to contribute a relatively simple way of differentiating one disorder from the other [27].

Dementia

Brain insufficiency, being a common occurrence in advanced age, contributes importantly to the deterioration of sleep-wake rhythms. Approximately 10% of the elderly population suffers cognitive decline of a pathologic nature, contributing to the degradation of sleep in advanced age. There is more sleep disruption in demented patients than in normal aged control subjects, and in turn, the loss of sleep-wake rhythms adds to the mental decline. The clinician's responsibility is to analyze all the detrimental factors that contribute to poor quality sleep in the demented patient, in an effort to identify the ones that can be corrected, thus providing a window of opportunity to the amelioration of the mental deficit.

Typical findings in demented patients are decreased sleep efficiency, increased stage 1, and more fragmentation by arousals and awakenings. Specific patterns of sleep-wake alteration have not as yet emerged in relation to the different forms of dementia [28], and no studies have related sleep patterns to specific areas of brain pathology. However, suggestive signs and symptoms of sleep-wake alteration can be uncovered.

Delirium

Delirium is defined as a transient organic mental syndrome characterized by a global disorder of cognition and attention, a reduced level of consciousness, psychomotor agitation or retardation, and prominent sleep-wake cycle disturbance [29]. Thus, delirium is a genuine manifestation of sleep alteration that illustrates the close alliance between sleep and cognition. The elderly are specially prone to develop delirium as a result of a variety of predisposing and precipitating factors that include dementia, structural brain disease, medical illness, use of drugs, sensory deprivation, psychosocial factors, and sleep loss. The condition is frequently superimposed on dementia, and 25% of individuals who are delirious have dementia [30].

Delirium is a transient disorder, usually lasting less than 1 month. Symptoms fluctuate during daytime hours and reach a peak at night. The sleep-wake cycle disturbance is an essential component of delirium. Patients are lethargic during the day and tend to nap, whereas at night sleep is short, fragmented, and punctuated with hallucinations. Agitation, restlessness, and wakefulness dominate the nocturnal period in clear contrast with the subdued and drowsy state that prevails during the day. Cholinergic deficiency seems to be a major pathogenetic mechanism in delirium and thus patients with AD are particularly vulnerable. The treatment is directed to removal of the cause whenever possible, correction of homeostatic imbalances, and control of the symptoms. Haloperidol (0.5–5.0 mg at bedtime) or thioridazine (10–20 mg at bedtime or 20–100 mg in divided doses) can be used as a tranquilizer preferably at night, whereas benzodiazepines are the drugs of choice in withdrawal from alcohol and sedative-hypnotic agents. Medications with anticholinergic effects should be avoided.

Alzheimer's Disease

One-half of demented elderly patients suffer AD, a condition of unknown cause that is associated with progressive degeneration of cortical and subcortical cerebral structures. Sleep in AD is characterized by profound disturbance of the sleep-wake rhythm, fragmentation of sleep, insomnia, and nocturnal wandering. Disruption of the sleep-wake rhythm occurs earlier in the disease [31], progressing as the disease advances [32]. Observation of the 24-hour sleep pattern in patients with AD reveals frequent daytime napping and prolonged nocturnal awakenings. Time in bed spent awake increases as the disease progresses in severity. Patients with AD might spend up to 40% of their bedtime hours awake and 14% of their daytime hours asleep. The cognitive decline is paralleled by a decline in the percentage of time in bed spent in SWS and REM sleep. These changes might represent a progressive loss of the neuronal mechanisms responsible for the generation of non-REM and REM sleep.

In AD, there is a profound disturbance of central cholinergic systems including the nucleus basalis of Meynert in the basal forebrain. This finding is of interest since the cholinergic system is heavily involved in the generation of REM sleep. Some studies have shown that REM sleep percentage is decreased in patients with AD [33]. The finding [27] that REM sleep latency is prolonged is also of interest, because if confirmed it could help differentiate AD from pseudodementia caused by affective depression, in which REM latency is shortened. However, in at least one study, REM sleep percentages were increased and REM latency shortened in a neuropathologically verified patient with AD [34]. Nonetheless, the evidence strongly suggests that neuronal degeneration of sleep-promoting and maintaining centers underlies the profound disturbances in sleep and sleep-wake rhythms, serving as a biological marker of the severity of AD.

Sleep-related respiratory disturbances are not more abundant in AD patients than in elderly controls, but this association is important since sleep-related respiratory disturbances and oxygen desaturations could contribute to cognitive dysfunction [35]. Although few data are available, it appears that periodic leg movements are increased in AD. Central dopamine depletion and cholinergic deficit might contribute to this clinical phenomenon.

Sundown Syndrome

Degeneration of the SCN in AD patients might contribute importantly to the profound fragmentation of nocturnal sleep and development of the "sundown"syndrome [36]. This syndrome is a poorly understood clinical phenomenon characterized by nocturnal confusion, wandering, agitation, and in advanced instances, delirium. In the hospital and nursing home, the sundown syndrome can be manifested by loud vocalizations and vigorous attempts to remove restraints or climb over bed rails, an activity highly disturbing to other patients and nursing personnel. The syndrome has not been characterized with precision as yet. Some use the term *sundowning* when the disturbance appears in the early evening, whereas others include all events occurring during darkness. Sundowning and delirium share many common features but are separate clinical phenomena. Sundowning is not a diagnosis but the description of a behavior that describes nocturnal exacerbation of disruptive behaviors and agitation. Delirium, however, is an acute confusional state with transient global disorder of cognition and attention [29] that can occur at any age and in the context of various conditions including AD. Sundowning has been related to the REM sleep behavior disorder, to the severity of nocturnal oxygen desaturations in patients with sleep apnea syndrome, and to the deterioration of the SCN with temperature rhythm disregulation.

Sundown syndrome can be a common cause of institutionalization of the elderly. Caregivers endure many inconveniences and accept with great patience the aggravations of daily life unavoidably provoked by an uncomprehending, disorderly, and unclean human being; and yet, caregivers will not tolerate chronic disruption of their sleep. Nocturnal wandering, sundowning, and delirious behavior at night so extensively disturb the peace and quiet necessary to sleep, that they invariably force the drastic and many times unwanted solution of permanent internment of the patient. Management of the sundown syndrome includes improvement in sleep hygiene, restriction of daytime napping, exposure of patients to daytime sunlight, maintenance of a stable nocturnal environment, use of a bedroom soft light, and in severe instances of agitation, administration of haloperidol (0.5–1.0 mg at bedtime) or thioridazine (25 mg at bedtime).

Premature Aging

Disorders that feature premature aging as a prominent manifestation of disease also exhibit profound disturbances of the sleep-wake rhythm that mimic the alterations found in advanced age. Patients with Down's syndrome have a stable form of moderate mental retardation along with other somatic features characteristic of the condition, such as short stature and typical physiognomy linked to trisomy of chromosome 21.

If they live past the age of 40 years, they invariably develop a degenerative form of dementia that neuropathologically is undistinguishable from AD [37]. Excessive daytime sleepiness and disturbed nocturnal sleep are relatively early manifestations of this form of dementia; in fact, unexplained daytime sleepiness can be one of the first manifestations of onset of dementia in patients with Down's syndrome. Other early symptoms are apathy, withdrawal from social interactions, and loss of self-help skills that in conjunction with the daytime hypersomnia gravely impair the day-to-day management at home.

Fatal familial insomnia is a newly recognized familial disorder with striking manifestations of premature aging among other progressive neurologic alterations that eventually converge in the death of the patient. Loss of neuroendocrine regulation and vegetative circadian rhythmicity [38] appear *pari passu* with severe progressive insomnia, impotence, loss of libido, orthostatic sweating, lacrimation, salivation, and increased body temperature; daytime stupor alternates with wakefulness. In the terminal stages, there is increasing agitation, confusion, disorientation, progressive stupor from which the patient is only transiently arousable, coma, and death. At autopsy, there is severe degeneration and gliosis of the anterior and dorsomedial nuclei of the thalamus. Rancurel's patient [39] developed marked facial aging and appeared 20 years older 18 months after the onset of the disease at the age of 62 years.

Patients with myotonic dystrophy exhibit muscle weakness and wasting of acral and facial muscles along with skin atrophy, bone demineralization, cataract formation, frontal balding, and hypogonadism that suggest premature aging. They also develop a slowly progressive neurologic syndrome characterized by mental decline, apathy, hypersomnia, and "slow alpha" rhythms consistent with subcortical dementia. Histologic study of the brain reveals abundant cytoplasmic inclusion bodies in neurons of the thalamic dorsomedial nuclei indicative of neuronal degeneration [40] and dysfunction that are probably responsible for the neurologic manifestations observed in patients with moderately advanced disease. Sleep laboratory investigation shows a high incidence of obstructive and nonobstructive sleep apnea syndrome, excessive daytime somnolence, and paucity or loss of plasma growth hormone increases that normally are associated with SWS, an alteration that has been linked to damage of dorsomedial nuclei. The loss of nocturnal growth hormone secretion, normally the largest burst in the 24 hours, might be related to signs of premature aging observed in patients with lesions of thalamic dorsomedial nuclei [41].

Werner's syndrome is the archetypical disorder of premature aging in the adult and is characterized by early senility, graying hair, baldness, cataracts, hypogonadism, scleroderma-like skin changes, and short stature. Neurologic evaluations of these patients are rare, but the ones that do exist indicate early mental impairment with memory disturbance, poorly organized EEG rhythms [42], delayed event-related evoked potentials, and marked ventricular dilatation as well as cortical atrophy in MRI of the brain. There are no published reports of formal sleep studies in patients with this disorder. The study of sleep parameters in this syndrome would yield important clues regarding the aging process of sleep as a cerebral function.

Cerebrovascular Disease

The cumulative effect of vascular damage in susceptible older persons is associated with a form of cognitive degradation that is known as vascular dementia. Nocturnal polygraphic studies in patients with multi-infarct dementia (MID) have shown sleep-related apneas and hypopneas [43]. Such changes have led to the hypothesis that nocturnal hypoxemia could worsen the intellectual capacity of these patients and cause hemodynamic alterations, such as cardiac dysrhythmias, hypotension, and decreased cardiac index, that would perpetuate the risk of additional brain damage [44].

In patients with lacunar infarctions involving the tegmentum of the pons, particularly if associated with periventricular white matter damage, the syndrome of REM sleep without atonia and phantasmagorias (REM sleep behavior disorder [RSBD]) can develop [45–47]. The disturbance is characterized by bizarre behavior during REM stage that suggests enactment of a dream. In some older individuals with risk factors for stroke, MRI studies have shown the presence of ischemic lesions in the tegmentum of the pons in a location that indicates damage to the muscle tone inhibiting system that normally generates muscle atonia during REM stage. This system originates in the peri-locus ceruleus area of the rostral tegmentum of the pons and activates the medullary inhibitory zone of Magoun and Rhines via the tegmentoreticular tract. In turn, the medullary inhibitory zone produces neuronal hyperpolarization by way of the reticulospinal tracts. Loss of atonia during REM sleep facilitates motor behaviors, that depending on the extent of the infarcted pontine area, range from simple limb movements to complex quasi-purposeful acts. Periventricular white matter lesions, also of an ischemic nature, contribute to this syndrome, perhaps by damaging a supratentorial system that modulates REM sleep related muscle atonia and inhibits stereotyped behaviors originating in brain stem structures. Patients with ischemic subcortical leukoencephalopathy or Binswanger's disease can have increased risk of developing RSBD.

RSBD has also been reported in patients with fatal familial insomnia who exhibit extensive thalamic damage. Patients with Parkinson's disease and Shy-Drager syndrome can suffer RSBD years before apparition of the florid disorder, perhaps because of the neurochemical alteration of specific brain stem systems. However, in addition, patients with Shy-Drager syndrome are at high risk of developing brain stem ischemia through nocturnal hypotensive episodes that could potentiate their tendency to develop RSBD.

Use of Hypnotics

In the United States, elderly persons receive 66% more medication with sedative and hypnotic effect than individuals between the ages of 40 and 59 years [48]. Although the practice has declined, in the United States in one single year (1985), 20 million prescriptions were extended for the benzodiazepines triazolam, temazepam, and flurazepam, which were generally used to counteract insomnia. It is acceptable to administer such medications for the alleviation of transient insomnia, but they should not be recommended for treatment of chronic insomnia, particularly if there is past history of drug abuse or alcoholism. Dependence and excessive sedation are common, particularly with the long-acting benzodiazepines propitiating falls and inducing psychomotor retardation that might be interpreted as an early dementia. Short-acting benzodiazepines such as triazolam can precipitate rebound insomnia [49] when the hypnotic effect dissipates in the middle of the night, thus aggravating the insomnia for which it had been prescribed. Benzodiazepines, like most medications with a CNS depressant effect, can worsen or bring to the fore a sleep apnea syndrome.

Toxicity and adverse reactions are more common and intense with the administration of sedatives and hypnotics in advanced age. This difference is related to changes in the absorption rate, metabolism, and excretion of these compounds that take place as age advances. Toxic reactions in the elderly person might have manifestations that are quite different from the ones observed in younger age groups. It is common to find hypotension, disinhibition, restlessness, hyperactivity, and even aggression. In addition, one might observe excessive daytime somnolence, confusion, hallucinations, gait ataxia, and falls. Hypnotics can also increase the risk of falls at night when the individual gets up to go to the bathroom or awakens in a state of confusion. It remains unclear whether the faster induction of sleep and the reduction in the number of nocturnal arousals caused by hypnotics improves the quality of the ensuing daytime vigilance. Traveler's amnesia has been reported in susceptible individuals who took triazolam to counteract the insomnia of jet lag syndrome and were awakened or started functioning before full clearance of the drug from the body was achieved. Memory impairment with the continued use of benzodiazepines can be more marked in older susceptible individuals, particularly if associated with other drugs or alcohol.

General Clinical Approach and Management Implications

Quality of life in advanced age can be determined by the ability to sleep restfully at night and the capacity to stay fully awake during the day. Severe fragmentation of nocturnal sleep and early awakenings, along with chronic fatigue and a tendency to fall asleep inappropriately during the best part of the day, disturb the well-being of many elderly individuals and limit their activities of daily living. Excessive somnolence while driving limits social interactions in concerned and responsible individuals and finally forces them to seek medical attention. A thorough investigation of the patient with a sleep-related complaint is warranted since detrimental factors acting on a sleep that is excessively vulnerable to extrinsic disturbances might be amenable to correction. Medication intake, sleep apnea syndrome, excessive nocturia, night pain syndromes, depression, and myriad other conditions might be identified and corrected not only in the otherwise healthy elderly individual but also in the patient with an early form of dementia. The mismanagement of a sleep disorder in an elderly person could have more serious adverse ramifications than in the middle-aged individual. Inappropriate administration of hypnotic or sedative medications might affect memory mechanisms, contribute to disorientation and falls during nocturnal awakenings, and aggravate daytime fatigue, apathy, and somnolence. Thus, for the elderly patient with a sleep-wake disturbance, professional and thorough investigation including the performance of sleep laboratory studies is medically indicated and fully justified. "Old age" as a diagnosis and as a justification for a nihilistic approach is no longer tenable.

The architecture of nocturnal sleep and the circadian rhythmicity of sleep-wake cycles are complex functions that suffer in early global brain dysfunction. A change in the sleep pattern might be one of the first manifestations of early dementia. In patients with Down's syndrome, hypersomnia is an indicator of dementia. In elderly individuals, persistent unexplained insomnia might herald a degenerative disorder such as Parkinson's disease or a dementing illness, whereas sundowning is the most common cause of institutionalization of the elderly with dementia.

Sleep architecture disturbances, as we know them today, are not specific enough to be of diagnostic value in the differential diagnoses of the various dementias, but the identification of a sleep disorder and the measure of its intensity is becoming important in the clinical management of a dementing disorder. By reducing the level of alertness, sleep disorders such as sleep apnea and periodic leg myoclonus can contribute to the cognitive disturbance. The investigation of a sleep disorder in a demented person is well justified, since it might uncover detrimental factors that contribute to the mental decline. Some of these detrimental factors, along with alcohol and CNS depressants, are controllable and correctable.

Sleep disorders in the elderly can be managed initially by the primary care physician with an understanding of sleep alterations in the context of the global physical and mental disturbances affecting the patient. The physician can effectively manage the problem by going over a checklist of items that commonly disturb sleep in advanced age. The generalist can effectively change medications and instruct the patient in sleep hygiene measures. A referral to a sleep center is indicated when a specific sleep alteration is suspected, including sleep apnea syndrome, leg myoclonus, and nocturnal seizure disorder, or when unexplained symptoms of insomnia or hypersomnia alter the quality of life of the individual and affect cognitive abilities. A patient who relates having fallen asleep at the wheel while driving should always be referred for complete evaluation of the sleep disorder.

Sleep Hygiene

The elderly person has a tendency to shorten days by retiring early and getting up early. This tendency is acceptable as long as the sleep-phase shift is not excessive, interfering with daily activities. It is important

Table 12-1. Sleep Hygiene in the Elderly

1. Maintain a regular sleep-wake schedule.
2. Exercise moderately and regularly before 5 P.M.
3. Take one nap in mid-afternoon not to exceed 1 hour, only if needed.
4. Improve comfort in the bedroom: temperature, lighting, noise level, bed, bed-mates, roommates.
5. Ban pets from bedroom.
6. Do not keep the TV set on at night while asleep.
7. Avoid spending excessive amount of time in bed.
8. Avoid copious meals or excessive alcohol shortly before bedtime.
9. Avoid caffeine past 12 noon.
10. Avoid shift work.
11. Avoid medications with alerting effect.
12. Use hypnotics sparingly and only for transient situations.

to maintain a well-disciplined sleep-wake schedule; individuals should go to bed and get up at the same time each day including weekends and holidays. The elderly person should adhere to other sensible norms of health hygiene (Table 12-1) such as avoiding copious meals, excessive alcohol, and caffeine-containing substances before going to sleep, a recommendation that should prevail in advanced age with even more strength than at other ages when sleep is less vulnerable. One daytime nap is acceptable and even recommendable when fragmentation of nocturnal sleep prevents the fulfillment of sleep needs. One or even 2 hours of sleep in the early afternoon can compensate for nocturnal sleep loss and restore full vigilance for the remainder of the day. The amount of sleep to be consumed in the 24 hours is fixed so that more sleep than necessary cannot be forced. A daytime nap that is too prolonged might steal sleep from the ensuing night, delaying sleep onset or increasing fragmentation. Notwithstanding such limitations, a reasonable daily siesta in the early afternoon is generally beneficial in the elderly person who does not have the impositions of a work schedule to respect.

The elderly person is more sensitive to schedule changes than the younger individual and endures with great difficulty modifications in circadian rhythmicity. As age advances, it becomes increasingly difficult to adapt to work shifts. Past the age of 45 years, tolerance of shift work is unpredictable. From a laboral perspective, it might become onerous to force nocturnal work, risking a deterioration of productivity and increasing workers' tendency to suffer work-related accidents as the attention, interest, and enthusiasm for work decline. Accommodation to the changes imposed by transmeridian flights becomes increasingly difficult as age advances. The elderly traveler should adapt to time zone changes by gradually introducing shifts in sleep-wake schedules before departure. East-west travelers should try to go to bed and get up later each day, whereas the west-east traveler should attempt the reverse modification, although success with this latter change is more difficult to achieve. At their destination, experienced travelers might consider taking small amounts of a short-acting benzodiazepine, such as triazolam (0.125 mg) or zolpidem (5 mg) before going to bed, over the first 2 or 3 days following arrival.

In general, circadian rhythmicity in the elderly person is of less amplitude and shorter duration than in younger individuals. The relative advanced sleep phase observed in the elderly can be modified with luminotherapy [50]. Body temperature remains higher at night in senescence, a phenomenon also observed in depressed subjects and in insomniacs. Bedridden adults exhibit similar changes along with sleep alteration, suggesting that lack of exercise, a common loss in advanced age, might have notable influence over sleep-wake phenomena. Vigorous exercise improves the quality of nocturnal sleep and increases SWS percentage. The production of growth hormone in association with SWS is stimulated with proper amounts of regular exercise and a restful sleep even in advanced age. This hormone has an anabolic effect on protein metabolism, helping to restore muscle mass, accelerating cicatrization, and enhancing the production of high-density lipoproteins. Its deficit could be associated with protracted healing, decubiti ulcers, skin atrophy, and muscle wasting.

References

1. Ramón y Cajal S. Conversations in the Coffee Shop. Madrid: Colección Austral, Espasa-Calpe, S.A., Décima Edición, 1978; 57.
2. Prinz PN. Sleep patterns in the healthy aged: Relationship with intellectual function. J Gerontol 1977;32:179.
3. Miles LE, Dement WC. Sleep and aging. Sleep 1980;3:119.
4. Foley DJ, Monjan AA, Brown SL, et al. Sleep complaints among elderly persons: An epidemiological study of three communities. Sleep 1995;18:425.

5. Saradzhisvil P, Geladze TS, Bibileishvili SI, et al. Clinical sleep patterns of long living males. Soobshenheniya Akademii Nauk Gruzinskoy SSR (Tbilisi)1974;75:693.
6. Principe JC, Smith JR. Sleep spindle characteristics as a function of age. Sleep 1982;5:73.
7. Guazzelli M, Feinberg I, Aminoff M, et al. Sleep spindles in normal elderly: Comparison with young adult patterns and relation to nocturnal awakening, cognitive function and brain atrophy. Electroencephalogr Clin Neurophysiol 1986;63:526.
8. Feinberg I, Floyd TC. Systematic trends across the night in human sleep cycles. Psychophysiology 1979;16:283.
9. Carskadon MA, van den Hoed J, Dement WC. Sleep and daytime sleepiness in the elderly. J Geriatr Psychiatry 1980;13:135.
10. Carskadon MA, Brown ED, Dement WC. Sleep fragmentation in the elderly: Relationship to daytime sleep tendency. Neurobiol Aging 1982;3:321.
11. Bliwise DL. Normal Aging. In MH Kryger, T Roth, WC Dement (eds), Principles and Practice of Sleep Medicine (2nd ed.). Philadelphia: Saunders, 1994;26.
12. Swaab DF, Fliers E, Partiman TS. The suprachiasmatic nucleus of the human brain in relation to sex, age, and senile dementia. Brain Res 1985;342:37.
13. Prinz PN, Vitiello MV, Raskind MA, et al. Geriatrics: Sleep disorders and aging. N Engl J Med 1990;323:520.
14. Ancoli-Israel S, Kripke DF, Mason W, et al. Sleep apnea and periodic movements in an aging sample. J Gerontol 1985;40:419.
15. Ancoli-Israel S, Klauber MR, Kripke DF, et al. Sleep apnea in female patients in a nursing home: Increased risk of mortality. Chest 1989;96:1054.
16. Mant A, King M, Saunders NA, et al. Four-year follow-up of mortality and sleep-related respiratory disturbance in nondemented seniors. Sleep 1995;18:433.
17. Palomaki H, Partinen M, Erkinjuntti T, et al. Snoring, sleep apnea syndrome, and stroke. Neurology 1992;42:75.
18. Dyken ME, Rodnitzky RL. Periodic, aperiodic, and rhythmic motor disorders of sleep. Neurology 1992;42:68.
19. Montamat SC, Cusack BJ, Vestal RE. Management of drug therapy in the elderly. N Engl J Med 1989;321:303.
20. Weitzman ED, Moline NL, Czeisler CA, et al. Chronobiology of aging: Temperature, sleep-wake rhythms and entrainment. Neurobiol Aging 1982;3:299.
21. Reynolds CF, Kupfer DJ, Taska LS, et al. EEG sleep in elderly depressed, demented and healthy subjects. Biol Psychiatry 1985;20:431.
22. Reynolds CF, Kupfer DJ, Hoch CC, et al. Two-year follow-up of elderly patients with mixed depression and dementia. J Am Geriatr Soc 1986;34:793.
23. Prinz PN, Vitiello MV, Smallwood RG, et al. Plasma norepinephrine in normal young and aged men; relationship with sleep. J Gerontol 1984;39:561.

24. Buysse DJ, Reynolds CF, Kupfer DJ, et al. Electroencephalographic sleep in depressive pseudodementia. Arch Gen Psychiatry 1988;45:568.

25. Reynolds CF, Kupfer DJ, Taska LS, et al. EEG sleep in elderly depressed, demented and healthy subjects. Biol Psychiatry 1985;20:431.

26. Reynolds CF, Kupfer DJ, Hoch CC, et al. Two-year follow-up of elderly patients with mixed depression and dementia. J Am Geriatr Soc 1986;34:793.

27. Bliwise DL, Tinklenberg J, Yesavage JA, et al. REM latency in Alzheimer's disease. Biol Psychiatry 1989;25:320.

28. Allen SR, Seiler WO, Ståhelin HB, et al. Seventy-two hour polygraphic and behavioral recordings of wakefulness and sleep in a hospital geriatric unit: Comparison between demented and nondemented patients. Sleep 1987;10:143.

29. Lipowski ZJ. Delirium in the elderly patient. N Engl J Med 1989;320:578.

30. Erkinjuntti T, Wilkstrom J, Palo J, et al. Dementia among medical inpatients: Evaluation of 2,000 consecutive admissions. Arch Intern Med 1986;146:1923.

31. Prinz PN, Vitaliano P, Vitiello M, et al. EEG and mental function changes in mild, moderate and severe senile dementia of the Alzheimer's type. Neurobiol Aging 1982;3:361.

32. Vitiello MV, Bliwise DL, Prinz PN. Sleep in Alzheimer's disease and the sundown syndrome. Neurology 1992;42:83.

33. Vitiello MV, Bokan JA, Kukull WA, et al. REM sleep measures of Alzheimer's-type dementia patients and optimally healthy aged individuals. Biol Psychiatry 1984;19:721.

34. Bliwise DL, Nino-Murcia G, Forno LS, et al. Abundant REM sleep in a patient with Alzheimer's disease. Neurology 1990;40:1281.

35. Bliwise DL, Yesavage JA, Tinklenberg JR, et al. Sleep apnea in Alzheimer's disease. Neurobiol Aging 1989;10:343.

36. Evans LK. Sundown syndrome in institutionalized elderly. J Am Geriatr Soc 1987;35:101.

37. Evenhuis HM. The natural history of dementia in Down's syndrome. Arch Neurol 1990;47:263.

38. Lugaresi E, Medori R, Montagna P, et al. Fatal familial insomnia and dysautonomia with selective degeneration of thalamic nuclei. N Engl J Med 1986;315:997.

39. Rancurel G, Garma L, Hauw JJ, et al. Familial Thalamic Degeneration with Fatal Insomnia: Clinico-Pathological and Polygraphic Data on a French Member of Lugaresi's Italian Family. In C Guilleminault, E Lugaresi, P Montagna, et al (eds), Fatal Familial Insomnia: Inherited Prion Diseases, Sleep and the Thalamus. New York: Raven, 1994;15.

40. Culebras A, Feldman RG, Merk FB. Cytoplasmic inclusion bodies within neurons of the thalamus in myotonic dystrophy. J Neurol Sci 1973;19:319.

41. Culebras A. Thalamic Lesions and the Endocrine System. In C Guilleminault, E Lugaresi, P Montagna, et al (eds), Fatal Familial Insomnia: Inherited Prion Diseases, Sleep and the Thalamus. New York: Raven, 1994;87.

42. Kakigi R, Endo C, Neshige R, et al. Accelerated aging of the brain in Werner's syndrome. Neurology 1992;42:922.

43. Erkinjuntti T, Partinen M, Sulkava T, et al. Sleep apnea in multi-infarct dementia and Alzheimer's disease. Sleep 1987;10:419.
44. Palomaki H, Partinen M, Erkinjuntti T, et al. Snoring, sleep apnea syndrome, and stroke. Neurology 1992;42:75.
45. Culebras A. REM sin atonía y fantasmagorías. Rev Neurol Arg. 1988;-14:151.
46. Culebras A, Moore JT. Magnetic resonance findings in REM sleep behavior disorder. Neurology 1989;39:1519.
47. Culebras A. Neuroanatomic and neurologic correlates of sleep disturbances. Neurology 1992;42:19.
48. Montamat SC, Cusack BJ, Vestal RE. Management of drug therapy in the elderly. N Engl J Med 1989;321:303.
49. Kales A, Soldatos CR, Bixler EO, et al. Early morning insomnia with rapidly eliminated benzodiazepines. Science 1983;220:95.
50. Czeisler CA, Kronauer RE, Allan JS, et al. Bright light induction of strong (type O) resetting of the human circadian pacemaker. Science 1989;244:1328.

13

General Management and Therapy of Sleep Disorders

Not poppy, nor mandragora, nor all the drowsy syrups of the world, shall ever medicine thee to that sweet sleep, which thou ow'dst yesterday.

William Shakespeare
Othello [1]

Sleep disorders, like other alterations of the body, are subject to alleviation and even cure with the implementation of a rational management based on the understanding of their manifestations and mechanisms. Therapeutic interventions can be classified in four broad groups: (1) sleep hygiene and prophylaxis of sleep disorders, (2) psychotherapy, (3) pharmacology, and (4) physical and surgical interventions. Whenever possible, it is desirable to start with the treatments that are least aggressive and onerous, without forgetting that simple measures of sleep hygiene and the elimination of risk factors are as important if not more so than pharmacologic therapy.

General Sleep Hygiene

The widespread lack of knowledge about sleep hygiene is notorious. It has been estimated that in the United States alone, 40% of the population, or approximately 100 million people, are sleep deprived and have developed a sleep debt that in some way they will have to repay.

Lack of regularity in the sleep-wake schedule and the common practice of cheating hours from sleep lead to a state of chronic fatigue that reduces an individual's physical and mental abilities. Students lose memory along with concentration and attention span, the commercial driver fights sleepiness on the job, the executive falls asleep at meetings, the elderly person nods repeatedly in church, and the guest has to make a great effort to stay awake following the first glass of wine. These are but a few examples of situations in which there is loss of productivity, social embarrassment, risk of accident, and decline in the quality of life as a result of sleep deprivation. It has been estimated that 50,000 traffic accidents occurring annually in the United States are related to sleepiness and mental fatigue (see Chapter 14).

Sleep needs should not be deceived. Sleep hygiene should acquire as much importance as balanced nutrition and the proper amount of exercise. A lack of order in this basic function of our lives leads to decreased longevity, increased risk of accidents, decline in work productivity, and degradation of the quality of life. The scope of sleep and its disorders goes beyond the reach of the specialist, whereas its understanding exerts an increasing influence on the planning of the educator, the sociologist, and the administrator.

Sleep-Wake Schedule

By 4 months of age, sleep consolidates to the nocturnal period coinciding with the establishment of non-REM sleep. Until the age of 5 or 6 years, the child needs a nap in the middle of the day despite a night sleep that is long, deep, and well structured. Past that age, most children are capable of satisfying all their sleep needs during the night period, and it is a well-known fact that adolescents despise daytime naps. However, as the individual ages and nocturnal sleep loses depth and continuity, the number of hours in bed increases to absorb the effect of episodes of nocturnal awakening; otherwise, sleep deprivation appears and affects the quality of daytime vigilance. Beyond middle age, most individuals welcome with increasing satisfaction a short nap in the middle of the day, and in senescence that satisfaction becomes a necessity for most people.

Each individual requires a specified number of hours of sleep in the 24-hour cycle, ranging between 6 and 9, with an average need of 8 hours. Differences among subjects are notable, and each person must find the number of hours needed by gauging the level of satisfaction with sleep. Many patients ask their physician how many hours they need to sleep at night, and the answer is quite simple: as many as required to be satisfied in the morning on waking up. It is not possible to extend the amount of sleep within the 24-hour period unless the individual is sleep deprived or suffers a sleep disorder. It is desirable to maintain the same schedule continuously; individuals should go to bed and get up at the same time each day, including weekends and holidays, and stay in bed only the amount of time necessary to sleep. Some people have noticed that they can facilitate consolidation of nocturnal sleep without noticeably affecting the quality of daytime alertness by cutting their sleep time 30–45 minutes.

It is possible to satisfy sleep requirements by dividing sleep into two periods, a major one at night and a minor period during the day lasting 1–2 hours. The sum of both should equal the total number of hours needed in the 24 hours. Generally, the daytime nap, or siesta, is taken after lunch, coinciding with a physiologic nadir in vigilance experienced by most persons. In fact, individuals who habitually take a siesta observe that the quality of alertness improves in the second half of the day.

Some individuals, like the owl, prefer to stay up late, work until late, go to bed late, and get up late in the morning. Others, like the lark, wake up with the break of dawn, work more efficiently in the early morning hours, and find it pleasant to retire early to bed. As age progresses, the internal biological clock tends to advance the sleep phase and the individual becomes increasingly inclined to implement an early sleep-wake schedule.

Environment

A well-known phenomenon in sleep laboratories is the "first-night effect" (Figure 13-1) [2], which consists of diminished sleep efficiency and reduction of stages 3, 4, and REM on the first night of testing relative to ensuing nights. This phenomenon is the result of lack of familiarity with the environment, the same factor that alters the sleep efficiency of travelers who stay overnight at unknown hotels, notwithstanding jet lag, even if relatively close to home. A few travelers sleep better away from home, but this is a pathologic manifestation of anxiety (see Chapter 5). To sleep properly, the individual needs an ambient that is free of noise, low in lighting, and neither cold nor hot.

Noises interrupt sleep with increasing ease as the night progresses since the arousal threshold decreases as nocturnal sleep is consumed and the pressure to sleep decreases. Children are more resistant than

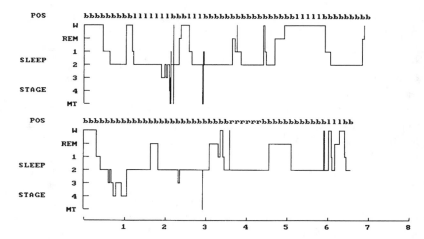

Figure 13-1. *Hypnogram showing the "first-night effect" in a 24-year-old man, free of sleep disorders, being tested for erectile impotence. On the first night (above), sleep architecture shows virtual absence of stages 3 and 4, scarce generation of REM sleep, and prolonged awakenings. On the second consecutive night of testing (below), there is a distinct cycle of slow wave sleep, and four cycles of REM sleep with appropriately spaced latencies and few awakenings. Postural shifts occurred less frequently on the second night as noted by the position indicator (POS). W = wake; MT = movement time. (Reprinted with permission from A Culebras. La Medicina del Sueño. Barcelona: Ed Áncora, 1994.)*

adults to being awakened by extraneous noises and middle-aged individuals are more so than the elderly [3]. Noises of similar intensity awaken women more easily than men. In general, the arousal threshold is low in stage 1 and high in slow wave sleep (SWS). The highest arousal threshold to noise is reached in REM sleep, at least in the experimental animal. Selective thresholds in humans allow nursing mothers to be awakened only by the whimper of the infant. Noises generated by automobile traffic and airplane approaches are particularly disturbing because of their irregular pitch and volume. A study performed among residents of a community adjoining the Los Angeles airport showed that their sleep was reduced on the average of 45 minutes per night relative to other residential areas [4]. On the other hand, background, or "white" noise, as experienced when traveling by airplane or hearing an air conditioner, helps individuals sleep by dampening sudden loud noises. The Los Angeles study showed that partial adaptation to noisy environments is possible. Ear plugs, a white noise background, or in extreme instances windows insulated against sound, attenuate noises and are solutions to keep in mind when noisy intrusions from the exterior cannot be controlled.

Temperature

Body temperature decreases during non-REM sleep reaching a nadir (1°C lower than basal awake) 3 hours after falling asleep. In REM sleep, the body ceases to regulate temperature and reduces perspiration, entering a state akin to poikilothermia. By early morning, as REM sleep becomes increasingly prevalent, ambient temperature exerts more influence over sleep. Studies in humans have shown that maximum amounts of both REM and non-REM sleep are achieved at the environmental temperature of 29°C, decreasing when the temperature deviates in either direction of this thermoneutral level [5]. At excessively high and low temperatures, there is significant fragmentation of sleep. REM sleep is more sensitive to temperature changes than non-REM sleep. As age advances, sleep sensitivity to external temperature deviations increases, as shown in elderly animals that exhibit more arousals with cold temperatures. Ambient temperatures below 22°C can influence the intensity and content of dreams [6], whereas very cold temperatures (0–5°C) can cause REM sleep to disappear as a defensive arousal occurs.

Meteorologic conditions, such as the extremes of barometric pressure that produce somnolence, influence the progression of sleep [7]. The seasons with long and short days also contribute to sleep variations. In the arctic environment, where days can be extremely short, inhabitants complain of daytime somnolence and difficulty initiating sleep.

Bed

Individuals who sleep on a hard bed tend to change position more often than ones who sleep on a soft one. Young couples sharing a matrimonial bed sleep more deeply than older couples under the same conditions [8]. As age advances and the arousal threshold decreases, individuals become increasingly sensitive to position changes by the bedmate, experiencing more frequent arousals with lesser intensity of movement by the companion, so that separate beds might be advisable for certain couples beyond middle age.

Meals, Drinks, and Tobacco

Satiety is conducive to sleep, and a good meal facilitates the siesta in midday. Animals in the wild, such as the felines, that feed irregularly and consume large amounts of food at each setting also sleep after being fed. Teleologically, the well-fed animal has no need to move in search for food, so that the postprandial time can be well served by sleeping. Early experiments in humans showed that dilatation of the jejunum with a balloon produces sleepiness [9], and that instillation of milk in the duodenum of kittens also produces somnolence. These observations led to the thought that hypnotic substances liberated in the gut could promote sleepiness, and indeed tryptophan, which occurs in relatively large proportions in milk products, is a precursor of serotonin, a well-known neurotransmitter that intervenes in the production of sleep.

Later, L-tryptophan was introduced as a popular remedy for sleeplessness among individuals desperate for a solution to their plight. The demand for a legendary cure for insomnia precipitated a hurried production of L-tryptophan in large scale for therapeutic purposes with disregard to safety precautions. In susceptible patients, massive consumption of over-the-counter L-tryptophan contaminated with noxious products led to the development of a serious myositis with myalgia associated with eosinophilia, the eosinophilia-myalgia syndrome [10]. Symptoms reported included incapacitating muscle pains, rash, shortness of breath, peripheral edema, congestive heart failure, and scleroderma; eosinophilia counts in blood reached 10,000–30,000 per ml. An expanded recall for L-tryptophan was issued by the FDA [11], and alerts to physicians were issued by the Centers for Disease Control (CDC) and by the American Sleep Disorders Association requesting the immediate discontinuation of L-tryptophan as a medical remedy. By 1991, 28 deaths had been reported by the CDC [12] in Atlanta. At the present time, L-tryptophan is not used for the treatment of insomnia and the eosinophilia-myalgia syndrome has vanished, but the history remains as a reminder of the dire consequences of hurriedly introducing without proper supervision a product demanded by millions of desperate individuals.

Acute loss of weight is typically associated with insomnia and weight gain with sound sleep. Individuals engaged in a weight-loss diet complain of sleep difficulties, since hunger is an enemy of sleep. In hyperthyroidism and in mania, weight loss is prominent along with profound sleep alteration. Patients with anorexia nervosa also exhibit insomnia, and depressed patients with poor sleep tend to lose weight, whereas individuals who complain of hypersomnia gain weight. Several mechanisms can be at play in this association, and one should remember that excessive weight gain leads to sleep apnea syndromes, although this liaison has a different mechanism of action. In hypothyroidism, weight gain is a manifestation of the disorder, and some patients complain of hypersomnia in part caused by sleep apnea. In general, foods rich in carbohydrates facilitate sleep. A meal at the end of the day also promotes sleep, but consumption of a large amount of heavy food immediately before retiring can alter sleep. Severe malnourishment produces somnolence, as noted in concentration camps during the Second World War.

Alcoholic beverages have a paradoxic effect over sleep. When the evening consumption exceeds three generous glasses of wine, representing approximately 420 g of wine or three shots of whiskey (84 g), there is an initial hypnotic effect that facilitates sleep, but several hours later withdrawal phenomena take hold as the hypnotic effect dissipates. The sympathetic tone increases and the level of catecholamines rises, provoking arousals that fragment nocturnal sleep. Ingestion of large amounts of alcohol causes sedation of neurologic functions including respiratory center activity that worsens a preexisting sleep apnea syndrome and increases snoring phenomena.

Caffeine-containing infusions or drinks (e.g., coffee, tea, chocolate, and sodas) alter the initiation and continuity of sleep, particularly if consumed at the end of the day [13]. Some individuals who consume large amounts of coffee during the day need to drink coffee before retiring to avoid caffeine withdrawal effects. Caffeine is an alkaloid that competes in the CNS with receptors of adenosine, a neuromodulator with inhibitor effect. A cup of regular coffee contains 100 mg of caffeine; a cup of tea, 50 mg; and a popular caffeine-containing soda, 75 mg. A daily dose exceeding 500 mg has a predictable inhibitory effect over sleep independently of the time of ingestion, since the half-life of caffeine has a range of 8–14 hours.

Liquid in any form taken in abundance immediately before retiring to bed can interrupt sleep by creating a need to urinate during the night. Individuals with significant leg edema experience a similar phenomenon, because edema fluid is reabsorbed in the supine posture. Indeed, a complaint of repeated urination at night suggests leg edema. Diuretic ingestion late in the day promotes repeated urination at night; administration to ambulatory patients should be ordered for the morning and never past 5:00 P.M.

Inhalation of tobacco smoke containing nicotine, a CNS stimulant, also influences sleep architecture [14]. On the other hand, suppression of tobacco use can have a paradoxic effect by causing anxiety and other psychological manifestations. The morning cough of the inveterate smoker indicates pooling of excessive bronchial secretions at night when the physiologic reflex is abolished. Indeed, nocturnal coughing indicates an arousal.

In general, food has a healthy, soporific, postprandial effect, and alcohol in small quantities has a welcome hypnotic action. Stimulant beverages and tobacco tend to alter sleep.

Reading, Radio, and Television

Pleasant reading before turning the lights off is recommended. The monotony of reading along with the deviation of attention to enjoyable subjects that permit escape to an imaginary world of chosen figments and figurations breaks the daily routine, interrupts the chain of stressing factors and facilitates the mental relaxation that is required to make a transition to sleep. Soft background music without stridence has a similar effect and camouflages intruding noises.

Television, however, can have an alerting effect. Continuous visual stimulation, both in color and in black and white, and the accompanying sound can stimulate wakefulness. Furthermore, the subject of many television programs is inappropriate to achieve mental relaxation.

Transoceanic Travel and Hotels

Some persons have difficulty initiating sleep in a strange environment; others sleep better away from home. The latter are usually neurotic individuals with an inclination to associate stressing factors with their bedroom, where going to bed elicits an alerting conditioned response that obstructs the entry to sleep. In alien bedrooms, the conditioned response fails to occur and the subject, at least during the first few days, is capable of sleeping with tranquility. Persons who do not sleep well away from home find solace in following the prebed rituals that they have instituted at home: brushing their teeth, using their own pajamas, and reading a favorite book are among some of the most common established forms of prebed activity that help promote sleep in and out of the home.

Transcontinental and transoceanic travel can cause insomnia and jet lag syndrome (see Chapters 9 and 14). East-west travel, such as from Paris to New York, is more tolerable than the contrary since it is tantamount to prolonging the day by 6 hours and going to bed very late. On the other hand, west-east travel, such as from New York to Paris, shortens the day by 6 hours, which means retiring to bed on destination 6 hours earlier than is customary. Fatigue might allow the traveler to fall asleep right after retiring, but sleep discontinuation will appear 2 or 3 hours later causing a transient form of insomnia. The countermeasure is to implement some form of progressive adjustment by going to bed increasingly early each day for 1 or 2 weeks before traveling, a strategy that is poorly accepted by younger individuals. Pharmacologic management of jet lag syndrome can be achieved by taking a short-acting benzodiazepine such as triazolam, 0.125 mg, or zolpidem, 10 mg, at bedtime. The passenger should not abuse alcoholic beverages during transcontinental and transoceanic air travel.

Exercise, Physical Health, and Mental Health

Vigorous physical exercise increases nocturnal deep sleep and stimulates the secretion of growth hormone during SWS, particularly in regular athletes of any age. Thus, exercise facilitates sleep of higher restorative value mentally and physically, the latter through the anabolic activity of growth hormone. In a study performed in Finland [15], a questionnaire was sent to 200 middle-aged individuals of both sexes. One-third of the respondents asserted that exercise had a positive beneficial effect, facilitating sleep onset at night, while increasing its depth and in general improving well-being and level of alertness.

The closer it gets to bedtime, the more intense the influence of sleep on sleep parameters. Very vigorous exercise immediately before retiring has an alerting effect that retards the onset of sleep. At any time during the day, exercise stimulates wakefulness, a phenomenon narcoleptics use to remain awake. Although it appears clear that regular exercise has influence over sleep, authors disagree on the amount of influence and not everyone admits a direct effect. Some suggest that exercise raises corporal temperature, causing warming of the hypothalamus, a phenomenon that is known to increase SWS. There is agreement to recommend daily regular exercise at approximately the same time every day before 6:00 P.M. as a factor contributing to a healthy sleep hygiene.

When a patient complains of insomnia, it is important to review the medication intake to investigate potential alerting actions and introduce the necessary adjustments (Table 13-1). Many medications stimulate alertness and delay sleep; among this group are the sympathomimetic drugs (e.g., amphetamine, methylphenidate, and pemoline), xanthines that compete for the adenosine receptor (e.g., caffeine and teophilline), and anorectics that have a central adrenergic action. Beta-blockers such as propranolol inhibit REM sleep and can cause fragmentation of nocturnal sleep, precipitating nightmares if there is a rebound phenomenon on withdrawal.

Daytime sedation is a common phenomenon with neuroleptic medication, benzodiazepines, tricyclic antidepressants, antihistaminics, opioids, and analgesics, including aspirin. Some are used to facilitate nocturnal sleep.

Stressing factors occurring during the day alter sleep. Included in this group are habitual occurrences such as final examinations, deadlines, financial loss, grieving, conjugal conflicts, family pathology, work crises, travel, and other incidents and accidents of daily life. If sporadic and transient, little or perhaps nothing should be done while awaiting their extinction, but when occurring frequently, chronification of their effect can result, in which case a therapeutic strategy should be implemented to counteract the stressful action. Sometimes, the administration of a hypnotic medication over a few days is sufficient to overcome the crisis.

Deterioration of physical health is also a source of poor sleep. Acute or chronic pain, functional incapacity, paralysis, difficulty breathing, diarrhea, incontinence, nocturia, and other pathologic sensations interrupt sleep, altering its architecture and decreasing its quality, resulting in secondary daytime fatigue and sleepiness. Alleviation of physical infirmities improves sleep and the well-being of the patient and relatives.

Psychotherapy

Psychotherapeutic and behavioral modification interventions are based on the unquestionable relationship that exists between wakefulness, sleep, and cognitive phenomena. The most common interventions are geared to control anxiety, tension, and chronic stress with the understanding that these factors are amenable to psychotherapeutic intervention and behavioral modification independently of their response to other therapeutic mechanisms, whether they are hygienic, pharmacologic, physical, or surgical (Table 13-2).

Table 13-1. Sleep Hygiene—Dos and Don'ts

Do

1. Adhere to a sleep-wake schedule that is the same for every day of the week, including weekends and holidays.
2. Get enough sleep to be satisfied in the morning.
3. Exercise daily but not before going to bed or late in the evening.
4. Adhere to a meal schedule.
5. Read or listen to soft music before turning the lights out.
6. Use a twin bed if your bedmate is a restless sleeper.
7. Eliminate or alleviate physical disturbances (e.g., noise, light, heat, and cold). Use ear plugs and eye shades if necessary.
8. Review with your physician medications you take and discontinue the ones with an alerting effect.
9. Use a medium-soft mattress and a comfortable soft pillow.
10. Take a nap at the same time every day, if this is your habit. Do not sleep more than 45 minutes; after lunch is the best time.

Don't

1. Stay out late on weekends and holidays.
2. Exercise in the late evening or before bedtime.
3. Eat or drink heavily in the late evening or before going to bed.
4. Drink caffeine-containing beverages past 12 noon.
5. Use alcohol as a hypnotic or sedative; more than one glass of wine in the evening or its equivalent can cause rebound insomnia in the second half of the night.
6. Watch television in the bedroom.
7. Bring paperwork to bed.
8. Turn on bright lights if you get out of bed at night.
9. Nap irregularly or frequently during the day.
10. Nap in the evenings.

Mental Relaxation and Biofeedback

The objective of mental relaxation and biofeedback is to influence sleep by modifying the character of the preceding wakefulness (Figure 13-2). Mental relaxation techniques reduce the level of stimulation and exci-

Table 13-2. Goals of Psychotherapy

Desired changes

1. Manage stress
2. Improve emotional expression
3. Develop insight
4. Improve interpersonal relationships
5. Restructure lifestyle away from complaints of insomnia

Specific adjuvant measures

1. Treatment of withdrawal states from drugs and alcohol
2. Treatment of medical and psychiatric causes of insomnia
3. Chronotherapy in sleep phase asynchronies

tation during wakefulness, facilitating sleep onset. The technique is to focus the attention of the patient on the level of muscular tension, while requesting contraction and relaxation of certain muscle groups in a predetermined sequence. Biofeedback techniques [16] add sensorial information to the muscular effort by incorporating an electromyographic receptor that triggers a sound at a specified frequency. This frequency depends on the degree of tension in a muscle that is sensitive to mental stress, such as the temporal muscle. Eventually, the patient learns to modify the tone of the sound acting on the tension of the muscle. Other biofeedback techniques use an EEG tracing to teach the patient to reach theta frequencies that indicate transition from wakefulness to sleep.

Cognitive Treatments

Stress management is paramount in patients with emotional and cognitive arousal under real or perceived psychological stress. Meditation and cognitive refocusing are taught to patients with persistent rumination of thought preventing sleep onset. Desensitization consists of executing muscle relaxation exercises of an increasing level of difficulty eventually reaching a threshold that causes anxiety. Learned habits and conditioning to the bedroom and its environment can be reformed with stimulus control techniques that attempt to interrupt the negative bond between the patient and the bedroom [17]. The procedure requires the patient to

Figure 13-2. *Serenity, tranquility, and placidity along with freedom from pressures, stress, and anxiety are conducive to a restful sleep.*

leave the bedroom when not sleepy and use the bedroom exclusively for sleep. It has been stated that the efficacy of behavioral therapy for insomnia occurs beyond any placebo effect, although polysomnographic objective measures have failed to show a difference [18].

Chronotherapy

Chronotherapy was devised to treat patients with delayed sleep-phase syndrome and later adapted to treat advanced sleep-phase syndrome. It is an attempt to reset the circadian clock by inducing a drift of sleep times over a period of days until an acceptable match is obtained between the internal and external cycles. In delayed sleep-phase syndrome, sleep is scheduled later and later each day [19]. The therapeutic goal of chronotherapy is to achieve and maintain a desired phase that matches the geocosmic 24-hour cycle. The method is to impose a 27-hour day on successive days by delay-shifting scheduled bedtimes and wake times until the desired position is reached. For instance, patients are instructed to enforce a schedule as follows: day 1, 3:00 to 11:00 A.M.; day 2, 6:00 A.M. to 2:00 P.M.; day 3, 9:00 A.M. to 5:00 P.M.; day 4, 12 noon to 8 P.M.; day 5, 3:00 to 11:00 P.M.; day 6, 6:00 P.M. to 2:00 A.M.; day 7, 9:00 P.M. to 5:00 A.M. Thereafter, patients are maintained on the final schedule allowing less than 1-hour deviations from the time frames. Naps are not permitted, and patients are instructed to maintain the discipline every day including weekends and days off. Many individuals are helped by keeping a logbook or diary. Strengthening of time cues along with enforcement of strict schedules is critical to maintain a socially acceptable timetable.

The successful phase-advance of schedules in a patient with advanced sleep-phase syndrome has also been reported [20]. The technique is similar to that used in phase-delay except that the patient is asked to go to bed and wake up 3 hours earlier each day until a desired schedule is reached.

Sleep Restriction Therapy

Sleep restriction therapy, by producing a daily sleep debt of modest proportions, can help some individuals with a weak homeostatic drive to initiate sleep [21]. An excessive amount of time in bed can retard the onset of sleep in the ensuing cycle. Although the immediate effect is to increase restfulness, the long-term effect causes a slight drift of the circadian rhythm. Individuals with a tendency to develop insomnia might find it easier to fall asleep when excessively tired, a situation best achieved when short on sleep. The individual should avoid daytime naps and should try to reduce nocturnal sleep by 45 minutes each day, either by going later to bed and getting up at the same time or the reverse. The patient stays in bed only the time necessary for sleep. Initially, there will be increased fatigue as a result of sleep deprivation, but as the treatment strategy continues the individual will find that nocturnal sleep is better consolidated, resulting in improved restoration of daytime vigilance. When this level is reached, the sleep schedule is adjusted to avoid excessive sleep deprivation while final fixed time frames are issued.

Luminotherapy

The intensity of light is measured in lux units of illumination. Indoor light has approximately 150 lux, whereas therapeutic bright light has a potency of 2,500–10,000 lux. Bright light treatment for circadian dysrhythmias with sleep-wake alteration has been in use since the discovery that bright light is an effective zeitgeber. Bright light of any source is a suppressor of melatonin, the mechanism by which luminotherapy is physiologically effective (see Chapter 9) [22]. Information on commercially available light boxes can be obtained from ad hoc societies [23]. An effective regimen has a range of 2,500 lux for 2 hours to 10,000 lux for 30 minutes, emitting fluorescent cool white light with ultraviolet rays filtered out to prevent damage to the lens and retina. The light box is placed at eye level at a distance of 3 feet. Treatment overdose is manifested by headache, dizziness, and hyperactivity. Following the principles of the phase response curve hypothesis, bright light can be applied in the morning or in the evening to achieve maximal therapeutic value.

Light therapy can be useful in the future for management of shift work schedules [24], jet lag syndrome [25], and space flights [26].

Pharmacotherapy

Insomnia and hypersomnia are the objectives of pharmacologic treatment in sleep medicine. To combat insomnia, there is a long list of medications, each with particular characteristics and idiosyncrasies that are necessary to know in order to use them properly with the least risk of side effects and adverse reactions. Pharmacotherapy is an important component of the treatment of insomnia once the proper assessment of the condition has been established and defined goals have been determined. Therapy with hypnotics is perfectly adequate for the control of transient insomnias. Patients with chronic forms of insomnia can use hypnotic medication as an adjunct to therapy, administering the minimum effective dose for short periods of time and only when cognizant of the adverse reactions. Sometimes periods of severe insomnia are predictable in susceptible individuals, and these can be targeted for treatment with hypnotics. Dose escalation and frequency of use can be controlled with close supervision, although most specialists would agree that risk of dependency is related to the personality of the patient and not so much to the medication. Both the patient and the prescriber need to have a clear understanding of the duration of activity of the medication administered in order to achieve the desired primary effect at night and to avoid unwanted actions. Duration of activity is a function of distribution and elimination. Half-life is a relative estimate of the duration of activity but fails to predict accumulation, a factor that underlies toxicity.

Ultrashort-acting compounds with half-lives of 3 hours or less initiate sleep and do not accumulate in the body. Compounds with a half-life of 5 hours or more maintain sleep better than short-acting preparations but have a tendency to accumulate and cause toxicity over many days of administration, particularly in susceptible individuals and in elderly persons with slow metabolism. Before a hypnotic is recommended, it is desirable to establish the goals of therapy. Three different actions can be sought: facilitate onset of sleep, maintain sleep, and produce daytime sedation following sleep.

Insomnia can be treated with a variety of compounds with differing actions. The compound can be a sedative with hypnotic effect, such as the barbiturates; or a sedative with anxiolytic and hypnotic action, such as the benzodiazepines; a tranquilizer, such as the phenothiazines and haloperidol; an antidepressant with hypnotic action, such as the tricyclic compounds; an anxiolytic, such as the beta-blockers; an antihistaminic; an anticonvulsant; or even an analgesic, such as aspirin. When to use, how long to prescribe, and in what amount depend on a series of factors that emanate from the proper medical assessment of the patient.

Hypersomnolence can be a secondary consequence of sleep deprivation or the direct effect of an intrinsic disorder. There is only one form of somnolence characterized by the tendency to fall asleep, but the treatment will vary depending on the underlying mechanism. Thus, as in the management of insomnia, the treatment of excessive sleepiness also depends on the proper assessment of the patient, using a medical perspective. Various products can be considered such as the amphetamines, which are potent monoaminergic stimulants; caffeine and xanthines, which compete for adenosine receptors; and gamma-hydroxybutyric acid, which has a dopaminergic effect. REM sleep inhibitors such as the tricyclic compounds act indirectly on alerting mechanisms and are used in narcolepsy and depression.

Hypnotics

Until 1970, the hypnotics most frequently used were the barbiturates with short and intermediate action. Starting with the introduction of flurazepam as a hypnotic in 1970, the use of benzodiazepines became widespread, and by 1985, virtually the only products used to combat insomnia in North America were flurazepam, temazepam, and triazolam, all benzodiazepine derivatives.

Benzodiazepines

Benzodiazepines are heterocyclic compounds known since 1891 but only used in clinical medicine since Leo H. Sternbach's introduction of chlordiazepoxide as an anxiolytic in 1960 [27]. Modifications of the chemical structure gave way to a variety of compounds with differing actions. By 1990, there were 13 different preparations of the benzodiazepine family available to the physician in North America (Table 13-3), with a wide spectrum of indications including epilepsy, movement disorders, psychiatric conditions, and sleep disorders.

Benzodiazepine derivatives have three distinct actions in addition to the hypnotic effect: anxiolytic, muscle relaxant, and anticonvulsant. Benzodiazepines differ from one another by their diverse clinical effect in any of these properties and by the speed of action, although in general they have a low level of toxicity. In the CNS, the benzodiazepines act directly on neuronal receptors that also include binding sites for picrotoxine and gamma-aminobutyric acid (GABA). These sites determine the frequency of opening of the chloride channel that leads to neuronal hyperpolarization, a final common mechanism that underlies the hypnotic, sedative, muscle relaxant, and anticonvulsant action of the benzodiazepines. Forty percent of neuronal synapses are GABAergic. Alcohol and barbiturates also bind to receptors that act on chloride channels, so that the general pharmacologic action is similar for all these compounds. Substances that antagonize the benzodiazepine action such as flumazenil (RO 15-1788) produce states of anxiety with tremors and insomnia in human volunteers, as well as convulsions in the experimental animal model.

The time-course of action of the benzodiazepines is determined by physicochemical and pharmacokinetic differences; there is no difference in the qualitative character of the drug-receptor interaction. To reach the neuronal binding site, the drug must diffuse out of the capillary circulation and through the lipoidal blood–brain barrier. Highly lipophilic derivatives such as diazepam attain tissue equilibration and receptor occupation very rapidly, with onset of clinical action that is likewise rapid if given intravenously. Less lipophilic substances such as lorazepam require more time for brain tissue equilibration and receptor binding, and thus the onset of clinical action can be delayed for 30 minutes. Clonazepam is even less lipophilic than lorazepam, with a correspondingly slower onset of clinical action following intravenous administration.

The clinical action starts to decline as the benzodiazepine molecules leave the neuronal receptor. The rate of removal is determined by the

Table 13-3. Pharmacokinetic Characteristics of Some Benzodiazepine Derivatives*

Benzodiazepine (Trade Name)	Daily Dose (mg)	Maximum Action (hrs)	Duration (half-life hrs)
Midazolam (Versed)	7.5–15	0.30 ± 0.11	1.9 ±0.4
Triazolam (Halcion)	0.125–0.250	—	—
Young	0.25	0.96 ± 0.10	2.43 ± 0.16
Elderly	0.125	0.95 ± 0.11	3.03 ± 0.25
Oxazepam (Serax)	15–30	2.2 ± 1.0	7.8 ± 1.7
Temazepam (Restoril)	10–30	0.8 ± 0.3	8
Lorazepam (Ativan)	0.5–2.0	2	10–22
Alprazolam (Xanax)	0.75–1.50	1–2	16
Young	0.5–10	1–2	11.2
Elderly	0.75–1.50	—	16.3
Estazolam (Prosom)	1–2	2.7	17.1 ± 1.3
Clonazepam (Klonopin)	0.5–1.0	1–2	18–50
Diazepam (Valium, Valrelease)	2.5–10.0	1.1 ± 0.3	21–43
Chlordiazepoxide HCL (Librium, Librax)	—	6	24–48
Adult	15–40	—	—
Elderly	10–20	—	—
Quazepam (Doral)	15	2	39–73 (metabolites)
Elderly	7.5	—	—
Flurazepam (Dalmane)	15–30	8.00 ± 8.00 (metabolites)	40–100 (metabolites)
Elderly	7.5	—	—
Clorazepate (Tranxene)	15.0–22.5	0.9 ± 0.3 (metabolites)	63.7 ± 9.5 (metabolites)
Elderly	7.5–15.0	—	—

*Arranged in order of their half-life duration.

rate of drug disappearance from brain tissue, which in turn depends on the rate of disappearance from peripheral blood. Hepatic clearance is ultimately responsible for elimination of benzodiazepine derivatives, but systemic blood concentrations also depend on distribution of drug in adipose tissue and muscle depots. Highly lipophilic substances such as diazepam are redistributed rapidly to peripheral tissues; clearance from the circulation is fast and the apparent clinical effect is short-lived. On the other hand, less lipophilic substances such as lorazepam appear to have a longer duration of activity because of less extensive peripheral tissue distribution and proportionately more availability of molecules for brain interaction. Benzodiazepine derivatives do not induce the production of microsomes in the liver, like the barbiturates that accelerate the degradation of other products and their own through this mechanism. However, the benzodiazepine catabolism can be enhanced by the administration of microsome-producing compounds.

Benzodiazepine derivatives reduce the cycles of SWS while decreasing the amplitude of slow waves. Beta activity at 25–30 Hz increases in all cerebral locations and remains identifiable as many as 5 days following discontinuation of the drug. Hypnograms show shortening of sleep latency and reduction in stage transitions. Stage 2 increases at the expense of stages 1, 3, 4, and REM, which are proportionately reduced. The effect on sleep architecture can be independent of subjective perceptions of satisfaction with sleep and restoration of alertness. Short-acting benzodiazepines tend to improve the ensuing level of alertness and even of anxiety, whereas long-acting compounds produce daytime sedation and decrease motor performance. Discontinuation of the medication must be gradual to avoid withdrawal phenomena with extreme anxiety, persistent insomnia, and agitation. When using ultrashort-acting compounds, the clinician should be aware of symptoms of mini-withdrawal manifested by anxiety between doses.

Ultrashort- and short-acting benzodiazepines (midazolam, 7.5–15 mg; triazolam, 0.125–0.250 mg) facilitate the onset of sleep and do not cause daytime sedation. The dose of ultrashort- and short-acting benzodiazepines should not be increased in search of a more potent effect, since higher doses can indeed cause a desirable short latency to sleep but pose the risk of rebound insomnia during the second half of the night once the effect is gone. Intermediate-acting benzodiazepines (temazepam, 10–30 mg) are effective to initiate, maintain, and consolidate fragmented sleep. Long-acting benzodiazepines (diazepam, 2.5–10 mg; flurazepam, 15–30 mg; clorazepate, 7.5–22.5 mg; quazepam, 7.5–15 mg ; estazolam, 1–2 mg) have a sedative effect beyond the nocturnal period and serve to consolidate sleep as well as to bring sedation to anxious patients the following day. Clonazepam (0.5–1.0 mg) is used to eliminate the cortical arousals of PLMS. All benzodiazepine derivatives should be administered in interrupted doses, for instance 5 days of the week, resting 2 days, in cycles not to exceed 1 month. Some patients use the hypnotic medication only on nights before important events, even though there is no proof that the quality of alertness improves following a pharmacologically induced, better night sleep.

The toxicity of benzodiazepine derivatives is much lower than that of other products with similar clinical action. Indeed, not long after their introduction in clinical practice, it was seriously proposed that they be dispensed as an over-the-counter product. However, as clinical experience accumulated, it became clear that despite their low toxicity there was a potential for habituation and dependence, particularly in predisposed individuals. Even more of an issue was the risk of serious toxic states when benzodiazepines are combined with the administration of other sedatives including alcohol [28]. Furthermore, benzodiazepines showed an untoward sedative effect over respiratory centers, aggravating sleep apnea syndrome and other respiratory disturbances of central origin.

Until the early 1990s, triazolam was the most popular and most widely prescribed hypnotic medication around the world. It was so popular because of its ultrashort action without residual effect when taken interruptedly. However, episodes of anterograde amnesia were described in susceptible persons taking triazolam, similar to the amnestic episodes described with other benzodiazepines. The world press reported instances of violence and even homicide caused by individuals under the influence of triazolam [29]. In subjects with a past history of psychopathology, triazolam in therapeutic doses has induced delirium, agitation, and bizarre behavior that given their sensationalism contributed to the prohibition of the hypnotic in some countries. The FDA has ruled that triazolam is safe when administered under proper supervision and instructions for proper usage are followed.

Benzodiazepines should not be administered to patients with sleep apnea syndrome unless the respiratory condition is controlled with nasal continuous positive airway pressure (CPAP) or bilevel positive airway pressure (Bi-PAP). The adverse effects of benzodiazepines mentioned in the popular press can occur with abuse of the preparation, when given for too long in doses that are too high, or when administered to susceptible individuals. Judicious use by knowledgeable physicians will preempt development of anterograde amnesia, frequent falls, and dependence. These drugs are not indicated for the treatment of insomnia in patients with a history of alcohol or drug abuse, or patients with untreated depression or psychosis. As with most other preparations, the use of hypnotics is not indicated during pregnancy.

In the elderly, particularly when there is a component of early dementia, the benzodiazepine derivatives exhibit toxic activity with doses much lower than in younger persons, because of a slower elimination that maintains higher plasma concentrations for a longer period of time. In demented patients, the reduced number of cerebral receptors become saturated with relatively low amounts of the drug. Furthermore, elderly persons generally take other medications that potentially modify the pharmacologic action of the benzodiazepines. As age advances, the half-life of flurazepam increases in men but not in women. Potential states of confusion, gait instability, and falls are of particular concern in the very elderly. The dysfunction of other organs alters the action and toxicity of the benzodiazepines. Hepatic insufficiency can delay their catabolism and patients thus afflicted become very sensitive to their action. There is some evidence that the neurologic component of hepatic coma is the result of toxic compounds acting on benzodiazepine receptors. Renal failure delays elimination, and cardiovascular failure slows transportation.

The administration of benzodiazepine derivatives and the concomitant ingestion of large amounts of alcohol produce highly toxic clinical effects that should be avoided. When individuals drink any amount of alcohol and take benzodiazepines, mental abilities and motor performance are expected to decrease even after discontinuation of the drug, particularly with long-acting derivatives that tend to accumulate in the body. For instance, flurazepam has a half-life of over 24 hours; should alcohol be ingested the day following its discontinuation, the presence of the benzodiazepine in the body will potentiate the effects of alcohol, a phenomenon that is of particular concern in drivers.

Barbiturates

Since the introduction of benzodiazepine derivatives, barbiturates are no longer used as hypnotics. Nonetheless, there remains some use for them in patients who do not tolerate or do not respond properly to benzodiazepines. Barbiturates also act on the chloride channel but on a receptor different from the benzodiazepine location. Phenobarbital (100–200 mg at bedtime) is a long-acting barbiturate with low lipid solubility. Its onset of action is 1 hour and the duration 12 hours with a mean plasma half-life of 79 hours. Pentobarbital (100 mg at bedtime) has a fast onset of action (10–15 minutes) and a short duration (3–4 hours). Both derivatives have a potent hypnotic action reducing sleep latency and the number of nocturnal arousals. Barbiturates decrease REM sleep proportion while increasing its latency, provoking a REM sleep rebound when discontinued after prolonged administration. Under the influence of barbiturates, stage 2 increases and stages 3 and 4 decrease. The EEG shows low-voltage, high-frequency beta activity that reaches a fixed frequency of 22 Hz with phenobarbital. Barbiturates are far more toxic than benzodiazepine derivatives. In addition to causing dose-dependent respiratory depression, barbiturates can be habit-forming. The sleep-inducing effect is lost after 2 weeks of continued administration. They potentiate the formation of hepatic microsomal enzymes that catabolize and alter the metabolism of other compounds.

Other Hypnotic Drugs

Chloral hydrate (0.5–1.0 g) is an old hypnotic compound that is still used to induce sleep in children undergoing EEG testing. It does not generate beta activity and sleep shows a relatively normal architecture. It has few adverse effects, and the half-life is 6–8 hours.

The tricyclic antidepressants (amitriptyline sodium, 50–100 mg; and protriptyline, 5–10 mg) administered at bedtime have shown some efficacy in idiopathic insomnia, and in overcoming the sleeplessness of Parkinson's disease and depression. These compounds suppress REM sleep; protriptyline, in particular, has a therapeutic anticataplectic effect in patients with cataplexy-narcolepsy.

The histamine system enhances alerting mechanisms, as illustrated by the highly desynchronized EEG that results from the cerebral intraventricular injection of histamine. Antihistamine preparations with a hypnotic effect (diphenhydramine hydrochloride, 50 mg at bedtime) are useful in Parkinson's disease because of the added mild antiparkinsonian action. Antihistamines produce daytime sedation and increase non-REM sleep at night.

Beta-blockers, such as propranolol, have anxiolytic effect and are used by performers to overcome stage fright and excessive perspiration; they reduce REM sleep also. Propranolol can be used as an anticataplectic medication in patients with intolerance or lack of response to other compounds.

Alcohol has a definite hypnotic effect along with a sedative action. An increase in the dose before bedtime shortens sleep latency, increases the duration of sleep, increases SWS, and suppresses REM sleep, particularly in the early part of the night. This phenomenon can cause a compensatory increase of REM sleep by the end of the night, with intense dreaming and even nightmares. Alcohol also depresses central respiratory activity and can potentiate snoring and the sleep apnea syndrome. Withdrawal experienced by chronic alcoholics after continued use in high quantities can cause delirium with intense REM sleep rebound, a state known as delirium tremens, which is characterized by agitation, confusion, and hallucinatory activity.

Anticonvulsants are not used as hypnotics but have an effect on sleep. Ethosuximide increases stage 1 and reduces SWS and REM sleep. Valproic acid increases SWS in children and reduces the number of arousals in adults. Phenytoin reduces REM sleep and increases stage 4. These effects are particularly important in children, since reduction of SWS can affect the nocturnal liberation of growth hormone and stunt somatic growth.

Neuroleptic compounds, such as phenothiazines and butyrophenones, are antipsychotic compounds used in the treatment of patients with agitated, violent behavior, as well as for the management of confusion, hallucinations in schizophrenia, mania, and dementia. The antipsychotic effect improves sleep architecture, but the secondary effect of sedation can affect motor performance during wakefulness. The butyrophenones, such as haloperidol and piperidine derivatives, produce less sedation than chlorpromazine and promazine. Neuroleptic compounds with pronounced anticholinergic effect reduce REM sleep. Lithium used in the treatment of mania and for prevention of the manic-depressive crisis inhibits REM sleep while increasing SWS.

Nonopiate analgesics, such as aspirin, improve sleep architecture and the quality of nocturnal sleep in patients with chronic pain of rheumatic origin. Aspirin also exhibits a soft hypnotic effect and improves somewhat the sleeplessness of chronic insomniacs. In large amounts, it increases stage 2, decreases SWS, and tends to increase sleep fragmentation. Inhibition of prostaglandins might be the mechanism of action.

Opiate analgesics, such as morphine, have a sedative effect and reduce REM sleep. Cocaine and heroin also reduce REM sleep. Anticholinergic compounds, such as scopolamine, delay the onset and decrease the total amount of REM sleep, increasing the duration of stage 2. Withdrawal causes REM sleep rebound.

L-Tryptophan, a serotonin precursor amino acid, has shown variable effects on sleep in humans. Some reports describe an increase in total sleep, increase in SWS, and elimination of transient sleep disturbances. L-Tryptophan also tends to reduce the latency and increase the duration of REM sleep, although the effect tends to disappear on consecutive nights. L-Tryptophan was prohibited as an over-the-counter remedy for insomnia following reports of eosinophilia-myalgia syndrome caused by contaminants in the preparation [30].

New Hypnotics

A new hypnotic, zolpidem (5–10 mg) is a benzodiazepine receptor ligand imidazopyridine that has received a great deal of attention. It potentiates deep sleep and has an ultrashort half-life of 2–3 hours that prevents accumulation in the body [31]. Zolpidem, like triazolam and flurazepam, might improve the perception of being asleep in insomniacs [32] and can be useful to counteract the effects of jet lag syndrome. Adverse effects are mild and include dizziness, somnolence, headaches, gastrointestinal distress, and dry mouth. There is no reported worsening of sleep apnea syndrome, and there are no reports of drug dependence with serious consequences.

Zoplicone is a ciclopirrolone with a mechanism of action similar to that of the benzodiazepine derivatives. Although used as a hypnotic, it also has anxiolytic, muscle relaxant, and anticonvulsant properties. It can act on the benzodiazepine receptor or close to this site. It has an ultrashort half-life of 5 hours and no known active metabolites [33]. Clinical reports indicate that zoplicone is well tolerated without causing respiratory center depression when administered at the therapeutic dose of 7.5 mg at bedtime. Some patients complain of dry mouth, daytime somnolence with tiredness, and decreased motor performance. It should not be administered to patients with liver damage.

Stimulant Drugs

Amphetamines

The amphetamines have been known since the latter part of the nineteenth century and introduced to clinical use in 1927 as an alternative to ephedrine. Amphetamines are potent stimulants of the central catecholamine and peripheral sympathetic systems (Table 13-4). They cause desynchronization of cortical electrical activity through activation of the reticular system. Clinically, they stimulate vigilance with an increase in mental and physical performance, enhanced confidence, better concentration, more resistance to fatigue, decreased need to sleep, heightened mood, euphoria, and loquacity. At therapeutic doses, adverse effects can include irritability, insomnia, headache, palpitations, nervousness, and myokimias. At high doses, amphetamines can

Table 13-4. Clinical Characteristics of Some Amphetamine Derivatives

Amphetamine (Trade Name)	Daily Dose (mg)	Stimulation Central	Stimulation Peripheral	Anorexia
Dextroamphetamine (Dexedrine)	10–60	++	++	++
Methylphenidate (Ritalin)	10–40	++	+	+
Phenmetrazine (Preludin)	25–75	++	+	+++
Fenfluramine (Pondimin)	20–60	Scarce	Scarce	+++

+ = mild intensity stimulation; ++ = medium intensity stimulation; +++ = strong intensity stimulation.

provoke aggression, agitation, and violence. When consumed in toxic amounts, amphetamines trigger psychotic states that are undistinguishable from paranoid schizophrenia. The amphetamines also have an anorexic effect through their action on the lateral hypothalamic center, and exhibit respiratory stimulant activity as well as mild antiparkinsonian action. Some persons develop a fine tremor and in rare instances facial dyskinesias and choreoathetosis have been reported. Amphetamines might fail to stimulate alertness in patients with schizophrenia. These stimulants have a more noticeable effect when the individual is physically tired, mentally fatigued, or somnolent [34]. Polysomnographic studies have shown an increase in REM sleep latency, reduction of REM sleep in approximately 50% of patients, and reduction of SWS.

Typically, the amphetamines induce tolerance and tachyphylaxis in 30–40% of subjects. Following abrupt discontinuation, there is REM rebound that can last up to 2 months. Intracranial hemorrhages secondary to cerebral angiopathy have been described in amphetamine abusers.

Dextroamphetamine is a CNS stimulant that is more potent than levo-amphetamine. At high doses, it produces peripheral sympathetic hyperactivity manifested by high blood pressure, increased heart rate, hyperthermia, mydriasis, and bladder sphincter contraction. Methylphenidate was introduced for the treatment of narcolepsy by Yoss and Daly [35] because of lessened peripheral sympathomimetic activity.

The amphetamines are typically used for the management of narcolepsy and other primary hypersomnias. The tricyclic antidepressants inhibit amphetamine catabolism and potentiate their behavioral effects. The tricyclic compounds can reduce by one-third the clinically effective dose of amphetamines. The amphetamines are well absorbed by the gastrointestinal tract; one-third is eliminated via the urine and the rest hydroxilated by the liver. Sodium bicarbonate, which induces an alkaline urine, delays the elimination of amphetamines. The dose range for dextroamphetamine is 10–60 mg daily and for methylphenidate is 10–40 mg daily. Some authors use higher doses, but the clinical experience indicates that beyond those levels patients develop unacceptable behavioral modifications that negate their clinical usefulness. Methylphenidate is also used for the treatment of hyperactivity in children with attention deficit disorder and minimal brain damage because it produces paradoxic sedation.

Xanthines

Xanthines are the most commonly used stimulants of wakefulness. They include caffeine and theophylline, which compete for receptors occupied by adenosine, an inhibitor neuromodulator that intervenes in sleep mechanisms. The effects of caffeine can last from 12–14 hours. A cup of strong coffee contains 200 mg of caffeine; 500 mg of caffeine, or more, taken at any time of the day will interfere with the generation of sleep.

Ephedrine

Known since antiquity, ephedrine has some clinical efficacy in the treatment of narcolepsy and in the general treatment of somnolence when taken in amounts of 30–60 mg three times per day. It is more potent than caffeine but less than the amphetamine derivatives. Toxic effects are manifested by tachycardia, perspiration, and headache.

Physical Treatments

Continuous Positive Airway Pressure

CPAP application during sleep is the treatment of choice for obstructive sleep apnea syndrome (see Chapter 7). The goal is to eliminate apneas, hypopneas, oxygen desaturations, arousals, and snoring. The CPAP apparatus consists of a mask adapted to the face, covering the nose but not the mouth (see Figure 7-8). It delivers air through a flexible hose connected to a compressor that generates air flow at a continuous specified pressure. With pressures of 5–20 cm H_2O, the airway remains open in most patients; higher pressures tend to arouse the patient. The system functions primarily as a pneumatic splint. The equipment weighs 7–9 lbs and is portable in an executive briefcase. Current versions are adaptable to most power sources. In general, tolerance and compliance to CPAP increase with severity of the sleep apnea syndrome and of daytime sleepiness. There is suggestive evidence of continued improvement after several weeks of optimal use of CPAP [36].

Complications, adverse reactions, and side effects are benign. Poor mask fits result in leakage of air toward the eyes and skin abrasions over the bridge of the nose. As the mask pressure increases, the risk of leakage also increases. Nasal and upper respiratory dryness are common complaints that respond favorably when a humidifier is added to the unit or when a vaporizer is used in the bedroom. Temporary nasal congestion and rhinorrhea such as caused by a cold can be controlled with a nasal spray with vasoconstrictor effect. CPAP application should be discontinued following head trauma until there is assurance that cerebrospinal fluid leakage is not present. The application of CPAP to patients with sleep apnea syndrome and advanced chronic obstructive pulmonary disease or congestive heart failure could compromise cardiac function and output [37]. Extreme caution should be exercised in patients with bullous emphysema or cystic lung lesions that might be ruptured by the delivery of external positive air pressures.

The conventional mask covering the nose can be substituted by a full-face mask in patients who are unable to maintain the mouth closed while asleep, or when there is risk of vomiting leading to aspiration of gastric contents. The apparatus should have a safety system to deliver fresh air in case of power failure. Nasal pillars or prongs adapted to the nares with silicon rubber can be used instead of the mask. Patients with excessively sensitive skin over the bridge of the nose or with a tendency to leak air in the direction of the eyes should consider nasal prongs. A useful addition is the ramp mechanism that delivers pressure increments during an initial period of time permitting initiation of sleep before the pressure reaches its maximal strength. It is expected that during this period patients will show desaturations and apneas. "Ramping" has not been validated formally. Although it appears useful, a measure of caution should be exercised in patients with severe forms of sleep apnea syndrome.

Bilevel Positive Airway Pressure

The Bi-PAP apparatus delivers differential inspiratory positive air pressure (IPAP) and expiratory positive air pressure (EPAP). Optimal positive pressure can be applied during inspiration only and lowered during expiration to prevent excessive expiratory effort. Inspiratory pressure sufficient to maintain airway patency is triggered by a low inspiratory airflow, whereas the expiratory level is reached when the inspiratory airflow falls below a set value. Modern devices have a safety feature that provides a timed trigger of IPAP in case of total failure of inspiratory airflow and of triggered delivery; this feature is particularly useful in patients with neuromuscular disorders or with predominantly central apneas of long duration. The combination of spontaneous and timed trigger allows comfortable physiologic breathing while the patient is awake and avoids frightening long-duration respiratory arrests in sleeping patients with central sleep apnea. The differential pressures provide a more physiologic delivery of air that is more comfortable and helpful in a variety of clinical situations. The Bi-PAP apparatus is useful in patients with restrictive neuromuscular disorders, kyphoscoliosis, or nonobstructive sleep apnea, and when CPAP is not tolerated. It is also indicated in bullous and cystic lung conditions in which high pressures could traumatize the lungs.

Titration of pressures for both CPAP and Bi-PAP should be done in the sleep laboratory, at night, under the close supervision of an experienced technician. It is performed by introducing small 2.5-cm H_2O increments of pressure until the optimal pressure is reached. Occasionally, there is a fine borderline between virtual elimination of respiratory interruptions and arousals caused by excessive airflow and pressure, forcing a compromise between less than optimal goal achievement and patient comfort. When this circumstance arises, a trial on Bi-PAP can be warranted.

Laser-Assisted Uvulopalatoplasty

In laser-assisted uvulopalatoplasty (LAUP), the carbon dioxide laser beam is used to vaporize the uvula and adjacent soft-palate tissue with linear incisions of the palate; only topical anesthesia is used. LAUP does not excise the tonsils or the lateral pharyngeal tissues. The intervention is an office-based procedure for the treatment of habitual snoring and is done in a series of one to five sessions spaced at weekly or biweekly intervals. The procedure is not indicated for patients with snoring and obstruction at sites other than the pharynx, for instance the nose or the hypopharynx. LAUP has a limited role in the treatment of obstructive sleep apnea because the obstruction is often located at multiple sites. Complications include pain that can last up to 8 days and other complications resulting from the use of analgesic drugs with sedative and narcotic action in the presence of postoperative inflammation. The Standards of Practice Committee of the American Sleep Disorders Association (ASDA) has published recommendations for the use of LAUP [38] (see Chapter 7).

Oral Appliances

Oral appliances are intended to eliminate snoring and improve sleep apnea. This goal is achieved by modifying the anatomy and changing the dynamics of the mandible, intraoral cavity, and upper airway sufficiently to improve the passage of air while the subject is asleep. There is some evidence that the cross-sectional area of the tongue increases and the cross-sectional area of the oropharynx decreases in the supine posture [39]. Furthermore, the volume of the tongue and of the soft palate increases with the body mass index [40]. On the basis of these observations, there appears to be some rationale for the modification of the intraoral anatomy in obese patients with sleep apnea syndrome. Oral appliances have been devised to move the mandible forward, lift the soft palate, or move the tongue forward, or effect a combination of these changes. As many as 13 oral and dental appliances have been introduced in clinical practice [41]. In general, oral appliances are safe and can be considered for individuals with snoring and for patients with obstructive sleep apnea syndrome of any degree of severity who refuse or do not tolerate CPAP and show anatomic reductions in the posterior space and oropharynx. Oral appliances should be fitted by qualified personnel. The ASDA recommends [42] that patients with moderate-to-severe obstructive sleep apnea receive follow-up polysomnography, or another objective measure of respiration during sleep, with the appliance in place, to ensure satisfactory therapeutic benefit. The precise indications for dental appliances have not been validated with reliable clinical studies. Dental appliances are not indicated for patients with temporomandibular arthrosis or for uncooperative individuals.

Surgical Treatments

There are several forms of surgical intervention used for patients with obstructive sleep apnea syndrome, all intended to alleviate or correct the obstruction.

Tracheostomy

Tracheostomy was originally performed in patients with advanced obstructive sleep apnea to by-pass the pharyngeal obstruction. It consists of creating an artificial opening in the anterior trachea immediately below the larynx. Today, tracheostomy is rarely used but remains as a back-up intervention for severe instances with high risk of death.

Nasal Reconstruction

Nasal obstruction contributes to increase the negative pressures generated more distally in the airway during inspiration and can be an impediment for the use of CPAP. Septal deviation and turbinate hypertrophy interfering with the adequate passage of air might have to be corrected surgically.

Tonsillectomy

The presence of large tonsils obstructing the oropharynx, particularly in children with sleep apnea syndrome, is the most common determinant of tonsillectomy. Hypertrophic tonsils are the most frequent cause of sleep apnea syndrome in children and young adults.

Uvulopalatopharyngoplasty

Uvulopalatopharyngoplasty (UPPP) was originally introduced to alleviate snoring by reducing the tissues of the soft palate and uvula along with resection of tonsillar tissue. Later, the indications were extended to obstructive sleep apnea syndrome. The selection of patients improves the results, and in the hands of experienced surgeons the discomfort, complications, and hospital stay are lessened. The procedure causes local pain and difficulty swallowing that can last up to 8 days. Patients with obstructive sleep apneas and large tonsils, redundant lateral pharyngeal walls, and patients with long, soft palate benefit the most. Complications usually relate to postoperative swelling or excessive reduction of tissue, and include nasal reflux that is transient in most patients [43], partial wound dehiscence, and rarely palatal incompetence. Failure occurs in patients with multiple sites of obstruction that had remained occult before the operation, a phenomenon that has introduced the stepwise approach in the surgical treatment of obstructive sleep apnea [44].

Mandible, Tongue, and Hyoid Reconstructions

Mandible, tongue, and hyoid reconstructions are interventions that are intended to improve airflow at the base of the tongue and hypopharyngeal level. There are several degrees of complexity in these operations that range from genioglossus advancement, including hyoid bone myotomy in some instances, to mandibular advancement. Patients are selected on the basis of radiographic analysis and cephalometric measurements showing stenosis of the hypopharynx. Advancement of the mandible 1 or 2 mm might be sufficient to improve airflow. The interventions can be indicated in young patients with moderate-to-severe sleep apnea syndrome and loud snoring caused by hypopharyngeal stenosis, particularly if associated with craniofacial malformations, retrognathia, or malocclusions. Specialized maxillofacial interventions are available only in selected centers. Complications appear to be few and range from surgical edema of the floor of the mouth to mental nerve dysesthesias. Contraindications are psychiatric disorders, advanced age, and drug dependency.

Liposuction

Liposuction, the surgical removal of fat tissues by suction, can be an acceptable option for rapid elimination of excessive abdominal tissue. This procedure might be particularly indicated for patients with a large accumulation of fat in the abdomen that creates a mechanical disadvantage to diaphragmatic function in REM sleep. Liposuction of fat tissue deposits in the anterior neck region is an alternative to consider when the abnormal accumulation threatens the viability of the trachea while the patient is supine.

References

1. Shakespeare W. Othello. Act III, Sc. 3, Line 323. In Bartlett J (ed), Familiar Quotations. Boston: Little, Brown, 1955;188.
2. Browman CP, Cartwright RD. The first-night effect on sleep and dreams. Biol Psychiatry 1980;15:809.
3. Roth T, Kramer M, Trinder J. The effect of noise during sleep on the sleep patterns of different age groups. Can Psychiat Assoc J 1972;(Suppl 2):197.
4. Globus G, Friedmann J, Cohen H. The Effects of Aircraft Noise on Sleep Electrophysiology as Recorded in the Home. In WD Ward (ed), Proceedings of the International Congress on Noise as a Public Health Problem. Washington, DC: US Environmental Protection Agency, 1974;587.
5. Haskell EH, Palca JW, Walker JM, et al. The effects of high and low ambient temperatures on human sleep stages. Electroencephalogr Clin Neurophysiol 1981;51:494.
6. Parmeggiani PL, Rabini C. Sleep and environmental temperature. Arch Ital Biol 1970;108:369.
7. Webb WB, Ades H. Sleep tendencies: Effects of barometric pressure. Science 1964;14:263.
8. Monroe LJ. Transient changes in EEG sleep patterns of married good sleepers: The effects of altering sleeping arrangements. Psychophysiology 1969;6:330.
9. Álvarez WC. Physiologic studies on the motor activity of the stomach and bowel in man. Am J Physiol 1920;88:658.
10. Thacker HL. Eosinophilia-myalgia syndrome: The Cleveland Clinic experience. Cleve Clin J Med 1991;58:400.
11. Expanded recall for L-Tryptophan. FDA Drug Bulletin 1990;20:2.
12. Auerbach SB, Falk H. Eosinophilia-myalgia syndrome: CDC update. Cleve Clin J Med 1991;58:215.
13. Curatolo PW, Robertson D. The health consequences of caffeine. Ann Intern Med 1983;98:641.
14. Soldatos CR, Kales JD, Scharf MB, et al. Cigarette smoking associated with sleep difficulty. Science 1980;207:551.
15. Vuori I, Urponen H, Hasan J, et al. Epidemiology of exercise effects on sleep. Acta Physiol Scand 1988;133:3.
16. Hauri P. Treating psychophysiological insomnia with biofeedback. Arch Gen Psychiatry 1981;38:752.
17. Bootzin RR, Epstein D, Wood JM. Stimulus Control Instruction. In PJ Hauri (ed), Case Studies in Insomnia. New York: Plenum, 1991;19.
18. Stepansky EJ. Behavioral Therapy for Insomnia. In MH Kryger, T Roth, WC Dement (eds), Principles and Practice of Sleep Medicine (2nd ed). Philadelphia: Saunders, 1994;535.
19. Czeisler CA, Richardson GS, Coleman RM, et al. Chronotherapy: Resetting the circadian clocks of patients with delayed sleep phase insomnia. Sleep 1981;4:1.
20. Moldofsky H, Musisi S, Philipson EA. Treatment of a case of advanced sleep phase syndrome by phase advance chronotherapy. Sleep 1986;9:61.

21. Spielman AJ, Saskin P, Thorpy MJ. Treatment of chronic insomnia by restriction of time in bed. Sleep 1987;10:45.
22. Lewy AJ, Wehr TA, Goodwin FK, et al. Light suppresses melatonin secretion in humans. Science 1980;210:1267.
23. Society for Light Treatment and Biological Rhythms. P.O. Box 478, Wilsonville, OR 97070.
24. Czeisler CA, Johnson MP, Duffy JF, et al. Exposure to bright light and darkness to treat physiologic maladaptation to night work. N Engl J Med 1990;322:1253.
25. Czeisler CA, Allan JS. Acute circadian phase reversal in man via bright light exposure: Application to jet lag. Sleep Res 1987;16:605.
26. Czeisler CA, Chiasera AJ, Duffy JF. Research on sleep, circadian rhythms and aging: Applications to manned spaceflight. Exp Gerontol 1991;26:217.
27. Wyllie E. The expanding role of benzodiazepines in neurology. Cleve Clin J Med 1990;57:S1.
28. Mendelson WB. Pharmacotherapy of insomnia. Psychiatr Clin North Am 1987;10:555.
29. Sweet dreams or nightmares? Newsweek, August 19, 1991;44.
30. Expanded recall for L-Tryptophan. FDA Drug Bulletin, April 1990.
31. Langtry HD, Benfield P. Zolpidem. A review of its pharmacodynamic and pharmacokinetic properties and therapeutic potential. Drugs 1990;40:291.
32. Mendelson WB. Effects of flurazepam and zolpidem on the perception of sleep in insomniacs. Sleep 1995;18:92.
33. Goa KL, Heel RC. Zoplicone. A review of its pharmacodynamic and pharmacokinetic properties and therapeutic efficacy as an hypnotic. Drugs 1986;32:48.
34. Hartmann E, Orzack MH, Branconnier R. Sleep deprivation deficits and their reversal by D- and L-amphetamine. Psychopharmacology 1977;53:185.
35. Yoss RE, Daly DD. Criteria for the diagnosis of the narcoleptic syndrome. Proc Mayo Clin 1957;32:320.
36. Lamphere J, Roehrs T, Wittig R, et al. Recovery of alertness after CPAP in apnea. Chest 1989;96:1364.
37. Krieger J, Weitzenblaum E, Monassier JP, et al. Dangerous hypoxemia during continuous positive airway pressure treatment of obstructive sleep apnea. Lancet 1983;2:1429.
38. Standards of Practice Committee of the American Sleep Disorders Association. Practice parameters for the use of laser-assisted uvulopalatopharyngoplasty. Sleep 1994;17:744.
39. Pae E, Lowe A, Sasaki K, et al. A cephalometric and electromyographic study of upper airway structures in the upright and supine position. Am J Orthod Dentofacial Orthop 1994;106:52.
40. Lowe A, Fleetham J, Adachi S, et al. Cephalometric and CT predictors of apnea index severity. Am J Orthod Dentofacial Orthop 1995;107:589.
41. Cartwright R, Samelson C. The effects of a non-surgical treatment for obstructive sleep apnea—The tongue retaining device. JAMA 1982;248:705.

42. Lowe AA. Dental Appliances for the Treatment of Snoring and Obstructive Sleep Apnea. In MH Kryger, T Roth, WC Dement (eds), Principles and Practice of Sleep Medicine (2nd ed). Philadelphia: Saunders, 1994;722.
43. Powell NB, Guilleminault C, Riley RW. Surgical Therapy for Obstructive Sleep Apnea. In MH Kryger, T Roth, WC Dement (eds), Principles and Practice of Sleep Medicine (2nd ed). Philadelphia: Saunders, 1994;706.
44. Nordlander B. Long-term studies addressing success of surgical treatment for sleep apnea syndrome. Sleep 1993;16:S100.

14

Sociopathology, Medicolegal, and Work-Related Issues

Sleep disorders have always existed, but the fabric of modern society has brought them to the fore. Almost everyone has a driver's license; many workers labor the night shift; people are commonly overworked and sleep deprived by choice or by necessity; the fast pace imposed on our work demands increasing attention and concentration; and the heavy equipment, large machines, and huge transport vehicles with sophisticated operating gears require constant vigilance. A brief distraction could be fatal or very costly, and when it happens society demands retribution and correction. Physicians and specialists in sleep disorders medicine have been asked to serve as healers, educators, mediators, and in some instances even gatekeepers to protect society from the tide of sleepiness that lurks behind the wheel, the computer screen, or the command center. This chapter outlines some of the problems related to sleepiness, identifies known factors, and provides recommendations to correct them.

Sleep and Driving

The New York State Governor's Task Force on the Impact of Fatigue on Driving [1] has indicated that 25% of New York State drivers admit

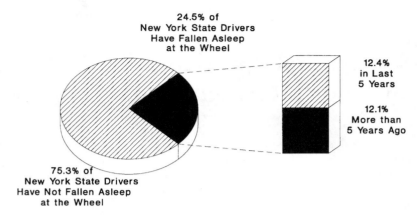

Figure 14-1. *Drivers falling asleep at the wheel. (Reprinted with permission from the Results of the Drowsy Driving Survey of the Governor's Traffic Safety Committee of New York State conducted in 1994 by Fact Finders, Inc., and the Team on Nature and Scope of Drowsy Drivers' Crashes for the New York State Task Force on the Impact of Fatigue on Driving. Albany, December 1994. Institute for Traffic Safety Management and Research, Albany, NY.)*

having fallen asleep at the wheel at some point in their lifetime (Figure 14-1). The information was gathered through a survey of 1,000 randomly selected drivers in New York State in the summer of 1994. Half of the group (54.6%) acknowledged having driven while drowsy during the previous year (Figure 14-2), and a small fraction (2.5%) were driving very often in a state of drowsiness. The reported conditions that led the drivers to drowsiness are shown in Figure 14-3. Miraculously, only a smaller percentage (4.7%) of the 1,000 drivers had been involved in a crash caused by their falling asleep or their drowsiness, but still this translates into 2,500 accidents per year in the state of New York alone. The figures are significant and cause for deep concern because the potential for fatal or costly accidents is always there when vigilance is reduced or absent.

Nationwide, the National Highway Traffic Safety Administration [2] reported that in 1992 there were 50,000 crashes because of driver drowsiness, which represent 1% of all crashes. There were 1,500 fatalities, and the circumstances of the accidents were quite similar to the ones reported by the New York State Task Force. Seventy-seven per-

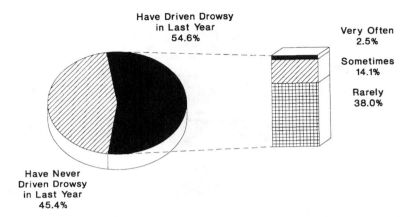

Figure 14-2.   *Driving while drowsy. (Reprinted with permission from the Results of the Drowsy Driving Survey of the Governor's Traffic Safety Committee of New York State conducted in 1994 by Fact Finders, Inc., and the Team on Nature and Scope of Drowsy Drivers' Crashes for the New York State Task Force on the Impact of Fatigue on Driving. Albany, December 1994. Institute for Traffic Safety Management and Research, Albany, NY.)*

cent of the drivers were male, 62% were younger than 30 years, 66% were driving alone, and most involved a single vehicle. The figures were obtained from the police accident report, which usually underreports drowsiness as a factor, since police are not trained to specifically search for or inquire about drowsiness.

The characteristics of the New York State crashes caused by drivers falling asleep revealed a profile that is almost predictable. Half of the accidents occurred between 1:00 and 7:00 A.M., and 40% occurred on a highway or expressway. Eighty-three percent of the drivers were alone and had been driving for an average of 4 hours. Approximately one-half had been working a night shift or had worked many hours overtime during the week that preceded the crash. Surprisingly, only one-third had consumed alcohol before the accident occurred, and 10% had taken medication. Most of the drivers were male and one-third snored during sleep, an interesting finding that brings about the specter of sleep apnea.

The Task Force identified groups that were at higher risk than others. Shift workers and overworked individuals are particularly vulner-

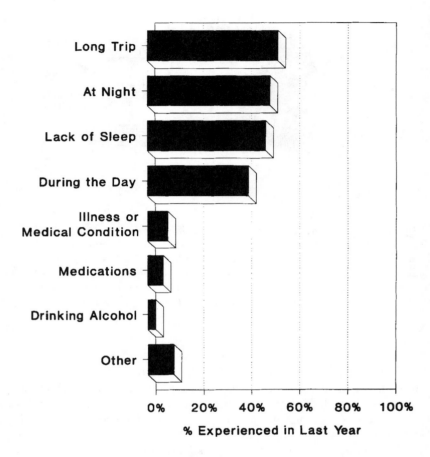

Figure 14-3. *Conditions associated with drowsiness. (Reprinted with permission from the Results of the Drowsy Driving Survey of the Governor's Traffic Safety Committee of New York State conducted in 1994 by Fact Finders, Inc., and the Team on Nature and Scope of Drowsy Drivers' Crashes for the New York State Task Force on the Impact of Fatigue on Driving. Albany, December 1994. Institute for Traffic Safety Management and Research, Albany, NY.)*

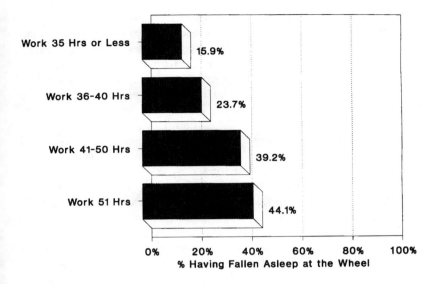

Figure 14-4.   *Profile of hours worked by people falling asleep at the wheel. (Reprinted with permission from the Results of the Drowsy Driving Survey of the Governor's Traffic Safety Committee of New York State conducted in 1994 by Fact Finders, Inc., and the Team on Nature and Scope of Drowsy Drivers' Crashes for the New York State Task Force on the Impact of Fatigue on Driving. Albany, December 1994. Institute for Traffic Safety Management and Research, Albany, NY.)*

able. The numbers indicate that members of this group drive more frequently while drowsy (Figure 14-4) and have a higher incidence of accidents than subjects in the other groups. Younger men also have a higher tendency to be involved in accidents caused by drowsiness, perhaps because of lifestyles that incorporate poor sleep hygiene.

Patients with sleep disorders such as sleep apnea syndrome and narcolepsy represent a small segment of society, but within each of these groups the crash rate is higher than in other subgroups. These conditions, if untreated, should be considered risk factors for the occurrence of highway accidents. Sleep apnea syndrome is probably the most common medical condition causing excessive daytime sleepiness. In a preliminary report discussed at the Eighth Annual Meeting of the American Professional Sleep Societies (APSS), the American Thoracic Society and its Assembly on Respiratory Neurobiology and Sleep [3] concurred with literature reviews that patients with severe sleep apnea syndrome have two to three times more automobile accidents than other drivers [4]. In a survey of 253 patients with driver's licenses referred to a sleep disorders center in California, 173 were diagnosed with sleep apnea syndrome after polysomnography was conducted. A questionnaire indicated that 31% of sleep apnea patients had suffered motor vehicle accidents, whereas only 15% of the non–sleep apnea group had been involved in accidents. Falling asleep at inappropriate times and driving past destination points with no recollection were considered indicators of risk of motor vehicle accidents [5]. The high-risk driver has a profile that is characterized by severe daytime sleepiness and a history of motor vehicle accidents. Unfortunately, the current statistics do no provide accurate figures on the proportion of patients who have this combination of factors.

In a review of 424 adults with sleep disorder and sleep-related accidents compared with 70 adults with sleep-related accidents but no sleep disorder, Aldrich [6] found that the proportion of individuals with sleep-related accidents was 1.5–4.0 times greater in the hypersomnolent group than in the control group. The proportion of narcoleptics reporting sleep-related accidents was more than four times as great as controls and was higher than any other patient group.

Commercial drivers suffer fewer accidents than noncommercial drivers (only 3% of the total), but the scope of the accidents is of larger magnitude and some are spectacular because of the lives lost or the destruction caused. Furthermore, the combination-unit trucks have more exposure (60,000 miles per year compared with 11,000 for passenger vehicles), and their expected number of involvements per vehicle lifecycle is four times greater [7]. The trucking industry employs two million drivers who operate one million carriers that travel 10 billion miles a year on the United States highways. There are approximately 4,800 fatal accidents involving trucks each year, and 57% are probably caused by fatigue [8], a term that indicates human performance failure and suggests drowsiness. The cost of a crash in which fatalities are involved is $2,700,000; the cost benefits of countermeasures in this particular subgroup are quite obvious. Despite allegations that commercial drivers are safer, the magnitude of the accidents is such that this subgroup merits particular attention in highway safety studies.

Analysis within the group has shown that obese long-haul truck drivers have two times more accidents per mile driven than nonobese truck drivers. Obese drivers have a higher prevalence of excessive daytime sleepiness, and this ominous symptom is probably the result of sleep-

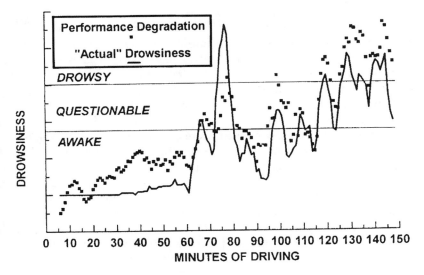

Figure 14-5. *Driving performance begins to degrade after 60 minutes of driving. (Reprinted with permission from RR Knipling, WW Wierwille. Vehicle-based drowsy driver detection: Current status and future prospects. Proceedings of the Fourth Annual Meeting of IVHS America. Atlanta: IVHS America, 1994.)*

disordered breathing. In a study of long-haul truck drivers, Stoohs and colleagues [9] found a clear trend of a higher accident frequency in truck drivers with sleep-disordered breathing, although complete congruency was not found. The authors suggested that the increased upper airway resistance syndrome along with obstructive sleep apnea syndrome contributed to the trend, explaining the modest incongruencies of their study.

An interesting study by the Office of Crash Avoidance Research of the National Highway Traffic Safety Administration [7] showed that driver performance started to degrade after 60 minutes of driving and reached a peak at approximately 80 minutes (Figure 14-5). A distinction was made between drowsiness, referring to a state of reduced alertness, and physical fatigue, emphasizing that drowsiness and not fatigue should be the principal concern in relation to driving. The report also indicated that reduced alertness should not be confused with distraction that results from a loss of attention, another major cause of traffic accidents.

The New York State Task Force asked drivers in focus group sessions what strategies they found useful to maintain alertness while driving. Invariably, they responded that driving over a grooved surface or rumble strip would immediately awaken them to full alertness. This statement fits well with observations that vehicle accidents decrease or disappear in segments of highway with rumble strips. Drivers also indicated that stopping at a rest area and walking around the vehicle or taking a short nap had a powerful alerting effect. Unfortunately, many drivers, particularly women, were concerned about safety in isolated, dark rest areas and most indicated that they would rather continue driving even if drowsy, than stop.

The Task Force concluded that public awareness of this epidemic is underemphasized and drowsiness as a cause of accidents is probably underreported. Education of trainers and drivers through drivers' manuals, special training classes, insurance rewards, public campaigns, and recommendations on specific countermeasures should have an effect similar to that achieved with previous campaigns enforcing seat belts and removing drunk drivers from the highway.

Psychophysiologic monitoring of driver performance in relation to vigilance and attention might lead to the development of countermeasure strategies such as warning signals when the blinking rate changes; detection of eyelid closure using miniaturized, glasses-mounted, optoelectronic emitters and sensors; steering-related signals; and lane position signals. However, perhaps the most efficient measure will be emphasizing public and official awareness of this epidemic.

Legal sanctions should be restricted to individuals who show poor judgment and lack of common sense despite efforts toward education. Drivers who insist on operating vehicles while under the influence of sleep deprivation, sedative medication, or alcohol, as well as drivers who reject therapeutic efforts to overcome an intrinsic sleep disorder, should come under the scrutiny of the authorities.

Railroad and Other Transportation Catastrophes

Railroad accidents can be spectacular in their magnitude and scope. In late 1991, two trains collided in Eugene, Oregon [10]. There were no fatalities, but the spillage of 8,000 tons of diesel fuel and its subsequent ignition stopped all traffic and caused major disruption to the local community. The engineer of the misguided train admitted that he had fallen asleep to awaken only a few instants before 7:30 A.M.

when the accident occurred. He had time to activate the emergency brakes, but it was too late to avoid the accident. Alcohol and drugs were eliminated as possible concurrent factors. In 1984, two Burlington Northern trains collided [11], causing deaths and millions of dollars worth of damage. The engineer of one of the trains had fallen asleep. In 1990, a Santa Fe railway crash [12] killed four members of the crew and caused $4.4 million in damages. All crew members of the train were asleep when the accident occurred.

Recent maritime accidents caused by human performance error have been linked to fatigue and sleepiness. The best known and most costly accident of modern times was the *Exxon Valdez* disaster [11] on March 24, 1989. The oil tanker hit a reef off the pristine coast of Alaska, spilling oil and causing environmental damage that changed the ecosystem for years to come. The captain had retired to his quarters while the third mate maneuvered the ship through difficult waters. Shortly after midnight, despite two warnings from the lookout, the tanker made contact and was cut open by the reef. The National Transportation Safety Board concluded that the third mate failed to maneuver the vessel properly because of fatigue and excessive workload.

Two other recent maritime accidents might have been caused by human performance error resulting from drowsiness and mental fatigue [12]. In 1989, a Greek tanker ran aground off the coast of Rhode Island spilling 7,000 barrels of diesel oil and causing major damage to the ship and the Rhode Island Sound. The ship's captain had been on duty for 33 hours, and the National Transportation Safety Board determined that acute fatigue impaired his judgment. In a separate accident, a ferry was lost off the coast of Puerto Rico while the ship's master had assumed watch under conditions of mental fatigue and sleep deprivation that impaired his judgment.

Sleeplessness and mental fatigue might have been concurrent negative factors in some airplane accidents, nuclear plant disasters, and derailed military operations. A great deal of the maintenance activity sustaining such operations occurs at night in preparation for daytime activities. Inattention, low vigilance, and poor performance might have contributed to the near meltdown of the Chernobyl nuclear plant in the Ukraine [13], which started at 2:00 A.M., and of the Three Mile Island nuclear plant accident in Pennsylvania, also occurring at night [14]. The airline industry has recognized the risk of sleepiness in transmeridian flights. Results of ongoing studies have indicated that 40-minute naps during nocturnal transcontinental flights relieves some of the mental fatigue that can impair aircrew alertness.

Jet Lag

Jet lag occurs when several time zones are crossed over rapidly in an eastward or westward direction (see Chapter 9). The manifestations of jet lag syndrome include sleep fragmentation caused by awakenings, poor quality nonrestorative sleep, difficulty maintaining sleep, daytime fatigue, apathy, depression, moodiness, and malaise along with somatic complaints such as gastrointestinal changes, muscle aches, and headaches. Some travelers complain of poor psychomotor coordination, decreased cognitive performance, and memory disturbance. Travelers past the age of 50 years suffer more intense complaints that take longer to disappear.

Jet lag is the consequence of a misalignment of internal circadian rhythm drives with external cues. The intensity of the manifestations depends on the distance traveled, the direction of flight, and idiosyncratic factors that determine the circadian rhythm inertia for each individual. Eastward flights shorten the day by as many hours as time zone changes are crossed, so that recovery is accomplished by a phase advance; it is the equivalent of going to bed very early in the day. Westward flights lengthen the day by as many hours as time zone changes.

Aircraft crews are also subject to the effects of jet lag. Studies by the Federal Aviation Administration (FAA) have shown that pilot crews were able to enhance alertness with 40-minute naps in flight without compromising safety [15]. Crews experienced temporary refreshment during night flights without reducing the sleep debt. These studies are important to help overcome social resistance to the use of sleep as a therapeutic tool. Falling asleep on the job when piloting an aircraft full of passengers might seem a bizarre proposition, and yet with evidence at hand that appropriate dosification of sleep will improve job performance, it follows that sleep should be allowed as a countermeasure in the workplace.

Shift Work Issues

Shift work issues have increasingly attracted the attention of health workers, employers, and sociologists because of the potential impact on individual health, and on workers' job performance and satisfaction. Twenty percent of the workforce in the United States is engaged in shift work. Shift work disturbs sleep, circadian rhythms, and social and family structures. Most shift workers are partially sleep deprived and therefore will complain of sleepiness. In addition, their circadian rhythms might be out of synchrony, leading to complaints of malaise, gastrointestinal upset, and poor work performance. A better understanding of the biomedical problems underlying shift work improves the ability to develop coping strategies.

Focus group sessions conducted in Syracuse by the New York State Task Force on the Impact of Fatigue on Driving [1] revealed that shift workers sometimes did not remember driving home after work. Analysis of vehicle crashes included in the Task Force Survey showed that 46% of drivers had been working the night shift or a great deal of overtime during the week preceding the crash. Of all drivers who worked rotating shifts, 24% admitted being drowsy while driving. The Survey also revealed that there was a direct correlation between hours worked and percentage of individuals admitting having fallen asleep at the wheel. Forty-four percent of individuals who worked 51 hours or more per week had fallen asleep while driving, whereas only 15.9% of individuals working 35 hours or less had fallen asleep while driving. Clearly, working the night shift and being overworked are risk factors for falling asleep and being involved in accidents.

Drivers are not the only individuals at risk of accidents. In 1984, a young woman died in a New York City hospital [16]. Her death was caused by an infection that if properly diagnosed could have been eliminated. The significant events occurred in the late evening and night, leading a grand jury to an extensively publicized conclusion that sleep deprivation and mental fatigue of the resident physicians on call had unavoidably contributed to the patient's death. As a result, the State of New York enacted laws limiting the number of hours that house staff are permitted to work in the course of 1 week.

Concerned over the safety of night workers, the Commission of the European Union has limited the number of hours they are permitted to work at night. A recent study conducted in Europe [17] analyzed 4,645 accidents occurring over the course of 1 year in a rotating three-shift system in an engineering company. The relative risk of sustaining an injury was 1.23 times higher on the night shift than on the morning shift—36.4% of injuries occurred at night compared with 29.6% that occurred in the morning. The results pointed to a significant increase in the frequency of injuries from the morning shift, through the afternoon shift, to the night shift. The study also revealed some evidence that the number of injuries rose as the week progressed toward Friday. Curiously, morning shift workers were not sleeping any more hours than night shift workers, suggesting that sleep deprivation was not the only factor contributing to the higher accident rate. The authors hypothesized that circadian rhythm maladjustment to the night shift had contributed to poor performance capabilities and alertness. Family life and social interactions are commonly disturbed. The daytime sleep of individuals is easily disturbed by household activity during daytime hours, adding to sleep deprivation, irritability, and accusations. Family obligations are not met, sexual behaviors are altered, and spouses might feel isolated and lonely on nights without their mate.

Disability and Job Loss

Not uncommonly, the sleep specialist and the family physician are confronted with a patient who is on probation at work because of falling asleep. The health professional is asked to correct the problem or else the patient might lose the job. Patients might also apply for disability benefits because of a sleep problem, and the physician needs to resolve whether the claim is genuine.

When workers fall asleep on the job, peers are disgusted, supervisors are annoyed, and the worker is greatly concerned. To be caught asleep while at work can lead to a stern counseling session, a negative report on the performance evaluation, or not infrequently dismissal from employment. Some sympathetic and reasonable supervisors suspecting a health issue might request a physician's examination and correction of the problem before taking action. This situation is particularly true for commercial and school bus drivers who are found dozing and perhaps snoring during recesses and meetings, while waiting for traffic lights to change, or who have been involved in accidents where sleepiness was suspected. The sleep specialist might be asked to intervene in situations in which shift workers have shown a poor work performance or have been observed to fall asleep, particularly if the job requires manipulation of heavy machinery or dangerous tools.

The sleep specialist's approach to the care of these individuals should be no different from that applied to any of the other patients referred to the sleep center. Particular attention should be paid to the interaction of circadian dysrhythmia and sleep deprivation along with potential complicating factors such as alcohol abuse and medication regimens. Detailed documentation of medical and sleep pathology data, explanation of facts and counseling to the patient and involved parties, as well as prompt evaluation in the sleep laboratory are the pillars of the initial assessment. This assessment should be followed by vigorous attempts at correcting the problem and proper follow-up of the patient. It is only after a full evaluation has been completed and the response to treatment has been evaluated that the physician can extend a reasonable judgment on whether the patient should continue on the current job or seek vocational rehabilitation.

Medicolegal Issues

Litigation and liability are gradually connecting with sleep pathology and the sleep specialist. Spectacular crashes with fatalities in which sleepiness is suspected, work-related accidents in the darkest hours of the night, accidental injuries involving individuals with well-established sleep disorders, and even sleep-related violence, beg the expert opinion of the sleep specialist. On other occasions, the sleep specialist is named as a codefendant in medical malpractice tort litigation and other claims related to criminal or workers compensation issues in which patients are involved.

Sleepiness that is severe and disabling is more prevalent than anticipated by the general public or recognized by the primary care physician. Severe sleepiness affects a significant number of individuals in the general population, most night shift nurses, and virtually all hospital house-staff. Individuals are at risk of suffering accidents in a variety of different circumstances. The accident risk is compounded if there is comorbidity such as alcohol abuse and intoxication, medication ingestion and toxicity, poor sleep hygiene, or infirmity caused by advanced age. Although quantification of sleepiness is possible by means of the widely used multiple sleep latency test, there is no correlation between the sleepiness measurements obtained in the laboratory and the accident rate. In other words, an index of predictability cannot be extrapolated from the test results. Nevertheless, a linkage is known to exist, and it behooves the sleep specialist to come as close as is reasonable and prudent to establish that linkage in an effort to take preventive and corrective action.

Physicians' Legal Obligations

Physicians are responsible for the medical welfare of their patients and are obligated to reduce or prevent foreseeable risk. The level of awareness of sleep-related problems is very low or even nonexistent among general practitioners. The subject of sleep disorders medicine has not penetrated medical school curricula or continuing medical education courses widely enough to expect an acceptable level of awareness among the profession in general. Therefore, it is reasonable to expect that generalists will not be held at the high standard of preventive and therapeutic care that specialists are obligated to provide. However, in the multidisciplinary integrative model of provision of medical care, there is an obligation to adhere to current and prevailing standards of care, suggesting that the general practitioner is required to seek the help of the sleep specialist.

On encountering a patient at risk of sleep-related accidents, the sleep specialist acquires various responsibilities. One profile that triggers an alarm response is that of a driver who complains of daytime sleepiness and has been involved in a motor vehicle accident. Some practitioners upgrade near-miss events to the same level of significance that actual accidents have. On identifying such a patient, the physician should describe the risk inherent in continued operation of the vehicle and issue a warning to the patient, and ideally to relatives also, about the perils involved in the operation of the vehicle or machinery, should the patient decline to adhere to accepted standards of care extended by the practitioner. Such a warning to the patient should be clearly documented in the clinical chart (Table 14-1). As a result of this action, the legal status of the patient is transformed, since the patient can no longer claim that a sleep-related accident was unexpected. The physician can acquire a liability toward third parties injured in case of an accident involving patients impaired in their abilities if the patients have not been appropriately warned and managed. It is not clear whether the physician should also be held legally accountable for monitoring adherence and compliance to the therapeutic regimen. The general advice is that reasonable follow-up should be provided until the condition comes under acceptable control.

Reporting the Condition

In an effort to extend protective action to third parties and the public in general, some states require physicians to report the names of patients with certain medical conditions. In some instances, the requirement is to report directly to the licensing bureau, in others the obligation is to inform a medical panel that advises the licensing bureau. Where such regulations apply, a failure to extend the appropriate report might establish the basis for tort liability to the patient or to an injured third party.

Table 14-1. Recommendations to Physicians Regarding Driving Restrictions

Make entries in the file of:

Information given to patient

Sources of information provided to the patient (e.g., handout, brochure, videotape)

Warnings and restrictions issued

Evidence of patient's noncompliance

Telephone calls made involving warnings and information provided

When mandatory reporting is based on a diagnosis alone, it is called categorical reporting. States under such regulation publish through their licensing bureaus the diagnoses to be reported. In other states, the regulation requires reporting only if the physician believes that the medical condition impairs the driving abilities of the individual; this approach is the functional one. A third approach is called permissive reporting and limits the involvement of the regulatory agencies to exempting physicians from any breach of confidentiality obligations, should physicians choose to report the name of a patient who in their judgment is at risk of accident. In general, states are more restrictive in granting and continuing driving licenses to passenger transport, occupational, or commercial drivers. The reason is that commercial drivers spend more time on the road and therefore have more exposure to risk. Furthermore, should they be involved in an accident the consequences would usually be of a larger magnitude in terms of human suffering and cost.

Regulations vary widely from state to state and from time to time. Physicians are encouraged to consult the Department of Motor Vehicles' regulations in their state. However, two general principles apply: (1) if a physician is obligated to file a report, failure to do so establishes a basis for tort liability to the patient or to a third party if there are injuries as a result of a crash, and (2) the physician is still liable in a tort suit even if the statutory reporting obligation does not specify the name of the sleep disorder under consideration.

Although general principles apply, many uncertainties still remain regarding reporting specific sleep-related diagnoses. Categorical reporting of sleep-related conditions is undesirable since it would include many patients who carry a diagnosis but are not impaired in their driving abilities. On the other hand, physicians have an ethical and perhaps legal obligation to be proactive when they encounter a patient whose medical condition anticipates a high level of risk of injury. Professional societies studying the problem have extended some guidelines to help physicians find the ecumenical approach [18]. There is consensus in noting that if a severely sleepy patient has been involved in a crash, the potential for more accidents is high. Such patients should be informed and their relatives apprised. Documentation of the warning issued to cease operating vehicles or machinery until the condition comes under satisfactory control should be filed. The physician should examine, assess, treat, and monitor the condition until it ceases to pose a risk to the patient and to society.

In 1990, the U.S. Federal Highway Administration recommended [19] that operators with sleep apnea, suspected or proven but not corrected, "should not be medically qualified for commercial vehicle operation until the diagnosis has been eliminated or accurately treated." The diagnosis was defined as occurring "when an individual has greater than 30 episodes of apnea during each hour of sleep or has hypersomnolence during waking hours associated with any apneic activity (greater than 5 per hour)." The report recommended that successful therapy be continuous for 1 month before restoring the license. The states of California and Texas mention sleep apnea in their Department of Motor Vehicles' guidelines. Maine has proposed guidelines and specific recommendations regarding sleep abnormality in relation to respiratory disturbance. Maryland, North Carolina, Oregon, and Utah have guidelines for narcolepsy but not for sleep apnea. Regulations are much stricter for commercial drivers. In New Hampshire, commercial drivers are prohibited from driving while sleepy, and in Texas, a sleep disorder precludes operation of cargo and passenger transport vehicles.

It is interesting to note that some other countries have passed regulations regarding the sleepy driver. In Canada, the National Safety Code for Motor Carriers indicates that patients with narcolepsy should not be allowed to drive any type of motor vehicle unless the condition responds favorably to treatment, in which case the individual might be allowed to drive a private vehicle after 3 months of sustained control. Patients with sleep apnea are also prohibited from driving if they have pathologic sleepiness. These patients are allowed to operate any class of vehicle after the condition has been adequately treated and controlled. In Europe, patients with narcolepsy and sleep apnea syndrome are limited or prohibited from driving in the United Kingdom, the Netherlands, and Sweden. Other countries have no regulations specifically directed at these conditions. Patients with narcolepsy are not permitted to drive commercial vehicles in Australia, but can drive private vehicles if the condition comes under satisfactory control that is sustained over 3 months of therapy.

In the United States, the FAA requires that commercial pilots report at any time any new medical diagnosis or condition, a change in therapy, or administration of new medication. Pilots are assigned to physicians who monitor their health status and become responsible for evaluation of the pilot. A letter from the FAA [20] specifies that complications of obstructive sleep apnea such as "daytime hypersomnolence, also referred to as excessive daytime sleepiness . . ." present a risk to flying safety, and the FAA recommends evaluation and treatment until the patient can sustain wakefulness as specified by the document. The importance of this statement is that it limits the scope of the restrictions to "complications" and not to the wide-based diagnosis of sleep apnea.

The driver of a vehicle, the operator of machinery, or the pilot of an airplane have the responsibility of being truthful with the physician and responsible for their behavior. Patients who continue to operate despite warnings become liable for the consequences. Some professional societies recommend that the physician report the name of the irresponsible driver to the Department of Motor Vehicles, particularly if the driver operates a commercial vehicle or if there is risk of a significant accident of spectacular magnitude, for instance a commercial jet pilot, a propane gas transport driver, or a school bus driver. The form and mechanism of the report can differ from one state to another.

State licensing agencies issue permits to operate vehicles and thus have a responsibility to maintain a safe environment. Specific names of sleep-related conditions are not mentioned in most statutes and regulations, but the concept of a medical condition that impairs the ability to operate a vehicle still applies. Requirements of categorical reporting of sleep-related conditions, particularly the ones that like sleep apnea respond effectively to treatment, should be discouraged. Recordkeeping and performance tests of sleep-related conditions by licensing agencies should be complemented by medical evaluations in sleep centers. However, sleep evaluations are expensive and insurance carriers might not approve testing for purposes of maintaining or obtaining a driver's license, so that a compromise or intermediate solution might have to be found between drivers, third-party payers, and state licensing agencies.

States might also want to improve safety on the highway through other actions. The New York State Thruway Authority has information indicating that rumble strips, or strips of corrugated pavement on the margins of the road, prevent accidents. Cars drifting off the highway when the sleepy driver loses control tend to invade the rumble strip causing a vibration of the wheels and a noise that alerts the driver. At a meeting of the APSS [21], Patricia B. Aducci, Commissioner of Motor Vehicles of the State of New York, indicated in a keynote lecture that the installation of rumble strips in a high-risk segment of a New York State highway coincided with the cessation of all accidents in that particular segment, suggesting that sleepiness was causing the accidents and that rumble strips were highly effective in their prevention.

Public Education

Sanctions should not be imposed before an effective public education campaign takes place. Ignorance of the law does not exempt the driver and the physician from obeying, but there is an aspect of unfairness in recommending sanctions based on regulations divested from widespread public knowledge. The New York State Task Force subcommittee on Public Education and Information [1] indicated that lack of awareness of the problem posed by sleepy drivers is prevalent not only among the public in general but also among physicians and authorities. Sleep-related crashes are probably underreported because guidelines have not been given to police officers. Trainers spend well-used time explaining the hazards of operating vehicles under the influence of alcohol and lecture continuously on the importance of using a seat belt, but perhaps fail to mention with sufficient ardor the risks of falling asleep at the wheel. Programs that are intended to educate and license commercial drivers should incorporate specific sections devoted to the issues of sleepiness and driving, along with education on sleep hygiene measures and the interactions of insufficient sleep, alcohol, drugs and overwork. The public in general, although acknowledging the significance of falling asleep at the wheel, fails to grant it priority status. Such issues need to be addressed as a preface to future regulations that are fair, well-defined, and effective.

Sleep-Related Violence

The asleep individual, although being in a state of suspended consciousness and animation, might from time to time engage in motor activities without regaining consciousness. In this twilight state in which motor acts are divested of purposeful guidance and reason, violent and harmful behavior can be inflicted by susceptible individuals. The physician is confronted with a clinical situation in which recurrent events need to be diagnosed and treated appropriately, not only to prevent injury to the patient and bedmate but also to dispel notions of malicious violent behavior, which, if important in magnitude and scope, can conjure intervention by the law.

Automatic status in sleep can be associated with complex violent behavior that can cause accidental destruction, harm, or injury. This state should be distinguished from aggression in which actions are guided and executed according to a premeditated plan that has an identifiable objective. Aggression is not compatible with sleep. Sleep-related violent behavior, independently of how complex or catastrophic it might be, is perpetrated in an automatic state and is characterized by senseless, inexplicable acts that translate no planning, motive, or objective. Amnesia for the event is the rule. Such acts include homicide, murder, apparent suicide, attempted strangulation, automobile crashes, infliction of fractures or bruises, nudity, and destruction of property. In some instances, such as in REM sleep behavior disorder (RSBD), patients are driven by a dream; in others, such as in somnambulism, there is no dream content. The following sleep-related diagnoses have been associated with automatic behavior and violence: somnambulism, sleep terrors, confusional arousals or sleep drunkenness, RSBD, episodic nocturnal wandering, paroxysmal dystonia, sleep-related seizures, and dissociative states.

Description and Differential Diagnosis

Somnambulism, night terrors, and confusional arousals are disorders of arousal. Somnambulism, or sleepwalking, and night terrors, also known as pavor nocturnus and incubus, are common in children (17%) [22], although adults can be occasionally affected (0.5–2.5%). Episodes of sleepwalking and night terrors are facilitated by daytime stress, febrile illness, alcohol, psychotropic drugs, and sleep deprivation, and can be precipitated by deep sleep of long duration. During the sleepwalking episode, individuals keep their eyes open and are capable of sorting out objects, although clumsily, and are at risk of falling. Windows might be mistaken for doors and individuals might attempt to go through them. Elaborate behaviors have been observed, and there are descriptions of individuals crashing through windows [23] and of killing people [24] while in this state.

There is some debate whether seemingly complex motor behaviors, particularly if associated with violence, represent confusional arousals or, rather, prolonged episodes of reticent somnambulism. A sleepwalking episode can turn into a confusional arousal, and both are conditions featuring an arousal disorder in which a subvigilant state is associated with motor activity. Therefore, the argument might be moot. In any event, it is hard to characterize as somnambulism episodes in which the individual drives a car or commits acts that are beyond the ability to walk [25]. Such states are perhaps better categorized as confusional arousals. Individuals walking in their sleep commonly exhibit a docile behavior that allows others to turn them back to bed without confrontation.

Night terrors are more prevalent in children, becoming increasingly rare in the adult years when they are frequently associated with psychopathology. Episodes are characterized by piercing screams, inconsolable crying, signs of autonomic discharge, and purposeless motor activity that can lead to violence if the patient falls out of bed or collides against sharp objects. Individuals appear to be awake but are clearly unaware and unresponsive to external stimuli. Dream content is nonexistent, and amnesia for the episode is the rule.

Confusional arousals, or sleep drunkenness, are characterized by episodes of motor activity without conscious awareness that occur when the individual is awakened out of deep sleep. The events appear in subjects who are severely sleep deprived or who are afflicted with intrinsic hypersomnia such as in narcolepsy and idiopathic CNS hypersomnia, or who have intense secondary hypersomnia such as in the advanced sleep apnea syndrome. Ingestion of alcohol and administration of psychotropic drugs can facilitate the occurrence of events. Confusional episodes are common in children awakened from deep sleep. Attempts to awaken adults with sleep pathology can trigger elaborate behaviors such as driving a car, using tools, or committing murder in what appears to be a purposeful, although senseless act.

The literature contains accounts of horrendous episodes that suggest a confusional arousal. In his book of tales of clinical neurology and the law [26], the neurologist Harold Klawans recounts the case of an overworked lawyer who pulled off the road at 1:00 A.M. to take a nap. Two hours later, he was arrested and charged with murder. A witness reported that he had driven several times over the body of a girl who had tried to awaken him to ask for a lift. The patient had no recollection of the event. Sleep laboratory testing revealed motor activity with violent behavior when the patient was awakened out of slow wave sleep (SWS). This event was characterized by a slow wave EEG, despite apparent wakefulness,with purposeless acts and unresponsiveness to orders given by the technician. A diagnosis of sleep drunkenness was made, and the charges were dismissed after expert witnesses for both the defense and the prosecution reached the same medical conclusion.

Harold Klawans points out that reports of impulsive, senseless behavior with elaborate violence leading to murder while the individual is asleep have been accepted in court for centuries. The term sleep drunkenness was introduced in Silesia in 1791 by J. F. Meister, a professor of law arguing in defense of a laborer who had killed his wife with an ax after being awakened from sleep by a noise. The following case study came under our management:

Case Study 14-1

A 46-year-old telephone repairman was evaluated because of an incident involving his car. The patient had attended a jazz festival where he consumed eight cans of beer from 5:00 P.M. to midnight. At 3:00 A.M., he headed for home driving his own car. Feeling very tired and sleepy, he pulled into a rest area off the southbound lane at approximately 3:25 A.M., parked his car, removed the keys from the ignition, and placed them in a box next to the driver's seat; he then reclined the seat and went to sleep. At 4:40 A.M., he was easily awakened by a sheriff deputy knocking on the car window with a flashlight. The patient immediately realized that his car was parked heading north on the southbound lane, not far away from the rest area (Figure 14-6); he had no idea how he got there. The patient was charged with driving while intoxicated, and his driver's license was suspended. His past medical history was relevant for episodes of childhood sleepwalking that continued into adulthood. As an adult, he occasionally found himself at night sitting or lying in odd places in the house. He never experienced dreams with such episodes. He also complained of having deep sleep from which it was difficult to be aroused. As a telephone repairman, he sometimes got emergency telephone calls at night, but on the following day he would have no recollection of the conversation. His alcohol consumption had been heavy in the past. The physical examination was normal. Testing in the sleep laboratory over two consecutive nights with the

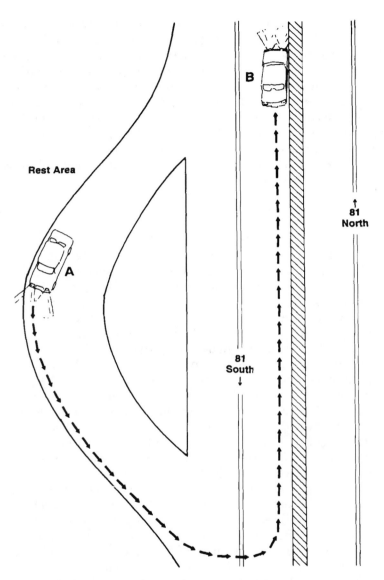

Figure 14-6. *Diagram of rest area on Interstate Highway 81, showing (A) the starting position and route (arrows) that the patient drove in an alleged state of confusional arousal. (B) When found by the state police, the car was parked heading north in the southbound lane of I-81. (Modified from A Culebras. La Medicina del Sueño. Barcelona: Ed Áncora, 1994.)*

seizure protocol revealed aperiodic jerk activity through phasic REM, mild enhancement of muscle tone in REM stage, and excessive amounts of SWS for his age relative to the standards of the laboratory. On three occasions, the technician intentionally awoke the patient out of stages 3 and 4 without difficulty. The patient contested the suspension of his driver's license claiming that he was not intoxicated when the incident occurred. He alleged that the episode was the consequence of his sleep disorder. In a note to the judge, we supported the patient's contention and suggested that the patient had suffered an episode of confusional arousal. In our opinion, this notion was supported by the patient's history of somnambulism, episodes of automatic wandering, and polysomnographic findings of excessive SWS. Alcohol had probably served as a facilitator of the event.

Rapid Eye Movement Sleep Behavior Disorder

RSBD is characterized by bizarre behavior in response to the dictates of a dream that is usually confrontational or features persecutions and chases by animals or human beings (see Table 10-3). The disorder is more common in older men with risk factors for stroke [27]. It has also been described in individuals with neurologic conditions affecting brain stem structures. It is believed that lesions of the tegmentum of the pons or mesencephalon disconnect the muscle atonia-generating centers, preventing the occurrence of this natural phenomenon during REM sleep. Enactment of dreams is facilitated in REM sleep without atonia as the constraint of atonic paralysis disappears. Individuals affected with the condition recount being driven by their violent dreams to beat their wives, jump out of bed, move furniture, open windows, and so forth. Surprisingly, individuals physically diminished by their infirmities exhibit great force and agility during the enactment of dreams. Their jumps out of bed are spectacular and their strength while moving furniture or opening windows appears to be inordinate in relation to their physical appearance. Injuries to both the patient and bedmate are common, and occasionally patients resort to tying themselves to the bed, putting up barriers with pillows, or sleeping on the floor to prevent injury at night. The condition is easily distinguished from somnambulism, night terrors, and even sleep drunkenness because of the presence of a vivid dream that precipitates the event. Although reports indicate that it can occur at any age, RSBD is more common in advanced age. The condition responds promptly to the administration of clonazepam. The following patient was studied by us:

Case Study 14-2

A 70-year-old man recounted the recurrent dream of an alligator chasing him. In order to prevent a bite he would grab the animal's snout with great force, at which point he would be awakened by the screams of his wife saying, "Let me go! Let me go!" To his horror and to the terror of his wife he would be clutching her arm and on occasions her neck. The spouse, a frail old woman, had hematomas that verified the events. During wakefulness the patient was a loving husband with a placid disposition. There was a medical history of hypertension and diabetes, and the magnetic resonance images of the head showed ischemic lesions in the tegmentum of the pons. A polysomnographic evaluation revealed REM sleep without atonia. Administration of clonazepam, 0.5 mg at bedtime, eliminated further episodes.

Episodic Nocturnal Wandering

Episodic nocturnal wandering is characterized by episodes of moving around in the middle of the night without a fixed course or aim while uttering unintelligible speech, sometimes screaming, and exhibiting violent behavior (see Table 10-2). Individuals appear to be driven by an internal force that takes them to different areas of the house to perform elaborate tasks. Their transfigured but vacuous expression reveals a senseless intent that when confronted might result in violence. The following day, the individual has no recollection of the episode except for vague traces in memory of static images. The disorder is more common in young men between the ages of 10 and 20 years. Some authors have identified epileptiform activity in frontal regions of the brain [28, 29] and treatment with carbamazepine has arrested the episodes. Montagna [29] and others [30] consider that episodic nocturnal wanderings, paroxysmal dystonia, and paroxysmal awakenings are gradations of the same epileptogenic disorder.

Attacks arise in clusters, more commonly in stage 2 of sleep in the second half of the night or early morning hours. Polysomnography has failed to show abnormal electrographic features, but interictal EEGs in some patients have revealed focal epileptiform activity.

Fugue States

Long duration complex behavior with compulsive aimless wandering and amnesia related to seizures characterizes a fugue state [31]. Patients might find themselves traveling many hundreds of miles away from home. The condition is also called poriomania, and when short in duration is difficult to distinguish from episodic nocturnal wandering, except that fugues are not related to sleep and can occur in temporal relation with a genuine seizure. Fugue states respond to carbamazepine and other anticonvulsants; the ictal EEG is abnormal.

Malingering

Reliable witness reports are important to obtain an accurate description of events and conduct a differential diagnosis. In general, sleep-related automatisms and epileptic fugue states are associated with clouding of consciousness that preempts any careful planning of motor behaviors. Violence committed without conscious input is senseless, misguided, unreasonable, and motiveless. It occurs when objects or persons interfere or obstruct the way of the affected individual. In malingering, despite individual claims of uncontrollable forces driving the action, or of clouding of consciousness obfuscating reason, there are identifiable elements of premeditation, planning, and direction.

Absence of volition is the cornerstone of sleep-related violence and the principle that determines the defense to a crime. In fact, sleep-related violence should be considered a form of noninsane automatism that rules out volition, premeditation, and malice. Mahowald and colleagues have developed a series of criteria that help differentiate sleep-related violence from malingering [32] as follows:

1. The history and sleep laboratory evaluation lend support to the diagnosis of sleep-related behavior.

2. The duration of the event is compatible with the presumed diagnosis.

3. The behavior is seemingly senseless and without motivation.

4. Immediately following the episode, there is perplexity and horror with no attempt to conceal or cover up the events.

5. There is amnesia for most of the event.

6. The event fits the timing after sleep onset and the duration of the proposed explanation.

7. The event is related to preceding sleep deprivation that can facilitate attacks.

Dissociated States

Admixtures of wakefulness into sleep and intrusions of REM or non-REM sleep into wakefulness result in what Mahowald has termed *dissociated states* [33]. These abnormal phenomena manifest partial invasions of one state of being into the domain of the other, or inappropriate partial generation of one state while the other is prevailing. The concept of dissociated states helps to explain alterations such as cataplexy (generation of REM sleep–related muscle atonia while the individual is awake), RSBD, some hallucinatory phenomena (invasion of the conscious mind by dreams), automatic behaviors, and arousal disorders.

Intrusion of some REM sleep components into wakefulness accounts for cataplexy, hypnagogic hallucinations, and sleep paralysis. Inappropriate activation during wakefulness of brain stem centers controlling REM sleep muscle atonia is the cornerstone of cataplexy. Inappropriate activation of REM dream generating centers might account for various forms of hallucinosis and delirious states. Vigorous REM sleep rebound following withdrawal of alcohol might explain the hallucinations of delirium tremens [34].

Polysomnograms performed during automatic states have shown episodes of very brief sleep, or microsleeps, that represent invasion of non-REM stages into wakefulness. This invasion can result in complex behaviors without adequate supervision by consciousness along with amnesia for the episode.

Lucid dreaming is characterized by intrusion of a domineering consciousness in REM sleep. Patients relate how they control their dreams and even manipulate the outcome of the story. Loss of H-reflex reactivity during such bizarre episodes attests to the presence of REM stage [35].

RSBD manifests an incomplete generation of REM sleep with muscle atonia missing. The presence of muscle tone during REM sleep facilitates the enactment of dreams and potentiates complex motor behaviors driven by the dream.

The disorders of arousal are exponents of dissociated states in which non-REM sleep coexists with a crude form of wakefulness. Patients are awake enough to perform elaborate motor behaviors such as screaming, walking, and talking unintelligibly, although they are not sufficiently aroused to judge their acts. In sleep drunkenness, wakefulness is associated with clouding of consciousness.

Chaotic admixtures of all three states occur in fatal familial insomnia, a condition in which a state of stupor features elements of wakefulness and RSBD without a clear polygraphic pattern of REM sleep.

Polysomnography

Testing in the sleep laboratory is a critical step toward the elucidation of the sleep alteration in sleep-related violence. In 100 consecutive instances of sleep-related injury studied in a sleep laboratory, Schenck and colleagues [36] identified the following disorders: night terrors and somnambulism (54), RSBD (36), dissociative disorders (7), nocturnal seizures (2), and sleep apnea (1). Unfortunately, episodes are transient and might not appear during the night of testing. The polysomnographer should be able to identify interictal signs to make a diagnosis. Video recording in conjunction with polysomnography assists significantly should episodes occur.

When getting out of bed and walking around are the patient's cardinal complaints, the sleep specialist needs to differentiate between somnambulism, RSBD, episodic wandering, confusional arousal, and postictal confusion after a genuine seizure event. Patients with somnambulism generally exhibit large amounts of SWS in the polysomnogram. The episode itself appears in the first third of the night during SWS and is facilitated by a prolonged episode of stage 4. Occasionally, high-voltage synchronous slow waves appear in EEG channels immediately before the event begins, or traces are observed before an awakening arising from a prolonged episode of stage 4. RSBD is characterized by REM sleep without atonia occurring intermittently during REM stage or continuously in severe instances. Myoclonic jerking in REM sleep and aperiodic muscle contractions in other stages manifest restlessness and motor facilitation. Episodic wandering occurs out of stage 2 of sleep. In some instances, frontotemporal epileptiform discharges are identified in interictal EEGs. Confusional arousals arise from stage 3 or 4 of sleep. Although the patient's eyes are open and the behavior appears to be that of an awake person, the EEG continues to show generation of central slow wave rhythms without the background typical of the alert state. Recordings during automatic behavior such as is seen in narcolepsy or in severe forms of sleep apnea syndrome have shown microsleeps, which are characterized by sudden episodes of stage 1 or 2 briefly invading the conscious state. Genuine seizures are associated with paroxysmal epileptiform discharges occurring predominantly during stages 1 and 2 and rarely in the REM stage. Occasionally, the surface EEG fails to show genuine seizure activity and instead exhibits one or more brief bursts of what appears to be an arousal or nonfocal paroxysmal slowing. Repeated surface daytime EEGs and polysomnography might be needed to determine the diagnosis.

Sudden Infant Death Syndrome

Sudden infant death syndrome (SIDS) is characterized by the unexpected death of apparently normal infants during nocturnal or daytime sleep. It is more common in lower socioeconomic classes, giving rise to hypotheses related to poor hygiene, parental ignorance, and alcoholism to explain the mysterious deaths. SIDS occurs between the ages of 4 weeks and 6 months, and occurs more frequently from October through March. Autopsy studies have shown few pathologic signs. The syndrome has caused great public concern because of the drama surrounding the unexpected death of a child, sometimes with repeated incidence in the same family, which raises suspicions and accusations.

In a celebrated case tried in the courts of Upstate New York, a 49-year-old woman was convicted of suffocating five of her infant children and sentenced to serve 75 years in prison. The woman claimed innocence. Ironically, the infants had been the subject of a landmark medical study 27 years before that helped establish SIDS as a genuine medical condition. A county prosecutor heard the story 20 years later, became suspicious, tracked down the woman whose children had been identified in the scientific articles by their initials, and brought the case to the attention of the Tioga County authorities (Figure 14-7).

Baby Killer Gets 75 To Life

■ A judge urges Waneta Hoyt to tell her adopted son the truth about murdering her five young children.

By JOHN O'BRIEN
The Post-Standard

Waneta Hoyt kept a secret for a quarter-century about the deaths of her five young children.

In Tioga County Court Monday, a judge urged her to come clean with her only living child, now 19 years old and seated behind her in court.

"Consider your sixth child," Judge Vincent Sguegla said, looking at Hoyt. "That boy is entitled to the truth. Whatever you tell anybody in this life — whatever you tell your husband, whatever you tell your lawyer, whatever you tell me, whatever you tell your God — you owe it to that boy to tell him the truth."

Hoyt's adopted son, Jay, lowered his head and appeared to choke back tears.

Hoyt must serve 75 years in prison for smothering her five naturally born children from 1965 to 1971. Sguegla gave her the minimum sentence of 15 years to life on each of five murder convictions, citing her age and ill health.

The judge could have had Hoyt serve all five sentences at once, meaning the 49-year-old Hoyt would have been eligible for parole at age 64. But in consideration of the murdered babies, Sguegla said, Hoyt had to serve the sentences one after the other. Her parole won't come up until the year 2070.

Hoyt, with her husband Timothy by her side, told Sguegla in a meek voice she was wrongly convicted of murdering her babies. Their deaths had been attributed to sudden infant death syndrome.

"I tried very hard to save my children," Hoyt said, crying as she spoke. "Why this story has come out like this, I don't know. I loved all my kids. And I'll love them till the day I die. All I can say is, God forgive all of those who have done this to me."

Her lawyer, William Sullivan, said any prison term would be a death sentence for Hoyt. He said she's been hospitalized repeatedly since she was jailed following her conviction in April. Hoyt has said she suffers from high and low blood pressure and diabetes, among other ailments.

"I hope she lives long enough so she can succeed on appeal," Sullivan said. He accused Hoyt's trial lawyers of ineffectively representing her by not calling witnesses they should have.

Prosecutor Margaret Drake said Hoyt's children, ranging in age from 2 months to 2 years old, had a right to expect their mother would protect them.

"Eric, James, Julie, Molly and Noah would've been young adults today had they survived — had they been permitted by their mother to survive," Drake said. "Their mother should've protected them, their mother should've cared for them, their mother should've nurtured them. They had a right to expect that she would do this. Instead, she took their lives because they were crying, and she could not stand their crying."

Hoyt's two youngest children were the subject of a landmark 1972 study on SIDS by former Syracuse pediatrician Dr. Alfred Steinschneider.

In 1986, Onondaga County prosecutor William Fitzpatrick saw the study, which only identified the children by their initials. He tracked down Hoyt and turned the case over to Tioga County authorities in 1992.

■ **Fighting back:** Hoyt's attorney attacks the credibility of the lead state police investigator in her case/B-1.

Figure 14-7.   *Sudden infant death syndrome (SIDS) has caused great public concern because of the drama surrounding the unexpected death of a child, sometimes with repeated incidence in the same family, which raises suspicions and accusations. In a celebrated case tried in the courts of Upstate New York, a 49-year-old woman was convicted of suffocating five of her infant children and sentenced to serve 75 years in prison. Ironically, the infants had been the subject of a landmark medical study 27 years before that helped establish SIDS as a genuine medical condition. (Reprinted with permission from The Post-Standard, Tuesday, September 12, 1995, Syracuse, NY. The Herald Company.)*

References

1. New York State Task Force on the Impact of Fatigue on Driving. Albany, December 1994. Institute for Traffic Safety Management and Research, Albany, NY.
2. National Highway Traffic Safety Administration General Estimates System. Statistical Report for 1992.

3. Strohl KP. Overview of the problem: Sleepiness, its assessment and the players in the equation. In Legal Implications of Sleep Disorders handout. Eighth Annual APSS Meeting, Boston, June 4, 1994.
4. Findley LJ, Fabrizio M, Thommi G, et al. Severity of sleep apnea and automobile crashes. N Engl J Med 1989;320:868.
5. Wu H, Yan-Go FL. The association of sleep apnea syndrome and risk of motor vehicle accidents. Neurology 1995;45(Suppl. 4):A269.
6. Aldrich MS. Automobile accidents in patients with sleep disorders. Sleep 1989;12:487.
7. Knipling RR, Wierwille WW. Vehicle-based drowsy driver detection: Current status and future prospects. Proceedings of the Fourth Annual Meeting of IVHS America. Atlanta: IVHS America, 1994;245.
8. National Transportation Safety Board. Safety Study: Fatigue, Alcohol, Other Drugs, and Medical Factors in Fatal-to-the-Driver Heavy Truck Crashes (Vols 1 and 2). Washington, DC: NTSB/SS-90/01 and 021.
9. Stoohs RA, Guilleminault C, Itoi A, et al. Traffic accidents in commercial long-haul truck drivers. The influence of sleep-disordered breathing and obesity. Sleep 1994;17:619.
10. Wake Up America: A National Sleep Alert. A report of the National Commission on Sleep Disorders Research. Volume 1: Executive Summary and Executive Report. Washington, DC: National Institutes of Health, January 1993;1.
11. National Transportation Safety Board. Marine Accident Report—Grounding of the U.S. Tankship *Exxon Valdez* on Bligh Reef, Prince William Sound, near Valdez, Alaska, March 24, 1989. Washington, DC: NTSB/Mar-90/04, 1990;1.
12. National Transportation Safety Board. Marine Accident Report—Grounding of the Greek Tankship *World Prodigy* off the coast of Rhode Island, June 23, 1989. Washington, DC: NTSB/Mar-91/01, 1991;1.
13. U.S. Nuclear Regulatory Commission: Report on the Accident at the Chernobyl Nuclear Power Station. Washington, DC, U.S. Government Printing Office, 1987.
14. Moss TH, Sills DL. The Three Mile Island nuclear accident: Lessons and implications. Ann N Y Acad Sci 1981;365:1.
15. Rosekind MR, Graeber RC, Dinges DF, et al. Crew factors in flight operations, IX. Effects of cockpit rest on crew performance and alertness in long-haul operations. Washington, DC, NASA Technical Memorandum Report, 1992.
16. Asch DA, Parker RM. Sounding Board: The Libby Zion case. N Engl J Med 1988;318:771.
17. Smith L, Folkard S, Poole CJM. Increased injuries on night shift. Lancet 1994;344:1137.
18. Ad Hoc Committee of the Assembly on Respiratory Neurobiology and Sleep, Strohl KP (chairman). Sleep apnea, sleepiness, and driving risk. Am J Respir Crit Care Med 1994;150:1463.
19. Conference on Pulmonary/Respiratory Disorders and Commercial Drivers. Washington, DC: U.S. Department of Transportation. Report No. FHWA/MC/91/004, March 1991.

20. Federal Aviation Administration. Sleep Apnea Evaluation Specifications, FAA Specification Letter. October 6, 1992.
21. APSS Eighth Annual Meeting, Boston, Opening Ceremonies, June 6th, 1994.
22. Klackenberg G. Somnambulism in childhood: Prevalence, course and behavior correlates. A prospective longitudinal study (6–16 years). Acta Paediatr 1982;71:495.
23. Oswald I, Evans J. On serious violence during sleep-walking. Br J Psychiatry 1985;147:688.
24. Luchins DJ, Sherwood PM, Gillin JC, et al. Filicide during psychotropic-induced somnambulism: A case report. Am J Psychiatry 1978;135:1404.
25. Broughton R, Billings R, Cartwright R, et al. Homicidal somnambulism: A case report. Sleep 1994;17:253.
26. Klawans HL. The Sleeping Killer. In HL Klawans (ed), Trials of an Expert Witness. Boston: Little, Brown, 1991;130.
27. Culebras A, Moore JT. Magnetic resonance findings in REM sleep behavior disorder. Neurology 1989;39:1519.
28. Pedley TA, Guilleminault C. Episodic nocturnal wanderings responsive to anticonvulsant drug therapy. Ann Neurol 1977;2:30.
29. Montagna P. Nocturnal paroxysmal dystonia and nocturnal wandering. Neurology 1992;42:61.
30. Peled R, Lavie P. Paroxysmal awakenings from sleep associated with excessive daytime somnolence. A form of nocturnal epilepsy. Neurology 1986;36:95.
31. Engel J, Jr. Differential Diagnosis. In Seizures and Epilepsy. Contemporary Neurology Series. Philadelphia: FA Davis, 1989;353.
32. Mahowald MW, Bundlie SR, Hurwitz TD, et al. Sleep violence: Forensic science implications: Polygraphic and video documentation. J Forensic Sci 1990;35:413.
33. Mahowald MW, Schenck CH. Dissociated states of wakefulness and sleep. Neurology 1992;42:44.
34. Hishikawa Y, Sugita Y, Teshima Y, et al. Sleep Disorders in Alcoholic Patients with Delirium Tremens and Transient Withdrawal Hallucinations—Reevaluation of the REM Rebound and Intrusion Theory. In I Karacan (ed), Psychophysiological Aspects of Sleep. Park Ridge, NJ: Noyes Medical Publishers, 1981;109.
35. Brylowski A, Levitan L, LaBerge S. H-reflex suppression and autonomic activation during lucid REM sleep: A case study. Sleep 1989;12:374.
36. Schenck CH, Milner DM, Hurwitz TD, et al. A polysomnographic and clinical report on sleep-related injury in 100 adult patients. Am J Psychiatry 1989;146:1166.

15

Organization of a Sleep Center and Laboratory

Antonio Bové-Ribé, Robert E. Westlake, Jr., and Antonio Culebras

Before 1960, medical interest in the field of sleep disorders was very limited, existing only in the area of psychology. The observation that sleep could be measured and objectively described through the simultaneous recording of different physiologic phenomena (polysomnographic recording) and, especially, the discovery of REM sleep, created a growing interest in sleep research. Still, the 1960s saw few sleep studies other than the ones performed in patients with parasomnias or mental illness and for the clinical investigation of hypnotic agents. During that initial decade of sleep research, there were no references to the entity that is considered today the most prevalent and perhaps most serious problem in sleep disorders: the sleep apnea syndrome. The subsequent discovery of sleep-related respiratory disorders gave rise to the development of sleep laboratories and additional research.

In 1977, the first three sleep centers were accredited in the United States. In the early 1980s, a consensus was reached regarding the methodology for performing sleep studies, and sleep disorders were recognized as an important aspect of medicine. Sleep units are now distributed worldwide. Polysomnography is the basic diagnostic procedure and, despite being an intensive and time-consuming technique in our diagnostic arsenal, it is now considered an indispensable part of the evaluation of the patient with sleep disorders. Many medical alterations that were previously unrecognized can now be successfully diagnosed and treated; sleep disorders medicine is one of the few areas of real growth in the clinical medical sciences.

In 1991, the American EEG Society published the following indications for sleep monitoring of patients [1]. Evaluations should be pursued when patients complain of the following:

1.   Episodes of sleep occurring at inappropriate times

2.   Difficulty sleeping during scheduled sleep periods (insomnia)

3.   Difficulty staying awake during scheduled awake periods (hypersomnia)

4.   Atypical behavioral events occurring during sleep (e.g., sleepwalking, loud snoring, respiratory difficulties, excessive movements, and possible seizures)

5.   Measurement of the effectiveness of various therapeutic regimens that can be instituted for the management of sleep disorders

To illustrate the ecumenical reach of sleep disorders medicine the following are the recommendations of the Australian and New Zealand Thoracic Society regarding polysomnography [2]:

1.   Sleep is a unique state in which physiologic regulation differs from wakefulness. Some pathologic events, such as sleep apneas and periodic leg movements, are state specific and cannot be diagnosed without the help of polysomnography.

2.   Sleep can modify functions that are abnormal during wakefulness. Chronic pulmonary diseases, neuromuscular disorders, and some forms of epilepsy are good examples. Polysomnography can be desirable or might be essential for adequate treatment.

3.   Alterations in sleep architecture can be diagnostic of specific disorders such as narcolepsy.

The evaluation of sleep and its disorders has broad applications in all fields of medicine. Sleep medicine is a multidisciplinary subspecialty, drawing its practitioners to the discipline primarily from the ranks of neurology, pulmonary medicine, psychiatry, and psychology, reaching beyond the frontiers of any single medical specialty.

The Sleep Center and Sleep Laboratory

Objective measurement of sleep parameters using methodology and recording techniques derived from the EEG laboratory is conducted in the sleep laboratory. A sleep center includes patient evaluation in addition to testing of sleep parameters. In order to function properly, a sleep center should:

1.   Perform administrative functions that coordinate the reception and evaluation of patients.

2.   Perform polysomnographic studies and the multiple sleep latency test.

3.   Accurately collate and interpret polysomnographic data.

4.   Formulate treatment recommendations.

5.   Communicate the results of the evaluation and the resultant recommendations for therapy to the referring physician in a timely manner, established at 5 working days from the performance of the laboratory study.

Patients should be assigned to any one of the physicians affiliated with the center. In order to establish a standard database, patients are asked to complete a questionnaire related to sleep-wake disorders. Daytime sleepiness can be assessed with the Visual Analogue Scale [4], the Stanford Sleepiness Scale [5], or the Epworth Sleepiness Scale [6] (see Chapter 6). These subjective measures have proven useful and are routinely used in many sleep centers.

The sleep log (see Chapter 5) is a useful tool to record the time at which the patient goes to bed, periods of wakefulness, rise time, and daytime sleep episodes. Bedtime rituals and the subjective assessment of sleep quality can also be recorded. Reference can be made to other phenomena associated with a particular night, such as snoring, morning headache, or daytime irritability.

Evaluation of the patient with a sleep disorder can require complementary studies such as pulmonary function tests, arterial blood gases, echocardiography, electrocardiography, and radiologic and hormonal studies. These tests, as well as pulmonary, psychiatric, and neurologic consultations, should be readily available.

Integration of information from the medical history, results of the physical examination, and results of complementary tests permit the formulation of a recommendation regarding polysomnography. A number of sleep disorders do not require polysomnographic studies for satisfactory management. For example, jet lag syndrome, delayed sleep phase syndrome, advanced sleep phase syndrome, and shift work–related sleep disorders can be defined with a meticulous diary. In some instances, actigraphy can be helpful to detect active and inactive periods, allowing inference of sleep and wakefulness periods. However, there are circumstances in which a polysomnographic evaluation should be performed to resolve a complex differential diagnosis, define the severity of the disorder, and indicate a treatment plan. Polysomnography in the absence of a full evaluation that permits proper interpretation of the findings in the clinical context is insufficient.

A fully accredited sleep center offers more comprehensive diagnostic and treatment services than a sleep laboratory. The sleep laboratory might be certified solely for the evaluation of sleep-related respiratory disorders. The sleep center performs nocturnal and daytime studies pertinent to the full spectrum of sleep disorders, limited only by the availability of technical support. Evaluations performed routinely include the ones for the assessment of excessive daytime somnolence, sleep-related respiratory disorders, abnormal nocturnal motor behavior, nocturnal seizures, nocturnal heart dysrhythmias, sleep-related penile tumescence, gastroesophageal reflux, nocturnal asthma, and hormonal levels in plasma. In addition, cardiac studies related to ischemia can be performed. Clinical research projects such as investigation of the effects of pharmacologic agents on sleep are encouraged, given the continued need to develop knowledge about sleep disorders and their management. However, not all sleep centers can invest the time and economic resources necessary for clinical research. Patient support groups for specific sleep disorders often use sleep centers as educational resources for sleep-related programs.

Sleep units should have exclusive dedication to sleep disorders. Studies done haphazardly or irregularly in units that double up as EEG or telemetry laboratories are generally of low quality. To maintain appropriate levels, studies should be conducted by specialized personnel in units with known working standards and programs of quality control.

Organization and Requirements

Physicians should not feel disappointed by the many requirements needed for the development of a sleep unit. This process can be achieved step by step, provided that a preestablished general scheme is followed. Limiting the clinical and polysomnographic evaluations to a subset of patients such as the ones with nocturnal breathing disorders (i.e., sleep apnea only) or neurologic conditions (i.e., epilepsy) should be avoided. Sleep and its disorders must be considered in a broad dimension to avoid false diagnoses.

Important factors that affect the development of a sleep unit include (1) size of patient catchment area or area of influence, (2) location of the unit, (3) equipment, and (4) personnel.

Catchment Area

The area of influence should comprise a minimum of 100,000 persons [7]. It is unlikely that a unit with a smaller catchment area will remain solvent and be able to survive by its own means. It is recommended to situate the sleep center in a hospital setting in order to facilitate relations with other medical departments, although extramural locations are acceptable provided that all necessary requirements are fulfilled. Cardiopulmonary resuscitation equipment is required for a possible emergency, and physicians on call should be available at all times. Offsite facilities should have access to an efficient ambulance service to be able to transfer a patient to the emergency room.

Location and Space

A sleep center requires space to accommodate staff in professional offices, as well as an examining room, individual bedrooms, and an independent equipment or control room. In its basic form, the laboratory is integrated by two rooms; one contains the equipment and control instruments necessary to perform recordings while the technician observes the sleeping patient on closed-circuit television; adjacent is the bedroom equipped with an infrared or low-level light television camera. The bedroom should be approximately 10 by 14 feet in size, easily accessible from the control room, and comfortable and private, providing an environment and amenities comparable to the ones found in a moderately priced popular chain motel. It should be silent, sound and light-attenuated, and have temperature control and an adjoining individual bathroom with shower. A wardrobe, table, armchair, bedstand, and bedlamp complete the furniture. The bed should be comfortable, with a spring-box mattress, of the size and style found in hotels rather than in hospitals, and reinforced to accept large patients weighing as much as 500 pounds. An intercommunication system between the bedroom and the equipment room allows verbal exchanges between the patient and the technician without the need for the technician to enter the bedroom.

Research and teaching centers should have an adjoining meeting and conference room. A storage room is desirable to stock studies and various accessories, although storage of voluminous records can be done in microfilm or optical disk, saving a large amount of space. Samples of each study must be stored for medicolegal purposes.

The sleep center should be well posted and indicated with signs throughout the hospital or facility. It should have its own stationery as well as educational and sleep disorders evaluation materials. A dedicated telephone line and fax machine are required for prompt communication with referral sources, patients, and administration. It is a long and arduous enterprise to design a sleep center. It requires installation of appropriate equipment and proper training of technical staff who will be responsible for the day-to-day operation of the center.

Personnel

Sleep center technologists and technicians can have different educational backgrounds and come from the ranks of nursing service, pulmonary medicine, or EEG technology. All should have specialty training in the various polysomnographic techniques, as well as knowledge of cardiorespiratory resuscitation maneuvers. Many sleep centers have 1- and 2-year programs designed to train sleep technologists. Technologists should be ready to work at night and be capable of managing patients of all ages. Training includes knowledge of calibration and operation of electronic transducers, amplifiers, and devices that record sleep parameters and measure respiration, cardiac function, periodic leg movements, erectile function, and esophageal pH. Required expertise also includes application and adjustment of continuous positive and bilevel positive airway pressure devices for sleep apnea treatment. Training in manual and computer-assisted polysomnographic scoring is an important aspect of the technologist's education; scoring is a tedious but essential job traditionally performed by the most experienced individual.

A minimum of two technicians is required to conduct both nocturnal and daytime studies. Two polysomnographic studies can be supervised by one person simultaneously. The night technician works 10 hours, 4 nights per week. Duties include welcoming the patient at approximately 8:30 P.M., 1 or 2 hours before the scheduled sleep time. Basic personal and clinical data are obtained from the patient, who is subsequently asked to complete sleep-wake–related questionnaires. This step is followed by the application of scalp electrodes in accordance with the 10–20 System. During these steps, the patient is readied psychologically while other transducers are applied and the preparation is completed. Lights are turned off at 10:30 P.M., at which time the study officially begins. During the night, the technician maintains the equipment in working condition, observes the patient, attends whatever necessities arise, and annotates in the chart the night phenomena that might occur. Following completion of the study in the morning, at approximately 7:00 A.M., the technician administers another set of questionnaires inquiring about the patient's perception of estimated sleep time, estimated awake time, and subjective details relative to arousals if they occurred. The daytime technologist works 8 hours, 5 days per week and conducts multiple sleep latency test (MSLT) recordings. Responsibilities include equipment maintenance and scoring of polysomnograms. The technical staff is also involved in training courses and collaborates in sleep research studies when they are performed.

The secretarial staff answers the phone, provides information about the center, and schedules patients; they type reports, mail letters, and file documents. An important function of the secretarial staff is to guide the patient through the maze of insurance forms, reimbursement policies, and requirements in preparation for preauthorization of the procedure. Billing should be done by separate staff.

Professional Staff

Under the guidance of the medical director, the center should strive to incorporate the professional services of interested specialists in neurology, pulmonary medicine, cardiology, internal medicine, surgery, urology, psychiatry, pediatrics, otorhinolaryngology, and psychology. The medical director should be well versed in the basics of neurology, applied neurophysiology, pulmonary medicine, cardiology, pediatrics, electroencephalography, and psychiatry as applied to sleep disorders medicine. In addition, the medical director should be knowledgeable about laboratory equipment and be experienced in scoring records and interpreting polysomnograms. Other functions include orienting and guiding referring physicians in the management of sleep disorders. Medical directors generally have a background in neurology or in pulmonary medicine and are commonly board certified in their original specialty, as well as in sleep disorders medicine. Sufficient experience and appropriate background in sleep disorders permit the medical director to ensure that patients receive the appropriate diagnostic evaluation, discussion of results and treatment options, as well as adequate follow-up. The American Sleep Disorders Association (ASDA) requires that at least one board-certified sleep specialist be on staff for purposes of center accreditation.

Well-rounded centers offer fellowships in sleep medicine and prepare physicians for specialty board examinations.

Standards for Board Certification of Polysomnographic Technologists, Sleep Specialists, and Center Accreditation

Board certification of polysomnographic technologists and sleep specialists along with ASDA accreditation of the center provide validation of the level of quality service that should be delivered.

Board of Registered Polysomnographic Technologists

The Board of Registered Polysomnographic Technologists [8] commissioned by the Association of Polysomnographic Technologists (APT) awards certificates (RPSGT) to worthy candidates who pass the combined basic and practical examinations. The eligibility requirements are:

1. Part I, 150 multiple-choice test questions in theory and application; and Part II, 100 multiple-choice test questions in record review and scoring. Prerequisites for the test are:

    A. A minimum of 1 year of clinical or research laboratory human polysomnography experience by the last day of the calendar month in which the examination is to be taken.

    B. A current certification in Basic Cardiac Life Support.

2. Part III, Clinical performance test with hands-on simulation of subjects set-up, equipment calibration, and conduct of overnight polysomnographic study. Prerequisites for the test are:

    A. Successful completion of Parts I and II multiple-choice tests.

    B. Current certification in Basic Cardiac Life Support.

American Board of Sleep Medicine

In the United States, the American Board of Sleep Medicine (ABSM) [9] was established in 1978 by the Association of Sleep Disorders Centers (now ASDA) and incorporated in 1991 as an independent entity, based on the cornerstone assumption that "mastery of specific clinical skills and procedures is essential for the practice of sleep medicine." The eligibility criteria for applicants includes 1 year of full-time training in an accredited sleep medicine training program or in a comparable program supervised by a board-certified specialist in sleep medicine. Waivers are considered on an individual basis for candidates with training and experience comparable to that obtained in structured programs. MD and DO candidates must be certified in a primary specialty such as neurology, pulmonary medicine, or psychiatry. PhD candidates must complete 2 years of full-time supervised clinical training or its equivalent with at least 1 of the years devoted to comprehensive full-time training in sleep medicine.

The examination consists of two sections. Part I, a multiple-choice questionnaire, tests knowledge in basic and clinical sciences relevant to sleep medicine; pass rates are 60–80%. Part II is administered to candidates who have successfully passed Part I. It tests competence in the diagnosis and treatment of sleep disorders, using clinical simulations of case histories and polygraphic records. Pass rates are 60–80%.

Although the ABSM is not affiliated with the American Board of Medical Specialties, one of its long-term goals is the establishment of a subspecialty board under its sponsorship. This goal is a desirable objective that will sanction and ordain the jurisdictional stature of the specialty.

Center Accreditation

The ASDA Accreditation Committee has issued a series of guidelines to prepare a center for accreditation [10]. Center accreditation by the ASDA requires documentation of the history and evolution of the center as well as a detailed description of its structure, professional staff, and functioning according to the following guidelines:

1.   History and goals of the facility

2.   Administration of the center and relationship to the host institution

3.   Medical structure with description of medical supervision, patient assessment, and access to consultative evaluations and procedures

4.   Physical plant of the facility

5.   Budget, finances, subventions, fees, and billing procedures

6.   Personnel, itemizing and describing functions of center-based specialists, consultants, technical staff, and clerical assistance

7.   Patient referral, handling, and follow-up. The documentation should detail the nature of patient contacts, acceptance criteria, referral sources, scheduling procedures, follow-up plans, and patient charts.

8.   Polysomnography, recording techniques, and use of the MSLT

9.   Scoring and interpretation of records. Automated scoring techniques used. Storage of polysomnographic data

10.   Equipment. Description of polygraphs, audiovisual monitoring equipment, emergency resuscitation equipment, and fire detection

11.   Experience of the center. Record of types of patients seen and major diagnostic categories evaluated

12.   Educational and research activities with description of continuing education activities directed at center staff and noncenter professionals including public. Public relations and techniques to avoid unethical advertising

Financial Study

Good organization and multiple steps are required to set up a sleep unit. High-quality output feeds a demand for clinical services that is required to retain the critical mass of procedures minimally necessary to ascertain viability and solvency. Since not all medical centers achieve this status, an alternate solution can be found in the concept of regionalization, provided that the different medical systems referring to a central location can keep a good level of collaboration among them. Before developing a sleep center or laboratory, it is necessary to complete a marketing and financial analysis, projecting the financial model over a period of 5–7 years. Underestimation of initial costs and required staff is a common mistake that should be avoided. The sleep center should be a stand-alone operation not sharing space and equipment with other medical departments as a cost-saving strategy.

Hospitals and medical facilities should identify the location of the sleep laboratory in consideration of various factors that include daytime human traffic, internal and external noise level, electrical interference, and ease of access. The ideal location is on the upper levels of the building where the tumult of street traffic, emergency room sirens, and parking lot noise does not reach. The optimal situation is at the end of a corridor or hospital wing where human traffic is minimal, far away from elevators, and distant from electrical interference by heavy electronic equipment or motors. Easy access for patients and staff is also important to avoid stressful adventures through endless hospital corridors.

Basic considerations in the development of a center include: maximum capacity of the center, working days and hours, fees charged, revenues, expenses, accounts receivable, and annual increments because of cost-of-living increases. The number of staff, job descriptions, salaries, and annual salary increases are necessarily estimated expenses (Table 15-1). The cost of staff replacement and overtime work should be evaluated as well, along with marketing activities and methods of staff and equipment acquisition.

Building and renovation expenses are considered capital expenses to be later depreciated. Operating expenses are fixed and variable (Table 15-2). Variable expenses depend on the volume of the service, and fixed expenses remain constant in the short-term. There are also semivariable expenses that remain constant within a fixed volume of service; below a certain threshold these expenses increase and above they decrease.

Examples of variable expenses are recording paper, chemical products, thermocouples, office supplies, laser disks (for centers with computerized equipment), and printed forms. Fixed expenses include general laboratory services (electricity and equipment), rent, depreciation, books, subscriptions, travel, and marketing. Personnel cost is an example of a semivariable expense.

Income depends on the volume of service offered, which is in turn determined by the capacity of the center, patient population, medical support, number of working days, marketing, and the competition.

Table 15-1. Patient Volume and Staffing of a Sleep Center Operating with Two Beds

Volume	Units
Testing beds	2
Testing nights	4
Testing weeks per year	50
Maximum patient/procedure capacity per year	400
Percentage occupancy	99
Patient volume per year	398
Patients per week	7.9

Staffing	Units
Clinical supervisor	1.0 FTE
Night technician	1.0 FTE
Clerical	1.0 FTE

FTE = full-time equivalent.

Possible subventions and contracts should be tabulated along with write-off studies. Operational expenses, fixed expenses, and depreciation are deducted from the revenues to calculate the net benefit (Table 15-3). Opportunity cost indicates the dividends that could have been generated if the funds had been deposited in the bank. These amounts are tabulated as an expense. Insolvent projects must become subsidiary in order to continue to be operational.

A negative financial analysis could be approved depending on other factors. A sleep center can be accepted because of work added to the medical institution even in the absence of solvency. This practice offers a service in order to attract clients to other services.

Should the project not progress along the planned direction, one would have to investigate the failed premises and introduce the necessary adjustments to find the right way. If in spite of a corrected course the project continues to deviate from the desired pathway, a decision must be made to close the center or to continue operating after reorganization. Investment return is advisable if the funds are available, even in a not-for-profit medium. If the investment return is less than the cost of initial investment plus maintenance, some form of subvention must be found in order to keep the project viable.

Table 15-2. Typical Capital, Variable, and Fixed Expenses in the Development of a Two-Bed Sleep Laboratory

Expenses	Cost (U.S. dollars)
Capital expenses	
Construction, 1,000 sq. ft.	51,600
Sleep computer testing system	80,621
Polysomnograph recorders (2)	46,564
Pulse oximeters (2)	3,360
Video cameras and miscellaneous electronics	9,500.
Office equipment: examination table, chairs, fax, two computer systems, printer, filing cabinets, phones	12,000
Data acquisition equipment	3,696
Bedroom furniture	4,020
Total capital expenses	211,361
Variable expenses	
Supplies	20,250
Laundry	1,125
Printing	500
Nourishment	550
Miscellaneous (phone calls, photocopying, microfilm)	1,140
Total variable expenses	23,565
Fixed expenses	
Salaries	79,862
Depreciation	20,000
Fees	6,323
Advertising	20,000
Repairs	4,250
Total fixed	130,435
Total operating expenses	154,000

There are few self-paying patients because of the high cost of the procedures. Third-party payers whether conventional insurance companies, HMOs, Medicare, or Medicaid entitlements absorb the cost of procedures in part or in full. Some companies authorize only studies to

Table 15-3. Net Benefit of a Two-Bed Sleep Laboratory Operating at Maximum Capacity (1995)

Item	U.S. dollars
Gross revenue	433,798
Operating expenses	154,000
Overhead	84,591
Net benefit	195,207

Table 15-4. Typical Hospital and Interpretation Fees for Sleep Studies in the United States (1995)

Center	Cost (U.S. dollars)
Apnea study	887
MSLT	428
CPAP study	818
Basic protocol	564
Siezure protocol	1080
Interpretation fees	
Apnea study	300
MSLT	150

MSLT = multiple sleep latency test; CPAP = continuous positive airway pressure.

evaluate sleep apnea and narcolepsy, rejecting insomnia-related studies performed for the assessment of patients with conditions such as psychophysiologic sleeplessness, restless legs syndrome, fibromyalgia, and similar nosological entities. Private for-profit centers require patient solvency and demand payment of all services. In the United States, the cost of a nocturnal test—exclusive of the professional component charged for interpretation of the record—ranges between $700 and $1,000. An MSLT study adds another $400–500. The second consecutive night increases the cost to $1,200–1,500 (Table 15-4). Some centers offer a package that includes medical consultation, polysomnography, and interpretation. Third-party payers might require ASDA center accreditation and a letter of justification including clinical documentation of the condition before authorizing payments.

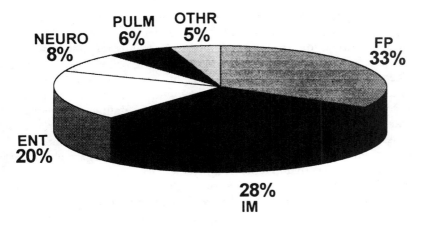

Figure 15-1. *Breakdown of physician group referrals to an accredited sleep center. (ENT = Ear, nose, and throat; NEURO = neurology; PULM = pulmonary; OTHR = other; FP = family practice; IM = internal medicine.)*

Although at first glance sleep studies appear expensive, there is a distinct cost-effective social gain considering the medicosocial complications, reduced quality of life, risk of accidents, and decline in work productivity of the patient with an uncontrolled sleep-wake disorder.

Marketing and Public Relations

The public should know about the existence of the sleep center. Time and effort should be dedicated to continuing education programs on sleep disorders targeting the medical establishment and the general community as well. This goal can be accomplished with seminars, conferences, and open meetings. Marketing techniques such as newspaper advertisements, television and radio programs, and mailings with informative brochures are recommended as long as they remain respectful of ethical considerations. A budget should be set aside for these activities.

Patients are referred by family physicians, internists, otorhinolaryngologists, pulmonary specialists, neurologists, psychiatrists, and pediatricians. A typical breakdown of patient referral patterns for a community sleep disorders center is illustrated in Figure 15-1, showing that 61% of referrals come from primary care physicians.

As the general public and primary care physicians become increasingly educated in sleep alterations, the demand for services will increase. Long gone are the days when physicians responded with a smirk to a patient's complaint of heavy snoring or excessive daytime sleepiness. The educated primary care physician understands the serious consequences of falling asleep at the wheel of a vehicle and is very much aware of the medicolegal responsibilities befalling on the physician who has been informed of that ominous risk. The physician needs to issue a serious warning to the patient and take the appropriate steps to prevent an accident waiting to happen. The primary care physician should also know that loss of work productivity, academic decline, and laboral accidents can be the result of fatigue and sleepiness at school or on the job, and that family pathology lurks behind heavy snorers (see Case Study 15-1), inveterate insomniacs, and individuals with bizarre nocturnal behavior. Genuine sleep pathology such as sleep apnea syndromes, narcolepsy, and the parasomnias are conditions that have emerged with renewed vigor as prominent causes of the ubiquitous human fatigue, as well as factors that increase the risk of vascular disease, accidental fatality, and unexplained nocturnal death. Since this is the case and because the evidence at hand shows that a sleep disorders assessment will probably lead to the satisfactory resolution of the patient's complaint, it is not surprising, it is in fact predictable, that sleep disorders medicine will continue to expand as primary care physicians are asked to take the helm once again of the health care boat.

Case Study 15-1

This is a letter sent by a patient awaiting preauthorization of laboratory sleep studies by Managed Care.

Dear Dr. —:

I am writing to inform you that my snoring problem continues to affect my personal life. My wife is unable to get a complete night's sleep because of my snoring. As a result, she became extremely run down, has been sick with a bad virus this fall, and has been under medical treatment. The alternative is not to sleep with her, which given that we are young and have a good marriage, has led us to feel very isolated and lonely. We are unable to accept this alternative as a long-term solution for ourselves and for our marriage. My children have also been awakened through the night complaining that my snoring is waking them up; they can hear it through the walls. Recently, guests in our home who should have been sleeping three bedrooms down the hall were found in the morning on the downstairs couches instead of in the guest room. Their explanation was that my snoring was so loud that they couldn't sleep.

While I realize that you have an obligation to ———— Managed Care not to recommend unnecessary treatments, I believe that the aforementioned description of our family pathology suggests that my situation warrants immediate attention and corrective action.

Thank you for your consideration.

References

1. Polygraphic assessment of sleep-related disorders (polysomnography) 1991. Bloomfield, CT: American EEG Society, 1991.
2. Grunstein R. Availability of sleep studies. Med J Aust 1992;156:137.
3. Johns MW. Polysomnography at a sleep disorders unit in Melbourne. Med J Aust 1991;155:303.
4. Folstein MF, Luria R. Reliability, validity, and clinical application of the visual analogue model scale. Psychol Med 1973;3:479.
5. Hoddes E, Zarcone V, Smythe H, et al. Quantification of sleepiness: A new approach. Psychophysiology 1973;10:431.
6. Johns MW. A new model for measuring daytime sleepiness: The Epworth Sleepiness Scale. Sleep 1991;14:540.
7. Burford SW, Adams ME, Vanderburg R. A model for the assessment and development of sleep disorders centers. Journal of Polysomnographic Technology 1991:21.
8. Board of Registered Polysomnographic Technologists, P.O. Box 14861, Lenexa, KS 66285-4861. Phone (913) 541-0400.
9. American Board of Sleep Medicine, 1610 14th Street N.W., Suite 300, Rochester, MN 55901-2200. Phone (507) 287-9819. Fax (507) 287-6008.
10. Standards for Accreditation of Sleep Disorders Centers. American Sleep Disorders Association Accreditation Committee, 1610 14th Street N.W., Suite 300. Rochester, MN 55901. Phone (507) 287-6006, Fax (507) 287-6008.

Glossary of Terms Used in Sleep Disorders Medicine

Actigraph	A biomedical instrument for the measurement of body movement.
Active sleep	A term used in the phylogenetic and ontogenetic literature for the stage of sleep that is considered to be equivalent to REM sleep. *See* REM Sleep.
Agrypnia	Insomnia.
Alpha activity	An alpha EEG wave or sequence of waves with a frequency of 8–13 Hz.
Alpha–delta sleep	Sleep in which alpha activity occurs during slow wave sleep. Because alpha-delta sleep is rarely seen without alpha occurring in other sleep stages, the term alpha sleep is preferred.
Alpha intrusion (or infiltration, insertion, or interruption)	A brief superimposition of EEG alpha activity on sleep activities during a stage of sleep.
Alpha rhythm	An EEG rhythm with a frequency of 8–13 Hz in human adults, which is most prominent over the parieto-occipital cortex when the eyes are closed. The rhythm is blocked by eye opening or other arousing stimuli. It is indicative of the awake state in most normal individuals. It is most consistent and predominant during relaxed wakefulness, particularly with reduction of visual input. The amplitude is variable, but typically is below 50 μV in the adult. The alpha rhythm of an individual usually slows by 0.5–1.5 Hz and becomes more diffuse during drowsiness. The frequency range also

varies with age; it is slower in children and older age groups relative to young and middle-aged adults.

Alpha sleep
Sleep in which alpha activity occurs during most, if not all, sleep stages.

Apnea
Cessation of airflow at the nostrils and mouth lasting at least 10 seconds. There are three types of apnea: obstructive, central, and mixed. Obstructive apnea is secondary to upper airway obstruction; central apnea is associated with a cessation of all respiratory movements; mixed apnea has both central and obstructive components.

Apnea-hypopnea index
The number of apneic episodes (obstructive, central, and mixed) plus hypopneas per hour of sleep as determined by all-night polysomnography.

Apnea index
The number of apneic episodes (obstructive, central, and mixed) per hour of sleep as determined during all-night polysomnography. Sometimes a separate obstructive apnea index or central apnea index is stated.

Arise time
The clock time that an individual gets out of bed after the final awakening of the major sleep episode. Distinguished from final wake-up.

Arousal
An abrupt change from a "deeper" stage of non-REM sleep to a "lighter" stage, or from REM sleep toward wakefulness, with the possibility of awakening as the final outcome. Arousal may be accompanied by increased tonic EMG activity and heart rate as well as body movements.

Arousal disorder
A parasomnia disorder presumed to be due to an abnormal arousal mechanism. Forced arousal from sleep can induce episodes. The "classical" arousal disorders are sleepwalking, sleep terrors, and confusional arousals.

Automatism
Quasi-intentional behavior in sleepy subjects, usually affected by severe hypersomnolence or sleep deprivation.

Awakening	The return to the polysomnographically defined awake state from any non-REM or REM sleep stages. It is characterized by alpha and beta EEG activity, a rise in tonic EMG, voluntary rapid eye movements, and eye blinks. This definition of awakenings is valid only insofar as the polysomnogram is paralleled by a resumption of a reasonably alert state of awareness of the environment.
Axial system	A means of stating different types of information in a systematic manner by listing on several "axes," to ensure that important information is not overlooked by the statement of a single major diagnosis. The International Classification of Sleep Disorders uses a three-axial system: axes A, B, and C.
Axis A	The first level of the International Classification of Sleep Disorders axial system on which the sleep disorder diagnoses, modifiers, and associated code numbers are stated.
Axis B	The second level of the international Classification of Sleep Disorders axial system on which the sleep-related procedures and procedure features, and associated code numbers, are stated.
Axis C	The third level of the International Classification of Sleep Disorders axial system on which International Classification of Diseases nonsleep diagnoses and associated code numbers are stated.
Baseline	The typical or normal state of an individual or of an investigative variable prior to an experimental manipulation.
Bedtime	Defined as the clock time when one attempts to fall asleep, as differentiated from the clock time when one gets into bed.
Beta activity	A beta EEG wave or sequence of waves with a frequency of greater than 13 Hz.
Beta rhythm	An EEG rhythm in the range of 13–35 Hz, when the predominant frequency, beta

rhythm, is usually associated with alert wakefulness or vigilance and is accompanied by a high tonic EMG. The amplitude of beta rhythm is variable but usually is below 30 µV. This rhythm may be drug induced.

Bi-PAP
Bilevel positive air pressure apparatus that delivers differential positive pressures during inspiration and expiration. Used for control of sleep apnea disorders.

Brain wave
Use of this term is discouraged. The term suggested for use is EEG wave.

Bruxism
Repetitive grinding of teeth during sleep, causing unpleasant noises that disturb the sleep of others.

Cataplexy
A sudden decrement in muscle tone and loss of deep tendon reflexes, leading to muscle weakness, paralysis, or postural collapse. Cataplexy usually is precipitated by an outburst of emotional expression—notably laughter, anger, or startle. One of the tetrad of symptoms of narcolepsy. During cataplexy, respiration and voluntary eye movements are not compromised.

Cheyne-Stokes respiration
A breathing pattern characterized by regular "crescendo-decrescendo" fluctuations in respiratory rate and tidal volume.

Chronobiology
The science relating to temporal, primarily rhythmic, processes in biology.

Circadian rhythm
An innate daily fluctuation of physiologic or behavioral functions, including sleep-wake states generally tied to the 24-hour daily dark–light cycle. It sometimes occurs at a measurably different periodicity (e.g., 23 or 25 hours) when light and dark and other time cues are removed.

Circasemidian rhythm
A biologic rhythm that has a period length of about half a day.

Conditioned insomnia
An insomnia that is produced by the development, during an earlier experience of sleeplessness, of conditioned arousal. Causes of the conditioned stimulus can include the cus-

tomary sleep environment or thoughts of disturbed sleep. A conditioned insomnia is one component of psychophysiologic insomnia.

Constant routine A chronobiological test of the endogenous pacemaker that involves a 36-hour baseline monitoring period, followed by a 40-hour waking episode of monitoring with the individual on a constant routine of food intake, position, activity, and light exposure.

CPAP A continuous positive air pressure apparatus used to control obstructive sleep apnea disorder.

Cycle Characteristic of an event exhibiting rhythmic fluctuations. One cycle is defined as the activity from one maximum or minimum to the next.

Deep sleep Common term for combined non-REM stages 3 and 4 sleep.

Delayed sleep phase A condition that occurs when the clock hour at which sleep normally occurs is moved back in time within a given 24-hour sleep-wake cycle. This results in a temporarily displaced, that is delayed, occurrence of sleep within the 24-hour cycle. The same term denotes a circadian rhythm sleep disturbance, called the delayed sleep phase syndrome.

Delirium Acute confusional episode with prominent sleep-wake inversion. Duration is less than 30 days.

Delta activity EEG activity with a frequency of less than 4 Hz (usually 0.1–3.5 Hz). In human sleep scoring, the minimum characteristics for scoring delta waves are conventionally 75 μV (peak to peak) amplitude, and 0.5-second duration (2 Hz) or less.

Delta sleep stage Indicative of the stage of sleep in which EEG delta waves are prevalent or predominant (sleep stages 3 and 4, respectively). *See* Slow Wave Sleep.

Diagnostic criteria Specific criteria established in the International Classification of Sleep Disorders to aid in determining the unequivocal presence of a particular sleep disorder.

Diurnal
Pertaining to the daytime; denotes cyclic or periodic occurrence.

Drowsiness
A state of quiet wakefulness that typically occurs prior to sleep onset. If the eyes are closed, diffuse and slowed alpha activity usually is present, which then gives way to early features of stage I sleep.

Duration criteria
Criteria established in the International Classification of Sleep Disorders for determining the duration of a particular disorder as acute, subacute, or chronic.

Dyssomnia
A primary disorder of initiating and maintaining sleep or of excessive sleepiness. The dyssomnias are disorders of sleep or wakefulness per se, not a parasomnia.

Early morning arousal (early A.M. arousal)
Synonymous with premature morning awakening.

Electroencephalogram (EEG)
A recording of the electrical activity of the brain by means of electrodes placed on the surface of the head. With the EMG and EOG, the EEG is one of the three basic variables used to score sleep stages and waking. Sleep recording in humans uses surface electrodes to record potential differences between brain regions and a neutral reference point, or simply between brain regions. Either the C3 or C4 (central region) placement according to the International 10-20 System is referentially (referred to an earlobe) recorded as the standard electrode derivation from which state scoring is done.

Electromyogram (EMG)
A recording of electrical activity from the muscular system; in sleep recording, synonymous with resting muscle activity or potential. The chin EMG, along with EEG and EOG, is one of the three basic variables used to score sleep stages and waking. Sleep recording in humans typically uses surface electrodes to measure activity from the sub-

mental muscles. These reflect maximally the changes in resting activity of axial body muscles. The submental muscle EMG is tonically inhibited during REM sleep.

Electro-oculogram (EOG)

A recording of voltage changes resulting from shifts in position of the ocular globes, as each globe is a positive (anterior) and negative (posterior) dipole; along with the EEG and the EMG, one of the three basic variables used to score sleep stages and waking. Sleep recording in humans uses surface electrodes placed near the eyes to record the movement (incidence, direction, and velocity) of the eyeballs. Rapid eye movements in sleep form one part of the characteristics of the REM sleep state.

End-tidal carbon dioxide

Carbon dioxide value usually determined at the nares by an infrared carbon dioxide gas analyzer. The value reflects the alveolar or pulmonary arterial blood carbon dioxide level.

Entrainment

Synchronization of a biological rhythm by a forcing stimulus such as an environmental time cue (zeitgeber). During entrainment, the frequencies of the two cycles are the same or are integral multiples of each other.

Epoch

A measure of duration of the sleep recording that typically is 20 or 30 seconds in duration, depending on the paper speed of the polysomnograph, and corresponds to one page of the polysomnogram.

Excessive sleepiness (or somnolence or excessive daytime sleepiness)

A subjective report of difficulty in maintaining the alert awake state, usually accompanied by a rapid entrance into sleep when the person is sedentary. May be due to an excessively deep or prolonged major sleep episode. Can be quantitatively measured by use of subjectively deemed rating scales of sleepiness, or physiologically measured by electrophysiologic tests such as the multiple sleep latency test (see MSLT). Most commonly occurs during the daytime; however, excessive sleepiness may be present at night in a person who has the major sleep episode during the daytime, such as a shift worker.

Extrinsic sleep disorders
Disorders that either originate, develop, or arise from causes outside of the body. The extrinsic sleep disorders are a subgroup of the dyssomnias.

Final awakening
The amount of wakefulness that occurs after the final wakeup time until the arise time (lights on).

Final wake-up
The clock time at which an individual awakens for the last time before the rising time.

First-night effect
The effect of the environment and polysomnographic recording apparatus on the quality of the subject's sleep the first night of recording. Sleep is usually of reduced quality compared to that which would be expected in the subject's usual sleeping environment, without electrodes and other recording procedure stimuli. The subject usually will habituate to the laboratory by the time of the second night of recording.

Fragmentation (pertaining to sleep architecture)
The interruption of any stage of sleep due to the appearance of another stage or to wakefulness, leading to disrupted non-REM–REM sleep cycles; often used to refer to the interruption of REM sleep by movement arousals or stage 2 activity. Sleep fragmentation connotes repetitive interruptions of sleep by arousals and awakenings.

Free-running
A chronobiological term that refers to the natural endogenous period of a rhythm when zeitgebers are removed. In humans, it most commonly is seen in the tendency to delay some circadian rhythms, such as the sleep-wake cycle, by approximately 1 hour every day, when a person has an impaired ability to entrain or is without time cues.

Hertz (Hz)
A unit of frequency; preferred term to the synonym cycles per second (cps).

Hypercapnia	Elevated carbon dioxide level in blood.
Hypersomnia (excessive sleep)	Excessively deep or prolonged major sleep period. The term is primarily a diagnostic term, e.g., idiopathic hypersomnia
Hypnagogic	Occurrence of an event during the transition from wakefulness to sleep.
Hypnagogic imagery (or hallucinations)	Vivid sensory images occurring at sleep onset, but particularly vivid with sleep-onset REM periods. A feature of narcoleptic naps when the onset occurs with REM sleep.
Hypnagogic startle	A "sleep start" or sudden body jerk (hypnic jerk), observed normally just at sleep onset and usually resulting, at least momentarily, in an awakening.
Hypnogram	A histogram exhibiting parameters of sleep usually in temporal correlation with sleep architecture.
Hypnopompic	Occurrence of an event during the transition from sleep to wakefulness at the termination of a sleep episode.
Hypopnea	An episode of shallow breathing (airflow reduced by at least 50%) during sleep lasting 10 seconds or longer, usually associated with a decrease in blood oxygen saturation.
ICSD sleep code	A code number of the International Classification of Sleep Disorders (ICSD) that refers to modifying information of a diagnosis, such as associated symptom, severity, and duration of a sleep disorder.
Insomnia	Difficulty in initiating or maintaining sleep. A term that is employed ubiquitously to indicate any and all gradations and types of sleep loss.
Into bed time	The clock time at which a person gets into bed. The into bed time (IBT) will be the same as the bedtime for many people, but not for those who spend time in wakeful activities in bed, such as reading, before attempting to sleep.
Intrinsic sleep disorders	Disorders that either originate or develop from within the body, or arise from causes

	within the body. The intrinsic sleep disorders are a subgroup of the dyssomnias.
Jactatio capitis	Stereotypical and rhythmic movements of the head at sleep onset in susceptible children, rarely in adults.
K-alpha	A K complex followed by several seconds of alpha rhythm; a type of microarousal.
K complex	A sharp, negative EEG wave followed by a high-voltage slow wave. The complex duration is at least 0.5 seconds and may be accompanied by a sleep spindle. K complexes occur spontaneously during non-REM sleep, and begin and define stage 2 sleep. They are thought to be evoked responses to internal stimuli. They can also be elicited during sleep by external (particularly auditory) stimuli.
Light-dark cycle	The periodic pattern of light (artificial or natural) alternating with darkness.
Light sleep	A common term for non-REM sleep stage 1, and sometimes stage 2.
Lucid dream	A dream controlled, directed, and even manipulated by the sleeping subject.
Maintenance of wakefulness test (MWT)	A series of measurements of the interval from "lights out" to sleep onset that is used in the assessment of the ability to remain awake. Subjects are instructed to try to remain awake in a darkened room while in a semireclined position. Long latencies to sleep are indicative of the ability to remain awake. This test is most useful for assessing the effects of medication on the ability to remain awake.
Major sleep episode	The longest sleep episode that occurs on a daily basis. Typically the sleep episode dictated by the circadian rhythm of sleep and wakefulness; the conventional or habitual time for sleeping.
Microsleep	An episode lasting up to 30 seconds during which external stimuli are not perceived. The polysomnogram suddenly shifts from

waking characteristics to sleep. Microsleeps are associated with excessive sleepiness and automatic behavior.

Montage

The particular arrangement by which a number of derivations are displayed simultaneously in a polysomnogram.

Movement arousal

A body movement associated with an EEG pattern of arousal or a full awakening; a sleep scoring variable.

Movement time

The term used in sleep record scoring to denote when EEG and EOG tracings are obscured for more than half the scoring epoch because of movement. It is only scored when the preceding and subsequent epochs are in sleep.

Multiple Sleep Latency Test (MSLT)

A series of measurements of the interval from "lights out" to sleep onset that is used in the assessment of excessive sleepiness. Subjects are allowed a fixed number of opportunities to fall asleep during their customary awake period. Excessive sleepiness is characterized by short latencies. Long latencies are helpful in distinguishing physical tiredness or fatigue from true sleepiness.

Muscle tone

A term sometimes used for resting muscle potential or resting muscle activity. *See* Electromyogram (EMG).

Myoclonus

Muscle contractions in the form of abrupt jerks or twitches generally lasting less than 100 ms.

Nap

A short sleep episode that may be intentionally or unintentionally taken during the episode period of habitual wakefulness.

Nightmare

Used to denote an unpleasant and frightening dream that usually occurs in REM sleep. Occasionally called a dream anxiety attack, not a sleep (night) terror.

Nocturnal confusion

Episodes of delirium and disorientation close to or during nighttime sleep; often seen in the elderly and indicative of organic central nervous system deterioration.

Nocturnal dyspnea	Respiratory distress that may be minimal during the day, but becomes quite pronounced during sleep.
Nocturnal penile tumescence (NPT)	The natural periodic cycle of penile erections that occurs during sleep, typically associated with REM sleep. The preferred term is sleep-related erections.
Nocturnal sleep	Indicative of the typical "nighttime" or major sleep episode related to the circadian rhythm of sleep and wakefulness; the conventional or habitual time for sleeping.
Non-rapid eye movement (NREM, non-REM) sleep	*See* Sleep Stages.
Non-REM–REM sleep cycle (synonymous with sleep cycle)	A period during sleep composed of a non–REM sleep episode and the subsequent REM sleep episode; each non-REM–REM sleep couplet is equal to one cycle. Any non-REM sleep stage suffices as the non-REM sleep portion of a cycle. An adult sleep period of 6.5–8.5 hours generally consists of four to six cycles. The cycle duration increases from infancy to young adulthood.
Non-REM sleep intrusion	An interposition of non-REM sleep, or a component of non-REM sleep physiology (e.g., elevated EMG, K complex, sleep spindle, delta waves), in REM sleep; a portion of non-REM sleep not appearing in its usual sleep cycle position.
Non-REM sleep period	The non-REM sleep portion of non-REM–REM sleep cycle; such an episode consists primarily of sleep stages 3 and 4 early in the night and of sleep stage 2 later. *See* Sleep Cycle; Sleep Stages.
Obesity-hypoventilation syndrome	A term applied to obese individuals who hypoventilate during wakefulness. Because the term can apply to several different disorders, its use is discouraged.
Ondine	Greek mythology divinity condemned to stay awake in order to breathe. Gave name

	to Ondine's curse, an obsolete term for central sleep apnea with severe hypoventilation.
Paradoxical sleep	Synonymous with REM sleep, which is the preferred term.
Parasomnia	Disorder of arousal, partial arousal, or sleep stage transition. It represents an episodic disorder in sleep (such as sleepwalking) rather than a disorder of sleep or wakefulness per se. May be induced or exacerbated by sleep; not a dyssomnia.
Paroxysm	Phenomenon of abrupt onset that rapidly attains a maximum and terminates suddenly; distinguished from background activity. It commonly refers to an epileptiform discharge on the EEG.
Paroxysmal nocturnal dyspnea (PND)	Respiratory distress and shortness of breath due to pulmonary edema, which appears suddenly and often awakens the sleeping individual.
Penile buckling pressure	The amount of force applied to the glans of the penis sufficient to produce at least a 30-degree bend in the shaft.
Penile rigidity	The firmness of the penis as measured by the penile buckling pressure. Normally, the fully erect penis has maximum rigidity.
Period	The interval in time between the recurrence of a defined phase or moment of a rhythmic or periodic event, that is, between one peak or trough and the next.
Periodic leg movement (PLM)	A rapid partial flexion of the foot at the ankle, extension of the big toe, and partial flexion of the knee and hip that occurs during sleep. The movements occur with a periodicity of 20–60 seconds in a stereotyped pattern lasting 0.5–5.0 seconds, and are a characteristic feature of the periodic limb movement disorder.
Periodic limb movements of sleep (PLMS)	An all-inclusive term to incorporate rare periodic arm movements of sleep. *See* Periodic Leg Movement.

Phantasmagoria	Complex succession of imagined perceptions of the senses and illusions of the mind with excessive, quasi-intentional motor behavior during sleep that suggest enactment of a dream.
Phase advance	The shift of an episode of sleep or wake to an earlier position in the 24-hour sleep–wake cycle. A shift of sleep from 11 P.M. to 7 A.M. to 8 P.M. to 4 A.M. represents a 3-hour phase advance. *See* Phase Delay.
Phase delay	A shift of an episode of sleep or wake to a later time of the 24 hour sleep–wake cycle. It is the exact opposite of phase advance. These terms differ from common concepts of change in clock time: to effect a phase delay, the clock is moved ahead or advanced. In contrast, to effect a phase advance, the clock moves backward. *See* Phase Advance.
Phase transition	One of the two junctures of the major sleep and wake phases in the 24-hour sleep-wake cycle.
Phasic event (or activity)	Brain, muscle, or autonomic events of a brief and episodic nature occurring in sleep; characteristic of REM sleep, such as eye movements, or muscle twitches; usually the duration is milliseconds to 1–2 seconds.
Photoperiod	The duration of light in a light–dark cycle.
Pickwickian	A term applied to an individual who snores, is obese and sleepy, and has alveolar hypoventilation. The term has been applied to many different disorders and therefore its use is discouraged.
PLM-arousal index	The number of sleep-related periodic leg movements per hour of sleep that are associated with an EEG arousal. *See* Periodic Leg Movement.
PLM index	The number of periodic leg movements per hour of total sleep time as determined by all-night polysomnography. Sometimes expressed as the number of movements per

hour of non-REM sleep because the movements are usually inhibited during REM sleep. *See* Periodic Leg Movement.

PLM percentage
The percentage of total sleep time occupied with recurrent episodes of periodic leg movements.

Polysomnogram
The continuous and simultaneous recording of multiple physiologic variables during sleep, i.e., EEG, EOG, EMG (these are the three basic stage scoring parameters), EKG, respiratory air flow, respiratory movements, leg movements, and other electrophysiologic variables.

Polysomnograph
A biomedical instrument for the measurement of physiologic variables of sleep.

Polysomnographic (as in recording, monitoring, registration, or tracings)
Describes a recording on paper, computer disc, or tape of a polysomnogram.

Premature morning awakening
Early termination of the sleep episode, with inability to return to sleep, sometimes after the last of several awakenings. It reflects interference at the end rather than at the commencement of the sleep episode. A characteristic sleep disturbance of some people with depression.

Proposed sleep disorder
A disorder in which there is insufficient information available in the medical literature to confirm the unequivocal existence of the disorder. A category of the International Classification of Sleep Disorders.

Protocol
A polygraphic montage to study a specific sleep alteration or disorder.

Quiet sleep
A term used for describing non-REM sleep in infants and animals when specific non-REM sleep stages 1–4 cannot be determined.

Rapid eye movement sleep (REM sleep)
See Sleep Stages.

Record
The end product of the polysomnograph recording process.

Recording	The process of obtaining a polysomnographic record. The term is also applied to the end product of the polysomnograph recording process.
REM density (or intensity)	A function that expresses the frequency of eye movements per unit time during sleep stage REM.
REM sleep episode	The REM sleep portion of a non-REM–REM sleep cycle; early in the night it may be as short as a half minute, whereas in later cycles longer than an hour. *See* Sleep Stage REM.
REM sleep intrusion	A brief interval of REM sleep appearing out of its usual position in the non-REM–REM sleep cycle; an interposition of REM sleep in non-REM sleep; sometimes appearance of a single, dissociated component of REM sleep (e.g., eye movements, "drop out" of muscle tone) rather than all REM sleep parameters.
REM sleep latency	The interval from sleep onset to the first appearance of stage REM sleep in the sleep episode.
REM sleep onset	The designation for commencement of a REM sleep episode. Sometimes also used as a shorthand term for a sleep-onset REM sleep episode. *See* Sleep Onset; Sleep-Onset REM Period (SOREMP).
REM sleep percent	The proportion of total sleep time constituted by the REM stage of sleep.
REM sleep rebound (recovery)	Lengthening and increase in frequency and density of REM sleep episodes, which result in an increase in REM sleep percent above baseline. REM sleep rebound follows REM sleep deprivation once the depriving influence is removed.
Respiratory Disturbance Index (RDI) (Apnea-Hypopnea Index)	The number of apneas (obstructive, central, or mixed) plus hypopneas per hour of total sleep time as determined by all-night polysomnography.
Restlessness (referring to a quality of sleep)	Persistent or recurrent body movements, arousals, and brief awakenings in the course of sleep.

Rhythm	An event occurring at an approximately constant period length.
Saw-tooth waves	A form of theta rhythm that occurs during REM sleep and is characterized by a notched appearance in the wave form. Occurs in bursts lasting up to 10 seconds.
Severity criteria	Criteria for establishing the severity of a particular sleep disorder according to categories: mild, moderate, or severe.
Siderealism	Disconcerting impression of falling in space.
Siesta	An afternoon nap, particularly after lunch.
Sleep architecture	The non-REM–REM sleep stage and cycle infrastructure of sleep understood from the vantage point of the quantitative relationship of these components to each other. Often plotted in the form of a histogram.
Sleep cycle	Synonymous with the non-REM–REM sleep cycle.
Sleep efficiency (or Sleep Efficiency Index)	The proportion of sleep in the episode potentially filled by sleep, i.e., the ratio of total sleep time to time in bed.
Sleep episode	An interval of sleep that may be voluntary or involuntary. In the sleep laboratory, the sleep episode occurs from the time of "lights out" to the time of "lights on." The major sleep episode is usually the longest daily sleep episode.
Sleep hygiene	The conditions and practices that promote continuous and effective sleep. These include regularity of bedtime and arise time; conformity of time spent in bed to the time necessary for sustained and individually adequate sleep (i.e., the total sleep time sufficient to avoid sleepiness when awake); restriction of alcohol and caffeine beverages prior to bedtime; and employment of exercise, nutrition, and environmental factors so that they enhance, not disturb, restful sleep.
Sleepiness (somnolence, drowsiness)	Difficulty in maintaining alert wakefulness with a tendency to fall asleep. It is not simply a feeling of physical tiredness or list-

lessness. When sleepiness occurs in inappropriate circumstances, it is considered excessive sleepiness.

Sleep interruption Breaks in sleep resulting in arousal and wakefulness. *See* Fragmentation; Restlessness.

Sleep latency The duration of time from "lights out," or bedtime, to the onset of sleep.

Sleep log (or diary) A daily, written record of a person's sleep-wake pattern containing such information as time of retiring and arising, time in bed, estimated total sleep time, number and duration of sleep interruptions, quality of sleep, daytime naps, use of medications or caffeine beverages, and nature of waking activities.

Sleep-maintenance DIMS (insomnia) A disturbance in maintaining sleep, once achieved; persistently interrupted sleep without difficulty falling asleep. Synonymous with sleep continuity disturbance.

Sleep mentation The imagery and thinking experienced during sleep. Sleep mentation usually consists of combinations of images and thoughts during REM sleep. Imagery is vividly expressed in dreams involving all the senses in approximate proportion to their waking representations. Mentation is experienced generally less distinctly in non-REM sleep, but it may be quite vivid in stage 2 sleep, especially toward the end of the sleep episode. Mentation at sleep onset (hypnagogic reverie) can be as vivid as in REM sleep.

Sleep onset The transition from awake to sleep, normally to non-REM stage 1 sleep, but in certain conditions, such as infancy and narcolepsy, into stage REM sleep. Most polysomnographers accept EEG slowing, reduction, and eventual disappearance of alpha activity, presence of EEG vertex sharp transients, and slow rolling eye movements (the components of non-REM stage 1) as sufficient for sleep onset; others require appearance of stage 2 patterns. *See* Latency; Sleep Stages.

Sleep-onset REM period (SOREMP)	The beginning of sleep by entrance directly into stage REM sleep. The onset of REM sleep occurs within 10 minutes of sleep onset.
Sleep paralysis	Immobility of the body that occurs in the transition from sleep to wakefulness that is a partial manifestation of REM sleep.
Sleep pattern (2-hour sleep-wake pattern)	A person's clock hour schedule of bedtime and arise time as well as nap behavior; may also include time and duration of sleep interruptions. *See* Sleep-Wake Cycle; Circadian Rhythm; Sleep Log.
Sleep-related erections	The natural periodic cycle of penile erections that occur during sleep, typically associated with REM sleep. Sleep-related erectile activity can be characterized by four phases: T-up (ascending tumescence), T-max (plateau maximal tumescence), T-down (detumescence), and T-zero (no tumescence). Polysomnographic assessment of sleep-related erections is useful for differentiating organic from nonorganic erectile dysfunction.
Sleep spindle	Spindle-shaped bursts of 12–14-Hz waves lasting 0.5–1.5 seconds. Generally diffuse, but of highest voltage over the central regions of the head. The amplitude is generally less than 50 μV in the adult. One of the identifying EEG features of non-REM stage 2 sleep; may persist into non-REM stages 3 and 4; not seen in REM sleep.
Sleep stage demarcation	The significant polysomnographic characteristics that distinguish the boundaries of the sleep stages. In certain conditions and with drugs, sleep stage demarcations may be blurred or lost, making it difficult to identify certain stages with certainty or to distinguish the temporal limits of sleep stage lengths.
Sleep stage episode	A sleep stage interval that represents the stage in a non-REM–REM sleep cycle; easiest to comprehend in relation to REM sleep, which is a homogeneous stage, i.e., the fourth REM sleep episode is in the

fourth sleep cycle (unless a prior REM episode was skipped). If one interval of REM sleep is separated from another by more than 20 minutes, they constitute separate REM sleep episodes (and are in separate sleep cycles); a sleep stage episode may be of any duration.

Sleep stage non-REM   The other major sleep state apart from REM sleep; comprises sleep stages 1-4, which constitute levels in the spectrum of non-REM sleep "depth" or physiologic intensity.

Sleep stage REM   Desynchronized sleep, characterized by enhanced brain metabolism and vivid hallucinatory imagery or dreaming. There are spontaneous rapid eye movements, resting muscle activity is suppressed, and awakening threshold to insignificant stimuli is high. The EEG is a low voltage, mixed-frequency, non-alpha record. REM sleep is usually 20–25% of total sleep time. It is also called "paradoxical sleep."

Sleep stages   Distinctive stages of sleep, best demonstrated by polysomnographic recordings of the EEG, EOG, and EMG.

Sleep stage 1 (non-REM stage 1)   A stage of non-REM sleep that occurs at sleep onset or that follows arousal from sleep stages 2, 3, 4, or REM. It consists of a relatively low-voltage EEG with mixed frequency, mainly theta activity and alpha activity of less than 50% of the scoring epoch. It contains EEG vertex waves and slow rolling eye movements; no sleep spindles, K complexes, or REMs. Stage 1 normally represents 4–5% of the major sleep episode.

Sleep stage 2 (non-REM Stage 2)   A stage of non-REM sleep characterized by the presence of sleep spindles and K complexes present in a relatively low-voltage, mixed-frequency EEG background; high-voltage delta waves may make up to 20% of stage 2 epochs; usually accounts for 45–55% of the major sleep episode.

Sleep stage 3 (non-REM stage 3)	A stage of non-REM sleep defined by at least 20% and not more than 50% of the episode consisting of EEG waves less than 2 Hz and more than 75 µV (high-amplitude delta waves); a "delta" sleep stage. With stage 4, it constitutes "deep" non-REM sleep, so-called slow wave sleep (SWS); often combined with stage 4 into non-REM sleep stage 3/4 because of the lack of documented physiologic differences between the two, appears usually only in the first third of the sleep episode; usually comprises 4–6% of total sleep time.
Sleep stage 4 (non-REM stage 4)	All statements concerning non-REM sleep stage 3 apply to stage 4 except that high-voltage, EEG slow waves persist in 50% or more of the epoch; non-REM sleep stage 4 usually represents 12–15% of total sleep time. Sleepwalking, sleep terrors, and confusional arousal episodes generally start in stage 4 or during arousals from this stage. *See* Sleep Stage 3.
Sleep structure	Similar to sleep architecture. However, in addition to encompassing sleep stages and sleep cycle relationships, sleep structure assesses the within stage qualities of the EEG and other physiologic attributes.
Sleep talking	Talking in sleep that usually occurs in the course of transitory arousals from non-REM sleep. Can occur during stage REM sleep, at which time it represents a motor breakthrough of dream speech. Full consciousness is not achieved and no memory of the event remains.
Sleep-wake cycle	Basically, the clock hour relationships of the major sleep and wake episodes in the 24-hour cycle. *See* Phase Transition; Circadian Rhythm.
Sleep-wake shift (or change or reversal)	When sleep as a whole or in part is moved to a time of customary waking activity, and the latter is moved to the time of the major sleep episode; common in jet lag and shift work.

Sleep-wake transition disorder	A disorder that occurs during the transition from wakefulness to sleep or from one sleep stage to another. A form of the parasomnias; not a dyssomnia.
Slow wave sleep (SWS)	Sleep characterized by EEG waves of duration slower than 2 Hz. Synonymous with sleep stages 3 plus 4 combined. *See* Delta Sleep Stage.
Snoring	A noise produced primarily with inspiratory respiration during sleep due to vibration of the soft palate and the pillars of the oropharyngeal inlet. All snorers have incomplete obstruction of the upper airway, and many habitual snorers have complete episodes of upper airway obstruction.
Somnambulism	Sleep walking.
Somniloquy	Sleep talking.
Spindle REM sleep	A condition in which sleep spindles persist atypically in REM sleep; seen in chronic insomnia conditions and occasionally in the first REM period.
Sundown syndrome	Clinical phenomenon characterized by nocturnal confusion, wandering, agitation, and in some cases, delirium.
Synchronized	A chronobiological term used to indicate that two or more rhythms recur with the same phase relationship. In EEG it is used to indicate an increased amplitude and usually a decreased frequency of the dominant activities.
Theta activity	EEG activity with a frequency of 4–8 Hz, generally maximal over the central and temporal cortex.
Total recording time (TRT)	The duration of time from sleep onset to final awakening. In addition to total sleep time, it is comprised of the time taken up by wake periods and movement time until wake-up. *See* Sleep Efficiency.
Total sleep episode	This is the total time available for sleep during an attempt to sleep. It comprises non-REM and REM sleep, as well as wakefulness.

	Synonymous and preferred to the term total sleep period.
Total sleep time (TST)	The amount of actual sleep time in a sleep episode; equal to total sleep episode less awake time. Total sleep time is the total of all REM and non-REM sleep in a sleep episode.
Tracé alternant	EEG pattern of sleeping newborns, characterized by bursts of slow waves, at times intermixed with sharp waves, and intervening periods of relative quiescence with extreme low-amplitude activity.
Tumescence (penile)	Hardening and expansion of the penis (penile erection). When associated with REM sleep, it is referred to as a sleep-related erection.
Twitch (body twitch)	A very small body movement such as a local foot or finger jerk; not usually associated with arousal.
Vertex sharp transient	Sharp negative potential, maximal at the vertex, occurring spontaneously during sleep or in response to a sensory stimulus during sleep or wakefulness. Amplitude varies but rarely exceeds 250 µV. Use of the term vertex sharp wave is discouraged.
Wake time	The total time scored as wakefulness in a polysomnogram occurring between sleep onset and final wake-up.
Waxing and waning	A crescendo-decrescendo pattern of activity, usually EEG activity.
Zeitgeber	An environmental time cue that usually helps entrainment to the 24-hour day, such as sunlight, noise, social interaction, alarm clocks, and meals.

Index

10 0353202 3

Clinical Handbook
of Sleep Disorders